OXFORD MEDICAL PUBLICATIONS

THE GENETICS OF
MENTAL DISORDERS

OXFORD MONOGRAPHS ON MEDICAL GENETICS

THE GENETICS OF
MENTAL DISORDERS

ELIOT SLATER

C.B.E., M.A., M.D., F.R.C.P., D.P.M.

*Formerly Director, Medical Research Council Psychiatric
Genetics Research Unit, The Maudsley Hospital, London*

AND

VALERIE COWIE

M.D., Ph.D., D.P.M.

*Consultant Psychiatrist, Fountain and Carshalton Group Hospitals,
Queen Mary's Hospital for Children, Carshalton
Formerly Assistant Director, Medical Research Council
Psychiatric Genetics Research Unit, and Honorary
Consultant, The Maudsley Hospital, London*

LONDON
OXFORD UNIVERSITY PRESS
NEW YORK   TORONTO
1971

Oxford University Press, Ely House, London W. 1

GLASGOW NEW YORK TORONTO MELBOURNE WELLINGTON
CAPE TOWN SALISBURY IBADAN NAIROBI DAR ES SALAAM LUSAKA ADDIS ABABA
BOMBAY CALCUTTA MADRAS KARACHI LAHORE DACCA
KUALA LUMPUR SINGAPORE HONG KONG TOKYO

ISBN 0 19 264130 1

Made in Great Britain at the Pitman Press, Bath

CONTENTS

PREFACE   vii

ACKNOWLEDGEMENTS   viii

1. INTRODUCTORY   1

2. SCHIZOPHRENIA: THE OBSERVATIONS   10

3. SCHIZOPHRENIA: GENETICAL MODELS   45

4. AFFECTIVE PSYCHOSES   72

5. DEVIATIONS OF PERSONALITY AND NEUROTIC REACTIONS   92

6. SENESCENCE, SENILE AND PRE-SENILE DEMENTIAS   122

7. EPILEPSY   160

8. THE GENETICS OF MENTAL SUBNORMALITY   185

9. NORMAL (GAUSSIAN) VARIATION IN INTELLIGENCE   188

10. METABOLIC DISORDERS: THE AMINOACIDURIAS   201

11. OTHER NEUROMETABOLIC DISORDERS I   237

12. OTHER NEUROMETABOLIC DISORDERS II   256

13. DOMINANT ABNORMALITIES   275

14. MISCELLANEOUS CONDITIONS   286

15. SEX CHROMOSOME ANOMALIES   297

16. AUTOSOMAL CHROMOSOME ANOMALIES   324

APPENDIXES

    A. Twin Research; Theoretical Basis   345
    B. Diagnosis of Zygosity by Finger-Prints   349
    C. The Weinberg Proband Method   353
    D. The Weinberg Morbidity Table   354
    E. The Weinberg Shorter Method, and the
       Strömgren Method (Simplified)   356

REFERENCES   358

INDEX   399

PREFACE

In recent years there has been steady advance in the genetics of mental subnormality, which has gone hand in hand with better understanding of the biochemical and pathological basis of clinico-genetical syndromes. The literature, however, is scattered through many journals, and is not readily available to clinicians, teachers and research workers. It is time that it was provided with an explanatory summary; and we hope that the section of this book which is devoted to it will do justice to the firm scientific basis we enjoy here.

In adult psychiatry, where we are concerned with the psychoses and neuroses, we have to do with a narrower range of observations, supported only here and there by firmly founded biochemical or pathological understanding. The problems we face are, accordingly, less well defined here, so that there is room for disagreement even about their nature, not to speak of the answers which research has so far been able to provide. In this part of the work we have tried to put the reader in possession of the evidence and to acquaint him with the variety of interpretations which it has received. We believe there is a strong case for accepting a genetical contribution to nearly all forms of psychiatric disorder, though one which varies in nature and importance from syndrome to syndrome. It is for the reader to assess the value of this evidence, and to fit the information into the models which he uses to guide his thinking.

Although there are many differences between psychiatric modes of approach to adult mental disorders on the one hand and subnormality syndromes on the other, the ways in which genetical factors, chromosomal, major gene, polygenic, enter the picture are the same in both. Genetics, in fact, is one of the unifying disciplines which emphasizes relationships between biological fields of study, and helps to create channels of communication between psychiatry and the medical sciences, clinical, physiological, biochemical and pathological.

We have aimed at a reasonably comprehensive presentation, and have not hesitated to overstep possible bounds in covering, from our own point of view, areas where we overlap Dr. Pratt's companion volume on *The Genetics of Neurological Disorders*. There will, of course, be gaps and deficiencies too, we hope not too serious. The main emphasis has been on recent literature; references to the older literature have not always been documented where this did not seem necessary. We have written our book in the first place for the clinical psychiatrist, but we hope that it will be found useful in the many neighbouring territories, neurology, paediatrics, general medicine, and human genetics.

We have received the greatest help from Professor Sir Cyril Burt, Dr. L. Crome, Professor C. E. Dent, Professor P. E. Polani, Dr. John Fraser Roberts, Mr. James Shields, and Dr. J. Stern, who have read large parts of the manuscript during preparation, and have made most helpful comments and suggestions. They are not, of course, to be held responsible for any of the errors, or any of the opinions, which are to be set solely to the authors' account. We are grateful also to Dr. Crome for his kindness in supplying neuropathological photographs; to Dr. N. C. Myrianthopoulos for a histopathological photograph (Fig. 39); and, specially, to Mr. Norman Le Page, of the Department of Photography, Fountain and Carshalton Hospital Group, for many clinical photographs.

Institute of Psychiatry, London   E.S., V.C.

January 1971

ACKNOWLEDGEMENTS

We wish to thank those authors whose names are acknowledged in the illustrations for permission to reproduce their work in this volume, and grateful acknowledgement is made to the editors and publishers of the various books and journals from which they were taken for their co-operation:

Fig. 3. *Current Problems in Neuropsychiatry: Schizophrenia, Epilepsy, and the Temporal Lobe*, 1969. ed. R. N. Herrington, Headley Brothers Ltd., Ashford, Kent.

Figs. 4 and 19. *Annals of Human Genetics.*

Figs. 6 and 7. *The Biologic Basis of Schizophrenia*, 1966. J. L. Karlsson, Charles C. Thomas, Springfield, Ill.

Fig. 11. *British Journal of Psychiatry.*

Figs. 22, 37 and 38. *Acta Psychiatrica et Neurologica Scandinavica.*

Fig. 23. *Mental and Scholastic Tests*, 4th ed. 1962. Sir Cyril Burt, Staples Press Ltd., London.

Fig. 25. *American Journal of Human Genetics.*

Figs. 26 and 31. *American Journal of Diseases of Children.*

Figs. 27, 29, 35 and 46. *Pathology of Mental Retardation*, 1967. L. Crome and J. Stern, J. & A. Churchill, London.

Fig. 28. *Journal of Pediatrics.*

Figs. 30 and 32. *Archives of Diseases of Childhood.*

Fig. 36. *New England Journal of Medicine.*

Figs. 37 and 38. *Acta Psychiatrica Scandinavica.*

Figs. 40 and 61. *The Lancet.*

Fig. 44. *Medicine.*

Figs. 48 and 51. *Mental Deficiency*, 1957. L. T. Hilliard and B. H. Kirman, J. & A. Churchill, London.

Fig. 54. *The Biology of Mental Defect*, 3rd ed. 1963. L. S. Penrose, Sidgwick & Jackson Ltd., London.

Fig. 56. *Pediatrics.*

Fig. 60. *American Journal of Public Health.*

1

INTRODUCTORY

In order to view the perspectives of psychiatric genetics in relation to the larger dimensions of general human genetics, it is helpful to consider first some basic principles.

Genetical influences are transmitted to the child by elements within the parents' germ cells. Each parent makes a contribution in that a male and a female germ cell (or *gamete*) must fuse to produce the single cell (or *zygote*) from which the new individual develops. The chromosomes, which are linear bodies within the cell nucleus, appear to be primarily concerned with hereditary transmission, but there is evidence to suggest that cellular elements outside the nucleus, in the cytoplasm of the cell, may also play a part.

Chromosome Numbers

In man, there are 46 chromosomes in each cell of the body (somatic cells) excluding the gametes. This was first established in 1956 by Tjio and Levan. Until that time there had been uncertainty with respect to the chromosome number in man, mainly owing to technical difficulties in cell preparation.

The set of 46 chromosomes in man consists of 22 matched pairs of chromosomes (the *autosomes*, or non-sex chromosomes) and one pair of sex chromosomes. In the male the sex chromosome pair consists of an X chromosome and a smaller Y chromosome. In the female the sex chromosome pair consists of two X chromosomes.

Types of Cell Division: Mitosis and Meiosis

In somatic cell division (*mitosis*) throughout the body, the chromosome number of 46 is maintained by a division of each chromosome lengthwise into daughter *chromatids*, which separate from each other and pass into the two respective daughter cells in which each chromatid becomes a chromosome identical with that from which it was derived in the parent cell.

In order that the zygote should possess a set of 46 chromosomes, the two gametes from which it is formed each make a contribution of 23 chromosomes. The gametes arise by special cell division called *meiosis*, in which the chromosome number of 46 is halved.

In the production of germ cells by meiosis there are two divisions of the germ-forming cells. In the first there is longitudinal splitting of the chromosomes into chromatids, and it is believed that at this stage an exchange of material may take place between the chromatids by processes called *crossing over* and *recombination*. By this means the chromosomes resulting from this first division are not exact replicas of the chromosomes from which they are derived. This mixing of genetical material is considered to be an important mechanism in bringing about hereditary variation within a species.

In the second cell division in the formation of germ cells the chromosomes do not split lengthwise into chromatids. Instead a whole chromosome from each pair passes into the respective daughter cells. By this process each daughter cell has half the complement of chromosomes in the parent cell. When the germ cell formed in this way fuses with a germ cell from a member of the opposite sex, the two sets of 23 chromosomes together restore the chromosome number to 46 in the resulting zygote.

Genes and the Structure of the Chromosome

Modern concepts of the structure and reduplication of genetical material have their origins in the teaching of Sir Frederick Gowland Hopkins of about 30 years ago. He taught that nearly all metabolic processes are catalysed by enzymes, and that all enzymes are protein molecules. Since then abundant evidence has accumulated, from work with both animals and plants, to confirm that protein and enzyme synthesis is controlled by genes. Moreover, it has been indicated that a one-to-one relationship exists between genes and enzymes, in that one gene is responsible for the synthesis of one enzyme (Beadle, 1945).

Genes, therefore, have two basic functions. First, they must be able to replicate themselves. Secondly, they must be able to determine the architecture of protein molecules. Genes have been postulated as hypothetical units of genetical activity, each with a specific locus on a chromosome. As the chromosomes exist in matching pairs (with the exception of the XY pair in the male), the genes are correspondingly paired, and the partners of a particular pair of genes are known as *alleles*. Until recently the existence of genes was inferred indirectly from effects in inheritance, such as the distribution (or segregation) of characteristics in Mendelian ratios. Recently, however, fundamental work, mainly by Watson and Crick and their co-workers in the Cavendish Laboratory in Cambridge, has thrown light on the chemical structure of chromosomes and therefore of genes.

The fundamental chemical component of chromosomes is deoxyribonucleic acid (DNA). This is a long polymerized structure with a sugar-phosphate backbone which carries bases of four types: adenine and guanine (which are purines); cytosine and thymine (which are pyrimidines). It is believed that the sequence in which the bases are arranged provides the code by which genetical information is transmitted. The structural model of DNA constructed by Watson and Crick (1953 a and b) consisted of a double helix, like two strands of a piece of string coiled round each other. Each strand represented the linear arrangement described above of a sequence of bases upon a sugar-phosphate backbone, and the two strands were held together by a hydrogen bond between the base of one strand and a corresponding base on the other. The double helix was so constructed that each base on one strand was paired with its complementary base on the other, adenine going with thymine, and cytosine with guanine. This implied that the pattern of bases on one strand determined that on the other. This would provide the basis for self-replication. Thus, if the double helix split into two daughter strands, each daughter strand would provide a template for the formation of a new double helix identical with the parent helix, as each base would pick up its corresponding partner from the surrounding chemical medium.

The control of protein synthesis appears to be more complicated, involving *messenger* ribonucleic acid (RNA) which closely resembles DNA chemically. It is thought that DNA segments determine the pattern of the RNA templates. In turn specific protein molecules are built up from these, this process being mediated through another type of RNA known as *transfer* or *soluble* RNA and finally being carried out on the surface of small bodies within the cell known as *ribosomes*.

Mutation

The basic chemical structure of the chromosomes appears to be remarkably stable. No doubt this stability is due to the effects of natural selection over a very long evolutionary period, but nevertheless changes apparently occur in the DNA from time to time with effects that are usually harmful. These changes are called *mutations*. These most probably arise through faulty replication of a small segment of DNA, so that the sequence of bases is changed in that region. In consequence the instructions from that part of the genetic code are changed. Larger changes may involve the actual loss or deletion of a section of DNA.

Experimentally mutations have been produced in plants and animals by chemicals and by irradiation. In man, similar effects have been seen to follow accidental or injudicious exposure to uncontrolled irradiation and to certain chemicals. The presence of such mutagenic agents cannot, however, always be demonstrated, and in a large number of cases it is to be assumed that either the mutation resulted from a specific but unknown cause, or that it occurred spontaneously. It is estimated that a mutation at any one gene locus occurs in only about 1 in 100,000 of gametes in fertilization.

On the whole the effects of mutation are deleterious, and the condition arising is often self-limiting owing to its severity and the inability of the affected individual to reproduce. However, some harmful mutations can be transmitted through generations, for example by the symptomless carriers of recessive genes or on account of the variable degree of effect in the case of some dominant genes arising by mutation. It is supposed that all of us carry at least several very harmful but nevertheless 'silent' mutations.

On the other hand, very occasionally a mutation occurs which is of beneficial effect to the species. Such mutations, of biological advantage, may provide an important step forward in the process of evolution. Mutation, therefore, is an essential part of biological progress despite the heavy price exacted by its frequently disastrous effects.

Single Gene Inheritance

A considerable number of clinical conditions are attributed to the action of single genes. Many of these are associated with mental subnormality and are usually distinguishable by well-marked clinical signs or by specific biochemical features. These conditions are rare, and tend to be eliminated by natural selection on account of their severity and deleterious nature. The number of these recognized conditions is increasing, however, owing mainly to new discoveries in the field of inborn errors of metabolism.

It is presumed that such deleterious genes arise by mutation or change in the chemical structure at a specific point on the chromosome. These changes cannot be seen in the way that gross morphological changes in the chromosome can be seen, such as translocations or deletions. Their presence can only be inferred from features in the family tree or pedigree, the most critical being the distribution of the relevant condition in a Mendelian ratio in sibships. According to Mendelian theory, single gene inheritance may be of *dominant* or *recessive* type, when the gene is carried on an autosome. Evidence suggests, however, that in the case of at least some genes the hereditary pattern is intermediate between these two extremes.

Genes which produce their full effect when in double dose in the homozygote, and still have some effect in the heterozygote, are quite frequent phenomena. As a rule, as in phenylketonuria, effects in the heterozygote are so mild that no pathological state is produced. However, this is not always so; and the genes for sickle-cell anaemia and for thalassaemia produce in their heterozygotes the sickling trait and thalassaemia minor respectively. In such conditions one can expect that the heterozygote has had some balancing biological advantage for the gene frequency to be maintained. In the case of sickle-cell anaemia, it is an improved resistance to malaria; in the case of thalassaemia, it is unknown.

Recessive conditions are less prone than dominant ones to the eliminating action of natural selection, and the rarer they are the less easily are they eliminated. If the gene frequency is p, the frequency of the abnormality being p^2, then the distribution of the genes between heterozygote and homozygote will be as $2p(1-p)$ to $2p^2$, i.e. as $(1-p):p$. For instance, if the frequency of the condition is 1 in 10,000 of the population, then 99 out of every 100 genes will be carried by a heterozygote, will not be producing any effects of a biologically disadvantageous kind, and will be protected against natural counter-selection. In the case of dominant conditions the gene shows its effects in the heterozygote and so is exposed to natural selection; however rare it is, wherever it appears it is selected against. For this reason there are more recessive than dominant forms of mental subnormality.

A schematic representation of the main features of dominant and recessive inheritance, as they are likely to show themselves clinically, can be drawn up, as below.

If the gene is carried by one of the X chromosomes, its effects will show *sex-linkage*. Nearly all such genes are recessive, and accordingly show little or no effect in the heterozygous female, but show their full effect in the male. The pedigree of a family affected by such a condition is very characteristic. Sex-linked recessive conditions are often very severe and lethal. Sex-linkage must be distinguished from *sex-limitation*. Genes determining sex-limited conditions are carried on the autosomes, but produce their effects in one sex but not in the other. Complete sex-limitation is very rare, though certain genetically determined types of pseudohermaphroditism occur only in males (e.g. the XY 'female', the testicular feminization syndrome). Partial sex-limitation, in which effects are more frequent or shown more grossly in one sex than the other, is, on the

	Dominant	Recessive
Incidence in relatives of index case		
parents	50 per cent	small
sibs	50 per cent	25 per cent
children	50 per cent	small
Remoter relatives likely to show	ascendants	
the condition	collaterals	collaterals
	descendants	
Parental consanguinity	not specially frequent	much more frequent than expectation
Manifestation in phenotype		
age of onset	often late	usually early
severity	often mild	usually severe
variability of clinical features	often very variable	usually a clear-cut syndrome

other hand a common phenomenon, and one of great theoretical importance in understanding the mechanisms by which genes produce their effect.

Characteristics of Recessive Conditions

The manifestation of recessive conditions depends on the presence of two matching genes, one coming from each parent. An individual who possesses the gene in double dose in this way is called a *homozygote*. The parents of a homozygote possess only one of the genes in question, and they are called *heterozygotes*. It is characteristic for the parents to be unaffected, though in some cases the carrier state may be detected by special tests, as in phenylketonuria and galactosaemia. A proportion of roughly one in four sibs of patients with recessive forms of mental defect may be expected to be affected. On a theoretical basis there is a risk that two out of every four sibs in a sibship containing an individual with a recessive form of defect will be apparently symptomless carriers. Marriage between blood relatives increases the risk of mating between two carriers of rare genes because such people may be expected to have a number of genes in common. By such a mating the offspring would receive the gene in double dose, getting one affected gene from each parent, which is necessary for the manifestation of a recessive condition. Therefore cousin marriage is found more commonly between the parents of patients with rare recessive defects than in the general population.

This can be seen from the formula

$$c = \frac{a}{a+16p}$$

which relates c, the frequency of a first-cousin marriage in the parents of a trait-bearer, with a, the frequency of first-cousin marriages in the general population, and p, the gene frequency of the recessive gene determining the condition. It can be seen that as the magnitude of p diminishes, so the numerator and the denominator of the expression approximate towards one another, and c gets closer and closer to unity. If we take the frequency of phenylketonuria to be 25×10^{-6}, then the gene frequency will be 5×10^{-3}. We can estimate the frequency of first-cousin marriage in Britain today as being about 0·005; and combining these figures we find c to be $0·005/(0·005 + 0·08) = 0·06$. We would accordingly expect about one in every sixteen phenylketonurics to be the child of a first-cousin marriage, instead of about one in every two hundred. The figure found in practice is about 8 per cent.[1]

Characteristics of Dominant Conditions

Mendelian dominant conditions show their manifestations in the presence of one specific gene, the other gene of the pair being normal. Therefore these conditions are transmitted from one parent only to the child, and the parent who possesses and passes on the gene characteristically shows the clinical signs associated with the condition. The transmission of dominant genes can be traced in families without 'skipping' a generation. On a theoretical basis 50 per cent of the offspring of an affected parent may be expected to inherit the dominant gene, and 50 per cent to escape this inheritance.

Natural selection acts against the hereditary transmission of deleterious conditions, and one may ask why it is that deleterious dominant conditions are not eliminated from the population. Their propagation is not afforded the protection of the symptomless carrier state, as in the case of recessive genes. There are, however, three important mechanisms which keep the frequencies of deleterious dominant genes more or less level in a population. First, the manifestation of the gene may be variable, so that a number of individuals possessing it are only slightly affected and their fertility is not noticeably reduced. For example, the gene for neurofibromatosis (von Recklinghausen's disease) may be transmitted through several generations without noticeable clinical signs other than innocuous manifestations such as *café au lait* spots. Then an individual may appear in the family in which the gene causes severe effects, including neurological involvement and mental defect.

Secondly, the occurrence of fresh mutations is a major factor in keeping up the level of deleterious dominant genes. When a condition known to be associated with Mendelian dominant inheritance appears in a child of normal parents, and there are no signs of the condition in the sibs or other members of the family, it is not unlikely that a fresh mutation has occurred. Mutation rates are estimated per gamete (or gene, or chromosome), and the number of mutant individuals produced will be twice that figure. Mutation rates have been estimated in a number of conditions, notably in epiloia. Gunther and Penrose calculated that new cases of epiloia, arising by mutation, were appearing with a frequency between 1 in 60,000 and 1 in 120,000. In general, mutation rates lie in the neighbourhood of 1×10^{-5}.

---

[1] Penrose (1966) quotes figures from the United States (Jervis) 5 per cent, United Kingdom (Munro) 10 per cent, and Norway (Fölling) 14 per cent.

Thirdly, the effects of harmful dominant genes may be delayed until their possessors are well advanced into the reproductive period of their lives. In this way it is likely that before it is known that they carry the gene, they will have passed on the gene to at least some of their children. A good example of a condition in which this mechanism is seen to work is Huntington's chorea. The mean age of onset for the chorea and the dementia is around 44. In such conditions it would be of immense value in genetical counselling to discover prodromal signs or biochemical markers which could be detected early on denoting the presence of the meanwhile silent gene.

Polygenic Inheritance

Dominance and recessivity are not the rule when we are dealing with the effects of physiological genes. To take a well-known example, the genes determining the blood groups: AO heterozygotes manifest the A antigens, BO heterozygotes the B antigens, and AB individuals carry both antigens on their red cells. Furthermore, when we are dealing with characteristics in which there is quantitative variation (e.g. stature, intelligence, fertility, longevity, etc.), we can expect that a very large number of genes will be exerting some of their effects in contributing to variance. Genetical theories of natural selection usually suppose that a large contribution to evolutionary advance has been made by the accumulation of physiological genes causing minor differences in such biologically important variables.

It has been pointed out that our knowledge of human variation in intelligence, as measured in IQ tests, could be accounted for by no more than 5 gene pairs. We can assume that at each locus the two allelomorphs would be equally frequent, and neither would be dominant to the other. Giving positive deviations to genes indicated by capitals and negative deviations to genes indicated by lower case letters, we would have 11 classes of individuals from aabbccddee at the left extreme to AABBCCDDEE at the right extreme, the first scoring zero points, the latter 10 points. The relative numbers of persons scoring respectively 0, 1 ... up to 10 points will be the coefficients in the expansion of $(1+1)^{10}$, i.e. 1, 10, 45, 120, 210, 252, 210, 120, 45, 10, 1. This distribution is shown in FIGURE 1, and it will be seen how closely it resembles the Normal or Gaussian curve. We could regard this distribution as covering the spread of IQs in the general population within the limits of $\pm 3.3 \, \sigma$ either side of the mean, say from IQs averaging 45 up to IQs averaging 155. The mean would be at 100, and σ about 17·4 points of IQ.

We can be reasonably sure that polygenic factors provide the main genetical contribution to variance in intelligence, though there is some reason to think that dominance may also enter the picture. Dominance on any material scale is likely to cause an observed distribution to deviate from Normality; but differences in gene frequencies between two alleles, and variation in such differences from locus to locus, leave the curve still closely approximating to Normality if a large number of genes is involved; the expansion of $(p+q)^n$ is strongly skewed if p is much greater than q and n is small, but not so over the main body of the curve if n is large. Distributions of many kinds tend strongly towards Normality when many factors are involved; and as Normal distributions are very easy to handle statistically, this fact is a fairly firm foundation for a great deal of observational and experimental data, and the tests of statistical significance to which they are subjected. In practice, workers do not bother much with binomial distributions, and hypothesize the many (= infinite number of) factors which make the mathematics easy.

Polygenic inheritance is not only the preferred hypothesis for accounting for variation in intelligence, but also for variation in the predisposition to neurotic

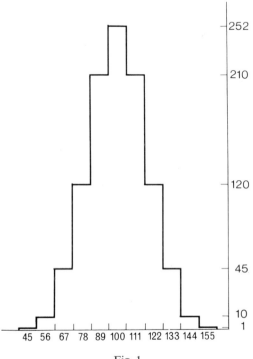

Fig. 1

reactions. Multifactorial inheritance, as it is also called, will be discussed in some detail in both the chapters of this book concerned with these topics. However, the possibility of applying multifactorial genetical theories is much wider than that. We now recognize that multifactorial variation may cause quantitative variations in bodily processes which may be subject to threshold effects. An elegant example is provided by the harelip cleft palate syndrome. In the normal individual the embryonic layers developing into buccal and nasopharyngeal regions join together at a certain developmental age so as to shut off the nasal cavities from the mouth. However, union may be delayed, if by a little, enough to produce a minor degree of hare-lip, if by more, enough to produce the full syndrome; intermediate degrees of delay producing intermediate degrees of failure of closure. The work of C. O. Carter and his colleagues has clearly demonstrated the multifactorial, or polygenic, basis of this phenomenon; and we have the resulting instructive example of quantitative variation producing an all-or-none effect (syndrome either present or absent, even though if present variable in degree). Many common disorders, in so far as they have a genetical basis, are likely to be based multifactorially; and threshold effects in medicine are widespread and important. Of particular importance to psychiatry is the possibility of a multifactorial basis (with threshold effect) for the predisposition to schizophrenia, which is dealt with in the chapters that follow.

2

SCHIZOPHRENIA: THE OBSERVATIONS

DEFINITION

'Schizophrenia', as the name for a category of mental illnesses, is somewhat differently used by different clinicians, and there are systematic differences between schools of psychiatry, between countries and between continents. In general, European countries, including the United Kingdom, Scandinavia, Mediterranean countries and Slavic countries, tend to use the term in a way which is still fairly close to the original Kraepelinian definition of 'dementia praecox' as it subsequently became modified by Eugen Bleuler under the name 'schizophrenia'. In the North American continent (but not in the Spanish and Portuguese cultures of South America), the term has become more and more widely extended, until now it has become very doubtful what it does mean. There are, for instance, very few European clinicians who would assert that (so-called) 'childhood schizophrenia' has any relationship with the schizophrenic illnesses of adult life, though some American clinicians would.

For the purposes of genetical research, it is clearly necessary to use an operational definition which will command a reasonable degree of agreement. Fortunately this has in practice been the case. Early workers on the genetics of schizophrenia, who composed the Munich school (Ernst Rüdin, Hans Luxenburger and Bruno Schulz as its foremost workers) kept to the established European usage, which was contemporaneously being strengthened and made more precise by workers of the Heidelberg 'phenomenological' school. Later investigators such as Kallmann had been trained in the same psychiatric background, to which also adhered the Scandinavians such as Strömgren and Essen-Möller.

American workers have adopted an entirely different standpoint. In so far as they came to genetical research from the field of clinical psychiatry, their background has been little if at all influenced by the phenomenological discipline imposed by Jaspers and Gruhle but much more affected by psychodynamic schools, especially the Freudian. However, in recent years genetical research in psychiatry has attracted interest from men with other backgrounds, such as psychology or brain chemistry, who, when they enter the clinical psychiatric field, try to satisfy both American and European requirements. Rosenthal and Kety, to mention two of them, while making personal use of a rather broad American concept of schizophrenia (accepting borderline schizophrenics and pseudoneurotic schizophrenics as index cases), provide the information on which the reader can make his own more restrictive limitations, if he wishes. In this way European and American standards in diagnosis have been brought closer together in psychiatric genetics.

For the purposes of this chapter, schizophrenia is to be regarded as an illness affecting the mind and the personality of the patient in a way which is seldom completely resolved. After an attack of illness there is nearly always some degree of permanent change of personality, even though there may be complete restitution of apparent mental health and social capacity. If there are repeated attacks of illness, or if a single illness continues for a longer time, the probability of personality change, and the degree of such change if it occurs, will be the greater. We conceive this personality change as basically organic in nature, so that we cannot expect to define it completely in solely psychological terms. Its main effect is to erode the capacity for functioning at the highest conceptual and affective levels, so that the patient is likely to be to some extent de-individualized and dehumanized; above all the capacity for normal affective response is likely to be diminished. Illnesses of this kind may at times be imperceptible in onset and insidious in development; but much more usually they occur in one or more acute attacks of relatively severe illness with florid symptomatology, followed by remissions in which restitution of the personality may proceed back to normality or near it. The symptoms of the acute illness are in many ways characteristic, focal disturbances of central nervous function occurring in a setting of general lucidity; hallucinations (especially in the auditory field), passivity feelings, primary delusional experiences, and rather typical forms of thought disorder.

GENERAL POPULATION RISKS

One may obtain an estimate of the expectancy (morbidity risk) of schizophrenia for a population group as the accumulated risk that faces the average member of that group, of developing a schizophrenic illness at some time in his life between birth and survival to the age of x years. It is convenient to ignore the way in which this estimate would be affected by the risk of mortality at intervening ages, as by leaving this out of account we can compare different populations with one another without making allowances for differences between the two populations in age-specific mortality rates.

The risk of a schizophrenic illness varies with age, as shown in TABLE 1. The table shows the mean values of admission rates per million of population

TABLE 1

ADMISSION RATE FOR SCHIZOPHRENIA

FIRST ADMISSIONS TO MENTAL HOSPITALS, PER MILLION OF THE
HOME POPULATION, ENGLAND AND WALES, 1952–1960

AGE GROUPS	ANNUAL ADMISSION RATE PER MILLION M	F	SEX RATIO M/F
10 to	13·2	15·2	0·87
15 to	228·8	193·4	1·18
20 to	427·0	290·8	1·47
25 to	415·4	341·2	1·22
35 to	223·2	235·8	0·95
45 to	96·4	165·4	0·58
55 to	53·4	111·2	0·48
65 to	26·2	61·8	0·42
75+	14·2	37·2	0·38

for the 5 years, 1952, 1954, 1956, 1958 and 1960, which are given by the Registrar General in his Review for the year 1960. These 5 years are roughly comparable, although there is a drop in admission rates in the youngest age groups and a rise in the admission rates in the oldest age groups, over the span of the decade, which holds good both for males and females. It will be seen from the table that the pattern of rates of admission by age differs a lot between the two sexes, the males tending to be admitted at younger ages than the females. The sex ratio, male admissions to female admissions, climbs to a peak between 20 and 25, and afterwards drops until at later ages about twice as many females as males are being admitted to hospital. If one were to assume that in a population at risk all age groups from 10 to 65 years were equally represented, one could calculate the mean age of first admission for males as 32 years and for females as 36 years. These are approximately the points at which 50 per cent of the total risk will have been survived, omitting consideration of the risk of a first illness after the age of 65.

For each sex separately we can calculate the probability of surviving from year to year without developing a schizophrenic illness sufficiently severe to require admission to hospital, and multiply these probabilities together to get a final survival rate by any given age [TABLE 2]. It seems reasonable to take the

TABLE 2

AGE DISTRIBUTION OF RISK OF SCHIZOPHRENIA

AGE-DISTRIBUTED RISK OF SCHIZOPHRENIA, ENGLAND AND WALES 1952–1960, CALCULATED FROM FIGURES OF TABLE 1

| | GENERAL POPULATION EXPECTANCY, ACCUMULATED RISK (PER CENT) | | PROPORTION OF TOTAL RISK TO AGE OF 55 SURVIVED (PER CENT) | |
BY AGE OF	M	F	M	F
15	0·0067	0·0077	0·6	0·8
20	0·1210	0·1044	11·4	10·6
25	0·3341	0·2495	31·4	25·3
30	0·5409	0·4197	50·8	43·5
35	0·7473	0·5896	70·2	59·7
40	0·8580	0·7067	80·6	71·6
45	0·9687	0·8237	91·0	83·4
50	1·0163	0·9056	95·5	91·7
55	1·0640	0·9875	100·0	100·0
60	1·0904	1·0427		
65	1·1168	1·0978		

age of 55 as a stopping point; after that age risks of a first schizophrenic illness are declining fast, and clinicians are becoming progressively less sure of a primarily schizophrenic and non-organic diagnosis. This final survival rate for the male is 0·98936 and for the female 0·99013. Subtracting these figures from 1, we find the total risk of becoming schizophrenic at some time in one's life before the age of 55, granted survival to that age, is just about the same for both sexes, i.e. 1 per cent (1·064 per cent and 0·987 per cent).

These figures correspond very closely with the figure obtained by Norris for the United Kingdom in 1959, based on national data, i.e. 1·07 per cent for males and 0·97 per cent for females. Norris also made a parallel investigation for the area of three mental hospitals, and obtained the very similar figures of 0·93 per cent for males and 1·16 per cent for females.

Some authorities regard national figures as liable to provide a somewhat distorted estimate of the expectancy of schizophrenia, since on the one hand there will have been no ascertainment of persons who have had a schizophrenic illness and who yet were never required to enter a psychiatric hospital; and one is also relying on diagnoses made in different hospitals at different times by clinicians of very varying experience and standards of diagnosis. Many attempts have accordingly been made to estimate the expectancy by the personal investigation of population samples, such as all persons born in a given region in a stated year, or the entire population of a delimited geographical area (such as Fremming's investigation of the island of Bornholm). In investigations of such kinds it is possible to obtain information from a variety of sources about every suspected schizophrenic, so as to make sure both of the diagnosis and of the approximate age of onset. Relatively small samples of the population surveyed are obtained; but as in some countries such as Germany, a number of different workers have tackled the problem from time to time by slightly different methods, and their samples have been found to be statistically compatible, summing of the samples eventually produces an impressive total. However large the total, it might be vitiated by systematic sources of bias and error. If they exist, these sources of systematic error have not been identified. One can only suspect that the differences between countries, and the differences between estimates made in one country in different eras, may be caused, not so much by real differences in the frequency of schizophrenic psychoses as by differences in the thoroughness of ascertainment, changes in clinical habits in formulating diagnoses, etc.

TABLE 3 shows mean values for estimated expectancies in a number of European countries, and it will be seen that there is statistically significant

TABLE 3

EXPECTATION OF SCHIZOPHRENIA IN VARIOUS COUNTRIES, FROM SUMMATED
RESULTS OF INVESTIGATIONS CONDUCTED OVER STATED TIME INTERVAL
(Data from Zerbin-Rüdin, 1967a)

DATE	COUNTRY	NUMBER OF INVESTIGATIONS	NUMBER OF INDIVIDUALS	WEIGHTED MEAN EXPECTANCY (PER CENT)	RANGE	STANDARD ERROR
1928–1950	Germany	8	26,409·5	0·42	0·35–1·40	0·0398
1929–1962	Switzerland	3	68,561	2·38	0·98–2·40	0·0582
1938–1951	Denmark	3	23,251	0·69	0·47–0·90	0·0543
1935–1956	Sweden	4	13,617	1·25	0·68–2·85	0·0952
1942	Finland	1	194,000	0·91		0·0216
1964	Iceland	1	4,913·5	0·73		0·1214
	Total	20	330,752	1·17	0·42–2·38	0·0187

The number of individuals observed is corrected for age by counting individuals as half only if within the limits of the hypothetical risk period, age 14 to age 40 with most authors.

variation between them. Some values are very high indeed, so that it may be improper to combine them with much lower estimates. Perhaps the estimate for all countries together, 1·17 per cent, is unrealistic; omitting the Swiss figures, we get a global estimate of the expectation of schizophrenia for the European general population as 0·85 per cent. It has been the custom in psychiatric genetical work in the past to take 0·8 per cent or 0·85 per cent as the general population risk.

It is of course quite possible that schizophrenia is commoner in Switzerland than in the other countries studied. There is every reason to believe that, in the isolated population studied by Böök in a remote part of Sweden north of the Arctic Circle, the population risk of schizophrenia, which he estimated as 2·85 per cent, is significantly higher than in southern Sweden. Local differences in gene frequencies in respect of rare pathogenic genes have been repeatedly demonstrated, and also in common genes causing physiological differences, e.g. in blood groups. One feature shown by Böök's population, which makes one feel reasonably sure that in that case differences in gene frequency are involved, is that the schizophrenic illnesses when they occurred conformed to a not very usual catatonic pattern, with a good deal of similarity from case to case. It is also noteworthy that in this population-isolate Böök found practically no manic-depressive illness.

INCIDENCE OF SCHIZOPHRENIA IN RELATIVES OF SCHIZOPHRENICS

There has been a considerable number of independent investigations into the occurrence of schizophrenia among the relatives of schizophrenic index cases, and the results of about twenty-five of them have been summarized by Zerbin-Rüdin (1967a). These statistics in simplified form are shown in TABLE 4. This

TABLE 4

EXPECTATION OF SCHIZOPHRENIA FOR RELATIVES OF
SCHIZOPHRENICS

(Figures extracted from tables of Zerbin-Rüdin, 1967a)

DATE	INVESTIGA-TIONS	RELATIONSHIP	N	SCHIZOPHRENIC	EXPECTATION %	S.E.
1928–62	14	Parents (uncorrected)	7675	336	4·38	0·23
1928–62	12	Sibs	8504·5	724	8·51	0·30
1932–62	10	Sibs (parents free of schizophrenia)	7535	621	8·24	0·32
1932–62	6	Sibs (parents not free of schizophrenia)	674·5	93	13·79	1·33
1921–62	5	Children	1226·5	151	12·31	0·94
1930–41	4	Uncles and aunts	3376	68	2·01	0·24
1916–46	3	Half-sibs	311	10	3·22	1·00
1926–38	5	Nephews and nieces	2315	52	2·25	0·30
1928–38	4	Grandchildren	713	20	2·81	0·62
1928–41	4	First cousins	2438·5	71	2·91	0·34

N is corrected for age distribution (= Bezugsziffer)

table includes only the 'certain' schizophrenics; if doubtful cases had been added, the calculated morbid risks would have been increased by about one-quarter proportionately. The table conceals the amount of variation between the results obtained by different investigators, but this can be illustrated by the data shown in TABLE 5. The range shown between minimum and maximum

TABLE 5

RESULTS OF INVESTIGATIONS INTO THE MORBID RISK FOR
SCHIZOPHRENIA IN RELATIVES OF SCHIZOPHRENIC INDEX CASES

RELATIONSHIP TO INDEX CASES	N	RANGE	MEAN	STANDARD DEVIATION
			ESTIMATES OF SCHIZOPHRENIA IN RELATIVES AS PER CENT	
Sibs	12	3·3–14·3	8·56	3·40
Children	6	7·0–16·9	11·52	3·66

N = number of independent investigations

estimates, and the standard deviation of grouped estimates, are uncomfortably high, and are presumably much influenced by different standards of diagnosis of secondary cases and of thoroughness of work in the field.

Turning to TABLE 4, and looking at the figures given for first-degree relatives, one sees that the expectation for the parents of schizophrenics is much lower than for either sibs or children. However, it is rare for a schizophrenic to produce a child after the onset of the schizophrenia, so that we can assume that there was a negligible risk of schizophrenia for the parent of the schizophrenic index case before the index patient was himself born. This means that, to calculate the number of risk-lifetimes observed, which will be the denominator in calculating the expectancy of schizophrenia for the parents, the numbers of mothers and fathers will each of them have to be reduced to a small fraction of themselves, a smaller fraction in the case of fathers than of mothers. The logic at the basis of these considerations has been explained by Essen-Möller (1955, 1963). In order to make an appropriate adjustment to allow for the part of the total risk of schizophrenia which will have been successfully survived at the time of the birth of the index case, information is needed about the ages of the parents at the time of the birth of the probands. This is not often available. Essen-Möller (1963) considered three sources of material (Alanen, 1958; Essen-Möller, 1955; and Goodman, 1957). A mean value for the proportion of the total risk survived was, in the case of mothers 0·58, in the case of fathers 0·80. If we say that for parents in general we can expect 0·69 of the total risk to have been survived at the time of the birth of the proband, then in the case of the average parent we are only observing the expectancy of schizophrenia in a fraction 0·31 of the risk-lifetime. If we multiply the number of parents in TABLE 3 by 0·31, we find that 336 have become schizophrenic in the course of 2379·25 lifetimes, an expectancy of 14·12 per cent. Although no great reliance can be placed upon this figure, we can be reasonably sure that the risk for the parents of schizophrenics is approximately the same as for their sibs and their children, and that this risk is in the neighbourhood of 10 per cent. There is, in fact, no reason to think that, from the genetical point of view, parents and sibs and children should not be regarded as more or less on the same footing. The fact that there is no reason to think that the risk is very different for the sibs of schizophrenics on the one hand and the children of schizophrenics on the other, must be counted as an argument against a mode of inheritance of the recessive type. It is compatible with either polygenic inheritance or a simple dominance.

In investigations on the sibs of schizophrenics some authors have classified their material according to the psychiatric status of the parents. It is therefore possible to give separately the risk for the sib of a schizophrenic given: (1) that his parents were free of a suspicion that either might have had a schizophrenic illness; and (2) that one was or might have been schizophrenic. It will be seen that the risk for the sibs in the two cases is not so very different, in (1) 8 per cent, in (2) 14 per cent. This difference will be discussed when we come to consider the mode of inheritance [p. 56].

Much interest has, very naturally, been taken in the risks of schizophrenia for the children when both parents are schizophrenic. Families where this has happened are, of course, rare; and if a fair estimate of the risks is to be made it is important that they should be ascertained without bias. Ascertainment via a schizophrenic child of such a union is likely to be biased. Only five investigators have studied this question, and their results (summarized by Slater, 1968) can be reduced to the following [TABLE 6]:

TABLE 6
CHILDREN OF TWO PARENTS BOTH SCHIZOPHRENIC,
OBSERVATIONAL DATA

N (= Bezugsziffer, i.e. corrected for age)	134·0
(a) of these definitely schizophrenic	49
(b) probably schizophrenic	13
expectancy of schizophrenia	
(a)	$0·366 \pm 0·0416$
(a+b)	$0·463 \pm 0·0431$

Probably the greatest interest these figures have is their bearing on the hypothesis that the genetic basis of schizophrenia is a single gene of major effect manifesting in the homozygote, i.e. recessive. If for all schizophrenic illnesses a single such gene was responsible, then all schizophrenics would be homozygous for it; all their children would be homozygous too, and accordingly all schizophrenic in the fullness of time. As this is obviously not the case, one must conclude that some more complex model will have to be thought of.

WORK ON TWINS

In Appendix A the reader will find an account of the theoretical basis of work with twins done with a view to obtaining information about the genetical background; and it is pointed out there that twin analysis can also make a contribution towards the detection of significant environmental factors. The most systematic work has been done by a group of workers at Bethesda, led by Pollin, who collected discordant pairs from all over the United States and took them into observation together with other members of their families. The results so far obtained (Pollin and Stabenau, 1968) are suggestive and interesting without being conclusive of the primary importance of any single environmental factor. Comparing index twins with the spared co-twins, Pollin and Stabenau report a preponderance in the former of lesser weight at birth, cyanosis at birth, neonatal medical complications, 'soft' neurological signs, and on the temperamental side dependence, submissiveness, fearfulness, compliance.

These findings run along much the same lines as those of earlier workers who were investigating systematically-gathered series of twins, regardless of concordance (Slater, 1953; Tienari, 1963; Kringlen, 1967). They, too, found that the relatively more severely affected member of an MZ pair was the one who had been less active, less energetic, less extraverted, had had a less successful premorbid social history, and had shown a relative passivity or submission in the intrapair relationship.

THE RISK OF SCHIZOPHRENIA FOR THE TWINS OF SCHIZOPHRENICS

Earlier Studies

It is convenient to discuss the work done on the twins of schizophrenics over two periods, earlier and later. While the methods of investigation have not changed very greatly, the selection of patients for study has changed a good deal, and there is a consistent difference between the results of earlier and later studies in respect of estimated risks of schizophrenia for co-twins. The principal concern of the earlier workers was to collect a sample of schizophrenic patients in whose cases there would be no possibility of quibble about the diagnosis. This meant that doubtful and borderline cases were not included, and a considerable part of the case material was made up of long-stay hospitalized cases. This does not apply to the Essen-Möller study (1941). Later workers have been less concerned to defend themselves against possible criticism on the basis of an insufficiently certain diagnosis of the index case, and more concerned to collect as representative a series of schizophrenics as possible. One method has been to take into the series patients serially admitted to a psychiatric service, however mild or transitory the illness which brought them under observation, provided a diagnosis of schizophrenia by a responsible clinician was attained (Gottesman and Shields). In Denmark (Fischer) and Norway (Kringlen) twins have been found by a systematic search of a national register of psychotics. Tienari's Finnish study started with twins and proceeded to the discovery of the schizophrenics among them.

The twin method requires one to ascertain by as reliable and fair a method as possible those in a series of patients who fill the clinical criteria, and who were born one of a pair of twins, or in a multiple birth. One will then select those who have a living twin of the same sex, or have had such a twin who survived up to a given age, say the lower limit of the age of onset of the disorder being investigated. The next step is to endeavour to make contact with this twin, since a personal interview is extremely important if it can be in any way attained, and to obtain all relevant psychiatric information about him from the patient who was the proband, from other relatives, from hospital records, and other sources of information. This work involves field work on an intensive level. When all the information is to hand, it will be possible to make a judgement whether the co-twin of the proband has or has not himself had a schizophrenic illness, or perhaps whether he shows 'schizoid' traits of personality.

It is not possible for the primary field investigator, if he is to do his work adequately, to be shielded from information about the proband, and about the type of twinship whether MZ or DZ, when he comes to see the co-twin. However, demands tend to be made nowadays that when the eventual diagnosis of the co-twin is made for statistical purposes it shall be guarded as far as possible against subjective biases. This may mean that the results of field work are collected by one worker and evaluated by another, the latter carrying out this task without knowledge of the psychiatric state of the other member of the twin pair. If these precautions are taken, concordance rates within twin pairs will tend to be rated somewhat lower than when field worker and evaluator are one and the same. Some clinicians will be inclined to diagnose an atypical psychosis as schizophrenic if they know that the co-twin had an illness which began very similarly and eventually went on to a typical schizophrenic state. Others may be tempted to go in the opposite direction, and to suspect a case of induced *folie à deux* where the illness of one twin has occurred in a close time sequence with that of the other. However that may be, one may doubt whether the figures obtained by the more elaborate procedure are actually to be preferred to the ones obtained when the evaluator is in possession of all the information, and not only a part of it.

TABLE 7, in which the older twin studies are shown, exhibits the observational data relating to twin pairs with one schizophrenic member in their simplest

TABLE 7

OBSERVATIONAL DATA RELATING TO TWIN PAIRS
WITH ONE SCHIZOPHRENIC MEMBER

		MZ PAIRS			SS DZ PAIRS		
INVESTIGATOR	DATE	N	C	%	N	C	%
Luxenburger	1928	19	11	58	13	0	0
Rosanoff	1934	41	25	61	53	7	13
Essen-Möller	1941	11	7	64	27	4	15
Kallmann	1946	174	120	69	296	34	11
Slater	1953	37	24	65	58	8	14
Inouye	1961	55	33	60	11	2	18

N shows the number of pairs investigated, and c the number found concordant, i.e. with a schizophrenic co-twin. Monozygotic pairs compared with same-sexed dizygotic pairs. (After Gottesman and Shields, 1966b.)

possible form. In some series some probable but not certain schizophrenic probands have been included. Age corrections, which have the effect of increasing concordance rates, have not been used; and the analysis is in terms of pairs observed. A logically correcter method, the proband method, demands that if both members of a twin pair have been independently ascertained as schizophrenic, the pair should be counted twice over. The difference this refinement makes to the final figures is not very large in most series, and on average yields concordance rates which are higher than the pairwise rates by about a quarter. The difference is due to the fact that each member of a doubly ascertained pair has to be taken as an independent propositus in the proband method, so that doubly ascertained pairs are counted twice. The logical basis of the proband method is shown in Appendix C.

It will be seen from the table that results from one series to another are remarkably consistent; the means for the six different investigators are respectively 63 per cent and 12 per cent. The risk for DZ twins of schizophrenics is not very much more than for sibs (9 per cent), and so does not suggest that the common factors in the background resulting from being born into a family at the same time, which hold for twins and not for sibs, have a very marked effect. The risk for MZ twins is more than five times as great; and the difference between the two series of twins gives great weight to the genetical hypothesis.

Recent Studies

TABLES 8 and 9 show the results obtained in recent twin series dating from 1968. The first involves some reconstruction of the primary data provided by the authors (and one re-diagnosis of a Tienari co-twin); the second gives the authors' own assessments of their minimum and maximum concordance rates. It will be seen that these rates are considerably lower than in the older series, ranging between 10 per cent and 40 per cent, with the mean concordance for all pairs taken together = 27 per cent. It is generally agreed that the principal reason for the difference in concordance rates between the older and the more recent series is due to a difference in the selection of the primary index cases. This has been discussed on an earlier page.

TABLE 8
RECENT TWIN STUDIES: MZ PAIRS

	BOTH STRICT SCHIZOPHRENIA			STRICT SCHIZOPHRENIA + PROBABLE SCHIZOPHRENIA − LIKE FUNCTIONAL PSYCHOSIS				INCLUDING ALL 'BORDERLINE' CO-TWINS		
	N	C	%	N	C	%	%*	N	C	%
Tienari (1968)	10	1	10	14	2	14	20	16	5	31
Kringlen (1968)	45	12	27	55	17	31	45	55	21	38
Fischer et al. (1969)	21	5	24	21	10	48	56	21	10	48
Gottesman and Shields (personal commn.)	20	8	40	22	11	50	58	22	11	50
Totals	96	26	27	112	40	36		114	47	41

N = number of pairs, C = those found concordant, with one co-twin in the Tienari series re-diagnosed by us as schizophrenic. %* shows the concordance rate calculated by the proband method. (With assistance from J. Shields.)

TABLE 9

RANGE OF RECENT SCHIZOPHRENIC TWIN STUDIES

	N	MZ %	N	DZ %
Tienari	16	6–36	22	5–14
Kringlen	55	25–38	90	4–10
Fischer	21	24–48	41	10–19
Gottesman and Shields	22	40–50	33	9–10

Uncorrected Pairwise Concordance, reported by investigators (various criteria) including 'borderline features' when diagnosed. (With assistance from J. Shields.)

There are strong reasons for thinking that evidence of genetical predisposition shows up more clearly in severely ill than in mild cases. Kringlen (1967) rated the severity of the incapacity of his twins, categories VII, VI and V being the most severe, in order of decreasing severity, but all involving gross impairment, chiefly of psychotic type. The concordance rate for schizophrenia or schizophreniform psychosis in the co-twins of index cases in these three grades was respectively 60, 31 and 25 per cent. It seems very probable that this relationship between severity of psychosis and concordance rate accounts for a large part of the differences in results between the older studies and the recent ones. Another factor which may have entered is the distribution of the sexes in the older studies, in which females preponderated in the index cases, and recent studies, in which the sexes have been more equally balanced. It is usually found that female pairs are more frequently concordant than male pairs, though this was not so in Kringlen's series. There are many possible explanations for the sex difference, including the consideration that a pair of brothers are likely to encounter much more various environments than a pair of sisters. Finally, it does seem to be the case that concordance rates run lower in the Scandinavian countries (Essen-Möller, Fischer, Kringlen, Tienari) than in the rest of Europe, or the United States.

In the modern series the greater vagueness of clinical definition of the index cases is paralleled by greater difficulty in determining what degree of mental abnormality is to be accepted as signifying schizophrenia in co-twins. As is shown in the table, if one includes psychotic states which were probably but not certainly schizophrenic, the mean concordance rate in MZ pairs goes up from 27 per cent to 36 per cent; and if one includes also cases with borderline psychotic features, the concordance rate goes into the range 36–50 per cent.

RISK OF SCHIZOPHRENIA AND SEX

There is no great difference between the sexes with respect to the total risk of schizophrenia; but this risk is rather differently distributed by age [see p. 11], being higher in males at early ages and higher in females later on. Most observers, however, have found a higher degree of concordance between members of female MZ pairs than between members of male MZ pairs, Kringlen being one of the few investigators who found no difference. Gottesman and Shields (1966b) have shown, however, that this sex difference depends on the mode of selection of the samples studied. Where patients have been selected from the standing populations of hospitals, female pairs have been found to outnumber male pairs, and the bulk of the female excess has been in long-standing chronic and severe cases. The greater concordance in female than in male pairs, there-fore, might be the result only of greater chronicity and severity of the case material in the females than the males. This is supported by the finding that, when series of patients are sampled by consecutive ascertainment on admission, the sex difference is no longer shown. This is exhibited in TABLE 10.

TABLE 10
CONCORDANCE BY SEX AND SAMPLING: STUDIES INVESTIGATING
BOTH SEXES AND REPORTING THE RESULTS SEPARATELY

SAMPLES (MZ PAIRS)	N		CONCORDANCE FOR SCHIZOPHRENIA (PER CENT)	
	M	F	M	F
Based on consecutive admissions	59	53	46	47
Not so based	55	84	51	71
All studies	114	137	48	62

(From Shields, 1968a)

On the whole it seems unlikely that there is a systematic difference between the sexes in respect of concordance within MZ pairs, or, indeed, in the penetrance of the schizophrenic gene or genes in the two sexes.

OTHER PSYCHIATRIC CONDITIONS IN THE MZ CO-TWINS

It would be very desirable to recognize, if we could, the schizophrenic genotype, even where there has as yet been no schizophrenic breakdown. Apart from schizophrenia, other mental illnesses occur in the families of schizophrenics, particularly affective illnesses. In the MZ co-twins of schizophrenics borderline states are common as well as deviations of personality and neurotic reactions; so far no one has reported a typical manic-depressive illness in the MZ co-twin of a schizophrenic. Numerous attempts have been made to define the 'schizoid' personality; the consensus view is that such personality traits are found in excess among first degree relatives of schizophrenics, and are also found in excess in the premorbid personality of the patient himself, i.e. tendencies to withdrawal, to sensitivity and a paranoid attitude, deficient initiative and energy, deficient warmth and responsiveness of affect. A modern attempt to describe the personality of the genetical schizotype is provided by Meehl (1962). Somewhat similar traits of personality have been found in investigations of MZ pairs to be shown in greater degree by that one of the pair who was eventually the more severely affected: less vigour, more passivity, more submissiveness, dependence and anxiety, more neurotic traits in childhood, more solitary or unsociable or eccentric lives later (Inouye, Kringlen, Slater, Tienari). Of course one is tempted to regard such traits of personality as manifestations of the schizophrenic gene or genes, short of showing as overt psychosis.

RELATION OF SCHIZOPHRENIA TO OTHER DISORDERS

At various times schizophrenia has been suspected of being related in some way to a number of other disorders, mental or physical. At one time the evidence that there was an association with tuberculosis seemed particularly strong. Not only was it found that there was a much higher risk of death from tuberculosis in hospitalized schizophrenics than in hospital patients suffering from other forms of mental illness, but also that there was an excess mortality from tuberculosis in their sibs. A parallel investigation (Manfred Bleuler) directed to estimating the risk of schizophrenia in patients suffering from tuberculosis and in their sibs did not find that the association showed up when approached from this side. In more recent years, since tuberculosis has become so much less of a scourge, this whole question has faded into insignificance; and together with it has gone one speculation (Kallmann) that the hereditary predisposition to schizophrenia was to be sought in an inadequacy of the reticulo-endothelial system.

Another association which has stimulated inquiry is that between schizophrenia and mental subnormality. The concept which was originally advanced was that there was a specific subtype of schizophrenia, *Pfropfschizophrenie*, in which mental subnormality in early years was combined with a schizophrenic development in later ones. This concept is now abandoned in that form. It was shown (Brugger, 1927) that among the relatives of pfropfschizophrenics could be found those who were mentally subnormal and those who became schizophrenic, but the combination was not propagated as such. Hallgren and Sjögren (1959) found that cases in which schizophrenia was combined with low-grade defect did tend to arise in the population in more than the expected number; but also that the incidence of schizophrenia in the sibs of defectives and the incidence of defect in the sibs of schizophrenics were not raised. There is accordingly no suggestion of any biological link.

In a more general form the speculation has been advanced that genes which in the duplex (homozygotic) state tended to cause mental defect might in single dose be responsible for one or another form of mental illness. It has, in fact, been particularly suggested that the heterozygotic carrier of the gene for phenylketonuria might be more than normally liable to depressive illnesses. Penrose (1935) had noted in the unaffected relatives of phenylketonurics a high incidence of paranoid illness in later life. Munro (1947) also found a high incidence of psychotic illness, which he classified as endogenous depression with paranoid features. The matter is discussed again on page 209.

Much attention has been given of late to what have been called the 'schizophrenic spectrum' disorders. It is undoubtedly the case that near relatives of schizophrenic patients, who may be supposed to carry some enhanced pre-disposition to schizophrenia, not only show an incidence of schizophrenic psychoses higher than in the general population, but also increased risks of other forms of mental illness, of suicide, of abnormalities of personality, and possibly also of alcoholism, criminality and other abnormalities of behaviour. Shields (1968a) has pointed out that in Slater's twin series nearly as many sibs of 158 schizophrenics (including atypical schizophrenics) had affective disorders as schizophrenia, and there were actually more parents with affective psychosis than schizophrenia—16 as against 12; 78 parents had other abnormalities, mostly personality disorders. If one takes pairs of relatives, both suffering from psychoses, all observers are agreed that concordance between members of the pair in respect of diagnosis is in excess of expectations on a random basis. This is shown in TABLE 11. However, in each of these series there is a considerable

TABLE 11

CONFORMITY OF DIAGNOSIS, SCHIZOPHRENIA OR NOT, IN PAIRS
OF RELATIVES BOTH HOSPITALIZED FOR PSYCHIATRIC DISORDER

| INVESTIGATOR | NO. OF PAIRS | RELATIONSHIP | DIAGNOSIS BY | SCHIZOPHRENIA DIAGNOSED IN | | | SIGNIF. LEVEL |
				BOTH	ONE ONLY	NEITHER	
Mitsuda	163	not specified	investigator	101	27	35	***
Ødegaard	197	first degree	hospital	55	65	77	***
Tsuang	71	sibs	hosp., ever	28	17	24	***
			hosp., final	13	25	33	*
			independent	9	27	35	n.s.

(After Shields, 1968a)

proportion of pairs in which one member was schizophrenic and the other not; in the two series of hospital diagnoses (Ødegaard and Tsuang) this is about one-third of the total material.

The question arises whether a considerable proportion of the psychoses occurring in the first-degree relatives of schizophrenics are, genotypically, schizophrenic, but not so recognized and diagnosed by the clinician. Owing to the uncertainties of the diagnostic method, and the variability of the sympto-matology, it would seem highly probable that this is the case. Schizophrenic illnesses have on the whole an earlier age of onset than affective psychoses; and in the single patient who has more than one attack during his life, schizo-phrenic symptomatology is likely to be shown more in the earlier than the later attack, and depressive symptomatology more in the later than the earlier one. It is, accordingly, not unexpected that when one proceeds from the schizo-phrenic patient back into the histories of his parents, one should find a fairly heavy incidence of affective illnesses, involutional depressions, and atypical pictures; and again, when one investigates the clinical histories of the children of patients who have suffered from affective psychoses, one should find a fair proportion who have become schizophrenic. The reverse situation does not occur: there is no excess of affective illness in the children of schizophrenics, and no excess of schizophrenia in the parents of affectively ill patients.

The most testing investigation of the relationship between schizophrenic and affective illness is provided by the study of the children of parents, both of whom have suffered from psychotic illnesses. TABLE 12 is adapted from Elsässer (1952), and shows the combined results obtained by three investigators, Elsässer, Schulz and Kahn. These show the psychoses running, on the whole, true to type. The psychotic children produced by purely schizophrenic matings are all schizophrenic; manic-depressive matings show more variability with one schizophrenic and three persons with atypical or unclear psychoses as well as the manic-depressive children. The matings between parents both of whom had an atypical psychosis produced a mixed bag of atypical, schizophrenic and manic-depressive psychotics. When a schizophrenic is mated to a manic-depressive, the main result is to produce schizophrenics and manic-depressives in equal numbers—and there is no larger number of atypical or doubtful psychoses than in the purely manic-depressive matings.

Summarizing the information available, we can say that the diathesis which supplies an enhanced risk of schizophrenia impairs the personality, the psychosomatic constitution or the capacity for adaptation in a more general and non-specific way. Above all, minor deviations of personality are likely, which may be recognizable as 'schizoid'; but in addition there is likely to be an increased risk of mental illnesses of a kind not readily diagnosable as schizophrenic.

This may be a convenient point to discuss briefly the problems which arise when atypical psychoses are observed in the first instance. We may think it probable that some of them are, genotypically, schizophrenic in nature, for the reason that such psychoses are found in the families of schizophrenics. However, atypical psychoses are also found in the families of manic-depressives; and as the Elsässer data have shown, atypical pictures may be common to both members of a parent-child pair. In the families of patients suffering from an atypical psychosis, it may be found (e.g. Smith, 1925) that the atypical manifestation seems to be the result of the merging of distinct and different strains; and, say, the 'schizo-affective' psychosis shown by the index case is associated with schizophrenic illnesses on one side of the family and affective illnesses on the other. It appears that this accounts for only a part of the clinical observations. There are families in which an atypical psychosis is repeated again and again down the generations, never distinctively schizophrenic or manic-depressive but showing a mixture of symptoms of a persistently specific quality. In such families each affected member in turn may have provided difficulties for the diagnostician, difficulties which disappear if one is content to diagnose yet another case of the family syndrome. Instructive pedigrees of this kind have been published by Leonhard (1959); and a very well observed family has been described by Kaij (1967), with the pedigree as shown [FIG. 2]. The pedigree is made a little complicated by the fact that two members of the family married consorts who became psychotic. These consorts and their children have to be dismissed from further consideration. But the psychoses of nine members, numbered in the pedigree, are available for clinical analysis. The psychosis shown by all these persons was one with an early onset, the age of first attack being from 18 to 31 with a mean of 24 years; the onset was nearly always acute; the illness had a tendency to recur, so that the nine individuals had a total of

TABLE 12

THE CHILDREN OF TWO PSYCHOTIC PARENTS

(After Elsässer, 1952)

NO. OF PARENTAL PAIRS	PARENTAL MATING	NO. OF CHILDREN OVER 16	NON-PSYCHOTIC CHILDREN			PSYCHOTIC CHILDREN (a CERTAINLY, b DOUBTFULLY)								
			NORMAL	DOUBTFUL	TOTAL	SCHIZ.		MAN. DEP.		ATYPICAL		? NATURE		TOTAL PERSONS
						a	b	a	b	a	b	a	b	
34	S×S	96	38	30	68	20	8	—	—	—	—	—	—	28
20	M×M	47	28	5	33	1	—	9	1	2	—	1	—	14
19	S×M	68	35	14	49	6	2	6	2	1	—	2	—	19
23	A×S	91	53	23	76	8	—	1	1	3	—	—	2	15
21	A×M	55	32	12	44	—	—	4	2	4	1	—	—	11
17	A×A	67	27	16	43	5	—	5	1	10	1	—	2	24

S = schizophrenic, M = manic-depressive, A = atypical; a = diagnosis certain, b = diagnosis uncertain. Among the 100 doubtfully normal children are 68 described as *mässig auffällig*, i.e. moderately conspicuous or deviant, 15 psychopaths, 10 persons with mental deficiency or neurological disease, and about 7 for whom there was insufficient information.

23 attacks; each attack tended to be of very short duration, 1–7 months, with mean of 3 months, with the exception of one attack in one case which went on for 18 months. The symptoms were those of agitation, often extreme, severe confusion or delirium, a markedly depressive or elated mood, hallucinations and delusions, bizarre behaviour and a more or less complete amnesia for the psychotic period. Recovery left the personality unaffected by the experience in most cases. The illness, in fact, was of an 'organic' rather than an atypically affective or schizophrenic kind; and organic causes (puerperium, infections, etc.) could be found in about half the cases. Stress was a factor, but in Kaij's

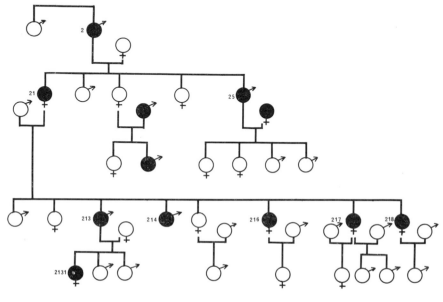

Fig. 2

opinion, a precipitant and not the main cause. The genetic basis was attributed to a single major (dominant) gene. This is not uncommonly the case where an atypical psychosis is repeated in the same form in several members of the one family. The clinical and family picture shown in Kaij's family is not unlike the psychotic states seen in porphyria, which is also due to a major gene manifesting as a dominant.

GENETIC HETEROGENEITY IN SCHIZOPHRENIA

Whatever genetical model we choose to adopt by which to understand the hereditary contribution to the causation of schizophrenia, we have to suppose that other factors will also play a part. These may be of two kinds, genetical and environmental. It is well known to general geneticists that the effects of a specific gene will be influenced by the genetical constitution of the individual as a whole, that is to say by all the other genes he has, or by the 'genotypic milieu'. It may well be that, if there is a specific gene for schizophrenia or some form or forms of schizophrenia, its manifestation as mental illness will be greater or less in certain types of bodily constitution (pyknic or leptosomatic, for instance) and in certain types of personality make-up (syntonic extraverted, for instance, or schizothyme introverted). Certain environmental stress factors, also, may tend to aid the manifestation of the hereditary predisposition, and certain environments may be equally protective.

It has been found that any factors which affect central nervous function, whether they are constitutional or environmental, may have an effect on gene manifestation. The onset of schizophrenia is obviously related to the age at which the individual finds himself; he is most in danger in early years after adolescence, and later in life tends to stabilize. However, there are late mani-festations of schizophrenia, e.g. late paraphrenia (Roth, 1957), which tend to be associated with a relatively low incidence of schizophrenia in first degree relatives, though one still higher than in the general population. One must suppose that in these cases the hereditary predisposition has in some way been attenuated, this attenuation however having been made good by reduction of adaptive reserves of the brain by an ageing process. It might be that the genetical pre-disposition in these cases was quantitatively reduced in degree; or it might be that, among these cases, the hereditarily predisposed individuals were mixed in with others in whom an apparently schizophrenic syndrome had been released by environmental stress. Roth and his co-workers have indeed shown that in these cases there were many in whom some form of sensory deprivation had played a part, especially in isolating the individual; but they also showed that a very high proportion of late paraphrenics exhibited lifelong traits of personality of a schizoid kind.

The same alternative presents itself when we consider the schizophrenic illnesses which arise after bodily illness or trauma. Schulz (1932) classified his very large group of sibships (according to the history of presence or absence of an effective stress factor in the index case) to make five groups: those in which there was no history of illness or trauma; those in which there was such a history, though thought to be improbable, either of a psychological or somatic kind, and those in which such a history was present and more probable, again either one of psychological or of somatic illness or trauma. The incidence of schizophrenia in the sibs of the index cases was not quite the same in each of these five groups, but there was no difference to speak of between the groups with less and with more probable causation. We can accordingly reconstruct his table to show a three-way classification [see TABLE 13]. In this table one can show that the difference in the incidence of schizophrenia in the sibs of the two groups with no trauma and with psychological trauma is so small as to be negligible $(0.50 > p > 0.30)$. But when these two groups are combined, and the third group with somatic trauma or illness is compared with them, we find that the incidence in sibs at 7·455 per cent is just twice what it is in the last (3·717 per cent). This difference is highly significant $(0.002 > p > 0.001)$. Again, one might think of attenuation of the predisposition, or of its dilution by non-hereditarily determined cases. In a further attempt to test the homogeneity of his material, Schulz (1934) calculated that such disparities as he found could be accounted for if out of a total of 512 cases with only one affected member in the sibship,

71 were attributed to non-hereditary exogenous causes. This work will be commented on again when we come to a discussion of genetical models in schizophrenia, particularly the polygenic model.

On the whole, it seems more probable that such findings as those of Schulz, and the work done on borderline schizophrenias and symptomatic schizophrenia, will be more satisfactorily explained by the hypothesis that the material has been diluted by exogenous cases, than by the hypothesis that the predisposition has been attenuated. In Hillbom's study (1960) of 395 brain-injured soldiers of the Russo-Finnish war, he reported the clinical histories of the 9 men who developed schizophrenia-like psychoses. One of them had an insane

TABLE 13

INCIDENCE OF SCHIZOPHRENIA IN SIBS OF SCHIZOPHRENICS, GROUPED FOR PRESENCE OR ABSENCE OF PSYCHOLOGICAL/SOMATIC CAUSATIVE FACTOR

(Data from Schulz, 1932)

INDEX CASES WITH/WITHOUT PSYCHOLOGICAL/SOMATIC CONTRIBUTORY CAUSE	BZ	SCHIZOPHRENIA IN SIBS		
		(a) CERTAIN	(b) NOT CERTAIN	(a) PER CENT
No such cause	1059·2	83	17	7·8
Psychological	376·0	24	8	6·4
Somatic	645·7	24	7	3·7

BZ = Bezugsziffer, i.e. number of sibs in sample, corrected for age distribution.

sister and a brother who had committed suicide, but otherwise the family histories were negative for anything suggestive of a schizophrenic predisposition. Moreover, the risk of a schizophrenia-like psychosis was related to the severity of the injury. There was no such case in the 70 patients with mild head injuries, 4 among the 264 men with moderately severe injuries (1·5 per cent), and 5 among the 81 men with severe head injuries (6·2 per cent). Everything suggests that hereditary predisposition did not play any role in the causation of these psychoses. The large material of schizophrenia-like psychoses following brain injury, described in great clinical detail by Feuchtwanger and Mayer-Gross (1938), leads to a similar conclusion. Psychotic states, for a time at least typically schizophrenic clinically, have been observed in association with a variety of cerebral disorders such as brain tumour, general paresis, temporal lobe epilepsy and amphetamine intoxication, conditions with immediate effects on brain function. In a study of schizophrenia-like psychoses associated with epilepsy, Slater and Glithero (1963) found an incidence of schizophrenia in the parents and sibs of patients which corresponded exactly with what one could have expected of a sample of the general population. It seems very likely, accordingly, that these 'symptomatic schizophrenias' are phenocopies of the genetically determined syndrome, and appear without any specific genetical contribution to their causation. This is most clearly demonstrated by the schizophrenia-like psychoses which have been repeatedly observed in association with Huntington's chorea [see Chapter 6, p. 136].

THE ORGANIC CONTRIBUTION TO SCHIZOPHRENIA

In an important critical review of the literature relating to this whole field, Davison and Bagley (1969) came to conclusions which must be discussed, and perhaps best at this point. If we discover that a patient, thought to be suffering from schizophrenia (the conventional endogenous concept), is in fact suffering from an organic illness, say an encephalitis, which must be held responsible for his symptoms, we are likely to discard the diagnosis of 'schizophrenia', or to qualify the illness as schizophrenia-like. This is an illegitimate way of thinking, since important questions are begged. In our minds we equate organic pathology with an 'organic' or 'psycho-organic' clinical picture. But in fact nearly all organic pathologies begin with 'non-organic' symptoms (e.g. neurotic symptoms, affective disturbances, etc.), and may so long continue. 'Cases of so-called functional psychoses exist in which the clinical manifestations of any organic component may be entirely lacking, but they nevertheless have as a basis a definite pathological process of the brain' (Ferraro, quoted by Davison and Bagley). The ambiguity of the term 'schizophrenia', in its many widespread uses, is even more notorious than the ambiguity of 'organic'. Davison and Bagley support the solution by Essen-Möller of the main problem, i.e. by making independent classifications of the syndrome and of the aetiology. In this sense there are 'organic schizophrenias', i.e. schizophrenic syndromes based on an organic brain process; there are 'psychogenic schizophrenias'; and others of unknown ('endogenous') causation. It is, of course, with the last group that we have been mainly concerned in this chapter. Davison and Bagley consider in some detail the symptomatological differences between the schizophrenias occurring in association with brain disease and those shown in the conventional syndrome. Some of the differences are very thought-provoking. Apart from a greater frequency of catatonic symptoms in the organic schizophrenias, their symptomatology was found to be much less rich, both in acute symptoms such as auditory and tactile hallucinations and passivity feelings, and also in thought disorder and flattening or incongruity of affect; all of these latter symptoms were commoner in the endogenous schizophrenias by factors varying from 1·3 to 3·8. A family history of schizophrenia was 3·5 and premorbid schizoid personality was 3·9 times as frequent in the non-organic as in the organic schizophrenias.

Davison and Bagley found the organic diseases which seemed to be particularly associated with schizophrenic syndromes (to a probably statistically significant extent) included Huntington's chorea, cerebrovascular disease, Parkinsonism, narcolepsy, certain brain tumours, and multiple sclerosis. Suggestions relating to the localization of the brain processes could also be pointed out—an association between left hemisphere and particularly temporal lobe lesions with primary delusions and catatonic symptoms, basal ganglia lesions with catatonic symptoms, diencephalic lesions (including basal ganglia) with auditory hallucinations, and brain stem lesions with thought disorder and Schneider's symptoms of the first rank.

Davison and Bagley conclude that these organic schizophrenias are genetically distinct from ordinary schizophrenia (showing, for instance, much lower morbidity risks in the sibs of probands), and that they are probably best to be regarded as without any genetic basis and, in effect, phenocopies, i.e. environmentally produced abnormalities which mimic disorders known to be usually genetically determined. The majority of these organic schizophrenias are to be regarded as caused by the organic process. This is no place to enter on their discussion of the modes of pathogenesis involved in the organic causation of schizophrenic syndromes; but they find a place in a simplified conceptual

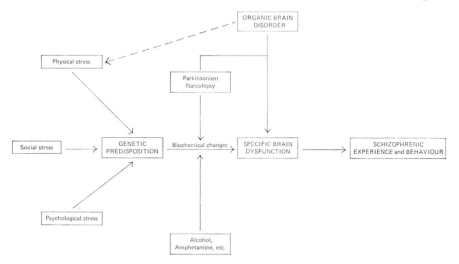

Fig. 3. The place of organic brain disorder in the aetiology of schizophrenia
(Davison and Bagley, 1969)

model [FIG. 3], self-explanatory, which is in effect a heuristic hypothesis offering a number of suggestions for future research.

FURTHER ASPECTS OF HETEROGENEITY

It follows from what we have said that schizophrenia, conceived as a clinical picture with certain distinctive features, persisting over some days, weeks, months or even years, shows itself as being a heterogeneous collection of different disorders when looked at from the aetiological point of view. However, the nuclear condition, aetiology unknown, distinguishes itself from clinically cognate states in the long run by having a long-term development which is different from the others. Most of the organically and psychogenically determined psychoses pass off after a relatively short interval into a state which has an understandable relation to the basic pathogenesis, psychological normality for instance after the clearing up of an amphetamine intoxication, or organic personality defect in the case of a temporal lobe epilepsy. All these symptomatic schizophrenia-like states, even when taken together, represent only a small part of the number of cases which are diagnosed as schizophrenic. We might liken the schizophrenic to the epileptic syndrome: in a proportion of cases specific causes can be found for the appearance of the syndrome, usually in the nature of an organic noxa, and these can be classified as symptomatic epilepsies or schizophrenias into which the hereditary factor has entered little if at all; in a larger proportion of cases no extraneous cause can be found, and we are inclined to speak of 'idiopathic' epilepsy or 'idiopathic' schizophrenia.

Next comes the question whether we should be seriously considering the possibility of heterogeneity of the very various psychoses, of early or late onset, of short or long duration, insidious or acute, single or relapsing and remitting or chronic and enduring, benign or causing extensive dilapidation of personality, of predominantly hebephrenic or catatonic or paranoid symptomatology. The belief that there is a heterogeneity which yet remains to be unmasked still obstinately persists and finds many followers, although at present no very satisfactory evidence in favour of such a heterogeneity can be produced.

Kallmann (1938) classified the type of schizophrenic illness, hebephrenic, catatonic or paranoid, shown by secondary cases observed in the families of probands, by the Kraepelinian type shown by the proband himself. From his tabulation the data relating to the children of probands have been extracted and are shown in TABLE 14. Kallmann rightly pointed out that since all types of

TABLE 14

DISTRIBUTION OF DIAGNOSES OF TYPE OF SCHIZOPHRENIA FOR
AFFECTED CHILDREN, BY DIAGNOSIS OF PROBAND

(Data from Kallmann, 1938)

| | CHILDREN | | | |
	HEBEPHRENIC	CATATONIC	PARANOID	TOTAL
Probands				
hebephrenic	34	8	14	56
catatonic	6	18	10	34
paranoid	5	9	7	21
Total	45	35	31	111

illness occurred in the relatives of patients of all types, there could be no question of these different forms of schizophrenia being genetically distinct conditions. However, it is to be noted that in these parent-child pairs there is a tendency of like to go with like: where 34 hebephrenic-hebephrenic pairs are observed only 22·70 were expected; and where 18 catatonic-catatonic pairs are observed only 10·70 were expected. The whole table gives a χ^2 of 15·32, which for 4 d.f. is significant at the ·01 level. Only the children of the paranoid probands are distributed pretty much as might have been expected.

Paranoid types of schizophrenia also distinguish themselves from hebephrenic and catatonic types in their familial relationships: the risk for the children of a schizophrenic proband is only about half in the case of a paranoid (or simplex schizophrenia) proband of that in the case of a hebephrenic or catatonic proband. This is shown very strikingly by Kallmann's data [TABLE 15]. The trend has been confirmed by Hallgren and Sjögren (1959). If one ranks the clinical types of schizophrenia in the patient by the magnitude of the risk of schizophrenia in

TABLE 15

INCIDENCE OF (DEFINITE) SCHIZOPHRENIA IN THE CHILDREN OF
SCHIZOPHRENICS, BY SEX OF PROBAND AND TYPE OF ILLNESS

(After Kallmann, 1938)

| PROBANDS: | CHILDREN OF | | | | | |
| | FEMALE PROBANDS | | | MALE PROBANDS | | |
	N	SCH	%	N	SCH	%
Hebephrenic⎱ Catatonic ⎰	241·5	42	17·4	130·5	24	18·4
Paranoid⎱ Simple ⎰	194·5	17	8·7	112·0	11	9·8

sibs, Hallgren and Sjögren's figures show—catatonics 8·5 per cent, hebephrenics
7·0 per cent, paranoid schizophrenics 4·7 per cent, atypical cases 2·3 per cent.

Schizophrenic illnesses, or schizophrenia-like illnesses, i.e. the symptomatic
schizophrenias, which occur on the basis of demonstrable organic pathology,
tend to take a paranoid form. In some of these instances [see TABLE 16] the

TABLE 16

GENETICAL PREDISPOSITION IN SOME DISORDERS RELATED TO
TYPICAL SCHIZOPHRENIA, POSSIBLY AS ATTENUATED FORMS

(After Shields, 1968a)

IN SIBS OF PATIENTS SUFFERING FROM:	RISK OF SCHIZOPHRENIA IN SIBS (AS PER CENT)
Paranoia (Kolle)	2·9
Recovered schizophrenia (Wittermans and Schulz)	3·3
Late paraphrenia (Kay and Roth)	3·4
Involutional psychosis (Kallmann)	4·2
Delusional climacteric psychosis (Knoll)	4·7
Schizophrenic reaction (Rohr)	5·3
Mixed psychosis (manic-depressive/schizophrenic) (Angst)	7·1

incidence of schizophrenia in first-degree relatives of probands is significantly
higher than the general population risk, but a good deal lower than the risk for
first-degree relatives of schizophrenics without organic pathology. In other
instances, e.g. the schizophrenia-like illness which may occur in temporal lobe
epilepsy, there is no increased risk of schizophrenia for the relatives of patients.

In 1938 Schwab reported an investigation into the families of 85 patients
whose illnesses had been classified as strictly catatonic after a thorough follow-
up survey. Among the sibs were found 14 certain schizophrenics, of whom all
but one had suffered from the catatonic form of the illness. There were 6 certain
schizophrenics among the parents, 4 of them catatonic. Among remoter relatives
58 per cent of the psychoses were schizophrenic, again predominantly catatonias.
The findings were such as to suggest some specificity in the genetic predisposition.

Even more remarkable findings were made when the case material was
classified by Leonhard (without knowledge of the family data) into 'typical'

and 'atypical' schizophrenias in his sense. Leonhard is a pupil of Kleist, and follows him in regarding schizophrenia as a congeries of different syndromes, which can be distinguished from one another in the generality of cases by a sufficiently exact clinical study. Adequate information for Leonhard's purposes was available in 41 of Schwab's cases, and they were classified into 20 'typical' and 21 'atypical' cases. Among the sibs of these 41 patients there were 10 schizophrenics, and among their parents 3 schizophrenics—all 13 of these secondary cases being related to the 'atypical' probands, and none to the 'typical' probands. Admitting the smallness of the numbers, Schwab felt inclined towards the conclusion that Leonhardian 'typical' and 'atypical' schizophrenias were genetically distinct; and that the former might perhaps be related to a recessive gene of low penetrance, and the latter to a dominant gene.

These striking findings stimulated Bruno Schulz to invite Leonhard to examine the case histories of schizophrenics whose families had been investigated from the genealogical department of the Psychiatric Research Institute in Munich, and to classify these cases according to his standards. Leonhard agreed, provided he was put in a position to see the patients for himself in a diagnostic interview. This could only be done in the cases of those patients still in psychiatric hospitals, and in the end only 75 out of the original 660 patients could be used. To these 75 another 24 could be added from another systematic research series, providing a total of 99.

The method of investigation is interesting as being one of the earliest 'double-blind' experiments. Both investigators saw the patient together. Schulz had the clinical record available, and could give Leonhard any clinical information he needed for the Leonhardian classification (while reserving all family data), but himself took no part in the diagnostic interview. In effect, the Schwab findings could not be confirmed; but on the other hand they were in no way rebutted, since the schizophrenias coming in question in the Schulz-Leonhard experiment were of all clinical varieties (in other senses than the special Leonhard dichotomy), and only a minority were catatonias. The results of both studies are shown in TABLE 17. If we allow ourselves to add the results of both studies together, and

TABLE 17

RISK OF SCHIZOPHRENIA IN SIBS AND IN PARENTS OF PROBANDS CLASSIFIED BY LEONHARD'S CLINICAL CRITERIA INTO TYPICAL AND ATYPICAL GROUPS

| SCHIZOPHRENIC PROBANDS | SCHIZOPHRENIA IN RELATIVES, NUMBER AND PER CENT | | | | | |
| | SIBS | | | PARENTS | | |
	BZ	N	%	BZ	N	%
Typical						
Schulz and Leonhard	161	9	5·6	108	1	0·9
Schwab	38	—	—	40	—	—
Atypical						
Schulz and Leonhard	122	8–11	7·8	90	4–6	5·5
Schwab	55	10	18·2	42	3	7·2

BZ = Bezugsziffer, i.e. corrected risk-lifetimes.

relatives of both kinds into one category, a 2 by 2 table gives a χ^2 for 1 d.f. of 8·7, for which $p < 0.01$, indicating a significant difference between the 'typical' and 'atypical' schizophrenias in respect of the familial incidence of schizophrenia.

One cannot explain this difference between the two Leonhardian groups on the basis that there were marked differences in severity of the two types of schizophrenic illness. In both groups the patients were severely affected patients, often with long histories of hospitalization; but on the whole the 'typical' defect schizophrenics were probably more severely affected than the 'atypical' ones, whose atypicality consisted in the main in tendencies to periodicity, partial remission and relapse. What one does observe about these figures is that, if we are postulating a genetical factor with reduced penetrance, the 'typical' group gives a suggestion, in the very low loading in the parents and relatively much higher loading in the sibs, of a recessive mode of inheritance; in the 'atypical' group dominance is much more probable, and would certainly fit the observations well enough. In general, genes which manifest in the heterozygote, i.e. dominantly, tend to be associated with milder and more variable clinical pictures than the conditions shown only in the homozygote with a double dose of a gene recessive in its manifestation. One concludes that the Schwab-Leonhard and Schulz-Leonhard investigations do support some genetical heterogeneity in the nuclear group of schizophrenias, but still leave the issue far from settled.

The Japanese worker Mitsuda has developed a conceptual scheme, and has founded it on a great deal of clinical, familial and other observations collected by himself and by many members of his school. In this scheme atypical psychoses, on the borderland between schizophrenia and other psychiatric genetical syndromes, find their natural place. One may conceive a triangle, with the three apices occupied by the typical epileptic, manic-depressive and schizophrenic syndromes; along the sides of the triangle one will find distributed illnesses with an admixture of symptoms, tending perhaps towards one or other apex but at some distance from each of them. Into these atypical psychoses the epileptic component will bring tendencies towards disorders of consciousness, EEG abnormalities, etc.; while the manic-depressive component brings tendencies to periodicity, symptoms toned with elation or depression, and a benign effect in protecting the personality against deterioration even after long disequilibrium; and the schizophrenic component brings the tendency towards the manifestation of the typical (Schneiderian 'first rank') symptoms of thought disorder and primary delusional experience. Ictal anxiety is a syndrome lying between the manic-depressive and epileptic poles; oneirophrenia between the epileptic and schizophrenic poles; and the schizo-affective psychoses between the schizophrenic and manic-depressive poles.

Mitsuda and his pupils have not as a rule carried out genetical investigations along the conventional lines, i.e. by estimating morbidity risks in various classes of relatives, but have used the cruder but still interesting method of classifying family histories accordingly as they show 'dominant', 'intermediate' or 'recessive' patterns. A family history of the 'dominant' type shows a taint of mental illness on one or the other side, paternal or maternal; a 'recessive' family history is one in which there is no recognizable taint in the pedigree or only in the sibs;

an 'intermediate' family history is one which fits readily neither into the 'dominant' nor the 'recessive' pattern, but includes, say, psychopaths in sibs of parents
or cousins.

When patients are classified as 'typical' or 'atypical' on clinical symptomatology according to Mitsuda's criteria, a large number of differences appear
between the two groups [see TABLE 18]. Some of these differences, e.g. in premorbid personality and mode of onset of psychosis, would appear to be closely

TABLE 18

FAMILIAL AND CLINICAL DIFFERENCES BETWEEN TYPICAL (NUCLEAR)
AND ATYPICAL (PERIPHERAL) TYPES OF SCHIZOPHRENIC ILLNESS
[Data from Mitsuda, 1967 (originally 1942), pp. 69, 71]

	TYPICAL (NUCLEAR) (N 78) %	ATYPICAL (PERIPHERAL) (N 37) %
Mode of inheritance		
dominant	6	35
intermediate	14	14
recessive	80	51
Other psychoses in family		
recovered	50	68
chronic	50	11
died in acute stage	—	21
Sex ratio (m/f × 100)	152	106
Body type		
pyknic	21	35
athletic	18	24
asthenic	61	41
Premorbid personality		
schizoid	72	38
sensitive	49	32
cyclothymic	22	28
epileptoid	6	34
Onset		
acute	—	49
subacute	21	32
chronic	79	19
Result of shock treatment		
full recovery	—	71
social remission	19	29
improvement	16	—
ineffective	56	—
Deterioration		
+++	34	—
++	47	—
+	19	28
−	—	72

related to the criteria of differentiation; and these same criteria would seem to
have very effectively discriminated between two groups of bad and good
prognosis. The differences in body type, in sex ratio, and in the familial background (type of inheritance pattern and natural history of other psychoses

occurring in the family) could not have been predicted, and can be regarded as observational data of considerable interest. The case for correlation between symptomatology, natural course of illness and familial background is a strong one, on these data, and provides justification for regarding the typical and atypical schizophrenias as being, to some extent, independent syndromes.

Rather similar findings have been made by the Japanese worker Inouye (1963), who however prefers to classify schizophrenic psychoses into three main groups. The way these relate the course of the illness with the family history of psychiatric illness and with twin concordance rates is shown in TABLE 19.

TABLE 19

PROBABLE HEREDITY OF THREE CATEGORIES OF SCHIZOPHRENIA
(From Inouye, 1963)

	MODE OF INHERITANCE OF SCHIZOPHRENIA	INHERITANCE OF OTHER DISORDERS	CONCORDANT RATIO OF MZ TWINS %
Chronic progressive	Recessive	Less	74
Relapsing	Often Dominant	Often	86
Chronic mild or transient	Often Recessive	Often	39

Mitsuda's work has been further supported in the Osaka school by electroencephalographic and pneumoencephalographic studies. In 111 patients studied by Yamada (1967), in over 40 per cent of the patients in the atypical and intermediate peripheral groups, seizure patterns were released by *Megimide*, which was possible with only one patient in the nuclear group. In the nuclear group there was no correlation, such as was found in the peripheral group, between the degree of deterioration of personality and EEG abnormality. There was also much more EEG abnormality in the peripheral than in the nuclear group [TABLE 20].

TABLE 20

DISTRIBUTION OF EEG ABNORMALITIES IN TWO CLINICAL TYPES OF
SCHIZOPHRENIA

SCHIZOPHRENICS	PERCENTAGE OF EEGS		
	NORMAL	BORDERLINE	ABNORMAL
nuclear (N = 50)	36	40	24
peripheral (N = 61)	13	20	67

Asano (1967) studied the pneumoencephalograms of 53 schizophrenics, 32 nuclear and 21 peripheral, and found rather marked differences between the two groups in respect of fairly gross changes. Morphological changes in the lateral ventricles (dilatation and asymmetry) were shown in 58 per cent of the nuclear group, 35 per cent of the peripheral group; dilatation of more than moderate degree of the third ventricle was found in 50 per cent and 29 per cent respectively; and definite widening of the cerebral fissures in 23 per cent as against 5 per cent.

These findings in the EEG and PEG, taken together, suggest that while focal cerebral pathology may play a significant part in the atypical or peripheral group of schizophrenics, it is of little significance in the nuclear schizophrenias. In the latter, on the other hand, there is more evidence of processes involving cell fall-out (or possibly congenital hypoplasia). Asano's findings favoured the former rather than the latter possibility, as the degree of pneumoencephalographic change was associated with the degree of personality deterioration.

In summary, there is a considerable body of data which suggest that schizophrenic psychoses will in due course be proved to be heterogeneous; but this position cannot be regarded as established as yet. We are very much more likely to make progress in this direction when we know more than we know now about the biochemical basis of these psychoses.

SCHIZOPHRENIA AND PSYCHOGENESIS

Rosenthal (1963) has classified theories of the aetiological basis of schizophrenia into three groups. The first are monogenic-biochemical theories. These postulate a single mutant gene, leading to an error of metabolism as yet unidentified, which in turn leads to mental illness. The second group of theories are named by Rosenthal diathesis-stress theories. A constitutional predisposition is postulated, but its nature is rarely specified. It might be that one had to deal with a variety of predispositions, which interacting with the same or different stresses, provided a variety of pathways to a group of different illnesses, subsumed under the generic title of 'schizophrenia'. Theories of this type suggest a wider distribution in the population of the predisposition to schizophrenia, with a consequently lower rate of manifestation of the predisposition in actual illness. As a corollary, environmental contributions to the precipitation of the illness would be greater. In this group of theories belong those which postulate a polygenic basis for the predisposition to illness; and both the degree of predisposition and the severity of the stressors are envisaged as being continuously distributed.

The third group of theories Rosenthal names life-experience theories. With them there is thought to be no inherited predisposition, and all persons are held to be equally liable to schizophrenia, as far as their genetic equipment is concerned. The cause of the illness is thought of as an excess or extreme of some common noxious influence, such as maternal over-protectiveness or rejection, or the insufficiency of some nearly universal benign influence such as maternal love or social contact.

It is not proposed in this chapter to discuss theories of the third group at any length. It seems to the authors that they could only be the product of totally unbiological thinking. It is extremely unplausible to suppose that the entire range of genetical variation in man should be without effect of any kind on the liability to schizophrenia, since there is no other disease known to us, in which there is a raised familial incidence, of which so much can be said.

On the life-experience basis, one would have to suppose that the liability to schizophrenia was universal, varying in degree somewhat from individual to individual, but entirely unspecific in nature; the specificity of the schizophrenic reaction would then be derived from specificity in the stressor or stressors. This would put schizophrenia on a par with the maladies caused by deprivations, intoxications, etc. There is much plausibility in the view that stressors of such a kind could play some aetiological role.[1] Occasionally reports appear implicating a hypothetical virus, or describing 'zooid bodies' in pathological preparations of the schizophrenic brain. These reports, however, remain without confirmation; and life-experience theories in a physical form are almost universally abandoned.

It is, therefore, somewhat remarkable that they not only survive in a psychological mode of expression, but dominate the thinking of many psychiatrists, particularly in the North American continent. Rosenthal has classified them into three types, in which the hypothetical psychogenic factors, which are left only vaguely defined, are supposed to exert their effects along one of the three pathways—failure of socialization, failure of cognitive integration, failure to contain anxiety. Applying these hypotheses to the observations made on the Genain quadruplets (1963), Rosenthal shows that each of them can be supported on the evidence. He doubts whether it is meaningful to ask whether one is valid and the others not. It would be possible to regard the three theories as different perspectives of a common disorganizing interpersonal process undermining social, cognitive and affective responses at the same time. However, if this were the case, it should be possible to formulate in words what this disorganizing interpersonal process was, and then to show that it was uniquely specific for persons developing a schizophrenic illness, and that it was derived from a uniquely specific psychogenic stress factor or combination of factors.

The strongest objection to psychogenic stress theories, and even to life-experience theories in the wider sense, is that, as they have been formulated so far, they have proved heuristically almost valueless. One psychogenic theory succeeds another in popular esteem, and is in its turn forgotten. No objective data are accumulated; no predictions are made, and none verified. Torsten Sjögren (1959) remarked that 'until the advocators of purely environmental hypotheses have shown with equally precise methods of investigation as those applied by the geneticists, that the morbidity risk of schizophrenia increases with particular environmental circumstances, such explanations remain speculations'.

From time to time facts emerge which would suggest that the role of the environment in the causation of the general run of schizophrenic illnesses is an important one. Thus in Britain the Registrar General's returns show an incidence of schizophrenia about three times as great in social class V as in the other classes; and in the United States, Hollingshead and Redlich (1954) have given prevalence rates of schizophrenia per 100,000 of the population, adjusted for age and sex, which are eight times as high in social class V (the semi-skilled

---

[1] The occurrence of schizophrenic phenocopies, i.e. environmentally determined schizophrenic or schizophrenia-like psychoses, is discussed on pages 26–30. It is to be noted that all these disorders, taken together in so far as they are known, constitute only a very small part of the totality of schizophrenic disorders of an ordinary kind. It is with the generality of schizophrenic psychoses that we are concerned in this part of the discussion.

and unskilled) as in class I. The immediate suggestion which arises is that there is some unfavourable factor in the environments of persons of less favoured socio-economic classes which puts them at greater risk. However, it has not proved possible to substantiate this. Goldberg and Morrison (1963), studying a national sample of schizophrenics aged 25–34, which showed this characteristic social class distribution, found that the fathers of these patients had had, at the same time of life, an occupational distribution corresponding to the general population. What had happened was that the patient had drifted downhill, either during the early stages of his illness, or in an insidious pre-hospitalization stage, or possibly even premorbidly. There is much to support the view that pre-psychotic drift, from whatever cause, genetic or environmental, does occur. Pollack *et al.* (1966), comparing the childhood pattern of development of schizophrenics with that of their sibs nearest in age, found not only temperamental differences between the two groups but also that scholastic performance was worse in the schizophrenics. Similar conclusions emerge from the work of Bower, Shellhamer and Daily (1960). Temperamental and personality differences between children who later become schizophrenic, and their sibs, certainly go back to quite early years (Prout and White, 1956).

Many psychodynamic theories of causation implicate the patient's mother, so much so that the concept of the 'schizophrenogenic mother' has become popular coinage. One of the most significant studies is that by Alanen (1958). In repeated psychiatric interviews he examined the mothers of 89 schizophrenic patients, currently in hospital, also all but 6 of the patients, the fathers of 19 of them and the sibs of 8. The findings he made were compared with those he got from the mothers of 20 neurotic patients and 20 normal controls, mostly medical and nursing students. The level of emotional and psychiatric disturbance in the mothers of the schizophrenics was very high, and much higher than in the mothers of either of the other groups. The mothers of schizophrenics showed much anxiety and inner insecurity, a proneness to unrealistic behaviour and thought patterns approaching the psychotic, schizoid traits, aggressiveness and poverty of affective life, lack of empathy, and proneness to dominating rather than submissive patterns of interpersonal relationships. These defects were shown particularly in their relationships with their children, and above all with those children who had eventually become schizophrenic. Their attitude towards these children had, indeed, been dominating and un-understanding, devoid of respect for the child as a person, loveless, cold, inimical towards him and deeply frustrating. The impression one obtains is, indeed, that these were wicked women. Alanen's judgement sounds so harsh that one wonders how far it was subjectively determined. Some support for the suggestion that the mothers of schizophrenics have been dominating in their attitudes has been provided by other workers; but a number of these investigations have shown the mother to be insecure and over-protective rather than directly inimical, and others have implicated fathers rather than mothers. In fact, no constant pattern either of the personality of the mother, or of her attitude and behaviour, has been described. The work in this field has been critically discussed by Kind (1966).

In Alanen's study and many of the others, part at least of the emotional tension and unhappiness observed in the parents, and their difficulties in coming to terms with their sick child, is understandable as a maternal reaction to the child's mental illness rather than as a cause of it. This has been brought out quite clearly in work on emotional disturbance in the mothers of so-called psychotic ('schizophrenic') or autistic children (Klebanoff, 1959; Mahler, 1961).

The trouble about the 'schizophrenogenic mother' hypothesis, when it is used to explain a raised incidence of schizophrenia in the children of schizophrenics, is that fathers seem to show just as much 'schizophrenogenicity'— an observation to be expected on the hypothesis that the connexion is along genetic lines, and not on the hypothesis that the connexion is along psychological (e.g. learning theory) or other environmental lines. In its early years the infant is very close to the mother, and mental abnormality in her could very plausibly be expected to produce a shift in its own psychological development; but in the early life of the child the father is at a much greater distance, psychologically and environmentally. Nevertheless, all investigators have found the risk of schizophrenia for the child of a schizophrenic patient is much the same whether the patient be male or female. Schizophrenic mothers are not more dangerous to their children, in this sense, than schizophrenic fathers. This comes out clearly from Kallmann's data, shown in TABLE 15.

When one proceeds along lines of investigation from child to parent, then one does indeed find more schizophrenic mothers than fathers; and for some time this was held to support the psycho-environmental hypotheses. However, it has been pointed out by Essen-Möller (1963) that this sex difference could be completely accounted for by the considerations that women marry at an earlier age than men, and if they become schizophrenic, tend to do so at a later age. Reproduction usually ceases after the onset of a schizophrenic psychosis, so that the interim between age of marriage and age of becoming schizophrenic is a longer one in the female than in the male, and gives a larger opportunity for having a child. If one makes the necessary arithmetical adjustments, the whole of the risk differences for fathers and for mothers can be accounted for in this way. This has been discussed in somewhat greater detail on page 15.

The most modern tendency has been to abandon the view that the mother herself is directly implicated in the causation of her child's schizophrenia, and to replace her as the *causa causans* by the organization of the family group as a single conceptual entity. Perhaps the strongest evidence that there is something to be found in this direction has been provided by Singer and Wynne (1965). Carefully controlled studies suggest that there is a thought-disordered pattern of intercommunication in the intimate families of schizophrenics which is not to be found in families of neurotic patients. This finding has not so far received confirmation by workers in other centres.

Sometimes it is possible to observe an experiment carried out by a whim of nature, which to some extent enables us to distinguish genetical effects from environmental ones. One such experiment is made when a pair of MZ twins is separated at birth or in very early years, each of the members being brought up in different environments. If, as is maintained by some of the authors we have discussed, the early environment is crucial for the development of a predisposition to schizophrenic illness, then the concordance rate in any collection of such pairs should be much lower than in pairs of MZ twins brought up together.

TABLE 21 shows the recorded cases in which the two members of an MZ pair have been separated and one eventually became a schizophrenic index case; in 11 out of the total of 17 cases the other twin became schizophrenic too, a concordance rate of 65 per cent which is very much the same as in pairs not separated in early years. All but one of these cases was ascertained in the course of comprehensive studies in a defined group of cases. The case reported by Craike and Slater was ascertained accidentally in an out-patient clinic; and one cannot be sure that the concordance between the members of the pair did not

TABLE 21
MZ TWINS REARED APART, ONE OR BOTH SCHIZOPHRENIC.
TOTAL CASES ON RECORD

DATE	INVESTIGATORS	AGE AT SEPARATION	NUMBER OF PAIRS CONCORDANT	DISCORDANT
1938	Kallmann	soon after birth	1	—
1941	Essen-Möller	7 y	1	—
1945	Craike and Slater	0 y 9 m	1	—
1956	Kallmann and Roth	not stated	1	—
1962	Shields	birth	1	—
1963	Tienari	3 y	—	1
	Tienari	8 y	—	1
1965	Mitsuda	infancy	5	3
1967	Kringlen	1 y 10 m	—	1
	Kringlen	0 y 3 m	1	—
	Total		11	6

play a part in leading to the publication. This was the case in none of the other pairs; so that, omitting this one, we are left with a concordance rate obtained on an unbiased series of $10/16 = 62.5$ per cent. The material is not large, but it constitutes a heavy item of evidence against the view that early home experiences play a major role in the causation of schizophrenia.

With foster-children observations of a complementary kind can sometimes be made. Here we are observing what happens when a group of individuals of very various genetical constitution are brought up in a rather uniform environment, from which the influence of the true parents has been eliminated. Heston (1966) made a very successful follow-up of children who had been born between 1915 and 1945 to schizophrenic mothers in an Oregon State psychiatric hospital, and who had not been brought up by their mothers or by any maternal relative, but, mainly, in foster-homes or foundling homes. They were matched for sex and age and type of eventual placement with a group of other children from the same foundling homes. The follow-up study began in 1964, and it was possible to get satisfactory information in a high proportion of cases in both groups. Some of Heston's data are shown in TABLE 22. It is noteworthy that all the five children who became schizophrenic were children of schizophrenic mothers, and that none of the control series of children of non-schizophrenic mothers became schizophrenic. It is also interesting to see the variety of other psychiatric abnormalities in the children of the experimental group. However, Heston observes that the 21 children of schizophrenic mothers who showed no significant

4

psychosocial impairment were not only successful, but in comparison with the control group were more spontaneous when interviewed, had had more colourful lives, had held more creative jobs and had had more imaginative hobbies; in the experimental group there was more variability of personality and behaviour. These differences between the experimental and control groups can be brought into a meaningful relation with the genetical background in the two cases, but could not be associated with environmental factors.

Studies along similar lines have been carried out in collaboration between Danish and American workers in Copenhagen (Kety et al., 1968; Rosenthal et al., 1968). Rosenthal et al. discovered many more schizophrenics and borderline schizophrenics in a group of adopted persons one of whose biological

TABLE 22

PSYCHIATRIC DISORDERS IN FOSTER-HOME REARED CHILDREN
(From Heston, 1966)

	MOTHER SCHIZOPHRENIC ($N = 47$)	CONTROLS ($N = 50$)
Mean age	35·8	36·3
Schizophrenia	5	—
Mental deficiency, IQ <70	4	—
Sociopathic personality	9	2
Neurotic personality disorder	13	7
Felons	7	2
Never married (aged 30+)	9	4

Categories not mutually exclusive.

parents was schizophrenic than in a group of matched adopted persons neither of whose parents was schizophrenic. Starting from schizophrenics known to be adopted, Kety et al. found more mental illness in their biological than in their adoptive families.

PSYCHOGENIC PSYCHOSES RESEMBLING SCHIZOPHRENIA

Much attention has been given to the question whether psychodynamic factors were capable of bringing about a schizophrenic psychosis in the absence of any hereditary predisposition. Labhardt (1963) has given an excellent clinical account of 53 patients suffering from acute schizophrenia-like psychotic reactions to severe stress, in which both bodily illness and emotional trauma had played a part. Symptomatologically these psychoses resembled acute paranoid or catatonic states, with anxiety and excitement, stupors, perhaps ideas of world catastrophe, vegetative symptoms and sometimes slight clouding of consciousness. Affective responsiveness was always well preserved, and all these patients responded well to treatment and recovered in a few weeks, 90 per cent in 4 weeks or less. No sequelae of a post-schizophrenic type were left. In the families of these patients there was relatively little in the way of schizophrenic illness. Labhardt attributes the reaction to an exhaustive state affecting meso-diencephalic functions.

A very similar group of patients was studied by Rohr (1961). These were patients who had been diagnosed as suffering from a 'schizophrenic reaction', with the criteria that they should have fallen ill in a close time relation with a severe psychotraumatic situation, that symptomatology should have been schizophrenic, and that the outcome should have been one of recovery in weeks or months. These cases were of relatively rare occurrence (as Labhardt found also), and there were only about 4–5 per annum out of an intake of 1000 to 1200 (of which one-third were schizophrenic). Nothing characteristic was found in the pre-psychotic personality, apart from some schizoid traits; the psycho-traumatic situation was of many different kinds, again with nothing specific. The response to treatment was, of course, very favourable. The genetical investigation showed 3 manifest schizophrenics in the 86 parents and also 2 ?schizophrenics. Among the 136 sibs (age-corrected $N = 90$) there were 5 schizophrenics. Rohr concluded that this syndrome lacked specificity. These reactions were not quite equivalent to schizophrenia, nor something quite different. The family loading was greater for schizophrenia than in the general population, but less than in the generality of schizophrenics.

A rather more definite negative, genetically speaking, was reached by Welner and Strömgren (1958) in their study of benign schizophreniform psychoses. This was really a follow-up study; and of the 107 patients after $1\frac{1}{2}$–20 years (average 9), 72 of them were either well or suffering from non-schizophrenic mental abnormalities. The expectancy of psychoses among the siblings of these 72 verified cases was significantly less than for a material of 'true' schizophrenics (expectancy for all schizophreniform illnesses 1·7 per cent); the expectancies for neuroses and character deviations on the other hand were significantly higher. The authors concluded that in these cases schizophrenic illnesses, quite typical by classical standards except for the lack of autism and the sustained capacity for rapport, had been precipitated in the absence of any specific genetical predisposition, but rather on the substrate of a relatively unspecific mental vulnerability.

On the basis of this work one might conclude that psychic trauma, like other noxae, is capable in favourable circumstances of precipitating a schizophrenic state without the contribution of any specific genetic factor. These psychogenic schizophrenias are of rare occurrence,[1] and are likely to provide not more than about 1 or 2 per cent of the general run of schizophrenic illnesses. In essence they do not distinguish themselves very much from other so-called symptomatic schizophrenias, such as those which occur with focal brain lesions and particular poisons; and it is probable that the pathogenic mechanisms involve interference with specific brain functions, very likely along physical lines. All symptomatic

---

[1] At least as so diagnosed in Switzerland (Rohr, 1961; Labhardt, 1963). In Scandinavia corresponding clinical usage is very different. There the diagnostic classification 'reactive psychoses' defines a major group of cases, most of which would fall into the main schizophrenic group in other countries. Atypicalities of a variety of kinds, especially significant precipitation, affective admixture in symptomatology and benign course, are the criteria invoked. The justification for regarding these cases as constituting a distinct diagnostic category has received some support from follow-up studies but is not generally regarded as established.

schizophrenias are reported by their investigators to distinguish themselves from endogenous schizophrenia by a relatively favourable prognosis, the schizophrenic state passing off after a fairly short period, and by a capacity for normal affective responses which is relatively much better retained. One does not feel inclined to deduce from these observations the conclusion that psychogenic mechanisms are likely to play a major role in the great majority of schizophrenic illnesses. Even where they might be thought to be obviously decisive, as in cases of *folie à deux*, further investigation may show that the genetical factors were there all along (Scharfetter, 1970).

3

SCHIZOPHRENIA: GENETICAL MODELS

DIATHESIS AND STRESS

On page 37 we noted that one of the alternatives to the hypothesis that schizophrenia was of solely environmental causation, indeed psychogenically caused, was that the causation might lie in an interaction between hereditary predisposition on the one side and environmental stress on the other. The hereditary contribution might, perhaps, be of a variety of kinds; or it might be of a quantitatively graded kind and universal distribution. Then those who carried a heavy degree of hereditary predisposition would be likely to fall ill under only minor degrees of stress, while even those who were relatively little predisposed could still be precipitated into a schizophrenic illness if the environmental stress were severe enough.

Reference has already been made to the 'symptomatic' schizophrenias which may be observed as sequelae of head injury or temporal lobe epilepsy [p. 28], and in the case of other focal brain damage [p. 29]. Similar observations have been made with some kinds of poisoning. In 1958 Connell described acute paranoid and paranoid-hallucinatory psychoses in association with amphetamine poisoning. The illness in many cases closely resembled an acute paranoid schizophrenia, but differed in its course in that recovery was complete in a few weeks once the further taking of the drug had been prevented. It is possible, though not very probable, that these patients had a latent predisposition to schizophrenia-like reactions. It would seem that in these forms of schizophrenia, the specifically schizophrenic-like qualities of the mental symptoms were not derived from the genetical constitution, but rather from an interference in particular functional systems of the brain (perhaps, say, the limbic lobe system).

A similar line of thought is encouraged by the observations recorded in Table 16. Here we see a number of forms of illness, clinically related to schizophrenia, showing a more than average incidence of (typical) schizophrenia in their sibs, but yet such an incidence as to be well below what would be expected if the index cases had been ordinary schizophrenics. The genetical background cannot be both qualitatively and quantitatively the same as for the general run of schizophrenics. Either the case material is heterogeneous, consisting of a mixture of genuine and pseudoschizophrenics; or it is homogeneous, but consisting of persons whose genetical predisposition is of a degree less than that of most schizophrenics but a degree greater than that of the average member of the general population. In a number of cases, e.g. that of late paraphrenia (Kay, 1963), the investigator has attributed the findings to a quantitatively variable predisposition, which is then linked with a hypothetically multifactorial polygenic hereditary basis.

There is a great weight of opinion, based on solid observational evidence, which now supports these views. The usual conception is that both heredity and environment are making their contributions to causation, and both to a degree which manifests continuous quantitative variation. The specific qualities of the schizophrenic reaction have then to be derived either from the hereditary predisposition, or from the environmental stressors, or from specificities in their mutual interaction. Manfred Bleuler (1963) has recently emphasized the importance of the third of these possibilities. He sees the genetical predisposition itself arising as an interactional phenomenon and being the result of a disharmony or clash between contrary gene-derived features of the personality. This is a concept which must make an appeal to the psychodynamically-oriented clinician, since it makes sense clinically: many of the troubles of his patients (but, one notes, even more of his neurotic or psychopathic than his schizophrenic patients) are derived from unresolved internal conflicts, mutually irreconcilable drives and lack of balance between different aspects of the personality. But the viewpoint is a clinical and not a biological one; from the geneticist's point of view it suffers from the defects that on the one hand it is heuristically unprofitable, not leading to any precise formulations which could be subjected to test, and on the other hand not accounting satisfactorily for the familial incidences such as we know them to be. For instance, as Shields has pointed out, one would not expect on a basis of genetical disharmony any markedly increased risk of schizophrenia over average expectations for the sibs of schizophrenics.

The range of disorders, in which familial relationships might be examined for the operation of multifactorial inheritance, has been greatly extended by the theoretical arguments advanced by Edwards (1960, 1963). The theoretical basis for estimating morbidity risks in the relatives of affected persons, for different population frequencies of the abnormality and for different degrees of 'heritability', has been developed along precise lines by Falconer (1965). And in the cases of a number of disorders, which manifest themselves clinically on an all-or-none basis, such as the hare-lip cleft-palate syndrome (Carter, 1965), convincing evidence has been provided that no single major gene came in question and that polygenic inheritance satisfactorily accounts for all the genetical findings.

Edwards pointed out that characteristics whose distribution appears to be discontinuous (quasi-continuous in Grueneberg's terminology) may yet be based on continuous variation if there is a threshold effect. The threshold then introduces a line of dichotomy, to one side of which all observations are regarded as negative for a given characteristic, while to the other side all observations are regarded as positive. We arbitrarily introduce such a dichotomy when we speak of people being thin, or being neurotic, or being hypertensive. But, to take the case already mentioned, a developmental abnormality such as cleft-palate (which must be counted in the adult as present or absent) is probably related to the unpunctual fusion of the margins of various grooves and holes, whose speed of development and timing in the embryo are determined by a number of genes of minor but additive effect. In other conditions the threshold is biochemical, the response to some substance showing a sudden discontinuity, as in the various hormonal switch mechanisms, or in the crystallization, incorporation or overflow which develops above a certain level, as in gouty deposits, atheroma, or glycosuria.

It is by no means out of the question that the development of schizophrenia might depend on such a biochemical threshold phenomenon; so that it becomes important to distinguish, if we can, the several expectations on a multifactorial and on a single-gene theory. In the latter case, the situation is complicated by the fact that no single-gene theory can account for the facts without supplementary hypotheses. The observations are such that we are bound to suppose that a proportion of people with a genotype adequate for the production of schizophrenia actually escape the disease, even over the course of a full lifetime. This introduces the concept of penetrance, and, on the hypothesis of a single gene, we have to concede that its penetrance is less than 100 per cent.

Edwards makes the important point that, in the case of rare diseases, such as Huntington's chorea, the use of the concept of penetrance is valid and indeed inescapable. The degree by which the incidence of Huntington's chorea in the first-degree relatives of Huntington choreics falls below the expected 50 per cent, when corrections are made for age, is small. By far the greater part of the variance among first-degree relatives is accounted for by the single-gene hypothesis; so that in assigning what remains to continuously varying factors we are being as economical in our assumptions as we can be.

The situation is different when we come to the common disorders. In this case the assumption that both a single specific gene is at work, and also other factors affecting penetrance, means that we have to say whether these other factors are hereditary or environmental in nature; in either case their effect is bound to be quasi-continuous with a threshold effect. 'In this case', writes Edwards, 'the difference between single gene concepts with penetrance, and quasi-continuous variation, is the difference between a single gene combined with multifactorial inheritance and multifactorial inheritance alone. The former hypothesis is more complex and shades into the latter as the single gene becomes of diminishing effectiveness or "lower penetrance".'

The further development of the mathematical argument leads to conclusions which can be applied practically. We can assume that first-degree relatives will resemble one another in regard to a continuous variable to a degree corresponding with a correlation coefficient of $+0.5$. If continuous is replaced by quasi-continuous variation, the proportions of pairs of first-degree relatives who are both positive, both negative, or one positive and the other negative, in respect of the threshold characteristic, will correspond to the four quadrants of a bivariate surface, with tetrachoric correlation coefficient of $+0.5$. If the threshold characteristic is shown by a proportion p of the population, then x, the proportion of first-degree relatives of a trait-bearer who also show the characteristic, approximates to $\sqrt{p}$ over a wide range of values of p. If p is less than 0.16, then x somewhat exceeds $\sqrt{p}$. Furthermore, the ratio of the incidence in first-degree relatives to the incidence in the general population approximates to $1/\sqrt{p}$. Our estimate of the morbidity risk for schizophrenia in the general population is likely to lie somewhere between 0.008 and 0.01; this means that the morbidity risk for the first-degree relatives of schizophrenics, including their children and their sibs, should be in the neighbourhood of 0·09–0·1. TABLE 4 shows an observed morbidity risk in pooled data of 0·085 for sibs and 0·123 for children, both of them compatible with the theoretically expected values within the limits of sampling and observational error. On this basis, then, multifactorial inheritance offers us a reasonably acceptable genetical theory.

A POLYGENIC MODEL OF HERITABILITY IN SCHIZOPHRENIA

The way in which hereditary factors underlying quasi-continuous variation might be investigated has been analysed in depth by Falconer (1965, 1967). The best way to introduce his model will be by a direct quotation (Falconer, 1965):

To overcome the difficulty of the all-or-none character of a disease we have to suppose that there is in fact an underlying gradation of some attribute immediately related to the causation of the disease. If we could measure this attribute, it would give us a graded scale of the degree of affectedness or normality, and we should find that all individuals above a certain value exhibited the disease and all below it did not. This hypothetical graded attribute will be referred to here as the individual's 'liability' to the disease . . . The term liability is intended to express not only the individual's innate tendency to develop or contract the disease, . . . but also the whole combination of external circumstances that makes him more or less likely to develop the disease . . . The point on the scale of liability above which all individuals are affected and below which all are normal will be called the 'threshold' . . . For the quantitative development of the idea it is necessary to define the variation of liability as being normally distributed. This gives a unit for the expression of the degree of liability, the unit being the standard deviation. This definition . . . (does) . . . exclude situations where the variation of liability is discontinuous, which would apply to diseases determined by a single major gene. The method of analysis . . . therefore applies only to diseases whose genetic component is multifactorial, or if there are few genes, where these have effects that are small in relation to the non-genetic variation.

With this introduction, we can now simplify Falconer's presentation to the simplest possible statement, taking the mathematical background for granted. We begin by ascertaining, by means of appropriate field investigations, the mean liability to a disease: (1) in the general population; (2) in the relatives (of a given degree) of propositi suffering from the disease. The regression (b) of relatives on propositi in terms of liability is then to be used to obtain an estimate of the heritability (h^2) of liability.

The reader is referred to FIGURE 4, which is taken from Falconer's article. We write:

q_g = the incidence of the disease in the general population, i.e. the proportion of the total population whose liability exceeds the threshold, i.e. the area of the tail of the normal distribution to the right of the threshold.

x_g = the distance in SDs from the population mean of the threshold value of the liability needed to provide a disease incidence of q_g. This is obviously a function of q_g.

q_r = the incidence of the disease in the relatives of propositi of the named degree.

x_r = the distance of the mean liability of these relatives leftwards from the threshold; this is obviously a function of q_r.

a = the mean liability (mean deviation) of affected individuals in the general population, i.e. in the tail end of the distribution to the right of x_g. The value of a can be obtained from the formula

$$a = z/q_g$$

in which z is the height of the ordinate at x_g. The corresponding equation giving the mean liability of individuals to the left of the threshold, i.e. normal individuals in the general population, is

$$n = z/(1-q_g).$$

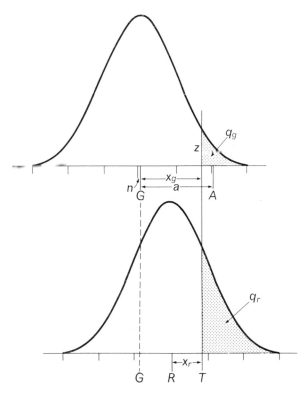

Fig. 4. Two distributions representing the general population above, and the relatives of affected individuals below, compared with reference to the fixed threshold, T.

    G = mean liability of general population
    A = mean liability of affected individuals in the general population
    R = mean liability of relatives
    q = incidence, i.e. proportion of individuals with liabilities exceeding the
          threshold
    x = deviation of threshold from mean, i.e. the normal deviate
    z = height of the ordinate at the threshold
    a = mean deviation of affected individuals from the population mean ($= z/q$)
    n = mean deviation of normal individuals from the population mean ($= z/(1-q)$)

Subscript g refers to the general population, subscript r to the relatives (Falconer, 1965).

It is to be noted that putting the mean of the normal distribution at zero gives a negative value for n.

The regression of relatives on propositi, which is equivalent (numerically equal) to the correlation between the propositi and their relatives in respect of liability, is given by the formula

$$b = (x_g - x_r)/a.$$

Heritability is defined as V_A/V_P, i.e. the ratio of additive genetic variance to total phenotypic variance. The contribution of heritability to liability can be derived from the formula

$$h^2 = b/r$$

in which r is the coefficient of relationship, i.e. 0·5 in first-degree relatives (parents, sibs, children), 0·25 in second-degree relatives (grandparents, uncles and aunts, half-sibs, nephews and nieces, grandchildren, double first cousins), 0·125 in single first cousins, etc. In the case of observations on children of conjugal pairs, both parents affected, the sib-sib correlation $r = 1$ and $h^2 = b$.

The use of empirical observations to form an estimate of heritability is aided by the tables provided by Falconer in an appendix to his paper. In these he gives for every value of q the corresponding value of x and a.

We may now use Falconer's method to estimate heritability in schizophrenia by using the empirically observed risks of schizophrenia for members of the general population and for various kinds of relatives of schizophrenic propositi, data taken from TABLES 3 and 4. Data on MZ twins are not suitable for the methods of calculation used here. The summed data of TABLE 3 gave a value of q_g of 1·17 per cent; on page 13 we gave reasons for preferring the estimate of 0·85 per cent. Whether we use the one estimate or the other, we find we get rather widely varying estimates of heritability, and that they tend to run rather high [see TABLE 23]. For comparison we may mention Falconer's own work

TABLE 23

ESTIMATES OF HERITABILITY (h^2) IN SCHIZOPHRENIA, BY FALCONER'S METHOD, AS AGAINST TWO ALTERNATIVE ESTIMATES OF THE INCIDENCE OF SCHIZOPHRENIA IN THE GENERAL POPULATION

	$q\%$	x	a	b_1	b_2	r	$h_1{}^2$	$h_2{}^2$
General population								
Estimate 1	0·85	2·387	2·720					
Estimate 2	1·17	2·267	2·612					
Relatives								
Sibs	8·51	1·371		0·3735	0·3430	0·5	0·75	0·69
Children	12·31	1·160		0·4511	0·4238		0·90	0·85
Uncles and aunts	2·01	2·052		0·1232	0·0823	0·25	0·49	0·33
Half-sibs	3·22	1·849		0·1978	0·1600		0·79	0·64
Nephews and nieces	2·25	2·004		0·1408	0·1007		0·56	0·40
Grandchildren	2·81	1·909		0·1757	0·1371		0·70	0·55
First cousins	2·91	1·894		0·1813	0·1428	0·125	1·45	1·14

(1967) on diabetes which yielded, in two independent samples, estimates of heritability of 0·34 and 0·35.

The heritability estimate provided by the data for first cousins stands at the impossible level of over 100 per cent. Falconer (1970) has also found in the case of diabetes that all first- and second-degree relatives give reasonably consistent estimates, but cousins give estimates over 100 per cent. Where information about first cousins is obtained by questioning propositi (as has been the case both in diabetes and schizophrenia investigations), a bias is likely to arise from a differential loss of information (Reich, 1970). While people can recall positive and negative data about all or nearly all their first- and second-degree relatives, they are likely to forget some of their cousins, and those who have the same disease are less likely to be forgotten than those who do not.

However, even leaving out the cousins, heritability estimates in schizophrenia average about 0·58, which still looks rather high. There are many reasons for this, all of which lead to the conclusion that the observational data we are trying to fit into Falconer's model may not be the appropriate ones.

1. It is important, in applying Falconer's model, that the affected relatives should be ascertained by the same criteria as the propositi. Thus, in the case of schizophrenia, if the propositi have all been hospitalized cases, only those affected relatives who have been hospitalized with a diagnosis of schizophrenia should be counted (Reich, 1970). In fact, psychiatric field workers have always included among affected relatives those who were recognizably schizophrenic on interview, or as shown by the report of a good informant, even if never hospitalized. If these cases were omitted, estimates of the morbidity risks in relatives would be considerably lower than those given in our tables, probably about only half as great, which would lead to lower heritability estimates.

2. Falconer's 'incidence' does not correspond exactly with the 'incidences' or 'morbidity risks' which we have been considering. The morbidity risk of schizophrenia for an individual we have taken as the probability that at some time in the course of a life-time, say of 70 years, he will have achieved a diagnosis (perhaps retrospectively) of schizophrenia. 'Incidence' in Falconer's terminology has rather the epidemiological meaning of prevalence; it means the frequency of affected individuals, 'i.e. the proportion of living individuals found to be affected in the population, or among the relatives. The incidence in a particular age-group is the proportion of people in that age-group who have the disease, irrespective of the age of onset.' So it is that Falconer's estimates of the heritability of diabetes mellitus are age-specific, and in the case of diabetes are higher for younger age groups than for older ones. The meaning of this is that environmental variance will have entered more largely into the observations at later ages. When we come to schizophrenia we might not find quite the same effect, as old-age schizophrenia makes up a very small part of the total picture of schizophrenia, whereas the diabetes of later ages constitutes a large part of the totality of diabetes. However, by using in the case of schizophrenia the life-time morbidity risk we are entering into Falconer's model numbers which are likely to be somewhat larger than the age-specific prevalences for which the model was designed. This might also lead to an exaggeration of the estimates of heritability.

3. Finally we have to bear in mind that if we are to regard the estimates of heritability as valid, we must be able to suppose that the correlation between propositi and relatives is not at all caused by similarity of environment. We know that there are often, perhaps always, environmental causes of resemblance, and so the estimate of the heritability can never be better than an upper limit to the true value. Falconer (1967) points out that it would be valuable to discover the incidence in people related to propositi by marriage only, such as brothers- and sisters-in-law, which could show whether the correlations estimated are seriously inflated by environmental similarity.

There are many epidemiological and family history similarities between diabetes and schizophrenia, and we cannot refrain from quoting here from Falconer's final paragraphs of discussion in his 1967 paper of monogenic and polygenic theories.

The single-gene hypothesis has been further modified by the supposition that there are minor, or modifying, genes at loci different from the major gene, which influence whether a person with the 'diabetic genotype' becomes diabetic or not. When modifying genes have to be introduced, the distinction between the two hypotheses themselves, as well as between their consequences, becomes very tenuous . . .

Thus the conflict—if there is still a conflict—is no longer between the hypotheses themselves but rather between the questions they lead the investigator to ask. Adherents to the single-gene hypothesis want to know if the gene is dominant or recessive, how frequently it leads to diabetes in those possessing it (i.e. its penetrance), whether the same gene is responsible for the diabetes in different families, what is the frequency of the gene or genes in the population, and what are the factors that determine whether the 'diabetic genotype' is expressed as overt diabetes or not. Adherents to the multifactorial hypothesis think that it is impossible at the moment to answer these questions because the individual genes cannot yet be unambiguously identified. The genetic properties that can be investigated are therefore the combined properties of all the genes in aggregate. The concept of the 'diabetic genotype' is replaced by that of liability, and the questions to be asked concern the causes of variation of liability. This approach can lead to a better understanding of the disease, but it is not a substitute for the study of the individual genes. Eventually it will be possible by biochemical means to identify some, at least, of the genes responsible for diabetes: the discovery of a biochemically different insulin in juvenile diabetics (Roy, Elliot, Shapcott and O'Brien, 1966) is an encouraging beginning. If this difference proves to be inherited as a single gene, as it seems likely to be, then one of the genes causing early-onset diabetes will have been identified. If one of the genes concerned is eventually identified and can be studied the question will arise of how 'important' this gene is in the aetiology of diabetes. Here the concept of liability and its variance will be needed, because the 'importance' of a gene will have to be assessed from its effect on liability and from the amount that it contributes to the variance of liability in the population.

In the same paper Falconer writes: 'The best test of the validity of the method as a whole is the practical one of whether it works; whether, that is to say, the results it gives are consistent with what is known about multifactorial inheritance in general, and also self-consistent when the heritability is estimated in different ways.' On this basis, the application of Falconer's model to the data on schizophrenia suggests that it does work. A hypothesis of multifactorial inheritance is adequate to the facts. However, we are entitled to demand a number of services from our working hypotheses, beyond the simple candidate qualification of not conflicting with well-established observations. We need them psychologically to give us a feeling that they 'explain' the manifold circumstances we are trying to grasp. But their real function is to provide us with clues to where we should go looking next, and tools to extract and sift information of a kind not previously envisaged.

ARGUMENTS FOR AND AGAINST
A POLYGENIC THEORY

A polygenic model of the contribution by heredity to the aetiology of schizophrenia has very practical merits. It is a model which is certainly applicable to a number of physical disorders, and may well be the best one for a variety of common ones; it is conceptually the simplest of all hypotheses at present available, and it should prove capable of being tested and refuted, or being made more likely, by further research and the accumulation of data of the right kind. Some of the data we already have fit in with it very well: the appearance of schizophrenics as the children of matings between two normal persons, a higher risk for close relatives of schizophrenics than for unselected members of the general population, and a risk for such relatives which is higher when the index case is severely affected than when he is mildly affected. Gottesman and Shields (1967), who regard this hypothesis as the most useful one at the present stage of our knowledge, have pointed out that with polygenic inheritance it is much easier to explain, than with any monogenic theory, the persistence and stability of the general population risk of schizophrenia when the fertility of schizophrenics themselves is a reduced one. In fact, observational data lead to an estimate of 'fitness' of the schizophrenic phenotype of only about 0·7. A major gene, manifesting dominantly with 100 per cent penetrance, with such a low chance of maintaining itself from one generation to the next, would decline to a very low gene frequency, unless it were maintained by a compensatory mechanism of large effect [see p. 69]. If the manifestation of schizophrenia depends on an unduly high dose of certain genes, which in a smaller dose do not affect fitness, the rate of elimination of these genes would in any case be low, and might quite easily be compensated by individual gene advantages of slight degree. Penrose (1949b) has shown that low fertility at the extremes of a normal distribution can be reconciled with a stable equilibrium in the population.

Polygenic (or multifactorial) inheritance for schizophrenia has been explicitly supported by Kay (1963). He investigated 57 cases of late paraphrenia, 48 of them being women, mean age at admission to hospital 69 years. The clinical characteristics of the group were such as to differentiate them from patients of the same age with other diagnoses; their survival and mortality rates, for instance, were closely similar to those of the general population and markedly different from those of organic psychotics. The expectancies of schizophrenia for their sibs was found to be 4·9±1·7 per cent, and for their children 7·3±4·2 per cent. The age of onset of schizophrenia among the relatives was in the large majority of the 22 secondary cases before the age of 40, i.e. approximating to that of schizophrenia in the general population. Kay argues that the paraphrenia of old age, together with the schizophrenia-like psychoses or symptomatic schizophrenias associated with epilepsy, head injury, amphetamine intoxication, etc., are clinically on a par with schizophrenia, and that there is no adequate reason for postulating distinctions on a genetical basis. There are also differences in the degree of familial loading to be seen within the universally accepted symptom-complex of schizophrenia, in that the relatives of paranoid patients show lower loading figures than those of catatonics and hebephrenics. The work by Davison and Bagley [p. 29] provides some arguments against this point of view.

Ødegaard (1970) has also supported the polygenic theory with statistical evidence. He points out that the monogenic and polygenic theories suggest rather different predictions about the risk of schizophrenia in the sibs of: (1) a single schizophrenic index case, and (2) two affected sibs constituting an index pair; by the monogenic theory the risks in the two types of family should not differ very much, on a polygenic basis the risk in the second case should be much greater than in the first. There should also be some difference between families in which apart from the index case there is an affected parent, uncle or aunt, and families where there is no other affected person outside the sibships inquired into. He provides the following tabulation:

TABLE 24
RISKS FOR SIBS WHEN NONE, ONE, OR MORE ANCESTORS AFFECTED
(Ødegaard, 1970)

NUMBER OF RELATIVES PSYCHOTIC IN PARENTAL GENERATION	N	SIBS PSYCHOTIC	PER CENT PSYCHOTIC
None	990	67	$8 \cdot 3 \pm 0 \cdot 97$
one	521	55	$14 \cdot 9 \pm 1 \cdot 85$
two or more	284	45	$20 \cdot 9 \pm 2 \cdot 77$

Certainly differences of such magnitude cannot be explained by a monogenic theory unaided, and are quite in conformity with polygenic causation. If these figures are confirmed, it would be necessary to suppose that the major gene of a monogenic theory was subject to a manifestation rate affected by other genes. The distinction between monogenic and polygenic theories in the last resort cannot be hard and fast, and just as the monogenic hypothesis may need support by postulating polygenic effects, so the polygenic hypothesis may be made more plausible by postulating some contribution by dominant or non-additive genetic factors.

It has always seemed to the present writers that multifactorial inheritance is much more plausible for manic-depressive illness than for schizophrenia (rather than the other way round). Underlying quasi-continuous variation, continuous variation is to be sought and found. Underlying the manic-depressive illness one can find a quality of temperament, usually called cyclothymic, tending to vary spontaneously in mood; and such a quality is capable of being shown to a greater or lesser degree. In the same way 'schizoid' traits of personality are to be found in the personalities of patients who become schizophrenic, and also in their relatives; but in this case the connexion is much less close, since about half, or perhaps even the majority, of schizophrenic patients show no very obvious features of personality before the illness, and a few days may transform an apparently very ordinary individual into a condition in which his personality has become changed almost beyond recognition. The majority of those who are concerned day by day with the diagnosis and treatment of schizophrenic patients find it difficult to believe that there is not something specific about the way things have gone wrong, whether that specificity is to be derived from genetic or environmental causes. To them, the model of quasi-continuous variation and a threshold effect has an unconvincing quality; and gout, atheroma and glycosuria seem models rather wide of the mark.

This is a clinician's viewpoint, and even as such is very far from being universally accepted. Gottesman and Shields (1967) say that 'although schizophrenia is necessarily viewed as an all-or-none character for record-keeping purposes, clinical contact with preschizophrenics or "recovered" cases shows clearly the artificiality of such a dichotomy.' Kay, also, thinks that there is little force in the argument that because schizophrenia presents as a clear-cut disease, sharply demarcated from normality, it is therefore likely to be due to a major gene. Remitted and borderline cases, and *formes frustes,* are not uncommon. He thinks that the frequency with which variants of personality occur both in the patients and in their relatives suggests transmission by polygenes; a polygenic hypothesis, he says, is now generally accepted as covering most epilepsies, except for a few rare cases; the low incidence of schizophrenia among the relatives of elderly schizophrenics is simply accounted for by a lowering of the threshold in their case.

Arguments of these kinds, then, though they have an immediate appeal to clinicians, are likely to pull them in opposite directions and to lead to no agreement, let alone a definitive solution of an important problem. We shall need to consider whether we have available any means of distinguishing the consequences of a polygenic theory with those of a modified major gene theory, which is the other significant candidate in the field. Edwards (1960, 1963) has drawn attention to two consequences of multifactorial inheritance which differ from those of single factor inheritance. With the former, the risk to the unborn increases with the number of relatives affected, while it does not do so with single factor inheritance. Secondly, when the arbitrarily dichotomized variate is measurable (e.g. in gout, feeblemindedness), there should be no bimodality in the scores; and, if dominant inheritance is simulated, the hypothetical non-carrier parent should tend to have above-average scores. In the case of schizophrenia we can get some data relevant to the first type of test; but with the second we shall have to wait for reliable measurement of some kind of substrate, whether this will be a psychological measurement of 'schizoidness' of personality or, perhaps, a biochemical measurement of variation in efficiency of an enzyme system.

Bruno Schulz (1934) carried out a test of the genetic homogeneity of his large material of sibs of schizophrenic patients. He went at this task in two ways. One was to find whether the secondary cases in the sibships tended to cluster in any way, or whether they were randomly distributed, in sibships of all magnitudes, as a consequence of the hypothesis that the risk for the sib of a schizophrenic was the same, independently of the state of other co-sibs. The computations were very elaborate and did not lead to a conclusive result. The other way, a much simpler one, was to single out the sibships in which there had been two or more probands, and to find whether the risk for sibs was greater or not than in the sibships in which there had been only one proband. Of course, for the purpose of this computation, each pair of probands counts as one double-proband; the single sibship in which there were three probands provided three doubles, and this sibship entered three times into the calculation. On this basis he had 20 double-probands with 57·5 sibs (adjusted for age distribution) of which 6 (10·4 per cent) were schizophrenic. In the sib material as a whole (BZ = 1959·5) there were 6·7 per cent of schizophrenics, or 8·2 per cent including probable but not certain schizophrenics. Schulz thought that the difference between the incidences in single-proband and double-proband was noteworthy;

TABLE 25

INCIDENCE OF SCHIZOPHRENIA IN SIBS OF SCHIZOPHRENICS, CLASSIFIED BY PSYCHIATRIC STATE OF PARENTS

(Data mainly from Zerbin-Rüdin, 1967b)

| | PARENTS | | | | | | |
| | FREE FROM SCHIZ. | | | NOT FREE FROM SCHIZ. | | | |
	BZ	N	%	BZ	N	%	RATIO
Schulz (1932)	1848·5	150	8·1	111·0	13	11·7	1·4
Luxenburger (1936)	237·0	26	11·0	41·0	6	14·6	1·3
Galatschyan (1937)	271·0	33	12·2	51·0	12	23·3	1·9
Kallmann (1938)	1630·5	169	10·4	366·0	61	16·7	1·6
Böök (1953)	222·0	20	9·0	55·0	7	12·7	1·4
Constantinidis and Garrone (1964)	not stated		13·5	not stated		28·5	2·1

BZ (Bezugsziffer) = size of sample adjusted for age; N = number of secondary cases of schizophrenia among sibs, certain or probable.

but in fact, owing to the smallness of the numbers in the double-proband sibships, the difference between 10·4 per cent in the double-proband sibships and 6·6 per cent in the single-proband sibships is well within the limits of small-sample error $(0·30 > p > 0·20)$.

The other test material we can use are the differential figures for the risk of schizophrenia in the sibs of schizophrenics from two types of mating, i.e. when neither parent has had a schizophrenic illness, and when one parent is or has been schizophrenic, definitely or probably. The figures available from a number of workers are shown in TABLE 25. From this we see that there is only a moderate increase in the risk to the sibs of a schizophrenic index case when one parent is affected than when neither is, an increase in fact of about 70 per cent. On the basis of a polygenic determination one expects a much larger risk for sibs of an index case when one parent is affected than when neither is affected; and Vogel and Krüger (1967) have estimated the expected ratio in the case of an abnormality with a population frequency of 0·01 as being about 2·5. Clearly, if the genetic determination is by a single major gene of diminished penetrance, one or other of the parents of a schizophrenic will be a gene-carrier, and it might not make much difference whether this was so manifestly or not. As we shall see when we come to discuss the monogenic theory, on the model there offered the theoretical ratio is 1·44.

THEORIES POSTULATING A SINGLE GENE

We have discussed theories of the aetiology of schizophrenia coming under Rosenthal's 'life-experience' and 'diathesis-stress' categories [see p. 37], and it remains to examine the third alternative, that involving a single major gene, dominant, recessive or intermediate, which may be supposed to lead to some disorder of metabolism, providing the physical predisposition for the mental illness. Theories of this type were the earliest in the field, being naturally the first to be thought of when efforts were made to apply Mendelism to psychiatric genetics. In a simple and unmodified form they proved unsatisfactory, and for serious consideration we can only use hypotheses which involve a less than 100 per cent penetrance or manifestation rate.

The hypothesis of a single major gene, intermediate between dominance and recessivity, i.e. manifesting in all homozygotes and in some but not all heterozygotes, was first advanced by Jan Böök (1953), as the simplest way of accounting for his findings in the course of a large-scale investigation of a Swedish population. These were people, about 9,000 in number in 1949, living in a very isolated region some hundred kilometres north of the Arctic Circle. The area occupied was approximately 5,000 square kilometres, so that the families in this population were isolated not only from the rest of Sweden by very poor communications, but also isolated from one another by the distances from home to home. Nearly half the population were farmers or lumbermen, only small numbers being employed in other trades or in the civil service. There had been very little immigration into the area for over 200 years, and nearly everybody living in these parts were the descendants of settlers of the period 1650–1730. Life was hard. The mean temperatures in January and July are respectively −14°C and +13°C, and the sun is not seen at all from the beginning of December to the middle of January. This population was of special genetical interest because of its social homogeneity, the inbreeding which made it more than usually genetically homogeneous, and the considerable but fairly uniform physical and psychological stress under which everyone lived.

In this isolated little world, aided by a wife who was herself native to those parts and extremely helpful in making contacts, Böök succeeded in ascertaining all the individuals who had had a schizophrenic illness among all residents and all who had been residents between 1902 and 1949. Some very remarkable findings emerged:

1. Of all psychoses schizophrenia was the only common one, and it predominated to an extent not hitherto met with. Out of the 183 psychotics ascertained 123 were schizophrenic and a further 33 were very probably schizophrenic. There were only 4 manic-depressives, all women, so that the schizophrenic manic-depressive ratio was 39:1, 95:0 in men and 61:4 in women.

2. The local incidence of schizophrenic illnesses was very high. Böök calculated the morbid risk for schizophrenia from birth to the age of 55 as 2·92 per cent for males and 3·20 per cent for females, 3·04 per cent for both sexes together,

i.e. about three times as high as other workers have found in other parts of the world.

3. Clinically, the schizophrenic illnesses ran very much to a pattern, predominantly catatonic in type, and usually with an insidious onset leading after some time to outbreaks of impulsive aggression.

4. The following morbidity risks for the relatives of schizophrenics could be calculated: parents 12·0 per cent, sibs of schizophrenics coming from parental matings of two non-schizophrenics 9·0 per cent, sibs where one parent was schizophrenic and the other not 12·7 per cent.

Böök interpreted his findings in a very cautious way, but he was concerned to offer a working hypothesis and for this he thought one could accept the view that the schizophrenic syndrome is caused primarily by major gene differences. At the time at which he was writing, the modification of polygenic hypotheses to allow for non-continuous distribution, as developed by Edwards, had not been proposed; it is quite possible that, if such a model had been available, Böök would have preferred it to the one he adopted. After showing that his findings could not be accounted for by either the theory of (recessive) manifestation in all homozygotes and in no heterozygotes, or by the simpler type of dominant hypothesis, he demonstrated that the hypothesis of a gene (with properties intermediate between dominance and recessivity), manifesting in some heterozygotes and in all homozygotes did meet the observations. He concluded:

I therefore venture to advance the hypothesis that the type of schizophrenia prevalent in the investigation area is primarily due to a major simple dominant gene with a heterozygous penetrance of about 20 per cent and a homozygous penetrance of about 100 per cent. The frequency of this gene in the population was estimated at about 7 per cent. The penetrance refers to a schizophrenic psychosis as defined in this paper.

He went on then to consider how this gene could maintain itself in the population at the very high frequency of 0·07 when it carried with it (in those carriers who became psychotic) a high selective disadvantage; and he showed mathematically that fresh mutation could only keep the gene frequency at this level if the mutation rate were almost impossibly high. We shall come at a later page to consider how relatively high gene frequencies of a disadvantageous gene may be maintained.

The next step taken, by Slater (1958a), was to examine the question whether Böök's hypothesis (which he applied only to the population isolate he studied, and only to the clinical type of schizophrenia there found to predominate) could be generally extended. It was found that when the morbidity risks of various classes of relatives of schizophrenics were considered, an intermediate gene behaves in a very different way from a dominant or a recessive gene, giving risks which over the greater part of the range of intermediacy are much lower than theirs.

If the frequency of the schizophrenic gene is p, then the frequency of the normal allelomorph is $(1 - p)$. Given mating at random in respect of the gene, the general population will consist of the three genotypes, normal homozygotes, heterozygotes and abnormal homozygotes, in the proportions given by the formula

$$(1-p)^2+2p(1-p)+p^2 = 1.$$

If the manifestation rate of the schizophrenic gene in the heterozygote is m, then the incidence of schizophrenia in the general population is given by the formula

$$s = 2mp(1 - p) + p^2.$$

If we take as a basic observational datum the value of s, the incidence of schizo-phrenia in the general population calculated as the morbidity risk of schizo-phrenia for the average member of the population over a life-span of, say, 55 years, then knowing s we can calculate the value of m for any given value of p, or calculate the value of p for any given value of m. Clearly m cannot be greater than 1, when manifestation is 100 per cent in all heterozygotes, nor can it be less than 0, when only the homozygotes will manifest the disease. When m is 1 we have the picture given by dominance, when it is 0 we have the picture given by recessivity; between its limits of 1 and 0 we have every possible intermediate value to consider. This can be seen from FIGURE 5.

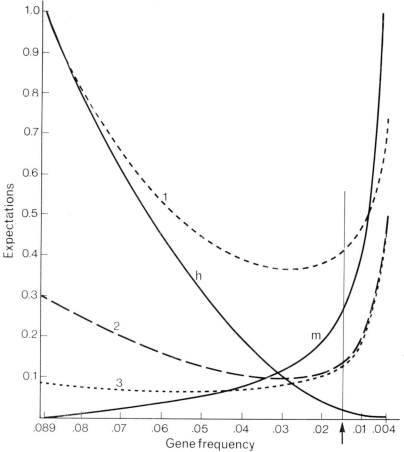

Fig. 5. 1 = Children of parents both schizophrenic; 2 = Children of parents, one schizophrenic; 3 = Sibs of schizophrenics

In this figure the conditions are shown when $s = 0.008$. At the extreme left of the figure we have the conditions of complete recessivity. This gives us the highest possible value for the gene frequency p at 0.089. The manifestation rate (in heterozygotes) is 0, and h, which is the proportion of all schizophrenics who are homozygotes is 1. At this point the expected observational data are a 30 per cent expectation of schizophrenia in sibs, an expectation of 8·9 per cent in the children of one schizophrenic, and an expectation of 100 per cent in the children of matings where both parents are schizophrenic. At the extreme right of the figure, where we have the conditions of simple dominance, the gene frequency p is at a minimum of 0.004, the manifestation rate has become 1, h the proportion of all schizophrenics who are homozygotes has dropped to 0.002, and the morbidity risks in sibs and in children of one schizophrenic parent are both 50 per cent, the risk for the child of two schizophrenics 75 per cent. Obviously the observational data were not to be matched with either of these extremes; but at the time of writing in 1958, Slater could provide a good match at just about the lowest point on the risk curves, where p was 0.015 and m 0.26. The data in TABLE 26 were thought to be about as good a fit as one could expect.

TABLE 26

FIT OF OBSERVATIONAL DATA TO THEORETICAL EXPECTATIONS ON
A MONOGENIC THEORY OF SCHIZOPHRENIA

(Slater, 1958a)

EXPECTATION OF SCHIZOPHRENIA FOR	EXPECTED	OBSERVED	OBSERVER
Children of one schizophrenic	0·143	0·164	Kallmann
Children of two schizophrenics	0·396	0·392	Elsässer
Sibs of schizophrenics	0·144	0·142	Kallmann

Since the time of this publication, Zerbin-Rüdin (1967b) has made available a compilation of the results collected by a multiplicity of workers, which is therefore based much more broadly than Kallmann's figures which were used by Slater in 1958. Making use of these collective data we take as our first fixed point a schizophrenia morbidity risk for the general population (based on a sample size of 330,752 individuals) of 0·85 per cent. The next most secure observational figure is the risk in sibs of schizophrenics, based on a sample size of 8505 individuals. Including both definite and probable schizophrenics among the secondary cases, the morbidity risk of schizophrenia in sibs is 10·2 per cent; taking only the certain cases, the risk is 8·5 per cent [see TABLE 24]. The best approximation we can get from theory is when $p = 0.03$, when with a manifestation rate of approximately 0.13 (0.13058) the risk for sibs is 10·2 per cent. Using these values of p and of m, by the method shown in TABLE 27, we can calculate the theoretical morbidity risk for all relatives, giving us a considerable number of theoretical values to compare with our observed ones. The comparison of observation with theoretical expectation is shown in TABLE 28, which gives two sets of observational data, based respectively on: (1) the number of diagnostically certain ('sicher') cases of schizophrenia found among the relatives; and (2) the total of both certain and probable ('fraglich') cases among relatives.

The way in which the calculation is made in the case of the sibs is as follows. We first note the frequencies of matings which are capable of producing schizophrenic children. As we begin our observations with a schizophrenic proband, the relative frequencies with which we ascertain parental matings of given genotypes will depend not only on the population frequency of the mating (on a hypothesis of random mating) but also on the frequency with which schizophrenic children result from it. It is the product of these two frequencies (the mating frequency and the weighting factor) which will determine the frequency with which schizophrenics and non-schizophrenics will be expected among the sibs of index cases. Following directly from theory we can draw up the following tabulations, in which A signifies the schizophrenogenic gene, p its population frequency and m its manifestation rate in the heterozygote.

TABLE 27

EXPECTATIONS, IN TERMS OF p AND m, IN OFFSPRING BY TYPE OF PARENTAL MATING

| | | | OFFSPRING | |
MATING	FREQUENCY	WEIGHTING	SCHIZOPHRENIC	NOT SCHIZ.
Indifferently of psychiatric status of parents				
AA×AA	p^4	1	1	0
AA×Aa	$4p^3(1-p)$	$\frac{1}{2}(1+m)$	$\frac{1}{2}(1+m)$	$\frac{1}{2}(1-m)$
AA×aa	$2p^2(1-p)^2$	m	m	$1-m$
Aa×Aa	$4p^2(1-p)^2$	$(1+2m)/4$	$(1+2m)/4$	$(3-2m)/4$
Aa×aa	$4p(1-p)^3$	$\frac{1}{2}m$	$\frac{1}{2}m$	$\frac{1}{2}(2-m)$
One parent schizophrenic				
AA×Aa	$4(1-m)p^3(1-p)$	$\frac{1}{2}(1+m)$	$\frac{1}{2}(1+m)$	$\frac{1}{2}(1-m)$
AA×aa	$2p^2(1-p)^2$	m	m	$1-m$
Aa×Aa	$8m(1-m)p^2(1-p)^2$	$(1+2m)/4$	$(1+2m)/4$	$(3-2m)/4$
Aa×aa	$4mp(1-p)^3$	$\frac{1}{2}m$	$\frac{1}{2}m$	$\frac{1}{2}(2-m)$
Neither parent schizophrenic				
Aa×Aa	$4(1-m)^2p^2(1-p)^2$	$(1+2m)/4$	$(1+2m)/4$	$(3-2m)/4$
Aa×aa	$4(1-m)p(1-p)^3$	$\frac{1}{2}m$	$\frac{1}{2}m$	$\frac{1}{2}(2-m)$

Looking at TABLE 28 in detail, we see that there is a fairly good fit between theoretical expectation and observation, with two exceptions: the observed morbid risk in the children of schizophrenics is about 40 per cent higher than theoretical expectation, but the observed risk in second-degree relatives is only about 75 per cent of the theoretical figure. Both of these deviations from expectation might be related to environmental factors affecting the manifestation rate.

On the basis of the polygenic theory also, the empirical risk for the children of a schizophrenic parent is uncomfortably high; but the figures for second-degree relatives fit the polygenic theory quite well, and indeed fit it better than the monogenic theory.

Taking the data as a whole, we can conclude that the hypothesis of a major gene, intermediate on the dominance-recessivity scale, is adequate for predictive and working purposes, and is a reasonably acceptable rival to the polygenic theory. The predictions which can be made with it as the basis are no less exact

TABLE 28
EXPECTANCIES OF SCHIZOPHRENIA IN RELATIVES OF INDEX CASES

RELATIONSHIP	N	OBSERVED SCHIZOPHRENIC NO.		%		THEORETICAL EXPECTATION %
		(a)	(b)	(a)	(b)	
Sibs (all)	8505	724	865	8·5	10·2	10·2
Sibs (neither parent schizophrenic)	7535	621	731	8·2	9·7	9·4
Sibs (one parent schizophrenic)	675	93	116	13·8	17·2	13·5
Children	1227	151	170	12·3	13·9	8·8
Children of mating schiz. × schiz.	134	49	62	36·6	46·3	37·1
Second-degree relatives						
Half-sibs	311	10	11	3·2	3·5	4·7
Uncles and aunts	3376	68	123	2·0	3·6	4·7
Nephews and nieces	2315	52	61	2·2	2·6	4·7
Grandchildren	713	20	25	2·8	3·5	4·7

(a) diagnostically certain cases only; (b) also including probable schizophrenics. The theoretical expectations are calculated on the values for best fit:
   general population risk of schizophrenia $s = 0.0085$
   frequency of schizophrenic gene $p = 0.03$
   manifestation rate of gene in heterozygote $m = 0.13058$.
For these values, the proportion of schizophrenics who will be homozygotes is about 10 per cent.

than with the polygenic theory, and in some cases may be much more easy to formulate and to calculate.[1]

ARGUMENTS FOR AND AGAINST A MONOGENIC THEORY

The monogenic theory is obviously, at best, an oversimplification of what must be a complexly interacting set of factors in determining the genetic predisposition and the frequency with which it manifests in recognizable and diagnosable schizophrenia. Apart from the hypothetical specific gene, it must be supposed that other genes of minor effect, the genotypic milieu, must come into the picture; and blood-related individuals will resemble one another in respect of these accessory genetic factors as well as in the possession (or not) of the major

---

[1] It is noteworthy that a monogenic (dominant) theory, differently formulated, has been adopted by Meehl (1962) and Heston (1970). But the phenotype with which each of them is concerned is not so much schizophrenia as what one might call a schizoid state, which should be recognizable, and which provides a necessary basis for the manifestation of the psychosis. Heston speaks of 'schizoid disease'; and Meehl considers the predisposition at three levels, 'schizotaxia', 'schizotypy' and 'schizophrenia'. As far as the testing of genetical hypotheses is concerned, this broadening of concepts adds to one's difficulties rather than helping. One might indeed say that the broader and more flexible one's hypothesis, the more probable it seems, and the better it appears able to cover observational data unlimited in their extent, the less 'falsifiable' it is in Popper's sense, and the less valuable it is heuristically.

gene itself. It may well be that factors of these kinds are the reason for the deviation of observation from theoretical expectation in some of the data shown in TABLE 28. However, it should not count against a hypothesis that it is an over-simplification. We need to know just how far we can get with the simplest possible theoretical structure before we start to modify it. The deviations mentioned are not as yet even reliable, let alone sufficiently so as to constitute a counter-argument. What we need are tests which will specifically discriminate between expectations on a polygenic and a monogenic basis. Carter (1969) has recently discussed this problem. It is an important one, since, as he points out, 'where inheritance is polygenic it is unlikely, in contrast to the situation with single-gene-determined diseases, that a search for a single biochemical abnor-mality underlying the condition will be profitable.' Among the tests he suggests, the following would seem to be relevant to schizophrenia:

1. With polygenic inheritance (unlike the usual situation with single genes), the risks to relatives will vary from family to family, and be bigger for instance where there are two affected.

2. The more severe the condition in the index case the greater the risk to a relative.

3. Where the sex ratio differs markedly from equality, the risk is higher in relatives of index cases of the spared sex.

4. Increase in parental consanguinity is expected, in the case of common conditions by about 50–100 per cent.

The first criterion has been discussed in earlier pages. Ødegaard's data, TABLE 24, show a risk 2·5 times as great to the sibs of a schizophrenic index case where there are two or more individuals affected in the parental generation than where there are none. This increase would be of the right order to support polygenic causation. On the other hand the data shown in TABLE 25 tend in the opposite direction. The empirical ratio of the risk to sibs when one parent is schizophrenic with the risk when neither parent is schizophrenic, which averaged over six observational series is 1·6, fits much better with the monogenic hypothesis (expectation 1·44) than with the polygenic hypothesis (expectation 2·5 according to Vogel and Krüger, 1967).

Slater (1966) examined the possibility of distinguishing the consequences of monogenic and polygenic hypotheses by observing whether secondary cases of schizophrenia observed among the ascendance (parents, grandparents, uncles and aunts, etc.) tended to be bilaterally distributed or predominantly unilateral, i.e. either on the paternal or on the maternal side. Use was made of a specification of the polygenic model in which a deviation of two standard deviations from the population mean (i.e. applying to about 2·3 per cent of individuals in the general population) brought the individual over the threshold with about a 37 per cent chance of manifesting as diagnosable schizophrenia. On this basis a pair of second-degree relatives would have about 22 chances of being either paternal or maternal to 10 chances of being one paternal and the other maternal. Slater and Tsuang (1968) then examined Bethlem-Maudsley case records to see what the empirical distribution was in the case of both schizophrenia and manic-depression. In schizophrenia the ratio was 37:10(N = 53), and was significantly deviated from expectation; in manic-depression it was 25:10 (N = 75), which was not a significant deviation. The finding is certainly suggestive of some element of dominance entering the picture in the case of schizophrenia, even if no very great reliance can be put upon it.

Probably the data which are most strongly suggestive of the significance of a major gene in the aetiology has been provided by Karlsson from his extended family studies in Iceland (1966). A beautiful example is given by his investigation of the descendants of a priest born in Iceland in the year 1781 and his wife who had a family of 13 children. Twelve of these 13 sibs married and had children, grandchildren and great-grandchildren to a total of 967 descendants who were traced by Karlsson, with ascertainment of whether or not any named individual had had a psychotic illness. Very strikingly it was found that the 23 psychotic descendants clustered into six of the twelve pedigrees. Two characteristic pedigrees are shown in FIGURES 6 and 7; perhaps even more strikingly it was found that the single psychotic member in a pedigree of 78 individuals (sib H) came from one of H's daughters who had married into a heavily loaded family.

These pedigrees do not fit a polygenic model at all well. On that theoretical basis one would suppose that the degree of predisposition of the 12 sibs A to L would be normally distributed about a common mean, and that the extent to which schizophrenia was manifested in their descendants would also be unimodally distributed. The fact that it is not, but is clearly bimodally distributed, suggests very strongly that there was a fifty-fifty chance of inheriting a major gene for the 12 children of the ancestral priest and his wife, and that 5 of them did inherit the gene and 7 did not. The observed and the expected distribution of the twelve pedigrees, in terms of number of psychotic descendants, is shown in FIGURE 8; and the comparison of observation with expectation in TABLE 29.[1]

TABLE 29

DISTRIBUTION OF PEDIGREES FROM A SIBSHIP OF TWELVE

PEDIGREES WITH SCHIZOPHRENIC DESCENDANTS NUMBERING	OBSERVED	EXPECTED
0	6	2·598
1 or 2	1	5·757
3 or more	5	3·645
Total	12	12·000

Observations against expectations on a polygenic basis. $\chi^2 = 8\cdot89$, 2 d.f., $0\cdot02 > p > 0\cdot01$.

Finally, we may briefly consider one of the objections which is advanced against a major gene hypothesis, namely that with the low fitness of schizophrenics, one might expect that the specific schizophrenogenic gene would be

Karlsson's own preference is for a theory involving two pairs of genes, i.e. two loci; but this does not differ as much as might be supposed from the simple monogenic theory, and, by postulating 9 different genotypes, is a theory which is difficult to test.

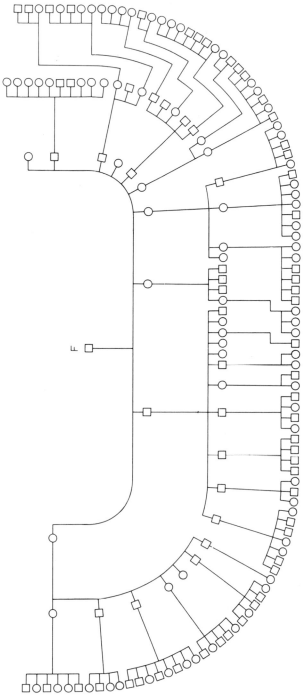

Fig. 6. From a sibship of 12, descendants of sib F. No schizophrenia is known in this branch of the family (Karlsson, 1966).

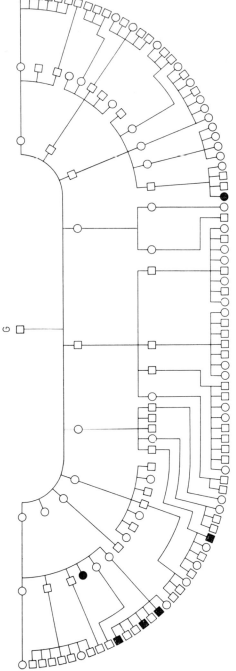

Fig. 7. From a sibship of 12, descendants of sib G. Schizophrenic individuals are shown in black (Karlsson, 1966).

eliminated from the population down to a point at which the disease itself became a rare one. Actually, with an intermediate gene the rate of elimination is not at all rapid. It can be calculated from the formula

$$p_2 = p_1[1 - u(m + p_1 - mp_1)]$$

in which p_1 is the gene frequency in the population from which we start, p_2 the gene frequency in the filial generation, u the 'unfitness', i.e. unity minus the 'fitness', and m the manifestation rate in the heterozygote. We take the 'fitness' of schizophrenics to be 0·7, from which $u = 0·3$; and p_1 is given as 0·03 and m as 0·13 by the theoretical model proposed on page 59. From the figures below,

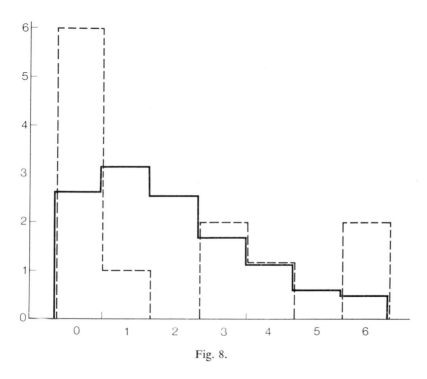

Fig. 8.

Generation	Gene frequency
1	0·0300
2	0·0286
3	0·0273
4	0·0260
5	0·0248
6	0·0237
7	0·0226
8	0·0216
9	0·0206
10	0·0197

it can be seen that the rate of decrement of p is slow even initially, and that it gets slower and slower. Nine generations are needed to bring a value of 0·03 down to one below 0·02, and at that stage the incidence of schizophrenia has only declined from 0·85 per cent to 0·54 per cent. If, as a result of a combination of circumstances, the gene frequency got pushed far above the point at which it could be maintained, by mutation or other processes, it would still take many generations to return to its equilibrium.

Of course, there is no reason to think that the fitness of schizophrenics has always been as low as 0·7; it is highly probable that there are variations from time to time and from place to place, depending on environmental circumstances. Erlenmeyer-Kimling and Paradowski (1966) compared fertility data for patients first hospitalized 1934–36 with those hospitalized 1954–56, and showed that the time interval, perhaps because of improved treatment and better acceptance by society of the individual patient, had been accompanied by increased fertility of the schizophrenic. Even more striking were the findings in the sibs of patients. The sibs of the 1934–36 group had much the same fertility as the general population at that time; the sibs of the 1954–56 sample, especially the sisters, showed a greatly increased fertility.

SCHIZOPHRENIA AS A BALANCED POLYMORPHISM
As we have just seen, the question is an open one whether the genetical factor or factors predisposing to schizophrenia carry with them some degree of genetic 'unfitness', but the evidence is strong that, at least during the first half of the twentieth century, those individuals who at some time in their lives suffered from schizophrenic illnesses, produced less than the average number of children. If we use the monogenic model offered in the preceding pages, with a gene frequency of 0·03 and a heterozygotic manifestation rate of 0·13, then we have to reckon with a 4·7 per cent gene mortality from generation to generation, this rate decreasing as the gene gets rarer. If the incidence of schizophrenia is stable, how can we suggest that this gene loss might be made good? There are two principal ways by which the gene frequency might be kept in balance: (1) fresh mutation, and (2) heterozygotic advantage.

We know that where there are two alternative states of the gene at any given locus, one state may spontaneously mutate into the other; the 'normal' gene may mutate into the 'abnormal' gene, and vice versa. Where we are concerned with genes which cause diseases or disadvantage states of the individual, the 'abnormal' state of the gene will be the rarer, and mutation from normal to abnormal will be a much commoner event than the back mutation from abnormal to normal. In the case of many rare genes, we can be sure that the main way in which their population frequency is kept at a standard figure is by fresh mutation balancing the weeding out of the gene by the selective disadvantages it brings with it. If we are dealing with a gene of 'intermediate' type, such as has been hypothesized for schizophrenia, then the rate of mutation α required to keep the gene frequency steady has been calculated by Moran (1969) as

$$\alpha = \frac{[p(1-p)-fp^2-p(1-2p)(1-m+fm)]}{[1-mp(1-f)]}$$

If we take f, which is the fitness of the schizophrenic individual, as 0·7, then the mutation rate α equals 0·0014, or, as we normally write such figures $1·4 \times 10^{-3}$. This is about two orders of magnitude greater than most established mutation rates, which are in the range 1×10^{-5}. Moran concludes, as Böök had concluded earlier, that such a mutation rate is highly improbable, and that accordingly mutation by itself is not likely to explain the stability of the incidence of schizophrenia over time and place. It is worth noting that when p is small and we can allow ourselves to neglect terms involving p^2, the balancing mutation rate approximates to $mp(1-f)$. If we give this a standard value of 1×10^{-5}, and put $m = 0·13$ and $f = 0·7$, then p is in the neighbourhood of 0·0001. We should have to have about 300 independent schizophrenogenic genes to balance their wastage with fresh mutation!

Moran next considers the possibilities of a hypothesis of heterozygotic advantage in accounting for the stability of the incidence of schizophrenia. If the fitness of the heterozygote is $1+a$, a being positive (i.e. if for every single child produced by the average member of the population the heterozygote produces $1+a$), and this factor is just sufficient to balance the unfitness of the schizophrenic, so that the gene frequency remains the same in the filial as in the parental generation, then

$$a = \frac{(1-f)}{(1-m)}\left[\frac{p}{(1-2p)+m}\right].$$

If we write $f = 0·7$, $m = 0·13$ and $p = 0·03$, then $a = 0·0558$. That is to say, the heterozygote must enjoy an advantage of appoximately 6 per cent. (In his discussion, considering other values of m and p, Moran arrived at an estimate of necessary advantage of about 10 per cent.)

In his further discussion, Moran pointed out the number of points in the life-cycle where such an advantage might be enjoyed, i.e. in the probabilities of: (1) the newly fertilized egg resulting in a pregnancy; (2) the resulting pregnancy coming to term; (3) surviving risks at birth; (4) surviving risks in early infancy, 0 to 1 year; (5) surviving risks from then till age of completed reproduction, say 40 years; (6) marrying; (7) producing surviving gametes; (8) these gametes resulting in a fertilized egg.

Clearly, a 10 or even 6 per cent advantage could only be looked for where 6 or 10 per cent of individuals, or more, are likely to fall by the wayside. The greatest wastage occurs at the phases (1) and (2); and a small relative advantage here might give us the differential survival expectancy we require. We know of such phenomena as maternal-foetal blood-group incompatibilities, and we could speculate that the extent to which these incompatibilities were tolerated by the embryo or foetus might be under genetic control; if the schizophrenic gene aided such tolerance, the advantage might indeed be of the necessary magnitude.

Another possibility of an intriguing kind is also discussed by Moran, i.e. the differential in social class fertilities. Social Class V, that of the unskilled workers, has in recent decades been afflicted by a higher fertility than higher social groups. There is also evidence to show that schizophrenics before they fall ill tend to slip down in the social scale so that, at their time of ascertainment (e.g. by admission to hospital) they are found to come disproportionately from the lower social classes. When the genotypes drift down in this way, it brings them into an area of increased fertility which may, in their own case or that of their children, enable them to compensate for the gene-wastage caused by the psychosis (Moran, 1965a). In his 1969 article, Moran observes that he does not find this possibility a very plausible one, since 'the incidence of schizophrenia does not seem to vary in any remarkable manner either between different large communities with different social structures, or historically (at any rate over the past 150 years)'; and this fact 'suggests that the true mechanism of the schizophrenic polymorphism must involve factors much more stable in space and time than class variations in fertility'.

In conclusion, it does not seem that the plausibility of a monogenic hypothesis is very greatly affected by the need to explain the remarkable frequency of schizophrenic disorders, which must be regarded as one of the severest of the common genetic syndromes, or one of the commonest of the severe ones. The trouble is that we do not have any widely based and reliable estimates of the genetic fitness of the schizophrenic patient, nor of the fitness of his sibs. The latest work in this field (Erlenmeyer-Kimling, 1968) showed a significantly lower mortality for the offspring of schizophrenic parents than for same-sexed infants in the population during the first year of life; and the mortality of female children of schizophrenics between the ages 0–15 was only 67 per cent of that of the United States population. We are not in a good position at present to estimate the degree of heterozygotic advantage required to keep the gene frequency steady.

MONOGENIC THEORIES UNDER A MATHEMATICAL TEST

Monogenic theories of schizophrenia have recently been examined mathematically by Wilson (1970). She developed new statistical methods of testing how far monogenic theories could account for observed expectations of schizophrenia in the relatives of schizophrenics, i.e. the data available in Zerbin-Rüdin's compilation and used here. These theories, dominant, recessive, and intermediate, are all covered by the general formula

$$s = 2mp(1-p)+kp^2$$

in which s is the morbidity risk of schizophrenia in the general population, and taken to be 0·008; p is the gene frequency as has been used earlier in this chapter; m is the rate of manifestation in the heterozygote; and k is the rate of manifestation in the homozygote. Wilson got the best fit with a hypothesis of an intermediate gene with $m = 0·27$ and $k = 1$, which was the hypothesis proposed by Slater (1958a) and which has been fully discussed in this chapter. However, she found that the sample sizes of the classes of relatives investigated were not sufficiently large to differentiate between this model and one of a partially dominant gene ($m = 0·06$, $k = 1$), or of a partially recessive gene ($m = 0$, $k = 0·5$). Clearly, the information available is not sufficient to test theories in which both m and k are non-zero and less than 1. Furthermore, the mathematical analysis is not addressed to testing polygenic theories, which may form the subject of later work.

CONCLUSION

From our examination of the evidence in the last chapter, and our consideration of possible genetical models in the present chapter, we can come to a few broad conclusions. Genetic variability in the predisposition to schizophrenia must be regarded as a secure hypothesis. This variability is widespread throughout the world, with local variations such as we are accustomed to finding in genetical syndromes. Two genetical models are available, either of which provides an adequate framework for the observations, so that the worker is entitled to choose the model which suits his purposes best. One of these is the polygenic model, involving the production of a schizophrenic disorder by a threshold effect; the other is a monogenic model, the single autosomal gene regarded as mainly responsible for the appearance of the disorder manifesting itself in all homozygotes (given adequate survival) and in approximately one-quarter of the heterozygotes. It is the latter hypothesis which is preferred by the present writers, since it permits of greater precision. In the case stated the gene frequency $p = 0.03$.

4

AFFECTIVE PSYCHOSES

DEFINITION

In recent years disorders in which a disturbance of mood appears to be the central symptom have become more and more readily recognized, and, despite the success with which they are customarily treated, have caused the admission of increasing numbers of patients from year to year into the wards of psychiatric hospitals and psychiatric units in general hospitals. This is probably true throughout western countries, but can readily be documented from British statistics. TABLE 30 shows the admission rates, by age and sex, for the years 1960 and 1966

TABLE 30

ENGLAND AND WALES: FIRST ADMISSION RATES: 1960 MANIC-DEPRESSIVE REACTION (REGISTRAR GENERAL), 1966 DEPRESSIVE PSYCHOSES (MINISTRY OF HEALTH)

| AGE FROM | FIRST ADMISSION RATES PER 100,000 | | | | | |
| | MALES | | FEMALES | | SEX RATIO (M:F) | |
	1960	1966	1960	1966	1960	1966
10 to	—	1	—	3		
15 to	7	20	14	35	0·50	0·57
20 to	18	44	35	80	0·51	0·55
25 to	27	48	59	!02	0·46	0·47
35 to	40	64	74	115	0·54	0·56
45 to	46	74	77	118	0 60	0·63
55 to	65	84	83	112	0·78	0·75
65 to	53	80	76	109	0·70	0·73
75+	27	57	30	62	0·90	0·92

from figures supplied by the Registrar General and by the Ministry of Health; and these figures, shown with comparable figures for schizophrenia-paranoia, are graphed in FIGURE 9. The change over this short space of time has been so marked that whereas the earlier admission rates for affective psychoses were calculated per million of the population in the respective age groups, the 1966 figures are calculated against the base of 100,000. Though the official terminology has been changed between 1960 and 1966, the same diagnostic groups of patients are covered by the two terms 'manic-depressive reaction' and 'depressive psychosis'; the change has, presumably, been determined by the recognition, on the part of the health officials, that the very large class of patients admitted for depressive psychoses include a majority of persons suffering from other conditions than what could be called 'manic-depressive', at least in the old Kraepelinian terminology.

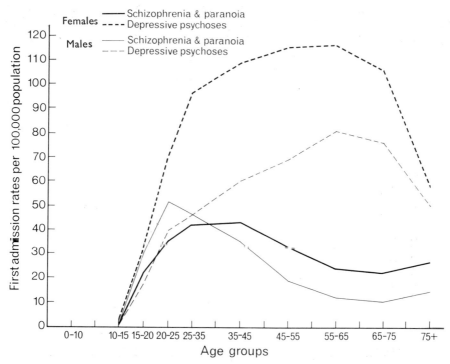

Fig. 9. First admissions, means for the 3 years 1964, 1965 and 1966. Continuous lines = schizophrenia and paranoia; broken lines = depressive psychoses

First admission rates per 100,000 home population

Age group	Depressive psychoses		Schizophrenia and paranoia	
	m	f	m	f
0–10	1	2	1	1
11–15	17	32	30	22
16–20	39	70	51	35
21–25	45	96	46	42
26–35	60	109	35	43
36–45	69	115	19	33
46–55	81	116	12	24
56–65	76	106	10	22
75+	50	58	14	27

(Ministry of Health)

From the 1960 figures, one can calculate an expectation for males of 2·4 per cent, and for females of 3·9 per cent, of admission to hospital for a manic-depressive reaction during a life-span of 75 years. From the 1966 figures, the total expectation of admission for a depressive psychosis at some time in a life-span of 75 years is for males 3·5 per cent and for females 5·8 per cent. This is a

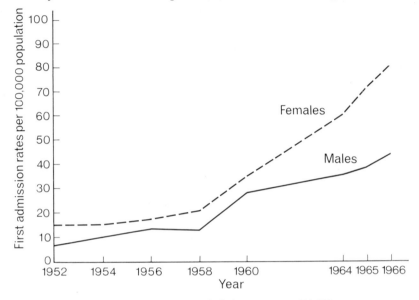

Fig. 10. Affective psychoses. First admission rates per 100,000, age group 20–24 inclusive.

	Males	Females
1952	7	15
1954	10	15
1956	13	17
1958	12	21
1960	28	35
—	—	—
1964	35	60
1965	38	71
1966	44	80

rise of 46–49 per cent for each sex. TABLE 30 shows us that the big increases are in the earliest years, i.e. both for males and females between the ages of 15 and 25. Such a large change in morbidity over such a short time must be attributed to a change in both public and medical attitudes; though one cannot exclude the possibility that the rapid social changes that are going on in the community are carrying with them an increasing real burden of psychiatric illness for young people, as well as an increasing probability of treatment in a psychiatric centre. The change that has gone on between 1952 and 1966, in the age group 20–24 inclusive, is shown in FIGURE 10.

It is clear that such rapid changes are independent of gene frequencies, which must be regarded as remaining very constant over a few decades. For an estimation of the general population risk of an affective psychosis of manic-depressive type we have to go back to a time before there was such a violent upsurge in hospital admissions, when, in fact, patients were not admitted to a mental hospital or psychiatric unit unless they constituted a danger to themselves, or a real problem to their families, or felt so much in need of help that they would face the rigours of hospital treatment.

In order to discuss the genetics of affective disorders of the manic-depressive group we need on the one hand a fairly strict clinical delimitation of what we are discussing, and then to estimate the population risk when this definition was the operative one in clinical practice.

For our purposes, then, the manic-depressive group of affective psychoses are conditions in which the central change in bodily metabolism shows itself either at the depressive or at the manic pole in a primary change of mood. The change is a phasic one, and tends to pass off spontaneously. Very often it also starts spontaneously, but it may also be precipitated by environmental causes. In the depressed phase there is some degree of psychomotor inhibition, leading for instance to slowing up of mental processes; in the manic phase there is correspondingly disinhibition with increased distractibility and flight of ideas. These changes generally spring from a personality which tends to be of the 'syntonic' extraverted type, often with mild tendencies to mood-swinging within a normal range. Some patients pass through life showing only depressive phases of such intensity that treatment is needed, their hypomanic phases either being undetectable or so slight that special control is not required; other patients show swings in both directions. Very rare are the patients who show only swings in the direction of mania. This syndrome is very readily recognizable when it is seen in a typical form, but it is quite often coloured by extraneous elements, when diagnosis is more difficult. It seems unlikely that we shall be able to solve the genetical problems presented by the condition until we have more reliable methods of diagnosis than purely clinical psychiatric ones, until in fact we have a much better understanding of the biochemical disorder that underlies the psychic changes.

BIOCHEMISTRY

The responsiveness of affective disorders in many patients has been a great stimulus to the search for possibly causative biochemical changes. A full and critical summary of this research was made by Coppen (1967), and later ones by Gibbons (1968) and Coppen (1969). Work in this area is beset by problems engendered by secondary effects of the condition itself, such as the altered dietary intake and activity of the patient; conflicting results have appeared and nearly every aspect of the subject is surrounded by controversy.

There is, however, evidence that in affective disorders there are biochemical disturbances in three main areas, those of amine metabolism, electrolyte distribution and adrenal cortical activity. Belief in a causal association between brain monoamines and affective disturbances has been stimulated and strengthened by the evidence that drugs such as imipramine and the monoamine oxidase inhibitors, which increase the activity of brain monoamines, alleviate depression. More direct evidence of disturbed amine metabolism in depression has been the observations of very significantly decreased excretion of tryptamine and decreased levels of 5-hydroxyindoles in cerebrospinal fluid, as well as changes in the metabolism of noradrenaline. Reduction in the levels of 5-hydroxytryptamine and its metabolite, 5-hydroxyindoleacetic acid, have been found in the brains of subjects who committed suicide while depressed. The evidence therefore points to an abnormality of indoleamine metabolism in patients suffering from depression, though there is little evidence about the role of the biogenic amines in mania (Coppen 1969).

Turning to changes in electrolyte distribution in the affective disorders, it is extremely difficult to judge whether the changes observed are causal or are secondary phenomena. Recently, isotope-dilution techniques have enabled estimates to be made of the relative concentrations of sodium and potassium in cells and in the extracellular space. The most consistent finding has been an increase in the amount of 'residual sodium', that is, mainly extracellular sodium together with a small but unknown amount of exchangeable bone sodium in depressed patients, the residual sodium returning to normal after recovery. In mania, similar but greater changes in the distribution of sodium have been observed (Coppen, 1969). The idea that electrolyte distribution may have a central role in the affective disorders is strongly supported by the therapeutic effects of lithium salts. The lithium ion is known to affect the transport of sodium across biological membranes.

The third area in which biochemical disturbances in affective disorders have attracted research is that of endocrinological studies. Research has been, however, much more limited in this area than in the areas of amine metabolism and electrolyte distribution, and the results are less striking. Endocrinological studies in affective disorders have been confined mainly to thyroid and adreno-cortical activity. Thyroid studies have yielded virtually negative results. Adreno-cortical activity in depressive illness has been repeatedly examined; Coppen (1969), in summarizing this work, expresses the view that although modest increases in hydrocortisone secretion have been found by many investigators, they did not bear a very close correlation with clinical state and the changes are probably secondary.

The evidence is convincing that changes involving the biogenic amines and electrolyte distribution play vital roles in affective disorders, but these changes are very likely only parts of a highly complex pattern which is not yet understood. Our present knowledge, however, is consistent with a constitutional element in the aetiology of affective disorders. It does not help us to decide whether one or many genes are involved, but does suggest the probability of coexisting genetically heterogeneous syndromes.

EXPECTATION IN THE GENERAL POPULATION

TABLE 31 shows such figures as are available of the expectation of illnesses of the manic-depressive group in males and females separately. Some further estimates are given by Zerbin-Rüdin (1967b); she comments that British and Scandinavian authors mostly accept a value of approximately 1·0 per cent (males

precise entities with clinical features, course and development and outcome of their own. So far it has not been possible to validate Leonhard's subclassification of schizophrenia by researches into the genetical background, but there has been greater success with manic-depression.

The first significant investigation along these lines was undertaken by Leonhard himself (Leonhard, Korff and Schulz, 1962). Starting with 104 female patients with affective psychoses, they found they could be classified into 42 women with manic-depressive, i.e. bipolar illnesses, showing mood swinging in both the hypomanic and the depressive direction, 22 women with 'reine Melancholie' and 40 with 'reine Depressionen', i.e. syndromes showing only mood swings into depressive states, which can therefore be called 'unipolar'.[1] The parents, the sibs, and the sibs of the parents of the bipolar patients all showed higher incidences of affective psychoses than the corresponding relatives of patients with unipolar syndromes [TABLE 33].

TABLE 33

RISK OF AFFECTIVE PSYCHOSIS IN RELATIVES OF BIPOLAR AND UNIPOLAR INDEX PATIENTS, AS PER CENT

(Data of Leonhard et al., 1962)

AFFECTIVE PSYCHOSIS IN RELATIVES	OF	
	BIPOLAR PATIENTS	UNIPOLAR PATIENTS
Parents	12	5
Sibs	11	5
Sibs of parents	7	2

These families also showed interesting differences in respect of the balance of affectively deviant temperamental types [see TABLE 34], the hypomanic temperaments being much commoner among the relatives of bipolar patients than among the relatives of the unipolar patients, while the distribution of subdepressive temperamental types in parents and sibs showed the opposite preponderance. The authors thought that cyclothymic traits of personality tended to be independent of the two types of deviation mentioned.

The authors hypothesize a specific genetic factor for manic-depressive illness which can show itself as cyclothymia; it comes to illness if there is in addition an affective temperamental deviation, melancholia and depressive psychoses occurring mainly in persons of subdepressive temperament.

This work has recently been followed by a later one from the same school (von Trostorff, 1968) with a considerable enlargement of the clinical material, i.e. with the 104 female probands being increased to 154 females and 53 males, constituting 105 manic-depressives and 102 unipolar psychotics. The incidence of affective psychoses in the parents and the sibs of these two groups differed

[1] The term used by Leonhard et al. is 'monopolar'. 'Unipolar', which is to be preferred on etymological grounds, has the same meaning, and will be used throughout this section. It is important that two different technical terms should not compete with one another in covering the same concept.

TABLE 34

TEMPERAMENTAL TYPES AMONG RELATIVES OF AFFECTIVE
PSYCHOTIC PROBANDS

(After Leonhard, Korff and Schulz, 1962)

TYPE OF DEVIATION CLASS OF RELATIVES	PERSONALITY DEVIANTS AMONG RELATIVES OF BIPOLAR/UNIPOLAR PROBANDS, AS %	
	BIPOLAR	UNIPOLAR
Hypomanic disposition		
Parents (N = 820, 120)	26	14
Sibs (N = 94, 143)	17	9
Sibs of parents (N = 205, 253)	20	6
Subdepressive temperament		
Parents	7·5	22·5
Sibs	5	13
Sibs of parents	10	5
Cyclothymic temperament		
Parents	15	11
Sibs	15	8
Sibs of parents	4	3

widely, the incidence in the bipolar groups of relatives being about twice as high as in the relatives of the unipolar groups [see TABLE 35]. Von Trostorff's material was also analysed for the sex distribution. In the manic-depressive families there were 9·2 per cent of the fathers and brothers affected, 8·7 per cent

TABLE 35

INCIDENCE OF AFFECTIVE PSYCHOSES IN RELATIVES OF BIPOLAR AND UNI-
POLAR AFFECTIVE PSYCHOTICS, ABSOLUTE NUMBERS OF PERSONS OBSERVED

(Data from Von Trostorff, 1968)

RELATIVES	AGE-CORRECTED N (BIP.)	(UNIP.)	PSYCHOTICS OBSERVED AMONG RELATIVES OF BIPOLAR PATIENTS	UNIPOLAR PATIENTS
Parents	190·0	177·5	18	10
Sibs	170·5	173·5	18	8

of the mothers and sisters, i.e. sex equality. In the relatives of patients with 'pure forms', there were affected 3·1 per cent of fathers and brothers as against 6·2 per cent of mothers and sisters, i.e. a sex ratio of 1:2.

The workers of the Leonhard school have had their main findings confirmed by other investigators in Sweden, Switzerland and the United States. The mode of approach has differed to some extent from country to country; and it seems best to report on each.

Angst (1966) reported on a family investigation into the 331 psychotic-depressives observed in Burghölzli 1959–1963. He separated the monophasic and periodic depressions from the cyclic psychoses, and started by considering involutional melancholias separately. Later, he rejected the autonomy of involutional affective illnesses and classified them with the monophasic and periodic depressions. There was significantly more affective illness in the fathers, mothers and brothers of the cyclic than of the monophasic probands, though in the case of the sisters the incidence was higher in the families of the monophasics. The sex ratio of those relatives who fell ill was close to parity in the case of the cyclic families, but showed a very high female preponderance in the relatives of monophasic patients (a 2·8 per cent risk in fathers and brothers as against a 16·4 risk in mothers and sisters). Angst thought his findings showed that cyclic and monophasic syndromes were genetically distinct, and these syndromes tended to run true in the families. The affected relatives of pure depressives were generally depressive and only exceptionally manic or cyclic;

TABLE 36

DIAGNOSTIC DISTRIBUTION OF AFFECTED RELATIVES BY DIAGNOSTIC CLASSIFICATION OF INDEX PATIENT

(Data from Perris, 1966)

RELATIVES EXHIBITING	BIPOLAR PROBANDS			UNIPOLAR PROBANDS		
	PARENTS	SIBS	CHILDREN	PARENTS	SIBS	CHILDREN
Bipolar psychoses	14	39	3	1	1	—
Unipolar psychoses	2	1	—	8	25	1

Figures show numbers of actual cases observed.

the illnesses in the cyclic group tended to have shorter phases and shorter intervals than in the depressive families; and pre-morbid personalities tended to run in the syntonic or cycloid-psychopathic direction in the first case, while in the families of depressives there were more personalities of a schizothyme, unsure or inhibited type. However, the ages of onset were about the same. Since pure depressions are quite common in the relatives of cycloid patients, one must suppose that the predisposition manifests about three times as a depression to once as manic. Angst thought of a major autosomal gene, manifesting in a proportion of heterozygotes, in the case of the cycloid syndrome, but of a multifactorial basis in the monophasic syndrome.

Perris (1966), publishing in the same year as Angst, from a continuous series of mental hospital admissions 1950–63, collected 57 males and 81 females who had bipolar psychoses, and 71 males and 68 females with multiphasic unipolar psychoses (i.e. not less than 3 attacks); there were also 17 patients who had had only manic episodes. He went a step further than Angst in subclassifying his secondary cases into bipolar and unipolar as well as the probands. The distribution, which is a very striking one, is shown in TABLE 36. The table does not include the considerable numbers of affected relatives with only single attacks of affective illness who could not be satisfactorily diagnosed as either bipolar or multiphasic unipolar, whom he left as a group of persons suffering from 'unspecified affective disorder'.

The findings of Perris and Angst, therefore, are in substantial agreement. Perris found, as Leonhard and Angst had done, that there were differences between the personalities of patients, but defines the difference in terms of the criteria proposed by Sjöbring, finding the bipolar patients tend to be 'substable', the unipolar patients 'subvalid'. Perris found mean ages of onset about 10 years younger in the cases of the bipolar probands (m 33·6, f 28·9) than in the unipolar probands (m 48·6, f 38·8). Angst found ages of onset about the same in the two groups, but this was after patients with 'involutional melancholia' had been eliminated.

These two authors, struck like every one else by the similarity of their findings, very sensibly compared notes (Angst and Perris, 1968) and gave an analysis of the findings they each made independently, and those in which they differed. Taking the 49 Angst patients who fulfilled Perris's criteria for inclusion, it was possible satisfactorily to compare the results of the one with those of the other [see TABLE 37]. It is clear that the findings run very close and are mutually

TABLE 37
COMPARISON OF THE ANGST-PERRIS DATA
(From Angst and Perris, 1968)

	MORBIDITY RISK OF AFFECTIVE ILLNESSES INCLUDING SUICIDE				
	PARENTS RISK AS %	SIBS RISK AS %	PARENTS AND SIBS TOGETHER		
			TOTAL BZ	TOTAL CASES	RISK AS %
Cyclic probands					
Angst	14·4	21·5	160	29	21·0
Perris	16·0	23·0	509	102	20·0
Phasic-depressives					
Angst	11·2	12·2	341	40	11·7
Perris	13·9	15·0	570	83	14·6

confirmatory; this happy result was no doubt in part due to the fact that the two clinicians had very similar diagnostic approach and standards.

The sex ratio of affected individuals among relatives of bipolar psychotics on the one hand and unipolar depressives on the other hand has already been referred to. Both Angst and Perris found near equality in the parents and sibs of cyclic probands (sex ratio 0·99 and 0·88 respectively) but a female preponderance among the relatives of 'phasic', i.e. unipolar probands on the other (sex ratio 0·17 and 0·64 respectively). It seems probable, therefore, that the marked female preponderance in affective disorders found in psychiatric clinics and hospitals all over the world does not depend on the no doubt relatively small admixture of bipolar cases in the general ragbag. The fact that the bipolar cases show no marked female preponderance, as Perris has pointed out, counts against the plausible hypothesis that a cyclothymic tendency is more likely to find expression when superimposed on the spontaneously varying female biological rhythm than when superimposed on the more invariant affective state of the male.

Repeated suggestions have been made by Winokur and his colleagues that a sex-linked (dominant) gene may be playing a part in predisposing to manic-depression, i.e. cyclothymic or bipolar affective disorders. If such a gene were both necessary and sufficient for the production of a diagnosable manic-depressive illness, then: (1) the illness should be twice as common in the female as in the male; (2) the affected parents or children of affected females should be males and females in equal proportion; (3) the affected parents or children of affected males should be females exclusively; (4) the affected sibs of affected males should be male and female in equal proportion; and (5) the affected

TABLE 38

DISTRIBUTION BY SEX OF AFFECTED RELATIVES OF BIPOLAR AND UNIPOLAR MULTIPHASIC PROBANDS, SUB-CLASSIFIED BY SEX, AGAINST EXPECTATION OF SEX RATIO ON A THEORY OF A DOMINANT SEX-LINKED GENE

| | AFFECTED RELATIVES | | THEORETICAL |
	MALE	FEMALE	M:F
Bipolar group			
Male probands			
sibs	10	17	1:1
children	6	7	0:1
Female probands			
sibs	18	19	1:3
children	1	2	1:1
Unipolar multiphasic group			
Male probands			
sibs	14	11	1:1
children	1	9	0:1
Female probands			
sibs	11	16	1:3
children	3	2	1:1

sibs of female patients should be male and female in the proportion 1:3. Perris (1968) has provided the data from his material on which dominant sex-linkage can be tested. The absolute numbers of affected relatives in each group are shown, for bipolar and unipolar probands by sex, against the proportions suggested by dominant sex-linkage, in TABLE 38. From this it will be seen that there is no resemblance between the observed and the expected figures in the bipolar group; but that in the families of patients with unipolar multiphasic affective disorders there is some approximation to theory.

Reich, Clayton and Winokur (1969) made findings which run in a somewhat contrary direction. Taking as index cases 20 men and 39 women who had manic attacks, they found family relationships [TABLE 39] which supported the

TABLE 39

DISTRIBUTION BY SEX OF PROBAND × SEX OF AFFECTED RELATIVE IN MANIC PATIENTS

| | AFFECTED RELATIVES | | THEORETICAL |
	MALE	FEMALE	M:F
Male probands			
parents	1	14	0:1
sibs	4	3	1:1
Female probands			
parents	13	21	1:1
sibs	—	9	1:3

hypothesis of a dominant sex-linked gene. However, 49 of these 59 patients had had previous affective illnesses, and clinically they correspond rather with Perris's bipolar than with his unipolar group. Apart from this anomaly, the findings of Winokur and colleagues (Winokur and Pitts, 1965; Winokur and Clayton, 1967; Winokur, 1967) have agreed fairly well with those of other recent investigators.

Brief mention should be made of other work in the field of heredity in the affective psychoses. Constantinidis (1967) investigated the families of 100 manic-depressives of Swiss origin who had been hospitalized in Geneva over 50 years. His figures are shown, with those of others, in TABLE 40. Hopkinson

TABLE 40

RECENT ESTIMATES OF THE RISK OF AFFECTIVE PSYCHOSES IN THE
RELATIVES OF MANIC-DEPRESSIVES

AUTHOR	PROBANDS	RISK OF AFFECTIVE PSYCHOSIS IN RELATIVES AS %	
		PARENTS	SIBS
v. Trostorff	bipolar	9·5	10·6
	unipolar	5·6	4·6
Angst	bipolar	14·4	21·5
	unipolar	11·2	12·2
Perris	bipolar	16·0	23·0
	unipolar	13·9	15·0
Constantinidis	all	19·5	11·9
Hopkinson	early onset	25·5	17·2
	late onset	10·0	6·8
	all	15·9	11·0
Winokur and Clayton	early onset	25·8	15·4
	late onset	12·6	15·1
	all	21·6	15·3

Hopkinson also shows risks of 23·5 and 12·8 per cent respectively in the children of early onset and late onset cases.

(1964) made a special study of 100 patients who developed affective illnesses after the age of 50; 39 of them had had previous attacks, 61 had not. Clinically, there were no differences between the two groups, but there was significantly more affective illness in the families of the early onset group. This difference was also found by Winokur and Clayton (1967) in the parents but not in the sibs of early- and late-onset cases.

RESULTS OF TWIN RESEARCH

The results of twin research are rather difficult to evaluate. A conspectus of the findings made in the principal investigations to date are shown in TABLE 41 from the monograph by Kringlen (1967). Even the larger series shown in this table include no large number of MZ pairs, and in some of the series numbers are very small. The series reported by Rosanoff, Handy and Plesset (1935) and by Kallmann (1950) are not well documented, and the recent series of Harvald and Hauge (1965) has not been reported in detail. The work of da Fonseca

TABLE 41

CONCORDANCE RATES IN TWINS OF MANIC-DEPRESSIVE PATIENTS
(Data summarized by Kringlen, 1967)

| | | | MZ | | DZ | |
			N	% CONC	N	% CONC
Luxenburger	1928	Germany	4	75	13	0
Rosanoff et al.	1935	United States	23	70	67	16
Kallmann	1950	United States	23	96	52	26
Slater	1953	England	8	50	30	23
da Fonseca	1959	England	21	75	39	39
Harvald and Hauge	1963	Denmark	15	60	40	5
Kringlen	1967	Norway	6	33	9	0

(1959), though reported in complete detail, is made difficult of study by most readers by the fact that it is in Portuguese. If we were to endeavour to summate the results of all these figures, we should be led to concordance rates of approximately 72 per cent in MZ pairs, 19 per cent in same-sexed DZ pairs. This can be regarded as a plausible estimate, but it cannot be justified logically. All these researches involved somewhat different types of samples, different methods of clinical approach, different degrees of liberality in diagnosis.

In a valuable piece of bibliographic research, Zerbin-Rüdin (1969) has examined the clinical information published both in systematic twin series (Essen-Möller 1941; Slater 1953; da Fonseca 1959) and in single case reports given in other systematic investigations (e.g. the major work of Stenstedt 1952, 1959, 1966), in so far as sufficient information was available for discriminating between unipolar and bipolar syndromes. From her report it is clear that there are no significant differences between the twin series and the twins netted in systematic family studies, and in the figures of TABLE 42 the two are combined. As Zerbin-Rüdin points out, these results speak strongly in favour of there being a genetical

TABLE 42

DISTRIBUTION OF CLINICAL TYPES OF MANIC-DEPRESSIVE DISORDER
IN PAIRS OF TWINS COLLECTED FROM THE LITERATURE
(After Zerbin-Rüdin, 1969)

| | NUMBERS OF PAIRS | |
TWINS	MZ	DZ
Both unipolar depressive	22	8
Both bipolar	16	—
Both manic	5	—
One manic, one manic-depressive	—	1
One unipolar, one bipolar	5	3
One manic, one depressive	2	1
Incompletely concordant	9	7
Discordant (co-twin normal)	24	36
Total	83	56

difference between unipolar and bipolar syndromes. Indeed, there could possibly be no overlap between the genetic predispositions to bipolar and unipolar syndromes; and the 5 MZ pairs and the 3 DZ pairs classified as one unipolar, one bipolar, could be occupying that place in the table because the bipolar predisposition may fortuitously manifest only once in a lifetime, or if more than once only in the depressive direction.

INVOLUTIONAL MELANCHOLIA AND THE AFFECTIVE PSYCHOSES OF LATER LIFE

The nosological position of these syndromes has persisted as a problem as long as psychiatry has been a scientific study. It is not to the point to go over

TABLE 43

RISK OF AFFECTIVE PSYCHOSES (INCLUDING INVOLUTIONAL MELANCHOLIA) AMONG THE RELATIVES OF INVOLUTIONAL MELANCHOLICS: MEANS OF RISKS CALCULATED IN 11 INVESTIGATIONS 1937–1959

(Based on data in Table 28, Zerbin-Rüdin, 1967b)

RELATIVES OF INVOLUTIONAL MELANCHOLICS	RISK (AS PER CENT) OF PSYCHOSES AMONG RELATIVES			
	AFFECTIVE PSYCHOSES	INVOLUTIONAL MELANCHOLIA	RATIO $I/A\%$	SCHIZO-PHRENIA
Parents	4·9	3·7	76	0·9
Sibs	6·1	4·0	66	1·3
Uncles and aunts	2·3	1·8	78	1·0
First cousins	1·7	1·0	59	0·8

The figures of the third column are the means of available individual estimates of the proportion of all affective psychoses classified as of involutional type.

the older literature, especially the many studies which have not made a systematic approach along genetical lines. Most workers have found a lower risk of affective psychoses in the relatives of involutional and climacteric depressives, though among those relatives who do have such psychoses the proportion of those whose illnesses are also classifiable as involutional is high. From a table provided by Zerbin-Rüdin (1967b), giving the results of 11 investigations from 1937 down to Stenstedt's work in 1959, the above table [TABLE 43] can be drawn up. The data indicate some degree of specificity of the predisposition to affective illness in later life, but do not support the very general idea that some involutional affective psychoses are really masked schizophrenias.

Later workers have confirmed the finding that the risk of affective psychoses in the relatives of involutional and late-onset depressives is lower than in the relatives of manic-depressives (Angst, 1966; Hopkinson, 1964; Kay, 1959). The most striking work in this field has been provided by Hopkinson and Ley (1969). These workers investigated the family histories of 182 probands (122 women and 60 men) admitted to a psychiatric clinic and diagnosed as suffering from manic-depressive psychosis or endogenous depression; information by the patient and in 58 cases by other relatives was sufficient to diagnose the presence or absence of a history of 'marked affective change, with good prognosis and lasting three months or more' in the first-degree relatives, parents, sibs and children. All first-degree relatives were taken together (which is justifiable in view of the fact that risks differ but little between parents, sibs and children as long as adequate allowance for the age distribution is made). The 'Bezugsziffer', or age-corrected estimate of numbers of persons at risk, was calculated by the Weinberg exact method [see Appendix D], and the risk of affective disorder in

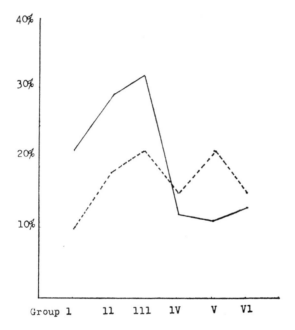

Fig. 11. Age distribution of initial attack in probands and morbidity risk in first degree relatives.

————————Percentage risk in relatives.
.................Distribution of probands according to age of onset.
(Hopkinson and Ley, 1969)

relatives was brought into relation with the age of onset of the psychosis in the proband. What emerged was that, for probands whose first illnesses came at any age under 40, the risk for first-degree relatives varied in successive decades between 21 and 32 per cent; for probands whose first illnesses came at ages 40+, the risk in relatives varied between 11·8 and 13·5 per cent [see FIG. 11]. There was no significant difference between the three estimates for the earlier decades, and none between the three estimates for the later decades; but the difference between the early and the late groups was highly significant as can be seen from TABLE 44.

Fig. 12. Fitting normal curves to ages of onset of affective psychoses (data from Slater, 1938, and re-worked). Note flattening of curves and double peaks, suggesting bimodality.

Admission rates, observed and expected (by fitting normal curves)

Age triennium centring on	Males Observed	Males Expected	Females Observed	Females Expected
23	23	13·1	58	28·2
26	31	19·9	70	41·8
29	42	28·4	78	58·5
32	48	38·3	83	77·4
35	52	48·9	94	96·9
38	52	59·0	98	114·6
41	43	67·3	94	128·2
44	49	72·5	91	135·7
47	49	73·9	105	135·8
50	53	71·2	109	128·5
53	62	64·8	103	114·9
56	58	55·8	91	97·3
59	48	45·4	94	77·8
62	52	34·9	77	58·9
65	52	25·3	61	42·1
68	22	17·4	59	28·5

Admission rates were calculated as number of admissions over 3 years, e.g. 46–48, 49–51, etc. to the University Clinic per 100,000 of the Bavarian population.

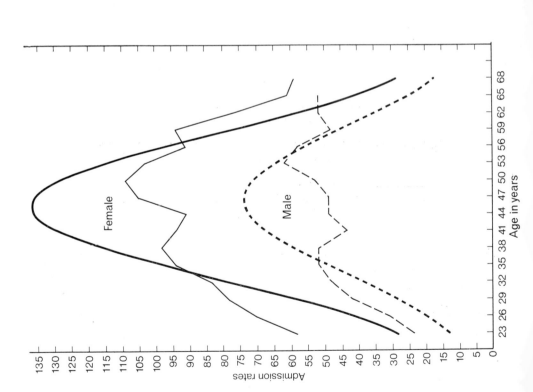

Hopkinson and Ley point out that the age-related incidence of manic-depressive disorders shows a bimodality in both sexes. This was demonstrable in their own proband material [see FIG. 11] but could also be seen in the much larger Munich material published by Slater (1938) [see FIG. 12]. The early-onset syndrome would have its peak age of manifestation between 30 and 39, the late-onset syndrome having its peak some 10 years later. While these authors consider the possibility of two genetically caused syndromes, aetiologically distinct from one another, they find the hypothesis of two syndromes, one genetically and one environmentally caused, a more attractive one. These disorders would not be clinically distinguishable from one another; but if one took a sample of patients with early age of onset they would include a relatively

TABLE 44

INCIDENCE OF AFFECTIVE DISORDER IN FIRST-DEGREE RELATIVES OF AFFECTIVE PSYCHOTICS, BY AGE OF ONSET OF FIRST ILLNESS IN PROBAND

(Data from Hopkinson and Ley, 1969)

PROBANDS AGED	BZ	N	RISK AS PER CENT
Up to 39	232	67	28·9
40+	305	38	12·5

BZ = Bezugsziffer, i.e. total number of first-degree relatives corrected for age; N = number of first-degree relatives with affective disorder.

high proportion of genetically determined cases, whereas if one took a sample of patients with late age of onset, the reverse would be the case. This hypothesis is an attractive one, but it is not fully supported by their own data. It would suggest the expectation that the proportion of genetically determined cases, and therefore the morbid risk in relatives, would be a continuous function of age; the observation of a sudden drop as shown in FIGURE 11 runs counter to this and would be more easily explained if there was little admixture of the two types and fairly sharp cut-off points in their ages of onset.

MODE OF INHERITANCE

The mode of inheritance in the affective psychoses must be regarded as a yet unsettled question. The view reached by the older workers (Kallmann, Slater, Stenstedt, etc.) that a major autosomal gene was involved, manifesting in a proportion of heterozygotes, say about 30 per cent, has been adopted by Angst for the bipolar psychoses, and has been endorsed (though with the modification of a constitutional personality contribution, probably multifactorial) by workers of the Leonhard school. Perris thinks in terms of multifactorial inheritance for both types of affective psychosis, and thinks a major gene involvement unlikely. Winokur and his colleagues support the idea that a sex-linked dominant gene is playing a role, a view which has not found much support at other centres.

7

Hopkinson and Ley support a major gene for the early-onset syndrome, believing that the late-onset syndrome is mainly non-genetically determined.

A specific test for distinguishing between major-gene and polygene inheritance in conditions of about the 1 per cent frequency in the general population is not easy to find. Of those suggested by Carter (1969) the only one applicable is the relative frequency of the disorder in first- and second-degree relatives respectively. The major-gene hypothesis suggests that the ratio should be about 1:2, while the polygenic model suggests a ratio more nearly equal to 1:4. As can be seen from TABLE 45, the results are rather equivocal.

TABLE 45

ESTIMATES OF MORBIDITY RISK OF AFFECTIVE DISORDERS (CERTAIN AND PROBABLE CASES OF MANIC-DEPRESSION, SUICIDES AND DEPRESSIVE REAC-TIONS INCLUDED) AMONG RELATIVES OF MANIC-DEPRESSIVE INDEX PATIENTS, AS PER CENT

(Data collated from Zerbin-Rüdin, 1967b)

CLASSES OF RELATIVES	NUMBER OF INVESTIGATIONS	RANGE	MEAN	MEAN OF MEANS
First degree				14·0
Parents	9	·7·4–23·4	14·3	
Sibs	10	3·6–23·0	12·9	
Children	6	8·4–24·1	14·8	
Second degree				4·8
Half-sibs	2	1·4–16·7	9·0	
Uncles and aunts	1		5·0	
Grandchildren	2	1·3–3·6	2·5	
Nephews and nieces	2	1·9–3·3	2·6	
Third degree, first cousins	1		3·6	3·6

Slater (1966) suggested that, even in a common disorder showing itself in about 1 per cent of the general population, one would expect different distributions of secondary cases in the ascendance of patients on a monogenic dominant and on a polygenic model. On the basis of a major dominant one would expect a large preponderance of similarly affected relatives to show unilaterally, i.e. either on the paternal or on the maternal side, and only infrequently on both sides; on the polygenic model one would expect a more nearly balanced distribution. On the model he computed, supposing that individuals exceeding the mean liability by $+2\sigma$ would be those who would be likely to manifest the disorder, it appeared that one should find a unilateral distribution of affected relatives taken in pairs in approximately two-thirds of the families. In an investigation of 19 schizophrenic families and 24 manic-depressive families the figures shown in TABLE 46 were obtained. The schizophrenic families show a deviation from expectation in the unilateral direction which is significant at the 0·05 (one-tail) level; the manic-depressive families show no significant deviation, either in the Slater and Tsuang figures or in the Perris figures for bipolar psychoses.

In the present state of our knowledge a polygenic theory seems to be more probable than a major-gene theory, but the question remains an open one. The

TABLE 46
DISTRIBUTION IN PAIRS OF SECONDARY CASES IN THE ASCENDANCE OF SCHIZOPHRENIC AND MANIC-DEPRESSIVE FAMILIES
(From Slater and Tsuang, 1968)

	OBSERVATION	EXPECTATION
Schizophrenic families		
Unilateral pairs	41·8	35·3
Bilateral pairs	11·2	17·6
Total	53·0	53·0
Manic-depressive families		
Unilateral pairs	53·3	50·0
Bilateral pairs	21·6	25·0
Total	75·0	75·0

major-gene theory is still to be regarded as on the map, and it is the theory which offers the most testable consequences. Probably we shall not get much further along genetical lines without further understanding of the basic bio-chemical and metabolic processes of the affective psychoses.

5

DEVIATIONS OF PERSONALITY AND NEUROTIC REACTIONS

RELATIONSHIP TO OTHER PSYCHIATRIC DISORDERS

Deviations, from what we ordinarily regard as normal, in the development of the personality may arise from a great variety of causes, both genetic and environmental. Among the genetical causes, with which we are principally concerned in this book, we must include chromosome anomalies, particularly trisomy or monosomy of the sex chromosomes (47, XXY and 47, XYY and 45, XO), gene abnormalities (e.g. the personality deviations which may be the first sign of an oncoming Huntington's chorea), abnormalities probably due to specific genetical factors, monogenic or polygenic (e.g. the 'schizoid' personality which may be observable before the onset of a schizophrenia, or may succeed an attack), periodic disturbances of behaviour associated with genetically caused disturbances of brain physiology (e.g. as shown in the EEG). However, the genetical aspects of these deviations need no further discussion, since these subjects are covered elsewhere in this book.

But before we proceed further there is one fundamental question which has to be answered. Are we to regard the so-called endogenous psychoses on the one hand, and on the other hand the deviations of personality and neurotic reactions, as being all part of a single spectrum? Do they constitute a single mode of variation, with the neuroses and personality deviations being but attenuated forms of the psychoses? There is some evidence to suggest that this might be so; and certainly there is an area in our clinical observations in which differential diagnosis, e.g. psychosis vs. neurosis, is difficult. The 'schizoid' personality which seems to bear some relation to schizophrenia has already been mentioned; and in the same way a cyclothymic personality is related to the endogenous affective psychoses. Clinical examples of these kinds might be added to, to provide what might seem an impressive argument in favour of a unitary though quantitatively variable mental disorder. This is a matter which we cannot discuss here in the detail required; it must be sufficient to make two points. First, the hypothesis of a unitary mental disorder is a heuristically sterile one; secondly, the genetical evidence goes all against it. In support of the second point we can quote the investigation made by Cowie (1961) as one of the most crucial.

Cowie investigated the children of a continuous series of patients admitted to hospital and subsequently discharged with a diagnosis of affective psychosis with early onset, affective psychosis with late onset, schizophrenia, and obsessive-compulsive reaction. The psychiatric probands were matched individually with control subjects attending general hospitals and a neurological hospital, none of them with a history of one or other of the above psychiatric illnesses. Information was obtained about the children from one or both parents for the clinical rating, from the children themselves, if old enough, by sending the Maudsley Personality Inventory through the post, and from parents or teachers for the Teacher's Report Form. The more important results are summarized in TABLE 47.

TABLE 47
A COMPARISON OF THE CHILDREN OF PSYCHOTICS WITH THE
CHILDREN OF A CONTROL GROUP, AGED 0–55 YEARS
(Data from Cowie, 1961)

| | CHILDREN OF | |
	PROBANDS	CONTROLS
N	330	342
Mean age in years	19·6	19·8
Good adjustment, absent or negligible neurotic symptomatology, as per cent, by psychiatric diagnosis in proband		
Affective psychosis, early onset	64·5	
Affective psychosis, late onset	79·6	
Schizophrenia	72·9	
Obsessive-compulsive neurosis	44·7	
All	69·4	75·1
Maudsley Personality Inventory mean score		
Neuroticism	18·2	24·8
Extraversion	27·4	26·5
Adjustment scores on Teacher's Report Form, completed by parent,		
means	13·7	14·4

They show no significant differences between the children of the two series. For instance, on the clinical rating, which looks the most promising, if we leave out the obsessionals, 73 per cent of the children in the psychiatric series had a zero score, 75 per cent of the children of the controls ($\chi^2 = 0.5, 0.5 > p > 0.4$). Cowie showed that there was some evidence that psychosis in the parent tended to bring about a neurotic reaction in the child during the first 2 years after the onset of illness in the parent. But the figures go flatly against the hypothesis of any genetical connexion between psychosis and neurosis.

While it is certainly important for the clinician to remember that personality disorder, at the time it first presents, may be the only recognizable manifestation of a specific syndrome, genetical or non-genetical, it is only in a small minority of cases that this proves to be the case, e.g. when a systematic follow-up is carried out. The great majority of patients suffering from neuroses, personality disorders, behavioural disorders, disorders of interpersonal relationships, disturbed relationships with the communities in which they live, sexual fixations and disharmonies, and so forth, show deviations from normality of a quantitative rather than a qualitative kind; indeed the distinction between 'normal' and 'abnormal' in this area of psychiatry is a vague and shifting one. As he goes through his life, the individual may cross the indefinite boundary line between normal and abnormal many times; and, moreover, at one and the same time he may be seen to stand on opposite sides of the boundary by different observers from different view points.

A WORKING MODEL

In our discussions of the genetics of psychiatric syndromes, we have as a rule offered the reader a presentation of the available evidence before trying to fit it to a genetical model. When we come to the deviations of personality and the behavioural disorders connected with them (neuroses), it is more convenient to begin by proposing a genetical model, and then try it, as it were, against the data available in a variety of different states.

The genetical model which we think appropriate is, essentially, the same as that which is applied in discussing Normal variations in intelligence, and which in that field is almost universally accepted. This is the polygenic model, extended into a plurality of independent dimensions of variation. In the field of intelligence study, we are often content to consider only a single dimension ('general intelligence' or g); but in fact, the independent or partially independent dimensions are many, and any careful work has to make room for such different kinds of ability as verbal, spatial, numerical, etc.

Pluridimensional variation of a quantitative kind in the predisposition to neurotic disorders, dependent on a multifactorial genetical basis, was first suggested by Slater and Slater (1944). At this time these workers had been deeply concerned with war experiences. The circumstances then, in which a great body of men were subjected to physical and psychological stresses of a relatively stereotyped kind, to which they reacted in a variety of ways, were such as to highlight the contribution made by individual differences in personality and predisposition. Statistical investigation of a large case material (Slater, 1943) led to two conclusions.

The first of these in importance was the inverse relationship between the degree of stress undergone and the number of markers indicating abnormality of personality. The larger the number of these markers recorded in an individual case, the less the degree of stress which had been required to produce breakdown. From this the suggestion arose that variation in neurotic predisposition was quantitative in nature, and, on the genetical side, could most plausibly be attributed to polygenes. However, there was also a relationship between the type of personality and the type of symptom manifested suggesting the existence of qualitative as well as quantitative variation. This relationship could be close or distant, tetrachoric correlation coefficients varying from $+0.76$ down to $+0.19$, as shown below, suggesting contributions to variance in eventual symptoms all the way from 58 per cent down to a negligible 4 per cent.

However, the correlations in this table should not be credited with any contemporary validity. In recent years much systematic work has been done on the correlation of personality variable with clinical symptoms, perhaps most notably by Graham Foulds and his co-workers (see Foulds, 1965; Caine, 1970; Foulds, 1971). Well-controlled psychometric techniques have been used, and the scales devised (e.g. the Hysteroid-Obsessoid Questionnaire) have been validated. The effect of work along these lines has been to bring out significant correlations between personality traits and symptoms, but also to show that psychiatrists are influenced by their feeling for the personality of the patient when they come to making a diagnosis.

Clinical observations could be accounted for if the disposition to neurosis was regarded as due to a number of distinct qualities, each of them subject to normal variation. An individual who differed markedly from the mean towards either extreme, in respect of any single such quality, would be more than normally susceptible to stresses of a certain specific kind; and if the stress passed a certain level of intensity he would be likely to break down, and then to show symptoms of a specific and related kind. But the majority of men breaking down under stress would, by the laws of chance, be those who showed deviations along a

TABLE 48

CORRELATIONS BETWEEN PERSONALITY TRAITS AND SYMPTOMS, AS OBSERVED DURING WAR TIME ON A MATERIAL OF 2,000 NEUROTIC SOLDIERS

(Slater, 1943)

TRAITS/SYMPTOMS	CORRELATION
obsessional	+0·76
hysterical	+0·51
paranoid	+0·50
anxious	+0·40
depressive	+0·39
hypochondriacal	+0·19

number of different lines, rather than those who showed an extreme deviation along one line. They would be liable to break down under a mixture of stresses, and to respond with a variety of symptoms. Variation in the constitutional predisposition to such reactions should correspond to a normal surface in many dimensions.

This model, which is one of extreme generality, still holds the field; but its applicability varies from one type of reaction to another, and in a number of conditions we have to take into account important factors of an unrelated kind, such as the effects of single major genes, brain damage from environmental trauma, etc. The post-traumatic personality change, with its tendencies to depression, irritability, hypochondriasis and hysterical symptomatology, is well known to psychiatrists, and can readily be shown by a previously very well adjusted and normal individual if a serious head injury occurs.

Our working hypothesis is, then, that the general genetical make-up of the individual determines an inborn constitution which, from the time of conception, is subject also to influences from the environment. The intra-uterine environment is certainly important, but it is not easy to get any information about it. One of the ways it can show itself is often seen when a pair of MZ twins is born. Very commonly there will have been a number of anastomoses between the two placental circulations, so that if one twin gets a small lead in development, with a more powerfully acting heart, or with a larger share of the placenta, it will have an advantage over the other. This is likely to show itself in a weight difference at birth, and this difference may be critical for the subsequent development of the two twins.

At all stages in post-conceptional life there will be influences coming from the environment, sometimes directly traumatic in nature as in the case of perinatal accidents, which affect the development and maturation of the individual. When adult life is reached, the primary genetic contribution, and the way it has released its activating forces, will be indistinguishably bound up with the direct and secondary results of environmental agents. We suppose that the genetic (polygenic) contribution will be manifested in personality traits which can be inferred from the ordinary behaviour of the individual; we also suppose that some of these effects will provide predispositions which will not be manifested in ordinary

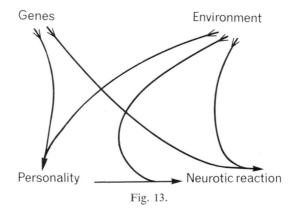

Fig. 13.

everyday life, but will show up when the individual is subjected to special, perhaps specific, stresses. Among these stress reactions we expect to find the symptomatology of the neuroses. It follows that different personality traits may be determined in very varying degree by the original genetical constitution, some being preponderantly so determined, and others much less. It follows also that these various personality traits will have varying degrees of association with varying kinds of neurotic symptomatology, some of them showing no measurable correlation with any particular kind of symptom induced by stress, while others show such a high degree of correlation between trait and symptom that the trait seems to be only a slightly masked form of a persisting symptom. It follows again that some neurotic symptoms, uncorrelated with any recognizable personality traits, will appear to arise in individuals under stress in an unpredictable way. And it follows finally that, when we attempt to measure the genetical contribution to neurotic manifestations, we are likely to come up against a very heterogeneous collection of data, some kinds of neurotic reaction appearing to have a genetical basis and others none. This is a simplified picture of a rather complex series of interrelationships. The accompanying diagram [FIG. 13] shows the way one might think about them, drawing the arrows thick or thin in one's imagination when one tries to quantify the contribution from the various factors in any individual case.

GENETIC FACTORS AND PERSONALITY VARIABLES

A large amount of work has been done in this field, of which an excellent recent summary has been provided by Shields (1971), nearly all of it by clinical psychologists. They have used a considerable number of tests of temperament, with a correspondingly varying list of concepts or traits, which, however, often show a kind of kinship from test to test. Nearly all of this work has been done on pairs of normal twins, and the estimates of heritability of the traits investigated

TABLE 49

SCHEMATIC DISTRIBUTION OF PERSONALITY TRAIT CONCORDANCES WITHIN PAIRS OF TWINS, CLASSIFIED BY THE STATISTICAL SIGNIFICANCE OF THE MZ:DZ DIFFERENCE

| | SIGNIFICANCE LEVEL OF INCREASED MZ CONCORDANCE | | | |
	0·01	0·05	n.s.	$r_{MZ} < r_{DZ}$
Introversion, social introversion, sociability, socialization, communality, social apprehension, shyness, social presence	4	4	4	—
Dominance/submission, self-assertion, dependence, dependency needs, need for affiliation, impatient dominance	3	1	4	2
Neuroticism, nervous tension, psychoneurotic complaints, psychosomatic complaints	3	1	4	—
Control/lack of control, self-control, will control, stable, impulsive, responsibility	—	2	5	—
Friendliness, empathy, likeableness, hostility, aggressiveness	2	—	2	1
Self-confidence, active, energetic conformity, vigorous, surgency	5	—	—	—
Cyclothymia/schizothymia, cyclothymia, depression, hypomania	1	1	2	—
Psychasthenia, orderliness, compulsion	1	2	—	—
Masculinity/femininity	—	1	2	—

Note: the numbers in this table refer to the number of appearances under the appropriate heading in Vandenberg's table of the results of twin research, quoted by Shields (1971), and do not directly relate to the total numbers of independent studies, of which there were 11 in all.

depend on the relationship between correlation coefficients in the MZ and the DZ pairs. The work has been summarized by Vandenberg (1967) and discussed by Shields (1971); and most of the information in the tabulated summary provided by the former has been restructured and simplified into the tabulation above [TABLE 49]. Personality features of the social extraversion-introversion type, which are focused on by a number of temperament tests, have provided the largest number of relevant results, tending strongly towards a significantly greater concordance in MZ than in DZ pairs. However, the feature which seems to be most consistently more concordant in MZ than in DZ pairs is something which seems to be related to energy of personality.

The Minnesota Multiphasic Personality Inventory (MMPI) is a psychometric temperament test which is of particular interest to psychiatrists, since it is formulated on the basis of psychiatric concepts, even if they have undergone somewhat of a 'sea-change' in being applied to normal rather than abnormal psychology. Gottesman (1962, 1963) investigated 34 MZ and 34 DZ twin pairs of normal school-children; and if the two sexes are combined (which might perhaps be objected to) then we have the following rank order of traits arranged in order of the magnitude of the estimate of the heritability, as a function of within-pair variances (assuming that MZ and DZ pairs are taken from the same population, or from populations with the same variance between individuals), so that $h^2 = (V_{DZ} - V_{MZ})/V_{DZ} = (r_{MZ} - r_{DZ})/(1 - r_{DZ})$.

TABLE 50

HEREDITY LOADINGS OF MMPI PERSONALITY TRAITS

		MMPI SCALE	h^2
3	Hy	hysteria	0·00
6	Pa	paranoia	0·05
5	Mf	pathological sexuality	0·15
1	Hs	hypochondriasis	0·16
9	Ma	hypomania	0·24
7	Pt	psychasthenia	0·37
8	Sc	schizophrenia	0·42
2	D	depression	0·45
4	Pd	psychopathic deviation	0·50
0	Si	social introversion	0·71

Gottesman remarked on these figures: 'It would appear that neuroses with hypochondriacal and hysterical elements have no or low genetic component, while those with elements of anxiety, depression, obsession and schizoid withdrawal have a substantial genetic component under the environmental conditions obtaining for this particular adolescent sample.' It is, however, far from sure that the MMPI scale factor, which is a closer approach to a personality trait than a symptom, is capable of being extended in an application to the eventual neurotic reactions to which the personality is liable. Here, it is more important to note that the genetical contribution to different aspects of the personality varies very much. There is no reason to think that some traits could not be strongly impressed on the individual by dint of the environmental circumstances through which he passes, without any genetical contribution of any importance or specificity.

Probably the most important investigations of the genetical contribution to variation in personality traits in normal individuals has been provided by the two major studies of MZ twins separated in early life, by Newman, Freeman and Holzinger (1937) 19 pairs, and by Shields (1962) 42 pairs. A third recent study by Juel-Nielsen (1965) is a detailed clinical investigation of 12 separated pairs of MZ twins, but does not provide material easily quoted in tabular form. Both the studies by Newman *et al.* and by Shields included control material of two kinds, MZ pairs and DZ pairs reared together. The correlations observed in these three kinds of twin pairs, in the two studies, and on three scales, are shown in TABLE 51. Shields was also able to rate personality resemblances and

TABLE 51

INTRA-PAIR CORRELATIONS FOR PERSONALITY QUESTIONNAIRE
SCORES IN MZ TWINS REARED APART, AND IN CONTROLS

(Quoted from Shields, 1971)

	MZ PAIRS		DZ PAIRS REARED TOGETHER (MOSTLY)
	REARED APART	REARED TOGETHER	
	r	*r*	*r*
Newman *et al.* (1937)			
Neuroticism (Bernreuter)	0·583	0·562	0·371
Shields (1962)			
Self-rating questionnaire (Eysenck)			
Neuroticism	0·53	0·38	0·11
Extraversion	0·61	0·42	0·17

differences within pairs of twins into five grades, partly by the developmental histories and information from third parties, and partly by personal interview. TABLE 52 shows that resemblances are somewhat less in the separated than in the

TABLE 52

MZ TWINS REARED APART, WITH CONTROL GROUPS; CLINICAL
ESTIMATES OF DEGREE OF PERSONALITY RESEMBLANCE OR DIFFER-
ENCE WITHIN PAIRS

(From Shields, 1962)

	DISTRIBUTIONS, AS PER CENT, OF		
	MZ PAIRS REARED		DZ
	TOGETHER	APART	PAIRS
Similarities outstanding			
Grade I	19	21	0
II a	36	15	9
II b	21	26	19
Differences outstanding			
III	17	28	25
IV	7	10	47

control MZ pairs, and differences markedly greater; but both kinds of MZ pairs are much more like each other than either is to the DZ pairs.

There is no large amount of work on resemblances and differences in personality traits in other relatives than pairs of twins. Cattell (1953) has proposed a method of analysing variances in paired relatives in family studies, so as to obtain estimates of genetical and environmental contributions. He and his colleagues have followed up this work by field studies (e.g. Cattell, Stice and Kristy, 1957), but with results that are rather difficult to interpret.

A recent methodological investigation by Elston and Gottesman (1968) was illustrated by an analysis of MMPI responses on the social introversion scale

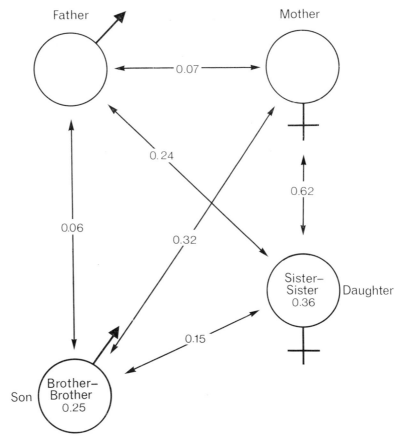

Fig. 14. Intrafamilial correlations (all positive) in estimates of neuroticism on the Bernreuter Personality Inventory, diagrammatized. (Data from Fuller and Thompson, 1960.)

given by 178 males and 233 females related to one another as parents, twins and sibs. A high estimate of heritability was obtained, but the data are not reported in the form of correlation coefficients.

Work with the Bernreuter Personality Inventory, quoted by Fuller and Thompson (1960) has provided intrafamilial correlations in respect of 'neuroticism', which are shown diagrammatically [FIG. 14]. Same-sexed pairs are more alike on the whole than opposite-sexed pairs; and females tend to provide much higher correlations than males. The only modern work known to us (Lienert and Reisse, 1961, quoted by Eysenck, 1968) showed positive correlations in neuroticism between parents 0·17, between father and child 0·13, between mother and child 0·31.

Work of considerable physiological interest has been reported by Abe and his colleagues (e.g. Abe, Shimakawa and Kajiyama, 1967). They found evidence to suggest resemblance between parents and children in respect of a variety of childhood behaviour traits: sleep-talking, teeth-grinding, sleep-walking, insomnia, and acquisition of bladder control.

GENETICAL FACTORS AND
NEUROTIC SYMPTOMATOLOGY

As will have been gathered from the presentation of our working model (see for instance the diagrammatic representation in FIGURE 13), genetical factors are capable of making a contribution to neurotic reactions and neurotic symptomatology at least at two different levels, i.e. in laying down the main lines of personality development, and also, independently, providing a predisposition capable of activation by environmental forces leading directly into manifestations of a neurotic type. Against this, the environmental contribution must be thought of as entering the picture at not less than three levels, so that we can expect its effects to be even more difficult to unravel. Some neurotic reactions will be predictable on the basis of knowledge about the personality and about the stresses to which it is subjected, but there will be other observations not capable of being so predicted. The variable and often loose association between personality traits and eventual symptoms was shown in TABLE 48. However, it will be possible to try to estimate the genetical contributions to symptom formation without presuppositions about the personality background.

Some of the complexity of these interrelationships comes out in an investigation by Coppen, Cowie and Slater (1965). These workers correlated ratings of 'neuroticism' and 'extraversion-introversion' on the Maudsley Personality Inventory given by 266 patients and 735 of their first-degree relatives and spouses. The N scores of the patients were raised, as had been expected; but contrary to expectation the scores of their relatives were not. Correlation coefficients within classes of relatives were generally low, and only significantly positive in the families of the male patients, and in them solely in the relationships between the mother and her children, and between the patient and his male siblings. However, the correlations between the scores of the mother of a male patient and her children were of a substantial kind, averaging +0·415 for extraversion and +0·405 for neuroticism. Correlations between spouses were significantly positive for N (+0·235), but not for E. It seemed obvious to the authors that these findings could hardly be accounted for on any genetical hypothesis unaided. They thought the results might suggest the possibility of some mothers being neurotogenic, to some sons but not to daughters. Low correlations involving females and their relatives might be in part accounted for by the extra variance in neuroticism shown by the female, connected with the menstrual cycle. Eysenck has criticized this work as being too vulnerable to changes in neuroticism accompanying illness. With the hindsight we now have, we might also think that the investigation involved the comparison of unlike subjects, in so far as patients were compared with their relatives. Referring to FIGURE 13, we see the environmental-genetical interactional pattern represented as being more complex for the neurotic manifestations than for the personality manifestation. These complexities are likely to obscure the meaning of the results, in all kinds of investigations of the genetical background of neurosis.

TWIN AND FAMILY STUDIES ON NEUROSES GENERALLY

An early study of neurotic symptomatology in twin school-children was carried out by Shields (1954) on 62 same-sexed pairs of twins, 36 MZ and 26 DZ, 27

TABLE 53

CONCORDANCES WITHIN TWIN PAIRS OF SCHOOL-CHILDREN IN RESPECT OF NEUROTIC SYMPTOMATOLOGY AND PERSONALITY TRAITS

(From Shields, 1954)

QUANTITATIVE CONCORDANCE AS %		QUALITATIVE CONCORDANCE AS %		
	MZ	DZ		MZ	DZ
Both 'neurotic'	47	35	Completely concordant	36	0
Both 'normal'	36	31	Essentially concordant	33	12
Discordant	17	35	Partially concordant	14	19
			Discordant	17	69

male pairs, 35 female pairs. These were normal children aged 12–15, but of course, as was to be expected, a good deal of neurotic symptomatology was found: nail-biting, enuresis, school problems, food fads, night terrors, fears, worries, etc. The most striking finding was that there was only a small difference between concordances shown by the MZ and the DZ pairs in respect of presence or absence of neurotic symptomatology, but a large difference between the two in the type of symptoms or personality traits shown [see TABLE 53]. Presence or absence of symptomatology, therefore, was much more closely related to environmental stresses than to genetical predisposition; but if symptoms were shown, then their nature was to a large degree determined by the hereditary factors. Other evidence supported these views. Poor family environments were closely associated with presence of symptoms.

Further research by the Maudsley genetics group leads to the conclusion that some kinds of symptoms are much more closely dependent on the genetical predisposition than others. This is made plain in TABLE 54. Both the anxiety states and the personality disorders show striking qualitative resemblances between members of MZ pairs, no large specific concordance in DZ pairs, and large differences between MZ and DZ concordances. However, when we come to the neuroses classified as 'other', which were mainly reactive depressions, there were no agreements in symptomatology between either MZ or DZ twins; and the general tendency to present with psychiatric symptomatology of some kind was apparently mainly determined by non-genetical causes, since MZ and DZ pairs showed exactly the same concordances.

TABLE 54

PSYCHIATRIC DIAGNOSIS AND CONCORDANCE IN SAME-SEXED TWINS

(Data from Slater and Shields, 1969)

| | N | | PSYCHIATRIC DIAGNOSIS IN CO-TWIN | | | |
| | | | ANY DIAGNOSIS | | SAME DIAGNOSIS | |
	MZ	DZ	MZ	DZ	MZ	DZ
Diagnosis in proband						
anxiety state	17	28	47	18	41	4
other neurosis	12	21	25	24	0	0
personality disorder	33	35	55	29	33	6
All probands	62	84	47	24	29	4

Probands (62 MZ, 84 DZ) accepted as neurotic or personality disordered on follow-up. Identity of diagnosis based on whole number of ICD classification. Figures on right are percentages of row totals.

The findings in Brown's 1942 study of the parents and sibs of neurotic patients [see TABLE 55] are also informative. Anxious personalities abound, not only in the relatives of neurotics, but also in a control population. But downright anxiety states were found most frequently in the relatives of anxiety neurotics, hysterical states among the relatives of hysterics, and obsessional neuroses most

TABLE 55

INCIDENCE OF NEUROTIC STATES, AS PER CENT, IN PARENTS AND SIBS OF NEUROTIC PROBANDS AND OF CONTROLS

(Data from Brown, 1942)

	PROBANDS			
	ANXIETY		OBSESSIONAL	
FIRST DEGREE RELATIVES	STATE	HYSTERIA	STATE	CONTROLS
N	365	107	101	189
Anxiety state	15	7	3	—
Hysteria	2	11	—	1
Obsessional state	1	—	7	—
Anxious personality	17	9	4	10
Manic-depressive	2	—	4	—

frequently in the relatives of the obsessional neurotics. There was no raised incidence of schizophrenia in the relatives of these neurotic probands; but 13 manic-depressives were found, 9 among the relatives of the anxiety neurotics and 4 among the relatives of the obsessionals. These findings suggest a certain degree of genetic specificity in the neuroses, which we can test further with data relating to particular neuroses.

Anxiety States

This field has recently been reviewed by Slater and Shields (1969). The family studies of McInnes (1937), Brown (1942) and Cohen et al. (1951) show incidences of anxiety neuroses in parents and sibs combined of 15·0, 15·1 and 15·8 per cent, respectively. Agreement between the three studies is not actually quite so good as that, since as a rule there was more anxiety neurosis in the parents than the sibs, and there is more variability from series to series when parents and sibs are handled separately. Cohen found an extremely high incidence, 55 per cent, of anxiety neurosis in the mothers of his chronic (male) patients, a finding which is reminiscent of the observations of Coppen *et al.*, mentioned on page 101.

The personal material reported by Slater and Shields (1969) was again a series of twins, covered in part by TABLE 54. TABLE 56, however, gives a much

TABLE 56

ANXIETY ILLNESSES AND SYMPTOMS IN CO-TWINS OF PATIENTS WITH ANXIETY STATES

(From Slater and Shields, 1969)

PROBAND ANXIETY STATE OR PHOBIC STATE (ICD CLASSIFICATIONS 310, 312 AND 320·3) CO-TWINS	MZ	DZ
Anxiety state (310)	8	1
Inadequate personality (320·3), anxious	2	—
Other neurosis or personality disorder	—	2
Other psychiatric diagnosis, anxious personality	—	1
Other psychiatric diagnosis, no mention of anxiety	—	3
Within normal limits, mention of anxiety	3	3
Within normal limits, no mention of anxiety	7	30
Total	20	40

Diagnoses of probands and of twins made independently, i.e. without knowledge of state in twin partner.

more complete picture of their findings in respect of the anxiety states. The most important finding of this study is that in the MZ pairs both twins showed marked anxiety symptoms in 13 out of 20 pairs, i.e. 65 per cent; in the DZ pairs only in 5 out of 40 pairs, or 13 per cent. The most interesting finding is, perhaps, that in the MZ pairs the co-twins showed psychiatric deviations only along the anxiety axis, but in the DZ twins in a number of other directions. Actual anxiety states were shown by 50 per cent of the MZ co-twins, by only 2·5 per cent of the DZ co-twins.

The authors conclude:

The anxiety state is best understood on an interactional model. The constitutional potentiality of becoming anxious could then be thought of as a normal component of personality, varying in degree and in that respect normally distributed through the population, and predisposing to neurotic illness if it is marked in degree or if adaptation is further hampered by obsessive-compulsive, depressive or hysterical tendencies. The environmental stress factor plays an equally important role. Genetic variability in respect of anxiety could well be of adaptive value to the species. The anxious reaction to stress must be regarded as basically healthy, and only likely to produce illness if it is extreme or if normal adaptation becomes impossible . . .

As we have seen in this twin series, stress may not only lead to an anxiety reaction, but precipitate one which continues irreversibly after the stress has passed off. It does not seem likely that such mechanisms as irreversibility will be explicable on a genetical basis.

Obsessive-Compulsive States

The findings made in the principal investigations are shown in TABLE 57. All

TABLE 57

INCIDENCE OF OBSESSIONAL DEVIATIONS, VARIOUSLY CATEGORIZED
IN RELATIVES OF PROBANDS WITH OBSESSIONAL ILLNESSES

INVESTIGATOR AND DATE	RELATIVES	FINDINGS	PER CENT
Luxenburger, 1930	fathers	anankastic features	15
Luxenburger, 1930	mothers	anankastic features	6
Luxenburger, 1930	sibs	anankastic features	14
Lewis, 1935	parents	obsessional traits	37
Lewis, 1935	sibs	obsessional traits	21
Brown, 1942	parents and sibs	obsessional neurosis	7
Rüdin, 1953	parents	obsessional illness	5
Rüdin, 1953	parents	obsessional personality	5
Rüdin, 1953	sibs	obsessional illness	2
Rüdin, 1953	sibs	obsessional personality	3

these investigations are rather old now, and it would be very desirable to have more modern work to refer to. Strömgren has criticized the Luxenburger study as relying on rather heterogeneous proband material, including psychotic cases, which may account for the high incidence of psychoses in his secondary cases. A rather high psychotic incidence was also found by Lewis, 4 per cent in parents and 6 per cent in sibs. Rüdin's study is the most modern and the most satisfactory in respect of index case material, and her results are to be preferred to all the others. Although the incidence both of schizophrenia and of manic-depressive illness was slightly higher in her secondary cases than was to be expected, there was no significant shift. She concluded that the predisposition to reactions involving obsessional symptomatology was to be thought of as distributed quantitatively and normally in the population, on a polygenic basis, with the hereditary factors playing an important role.

The twin literature on obsessive-compulsive states has recently been reviewed by Marks et al. (1969) in connexion with the publication of a concordant MZ pair of their own. The cases reported in the literature are by no means always systematically ascertained, and they are often reported incompletely, so that it is not easy to make any general statement. Perhaps one could say that of something like 40 MZ pairs, something like 30 were concordant in showing some obsessional symptomatology. The concordance rate of over 75 per cent is not to be relied on, since some of the literature selection may have been biased in favour of concordance. The co-twins of 6 systematically ascertained MZ twin pairs in the files of the genetics section at the Institute of Psychiatry,

8

London, were probably concordant in 3 cases (Shields, personal communication).

There is one significant study (Rosenberg, 1967) which tends in the opposite direction; in the first degree relatives of 144 obsessional neurotics there was indeed a 9–11 per cent incidence of psychiatric illness, but only two cases of obsessional neurosis were found among them. Apart from this the evidence suggests that the genetical contribution to the obsessional neuroses is an important one. There is no suggestion of any major gene playing a role, and polygenic inheritance is to be thought of.

'Hysteria'

'Hysteria' is a diagnosis which is quite commonly made, but one which has never been given any satisfactory definition. There are, of course, a variety of symptoms which are legitimately called hysterical, especially those involving the mechanisms of psychic dissociation and conversion, such as highly recoverable states of loss of memory, paralyses, anaesthesias, etc. However, follow-up studies have always shown, either that these symptoms have been temporary manifestations of some underlying disorder, such as an affective psychosis or an organic disorder of the brain, or that they have made up only a part of the clinical picture being accompanied by other diagnostically significant manifestations, or that they have been a temporary reaction to acute stress on the part of a normal, if often somewhat immature, individual. It is then hardly surprising that the evidence of a genetical contribution to the occurrence of such syndromes is slender and unreliable. The reader will have noted on an earlier page the conflicting findings of Slater [TABLE 48], Gottesman [TABLE 50], and Brown [TABLE 55].

The most important studies are those of Ljungberg (1957), and Slater (1961), a family study and a twin study respectively. Ljungberg accepted as his probands (N = 381), patients with bodily symptoms: difficulties in walking, fits, paralyses, anaesthesia, tremor, etc., and such psychic symptoms as memory disorders. It is noteworthy that 25 per cent of the men and 11 per cent of the women had suffered a cerebral injury. Psychopathy and abnormal personality were common in the probands, and Ljungberg classified the three commonest types of deviation as hysterical personality 21 per cent, psycho-infantile 10 per cent and psychasthenic 8 per cent. In the first-degree relatives the morbidity risk of hysteria was found to be, expressed as percentages:

fathers	1·7	mothers	7·3
brothers	2·7	sisters	6·0
sons	4·6	daughters	6·9
males	2·4	females	6·4

It was not possible for Ljungberg, nor is it possible for us, to give any estimate of the population risk of 'hysteria'; the vagueness of the diagnosis is an insurmountable barrier. However, these figures are certainly higher than one would expect to find, if one were to rely on clinic diagnoses. Ljungberg provides clinical epitomes of the doubtful diagnoses of hysteria in the relatives, which certainly leave these diagnoses still doubtful.

Ljungberg, very naturally considering his results, regards the findings as supporting a genetical contribution to 'hysteria', and 'on the basis of the hypothesis that every person is to a varying degree prone to hysteria, polygenic transmission seems to be a reasonable supposition.' The large preponderance of females, both in the proband material and in the secondary cases, a preponderance which is the general experience of clinicians, fits in well with polygenic determination. A finding that runs against the hypothesis is Ljungberg's observation that the risk of hysteria for the children of a parental mating unaffected × affected was not higher than for the children of a mating unaffected × unaffected.

Slater's investigation (1961) was made on a systematically ascertained unselected series of probands diagnostically classified as suffering from 'hysterical reaction without mention of anxiety reaction' (23 pairs) and 'pathological personality not otherwise specified, hysterical' (1 pair). There were 12 MZ pairs, 7 male and 5 female and 12 same-sexed DZ pairs, 1 male and 11 female. No single co-twin, either in the MZ or the DZ series, had at any time achieved a psychiatrist's diagnosis of 'hysteria'. Using other criteria of psychiatric deviation, none were found which showed a greater within-pair similarity in the MZ than in the DZ pairs. An excerpt from the conclusions may be permitted here:

Perhaps the most surprising feature of the follow-up statistics is their lack of uniformity. Some patients do well, others very badly indeed; and good or bad outcome bears little relation to the nature, the amount or the severity of the hysterical symptoms. To get a clue to the prognosis, we have to look, not at the hysterical mechanisms exposed, but to their aetiological basis, whether this is a brain lesion, an endogenous psychosis, a deviation in personality development, a temporary stress situation, or a built-in self-perpetuating mechanism.

We are compelled to ask, what is the justification for regarding hysteria as a syndrome? The aetiology appears to be very various; and the hypothesis of a genetical basis of a specific or indeed important kind has had to be discarded. Among the hysterics of the present series we have found patients suffering from a focal brain lesion, also probably from epilepsy, from schizophrenia, from endogenous depression, and from anxiety states falling more easily into the category of affective than hysterical illnesses. Comparative analysis of personalities shows the affected twin not so much more hysterical as more anxious than his partner.

The dissociative mechanisms of hysteria are known of old, and can lead to symptoms which deserve no other name. But the diagnosis of an illness as hysterical goes much further than the recognition of a symptom. The unreliability of the diagnosis indicates the unsatisfactoriness of a psychopathology which is based solely on a mental mechanism. The mere manifestation of a mental mechanism within the range of normal potentialities tells us little of consequence. If in our patient we find the signs of hysteria and no more, then these are signs that we have not yet looked deeply enough.

This purely negative conclusion has subsequently been both supported (e.g. by Slater, 1965, and by Slater and Glithero, 1965) in follow-up studies, and also controverted by Guze and his associates. Guze's work depends on a revised concept of 'hysteria'. Finding that conversion symptoms occur in a great variety of psychiatric states, Arkonac and Guze (1963) abandoned them as a criterion for the diagnosis of hysteria, and redefined the syndrome as one characterized by occurrence early in life, with few exceptions in women and very rarely in men, with recurrent symptoms in many organ systems, some at least of: varied pains, menstrual difficulties, sexual maladjustment, headaches, anxiety symptoms, conversion symptoms, repeated hospital admissions and operations. A syndrome so delimited was found to retain its identity over a follow-up of 6–8 years. In the first degree relatives of 25 women so diagnosed, Arkonac and Guze found a total of 5 secondary cases of 'hysteria' (by the same definition), all of them female, i.e. 9 per cent of all relatives interviewed, or 15 per cent of all the female relatives. Arkonac and Guze also made an attempt to estimate the frequency of 'hysteria' in the general population, which they put at between 1 and 2 per cent of the female population; they found the syndrome in 3 out of 167 women in a maternity hospital for normal full term delivery (2 per cent). In addition to the secondary cases of 'hysteria' there was an incidence of 9 per cent of anxiety neurotics in the relatives of their hysterical probands. Arkonac and Guze did not think that this was in significant excess of normal expectations. However, they did consider that the prevalence of alcoholism among the male relatives was probably raised.

An increased prevalence of hysteria in the female first-degree relatives of hysterics, and an increased prevalence of alcoholism or sociopathy in their male relatives, were also shown in a later study by Woerner and Guze, 1968. This study is particularly interesting for the information provided about the husbands of the probands, a psychiatrically abnormal group. However, the Guze definition of 'hysteria' is so restrictive, and so contingent on a multiplicity of rather heterogeneous abnormalities of behaviour, that it is very doubtful whether it can enshrine any genetical entity. The restrictiveness of definition means that it is not easy to find probands. It is surprising that 2 per cent of women in a normal lying-in hospital were found to be 'hysterics'; the frequency of 'hysterics', according to the same definition, in a psychiatric hospital would hardly be much higher. The difficulty in finding probands meant, of course, that the numbers investigated in both of Guze's two reports are very small. In the second report, there were only 23 female first-degree relatives of the probands whose condition could be diagnosed for psychiatric purposes.

Reactive Depression

On an earlier page [p. 102, and TABLE 54], we have referred to the fact that the psychiatric states found in a group of neurotic twin probands suffering from conditions other than anxiety states and personality disorders, were mainly in the nature of reactive depressions; and that in the co-twins of these probands there was none who had the same diagnosis as the proband. In this series there were 24 probands diagnosed as suffering from reactive depression, 8 of them belonging to MZ and 16 to DZ pairs. No co-twin achieved a diagnosis of reactive depression, and the numbers that achieved any psychiatric diagnosis at all were 3 of the MZ and 4 of the DZ pairs. If this can be called concordance, then it was present in 38 per cent of the MZ and 25 per cent of the DZ pairs (Price, 1968). This finding goes against the hypothesis that there is any specific genetical contribution to disorders of this kind, though a general susceptibility to emotional over-reaction may possibly be involved.

The only important study of the genetics of reactive depression has been carried out by Stenstedt (1966), who investigated the parents and sibs of 176 probands suffering from neurotic depression. The expectancy of mental disorder and abnormality among these relatives did not differ appreciably from controls.

Alcoholism

It might be thought that the investigation of the aetiology of alcoholism along genetical lines would be a forlorn task since, as Strömgren (1967) has pointed out, there are enormous group differences in the proclivity to alcoholism which can have nothing to do with genetics. Alcohol consumption varies very much from country to country, between social classes, between persons of different occupation, between the younger and the older. Strömgren says that no report of a genetical investigation can be acceptable without an account of the drinking habits of the population from which the group of probands was drawn. He points out, further, that in population groups in which a fairly heavy consumption of alcohol is very common, the individuals who succumb to a health-damaging addiction will be, by and large, people of fairly normal personality; in groups where alcoholic consumption is slight, those who deviate so far from the norm as to become addicts will much more often show pathological features. For the same reason, alcoholically addicted women will show more psycho-pathology than alcoholic men. When we come to discuss criminality we shall find that very similar arguments apply.

However, there are suggestions that some genetically determined biochemical difference might be involved in alcoholic addiction. There are indeed in all Western countries persons who drink so much alcohol that they damage their bodily or mental health, without ever being so enslaved that, under psychological pressure, they are unable to keep in some kind of balance. In most countries these people make up the majority of the alcoholics who constitute a health problem. However, most psychiatric specialists in the addictions agree that there are, much more rarely, patients who can quite easily remain teetotal for long periods of time, but, once having taken a drink, find it impossible to stop drinking, before a single prolonged bout, or a series of bouts, have brought them under external control. Jellinek classified drinking behaviour into continuous drinking (gamma and delta alcoholism) and bout drinking (epsilon alcoholism), and this classification is widely used by clinicians. It would seem probable that individuals with a genetically determined biochemical insufficiency, if they exist, would be found mainly in Jellinek's epsilon class. It is a common clinical impression that it is among the relatives of these individuals that one finds an excess both of alcoholics and of teetotallers, and a relative deficiency of slight and moderate drinkers.

On *a priori* grounds, it is probable that special susceptibilities to the effects of alcohol may exist, just as much as specific susceptibilities to other pharmacological agents. To support the view that a biochemical inquiry in human subjects might be rewarding, we have the experimental evidence (which has been reviewed by Partanen *et al.*, 1966), that strains of rats can be bred who are liable to alcoholism, and can be protected from it by dietetic controls (vitamins, amino acids). However, investigations along such specific lines have never yet been undertaken in man. We have instead quite substantial and important studies along more conventional lines, with results that are certainly interesting.

A work of fundamental importance is the model study of Finnish drinking habits by Partanen, Bruun and Markkanen (1966). Drinking habits in Finland differ from those in other countries chiefly in that there is a relatively low over-all consumption, low availability of alcohol, and alcoholic consumption is not a part of daily life. Most people drink only on special occasions, but then with the purpose of achieving some degree of intoxication. The social manifestations of drinking are strictly controlled by the community, so that drunkenness will incur a high risk of leading to police action and an arrest. In such a community, one would expect heavy drinkers and alcoholics to be markedly aberrant individuals.

Partanen *et al.* ascertained a series of same-sexed male pairs of twins from the birth registrations of the 1920–29 decade. Data about drinking habits were available for estimates of heritability in 172 MZ and 557 DZ pairs; additional analysis of tests of intelligence and personality traits could be carried out on smaller numbers, 157 MZ and 189 DZ pairs. Factor analysis of the various estimates of drinking behaviour led to the definition of three factors, Density (closely approximated to by frequency of drinking), Amount, and Lack of Control. Correlations between measurements of Density and the other two factors were negligible; but there was a correlation of 0·36 between Amount and Lack of Control. Heritabilities were estimated from intra-pair variances in MZ and DZ pairs as follows:

Density	0·39
Amount	0·36
Lack of Control	0·14

In their conclusions the authors make the following observations. Normal drinking, as well as abstinence and heavy use, show considerable hereditary variation, but not arrests, social complications or addictive symptoms. Heritability of Lack of Control was high in the younger age groups, but low in the older ones (there being no such age differences for Density or Amount, or for intelligence measures or personality variables). There was, surprisingly, little evidence for hereditary connexions between drinking and personality variables. Environmental factors which were found to play a part were age, age at separation of the members of the twin pair, marital status, and degree of urbanization of the area of residence. Hereditary factors were also found to play a part in the consumption of coffee and of alcohol.

The above study is of special importance because it investigated a normal population, with the aid of a fully representative series of twins, and by means of highly sophisticated statistical methods. To compare with it we have three significant studies of alcoholism as a psychiatric problem, by Åmark (1951), Bleuler (1955) and Kaij (1960).

Kaij's work is also a study of twins, ascertained by comparing the birth dates of the twin register with the registers of two County Temperance Boards in southern Sweden. Members of twin pairs so found (opposite-sexed pairs excluded) were followed up to interview or death. Kaij had to formulate quantitative categories of alcoholic abuse, and did so on a five point scale from 0 to 4. TABLE 58 shows the distributions in the MZ and the DZ pairs. From these figures, Kaij calculated a concordance (identity of degree of alcoholism) of 53·5 per cent in MZ and 28·3 per cent in DZ pairs. Looking at the figures rather more directly, one can calculate that in the MZ group for the 31 concordant pairs observed only 14·50 could have been expected by chance, in the DZ group for the 39 observed 29·44 could have been expected. There is a 32 per cent excess of concordance in the DZ group, and a 114 per cent excess in the MZ group.

A finding of a somewhat paradoxical kind was that there was no convincing evidence of intellectual deterioration being greater in the twin who drank more than in his partner. Kaij was inclined to think that in some cases the intellectual impairment was arising from other sources than alcoholism, but might have a contributing effect in the causation of alcoholism.

TABLE 58

CONCORDANCES AND DISCORDANCES IN SEVERITY OF ALCOHOLISM, GRADED 0–4, IN ALCOHOLIC PROBANDS AND THEIR CO-TWINS

(From Kaij, 1960)

MZ PROBANDS							DZ PROBANDS					
0	1	2	3	4	Total		0	1	2	3	4	Total
—	—	1	1	10	12	4	—	1	2	1	10	14
—	1	4	7	1	13	3	1	3	7	6	3	20
—	3	10	3	2	18	2	—	6	4	6	6	22
—	4	5	2	1	12	1	1	19	22	10	7	59
—	1	2	—	—	3	0	—	7	5	6	5	23
—	9	22	13	14	58	co-twins	2	36	40	29	31	138

The reports of Bleuler and Åmark relate to families. Åmark (1951) gathered his cases, all male, from three sources, a psychiatric clinic, ten different institutions for alcoholics, and from the Stockholm Temperance Board; and parents and sibs were followed up. No raised incidence of schizophrenia, manic-depression or other functional psychoses was found among the relatives, but the incidence of alcoholism was raised, both for fathers and for brothers: (in fathers 26 per cent, in brothers 22 per cent, as against a general population risk of alcoholism of 3·4 per cent, quoted from Fremming for the Danish population). There was also an increased incidence of 'psychopathy', of 15 per cent in parents (either sex), and from 12 to 21 per cent in sibs (either sex).

Probably the most interesting data are shown in the analysis of morbidity risks for sibs against parental constitution. This is shown in TABLE 59. There is a greatly raised risk of alcoholism in the sibs of alcoholics when one parent is alcoholic, as against the matings where neither is; the risk of psychopathy does not make such a big shift; and where the criterion is criminality, the difference is quite slight. This suggests a polygenic basis for the predisposition to alcholism, with some of the hereditary factors being capable of showing themselves in psychopathy.

One interesting point that emerged from Åmark's work is that the bout drinkers (periodic drinkers) did seem to differ from other chronic alcoholics, showing what Åmark thought was a clinically distinct syndrome. In those families where one parent was alcoholic, 42 per cent of the sibs of the proband were alcoholic; there were 14 alcoholic brothers, in fact, and 6 of them were also periodic drinkers like the proband.

Bleuler's two family studies (1955) are at least as interesting for the information about the personalities of chronic alcoholics, the wretchednesses of their home lives in childhood, etc., as for the genetical information. He found that the morbidity risk for schizophrenia was the same as for the general population, the risk for epilepsy somewhat lower, and the risk of manic-depressive psychoses somewhat higher, though not significantly so. The incidence of personality abnormalities in the probands was high: only 10 of the 50 probands were regarded as 'normal', 20 were borderline, 18 morbid but without psychosis, 2 psychotic. Among the morbid personalities were those who suffered from depressive moods, compulsive-obsessional neurotics, hysterical personalities,

TABLE 59

MORBIDITY RISK OF ALCOHOLISM, PSYCHOPATHY AND CRIMINALITY
IN SIBS OF CHRONIC ALCOHOLICS

(Data from Åmark, 1951)

	ALCOHOLISM AMONG BROTHERS (%)	PSYCHOPATHY AMONG BROTHERS AND SISTERS (%)	CRIMINALITY AMONG BROTHERS (%)
A. Neither parent alcoholic (252 brothers, 265 sisters)	17·1	12·8	16·3
B. One parent alcoholic (97 brothers, 100 sisters)	33·3	20·8	18·6
Ratio B/A	1·95	1·68	1·14

those who were shy, shut-in and seclusive. In other words, deviations along a number of different dimensions were observed, and the personality background for the development of chronic alcoholism would seem to be very heterogeneous. These results resemble those of Åmark (1951); he found psychasthenics, hyperthymics, anankasts, cycloid and cyclothymic persons, dysphoric and depressive ones, and types classified as psycho-infantile, affectively cool, schizoid, hysteroid and easily suggestible, ixoid and ixothymic, torpid, unstable and neurasthenic. This information may not seem helpful, but it does suggest that alcoholism can constitute a danger for any individual with personality difficulties of any kind.

Of Bleuler's two studies one was based on case material from the Payne-Whitney Clinic in New York. The second from Burghölzli, Zürich, was designed to act as checks on the first: the result was that the main familial findings were confirmed. The New York patients were much more intensively investigated than the Zürich ones, and only in New York could data about second-degree relatives be used. TABLE 60 shows the prevalence of alcoholism among the relatives over the age of ten. Bleuler also gives corresponding rates for the over-40, but this does not make much difference to their magnitude. One of the more interesting features of this investigation is the high incidence of alcoholism in the consorts of alcoholics.

Reviewing the statistics made available in the above twin and family investigations, one finds strong evidence of a contribution of hereditary factors to the predisposition to alcoholism, and a strong suggestion that this is along polygenic lines. There is a possibility of a type of alcoholism resulting from an inborn metabolic deviation, but nothing firm to go on. The genetical predisposition to alcoholism does not show itself in any specific type or types of personality deviation.

One very important factor has been relatively neglected in investigations carried out so far, Manfred Bleuler being the one worker who has provided differential distributions for the two sexes; this is the much greater liability of

TABLE 60

PREVALENCE OF ALCOHOLISM IN RELATIVES (AGED OVER 10 YEARS) OF CHRONIC ALCOHOLICS

(From Bleuler, 1955)

			ALCOHOLICS AMONG RELATIVES AS PER CENT			
	NO. INVESTIGATED		MALES		FEMALES	
RELATIVES	AMER.	SWISS	AMER.	SWISS	AMER.	SWISS
Parents	100	98	22	33	6	8
Sibs	114	162	12	8	8	2
Children	63	47	—	—	—	—
Half-sibs	17	32	17	—	13	—
Grandparents	168	*	11		4	
Uncles and aunts	333	*	15		2	
Wives and husbands	46	45	29	15	16	3
Step/foster parents	16	*	22		—	

* Not investigated.

the male than the female to become alcoholic. This fact underlines the desirability of making a large-scale and intensive study of alcoholism in women, since among them constitutionally deviant individuals, or persons subjected to graver stresses from the environment, are likely to make up a relatively high proportion. No one has done this yet.

Criminality

On page 92 we have mentioned the personality deviations and the tendencies to criminal behaviour which may be correlated with an aneuploid constitution, especially 47, XXY and 47, XYY. Our purpose here is to provide a brief account of the massive work that has been done on the non-specific genetical contribution to a predisposition to criminality. In this field, we are almost confined to reports made on series of twins; modern studies of prevalences and risks of criminality among the relatives of index cases are not available.

The earliest of these is that of Johannes Lange (1929). He collected his twins from several sources, and the ascertainment was not systematic. He studied only pairs of the same sex; and in 13 MZ and 17 DZ pairs, he found only 3 of the

MZ pairs who were *discordant* in the possession of a criminal record, only 2 of the DZ pairs who were *concordant*. His study is along clinical lines, and provides masterpieces of description of personalities and careers.

The three discordant MZ pairs are of interest. In one, both twin boys suffered from birth injuries, which however took a rather different form; one developed normally, the other into an individual of feminized bodily constitution and homosexual in orientation. In a second pair, both twins were mentally retarded,

TABLE 61

CONCORDANCE WITH REGARD TO BEHAVIOUR DIFFICULTIES, DELIN-
QUENCY AND CRIMINALITY IN MONOZYGOTIC AND SAME-SEXED
DIZYGOTIC TWIN PAIRS

(From the literature)

		MONOZYGOTIC PAIRS		DIZYGOTIC PAIRS		CONCORDANCE RATE AS %	
		CONC.	DISC.	CONC.	DISC.	MZ	DZ
Rosanoff, Handy and Plessett (1941) child behaviour difficulties:							
preneurotic and prepsychotic	males	14	5	10	9	77	12
types	females	8	2	11	21	80	34
child behaviour difficulties:							
predelinquent types	males	8	—	5	4	100	56
	females	14	—	8	11	100	42
juvenile delinquency	males	29	—	12	5	100	71
	females	11	1	9	—	92	100
adult criminality	males	29	9	5	18	76	22
	females	6	1	1	3	86	25
	all males	80	14	32	36	85	47
	all females	39	4	29	35	91	45
Adult criminality, sexes undifferentiated							
Lange (1929)		10	3	2	15	77	12
Le Gras (1933)		4	—	—	5	100	0
Kranz (1936)		20	11	23	20	65	53
Stumpfl (1936)		11	7	7	12	61	37
Borgström (1939)	Adult	3	1	2	3	75	40
Yoshimasu (1965)		14	14	—	26	50	0
Hayashi (1967)	Juvenile	11	4	3	2	73	60

but the one who became criminal also suffered from epilepsy; his crime, that of a bloody and unmotivated murder, was committed in an epileptic twilight state. In the third pair, it was the pathological twin who never lapsed into criminality; with a goitre and other signs of endocrine dyscrasia, he was too inert an individual to run the risk. His normal brother, a more energetic type, boastful and unsettled, became an embezzler.

Lange's work, which appeared as a monograph under the title *Crime as Destiny*, aroused great interest, and led to a number of parallel investigations, all of them rather better designed statistically, and less likely to be biased by case-selection or by differences between MZ and DZ pairs in thoroughness of

standards are the same for both sexes. In this field the liability of the female is very much less, and the increase in delinquency rates starts later than in boys and has a lower gradient. When all forms of misbehaviour are taken together, delinquent girls make up a much smaller proportion of their generation than delinquent boys; and they represent accordingly a more extreme selection.

We have discussed the nature of male-female differences in juvenile delinquency, and their biological background, in some detail elsewhere (Cowie, Cowie and Slater, 1968). In brief, we can regard the relative immunity of the female to delinquent behaviour as the result either of a lower liability, or of relatively better protection against the stresses that provoke delinquent behaviour, or both. It seems likely that the former factor is the more important. Sex differences in delinquency rates have remained fairly steady for many decades, despite a progressive approximation of the liberties allowed to growing girls to those permitted to boys. Moreover, in economically depressed classes, in over-large and problem families, where the upbringing of girls and boys is equally haphazard and undisciplined, the large male preponderance in delinquents is still maintained. Delinquent females are much more frequently psychotic, psychopathic or psychoneurotic than delinquent males; and this higher level of psychiatric abnormality also points to a greater constitutional resistance of the female to delinquent and criminal manifestations—and not to a lower incidence of stress, as the principal operative factor.

The explanation that lies nearest to hand, is that the male-female differences (both in delinquency rates and in the forms that delinquency takes) are closely connected with the masculine or feminine pattern in development of personality. This again would be related to biological and somatic differences, including differences in hormonal balance; and these would be ultimately derived from the chromosomal differences between the sexes.

Homosexuality[1]

The view that there is a genetical contribution to the aetiology of homosexuality (i.e. male homosexuality, since the genetics of lesbianism has not been investigated at all), relies mainly on twin studies. These have recently been reviewed, very informatively, by Heston and Shields (1968), in connexion with the report of a sibship of their own. This was a most interesting family, including in the same sibship no less than 3 male MZ pairs; two of these were concordant for homosexuality, and the third was concordant for heterosexuality. One pair of these twins was part of a systematically ascertained series which included also 4 other male MZ pairs and 7 male-male DZ pairs. Two out of 5 MZ pairs were concordant in respect of homosexuality, and one out of 7 DZ pairs.

The largest study of the twins of male homosexuals was made by Kallmann (1952). His study was carried out under difficulties, as the subjects were nearly all living in an underworld, liable to persecution by the police, and contacts had to be made in such places as cafés and places of homosexual resort rather than in the Institute of Psychiatry. Of the 37 MZ pairs investigated, all were concordant; of the 26 DZ pairs only 12 per cent. Kallmann subsequently gave

[1] The relationship with sex chromosome anomalies is discussed on page 315.

his view that the 100 per cent concordance in the MZ pairs was somewhat of an artificiality. Kallmann's colleagues (Mesnikoff *et al.*, 1963) were able to collect and report on four discordant MZ pairs, of which one was female.

Most of the other reports discussed by Heston and Shields have the defect of (probably) not having been systematically ascertained. One that was systematic gave a negative result. Koch (1965) in a systematic study of a normal population came on one female homosexual whose MZ partner was normal, and one male homosexual whose male DZ partner was also normal.

On the evidence available we can only make a guess at the probable concordance rate in male MZ pairs, but it seems more likely that it is in the neighbourhood of Heston and Shield's 50 per cent than Kallmann's original 100 per cent.

The genetical contribution to male homosexuality has also been investigated along other lines. Theo Lang, deriving his ideas from Goldschmidt's work on intersexes in butterflies, hypothesized that male homosexuals would include in their number a certain proportion of human intersexes, i.e. genetic females who were phenotypic males somatically but with a female rather than a male psychosexual orientation. The proportion of such individuals should be higher, he considered, in older homosexuals, since adolescents and young men seduced into homosexual behaviour would in many cases grow out of it by full maturity. Lang predicted that the sex ratio in the sibs of intersexual male homosexuals would be shifted towards the male side. He obtained the co-operation of the Hamburg and Munich police, and obtained figures of the sex distribution in the sibships of male homosexuals known to the police in those regions. He also stimulated a colleague, K. Jensch, to make similar investigations in Breslau and Leipzig. The findings were published in a series of papers by Lang from 1939 on; and he gave a compendious summary of the entire material in 1960.

This is shown in TABLE 62. It is interesting that the two sets of material, Lang's and Jensch's, are significantly different, but both show a statistically highly significant shift in the direction of male preponderance in the full sibs, both as compared with known distributions in general populations, and in a control group in which methods of ascertainment of the sex distribution in the sibships were duplicated. Both workers found a larger shift of the sex ratio in the sibs of the older than in the sibs of the younger homosexuals. Lang states that the male preponderance in the sibs of married homosexuals, in his material, was a good deal lower at 119·0, than in the older group (133·6). Jensch also applied a supplementary test, taking out of his Saxony material 244 homosexuals whose record (in respect of behaviour, occupation, kind and number of delinquencies) indicated a feminine element in the personality; their full sibs numbered 536 males and 351 females, with a ratio of 156·6:100.

The findings in the half-sibs, showing a male preponderance in the paternal half-sibs and a female preponderance in the maternal half-sibs, are striking, although the numbers are not large. Here the Lang and Jensch data agree very well; summing them, we find a difference between sex ratios in paternal and in maternal half-sibs significant at the 0·0005 level. Lang is right to point out the difficulty of explaining this finding on a psychogenic basis, e.g. on the theory that having a male sib to play with in childhood is likely to encourage a homosexual development in the growing boy. However, the difference is no easier to explain along genetical lines.

A very reasonable explanation of the difference between the sex ratios in paternal and maternal half-sibs has been offered by James (1970). Half-sibs will be born when a marriage has been broken and one of the parents marries again. In the event of the death of one parent, the children can be expected to continue

TABLE 62

DISTRIBUTION OF SEX RATIO IN SIBS OF MALE HOMOSEXUALS, AND OF A CONTROL GROUP OF MALES, BY AGE OF INDEX CASE AT TIME OF ASCERTAINMENT

(From Lang, 1960)

MATERIAL	M	F	M/F × 100
Full sibs of index cases			
Controls (1296)	3571	3349	106·6
Lang, under 25 (825)	1166	1006	115·9
over 25 (952)	1712	1281	133·6
Jensch, under 25 (683)	961	984	97·7
over 25 (1389)	2833	2349	120·7
Paternal half-sibs of index cases			
Lang	178	140	127·1
Jensch	156	119	131·0
Maternal half-sibs of index cases			
Lang	277	308	89·9
Jensch	164	200	82·0

to live with the survivor. But when the parents separate or are divorced, alternative possibilities arise, and the children may go to live with one or the other parent, or perhaps some to one and some to the other. Two hypotheses are necessary to provide a significant shift in the sex ratio of the half-sibs: (1) offspring of a disrupted marriage are subsequently more likely to live with their same-sex parent; and (2) half-sibs are sometimes unaware of one another's existence when they are not domiciled together. If the index individual is the child of a first marriage, or if both the parents marry again, no statistical shift occurs. However, if the index individual is the child of a second marriage, then a father entering this marriage will have brought with him any sons but not daughters from the first marriage; and if it was the index individual's mother who entered on a second marriage, she will have brought with her daughters rather than sons. The reader must note that James' ingenious suggestion has nothing whatever to do with the homosexuality (or other psychiatric abnormality) of the index individual. We should be able to confirm such an adventitious shift in sex ratios, if it occurs, by studies on the normal population.

James' suggestion greatly weakens the possible significance of the shift in sex ratios in the half-sibs of homosexuals, but it leaves the data relating to the full sibs untouched. Further evidence might be sought for from the sibships of female homosexuals, and from the children of homosexuals.

Lang had no material on female homosexuals of his own to report, but he could mention data passed to him by the Payne-Whitney Clinic in New York; 150 women attending that clinic for psychotherapeutic help for their homoerotic tendencies had 177 full sibs, 76 brothers and 101 sisters—a female preponderance (75·7) balancing the male preponderance in the sibships of male homosexuals.

The sex ratio in the children of male homosexuals was found to be 113·1 in Lang's material and 116·7 in Jensch's.

Later investigators, by and large, have not been able to confirm the Lang-Jensch results. This, however, does little to render them invalid, since all subsequent series have been so small that sampling errors can easily account for any difference between their figures and those of Lang-Jensch. Lang's theory, at least in its original form that the male homosexual was in a significant proportion of cases a genetic female, presumably therefore with a 46,XX constitution, has now been decisively disproved by studies of nuclear sex (Bleuler and Wiedemann, 1956; Pare, 1956; Pritchard, 1962; Raboch and Nedoma, 1958). However, this is very far from excluding the possibility of a sex chromosome deviation, perhaps of a minor kind, playing a part in disturbing the normal development of sexuality. The Lang-Jensch data still have to be taken seriously, and used to propose a working hypothesis (not necessarily chromosomal) for further investigation.

Evidence that suggests the possibility that chromosome anomalies may play a part in the aetiology of homosexuality was offered by Slater (1962). A consecutive series of 401 male homosexuals were found to have a mean birth order[1] of 0·58 (as against a control series of epileptics with a birth order of 0·51), and a mean maternal age of 31·3 years (general population 28·5 years). A small series of 53 female homosexuals showed the same shift, with a birth order of 0·62 and maternal age of 30·3. Slater concluded that the findings supported a hypothesis of heterogeneity in the aetiology of homosexuality in the male, and as suggesting that a chromosome anomaly, such as might be associated with late maternal age, may play a part in causation.

Of course, it goes without saying that late maternal age might contribute to the aetiology of homosexuality along psychogenic rather than genetic lines. A late-born son, the hypothesis suggests, would be likely to be over-dear to an elderly mother, to suffer from over-mothering, with the result that females might become sexually taboo. Theoretical constructs like this are extremely difficult to test, and need more precision to become working hypotheses for the purposes of investigation. The psychogenic hypotheses of the aetiology of homosexuality are manifold, and self-contradictory. J. H. Schultz, for instance (according to Koch, 1965) holds that it is a combination of the cold, hard, rejecting mother

---

[1] The birth order of an individual who comes mth in order in a sibship of children of the same mother n in number is defined as $(m-1)/(n-1)$, and will vary about a mean of 0·5. The theoretical variance of the distribution is $\Sigma[(n+1)/12(n-1)]$. The formula is applicable only to completed sibships, and, like all estimates of birth order, biases due to such factors as secular changes in birth rate can influence it (see Hare and Price, 1969, 1970).

plus the warm, soft, tender, loving and manly father which provides the most dangerous background.

Slater's data, which were systematically taken from Bethlem and Maudsley case records 1949–60 inclusive, were re-examined and re-analysed by Abe and Moran (1969). In 291 cases both paternal and maternal ages were known, and these were compared with general population expectations adjusted to the years of birth of the probands (i.e. eliminating any effect from secular changes in birthrate). The maternal age of the homosexuals was greater than a corresponding population sample (31·7 years as compared with 29·4 years), with a highly significant difference of 0·35 SD. However, the mean paternal age was found to show an even greater shift (34·9 years, with expectation between 31·4 and 31·8), a difference of 0·40 to 0·45 SD. The regression analysis then carried out showed that the shift in paternal age could not be accounted for as a reflection of a primary maternal age shift; but that the maternal age shift could be accounted for as a consequence of the paternal age shift. The social class of the fathers, which was known and could be brought into the analysis, was found to play no part in producing this very remarkable effect. In a second paper (Moran and Abe, 1969) the authors showed that it was most improbable that the death of fathers could be implicated; there was, in fact, no support for the view that it was the loss of a father which tended to predispose the son to homosexuality, and that the age shift was there only because more fathers would have died at later ages than earlier ones. Abe and Moran were not able to make any precise suggestion in answer to the question how such a paternal age shift could have arisen. They thought that an intrafamilial environmental factor was more likely than a chromosomal one, although a genetical contribution was possible. 'One might suppose, for instance, that in both fathers and sons there was a genetical predisposition to sexual deviance, manifesting in the fathers as a tendency to marriage at a later age than the norm.' No light on such problems could be thrown by the material available.

To sum up our knowledge about the genetical contribution to homosexuality, we can say that, in a Europeo-American culture in the present epoch, genetical factors do play some part. The way in which they enter the picture is entirely obscure, although there are some very interesting leads. We cannot leave the subject, however, without pointing out that any inborn constitutional sexual deviance can only be ascertained on the basis of behaviour, and that sexual behaviour, especially the sexual behaviour of the male, is open to a multiplicity of deviations, many of them acquired tastes, closely related to the culture in which the individual grows up. Homosexuality in Ancient Greece and homosexuality today are very different phenomena; in the ancient world it was not accounted a deviation from the norm at all, and presumably, in that era, the genetical contribution was completely submerged. One can imagine circumstances, such as increasing population pressure and increasing sexual permissiveness, in which homosexual behaviour will be so much in the repertoire of the average 'normal' individual, that the genetical contribution will become undetectable, even by sophisticated methods of investigation.

6

SENESCENCE, SENILE AND PRE-SENILE DEMENTIAS

Senescence

The biological background of senescence offers many unsolved problems and is at present so unclear that little of any certainty can be said. Noteworthy contributions to the literature have been made by Comfort (1956, 1963, 1965).

From the genetical point of view, senescence might be looked on as an almost obligatory accident of evolution. Medawar (1946) has pointed out that the forces of natural selection will tend to favour gene mutations which provide an advantage in the early life of the individual, even though it is compensated for by a disadvantage in later life. Consider a race of individuals, each of them potentially immortal and suffering no decrement in vitality or fertility whatever the age reached. As a cohort of such individuals ages, it will be diminished in number by the effects of predation, environmental disease and other accidents of all kinds. The age distribution of such a race, which is constantly replenishing itself by reproduction, will be pyramidal, with the youngest ages at the base of the pyramid, and the oldest ages towards the apex. Any gene mutation which now occurs, which provides a selective advantage for the young, even though at the same time handicapping the older members, will tend to spread through the population, since its advantages will be felt in the most numerously represented classes. Furthermore, owing to the fact that the young have the whole of their reproductive life ahead of them, a selective advantage shown by a gene in early years will cause its disproportionate representation in the succeeding generation. On this model, it would seem that in all races in which reproductive functions are retained by all individuals (and not reserved to members specialized for that function, such as the queen in an apiary), senescence would be an inevitable consequence of evolution.

It is not quite certain that this is actually the case, and the point is one which it would be very difficult to establish. Most species have such a high mortality rate that the individual never reaches senescence in the wild—and what happens in captivity is only doubtfully relevant to the question. While it seems likely that all Metazoa are subject to senescence (and even also pure lines of Protozoa), there are some in which it has not been shown to occur, despite the occurrence of very long life-times; this is the case with tortoises, with *Testudo sumeiri* holding the record at 152 years, and a marked specimen of *Terrapene carolina* having been recovered in the wild at an age of 129 years.

It is certain that genetical factors do play a part in longevity, in man no less than in other animals, as has been shown by the investigations of Kallmann and Sander (1948, 1949) on longevity in 1062 pairs of twins. In this series the within-pair difference in longevity was twice as great in DZ pairs as in MZ pairs. Interest attaches to the observation, discussed by Comfort, that the sib-sib correlation in longevity has been found to be twice as great as the parent-offspring correlation. Haldane pointed out that this type of correlation difference is to be expected where the heterozygote is fitter than either homozygote. It is quite possible that hybrid vigour, the covering up of deleterious recessives by heterozygosis, is one factor in longevity. Abnormally long-lived animals can regularly be produced by crossing certain pure lines, not themselves long-lived. Cytoplasmic and environmental factors may also contribute to 'vigour', since the vigour of pure-line ova is increased by transplantation to hybrid mothers.

Comfort considers that senescence is not an 'inherent' property of animal species, but has been many times acquired as a potentiality. Organisms have been provided by evolutionary selection with a programme of development and function, which is directional and finite. Progressive loss of the power to remain in stable function occurs towards the end of the programme. He quotes the view of Weismann that senescence is itself a functionally determined item in the programme. There is clearly much to be said for this idea. In some cases the system fails suddenly at a fixed point, as if programme-directed, although in mammals the decline of resistance and the rise of mortality are gradual and smooth. Weismann's idea would fit in with evolutionary processes. Two races in competition, one with ageing and so with rapid turn-over of the generations, the other not, might have very different survival chances in a rapidly changing environment, and the former might be favoured. However, Comfort believes, optimistically, in an undirected process, not a part of the programme, but a weakening of the directive force of the programme. Senescence has no function: it is the subversion of function, he considers.

The processes of senescence include a summation of the effects of previous injuries imperfectly repaired and the deterioration of irreplaceable structures. As humankind works against these processes, the removal of one cause immediately permits the operation of a later cause of damage. Most people who die in old age are found *post mortem* to show the effects of a number of other pathological processes, apart from the process that killed them. The cellular pathology at the basis of these processes is unclear. It has been suggested that genetic mutation including that caused by background and other environmental radiation, could cause divergence in tissue cells, with a shift to a higher and higher proportion of deviant and inefficient cells. A counter-argument to this suggestion is provided by the consideration that mutation processes are much too slow to mutate more than an infinitesimal proportion of all human cells, say 2×10^{-6}, in a span of 30 years. It may also be that the copying processes by which normal proteins are replaced are in any case subject to error, and the cell processes we see in senescence are attributable to a gradual accumulation of incorrect proteins. Auto-immune processes could be involved, if a mutated cell came to be recognized by the body as not-self; for if such cells were viable, they would excite auto-immune reactions. There may be a three-cornered mutual interaction between age processes, neoplastic processes and auto-immunization.

Evidence is accumulating that mitotic processes begin to go wrong with increasing age. This has been demonstrated by the Edinburgh team under Court Brown (Court Brown *et al.*, 1966). In age groups arranged in succeeding decennia from 15 to 24 up to 75 to 84, the proportion of hypomodal cells (i.e.

cells lacking one or more chromosomes) increases in the female from 5·9 per cent to 11·6 per cent, and in the male from 3·5 to 6·6 per cent. The proportions of hypermodal cells, with one or more extra chromosomes, show a sharper gradient, and in many ways provide a more reliable index, since their appearance is much less likely to be due to accidents and artefacts connected with culture and staining. In respect of the proportion of hypermodal cells, the Court Brown figures show no significant difference between the sexes at any age, with the exception of the age group 65–74 ($p<0.05$); and in TABLE 63 the two sexes

TABLE 63

PROPORTION OF HYPERMODAL CELLS AS A FUNCTION OF ADVANCING AGE

(Data from Court Brown et al., 1966)

AGE	TOTAL CELLS	% HYPERMODAL	S.E.
15–24	1050	0·10	0·10
25–34	1380	0·29	0·14
35–44	1016	0·30	0·17
45–54	1050	0·95	0·30
55–64	1288	1·16	0·30
65–74	4169	0·98	0·15
75–84	2467	1·26	0·18

have been combined. As will be seen, there is a rise in the proportion of hyper-modal cells from 0·10 per cent in the youngest age group to twelve times that figure, 1·26 per cent, in people over 75. The figures have also been shown in a graph [FIG. 15].

Hamerton et al. (1965) confirmed this trend in a systematic examination of the Tristan da Cunha population, who were brought to England after their island was made uninhabitable by the eruption of a volcano. They came to the conclusion that, with increasing age, there was a 'generalized lowering of mitotic efficiency leading to lagging of chromosomes or non-disjunction'. If the chromosome involved in such a faulty mitosis was an autosome, then the daughter cells, especially monosomic ones, would have at least greatly reduced viability. But gaining or losing one of the sex chromosomes, either X or Y, would give rise to viable aneuploid cells. It has in fact been found by all workers that the supernumerary or deficient chromosomes of older age groups are in the case of women in the C or 6-X-12 group, and in the case of men in the G or 21-22-Y group.

It is not easy to say whether these chromosomal changes are merely the result of an ageing process, or whether they can themselves be the cause of declining efficiency of a variety of organic functions. Jarvik (1963) pointed out that we must distinguish between the age of the cell and the age of the cell line. The neurones of the central nervous system do not undergo mitosis and are therefore individually old; the blood cells are, individually, only a few weeks old; but they come of an ancient cell line some hundreds of generations old at the time of life at which obvious processes of senescence are beginning to show. Accordingly, if as age goes on, we find an increasing proportion of aneuploid cells in the blood cells, this is no reason to think that the neurones show any parallel change. The progressive aneuploidy of ageing that shows itself in the brain will be confined to the interstitial cells, and if there are effects on the neurones, they will be secondary. It is not necessary to postulate such secondary effects, since the neurones are just as liable to an increasing inefficiency of copying processes occurring with age as any other cells.

Another possibility can be borne in mind. The most probable cause for an increasing blood mosaicism as life goes on is, as suggested by Hamerton *et al.*, a decreasing efficiency of the mitotic process. However, it is possible that

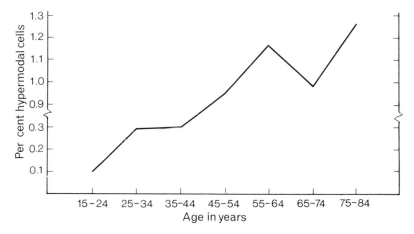

Fig. 15. Proportion of hypermodal cells as a function of advancing age.

aneuploid cells will be sufficiently efficient to start their own cell lines; and if these aberrant cell lines are not eliminated as frequently as they are started, they will gradually accumulate.

The possibility of increasing sex-chromosome aneuploidy being itself a cause of ageing is made unlikely by what we know of the life histories of the subjects of Klinefelter's and Turner's syndromes: there is no evidence for supposing that ageing processes begin earlier or proceed at a greater rate in these individuals than in the general population. On the whole it seems more probable that there is a primary ageing process (e.g. the deficient copying mechanisms mentioned earlier) which is responsible for the chromosomal changes of ageing, than that the latter is itself a primary cause. Perhaps there is some still more basic phenomenon which initiates both.

In man, the key tissues of the body, the kidneys, the muscles and the nervous system, are provided with a limited capital of units, which are gradually expended as life goes on. The fall-out of neurones, nephrons and muscle cells is never made good by regeneration. Bürger (1957), studying the brains of 2187 men and 1489 women, showed that the weight of the brain reached a peak between the ages of 20 and 30, declined subsequently, and declined very rapidly after the age of 70.

The brain in advanced ages shows atrophy, with widened sulci and enlargement of the ventricular system. The cytoarchitecture of the brain is preserved, but by a much reduced number of neurones. Among those that remain, shrinkage and chromatolysis is going on. Gross changes, e.g., senile plaques and the consequences of vascular degeneration will also be seen. It seems probable that the clinical signs of destruction of brain tissue will only become of such magnitude as to be capable of clinical assessment, when a certain marginal proportion of total brain tissue has gone. The vigour that some old people show is very much a function of good preservation of the central nervous system. Some mental capacities can be tested in a much more rigorous way than by ordinary clinical methods, and here we see a loss of efficiency beginning at quite early ages, e.g., in match play for the chess championship of the world. It seems quite likely that the decline, which begins to show itself in the thirties, is related to the quite minor proportionate neuronal loss which will have occurred by that age.

Werner's Syndrome

This syndrome, which has recently been discussed by Motulsky, Schultz and Priest (1962), is potentially of relevance to the ageing process, since its main feature is premature senescence of the adult. Onset is between the ages of 20 and 40 years, and involves the familiar changes of early greying, some hair loss and cataracts. Males and females are equally affected. In addition, there is an increased liability to the disorders whose frequency systematically increases with increasing age: diabetes, atherosclerosis and tumours. However, there are specific features also. The body build is described as characteristic with tapered extremities, a pinched face and usually short stature; the voice is squeaky. Skin changes typical of the disease include hyperkeratinization and scleroderma-like skin changes in the lower extremities.

Motulsky et al. had two cases of their own, and collected a further 106 from the world literature. Data in 72 families indicated a very high rate of consanguinity between the parents, something between a minimum of 21 per cent and a maximum of 44 per cent. In the sibships the proportion of affected persons indicated a morbidity risk between 17 and 34 per cent, i.e. centring on the 25 per cent one expects of an autosomal recessive gene. This, then, is the most probable genetic background. The parental consanguinity indicates a gene frequency of approximately 6×10^{-4}, from which the frequency of Werner's syndrome should be about 4×10^{-7}.

It is possible that the action of the gene is shown to some extent in heterozygotes, since among the apparently unaffected members of these families premature greying does occur, and there is also a raised incidence of diabetes, etc. Motulsky et al. think that the basic defect in Werner's syndrome may affect an 'anti-ageing' factor which is normally present. While variations in the onset and rate of senescence are usually attributed to multifactorial genes, the existence of such a specific gene intervention suggests that one or more major genes may play a role. However, it would not seem likely that there is genetic heterogeneity at the back of Werner's syndrome, and a working hypothesis would suggest only a single locus.

SENILE DEMENTIA

Definition, Clinical Features, Pathology

Largely owing to the work of Roth and his colleagues (Roth, 1955; see also Mayer-Gross, Slater and Roth, 1969), the clinical approach to the classification of the psychoses of the senium has been greatly advanced. Roth showed that these psychotic states were very various in aetiology, clinical appearances, course and outcome. Although in earlier times psychiatrists tended to regard all psychotic old people as probably suffering from an irreversible and eventually fatal process, evidence was brought to show that affective psychoses, late paraphrenia, psychoses due to cerebrovascular disease and delirious pictures could be defined. When these conditions had been eliminated, what remained did in the main correspond with a fairly homogeneous syndrome, a purified concept of senile dementia.

The main clinical features of this syndrome are a progressive disorganization of all aspects of the mind, personality being as early and as much affected as memory, intelligence, judgement and conceptual powers. Progress is unremitting, and as a rule fairly even, although exacerbations may occur, e.g. accompanying somatic illness. Larsson, Sjögren and Jacobson (1963), on their large Swedish material calculated that the mean age of onset was 73·4 years for males, and 75·3 for females; the mean age at hospitalization was respectively 76·4 and 78·4; and the average at death was 78·5 years for males and 80·5 for females.

Pathologically, the main change is a universal outfall of neurones, which show successively accumulation of lipochrome, chromatolysis and vacuolation, shrinkage and disappearance. There are neurofibrillary changes identical with those of Alzheimer's disease, and the development of argyrophilic tangles. Argyrophilic plaques, consisting in the first place in an accumulation of an amyloid substance, appear and accumulate in very large numbers in the grey matter, particularly of the cerebral cortex, but also in the basal ganglia and elsewhere (rarely in the cerebellum). There is an increase in astrocytes, but otherwise no marked reaction of the supporting tissues; the blood vessels small and large usually show no more change than would be appropriate to the age.

These changes are very different from those of cerebral vascular disease, which is the other most common cause of dementia in the senium. The differences between the two syndromes can be illustrated by TABLE 64, based on data from Corsellis (1962).

Mention has been made on page 124 of the tendency for an increasing proportion of aneuploid cells to appear among blood cells with increasing age. Nielsen (1968) has suggested that the loss of the X chromosome in females is a basic part of the aetiology and pathogenesis of senile dementia. This suggestion relies on the finding that in patients with senile dementia the proportion of hypomodal cells is higher than in controls even when the controls are taken from the same age group. The chromosome loss might interfere with metabolic functions of

TABLE 64

COMPARISON OF CLINICAL AND PATHOLOGICAL FEATURES IN ARTERIO-
SCLEROTIC PSYCHOSIS AND SENILE DEMENTIA

(Data from Corsellis, 1962)

	SENILE PSYCHOSIS VASCULAR	SENILE DEMENTIA
Clinically		
Sex ratio m:f	21:25	9:26
Duration in years		
onset to death	4·0	4·6
admission to death	2·5	2·6
Mean age at death	72	77
Per cent of patients		
hypertensive (sys. 209+)	70	25
Pathologically		
Per cent of patients with		
senile plaque formation	29	79
cerebral atrophy	39	71
neurofibrillary changes	13	46
macroscopic vascular changes	76	31
microscopic vascular changes	89	23
microscopic focal damage	79	14

TABLE 65

DIFFERENCES BETWEEN THREE GROUPS OF FEMALE PATIENTS: EACH GROUP
CONTAINED 10 INDIVIDUALS, AND FOR EACH PATIENT FROM 70 TO 80 META-
PHASES WERE COUNTED

(Nielsen, 1968)

	PERCENTAGE OF ANEUPLOID CELLS			P-VALUE OF DIFFERENCES		
	A SENILE DEMENTS (AGED 70+)	B CONTROLS (AGED 70+)	C CONTROLS (AGED 45)	A:B	B:C	A:C
Hypodiploid cells	16·9	10·1	3·9	0·001	0·001	0·001
Hyperdiploid cells	1·1	1·8	0·3	0·2	0·02	0·1
Cells lacking 6-X-12 chromosomes	11·1	4·9	1·1	0·001	0·001	0·001
Cells lacking other chromosomes	5·8	5·2	2·8	0·7	0·05	0·05

different kinds, leading to rapidly ingravescent age processes, senile dementia, and death.

The alternative hypothesis would be that ageing processes and the tendency towards disturbances of mitosis have a common cause. The accelerated fall-out among neurones, which certainly occurs in senile dementia, cannot be caused by aneuploidy of the neurones themselves. Furthermore, as has been mentioned earlier, individuals with atypical modal numbers of sex chromosomes (XXY, XO), do not appear to suffer from any unusually early or severe process of ageing.

Epidemiology

From the Ministry of Health Report (1969) one can calculate a three-year average of the years 1964–66 of the first admission rate per 100,000 home population by age and sex for 'psychoses of the senium'. These figures are:

AGE	MALES	FEMALES
45–54	2	2
55–64	11	11
65–74	67	71
75+	278	307

'Psychoses of the senium' is a loose grouping, but its principal contributors will be cerebrovascular disease and senile dementia. The schizophrenic group of disorders, the affective group, and 'other psychoses' (e.g. psycho-organic psychoses) are distinguished in the official records. After the age of 75 the risk of a first admission to a psychiatric hospital or unit is almost identical for the two sexes (502 for males and 513 for females per 100,000); but the proportion of these admissions taken up by the psychoses of the senium is somewhat greater for females (60 per cent) than for males (55 per cent). The age distribution of admissions for psychoses of the senium on the one hand and for depressive psychoses on the other are shown in FIGURE 16.

The figures provided by Larsson, Sjögren and Jacobson (1963) are much more reliable from the diagnostic point of view. In their own material they found the distribution of ages at onset of senile dementia to be:

AGE OF ONSET	MALES	FEMALES
56–59	5	2
60–64	12	8
65–69	27	27
70–74	32	50
75–79	34	60
80–84	23	27
85–89	9	12
90–94	1	4
Total	143	190

These authors do not provide an estimate of the population risks of a first hospital admission for senile dementia for the two sexes by age, which would be comparable with the British figures quoted in the previous table; but they do give us something which is of greater genetical interest, i.e. the aggregated morbidity risk of senile dementia providing there is survival to the stated age. These figures are shown in TABLE 66. It is to be noted that the risk is taken as being approximately the same for the two sexes, since figures calculated for

TABLE 66

AGGREGATED MORBIDITY RISK (AS PER CENT) FOR SENILE DEMENTIA
UP TO AGE STATED

(From Larsson, Sjögren, and Jacobson, 1963)

AGE	M, F
60	0·03
65	0·12
70	0·40
75	1·2
80	2·5
85	3·8
90	5·2

the two sexes separately show very little difference. The small difference between males and females is also clearly seen in FIGURE 16.

It is perhaps the final figure in this table, i.e. the expectation of a little over 5 per cent, which is the most significant one genetically. If senile dementia were the direct consequence of a single autosomal gene, dominant in the heterozygote, then there would have to be a minimum gene frequency of 0·05.

Very little is known about the geographical, ethnic and cultural distribution of senile dementia. It is almost impossible to compare one country with another, since the ascertainment of senile dementia depends on hospital admission, and hospital admission depends on the facilities available. Larsson, Sjögren and Jacobson found that there was some evidence that senile dementia was more common in some parts of Sweden than others, possibly indicating variation in gene frequency from one region to another; but that there was no suggestion that the morbidity risk was related to socio-economic class. This last observation was an important one from their point of view, since it reinforced the view that environmental factors were likely to be less significant than genetical ones.

Genetics

The earlier work on the genetical contribution to senile dementia pales into relative insignificance after the publication of the monograph by Larsson, Sjögren and Jacobson; but the fact that there is such a contribution has been recognized for many decades. Meggendorfer (1925), starting from 60 histopathologically verified cases of senile dementia, found a total of 18 secondary cases of senile dementia among first-degree relatives, parents, sibs and children, who were, however, clustered into relationship with 16 out of the 60 families. Meggendorfer hypothesized a complex mode of inheritance, and rejected the hypothesis of a single major gene, on the basis of an argument which nowadays

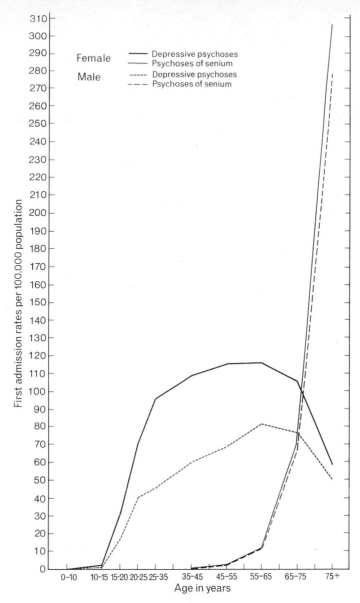

Fig. 16. First admission rates per 100,000 Home Population (Ministry of Health, 1969). Returns for 1964, 1965 and 1966 averaged.

Age	Depressive Psychoses		Psychoses of Senium	
	Males	Females	Males	Females
0–10	1	2	—	—
11–15	17	32	—	—
16–20	39	70	—	—
21–25	45	96	—	—
26–35	60	109	—	—
36–45	69	115	2	2
46–55	81	116	11	11
56–65	76	106	67	71
66–75+	50	58	278	307

would not be regarded as convincing. Weinberger (1926) also found the incidence of senile dementia among the relatives of senile dements higher than in the general population, and higher than in a control series of relatives of patients suffering from cerebral arteriosclerosis investigated by Schulz (1929) among whom there was only one instance of senile dementia. Cresseri (1948) has also made comparable findings. In each of these series the numbers of patients were relatively small.

One possible way of accounting for the excess of senile dements among the families of senile dementia index cases would be by hypothesizing that there was a family tendency to longevity, and the dementia showed up only because these relatives were unduly long-lived. This point has been gone into by the workers quoted but did not find support. Larsson, Sjögren and Jacobson (1963) also agree in finding no more than average longevity among the relatives of index patients.

Twin studies have been carried out by Kallmann and his colleagues (1948, 1949, 1950, 1956a, 1956b, 1959). In the series reported by Kallmann in 1956, there were 108 pairs in which the index twin suffered from a senile psychosis: in the MZ co-twins aged 60 or over the incidence of senile psychosis was 43 per cent, in the DZ co-twins 8 per cent, in full sibs 7 per cent, and in parents 3 per cent. Kallmann in 1956, and Kallmann and Jarvik in 1959, supported a hypothesis of genetic-environmental interaction, which on the genetic side was based on multifactorial inheritance. Larsson, Sjögren and Jacobson have, however, pointed out that the data are quite compatible with a major-gene theory. The difference between the concordance rates of 43 per cent in MZ pairs and 8 per cent in DZ pairs might be in part attributable to an unavoidable statistical bias. Kallmann and his colleagues have shown that the life-spans within MZ pairs are more alike than in DZ pairs, and indeed the average intrapair difference in life-span in MZ pairs is only about half the DZ value. Now if there is a higher correlation in age of onset of senile dementia within MZ than within DZ pairs, and dead and living twins are being collected in a continuous process of registration, concordance will be more correctly estimated in the MZ than in the DZ pairs, and in the latter will tend to be underestimated. What holds for the DZ pairs holds also, obviously, for sibs.

The investigation by Larsson, Sjögren and Jacobson (1963) is the critical one for the present state of our knowledge. They took a continuous run of admissions with the diagnosis dementia senilis from two large mental hospitals in Stockholm over a span of about 15 years. The case records were then scrutinized and classified by Roth's diagnostic scheme, and about half the cases were excluded as not falling within a strict application of the characteristic criteria. This left them with 377 probands. The genealogical investigation of the relatives was, as is possible and customary in Swedish psychiatric investigations, of great thoroughness and great reliability owing to the availability of excellent public records and information services on the one hand and on the other a long tradition of willing collaboration with medical research in a well educated and public spirited population.

Larsson and his colleagues found in the families in which field investigations were performed a total of 51 cases of senile dementia among parents, sibs and children of index cases, when 17 was the number to be expected on the basis of their epidemiological work. Their findings accordingly confirmed those of earlier workers, suggesting a significant genetical contribution to the causation of senile dementia. Careful analysis of their observations showed that information was most satisfactory and complete for the female sibs of female probands. Among these sibs the expectation of senile dementia was 4·3 times as great as for females of the same age in the general population. Taking this figure of 4·3 as the best estimate of the factor by which the morbidity risk was increased, they could then check it against observations based on the total sib material. This is shown in TABLE 67.

TABLE 67

OBSERVED RISK OF SENILE DEMENTIA AMONG SIBS OF INDEX PATIENTS, AS PER CENT, AGAINST EXPECTATION ON THE BASIS OF AN INTENSIFICATION FACTOR OF 4·3

(From Larsson, Sjögren and Jacobson, 1963)

	AGGREGATE MORBIDITY RISK UP TO AGE STATED, %				
	GENERAL POPULATION	DIRECT CALCULATION SIBS OF PROBANDS			ASSESSMENT SIBS AND PARENTS OF PROBANDS
AGE	M, F	M	F	M+F	M, F
70	0·4	0·8	2·3	1·6	1·7
75	1·2	3·3	6·4	5·0	5·2
80	2·5	7·5	9·6	8·6	10·8
85	3·8	9·6	19·7	15·7	16·3

The investigators found no increase in the morbidity risk of disorders other than senile dementia (e.g. schizophrenia, manic-depression). It is of particular importance that they found no single instance of Alzheimer's disease or Pick's disease among the relatives. This is strong evidence that the genetical predispositions to senile dementia and to the pre-senile dementias have little in common, this despite the fact that the histological pictures in senile dementia and in Alzheimer's disease are so similar. The morbidity risk for both Alzheimer and Pick taken together is estimated as being about 0·1 per cent in Sweden, so that it is not very surprising that no single case appeared even in so large a group as 2133 family members aged 50 or over. A curious finding is that there was a statistically significant shortfall in the number of relatives with arteriosclerotic psychosis. These findings led the authors to conclude that there are hereditary factors for senile dementia, and that (as Meggendorfer also concluded nearly 40 years earlier) they are specific. There was no evidence that sex-linkage or sex-limitation played any role; there was no deviation from population standards of mortality, nuptiality or fertility; birth order was randomly distributed.

The most important findings which emerge from this monumental study can be listed as follows:

1. The syndrome of senile dementia is shown to be autonomous, and un-connected either with senility or with the presenile dementias. No 'intermediates' between senile dementia and normal ageing were found among the relatives of index cases. Apart from those among them who showed the specific syndrome, the relatives of index patients exhibited normal fertility, normal senescence and normal mortality by population standards. Among these relatives the incidence of the Alzheimer-Pick syndromes was no greater than one might have expected of a similar sample from the general population.

2. The syndrome of senile dementia is a familial one, and is clinically homogeneous. The risk of senile dementia for the first-degree relatives of index patients is greater than the general population risk by a factor of 4·3. The affected relatives of index patients show a pattern of onset, course, clinical features and outcome which fits in with that shown by the proband material.

3. No evidence was found that environmental factors of a sociomedical nature play a part in the causation. Evidence was sought to show whether the population risk of senile dementia had changed over the course of decades. There had been no such change.

4. The morbidity risks for males and for females are approximately equal.

5. There is a steady approximately linear increase of the morbidity risk of senile dementia with age up to the most advanced ages. This holds true both for the general population and for the relatives of index cases. The factor of intensification by which the risk in relatives is greater than the risk in the general population remains steady at approximately 4·3 at all ages.

All these important findings have to be borne in mind when we come down to the problem of setting up a genetical model of the mode of inheritance: for the syndrome is clearly a genetically determined one, and we have no evidence on which to postulate an aetiological contribution by environmental factors. To be sure, the internal 'environment' is of cardinal importance; the onset of the disease is strictly age-dependent, and the manifestation of any gene or genes which we may hypothesize must be regarded as depending on the internal chemistry of the cells affected, i.e. a condition of the cell which has been arrived at by normal ageing processes.

Larsson, Sjögren and Jacobson consider the possibilities of polygenic inheritance, and of inheritance of a single major autosomal gene manifesting either as a dominant or a recessive. They prefer the hypothesis of dominance, which fits their facts very well, and support this view by arguments based on analogous findings in two other syndromes, torsion dystonia and essential tremor, both of them relatively rare conditions susceptible of genetical analysis along standard lines with a clear-cut result. The principal difficulty arises when weighing up the pros and cons of a polygenic and a dominant monogenic model. They argue as follows:

One should be cautious about applying a polygenic model to conditions occurring in later life merely because there are difficulties in reconciling the data with a single major-gene hypothesis on account of late manifestation, deficient registration, internal migration, atypical phenotypic manifestations, the occurrence of *formes frustes*, etc. Torsion dystonia (dystonia musculorum deformans) is certainly due to a single autosomal dominant (Larsson and Sjögren, 1961).

But it shows much phenotypic variability, a hyperkinetic and a myostatic type, many very mild pictures, much variability in age of onset and course. Without the genetic evidence (from 120 cases), it would have been difficult or impossible to prove that it was a unitary disease. Essential tremor (Larsson and Sjögren, 1960) has also been shown to be due to a monohybrid autosomal dominant with full penetrance, and only a single mutation is involved. The age of onset extends all the way from 10 to 70, with a mean about 50, i.e. after the end of reproductive life for the female. The symptoms and course are very variable. In the main part of the geographically affected area the gene frequency is very high, with 9 per cent of all males and 6–6·5 per cent of all females estimated as being gene carriers (from which it follows that the gene frequency would be about 0·05). Against this background one is impelled to suppose that there exist a number of diseases, beginning at advanced ages, determined by single genes. There must be many such widely spread, though presumably with local variations in prevalence. With such a large proportion of gene bearers dying before manifestation, owing to the late age of onset, genetic analysis cannot expect to disclose simple Mendelian ratios. But should one under such circumstances speak of 'reduced' or 'full penetrance'?

It seems to the present writers that Larsson, Sjögren and Jacobson have made out a fairly convincing case in favour of the single-gene hypothesis. All the available facts fit such a hypothesis, which has also the advantage of being the simplest possible working model and the one which is the easiest to test. The polygenic hypothesis, which has the disadvantage of being more difficult to test, is rendered most improbable by the absence of transition forms in the clinical borderland between senile dementia and normal senescence, as well as the independence of the syndrome from the pre-senile dementias. On the polygenic basis one would have expected some degree of sex preponderance, since some preponderance is shown by all other known polygenic syndromes (e.g. pyloric stenosis and talipes equinovarus on the male side and spina bifida and congenital dislocation of the hip on the female side). One would also have expected of a polygenic syndrome some connexion with sociomedical variables.

However, if we are inclined to attribute the genetical basis of senile dementia to a major autosomal gene, dominant in the heterozygote, a number of other questions arise which will require further research. Perhaps the most obvious is the question whether one or many loci are involved, whether one should think of only a single autosomal gene or of many different ones. The general discussion of the evolutionary aspect of deteriorative disorders of later life [p. 122] leads one to think that there have probably been many independent mutations, which have gradually accumulated in the species on an evolutionary time-scale. Senile dementia would then be a congeries of theoretically but not practically distinguishable disorders, each with its own specific genetic determinant.

HUNTINGTON'S CHOREA

The Clinical Syndrome

Huntington's chorea is a progressive disorder of the brain in which the primary change is degeneration and fall-out of neurones principally in the middle and posterior parts of the putamen, and in the caudate nucleus; the globus pallidus usually escapes. As a general rule, there are also abiotrophic changes in the cortex, especially the third, fifth and sixth layers, and preponderantly in the frontal lobes and anterior part of the brain. The nerve cells show chromatolysis, shrinkage, and excess of lipochrome and sometimes neuronophagia. Together with the nerve cells the nerve fibres disappear in stages. The interstitial reaction is shown in proliferation of astrocytes, changes in the small blood vessels and leptomeninges.

Clinically, the first changes, usually in early middle age, show up as a change in personality. 'The patient may become irritable, moody, ill-tempered, and show a morose and truculent discontent. He is over-sensitive to slights and may express ideas of reference or paranoid delusions. The picture may on the other hand be one of apathy, slowness, and increasing slovenliness' (Mayer-Gross *et al.*, 1969). The next change to be seen is the appearance of involuntary movements, usually in the face, hands and shoulders, looking at first like fidgetiness, but soon becoming recognizable as abrupt jerking and choreic movements. The neurological picture tends to differ somewhat with the age of onset. Finally, there come the evidences of a progressive dementia: increasing inertia, muddled thinking and inability to concentrate, distractibility, liability to catastrophic reactions, confusion and disorientation and, rather late in the course, memory impairment.

The course of the illness is frequently interrupted by psychotic episodes, and such an episode may be the first indication of illness. It is a matter of great interest that these acute psychoses may at times be clinically indistinguishable from an acute schizophrenia, usually of the paranoid type. Convincing clinical histories and reports have been published by Panse (1942). Depressive syndromes are also common, and any psychotic episode that occurs early in the course of Huntington's chorea practically always presents, not an organic psychosyndrome, but a typically 'endogenous' picture (Streletzki, 1961).

Streletzki studied Wendt's material from the clinical point of view. Wendt had collected more than 5000 Huntington patients from the entire German Bundesgebiet, and complete case histories from the clinical point of view were available in about 1200. Paranoid psychoses occurred in 53 cases, and in a further 14 there was sufficient information for certain purposes. Thus out of these 67 cases there were 20 in which the disease had its first onset in a paranoid state, and of these 20 patients, 10 were diagnosed as suffering from schizophrenia and two from schizophrenia-like psychoses. There were 4 patients who had a typically depressive psychosis, with ideas of sin, poverty and hypochondriasis. These early psychoses, with their typically endogenous type of picture, were very different from the psychoses occurring later on in the course of the illness, in which indications of dementia altered the picture and there was little difficulty in distinguishing the state from schizophrenia. The duration of the paranoid psychosis was shorter in the cases in which it appeared late. In general the paranoid state usually wore off into an organic picture after 2 years or so, though it might last longer when it had appeared early. The relation between the duration of the paranoid state and the year of illness in which it appeared is shown in TABLE 68. The mean duration is 1·7 years, and appears to be unrelated to the duration of overt symptoms before the onset of the psychosis. The paranoid state presents most often in the first year of illness, but there is much variation in this and the mean duration of illness before psychosis is 5·6 years.

The clinical form taken by Huntington's chorea varies to some extent with the age of onset, and may also have some consistency within families. Cases

TABLE 68

DURATION OF PARANOID STATE, IN RELATION TO THE YEAR OF THE DISEASE IN WHICH IT OCCURRED

(Data from Streletzki, 1961)

YEAR OF H.CHOREA IN WHICH PARANOID STATE APPEARED	DURATION OF PARANOID STATE IN YEARS						N
	1	2	3	4	5	6	
1st	6	6	3				15
2nd							—
3rd							—
4th	2						2
5th	4	5					9
6th	4	1	1	1			7
7th	2	1					3
8th	3	2				1	6
9th	1	2	1				4
10th		2					2
11th	1	1					2
12th	2						2
15th	1						1
Totals	26	20	5	1		1	53

with onset in the first 10 years of life are rare but have been reported by a number of authors (Jervis, 1963; Müller-Küppers and Stenzel, 1963; Schönfelder, 1966; Byers and Dodge, 1967). In these children choreic movements are not prominent and occur late or not at all. Intellectual impairment may show as mental subnormality or educational retardation; behaviour disorders are prominent and early; epileptic attacks are not infrequent. Instead of the appearance of choreic movements, one sees stiffening of the musculature and a tremor which becomes worse on movement.

Rigid and akinetic forms of Huntington's disease have been described by many authors (Bittenbender and Quadfasel, 1962; Barrows and Cooper, 1963; Neumayer and Rett, 1966; Perrine and Goodman, 1966; Tsuang, 1969). In all these families there was more than one case showing the atypical akinetic syndrome, and the onset tended to be much earlier than is the rule. Observations like this suggest the possibility that the Huntington gene is appearing at a locus where there is more than one kind of normal allelomorph, one normal gene having a somewhat greater protective effect than the other.

No radical treatment is possible for this disease, and it progresses ineluctably, though perhaps with interruptions lasting for months or years in which there is no further deterioration, until it leads to death in marasmus or from inter-current illness, or perhaps from suicide. The mean duration from onset to death is 12·4 years (Wendt, Landzettel and Solth, 1960); the mean age of onset in Wendt's material was 44·0 years, and the mean age at death 56·4 years.

Age of Onset

It is noteworthy that all workers previously to Wendt and his colleagues (e.g. Bell, 1934; Panse, 1942; Reed and Chandler, 1958) have reported a mean age of

TABLE 69

DISTRIBUTION OF AGES OF ONSET

(From Wendt *et al.*, 1959)

AGE PERIOD	NUMBER	PER CENT	CUMULATIVE
1–5	—	—	—
6–10	1	0·1	0·1
11–15	5	0·7	0·8
16–20	11	1·4	2·2
21–25	24	3·2	5·4
26–30	58	7·6	13·0
31–35	68	8·9	21·9
36–40	102	13·4	35·3
41–45	125	16·4	51·7
46–50	151	19·8	71·5
51–55	107	14·0	85·5
56–60	73	9·6	95·1
61–65	27	3·5	98·6
66–70	8	1·1	99·7
71–75	2	0·3	100·0

The ages shown are presumably ages at last birthday, the age period 0–1 being omitted. N = 762. The mean, 43·97, has presumably been calculated on ungrouped data, and if on age at last birthday, then the true mean = 44·47 years. S.D. = 10·9 years.

onset between 35 and 36. Wendt has pointed out that these estimates are subject to a systematic error: if one includes cases from an age cohort which is not yet extinct, one will ascertain all the cases of early onset but miss some of those of late onset. Wendt guarded against this error by studying the cases of patients born in successive decades and comparing these decades with one another. In the decades born 1830–9, 1840–9 etc., up to 1890–9 the mean age of onset fluctuated between 43 and 47; in subsequent decades it fell successively to 37, 31, 24, 16, and 11. Taking the material as a whole, the mean age of onset was 40·2; but if one used only the 1870–99 material, in which Wendt thought there was least risk of losing either earliest or latest ages of onset, the mean age of onset was for males 44·25, for females 43·69 and for both sexes together 43·97—or 44·0 for all practical purposes, with standard deviation 10·9.

The difference between the ages of onset in males and females, with the males half a year later, is not significant, and we can consider the sexes together.

and erythrocyte neutral lipids and phospholipids in 7 patients and 5 normal controls. Except for some minor deviations, the values obtained for the patients fell within the normal range.

Hooghwinkel, Borri and Bruyn (1966b) examined the plasma and erythrocyte glycolipids and the fatty acid composition of glycolipids in 10 patients with Huntington's chorea. Their findings suggested a marked increase in N-acetyl neuraminic acid, the significance of which they were reluctant to interpret from the biochemical or aetiological point of view, though they pointed out that this compound forms a chemical bridge between polypeptides and polysaccharides because of its ability to enter into both amide and glycosidic linkages; the observed increase may correspond to the increase of serum alpha-glycoproteins reported previously (Bruyn and Lequin, 1964).

Biochemical studies of the brain in Huntington's chorea are likely to show features relating to the effects of the disease rather than to its cause. Borri *et al.* (1967) found in the brains of patients with Huntington's chorea a decrease of total lipids and total protein in the caudate nucleus which was found to be related linearly to the shrinkage of that organ. There were various changes in the lipids in the caudate nucleus, including a relative decrease of phospholipids and a relative increase of sphingomyelin. An increase of glutamic acid was found in both putamen and caudate nucleus. These workers point out that the observed changes should be interpreted as reflecting the biochemical aspect of the neuropathological changes in Huntington's chorea rather than as constituting changes closely tied to the causative metabolic derangement.

A broadside attack was also made on the biochemical front in Huntington's chorea by Oepen and his co-workers. They also came up with essentially negative findings. Oepen and Bickel (1964) examined the urine of 6 patients with Huntington's chorea, and found no abnormalities of amino acids or sugar on filter paper partition chromatography. Oepen and Kreutz (1964) found no characteristic anomalies in the serum cholesterol level or other fatty serum compounds in 7 cases of Huntington's chorea. Deiwick and Oepen (1964) found no pathognomonic changes in the activity of main chain-enzymes in 8 Huntington's chorea patients and one clinically unaffected daughter of one of these patients. In a urine test of 7 Huntington's chorea patients, Delbrück and Oepen (1964) were unable to demonstrate any abnormality of acid mucopolysaccharides.

A possible connexion between a raised serum alanine level and the gene for Huntington's chorea was considered when a boy with increased serum alanine was found to be the son of a woman with Huntington's chorea (Cowie and Seakins, 1962). The boy (aged 15) came under observation in a survey of juvenile delinquents using the Phenistix test. His urine gave a positive result, but he was found not to be phenylketonuric. Three of his sibs were also investigated, and the propositus and one of his brothers had raised levels of serum alanine. The urinary alanine level was also raised in the case of the propositus. The question arose as to whether the raised serum alanine in these two sibs could be a manifestation of the gene for Huntington's chorea. Neither the propositus nor his sibs had reached an age when appearance of neurological signs would have been very likely; the mother's choreic movements had been noticed for 10 years before her death at 40 years of age. The urine and serum of

6 adults with Huntington's chorea (4 men; 2 women) were examined by paper chromatography. In 5 of the cases no abnormalities with respect to amino acids were detected, but in the sixth (that of a woman aged 55) the level of serum alanine was slightly raised though the urine amino acid pattern was normal. The possibility of a disturbance of pyruvate metabolism resulting, by transamination, in a raised level of serum alanine was considered. Glucose-pyruvate tolerance tests in the Huntington's chorea patients and in the brother of the propositus with raised serum alanine, were, however, normal. Unfortunately the propositus was not available for this test.

A line of approach which seemed as though it might be promising, but which so far has yielded little if anything to further our understanding of Huntington's chorea, is that of immunological studies. McMenemey (1961) suggested the study of immunity mechanisms in Huntington's chorea and other neurological diseases characterized by the degeneration of large numbers of nerve cells. He studied serum from patients with a variety of neurological diseases by electrophoresis, and reported a rather characteristic pattern with a raised β and a peculiar plateau-like γ on densitometric scans in sera from patients, in one of whom there was an established diagnosis of Huntington's chorea. More recently, Bruyn and Lequin (1964) observed quantitative differences in the immuno-electrophoresis of serum from 27 cases of Huntington's chorea when compared with samples of pooled normal human serum. They noted an elevation in five distinct protein fractions including γ_1-A-globulin and 7S-γ-globulin and the α_2-macroglobulin in a number of the Huntington's chorea cases, though the extent of the elevation of each fraction was not specified. Maughan and Williams (1966) in sera from a series of 19 Huntington's chorea patients, using immuno-electrophoresis and starch-gel electrophoresis, found an increase of α_2 macroglobulin in 7 of them. The only other abnormalities detected were an increase in the γ-G-globulin in two samples, increased haptoglobin in three, increased transferrin in four and increased β-lipoprotein in one sample.

The levels of the major protein fractions determined by the densitometric analysis of cellulose acetate electrophoretic separations in the serum from 14 hospitalized patients with Huntington's chorea were compared with those from 14 controls in the same hospital by Cowie and Gammack (1966). There were no obvious qualitative differences in the electrophoretic patterns obtained for the two groups, but a statistically significant elevation of γ-globulin in the group of Huntington's chorea patients was observed. In a later study, in collaboration with Professor Sydney Cohen, serum immunoglobulin fractions were measured in a series of 11 patients with Huntington's chorea, and the results were compared with those from a control series of 9 schizophrenic patients and 7 patients with Parkinsonism living in similar hospital-ward conditions (Cowie, 1969). The patients with Parkinsonism were included because they were suffering from a condition characterized, like Huntington's chorea, by a massive breakdown of nervous tissue. The three main classes of immunoglobulins were studied: immunoglobulin G (7S γ-globulin), immunoglobulin A (γ_1 A-globulin) and immunoglobulin M (γ_1 M-globulin). An agar plate diffusion method was used. No significant differences were found between the means of immuno-globulins G, A and M and total immunoglobulins for each group of patients, though the immunoglobulin M mean for the Huntington's chorea group was raised by the abnormally high reading from one patient which was three times as high as any other in the group. When this reading was excluded, the mean immunoglobulin M for the Huntington's chorea group was reduced to a value very much in line with the immunoglobulin M means for the other two groups.

The whole approach of immunological studies in a condition such as Huntington's chorea is beset with the imponderable effects of many known and probably many unknown influences. Maughan and Williams (1966) have suggested that the increase in so many different fractions in the serum from Huntington's chorea cases seen in the immuno-electric studies by Bruyn and Lequin (1964) and themselves make it likely that these changes are non-specific. They have put forward the view that the changes reflect tissue destruction and secondary infection or other complications, rather than being connected with the aetiology of the disease.

So far the various lines of biochemical research in Huntington's chorea seem to have led into blind alleys. False hopes of finding a metabolic disorder involving trace metals may have been raised by drawing a parallel between Huntington's chorea and Wilson's disease. Perhaps as a starting point for further research it would be better to disregard ideas prompted by the notion of Huntington's chorea as an analogue of other conditions affecting the central grey matter.

In an effort to understand the specific enzymopathy that underlies Huntington's chorea, it would seem worth while, moreover, to examine the central grey matter from fresh autopsy material rather than to look for more peripheral biochemical changes in living patients, which may be a number of steps removed from the primary change. There are, however, many practical difficulties in the way, not least the difficulty of reaching the central grey matter while it is fresh enough for enzyme studies. There is some hope, however, with improving neuropathological and histochemical techniques, that this difficulty may be overcome.

Genetics

The disease is the direct consequence of a single major gene, which manifests dominantly in the heterozygote with a penetrance which has been estimated (Kishimoto, Nakamura and Sotokawa, 1957) as 0·94, which for practical clinical purposes is negligibly less than 100 per cent. All the major investigators (Entres, 1921; Sjögren, 1935; Panse, 1942; Reed and Chandler, 1958) have found identically the same genetical picture, and there is no suggestion of more than one locus being involved or of multiple allelomorphy of the pathogenic gene (the possibility of alternative forms of its normal allelomorphy has been mentioned).

Reed and Chandler (1958) found that among sibs the ages at onset and the ages at death were significantly correlated with those of the index case ($r = 0·28$ and 0·47 respectively). However, the sib-sib correlation for rate of progress of the disease, as measured by the interval between onset and death, was not significantly different from zero. Further analysis showed that the sib-sib correlations were probably due to similar genetic backgrounds rather than to the possession in common of the same particular gene for Huntington's chorea, supposing that several such genes at one or more loci actually existed. Mono-zygotic twin pairs, culled by Myrianthopoulos from the literature in a valuable critical review (1966), show remarkable agreement in ages of onset: 35–35, 41–41, 45–45, 43–43, 22–22.

Many attempts have been made to discover the earliest manifestations of the gene before it shows itself in outright psychosis or chorea of a clinically diagnosable syndrome. In many cases, perhaps in young people more than in those of middle-age, personality changes and disorders of behaviour show first, and may be enough to direct suspicion on a member of a known Huntington family some years before a definite diagnosis can be made. However, such changes are the earliest manifestations of the disease and not a pleiotropic effect of the gene. EEG changes may also occur early in the disease, but attempts to use EEG abnormalities for predicting the later occurrence of the disease in members of Huntington families (Patterson, Bagchi and Test, 1948) were shown by an 18-year follow-up study to have been as often wrong as right (Chandler, 1966).

Selection and Mutation

In considering the population genetics of such conditions as Huntington's chorea, we need to know what the expectation of the gene is to survive from generation to generation, and either to spread through a population or to be gradually eliminated. The basic information is provided by an estimate of the 'fitness' of the gene bearer. The problems involved in making such an estimate have been considered by Reed (1959). Relative fitness (W) has usually, especially in Huntington's chorea, been calculated by relating the number of live-born children born to index patients with the number born to their sibs. However, the sibs do not provide good comparative material, since their fertility is not the same as that of the general population. Reed has shown that the comparison must be made with the general population from which the index subjects were drawn; the target series and the control series have to be matched in parental age distribution with or without the aid of corrections; the secular epoch over which reproductivity is being measured should be the same for the two series; and only completed or nearly completed fertilities should be used. There are indeed other requirements for a satisfactory comparison, but these are the main ones.

Working in this way, Reed and Neel (1959) found that Huntington choreics had a relative fitness of $1\cdot12\pm0\cdot12$ compared with their non-choreic sibs, but if one took heterozygotes whether they were choreic or not, the figure was about $1\cdot01\pm0\cdot11$. The fertility of male choreics or heterozygotes was significantly less than that of female choreics or heterozygotes. However, the fertility of the non-choreic sibs differed significantly from the general population figure and was only about $0\cdot77\pm0\cdot08$ of the latter; taken together, these findings suggest a relative fitness of the heterozygote of about $0\cdot81$.

An estimate of the mutation frequency could be made on the basis that enough mutation is occurring to keep the gene frequency in balance from generation to generation from the simple formula

$$\mu=(1-W)\,p$$

in which W is the relative fitness and p the gene frequency. Reed and Neel estimated that in Michigan the frequency of the heterozygotic constitution was 1.01×10^{-4}, which would mean that the gene frequency was half that figure. This gives for μ, the mutation rate, a value of 9.6×10^{-6}, which they consider very much too high. From examining their pedigree data they concluded that the mutation rate could not be higher than 5.4×10^{-6} and could lie at any figure between that and zero, almost certainly several times smaller than the observationally estimated maximum. Any approach to estimating the mutation rate, however, is rendered more difficult when one has to admit that the gene frequency may very well not be in equilibrium.

Epidemiology

In his critical discussion of the literature on the epidemiology of Huntington's chorea, Myrianthopoulos has pointed out that very wide variations from one geographical region to another in estimates of prevalence are frequently more likely to be due to the method of ascertainment by the investigator than to any likely local variation. Taking only the most reliable figures, Myrianthopoulos concludes that the prevalence rate is generally in the neighbourhood of 4–7 per 100,000 population. However, there are small population pockets, in which the figure may be accidentally high from the multiplication of a single family stock, as seems to have been the case in Tasmania (17 per 100,000), and in one of the two Swedish areas investigated by Sjögren in 1935. In Japan the condition seems always to have been very rare, and the first case report of a Japanese case came in 1927. In Japan, Kishimoto *et al.* found a prevalence of only 0·4 per 100,000 in a province of 4 million population. These two points together do suggest strongly that the prevalence, and the gene frequency, in Japan are only about one-tenth of the world figure. There is no evidence that other ethnic groups are relatively spared, and the prevalence in American Negroes and in American Jews is probably about normal.

Since at any one time only a proportion of heterozygotes will be ascertainable as suffering from the disease, the heterozygotic frequency is higher than the prevalence rate. Thus Reed and Chandler estimated the prevalence in Michigan as 4·1 per 100,000 and the heterozygote frequency as 10·1 per 100,000. The gene frequency will be one-half the heterozygote frequency, i.e., in most countries in the neighbourhood of $5-9 \times 10^{-5}$.

Genetic Counselling

Huntington's chorea offers a suitable model for consideration of the problems of genetic counselling in a condition of known genetical causation, in which there is a wide spread of age of onset. The pedigree shown in FIGURE 17 is a fairly typical example of a Huntington family, such as might be established by good clinical investigation, without deployment of all the research techniques that might be applied, such as follow-up over many years. We shall suppose that members of this family come for advice to a genetic counselling clinic, and consider what the adviser will say to them. To begin with the inquirer only says that there is mental disease in his family, leading to long-term stay and death in a mental hospital, and that he understands the condition is Huntington's chorea. The steps that are now taken can be ordered as follows:

1. The inquirer gives the completest information he can about his own parents and his sibs, and shows the relationship to the relative with supposed Huntington's chorea, or to as many such relatives as are known. In as many as possible of these cases, the doctor will wish to confirm the diagnosis, by writing to the hospitals or to the doctors who had these relatives in their medical care. Full names are needed, both married and maiden names in the case of women, dates of birth if possible, of all relatives, and in the case of those who come under treatment, the calendar year or age or both at which the named relative was under care, and the name and locality of the hospital where he was. These hospitals (or doctors, if in private care only) will be written to, with a request for a clinical summary or loan of the case-notes, and the diagnosis will be confirmed in as many cases as possible. It will be particularly important to

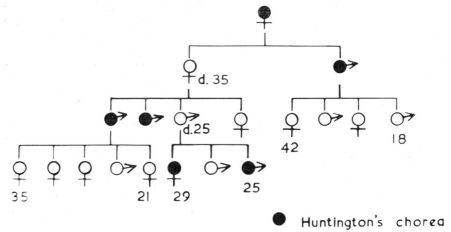

Fig. 17. Huntington's chorea.

establish or rebut the diagnosis of Huntington's chorea in the case of any unclear mental illness affecting a parent who is the connecting link between the inquirer and the rest of the affected family, unless there is an unequivocal history of Huntington's chorea in the case of one of his full sibs. In this connexion one should not forget the possibility of a mistaken paternity, although as a practical question the matter rarely arises.

We suppose that, in the family under discussion, all these inquiries are completed, with the result that the pedigree shown has been drawn up. Furthermore we may suppose that in more than one of the individuals shown as affected the diagnosis is quite unequivocal, and that in all the diagnosis is compatible with the known facts.

2. In the clinic, we shall be asked for advice about two distinct though related questions: what will the doctor's advice be about the inquirer getting married, and what will be his advice about having children? In both cases the best line to take is to give the inquirer the best estimate possible of what the morbidity risk is (a) for himself; and (b) for his children. The decision he ultimately takes will be his own responsibility, but it should be a well-informed one. Some

doctors go no further than that; but the present authors have no doubt that, in the case of a condition as disabling and ultimately lethal as Huntington's chorea, ethical considerations do arise, and should be made quite clear to the inquirer when the risks he faces are material ones.

3. We may suppose that the first inquirer who comes to us is IV 1, a single woman of 35, whose father died of Huntington's chorea. Since her father was a gene carrier, her own initial chance of being a gene carrier likewise was one in two. However, by now she has reached the age of 35, so that she has outlived a considerable part of the danger period. Consulting Wendt's table [p. 138] we see that she has now outlived 22 per cent of the total risk, so that her 50 per cent risk can be reduced to 39 per cent. It is still a substantial one. Any child she now has would have a one in two chance of inheriting the gene, if she were herself a carrier, so that any child would face a 19·5 per cent risk. In considering marriage for herself, the inquirer is obviously under an obligation of honour to inform her prospective spouse of these potential risks. If he were prepared to take the risk of seeing her fall eventually a victim to the disease, and still wished to marry her, no reasonable objection could be made. However, the 20 per cent risk for eventual children is more than a responsible pair would wish, or should take, and their marriage should certainly be childless unless they adopted a child.

4. Our next inquirer is someone not marked on the pedigree, the 35-year-old son of III 4, a woman who is still alive and well in her 62nd year. The inquirer's mother, though not the child of a Huntington choreic, was certainly the child of a gene carrier, and has choreic sibs. *Ab initio* her chance of being a gene carrier was one in two, but by now she has outlived 95 per cent of the risk period, and the remaining risk that she carried the gene is one-half of 5 per cent, i.e. 2·5 per cent. Her son, the inquirer, carries an *a priori* risk of half that figure, i.e. 1·25 per cent, which has itself to be further diminished by 22 hundredths, leaving him with a less than 1 per cent chance of developing the disease. Any child he were now to have would be faced by a risk of less than half a per cent, and could not be regarded as seriously endangered. Reassuring though these facts are, the inquirer should have them drawn to his attention, and be advised to put his prospective wife in possession of them.

ALZHEIMER'S DISEASE AND PICK'S DISEASE

The Distinction

These two conditions are certainly distinct and each of them has its own genetical basis independent of the other; nevertheless it will be convenient to discuss them together. Clinical appearances are very similar during life, and it is often impossible to make a differential diagnosis with any certainty if pathological findings are not available. Both conditions manifest themselves as a slowly progressing dementia with insidious onset usually in the fifth or sixth decades, i.e. well before the main danger period of senile dementia. Focal neurological signs, particularly those referable to the parietal lobes, are much commoner in Alzheimer's than in Pick's disease; and in Pick's disease frontal lobe symptoms usually dominate the picture. Nevertheless, in their definitive study *Morbus Alzheimer and Morbus Pick* (1952) the Sjögrens preferred to make only a provisional differentiation in those cases in which the pathological findings (studied by Lindgren) were not available. Hakon Sjögren, the clinician in this group of workers, found that the symptom of greatest differential value was a disturbance of gait, which he has described in detail; this was practically always present in the Alzheimer cases while absent in the Pick cases. TABLE 70 gives a schematic representation of the results of his clinical analysis.

TABLE 70

CLINICAL FEATURES OF 18 ALZHEIMER CASES AND 13 PICK CASES, ALL WITH NEUROPATHOLOGICAL CONFIRMATION

(From Sjögren, Sjögren and Lindgren, 1952)

	ALZHEIMER	PICK
Total of cases with satisfactory clinical examination	18	13
Progressive dementia	18	13
Sensory aphasia	15	13
Amnestic aphasia	18	5
Deterioration of speech faculty	17	12
Alexia	14	4
Agraphia	15	5
Dysarthria	12	4
Logoclonia	6	3
Perseveration	16	10
Tonus changes	14	1
Disturbance of gait	13	—
Epileptic fits	4	1

Pathology

Pathologically, the two conditions bear little resemblance to one another. In Alzheimer's disease there is brain atrophy affecting all areas, although the prefrontal and temporal regions may be more shrunken than others at the time of death. Histologically there is outfall of cells and the formation of plaques and neurofibrillary changes. These neurofibrils stain well with silver dyes (and are called argyrophilic) and form characteristic loops and tangles. However, none of these very striking appearances are very specific, and all of them are found in other degenerative disorders such as senility, senile dementia, motor neurone disease, etc.

In Pick's disease the outer three layers of the cerebral cortex are most severely hit by the atrophic process, and changes are maximal in the frontal and temporal regions, usually leaving the parietal lobes unaffected. There is a heavy outfall of cells, and those that remain are likely to show all stages of degeneration: ballooning of the nerve-cell body, disappearance of Nissl's bodies and finally extrusion of the nucleus; argentophil granules are seen in the fine texture of the cell. Senile plaques and Alzheimer's neurofibrillary changes do not occur; but glial proliferation and changes in the blood vessels are common.

Epidemiology

There is no useful information about the frequency of these conditions in the general population of any country apart from Sweden; but it seems likely that there is as much variation in this respect from country to country as in the case of Huntington's chorea. In Sweden Torsten Sjögren estimated a population risk of about 0·1 per cent for both conditions combined; but this may well be an over-estimate. Most clinicians see cases sufficiently infrequently to be cautious in diagnosis—and this would hardly be the case if we could expect to see one Alzheimer-Pick for every ten schizophrenics. Alzheimer's disease is, in the experience of most clinicians and neuropathologists, much commoner than

TABLE 71

DISTRIBUTION OF AGES OF ONSET OF 80 INDEX CASES (22 MALES AND 58 FEMALES) SUFFERING FROM ALZHEIMER OR PICK SYNDROMES FROM SJÖGREN *et al.*, 1952, COMPARED WITH AGES OF ONSET OF 89 ALZHEIMER AND PICK CASES COLLECTED FROM THE LITERATURE (41m, 48f)

AGE OF ONSET	SJÖGREN ET AL.	OLDER LITERATURE
20–29	—	7
30–39	3	18
40–49	12	40
50–59	42	16
60–69	20	7
70–79	3	1
Total	80	89

Pick's disease and the latter is definitely rare. It is therefore anomalous that Sjögren, Sjögren and Lindgren found equal numbers of the two conditions in their pathologically confirmed cases. However, their survey was not nation-wide, and, as often occurs with genetically caused conditions, there were obviously local variations in frequency: combining index patients and affected relatives, the majority of their Pick cases came from near Stockholm (A:P ratio 14:57), the majority of the Alzheimer cases from the neighbourhood of Gothenburg (A:P ratio 25:3).

In this Swedish study, in both Pick and Alzheimer cases, there was a marked preponderance of the female sex. Taking both index and secondary cases together, the male/female ratio was 0·22 in the Alzheimer series, 0·50 in the Pick series. However, the authors considered that there was some biased selection with regard to sex distribution, and if they restricted themselves to clinics where there was no reason to suspect an over-registration of female patients, then the sex ratio (both A and P together) was 19:35 probands = 0·57. Mean ages of onset were for males 52, females 56; for Alzheimer cases 55, for Pick cases 55. Mean ages at death were for males 59·5, for females 63; for Alzheimer cases 61, for Pick cases 62. The distribution of ages of onset is shown in TABLE 71. The ages of onset in this Swedish series are rather later than those reported in the literature. For comparative purposes the data on established cases reproduced in the tabulations of Zerbin-Rüdin, 1967a, supplemented by data from Schenk's family, are shown alongside. The literature data can be broken down by diagnosis and sex, and are shown in more detail in TABLE 72. If one can trust these findings (and it is always possible that they represent a biased selection), the mean age of onset in Alzheimer's disease is earlier than in Pick's disease, in both syndromes

TABLE 72

AGES OF ONSET WITH MEANS AND STANDARD DEVIATIONS OF 42 ALZHEIMER CASES AND 49 PICK CASES, BY DIAGNOSIS AND SEX
(Data compiled from Zerbin-Rüdin, 1967a, and Schenk, 1958–9)

AGE OF ONSET	ALZHEIMER CASES		PICK CASES	
	M	F	M	F
20–24	—	—	2	—
25–29	4	—	—	1
30–34	2	2	1	2
35–39	6	3	2	—
40–44	7	6	2	4
45–49	3	4	4	10
50–54	1	1	2	7
55–59	—	1	1	3
60–64	2	—	1	2
65–69	—	—	1	1
70–74	—	—	—	1
Total	25	17	16	31
Mean	40·2	42·6	44·5	49·5
S.D.	9·5	6·2	12·4	9·2

is earlier in males than in females, and in both syndromes shows more variability in males than in females. The variance ratio $F = 2·35$ in Alzheimer's disease, and is significant at the 0·05 level; in Pick's disease $F = 1·81$, which is not significant.

Genetics

The investigation by Sjögren, Sjögren and Lindgren is the only systematic study in depth on the genetics of Alzheimer's and Pick's diseases. They took two points of departure, from an inclusive series of diagnoses in certain mental hospitals on the one hand and on brain protocols in certain university departments of pathology on the other. Where possible, the two sets of records were married; and an investigation into the families yielded a series of secondary cases, some of which could again be pathologically verified. Their material of 80 index cases finally included: (1) histologically verified Alzheimer cases 18 (6 m, 12 f); (2) histologically verified Pick cases 18 (7 m, 11 f); (3) histologically not verified Alzheimer-Pick cases with verified cerebral atrophy 29 (7 m, 22 f); and (4) histologically not verified Alzheimer-Pick cases without verified cerebral atrophy 15 (2 m, 13 f).

No differences were found between these four groups in respect of age of onset, course and duration of disease; and no differences of importance in respect of family history. The total material could accordingly be brought into one whole, and then divided by means of H. Sjögren's diagnostic criteria into two series, the A series of 36 certain and probable Alzheimer cases and the P series of 44 certain and probable Pick cases. Needless to say, it was not possible to achieve any certainty in the differential diagnosis of the secondary cases found in the families of the two series of probands; so that what we finally have is a comparison of the incidence of Alzheimer-Pick syndromes in the one series and in the other.

The 36 A cases yielded 8 secondary cases among parents and sibs, the 44 P cases yielded 22 secondary cases, so that the family loading was much heavier in the Pick than in the Alzheimer group. The morbidity risk for parents was calculated as 10 per cent in the A series, 19 per cent in the P series; and for sibs 4 per cent in the A series, 7 per cent in the P series. Taking both groups together, the risk for parents was 15 per cent and for sibs 5 per cent; the risk for sibs where one parent was affected was 16 per cent as against 2·5 per cent where neither parent was affected. The ratio of one to the other, here 6·4, is evidence in favour of a polygenic theory and is not easy to reconcile with a single dominant gene.

From the genealogical part of the work, Torsten Sjögren came to only rather provisional conclusions. He thought the likelihood of multifactorial inheritance was greater in the case of Morbus Alzheimer than in that of Morbus Pick, and for the latter he preferred the hypothesis of a dominant major gene with polygenic modification of its manifestation. The preponderance of women could not be accounted for by a total or partial sex-linkage. The frequency of psychoses and severe oligophrenia among the relatives of these patients was according to population expectations. He thought that the frequency of these conditions was much higher than was usually thought probable, and assessed the contribution to morbidity they made as making up about 10 per cent of all senile and pre-senile psychoses.

Constantinidis, Garrone and Ajuriaguerra (1962) have reported on the literature relating to the hereditary factor in dementias of advanced age and have reported a family investigation of their own; together with Tissot (1965) they also studied the familial incidence of Alzheimer's neurofibrillary changes in the cortex. Their material is based on an inclusive series of elderly dementing patients admitted to the Bel-Air clinic over the years 1901–58. While their findings do not seem to have involved field work on the families, as the Swedish study just discussed, and so are not comparable with those of Sjögren, they confirm the existence of a hereditary component. Of the 814 cases in which they were able to make confident diagnoses, with the aid of 155 autopsy reports, 423 patients (52 per cent) suffered from cerebral arteriosclerosis, 229 (28 per cent) simple senility, and 60 on a mixed arteriopathic and atrophic-degenerative basis. The Alzheimer-Pick cases constituted just one-eighth of the total material, with 97 Alzheimer to 5 Pick cases. Constantinidis et al. found that each of the three conditions, Alzheimer's disease, senile dementia and dementia due to vascular disease, tended to run true in the families: among the sibs of the Alzheimer patients 3·3 per cent could be diagnosed as Alzheimer cases, but only half as many of either the parents or the children. These figures are lower than the Swedish ones, and are probably less reliable.

Apart from these studies, the main evidence about the heredity of the Alzheimer and Pick syndromes is to be drawn from the fairly large number of individual families which have been reported from time to time. Nearly all of these reports are on Alzheimer families, and the Pick families are relatively few and far between—hardly surprising if, as the figures of Constantinidis would lead us to suppose, Alzheimer's disease is twenty times as common as Pick's disease.[1] Some of these family reports are of individual sporadic cases without a positive family history, then usually communicated for neuropathological interest. The reports showing a family history (Bogaert, Maere and de Smedt, 1940; Bucci, 1963; Essen-Möller, 1946; Feldman et al., 1963; Grünthal and Wenger, 1939; Heston, Lowther and Leventhal, 1966; Lowenberg and Waggoner, 1934; McMenemey et al., 1939; de Risio, Conterio and Ridolo, 1965; Wheclan, 1959; Zawuski, 1960) uniformly exhibit typical dominant inheritance. The sex distribution is equal, there is no parental consanguinity, and the mode of inheritance is from affected parent to 50 per cent of the children. There does not seem to be any significant departure from the expected 50 per cent ratio of affected individuals in endangered sibships, and where direct inheritance fails, it can be explained by insufficiency of information. We must suppose that in these reported families we are seeing the manifestation of a major autosomal gene, whose manifestation rate is little diminished by accessory genes or by peristatic influences.

With regard to Alzheimer's disease, then, we are faced with a conflict of evidence. Systematic study reveals an uncharacteristic mode of inheritance, readily compatible with a polygenic basis; the reported pedigrees on the other hand show the undeniable manifestation of a major gene. We must conclude that in the majority of cases Alzheimer's disease (which Sjögren took to be quite a common condition) is attributable to multifactorial inheritance; but that there is also a relatively rare number of cases in which dominant inheritance is occurring. In the former there is a female sex preponderance, in the latter sex equality. The evidence tends to suggest that where polygenes are responsible, the affected male has a heavier genetical predisposition than the affected female. In the Sjögren material 3 of the 8 secondary cases were derived from the 6 male probands, 5 only came from the 30 female probands.

When we turn to the mode of inheritance in Pick's disease, there is no longer a conflict of evidence. Both the systematic Swedish studies and the relatively few family pedigree studies of the literature are in agreement in supporting a single gene hypothesis. One of the most instructive Pick pedigrees has been provided by Schenk (1958–9) after a follow-up 20 years later of a large family first reported by him and Sanders in 1939 [see FIG. 18]. Looking at this pedigree one will see that every certain, almost certain and probable case of the disease is the child of an affected parent, back to the original ancestor; furthermore that in the endangered sibships there are 26 affected individuals to 25 unaffected ones. The shift towards a female preponderance is slight and non-significant (11:16). There is a slight tendency for affected males to be a greater danger to

---

[1] A comprehensive review of the literature and its case material has been provided by Zerbin-Rüdin (1967a).

their children than affected females, but it is readily explainable as a chance phenomenon ($0.50 > p > 0.30$). In the case of Pick's disease we can be reasonably confident in rejecting a polygenic hypothesis and settling for a major autosomal gene. If there is a female preponderance it may be no more than can

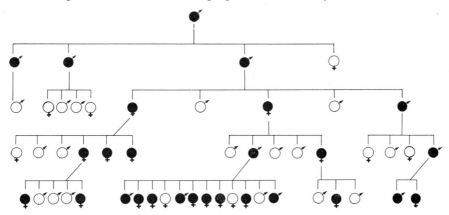

Fig. 18. Pedigree of a family with Pick's disease (modified from Schenk, 1958–9).

be accounted for by the greater longevity of the female sex. The distribution of ages of onset is shown in TABLE 72.

WILSON'S DISEASE (HEPATOLENTICULAR DEGENERATION)

This condition has been named after Wilson (1912), who published a monograph entitled *Progressive Lenticular Degeneration: A Familial Nervous Disease Associated with Cirrhosis of the Liver.* Six years previously Gowers (1906) reported a brother and sister with signs and symptoms now recognized as typical of hepatolenticular degeneration, and apparently reports of the condition had appeared from time to time earlier than this, but no systematic study had been made.

The essential pathological changes in Wilson's disease are in the liver, which undergoes nodular cirrhosis, and the brain. The basal ganglia particularly are affected, leading to extrapyramidal neurological signs including rigidity, athetosis, tremor, dysarthria and dysphagia. The chief neuropathological changes consist of degenerative changes, usually spongiform, of the striatum (Crome and Stern, 1967).

Wilson's disease frequently brings about personality changes fairly soon after the supposed onset; these are similar to those occurring in Huntington's chorea [see p. 135]. Like Huntington's chorea, Wilson's disease is particularly interesting to the psychiatrist by quite commonly being complicated by a temporary schizophrenia-like psychosis. Davison and Bagley (1969) have recently reviewed the literature and comment 'It is remarkable that such a rare disorder as Wilson's disease should so often be associated with a psychosis diagnosed (or mis-diagnosed) as schizophrenia'. They found in the accumulated literature 11 acceptable and 11 doubtful cases of schizophrenia (by their criteria of adequacy of the clinical data for the schizophrenic diagnosis), and note that of these only one had a family history of schizophrenia. We have ourselves observed one case, i.e. that reported by Beard (1959), over the greater part of his long illness. Subsequently to Beard's report, this patient passed out of his schizophrenia-like state into a typical organic deterioration, with personality changes and dementia without any residue of schizophrenic symptomatology. It seems that this is not an unusual mode of development of the disease, with personality change early on, sometimes a frank psychosis when neurological changes are well advanced, passing off into an organic defect, and finally progressive dementia in the terminal stages.

A curious feature in Wilson's disease is the Kayser-Fleischer ring. This is a greenish ring seen at the limbus of the cornea. It is usually most marked at the superior and inferior parts of the corneal circumference. Sometimes slit-lamp examination is necessary to exclude the presence of a Kayser-Fleischer ring, but in most cases rings are to be clearly seen by the naked eye. This sign is regarded as the single most important clinical diagnostic sign of Wilson's disease (Bearn, 1966).

The age of onset shows a wide range of variation. The first signs may be seen in childhood in some cases. In others, the patient may have remained symptom-free until well on into adult life. For example, Scheinberg and Sternlieb (1959) found the age of onset, in a series of 14 patients, to range between 8 and 34 years. This is quite typical of most series of patients. These authors draw attention to the fact that there are at least three types of clinical course that Wilson's disease may run. First, the patient may develop and die of severe neurological disease with little evidence of clinically significant hepatic disease. Secondly, the patient may die of liver disease with little, if any, evidence of neurological disease. Thirdly, he may run a clinical course characterized by both frank neurological and hepatic symptomatology. Scheinberg and Sternlieb point out that neither they nor others have been able to find variations in the fundamental hereditary and biochemical manifestations which correlate with one or another of these forms of Wilson's disease. In fact each of the different forms may appear in different members of the same sibship. The variation of manifestation of Wilson's disease in one sibship is well exemplified by a brother and sister reported by Warren and Broughton (1962). The sister, who was the elder, had an attack of jaundice at the age of 7, 5 years before she presented with the full clinical syndrome with severe neurological symptoms, hepatospleno-megaly and a Kayser-Fleischer ring. Her brother, on the other hand, was diagnosed biochemically as having Wilson's disease at the age of 6 when there was no other evidence of the disease. Three years later he was still without symptoms, but showed evidence of liver damage, electroencephalographic changes and accumulation of copper. He was considered to have the disease in an active but silent form.

There is a strong tendency for hepatic symptoms to be the first to appear in cases with onset in childhood. This is clearly seen in a study of the presenting symptoms of Wilson's disease by Walshe (1962). Cases presenting with an apparently pure hepatic illness may later develop the classical neurological lesions with an amelioration of the hepatic signs. Walshe considers it probable that environmental factors influence the varying clinical manifestations of Wilson's disease, but a role for the action of modifying genes in the hereditary structure of affected sibs cannot be entirely excluded.

It is believed that the basic defect in Wilson's disease is a genetically-determined error of copper metabolism. In normal individuals most of the copper in the serum is carried in combination with protein as caeruloplasmin. A small amount is carried as a copper-albumin complex. In patients with Wilson's disease, however, the reverse is the case (Walshe, 1961). As the copper in the copper-albumin complex is more loosely bound than copper in caeruloplasmin, copper becomes deposited in the tissues in Wilson's disease. Many of the clinical signs, including cirrhosis of the liver, are thought to be a direct result of this.

Two current hypotheses concerning the pathogenesis of Wilson's disease are very clearly expounded by Bearn (1966). Neither fits all the facts. The most favoured of the two suggests that the primary effect of the abnormal gene is to diminish the synthesis of normal caeruloplasmin and possibly of other closely related proteins. However, as Bearn (1966) points out, many experimental observations do not agree with this hypothesis. Thus, there is no correlation between the depression of caeruloplasmin synthesis and the amount of copper absorbed; administration of copper in animal experiments has failed to mimic the disease; some patients with Wilson's disease, especially those with hepatic involvement, have a caeruloplasmin level which is quantitatively normal; finally, there is relatively little correlation between the increased output of copper in the urine and the clinical improvement which may follow the administration of chelating agents such as British anti-lewisite and penicillamine.

The second hypothesis, however, has been criticized even more severely for several reasons. This hypothesis was put forward by Uzman (Uzman et al., 1956; Iber, Chalmers and Uzman, 1957). It ascribes the primary effect of the Wilson's disease gene to an abnormal protein with increased power for binding copper. This protein is presumed present in all tissues where the copper content is raised, and the low caeruloplasmin level is considered a secondary effect due to the by-passing of copper to the tissues. Moreover, according to this hypothesis, the abnormal protein metabolism leads to the production of specific oligopeptides which are in competition with amino acids and uric acid for reabsorption in the proximal renal tubules, thus giving rise to abnormal urinary findings. The changes in the liver are said to be due to nutritional deficiencies. Bearn (1966) summarizes the objections to this hypothesis as follows. On the basis of quantitative observations it is extremely unlikely that renal loss of amino acids could lead to cirrhosis of the liver; moreover, many patients with Wilson's disease have been reported in whom no aminoaciduria is present but in whom a diminished caeruloplasmin has been observed. According to this hypothesis, if copper was absorbed with greater facility into the tissues by virtue of the increased affinity of tissue proteins, one would expect intravenously administered radioactive copper to disappear more rapidly rather than more slowly from the circulation. The hypothesis is weak in its explanation of

aminoaciduria through competition of amino acids with oligopeptides for reabsorption in the proximal renal tubules, since at least 75 per cent of amino acids
liberated by acid hydrolysis of human urine is derived from compounds other
than peptides.

Genetics

Although in his original monograph Wilson drew attention to the familial
occurrence of the condition which now bears his name, he believed that this
was due to the effects of environment rather than to inherited causes, though
he did not rule out the possible role of heredity. This view was generally held

TABLE 73

THE CONSANGUINITY RATE IN 30 FAMILIES WITH WILSON'S DISEASE

	CONSANGUINITY RATE IN PARENTS OF PATIENTS WITH WILSON'S DISEASE					
NO. OF SIBSHIPS	FIRST COUSINS		SECOND COUSINS		UNRELATED	
	NO.	PERCENTAGE	NO.	PERCENTAGE	NO.	PERCENTAGE
30	11	36·7	3	10·0	16	53·3

Source: *The Metabolic Basis of Inherited Disease* by Stanbury,
Wyngaarden and Fredrickson. Table adapted from A. G. Bearn
(1960).

until quite recently, and our present understanding of the genetical basis of
Wilson's disease is owing largely to the classical work of Bearn.

Bearn (1960) carried out an extensive genetical analysis of data from 32
patients belonging to 30 families mainly from the New York area. The high
consanguinity rate in the series was good evidence that Wilson's disease is
inherited as an autosomal recessive trait [see TABLE 73]. This mode of transmission of the condition is now generally accepted. From the patients in Bearn's
series two groups from geographically circumscribed areas emerged. One
consisted of Jews (14 patients) of eastern European origin; the other consisted
of non-Jews from the Mediterranean (8 patients) [see FIG. 19]. The Jewish
group showed some interesting differences when compared with the Mediterranean group and the remaining patients of varied geographical origin in the
series. The Jews tended to have more consanguinity, a later age of onset of the
disease, milder symptoms, a better response to treatment, later age of death and
a wider variation of serum copper and caeruloplasmin levels. (The Jewish group
included patients with a normal level of caeruloplasmin.) Not all these differences
were statistically significant, and it was emphasized that the collection of more
cases was needed before firm conclusions could be drawn. The findings, however,
led Bearn to consider the possibility that the eastern European Jewish population may possess a modifying gene to bring about these differences in Wilson's
disease. These observations, together with the fact that in some sibships there is
similarity in the expression of the disease and in others considerable variation
may exist, could be due to a variety of factors, environmental and genetical.

Fig. 19. Map illustrating the geographical origins of parents of patients with Wilson's disease. Each solid circle indicates the birthplace of both parents. Where birthplaces of both parents are not identical, this is indicated by two capital letters, one for each parent, e.g. *A* and *A'* (Bearn, 1960).

Bearn suggested that environmental factors might possibly be dietary or hormonal in nature. Genetically, in addition to the idea that genetical modifiers may exist in some populations and not in others, Bearn put forward the possibility that the different expression of the disease in families might be supposed to result from a different allelomorphic gene at the same locus, or a mutation at a closely linked locus. Bearn emphasized that the evidence available is insufficient to state that caeruloplasmin is the primary gene product in Wilson's disease. If further evidence lent support to that view, he considered it would be necessary to perform structural studies on caeruloplasmin from patients with Wilson's disease of various geographical origins, in order to investigate the possibility of chemical allelism.

Wilson's disease appears to occur in individuals of all races. It is possibly slightly less common in females than in males. The hazards in estimating its gene frequency are discussed by Bearn (1966). First, it is not certain that the disease is genetically homogeneous. Secondly, if Dahlberg's method is used, it is necessary to know the frequency of first-cousin marriage in the population from which the sample is drawn. Little precise information is available concerning the first-cousin consanguinity rate in Eastern Poland or Sicily 50 years ago, whence came the two main geographical groups in Bearn's study. Bearn offers an argument based on assuming this rate to have been 0·1 at the time in question, but we are unable to follow it, and it leads (or does not lead) to results which Bearn himself does not accept.

Bearn estimates the first-cousin parental consanguinity as 0·367. Using Dahlberg's formula [see p. 5], $c = a/(a+16p)$, and substituting 0·367 for c and 0·100 for a, we find $p = 0·01$. This would give 1×10^{-4} as the frequency of the homozygote, and correspondingly of the Wilson case, in the population. The estimate of 0·1 for c is little better than a wild guess, and seems improbable, even in highly inbred groups, when we are considering first-cousin consanguinity only; if we drop the guess to 0·05, the estimate for p becomes approximately 0·005, and the frequency of Wilson's disease about 3×10^{-5}. It would be better to estimate the gene frequency from the best available estimate of the frequency of Wilson's disease in a large population, say that of the United States; the information for doing this does not seem to be available. Bearn (1966) estimates the heterozygote frequency as 1/500. This would give us a gene frequency of 0·001, and a homozygote frequency = estimate of Wilson's disease, of 1×10^{-6}. This would seem to be of about the right order.

The Detection of Genetical Carriers

A number of investigators have found abnormally low serum caeruloplasmin concentrations in parents of patients with Wilson's disease (e.g. Neale and Fischer-Williams, 1958; Sass-Kortsak et al., 1959). This suggests that in single dose the abnormal gene may have a detectable metabolic defect. This finding, though, in presumed heterozygotes has been variable. Sternlieb et al. (1961), however, found that measurements of the incorporation of a load of radioactive copper (Cu^{64}) into caeruloplasmin, can provide a fairly reliable means of distinguishing heterozygotes for the Wilson's disease gene from individuals who are homozygous for its normal allele. The quantitative measure of this incorporation of Cu^{64} into caeruloplasmin was the ratio of the concentration of Cu^{64} in serum at 48 hours to that at 1 or 2 hours, after oral ingestion of 2 mg. of copper[64]. In their series of 19 normal controls, 7 patients with Wilson's disease and 19 presumptive heterozygotes for the Wilson's disease gene (parents of patients), Sternlieb and his co-workers found the geometric means of these ratios to be 1·372, 0·171 and 0·510 respectively. The intermediate value for the heterozygotes reflected the diminished efficiency for incorporation of Cu^{64} into caeruloplasmin in the presence of a single Wilson's disease gene. Unfortunately the incorporation of labelled copper into caeruloplasmin appeared to be correlated with age. On account of this, accurate discrimination of the heterozygotes becomes less certain, and the application of the test to individual patients should be made with caution until more information is available with respect to this age effect (Bearn, 1966).

7

EPILEPSY

DEFINITION

Russell Brain (1951) defined the epileptic attack as 'a paroxysmal and transitory disturbance of the function of the brain which develops suddenly, ceases spontaneously', adding 'and exhibits a conspicuous tendency to recur'. Spontaneous neuronic excitation starts at a focus; it may remain limited to that focus, or spread from it; so that the observable phenomena and the subjective experiences may remain localized, or become general as in a major convulsion. It is very doubtful whether the potentiality of spontaneous neuronic excitation is ever manifested under normal conditions in the cerebral cortex; epilepsies which have a cortical focus of origin are nearly always related to a local lesion. To be sure, there seem to be some cases of temporal lobe epilepsy with a genetic basis and without known pathology [see p. 167]; but their status is not yet assured. On the other hand, the deep central masses of grey matter in the brain have retained to a much greater degree than the cortex the capacity to go into excitation autonomously or under relatively slight stimulation from other sources. If this occurs one may see the *petit mal* attack or a spread of excitation over the whole brain in a *grand mal* attack, each of them with a characteristic electroencephalographic (EEG) picture. It seems clear that (1) the potentiality of autonomous excitation in the centrencephalic region, and (2) the potentiality of its spread are basic physiological mechanisms.

The capacity to have epileptic attacks, minor or major, is then universal. It also seems probable that a large proportion of otherwise normal persons do in fact have an epileptic attack at some time in their lives, most probably in childhood, when the occurrence of a major convulsion is particularly common during such upsets as a specific fever. In adolescence, brain stability has increased to the point where such attacks are much less common; but this is the time of life when spontaneously occurring attacks, clinically indistinguishable from minor epileptic attacks with a temporal lobe focus, are experienced very commonly by normal people—in the form of short-lasting feelings of *déjà vu*, depersonalization and unreality.

However, in this book we are concerned with the genetics of psychiatric abnormalities, or deviations from population averages, of such a degree (or capable of becoming of such a degree) as to require medical help. To cover the field of epilepsy we have to adopt a definition which is operational and arbitrary rather than logical. We shall not be concerned with the epileptic-like manifestations of normal individuals, nor with the epileptic attacks which are a common and important symptom, but only a symptom, of brain pathology. We shall have something to say of these 'symptomatic' epilepsies, but mainly to contrast them with the epilepsies without known cause or lesion, the so-called idiopathic epilepsies. As has already been noted, these are the centrencephalic epilepsies.

PREVALENCE OF EPILEPSY AND GENERAL POPULATION MORBIDITY RISK

In the various epidemiological studies of epilepsy it is unusual to distinguish the 'symptomatic' from the 'idiopathic' groups, as we would wish to do; but most of the patients in whose cases there is known organic disease do get otherwise classified, so that the admixture of symptomatic cases in the general total is a small one until one gets on into the later age groups.

The Research Committee of the College of General Practitioners (1960) collected data from a large number of general practices, and found an over-all prevalence rate (of persons having treatment for epileptic attacks) of 419

TABLE 74
PREVALENCE OF EPILEPSY PER 100,000 POPULATION

Edwards *et al.*	1943	United States	515
Military authorities	1944	United States	900
W.H.O.	1955	—	400
Kurland	1959	United States	376
College of Gen. Practs.	1960	United Kingdom	419
Pond *et al.*	1960	United Kingdom	620

per 100,000. Broken down into age groups, there was very much the same figure all through life, though the peak prevalence was in the 15–24 age group. Another British study, very carefully done, by Pond, Bidwell and Stein (1960) defined epileptics as persons who had had a fit of any sort in the previous 2 years or who were on anticonvulsants, and estimated the prevalence in these terms as 620 per 100,000. Again, the figure was fairly steady throughout all age groups, but showed maxima at both extremes of life.

In the United States, Kurland (1959) investigated the incidence and prevalence of convulsive disorders (excluding persons who had had only single or febrile convulsions) in a population of 30,000 (Rochester, Minn.) over a 10 year period. The prevalence of persons so defined, who had had fits in the previous 5 years, or who were on anticonvulsants, was 365 per 100,000 over all age groups, with a peak of 579 per 100,000 in the first 5 years of life declining to 78 per 100,000 in the old age group, 70–79. Morbidity risks were not calculated. These estimates together with others quoted by Koch (1967) are shown in TABLE 74.

Important though the prevalence rate is for social medicine, the geneticist is more concerned with the morbidity risk, i.e. the probability that an individual chosen at random from the general population will become an epileptic (i.e. be known as such to doctors) at some time during his life.

The authors of the report of the College of General Practitioners concluded that about one person in 20 has a fit at some time in his life, and of these about one in 8 develops a chronic epilepsy. This would give a morbidity risk in the general population of 1 in 160. This may be compared with the other estimates in the following tabulation (data from Koch, 1967):

		MORBIDITY RISK AS PER CENT
Panse	1936	0·85
Conrad	1938	0·39
Alström	1950	0·50
Harvald	1954	0·50
General Practitioners	1960	0·625

AGE OF ONSET

If the probability of onset of an epilepsy does not vary so very greatly from one time of life to another, this may be due in part to the confounding of 'symptomatic' with 'idiopathic' cases. When they are separated from one another very different profiles are to be seen [FIG. 20] for these two kinds of syndrome, profiles which are remarkably complementary to one another. If we assume that epilepsies are 'cryptogenic' in about 80 per cent of cases, and 'symptomatic' in 20 per cent, then Peiffer's data enable one to estimate roughly how likely it is that an epilepsy arising at a particular age will have an organic cause for which a search should be made. This is shown in the lowest of the three histograms in FIGURE 20.

ELECTROENCEPHALOGRAPHIC PHENOMENA

As the disturbance of the epileptic fit is mediated electrically in the brain, one might reasonably assume that we would come somewhat closer to the genotypic constitution predisposing to epilepsy by the study of individual variation in electrical performance. This has proved to be true in fact, as has been shown in the study of twins.

Twin Investigations

The first of these was reported by Davis and Davis (1936): in 8 MZ pairs of normal individuals aged 18–58, EEGs taken under standard conditions showed (in the resting phase) as much similarity from twin to twin as in the same individuals between records taken at different times. Further reports of single cases followed from various authors, confirming the close similarity between twins in MZ pairs, and showing much greater differences between twins in DZ pairs. The next major study came from Lennox, Gibbs and Gibbs (1945): 85 per cent of the 55 MZ pairs had practically identical EEGs, 11 per cent doubtfully similar, and 4 per cent (two pairs) were different; on the other hand all but one of the DZ pairs were different.

A rather curious feature of the Lennox material was an incidence of abnormal records higher than might have been expected of a general population sample, perhaps due to the youthfulness of the subjects, perhaps also to unrepresentativeness of the sample. The suspicion that twins, as such, might show more abnormality in their EEGs than normal singletons has not been borne out in later studies.

Some of these have been on a large scale (Hanzawa, 1957: 34 MZ, 50 DZ; Vogel, 1957, 1958, 1965: 110 MZ, 98 DZ). In addition there have been more

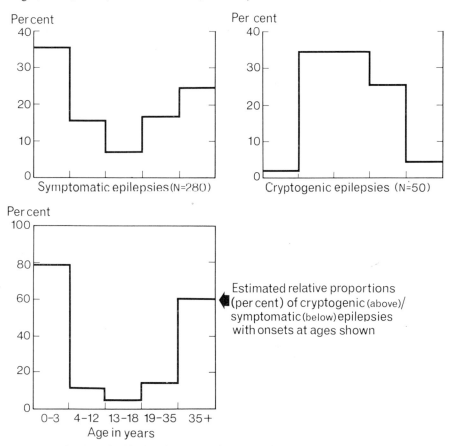

Fig. 20. Distribution (as per cent) of ages of onset of epileptic attacks.
(Data from Peiffer, quoted by Koch, 1967.)

specialized investigations: on 26 pairs of twins aged 50–79 (Heuschert, 1963), and on 8 MZ pairs whose members had been separated from one another in early childhood (Juel-Nielsen and Harvald, 1958). In this last group, the complete concordance within pairs in respect of all important features indicates the probably predominant contribution made by genetic predisposition to brain organization as reflected in the EEG. Shown pairs of records of normal twins, it is in fact an easy task for the electroencephalographer to classify them into MZ and DZ pairs with a low margin of misclassification.

There are a number of respects in which EEGs can be compared with one another: the amount of energy output at all frequencies and its relative distribution between them; and the quantitative aspects of reactions to eye closure and opening, hyperventilation, reduction of oxygen intake, barbiturates, natural sleep, etc. It has also been shown by studies on twins that the way the EEG characteristic for the individual develops, over the period from childhood into maturity, is largely a product of the genetical constitution.

Family Investigations

As well as their very important twin work, Vogel and his collaborators have carried out a series of family investigations, involving many hundreds of normal individuals and their relatives. (Vogel, 1965, 1966a, 1966b; Vogel and Götze, 1959; Vogel and Helmbold, 1959). In this work emphasis was placed not on the general features of EEG profiles, but on specific precisely (or nearly precisely) definable patterns. This work has proved exceptionally productive and interesting and should stimulate trials along parallel lines in other centres. A number of such patterns appear to be normal variants, shown by a small or very small minority of the general population, determined each by a major dominant autosomal gene, and not, it seems, predisposing to behaviour disorders or other psychopathology. They can be listed:

1. A low-voltage EEG with absence or reduction of occipital alpha (1959).
2. The 'Niederspannungs-EEG', characterized by the non-appearance of α-waves after eye-closure. Population frequency estimated at 7 per cent (1962).
3. 14 and 6/sec positive spikes in sleep in youthful individuals (a twin study, 1965).
4. High frequency (25–30/sec) β-waves of relatively low voltage, shown in frontal leads: population frequency 0·45 per cent (1966).
5. Another β-wave syndrome, at lower frequency (20–25) and higher voltage with a precentral maximum, more frequent in the EEG than type 4 above, great variability, may be almost continuous. Population frequency estimated as 1·47 per cent in young men (1966).
6. Replacement of the α-waves by 16–19/sec β-waves which show an occipital maximum and are blocked by opening of the eyes. Population frequency in young males 0·6 per cent (1966).

Rodin (1964) and Petersén and Åkesson (1968) have confirmed the occurrence of 14 and 6/sec spikes (No. 3 in the above list) in the families of index cases, and the latter found approximately 50 per cent of sibs showed the trait; they agree that dominant autosomal inheritance is the first possibility but other modes of transmission are not excluded.

Clearly much further work along these lines is needed. Although psychopathology has not been implicated so far, it seems most improbable that none of these normal variants are associated with particular psychological features, or with any variation in morbid risks.

ELECTROENCEPHALOGRAPHIC-CLINICAL SYNDROMES

Corresponding to the electroencephalographic normal variants, possibly controlled by a single major gene, we have the recent discovery of syndromes of some specificity manifesting both in the EEG and in recognizable clinical phenomena. Of these the most important is the centrencephalic petit mal syndrome.

In a series of papers (1960, 1961a and b) Metrakos and Metrakos have produced very striking evidence that this syndrome (centrencephalic spike and wave records and clinical petit mal) is predisposed to by a single major autosomal

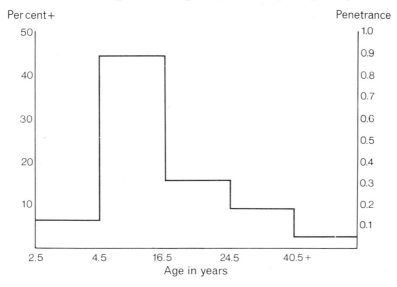

Fig. 21. Proportion of parents and sibs with positive EEGs within age limits shown. (Data from Metrakos and Metrakos, 1960, 1961.)

gene, with penetrance that varies with age. This can be seen from FIGURE 21 showing the proportions of first-degree relatives (parents and sibs) manifesting the same type of EEG at various ages, their observations being:

AGE LIMITS	NUMBER OF SIBS/PARENTS TESTED	EEG+	HYPOTHETICAL PENETRANCE
$2\frac{1}{2}$ years	16	1	0·13
$4\frac{1}{2}$ to $16\frac{1}{2}$	146	65	0·89
$16\frac{1}{2}$ to $24\frac{1}{2}$	26	4	0·31
$24\frac{1}{2}$ to $40\frac{1}{2}$	147	13	0·18
$40\frac{1}{2}$	40	1	0·05

The hypothesis seems to be a reasonable one; and when one considers that (1) the potentiality of convulsive phenomena is normal and (2) the petit mal syndrome of childhood is a very benign one, one might well feel like regarding this particular clinical syndrome as very much on a par with the normal electro-encephalographic deviants described above.

This genetical theory has been objected to by Koch on the grounds that, although concordance in MZ twins in respect of the centrencephalic spike and wave type record is very high, still it is not 100 per cent; he points out, however, that as the electrically recognizable state is so dependent on age and, presumably, so much under control from maturation processes, it is not unreasonable to expect even MZ twins to differ from one another to some extent in their maturation level at any one time. It is perhaps worth noting that Critchley and Williams (1939) have reported an MZ pair, both twins with abnormal EEGs but only one of them with petit mal. Manifestation will be even less complete as a clinically than as an electroencephalographically recognizable state.

The other objection made to the Metrakos theory was by Jung, who pointed out that this type of EEG is to be found at times in epilepsies whose symptomatic nature can be regarded as sure.

It seems to us that neither of these objections carries great weight. The gene must be a fairly common one, and if focal damage to the brain had any tendency towards releasing its effects even after it had become latent, a most plausible possibility, the Jung objection would be met. The twins discordant for the centrencephalic EEG abnormality do not greatly affect the issue, as it is not supposed that the gene reaches 100 per cent penetrance even at the most susceptible age.

Petit mal syndromes of childhood, if they do not clear up spontaneously, are likely to be continued into generalized convulsions in later life. Niedermeyer (1966) discusses the evidence that this syndrome can be attributed to a major autosomal dominant, with penetrance very low under the age of 4 and again after 16. He draws attention to the technical difficulties in distinguishing the EEG pattern in such cases, since the very occurrence of major fits is likely to bring about consequent changes in the EEG, both 'secondary temporalization' and 'secondary bilateral synchrony'.

A related but distinct syndrome has been described by Doose et al. (1967). They took EEG recordings from 161 sibs of children suffering from convulsive disorders and showing abnormal theta rhythms; these were compared with 149 healthy controls. Theta rhythms are found in normal children, equally frequently in boys and girls, and with maximum incidence between the ages of 2–4 years, tailing off after the age of 7 or so. In the control population studied they were found in 11–12 per cent, but in the sibs of the proband group in 35 per cent of those aged 2–7, in 54 per cent of those aged 2–4. The correlated special types of spikes and waves were registered in 8 per cent of the siblings of probands and in 0·8 per cent of the controls. Numbers were large enough to ensure the statistical reliability of these findings. The authors regard this theta rhythmicity as a symptom of a gene-controlled disposition to convulsive phenomena of the centrencephalic type; they think an autosomal dominant mode of inheritance possible. No relationships were found with other factors known to play a part in the aetiology of epilepsy.

Another syndrome which rests on a fairly solid observational basis is familial temporal-central focal epilepsy, so named by the first to describe it (Bray et al., 1965). Index cases were selected on a basis of a focal temporal lobe EEG spike abnormality, and 12 familes were found with affected relatives. The condition is attributed to an autosomal dominant gene with a penetrance low in the first 5 years of life, reaching approximately 50 per cent between the ages of 5 and 15, and dropping again to a low level after the age of 20. Vogel has pointed out that a multifactorial genetical model is not to be excluded.

In their report (1969) on an investigation sponsored by the French League Against Epilepsy, Loiseau and Beaussart gave an account of special studies conducted on 51 cases of 'partial epilepsy' in which there was a family history. The largest identifiable sub-group and the only one suggesting the manifestation of a single gene, consisted of 15 cases showing the following features: (1) clinical evidence of generalized or focal motor fits or unilateral seizures, often nocturnal; (2) in the EEG paroxysms of spikes or spikes and waves over the lower part of the Rolandic region; and (3) onset between the ages of 3–8 years, with the disappearance of both the seizures and the EEG abnormalities at puberty. Loiseau and Beaussart identify this syndrome with that described by Bray et al.

Barslund and Danielsen (1963) have given an account of three pairs of MZ twins, all female, all concordant or partially concordant for a syndrome which, from the account given, is indistinguishable from Bray and Wiser's. In the first pair both children were subject to temporal lobe epileptic attacks, one showing bilateral spikes, the other changes mainly in the temporal area; a daughter of twin 1 had temporal spikes but no clinical epilepsy. In the second pair both twins had major and minor attacks, a normal EEG record being made in only one while the other had sharp waves in the left temporal region; a cousin and a grandmother common to them all have had epilepsy. In the third pair one twin had first absences and later convulsions, the EEG showing long runs of spikes and waves; the twin had minor attacks and a bitemporally abnormal EEG, and she has two epileptic children. The authors describe also a sibship in which two sisters and a brother all have bitemporal abnormal EEGs and two of them have fits; and a pair of sisters both with temporal foci and attacks.

Perhaps further support for the existence of the Bray and Wiser syndrome can be found in the report by Rodin and Whelan (1960). They compared EEG findings in 27 children of 10 matings in which one parent exhibited a paroxysmal temporal dysrhythmia, with the 20 children of 10 pairs where neither parent showed such an anomaly; in the first group 14 of the 27 children, in the second group none of the 20 children, showed a similar temporal dysrhythmia.

Verner, Johnson and Merritt (1966) have described a syndrome combining temporal lobe dysrhythmia (and emotional instability) with café au lait spots. They found 60 patients with this combination, having at least one café au lait spot, and 52 of them had one or more similarly affected relatives. Twelve such relatives studied by EEG showed a temporal dysrhythmia, and over half of the children of the patients had café au lait spots. In the case of 15 patients an air encephalogram gave evidence of cortical atrophy. The familial findings lead the authors to suggest an autosomal dominant.

It seems probable, then, that there are quite a number of major genes in circulation whose most obvious effect is to produce a clinically recognizable epilepsy. Alström (1950), in his large-scale studies of the families of epileptics came across several in which the epileptic tendency seemed to be inherited as a

(1)

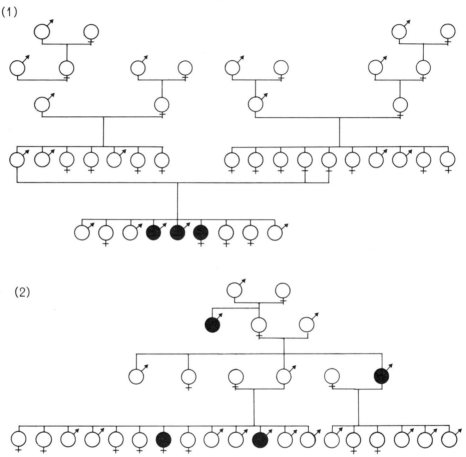

(2)

Fig. 22. Two pedigrees from Alström (1950)

1. Suggesting an autosomal recessive gene.
2. Suggesting an autosomal dominant with diminished penetrance.

dominant, irregularly manifesting dominant, autosomal or sex-linked recessive. Two of these pedigrees are shown in FIGURE 22. Other investigators have come across similar curiosities. Kimball and Hersh (1955) found a family in which the epileptic tendency had been transmitted as a dominant over 300 years; and another interesting family with presumable autosomal dominant inheritance has been reported by Ounsted (1955). The patient and four members of his family showed the trait, the boy's twin sister, another sister, their mother and her brother's daughter. In all five cases the disorder consisted in frequent generalized grand mal seizures, occurring mainly at night between the hours of 2 and 5 a.m. In all cases onset was in the first 2 years of life, and a full remission occurred within the next 2 years. All the relatives developed normally; but the patient himself was held back for a time by a hyperkinetic syndrome which came on after (presumable brain damage from) status epilepticus at the age of 17 months.

It must not be supposed that simple major gene inheritance is anything but unusual in epilepsy, even in somewhat specific special types. An inheritable predisposition is clearly demonstrable in such conditions as pyknolepsy, 'propulsive petit mal', 'impulsive petit mal', in the temporal lobe epilepsies by and large, and even in the established cases of 'symptomatic' epilepsy. There is no need to think in any of these of anything more specific than polygenic inheritable factors. The familial and clinical findings are in conformity with the view that, in the case of the symptomatic epilepsies, a sub-threshold predisposition can be brought into manifestation by the presence of a lesion.

One of the more interesting semi-specific epileptic predispositions is shown in one of the 'reflex' epilepsies, so-called photogenic epilepsy. This has attracted a good deal of experimental attention, as the epileptogenic stimulus can be quantified. What is critical for the subject is the alternation of relative light and darkness, and the rhythm with which it occurs. Members of the subject's family can usually be found who show the same tendency, though in perhaps lesser degree. Quantitative variation in the degree of the susceptibility can presumably be related to a quantitatively variable degree of predisposition, depending on multifactorial inheritance.

THE PROGRESSIVE MYOCLONIC EPILEPSY OF UNVERRICHT AND LUNDBORG

The literature was comprehensively reviewed by Novelletto (1958), since when there has been no important new acquisition of knowledge. For the literature relating to this and other myoclonic disorders, the reader should consult Pratt (1967). The syndrome is further discussed on page 254.

The Unverricht-Lundborg syndrome is a very rare condition. Novelletto collected 26 cases from the literature, which had been followed through from onset to death, and the individual particulars he presented in his Table 1 can be summarized as follows:

YEARS OF	RANGE	MEAN	S.D.
Age at onset of epilepsy	3–17	12·4	3·79
Age at onset of myoclonus	3–21	14·9	3·44
Age at death	6–33	20·3	6·34
Duration onset to death	2–26	7·9	6·25

The epilepsy is of the centrencephalic type, manifesting both as petit and grand mal seizures; and EEG studies show myoclonic and epileptic disturbances originating centrally, probably in the thalamic and mesencephalic regions of the

12

brain. Psychiatrically, the condition is interesting in that schizophrenia-like symptoms and states are not uncommon in the early stages, psycho-organic symptoms of all kinds occur during the course of the disease, and there is usually some degree of dementia before death.

The condition is determined by an autosomal recessive gene, which leads to an enzymic deficiency (presumably), since an amyloid-like substance is laid down, particularly in the central grey matter of the brain, but also later in the cerebral and cerebellar cortex. Edgar (1963) has suggested that a storage process is involved, and that the pathological basis is an alteration of glycogen metabolism. Sometimes very distinctive 'Lafora bodies' are observed in the brain, but not in all cases. It is possible that not one but two different genes at different loci (conceivably two allelomorphs at the one locus) may be held responsible. Yanoff and Schwarz (1965) claim that 'Lafora's disease' is a distinct genetical entity.

THE GENERALIZED SYNDROME

The history of genetical investigations in epilepsy enters the modern era with the classical papers of Klaus Conrad (1935–38). Up till this time there had been a number of investigations of the frequency of epilepsy in the parents, sibs and children of epileptics; but though they had all yielded consistent estimates in the neighbourhood of 3 or 4 per cent, this figure was too low to be reconciled with expectations on a Mendelian basis, and the studies were themselves unsystematic and on a restricted scale. There were indeed many clinical authorities who doubted whether heredity played any part at all. Conrad's work settled this point once and for all.

Twin Investigations

Conrad's most important contribution was a study of twins, and it is somewhat ironic that his first publication was just anticipated by another large-scale twin study from Aaron Rosanoff. The contribution by Rosanoff, with his collaborators, to psychiatric genetics has never received the honour it deserved. He succeeded in collecting large numbers of twin patients from State hospitals in the United States, and provided concordance figures which—despite the unsystematic way in which they were gathered—have stood in very fair conformity with later results. He was a pioneer in the field, who had entered it quite independently of the German school, deriving his inspiration (most probably) directly from the father of twin studies, Francis Galton. Three important twin studies, in epilepsy, manic-depression and schizophrenia respectively, all appeared in 1934; but despite the weighty evidence they offered, they made remarkably little impact. The dominant current of thought in the United States at that time stemmed from Adolf Meyer, in a conceptual scheme with which the idea of genetical determination was almost wholly incompatible. When a revolutionary change eventually took place, it was in the direction of Freudian psychoanalysis, and Rosanoff was left as heretical a figure as ever. Even American clinical psychology, which has salvaged so much of the ideas of European psychiatry, found little use for Francis Galton and his American disciple.

The work of Conrad could not be so lightly dismissed, at least among psychiatrists in Europe who read the German literature. Its outstanding features were the massive scale on which it was conducted and the scrupulous care that was taken to avoid the known sources of statistical bias. The basic material consisted of all the 12,561 epileptics in hospitals and institutions in the entire German Reich. This then was not a possibly biased sample but an entire national group. In later years it was criticized as not being representative of epileptics in the general population, since it was only those sufferers who were unable to carry on in the community, so severely affected as to have to be in hospital, who would be sampled for twins. This criticism, true though its factual basis is, does not in any way invalidate the results of Conrad's work; all that is necessary is to remember that his conclusions apply to a specially severely affected group of epileptics and can be generalized only with reservations.

At the time when Conrad did his work, a greater danger was seen in the possibility of selective bias in ascertaining the twins, especially the danger of a bias in favour of ascertaining MZ and concordant pairs. For this reason the enormous administrative labour was undertaken of finding the birth date and place of birth of all the 12,561 epileptics, going back to the local birth registers, discovering whether a twin had been born at the same time, and then following up this twin through all the agencies which might supply information. In this way a total of 253 epileptic proband members of a twin birth was obtained, a number higher than expected on the known twin birth rate. There was, in fact, a statistically significant excess of twins and, particularly, an excess of DZ twins. Perhaps a balanced excess of twins could have been expected in view of the greater perinatal risks attending a twin birth; but the excess of DZ pairs is hard to explain and has not yet been either confirmed in another large series or adequately accounted for.

Very many of the co-twins had died under the age of 5 years (and so before an arbitrarily assigned beginning of an age of risk), and were therefore discarded; a small number of co-twins had disappeared or had to be omitted for lack of information. For the clinical-statistical investigation there remained 30 MZ and 127 DZ pairs. Here a second stage of very punctilious work was entered on, in investigating all of the same-sexed twin pairs, in which both twins were alive, with the most approved methods of determining zygosity. Blood grouping was not available at this time, finger-prints had not been established as a useful discriminant, and Conrad relied on anthropological measurements.

He found that two-thirds (20 out of 30) of the MZ pairs were concordant for epilepsy, but only 3 per cent DZ pairs. Conrad's clinical work was as careful as his anthropometric work, and on its basis he classified the epileptic probands into 'symptomatic' cases and 'idiopathic' ones. On this basis he provides the following tabulation:

CONCORDANT FOR EPILEPSY OR EPILEPTIC EQUIVALENTS	'SYMPTOMATIC'		'IDIOPATHIC'	
	N	C	N	C
Opposite-sexed pairs	20	—	56	4
Same-sexed DZ pairs	14	—	41	—
Same-sexed ?Z pairs	1	—	2	1
MZ pairs	8	1	22	19

What stands out is the very large difference in respect of frequency of concordance between the MZ and DZ pairs in the 'idiopathic' group and the negligible difference in the 'symptomatic'; it would seem that heredity plays a massive role in the former syndrome, but only a very small part in the latter.

Conrad supported this part of the work with careful individual clinical studies of the concordant MZ pairs (1936a) and the discordant MZ pairs (1936b). It is of some interest to tabulate the findings in 15 pairs which he reports in detail [TABLE 75]. Conrad's further work on the children of epileptics is discussed on page 174.

TABLE 75

CONRAD'S CONCORDANT OR PARTIALLY CONCORDANT
MZ TWINS

CASE NO.	SEX	AGE OF ONSET OF ATTACKS MINOR/PRODROMATA	MAJOR	FIT FREQUENCY	PSYCHIATRICALLY	TWILIGHT STATES	NEUROL.	NOTES
54	M	5 to 6	10	++	p+, d±	+	—	
		5 to 6	12	++	p+, d±	+	—	
55	F	7 to 9	25	±	p+, d+, psychosis	+	—	t.l.s.
		7 to 9	23	±	p+	+	+	t.l.s.
56	F		5 to 6	±	m.def., p+ d+		—	
			5 to 6	+	m.def., p+ d+		+	
57	M	4	13	++	p+ d+		+	
		4	13	++	p+ d+	+	+	
58	F		15	+++	p++ d++	+	—	
			15	+++	p++ d+++	+	—	
59	M	6	15	++		+		d. 27
		6	15	++	p++ d+++	+	+	
60	M		18	++	p+ d+	+	—	
			19	+			—	
61	F		25	±			—	
			26	±		+	—	
6	F		9	+	p+ d+	+	—	
			9	+		+	—	
62	M		2	±	severe m. def.		+	
			2	±	severe m. def.		+	
63	M		14	+		+	—	
		14	15	++	p++ d++	+	—	
64	F		24	+	p+ d+	+	+	had meningitis
		12	13	++	p+ d+			d. 38
65	F		1½	++	m. def.		+	
			1½	±	m. def.		+	
66	M	1	3	++	? (psychotic)	+	—	
		1	3		normal			fits ceased at 3
67	M		2	++	severe m. def.		+	
			10	±	m. def.		+	

Clinical details summarized from his case histories (1936).
p = personality change; d = dementia; m. def. = mental deficiency; t.l.s. = temporal lobe syndrome.

All this gave the death-blow to the hypothesis that, if sufficiently careful investigation were made of every case, all epilepsies would prove to be 'symptomatic', and as a rule due to a local lesion which had been caused by some environmental noxa. This view was accepted very widely, and indeed almost universally by one of the leading schools, that of the French neurologists, in the earlier decades of the twentieth century. If there had been any survivors among its adherents, they would have been silenced by a stream of work on the genetical aspects of epilepsy which has followed on Conrad. A conspectus of the twin series which have been reported from time to time is given in TABLE 76, simplified from a more detailed table provided by Koch (1967).

TABLE 76

ACCUMULATED RESULTS OF STUDIES OF EPILEPTICS AND THEIR TWINS
(From Koch, 1967)

INVESTIGATORS	YEAR	MZ TWINS		DZ TWINS	
		N	CONCORDANT	N	CONCORDANT
Rosanoff et al.	1934	23	14	84	20
Schulte	1934	10	2	12	—
Conrad	1935	30	20	127	4
Alström	1950	2	—	14	—
Castellis and Fuster	1952	2	1	4	—
Ellebjerg	1952	7	3	12	—
Slater	1953	2	—	12	—
Schimmelpenning	1955	4	2	15	—
Bormann	1956	5	2	15	2
Lafon et al.	1956	7	5	—	—
Kamide, Inouye, Suzuki	1957–60	26	14	14	1
Lennox	1960	95	59	130	19
Braconi	1962	20	13	31	4
Totals		233	135	470	50

With the Japanese series we enter the era of EEG investigation. Kamide (1957) and Inouye (1960) reported the clinical findings, and Suzuki (1960) the EEG results. Inouye's report shows:

CONCORDANCE/DISCORDANCE	MZ		DZ	
	CONC	DISC	CONC	DISC
in respect of epileptic attacks	14	12	1	13
combining EEG with clinical findings	20	6	2	7

Clearly one is getting somewhat closer to the genotype if one penetrates into brain physiology rather more deeply than clinical expertise alone permits.

The same lesson can be learned from the work of Braconi, concordances going up [see TABLE 76] from 65 per cent to 80 per cent in the MZ, and from 12 per cent to 35 per cent in DZ pairs, when EEG findings were added to the clinical ones. Considering the 'idiopathic' pairs separately 11 of 12 MZ pairs and 8 of 16 DZ pairs were concordant.

The massive work of Lennox and his collaborators, the Gibbses, confirmed previous results. To them we owe the largest contribution to case material, but unfortunately not systematically ascertained. This means that selection may have been biased, but there is no positive evidence that it was. The concordances found by Lennox and Lennox (1960) in respect of EEG findings in the co-twins of epileptic patients are shown in TABLE 77.

TABLE 77

TWIN CONCORDANCES IN RESPECT OF EEG ABNORMALITIES

(Lennox and Lennox, 1960, quoted by Koch, 1967)

	MZ		DZ	
	N	CONC.	N	CONC.
3/sec Spike and wave	19	16	14	–
2/sec Spike and wave	6	3	3	–
High amplitude long waves or spikes	15	9	28	1
Total All changes	40	28	45	1

Family Investigations

Some scepticism about the genetical contribution to the causation of epilepsy has tended to persist in France, as may be seen from the papers contributed to the Symposium on Epilepsy and Heredity, Paris, 1967 (*Epilepsia*, 1969). Although this congress came to conclusions supporting a significant hereditary contribution, there were dissentients; and a number of papers were contributions to an attempt to define a 'hereditary epilepsy' which would be clinically distinguishable from non-hereditary epilepsies. Not unexpectedly, evidence accumulated in the course of the congress that there were not one but many hereditary epilepsies.

It is again to Conrad that we owe the first well-designed investigation into the families of epileptics, i.e. into the frequency of epilepsy and other psychiatric abnormalities in the children of epileptics. Conrad was particularly interested in the children because of the Nazi compulsory sterilization laws which were coming into force at the time he did his work. With the help of State registers he ascertained 553 epileptics each with not less than one child over the age of 20 years. Of the 2,599 children 655 had died in infancy. Classifying the epileptic parents into 'idiopathic', 'intermediate' and 'symptomatic' clinical types, the incidence of epilepsy in the children was found to be 6·0, 2·7 and 1·6 per cent respectively. The incidence of other abnormalities (mental deficiency, psychoses, abnormal personality) was also found to differ sharply from group to group, with the children of the 'symptomatic' group showing no departure from general population norms, while the children of the 'idiopathic' group were heavily handicapped in every way, showing among other things raised incidences of criminality and suicide. Current opinion discounts the significance of these findings. It seems probable that Conrad was sampling an extremely depressed social class, and that the high incidence of mental subnormality, etc. in the children reflected the restricted range of consorts available to these very handicapped patients and their disorganized home lives.

An investigation of unusual interest was carried out by Pohlisch, Tröger and Feige (Pohlisch, 1950, quoted by Koch, 1967), in that in order to get nearer to the genotype they chose as their *epileptic* index cases sib pairs, both members of the pair suffering from the condition. They balanced 50 such pairs with 50 *traumatic* epilepsy cases, in which epilepsy had begun after severe brain damage.

In the first, second and third-degree relatives of the *traumatic* cases there was no excess of epilepsy; but in relatives of corresponding degree in the *epileptic* series the incidence of epilepsy was estimated as between 4 and 8 per cent, 1 and 2 per cent, and about 0·6 per cent respectively. It is noteworthy that this epilepsy material showed only the usual increase of risk in relatives, a fact to be borne in mind when we come to consider genetical models for epilepsy.

A corrective to Conrad's gloomy picture of the outlook for the children of epileptics was provided by Alström (1950). His probands were 897 epileptics clinically investigated in the University Neurological Clinic, Stockholm. These patients were not severely affected and partially incapacitated like Conrad's patients, but much more nearly representative of the epileptics of the general population. Alström rejected the distinction between 'idiopathic' and 'symptomatic' cases, and grouped them into those of known (K), probably known (P) and unknown (U) causation, more than two thirds of all index cases being in the last category. The risk of epilepsy for first-degree relatives in each of these three groups can be tabulated as below:

RISK OF EPILEPSY (AS PER CENT) IN RELATIVES OF	GROUP K	GROUP P	GROUP U	ALL
Parents	1·2	1·8	1·7	1·7
Sibs	1·5	1·2	1·9	1·7
Children	3·2	5·4	4·0	4·1
All relatives				1·9

There are two noteworthy features about these results: (1) the very low morbidity risks, little more than might be expected of a general population sample; and (2) the lack of any sharp difference between the three clinical groups. Alström concluded that there was no support for a single-gene hypothesis, dominant or recessive, for the great majority of epilepsies. He thought the hypothesis of a dominant with a very low rate of manifestation was possible, but very unlikely in view of the way in which such a gene would be eliminated over the generations by natural selection. He thought, moreover, that multifactorial inheritance determining a 'seizure-threshold' could not be supported. He ends his discussion by saying that, presumably, 'all epilepsy may be focal'; 'epilepsy, even that in a so-called "nuclear group", is not a disease *sui generis* but must be interpreted as a neurological clinical symptom of a pathological irritation of the central nervous system. . . . The fact that no uniform mode of hereditary transmission is found for a symptom of so general a nature is then explicable.'

At the time when Alström was making his study epileptics in Sweden were under a serious civil disability, in that they were prohibited from marrying without a State permit. This restriction was a very ancient one and based rather on a taboo than on rational grounds. Alström's work showed that neither epileptic patients themselves nor their progeny had any very marked tendency to be mentally defective, psychopathic or criminal. He criticized the eugenic laws and recommended their repeal. As a consequence, the ancient prohibition was rescinded, and sufferers from epilepsy at last enjoyed the same civil rights as everyone else.

It is interesting to reflect on the change in public attitudes between those days and now. Compulsory provisions interfering with the reproductive lives of biologically handicapped individuals are now entirely out of fashion. Where they were once in force, as in some States of the United States, Denmark and Sweden, they have largely become inoperative. However, whereas at one time liberally minded people felt it was inhumane to deprive anyone, however unfortunate, of the elementary human right to parentage and the enjoyment of family life, now the pendulum has begun to swing back again. We shall not again be much worried by eugenic bogeys, but we are becoming more and more concerned that children should not be denied the elementary human right of being born to and brought up by healthy, normally intelligent, loving parents, living in harmony with one another.

Alström's negation of the hereditary factor was, we may think, pressed too far, even perhaps further than his own data warranted. In a review of his monograph by Steinberg and Mulder (1951) it was pointed out that in his material the risk of epilepsy in the sibs of propositi was 0·9 per cent when neither parent was epileptic, and 5·1 per cent when one parent was epileptic. Such a sharp difference is not to be accounted for very easily on any other than a genetical hypothesis.

Later workers have combined EEG investigation with clinical studies of the relatives of epileptics. The results of Harvald's extensive survey are shown in TABLE 78; and a table summarizing the principal results of other workers in TABLE 79.

TABLE 78

RELATIVES OF THREE GROUPS OF EPILEPTIC PROPOSITI (CLASSIFIED BY TYPE OF EEG ABNORMALITY); PERCENTAGE INCIDENCE BY SEX OF DIFFERENT GRADES AND KINDS OF EEG ABNORMALITY

(From Harvald, 1954, modified)

		NUMBER AND PER CENT OF RELATIVES WITH ABNORMAL EEG RECORDS, BY SEX							
PROPOSITI WITH		FIRST-DEGREE RELATIVES				SECOND-DEGREE AND REMOTER			
		N	S	M	F	N	S	M	F
1. Markedly abnormal	m	145	21	10	1	114	15	7	—
EEG (non-focal)	f	147	37	18	1	104	41	11	1
2. Normal or slightly	m	69	29	4	—	22	14	—	—
abnormal EEG	f	54	41	4	—	36	36	3	—
3. Focally abnormal	m	67	7	—	—	42	12	—	—
EEG	f	65	22	5	—	36	33	8	—
Controls	m	693	13	3	1				

s = slightly abnormal, m = markedly abnormal, f = focally abnormal.

TABLE 79

INCIDENCE OF EEG ABNORMALITY, INCLUDING BORDERLINE ABNORMALI-
TIES, IN FIRST DEGREE RELATIVES (PARENTS, SIBS, CHILDREN) OF EPILEPTICS
(Adapted from Koch, 1967)

| | | NUMBER OF | | PER CENT ABNORMAL EEG | |
INVESTIGATORS	YEAR	PROBANDS	RELATIVES	RELATIVES	CONTROLS
Löwenbach	1939	11	37	46	
Strauss *et al.*	1939	31	93	28	
Lennox *et al.*	1940	94	183	60	16
Harvald	1954	237	547	36	13
Vercelletto	1955	109	158	45	
Richter	1956	43	87	35	

The incidence of EEG abnormality in first-degree relatives is very much higher than the 5 or 6 per cent or so of first-degree relatives found subject to epileptic attacks. On the other hand, investigations of control populations show surprisingly high incidences of EEG abnormality judged by the same standards.

MODE OF INHERITANCE

The previous discussion has shown that the pattern of electrophysiologic activity in the brain can take on a variety of forms in normal individuals, and that these variant constitutional patterns tend to repeat in their relatives in a way that suggests a basis in major autosomal genes. We must consider the possibility that there are a relatively large number of such genes, each of them causing a departure from the norm, as regards EEG criteria, but not causing any enhanced tendency (as far as we yet can tell) to behavioural abnormalities, such as psychopathic or convulsive disorders.

There is also evidence of several single major genes, again dominant and autosomal, which cause both a recognizable deviation in the constitutional EEG pattern and also a tendency to petit and grand mal. The epileptic tendency in these cases tends to be relatively mild, to show up only in childhood or adolescence, and to be controlled in the mature brain. Again in such cases, there is no evidence to show that these single major genes cause anything one can call pathological.

An exception has to be made of the gene determining progressive myoclonic epilepsy (Unverricht—Lundborg): this is a recessive gene, and as with most such genes its effects are malignant. However, it stands almost alone in this. We can dismiss the possibility that recessive genes and (equally) sex-linked genes play any important part in the causation of epilepsy. Family histories show an equal excess of epileptics in all three types of first-degree relatives, parents, sibs and children, which can be fitted either to a dominant or a polygenic model—but it is incompatible with recessivity. Furthermore, the total lack of any increased rate of cousin marriage in the parents of epileptics is almost conclusive in the same sense.

In addition to the major dominant genes whose existence we suspect, we can be reasonably certain that polygenic inheritance plays a considerable role. The electrophysiological activity of the brain is responsive to a great variety of agents, both chemical and blood borne, and electronic, e.g. via signals along neuronic pathways. The ways in which the brain reacts to such stimuli differ from individual to individual by imperceptible degrees; and the only reasonable picture we can form of the genetic contribution to this reactivity has to be multifactorial. We must also expect interactions between gene effects. A single major gene, harmless in one individual, might be the cause of dangerous disequilibration in another individual, of somewhat different make-up in the polygenic respect.

This would seem a tenable hypothesis, rather more complex than one would wish to choose, and correspondingly flexible and difficult to test and rebut. But most of its complexities seem to be called for by the evidence, and nothing simpler suggests itself.

Both Alström (1950) and Harvald (1954) have pointed out the difficulties in the way of accepting a genetical theory of the epilepsies involving dominant genes. The argument is that epileptics are known to have a higher mortality, a lower mean expectation of life, a reduced marriage rate, and within marriage a lower fertility, than average members of the population; there has also been some suggestion that infant mortality is higher in the children they do have. There have been a number of estimates of the 'fitness' of the epileptic, in the main centring around a figure of 0·5 or 0·6. Given this reduced fitness of the gene, it should be rather rapidly eliminated by natural selection, even if it has a reduced penetrance. The fact that epilepsy is such a common condition is, then, a powerful objection to hypotheses involving dominance.

But who are the epileptics who have proved so 'unfit'? We must suppose that a large part of observed epilepsies are symptomatic, i.e. depending on a local brain lesion. Such cases are of relatively poor to bad prognosis, and the psychiatric complications of epilepsy (personality change, psychoses and dementia) occur mainly in this group of epileptics and not in the centrencephalic group. There is an important exception to this statement: a centrencephalic epilepsy persisting over a number of years and involving a considerable number of grand mal attacks, not infrequently becomes complicated by secondary brain damage, and by additional focal fits. However, such a change is very unusual in the centrencephalic epilepsies, which nearly always remit in later adolescence and early maturity. These milder epilepsies, accordingly, which include by far the greatest number of genetically determined epilepsies, do not require admission to hospital, do not suffer from psychiatric complications, and have escaped ascertainment in the series investigated by nearly all observers who have concerned themselves with mortality, marital state and fertility.

There is, in fact, no evidence that the centrencephalic epileptic has less than average biological 'fitness', and it is quite possible that he is above rather than below average in this respect. If the question is to be adequately investigated, a prospective study of a cohort of epileptics followed up over a reproductive lifetime would have to be made.

THE 'SYMPTOMATIC' EPILEPSIES

Niedermeyer (1966) has (very sensibly) suggested that the epilepsies should not be dichotomized into, let us say, idiopathic and symptomatic types, but 'trichotomized' into: (1) centrencephalic epilepsy; (2) epilepsy due to cerebral disorder; and (3) convulsions due to extracerebral causes.

Convulsive symptoms arising from causes in this last category are not our concern in this book at all, but a few words must be said about them. They are, of course, very common indeed, in that a large proportion of the population exhibit some symptoms of this kind at some time in their lives. Probably the commonest cause is the febrile reactions of children, but fits are very probable complications of such conditions as eclampsia, uraemia, hypoglycaemia, barbiturate withdrawal, alcohol withdrawal and delirium tremens, among a vast range of other conditions. There is no evidence worth discussing that genetic factors play a role of the slightest importance in predisposing the individual, who is so unlucky as to suffer from one of these conditions, towards either having fits or not having them. These patients do not come into the medical category of persons called 'epileptic' for sound and obvious reasons— aetiology, treatment and prognosis have no relationship with and no relevance to the like aspects of those conditions which are accepted as 'epileptic'.

However, a connexion in the lifetime of a single patient may arise. A grand mal attack causes a temporary cerebral hypoxia; and a series of grand mal attacks can cause very dangerous and probably damaging cerebral hypoxia. It is therefore possible for a normal individual, not predisposed to epilepsy but caused to have convulsive attacks from a non-cerebral cause, to develop small cerebral lesions (very likely in one or both temporal lobes); and further for these lesions to prove epileptogenic. In fact convulsive symptomatology can be the cause of a chronic epilepsy.

The same considerations apply, *a fortiori*, to the states in which convulsive attacks are caused by a brain lesion. Given the epileptogenic focus, repeated grand mal attacks are likely to occur; and unfortunately this convulsive tendency is usually more difficult to control by anticonvulsant drugs than the centrencephalic epilepsies. Repeated episodes of cerebral hypoxia cause multiplication of lesions, and a progressively disorganized cerebral electrophysiological state.

This danger exists even in the mild and benign centrencephalic epilepsies. Very often this type of epilepsy manifests only in petit mal attacks, which are without danger even when they occur repeated in large numbers over a short time interval (pyknolepsy). The petit mal attack does not involve interference with blood supply to the brain, and accordingly is not likely to lead to complications. However, if the brain is very unstable, if there is, perhaps, a more than normal tendency for the bilateral spread of fit frequencies, then petit mal attacks can go on into a petit mal plus grand mal syndrome. If the grand mal attacks are frequent and severe, the centrencephalic epilepsy can complicate itself with one or more focal epilepsies, once again very probably with a temporal focus (or foci).

While there is some evidence to suggest that the occurrence of a focal epilepsy, secondary to a local brain lesion, may be more probable in some genetical constitutions than in others, there is no reason to regard the genetical predisposition as of any pathological significance. As has been shown in the earlier discussion [pp. 162–4], there is a wide range of normal variation in basic aspects of brain physiology; and such variation would be quite enough to account for such findings as a slightly raised incidence of epilepsy in the relatives of patients suffering from 'symptomatic' epilepsies.

EPILEPTIC PSYCHOSES

Important and interesting psychotic phenomena are seen in some epileptics when they are observed over a long period of time. Psychomotor attacks and automatisms, twilight states and fugues can appear at any stage in the course of the disorder, even at its onset. Their occurrence is not random, since the majority of epileptics never have such manifestations, while others have repeated attacks. Most of the patients who have such attacks suffer from a focal epilepsy, especially one with origin in a temporal lobe. However, centrencephalic epileptics can suffer from altered psychic states accompanying petit mal status, confusional states after a series of major attacks, drug intoxications, etc.

Endogenous mood changes, especially short-lived, sudden and severe moods of depression, may be an important symptom in some epileptics; again, they are seen most commonly in patients with a cortical lesion, especially in the temporal lobe.

Chronic paranoid psychoses have attracted a good deal of attention because they may mimic schizophrenic psychoses very closely. Slater, Beard and Glithero (1963) investigated 69 such patients. Most of them had temporal lobe epilepsies. In the families of these patients there was no excess of schizophrenia, probably no excess of 'psychopathic personalities', possibly an excess of epileptics: the calculated risk figures for these three conditions were, respectively, 0·7 per cent, 3·7 per cent, and 2·4 per cent. It is interesting that the father of one of the probands had himself had an epileptic schizophrenia-like psychosis, probably caused by a temporal lobe epilepsy.

When epileptic major attacks have repeated themselves for years, there may be personality deterioration and even dementia, the amount of change being related to the number and severity of the convulsions. These symptoms can safely be attributed to brain changes, especially anoxic changes, produced by the fits; and they are therefore an accidental complication of the disorder. It seems certain that such complications are much commoner with the symptomatic (focal or cortical) epilepsies than with the centrencephalic syndromes.

There is no evidence that genetic factors play any important role in pre-disposing to any of the above conditions. However, genetical work on the subject is remarkably deficient. It seems [see p. 167] that some temporal lobe epileptic syndromes may arise from a single gene difference; and it is an ascertained fact that temporal lobe epileptics are more subject than epileptics with other sites of origin of the fits to psychiatric manifestations, especially short-lived psychoses and the chronic paraphrenic-like state. The father-son pair reported by Slater et al. might very well have been an example of hereditary temporal lobe epilepsy.

MENTAL SUBNORMALITY

A number of serious congenital anomalies and diseases of the brain cause syndromes in which both mental deficiency and epilepsy are among the clinical manifestations. A typical case is phenylketonuria. As a rule the mental deficiency is the more constant and the more clinically and socially important aspect of the syndrome, and the occurrence of epileptic fits is merely a disagreeable complication. These banal facts are of little theoretical interest. When a severe degree of mental subnormality is combined with epileptic fits, one can be sure that there is a basic gross brain pathology, which is the common cause of both manifestations.

What one would like to know is whether the centrencephalic epilepsies, e.g. those which would appear to be the consequence of a single gene difference, tend to be associated with mental subnormality. Once again it is possible that a purely adventitious and uninteresting association may arise. A child who develops early in life from a petit mal into a centrencephalic grand mal syndrome, whose fits are ill controlled, whose schooling suffers, whose mental activities are modified by drugs, who may perhaps suffer anoxic damage to the brain, such a child, after a normal start, may become mentally subnormal.

Apart from such accidents, there is no reliable evidence that the distribution of IQs in centrencephalic epileptics is shifted to the left; and there is no reliable evidence that dull and backward and borderline feeble-minded children include any excess of epileptics above population norms. Conrad's work, which is sometimes quoted in this connexion, is not relevant, since he sampled an extremely depressed socio-economic class.

THE 'EPILEPTOID' PERSONALITY

The basic clinical observation, which has contributed above everything else, to the need to formulate the concept of 'epileptoid' personality, is that persons who develop epilepsy have not infrequently shown temperamental traits of an 'epileptoid' kind, as defined later, at an earlier stage in their lives. These temperamental traits, moodiness, irritability, etc., are all of them the sort of clinical manifestation which is found to accompany epileptic types of cerebral dysrhythmia and the occurrence of ictal frequencies. The symptoms are, in fact, *formes frustes* of epileptic symptoms. When they are recognized in time, as they may be, for instance, when they occur in the sib of an epileptic already under treatment, they can be treated as successfully as any other epileptic symptom. This basic fact has been given greater theoretical consequence than is its due, and has been elaborated into what, is, almost certainly, a piece of mythology.

A great deal has been written about the so-called epileptoid psychopath, particularly by an older generation of clinicians, but very little systematic work has been done. The concept is ambiguous, since two quite different groups of personality traits have been called epileptoid: (1) liability to sudden unmotivated (or inadequately motivated, 'triggered') affective changes, especially in the direction of irritability, anger, aggression, or severe depression, or panic, impulsive actions, 'short-circuit' reactions, fugue states, etc.; and (2) a sluggish stolidity, rigid and inflexible habits of mind, love of routine, over-conscientiousness, meticulousness, pedantry.

Traits of both these kinds are liable to appear as direct or indirect consequences, along different pathways, of the epileptic 'process'. The changes of
mood, etc., covered by (1), are common in patients who are having epileptic
attacks, and when the EEG is taken during such a mood state, recognizable
deviations from the individual's personal norm are observed contemporaneously
(e.g. high voltage slow rhythms, ictal frequencies, or, perhaps, Landolt's
'forced normalization').

Among the relatives of epileptic index cases there are also persons who have
similar 'psychic equivalents', even though these people do not ever have a
typical fit. When observed with the EEG, they too show characteristic changes
when in one of the 'epileptoid' mood states, if not in the resting EEG, then when
stressed physiologically by hyperventilation, etc.

Wissfeld (1954) investigated 30 'epileptoid' patients with the EEG. They had
shown symptoms classified under (1) above, and had been brought into the
clinic for such reasons as an attempt at suicide. Wissfeld comments that the
clinical condition is not a very common one, and that it required one and a
half years to collect the 30. All but 2 of them showed an abnormal EEG, and
in 16 patients ictal frequencies were observed. None of these patients had ever
had an epileptic fit, and a history of epilepsy in other family members was
unusual. By and large, the patients felt themselves to be healthy individuals;
and it was only because of the catastrophic event that they landed in a clinic.
Control work carried out by Wissfeld with similar EEG studies on other types of
'psychopath', mainly pension and compensation neurotics, gave negative EEG
findings. Three patients referred to Wissfeld for EEG investigation with a
clinical diagnosis of epileptoid psychopathy, showed characteristic EEG
changes, including ictal frequencies; but the inquiries which were suggested
by these EEG findings led to the discovery that the patients had rare epileptic
attacks or absences, so that the diagnosis had to be changed from 'epileptoid
psychopathy' to 'epilepsy'!

A later investigation by Wissfeld and Kaindl (1961) covered 183 'psychopaths'
of eleven different clinical types (epileptoid, hysteric, irritable-excitable,
alcoholic, cyclothymic, irresponsible, etc.); it was only the 46 psychopaths in
the epileptoid group who showed anything more than slight dysrhythmic
changes. Of these 46 persons, 17 or 37 per cent, showed ictal potentials, perhaps
after provocation. The clear way in which the 'epileptoid' group distinguished
itself from all the others can be shown best in the tabulation below:

EEG	PSYCHOPATHS	
	EPILEPTOID (46)	OTHERS (137)
Normal	2	122
Slight dysrhythmia	15	14
Considerable dysrhythmia	10	—
Changes only on hyperventilation	2	1
Ictal potentials (in part under provocation)	17	—

It was, moreover, only the epileptoid group that showed on inquiry a family loading with epilepsy.

The only investigation of the epileptoid personality that has been carried out along genetical lines was Conrad's work on the children of epileptics. He pointed out the confusion of two concepts of 'epileptoid'; epileptoid manifestations can be taken to be those that have some resemblance to the known clinical manifestations of epilepsy; or they can be taken to be abnormalities of personality seen in persons genetically related to epileptics. One of the results of his inquiry was to show that clinical appearances classified under (1) [p. 181] did show up in excess in the children of epileptics, those classified under (2) did not.

Conrad classified his probands into idiopathic, intermediate and symptomatic. The distribution of abnormal personalities in the children of probands in these three groups was:

		CHILDREN			
	BZ	ABNORMAL PERSONALITIES			
INDEX CASES		M	F	TOTAL	PER CENT
Idiopathic group	911	47	30	77	8·4
Intermediate group	408	9	5	14	3·4
Symptomatic group	275	2	—	2	0·7

It was in fact only in the children of the 'idiopathic' group of probands that a marked excess of abnormal personalities showed up. In this group the criminality rate was four times the population norm; the incidence of suicide was raised, especially suicides carried out suddenly or impulsively. However, only 30 of the 77 psychopaths in the children of the idiopathic group could be classified as 'explosible' or 'stimmungslabile' (explosive or labile in mood), the two Schneiderian types of psychopathy which Conrad accepted as epileptoid (apart from only two individuals of the 'hypersocial' type (i.e. of type (1)).

Later workers have not been able to validate Conrad's results; both Alström and Harvald failed to do so.[1] It seems very probable that he found so much criminality, etc., because of the fact that his incapacitated epileptic probands, who despite their incapacities had produced children, certainly came from about the lowest socio-economic class. The sex ratio in the 77 psychopaths is male/female = 5:3 approximately; in the 28 'epileptoids' it is 20:8. Epilepsy is about as frequent in females as in males; and we must presume that the gene frequency, or gene frequencies, are about the same in the two sexes. One would

[1] Harvald (1954) is worth quoting: 'The conclusion seems warranted . . . that the relatives of epileptics do not differ in character and personality from the general population. In other words, psychosis, psychopathy and criminality do not, as previously supposed (*Conrad*, 1939), seem particularly frequent among the relatives of epileptics. The great frequency of dys-rhythmia among the mentally anomalous relatives, especially among the psychopaths, is in close accordance with the observation of other writers . . . that certain forms of psychopathy may be associated with markedly abnormal EEGs. As, however, the incidence of psychopathy is not particularly high among the relatives of epileptics, this cannot be taken as evidence in favour of a genetic relationship between epilepsy and psychopathy.'

therefore expect an equal distribution of psychopaths by sex, if the hypothetical epileptic gene is the cause of the trouble. The male preponderance does not fit very well with a genetical epileptoid personality syndrome.

On page 181 we referred to traits that Conrad called 'hypersocial' which had been incriminated as epileptoid under (2). There is no evidence at all that these traits have anything to do with a premorbid state in epileptics, or have any genetical relation with the syndromes we call epileptic; so much we can conclude from Conrad's work no less than that of Alström, Harvald and others. These traits have become associated with epileptic syndromes for reasons different from those which led to the association with (1) type symptoms. Epileptics who have repeated fits show insidious personality changes over the years, traits which may be quite obvious clinically even when there is no evidence of organic changes such as memory disturbances. These symptoms, orderliness, stickiness, pedantry, etc., are just those which the work of Goldstein showed were slight and early but highly characteristic symptoms of organic cerebral disease. We need think the mystery is no greater than that.

In conclusion, the present state of our knowledge seems to be in agreement with the conclusions of Wissfeld and Kaindl: there is an 'epileptoid' personality syndrome showing itself, in the (1) type features we have described above (which Wissfeld and Kaindl do not attempt to define in any exact form of words); the syndrome shows itself in the EEG in the form of epileptic-like frequencies, perhaps only under physiological stress; there is no clear distinction between 'epileptoid' persons and epileptics not yet clinically recognized as such; one can properly look on 'epileptoid' individuals as potential epileptics; the syndrome may be related genetically to epilepsy, in depending on a common gene; but it can also appear as a consequence of delayed or disordered maturation of cerebral physiology, brain trauma, etc. 'Epileptoid' and 'epileptic'—the distinction is one of degree and not of kind.

8

THE GENETICS OF MENTAL SUBNORMALITY

INTRODUCTORY

The terms mental subnormality, mental deficiency and mental defect are used to mean subnormality in the area of intellectual function. This condition may be regarded as the lower end of a continuum representing the distribution of levels of intelligence throughout the population. Two points of arbitrariness arise, however. First, the criteria by which levels of intellectual function are judged are themselves arbitrary. The problems of psychometric testing enter here, and the fact that any one individual may obtain wide ranging scores, if a number of tests are given, each testing a different facet of mental ability. For a long time attempts have been made to define and measure 'pure' intelligence, but without very much success; little advance if any has been made since the pioneering work of Spearman.

The second point of major arbitrariness comes with the decision where a cut-off point should be made on the continuum, below which an individual could be regarded as mentally subnormal. In practice, this rests largely on the requirements of educational and legislative administration. On the other hand, on a continuum based on psychometric scores, assuming the reality of a Gaussian distribution (see below), Penrose suggests that any score outside twice the standard deviation from the mean might be considered exceptional. Towards the left extreme of the Gaussian curve, these exceptional individuals would be likely to find themselves educationally and socially handicapped.

A classification of mental defectives into two groups was proposed by Lewis in 1933. He had carried out a survey of the prevalence of mental defect in the general population of England and Wales for the Departmental (Wood) Committee. He suggested that 'subcultural' mental defect might be regarded as part of normal variation (at the lower end of the distribution curve for normal intelligence) while 'pathological' defect was outside the range of normal variation, being due to some definite lesion or abnormality. This concept has been thoroughly tested by subsequent work and has stood up well. It was upheld by the findings of Penrose's extensive Colchester survey (Penrose, 1938b). Penrose (1963) considers Lewis's dichotomy the best so far devised, but thinks the term 'physiological' would be more natural than 'subcultural'.

In fact subcultural defect and pathological defect merge into one another on any psychological or social scale, but still show important group differences, in simplified terms stated on page 186.

Further important work on the differentiation of subcultural from pathological defect was carried out by Fraser Roberts and his colleagues in a series of surveys of the intelligence of the schoolchildren of Bath in the thirties. The

SUBCULTURAL DEFECT	PATHOLOGICAL DEFECT
mental defect usually of milder degree	mental defect of all degrees of severity, often very severe
approximately 2 per cent of the general population	approximately one-quarter of 1 per cent of the population
representatives of clinically classifiable syndromes very rare	in a number of cases clinical classification can be made on a basis of physical examination, history, biochemical investigation, etc.
fertility normal or increased	usually infertile
parents and sibs frequently of less than average intelligence, but not sharply distinguished from normal in this respect.	parents usually of normal intelligence. Sharp segregation with respect to intelligence between normal and affected sibs.

work is reviewed, and all the important evidence discussed, in Fraser Roberts' Galton Lecture of 1952 (Roberts, 1952). An examination of the Normality of the lower part of the frequency curve (Stanford Binet IQs) for a sample of 3361 children showed a good approximation to Normality down to an IQ of 45, below which, instead of the 0·7 of an individual expected there was an observed figure of 12·5.

In a later survey, Fraser Roberts and his colleagues ascertained 271 defectives with IQs from 35 to 60, i.e. over the critical boundary region centring on IQ 45, and 562 of their sibs were tested. The distribution of these sib IQs was far from normal; but when the probands were allotted to two contrasting groups of imbeciles and feeble-minded, an unmistakable bimodality of the sib IQs was demonstrated. On the one hand the IQs of the sibs of the feeble-minded produced a fairly Normal curve centring on IQ 80; on the other hand the IQs of the sibs of the imbeciles showed another Normal curve with peak at IQ 100—and also the expected hump at the lower end, representing the sibs who were also imbeciles. This striking piece of evidence is discussed by Fraser Roberts in his lecture, together with other important data on regression coefficients observed in his and also in Penrose's material, and the results of tests using social criteria. This work has made the foundation on which our understanding of the aetiology of mental defect is based, with respect to the role of genetics.

We have, then, two kinds of mental defect, subcultural defect which tails out rapidly at IQs below 45, pathological defect with rather few representatives in the IQ range over 45 and accounting for the great majority of defectives with IQs under that figure; clinically we have moderate mental defect against severe mental defect. However, 'subcultural' and 'moderate degree' do not entirely coincide, any more than 'pathological' and 'severe'.

'Pathological' defect of the Lewis classification is, by definition, due to a pathological state with causation outside the range of Normal variation. The causation may be an *environmental accident*, such as damage to the young embryo by maternal rubella, or by injury or anoxia at birth; or it may be genetical and due to a *rare single gene* with a massively damaging effect, or to a *chromosomal anomaly*. Accordingly, within this range, we find a number of clinical entities which are discussed in detail in later chapters. But it must be emphasized that the great bulk of severe mental defect is undifferentiated and does not fall into known entities or syndromes. The metabolic defects, with which we shall be closely concerned, are a small part of the total. Another small part of the total of severe undifferentiated mental defect is due to single genes, usually autosomal recessive, but, very rarely, also sex-linked. In the fullness of time we can expect to be able to identify them, one by one, most probably by biochemical investigation. It seems likely that the greater part of undifferentiated severe mental defect is the result of non-genetic, random and environmental factors.

Equally we must not forget that in the subcultural range with IQs over 45, there will be representatives of all the known genetical and non-genetical syndromes. These include the inborn errors of metabolism, recessive autosomal and sex-linked syndromes and chromosomal anomalies. Metabolic defects (e.g. phenylketonuria), usually associated with severe mental defect may sometimes be associated with no more than mild retardation, or even no retardation. In Norrie's disease, due to a sex-linked recessive, there is a variable degree of microphthalmia and a variable degree of mental subnormality, but the severity of the one is not closely correlated with the severity of the other (Fraser Roberts, 1937).

We discuss the known syndromes, producing mainly severe degrees of defect, a little later on. We must now turn to a more detailed consideration of what Penrose has called physiological variation in intelligence, described by the Normal or Gaussian curve. The reader must remember, however, that physiological variation produces a high proportion of the children and adults who by reason of their subnormality are regarded as 'abnormal' on social grounds, sometimes also on psychological grounds, and even at times on medical grounds.

9

NORMAL (GAUSSIAN) VARIATION IN INTELLIGENCE[1]

HUMAN VARIABILITY

The earliest approach to the study of human variability in intelligence was made by Darwin's half-cousin, Sir Francis Galton. In his Preface to *Hereditary Genius* (1869) he writes: 'I may claim to be the first to treat the subject in a statistical manner, to arrive at numerical results, and to introduce the "law of deviation from an average"'. He began by distinguishing between intellectual capacities and motivational characteristics ('zeal, interest, industry,' etc.), and maintained that his data indicated the superior importance of a 'general ability', over and above that of 'special aptitudes' (such as the traditional list of 'faculties'). Differences in this 'general ability', he contended, were largely innate and conformed in their distribution to the so called 'law of error'.

Binet made much the same assumptions, and adopted the method of standardized mental tests which Galton used for children in his 'Anthropometric Laboratory'. Since 'ability' has a different meaning in French, he substituted the word 'intelligence', which he used as a synonym for what Galton variously called 'general' or 'natural ability'. In his well-known scale of intelligence tests, he proposed to measure differences in terms of mental age. The application of such tests to representative samples of the school population revealed an unexpectedly wide range of variation, e.g., in a sample of one hundred 10-year-olds, from a mental age of 6 or less to one of 14 or more.

When the same children were tested year after year it was found that those who were ahead of their contemporaries on entering the primary school tended to maintain their advantage, while those who were behind their contemporaries (i.e. 'retarded') still tended as a rule to lag behind. Moreover, the range of variation in mental age itself increased approximately in proportion to the increase in chronological age, so that the ratio of mental to chronological age, the 'intelligence quotient' or 'IQ', remained fairly constant in the great majority of cases.

The first step was to refine the tests used to estimate intelligence in order to rid them, as far as possible, of the effects of environmental influences in early upbringing and in formal education. Tests of qualitatively different kinds (verbal, spatial, numerical, etc.) were correlated with one another, and with teachers' reports. Factor analysis appeared to confirm the hypothesis of a general factor, g, common to all the better tests; and it was possible to estimate the g-saturation of individual tests, so as to eliminate as completely as possible the

[1] The authors are particularly indebted to Sir Cyril Burt for a thorough-going critique of this section [pp. 188–200] and for major suggestions for its improvement.

effects of training. What resulted in the end was a number of tests which did seem to describe some kind of innate general ability, its degree varying much from child to child. The different kinds of ability have never given complete correlation with one another; and it has been shown that, in addition to the general factor, there are a number of group factors (e.g. verbal, spatial, musical, numerical, etc.).

It also emerged from further study that the child's mental age, after rising steadily for a number of years, tends to level out between the ages of 14 and 16; after that there is little if any increase in mental age though standards of attainment and education could continue to improve indefinitely. It was also found that the estimate of the child's intelligence provided by the IQ proved an extremely informative guide to his powers of responding to training and education. Estimates of a child's intelligence made before the age of 6 or 7 tend to fluctuate rather widely, but after that age the IQs obtained in successive years for the same child show as a rule only minor variations. Here perhaps we may see a justification for the 'eleven plus' and similar examinations, which permitted children to be sent on to 'grammar school', 'technical school' and 'secondary modern school' according to their potentialities. The big error in this administrative arrangement was not to make adequate arrangements for misclassification. In a single examination held on a single day some children naturally failed to do themselves justice, owing to temporary ill health, emotional upset, or the mild panic induced by the ordeal. These children would then very likely show their abilities at a later stage, but then find great difficulty in getting the education to which their abilities fitted them, and social justice would not be done. Educational theory and practice since that time have developed along lines which do not always seem to pay adequate regard to the facts that children do differ very widely in educability, and that the style and the tempo of education should be matched to the child's capacities.

Some educationists have taken the view that the innate contribution to intelligence is a small one, and that the relatively low intelligence which has been found to be so much commoner in the children of unintelligent parents has been caused by deficiencies in early upbringing. The child in his first few years picks up a great deal in the way of a vocabulary from his parents and sibs, or, in the case of dull and inarticulate families, very little. Despite all the efforts that have been made to purify the assessment of this contribution from the early environment, a certain element is bound to remain.[1] Nevertheless, tests have been improved so far that, in the best tests for this purpose, the genetic contribution to variance is larger than the environmental one, in some estimates by a factor as large as 4:1.

Regarding IQs, for the purpose of the present discussion, as moderately accurate estimates of innate general ability, one can see how far the known facts about their distribution in the population correspond with available genetical models. The distribution of IQs fits fairly well with the Normal (Gaussian)

---

[1] One should remember that in practice, whether it is a teacher or school doctor or school psychologist who is dealing with a dullard or a potential grammar school candidate, his clinical assessment of intelligence is not a mere test of IQ; the test (group or individual, verbal or non-verbal) is only one item in the examination, and is valuable chiefly for standardization.

curve, which is the one to be expected on a multifactorial basis. Most standard IQ tests have a standard deviation of approximately 15 points. Predictions based on the Normal curve would then show the following expectations:

σ	BELOW IQ	PROPORTION OF POPULATION
−2·0	70	0·02275
−2·5	62·5	0·00621
−3·0	55	0·00135
−3·5	47·5	0·00023

As can be seen from FIGURE 23, persons with IQs more than three standard deviations below the mean are markedly more frequent in the population than can be accounted for on the basis of Normal distribution. These are the rather low-grade mental defectives whose intelligence has been prevented from reaching normal values by specific pathological causes, both genetical and environmental. The genetical syndromes which contribute to this part of the intelligence distribution will be discussed in detail in later chapters.

Turning our attention now to the part of the distribution in FIGURE 23 which does not deviate markedly from Normality, we can see that the proportion of the population with IQs of 55 and over can be largely accounted for by normal variation. Environmental factors make a contribution to this, but the genetical factors a more massive one. The genetical factors involved can be conceived most simply as numerous (= infinite in number), additive, and without dominance or recessivity, each equally frequent in the population, and each causing an equal amount of variance. To satisfy empirical findings, as few as five independent genes would be sufficient; but the mathematics of the situation are rather easier if we postulate a large and indeterminate number of genes; and this larger number seems in better accord with *a priori* considerations. Such general biological functions as body build, fertility, neuromuscular co-ordination, 'vitality' and 'longevity', and intelligence too, are likely to be affected to some slight degree by genes whose main effects, perhaps specific effects, are shown elsewhere. Studies of experimental animals, such as *Drosophila*, have shown that nearly all genes, e.g. those determining eye-colour, or the number of veins in a wing, have effects on general functions, such as fertility and mortality, as well.

EXPECTATIONS DERIVED FROM THE POLYGENIC HYPOTHESIS

In man, males are more variable than females, in intelligence as well as in most other traits. This is something that might have been expected from the genetical constitution of the two sexes. Given two X chromosomes, the female has a large measure of protection against deviations from the norm caused by genes whose effects are in any way counterbalanced by their allelomorphs. Thus a sex-linked gene, recessive or not fully dominant, carried in a proportion p of all X chromosomes, will show its full effects in a proportion p of all males, but only in a proportion p^2 of all females. In fact, in most subnormality hospitals there are many more males than females, even though specific forms of subnormality known to be carried by X-linked genes are quite rare. At the other end of the scale, it is probable that there are more males than females whose intelligence exceeds three standard deviations above the mean. It is tempting to regard this

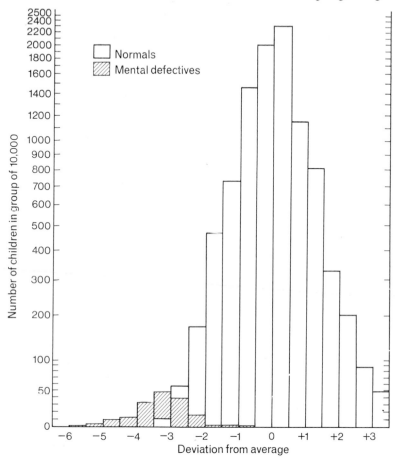

Fig. 23. Distribution according to general intelligence of children of ordinary elementary and special M.D. schools (by courtesy of Sir Cyril Burt).

as one of the main causes of the greater amount of work of 'genius' that has been done by men than by women; but there are other plausible causes for this.

The polygenic model predicts (on a basis of random mating) that the IQs of relatives will correlate to a degree determined by the closeness of the relation, i.e. $r = 0.5$ for first-degree relatives such as parents and children and sibs. These expectations are nearly fulfilled by the observations, but not completely [see TABLE 80]. We note that there is a positive correlation between the intelligence test scores of unrelated children brought up together, and also between foster-parent and child. This suggests that a significant part of the co-variance between sibs, between twins, and between parents and children is due to the common environment. So that although the observed correlations of 0·5 approximately between parent and child, between sibs, and between DZ co-twins, is exactly in accordance with the genetical hypothesis (that 50 per cent of the genetical factors determining intelligence are held in common between members of these pairs), yet, given an environmental contribution, this figure

TABLE 80

INTELLIGENCE TEST SCORES
MEDIAN CORRELATION COEFFICIENTS IN FAMILY, TWIN
AND FOSTER-CHILD STUDIES
(After Erlenmeyer-Kimling and Jarvik, 1963)

	REARED APART	REARED TOGETHER	
Unrelated	−0·01 (4)	0·23	(5)
Foster parent—child		0·20	(3)
Parent—child		0·50	(12)
Sibs	0·40 (2)	0·49	(35)
Twins—DZ:			
Like-sex		0·53	(9)
Unlike-sex		0·53	(11)
Twins—MZ	0·75 (4)	0·87	(14)

(Number of studies in brackets)

could well have been somewhat higher.[1] One also has to note that the correlation in MZ pairs, at 0·87, is significantly below unity. However, unity would be an unrealizable maximum, since every random error in giving or marking the tests, or produced in other ways, would act only to diminish the correlation and not to increase it. It can be taken that the figures of TABLE 80 bear out the polygenic hypothesis in respect of the genetical contribution to intelligence.

MALE–FEMALE DIFFERENCES

Penrose (1963) has given an account of the work which has shown that males are rather more variable in intelligence than females.[2] This has meant that observers have found rather more males than females at both extremes of the continuum, among those of very high intelligence and among the severely mentally sub-normal. In the Scottish Survey of 1932 (Scottish Council, 1949) the standard deviation for males was 17 points, for females 16. However, there is evidence, according to Penrose, that there is an excess of females among the mildly

---

[1] Assortative mating, causing parents to resemble one another in intelligence, should also tend to bring the correlation between sibs to a higher figure than 0·5. On the other hand, dominance would tend to lower the correlation.

[2] The sex difference in variability itself varies with age. Dunsdon and Fraser Roberts (1957) found that girls are more variable than boys in the younger age-groups. At about 8 or 9 years equality is reached; and thereafter boys become progressively more variable than girls up to the age of 11 or 12. Beyond this age the difference between the sexes is progressively reduced.

subnormal, for which no very plausible explanation has as yet been offered. Considering the very large numbers of school-children who have been subjected to intelligence tests, it is a little surprising that so little is known for sure about sex differences. It appears to be true that girls on average are rather higher than boys in verbality; but as intelligence tests are loaded, by the psychologists who devise and standardize them, in order to produce equality between the sexes, the results cannot be used to tell us about sex differences.

One of the few psychologists who has given serious attention to sex differences in intelligence is Sir Cyril Burt. In the following discussion we are much indebted to him for a valuable personal communication (27.11.1969). He found that, in a parallel case, the height of school children showed rather greater variability in boys up to prepubertal age; from 12 to 14 it was slightly greater among the girls; and after puberty the boys were again more variable. However, if, as some writers have suggested, we allow for the differences between the means, and calculate the relative rather than the absolute amount of variability (i.e. $100\sigma/m$, Pearson's 'coefficient of variability') the sex difference is greatly reduced.

Combining the data for a number of studies, Burt gives the following figures; means for each sex have been reduced to 100·0, and the standard deviation in the total population to 15·0 IQ.

STANDARD DEVIATIONS	BOYS	GIRLS
Group tests: verbal	14·8	15·3
non-verbal	15·8	14·1
Individual tests	15·6	14·4
Adjusted assessments	15·3	14·6

This would suggest that boys show about 5 per cent more variability in intelligence over tests of all kinds taken together. This is about the same as the 17:16 ratio concluded from the Scottish Survey of 1932. It is a good deal lower than the estimate made by Fraser Roberts (1945), that boys were 13 per cent more variable than girls. That estimate was made for 11-year-olds, and is to some extent superseded by later work (see footnote, page 192).

The consequences of these two estimates can be shown in contrast if we use the normal curve to predict the proportion of boys and girls expected 3 σ or more above the population mean in intelligence [TABLE 81]. These estimates go some

TABLE 81
PROPORTIONS OF BOYS AND GIRLS EXPECTED TO EXCEED $+3\sigma$ FROM THE POPULATION MEAN, ON TWO DIFFERENT ESTIMATES OF RELATIVE VARIABILITY

	DEVIATION IN EACH SEX TO CORRESPOND WITH 3σ IN TOTAL POPULATION		POPULATION FREQUENCY OF THIS DEVIATION		RATIO M:F
σ_M/σ_F	MALES	FEMALES	MALES	FEMALES	
1·05	2·93	3·08	0·00169	0·00104	1·64
1·13	2·83	3·20	0·00233	0·00069	3·39

way towards accounting for what seems to be the preponderance of males at the upper and lower extremes of the distribution of mental abilities.

However, a normal curve of distribution may be an unrealistic model. Sir Cyril Burt writes (1969):

> Since the frequency distributions are not strictly normal (being both asymmetrical and lepto-kurtic), it is important to make sure that the extreme cases are adequately represented. It is these that largely account for the divergences. My guess is that *large* deviations in either direction (but particularly in the lower) are partly due to so-called 'major genes', behaving as sex-linked alleles with dominance (as for colourblindness, etc.)—I don't believe in any sharp distinction between major genes and polygenes. . . . The peculiarities which I have noted in the distribution suggest a Type IV frequency-curve, and the calculations based on this type of curve yield a decidedly better fit to the data than the familiar normal curve.

ASSORTATIVE MATING

There is a large literature on the tendency of spouses to resemble one another ('homogamy' or, better, 'homoiogamy'), beginning with the calculations of Galton, Pearson and their followers. An early British study in the psychiatric field (Slater and Woodside, 1951, TABLE IXa) showed a (roughly estimated) correlation between husbands and wives in respect of intelligence of +0·44 in the neurotic group and +0·28 in the control series; there were also positive correlations in respect of neurotic features. In whatever variable it has been tested, correlations, if significant, are positive; and, apart from the sex difference itself, there is no general tendency of opposites to associate with one another in companionship, betrothal or marriage. This does not preclude the innumerable single cases in which a strong contrast has acted as an attractive feature for one or both of a pair; but it means that such contrast attractions exercise their effect against a general background of similarity. Perhaps it is that a feeling of similarity is an aid to instinctive feelings of understanding and tolerance; and that the lack of it may underlie tendencies to racial, cultural and language hostilities.

In his appreciation of the intensity of assortative mating in respect of intelligence, Sir Cyril Burt writes (1969):

> In Britain the degree of preferential mating for 'intelligence' is higher than that for any other characteristic, except socio-economic class and educational achievements (both of which are of course closely related to innate ability). In the main the figures reported range between 0·30 and 0·55. . . . Several American writers quote figures varying around 0·50; but these are nearly always based on group tests, particularly verbal tests, or in indirect deductions from educational and occupational level. Those who have relied on individual tests, particularly tests for more specialized intellectual aptitudes, report coefficients of 0·20 to 0·40 (Jones, H. E., Homogamy in intellectual abilities, *Amer. J. Sociol.*, XXXV, 1929–30, pp. 369–382; Conrad, H. S. and Jones, H. E., A second study of familial resemblance in intelligence, *39th Yearb. Nat. Soc. Stud. Educ.*, 1940, Pt. ii, pp. 97–141). . . .
>
> The foregoing correlations are the result of preferences based on phenotypic characteristics. They must vary widely with the mating customs prevailing at the time of the inquiry within the community studied. In Britain they seem to have diminished appreciably during the last half century. Owing to the difficulty of testing adults, my early figures are not very trustworthy: but most of the correlations obtained in 1910–20 for husband and wife (0·45 to 0·57) were slightly *higher* than those between brother and sister; since 1945 they have been consistently *lower* than the correlation for sibs (0·34 to 0·48). The change presumably is partly due to the progressive lowering of the barriers between different social classes.

In our later investigations on the heritability of intelligence my coworkers and I made special efforts to estimate the probable correlation between genotypes. For what we took to be a representative sample of the London population we obtained a correlation between spouses amounting to 0·387; the correlation between phenotypic assessments on which this was based amounted to 0·463, the excess being due to similarities in cultural background (Burt, C. and Howard, M., The multifactorial theory of inheritance and its application to intelligence, *Brit. J. statist. Psychol.*, IX, 1956, pp. 95–131). In correspondence Godfrey Thomson gave me similar figures for the Scottish population at the time of the survey: vis., 'about 0·45, reduced to 0·35, if allowance is made for non-genetic factors affecting the scores'.

For present-day conditions therefore I would suggest a figure of about 0·40: this is higher than Thomson's rounded estimate, but lower than the earlier American estimates.

Such a large correlation as 0·4 between spouses, estimated for genotypes, is of course of wide and deep significance. Sociologically, the tendency of spouses and parents to choose mates resembling themselves must make a stabilizing contribution to marital unions, and help to provide a harmonious atmosphere for the upbringing of the children. Children who differ too markedly in intelligence from their parents and their sibs, either upwards or downwards, have a more than average liability of finding their way to child psychiatric clinics and other facilities for the maladjusted.

Parental homoiogamy in intelligence, while tending to diminish differences between sibs within the sibship, tends to increase variability between sibships. This also makes a valuable social contribution, since by its means the proportion of extreme deviants in the population is multiplied. Society very largely relies on such extreme deviants (in an upward direction) for the immense variety of tasks for which quite exceptional intellectual capabilities are called for. It is to be borne in mind that the tendency to homoiogamy between spouses shows itself not only in general intelligence but also in respect of special gifts and talents. The tendency of musically gifted people to marry one another increases the proportion of the musically gifted in the general population, and helps to provide musically gifted children with home environments in which their talents will be recognized and encouraged.

From the evolutionary point of view, the additional variability caused by homoiogamy intensifies the effects of natural selection, if there is a selective difference in 'fitness' of persons of higher and of lower intelligence. A couple of decades ago there was general agreement on the existence of a negative correlation between intelligence and fertility (e.g. a negative correlation between the intelligence of one member of a sibship and the size of the sibship from which he came). It was accordingly expected that when the Survey of the intelligence of Scottish schoolchildren was repeated in 1947 in much the same way as it had been made in 1932, a decline in the intelligence of the schoolchildren would be found. When it was not found as expected, a question was left unanswered. The most probable answer has been provided by Higgins, Reed and Reed (1962). The investigations in sibships had taken no account of sibships of zero magnitude; taking data over two generations showed that though the dull and backward when they married did tend to have more than the average number of children, their reduced likelihood of marrying and founding a family more than offset this tendency. On the whole, the dull and backward were slightly less, rather than slightly more, prolific than the population average. If there is a consistent and persistent fertility differential in favour of intelligence, even if only slight, it can be regarded as favourable for the prospects of the human species. We can be sure that in the ever increasing complexity of our world both a greater level of average intelligence, and a higher incidence of people of outstanding and exceptional mental abilities will become more and more necessary.

THE RELATIVE CONTRIBUTIONS OF HEREDITY AND ENVIRONMENT

Estimates of the relative contributions of heredity and environment to intelligence can be made from the results of a variety of studies. What this amounts to is an attempt to partition the variance between individuals into those parts which can be attributed to the one source or the other, to their interaction, and to random or unclassifiable causes of variation and 'error'. It is important to recognize from the beginning that all such estimates are made with a limited population, often rather ill-defined. If this population is genetically homogeneous, then the environmental contribution will show up more readily; if the population is one reared in a uniform culture with little variation from individual to individual in environmental variables, then the genetical contribution will be emphasized. For instance, an experiment on boys at Eton College, all (presumably) coming from a socially favourable environment, might lead to an underestimate of the relative contribution of environmental factors, while the converse might be true of a study of intelligence in, say, a rural area of Scotland, with a good deal of in-breeding and wide variation from family to family in occupational and social level. One should also think of the likelihood that genetical vs. environmental variability will change in the course of time. As the material condition and the educational facilities available to the general population improve, environmental variance will tend to diminish while nothing is likely to make much of a dent for some time to come in genetic variability.

Studies of Foster-children

One of the types of investigation designed to provide direct evidence about the relative contributions of genetic and environmental sources of variation is the study of foster-children. Not much work of importance has been done recently in this field, more because of changes in taste and fashion than because such work is not informative and important. Educationists have recently tended to take the line that the hereditary contribution to educability is either non-existent, or should be so, and is best ignored if it exists. However, good work has been done here in the past, and a short discussion of the results of past work has been given by Shields and Slater (1960).

Children brought up from very early years in a residential institution or foster-home are exposed to a similar environment, but may have come from very different parentage. If the environmental contribution to the development of intelligence was the main source of variation, then these children should show much less scatter in intelligence quotients than samples of the ordinary school population. This has not been found: the variance in intelligence is just the same.

A more critical test can be made by comparing intelligence scores of children, their own parents, and their foster-parents. The correlations obtained in two groups: (1) adopted or fostered children and their foster-parents; and (2) a comparable sample of children brought up in their own homes with their (genetical) parents (data from Burks, 1928), are shown in TABLE 82.

TABLE 82

CORRELATIONS BETWEEN MENTAL AGES OF FOSTER-PARENTS AND CHILDREN COMPARED WITH CORRELATIONS BETWEEN MENTAL AGES OF GENETICAL PARENTS AND CHILDREN

(Data of Burks, 1928; quoted from Shields and Slater, 1960)

	FOSTER-GROUP PARENTS AND ADOPTED CHILDREN		CONTROL GROUP PARENTS AND OWN CHILDREN	
	r	N	r	N
Fathers	0·07	178	0·45	100
Mothers	0·19	204	0·46	105

There are several snags in these investigations, quite apart from the difficulty of getting a fair sample. Adoption societies try to match the social background of the adoptive infants, and their estimated genetic potentialities, with that of the adoptive parents; obviously it is important for the welfare of a potentially more than averagely intelligent child that it should be brought up in a reasonably intelligent family background. This would tend to bring about a spurious positive correlation between the intelligences of child and foster-parent. Another difficulty is that, by and large, foster-homes tend to be more than averagely prosperous and culturally superior, so that environmental variance is reduced. On the basis of her work Barbara Burks concluded that heredity accounted for about 75–80 per cent of the variance in intelligence.

Work with Twins

A more powerful and more satisfactory type of study for discriminating between the effects of heredity and environment is provided by work on twins. Here we can compare twins brought up together with twins brought up apart; we can compare, in both types of environment, monozygotic with dizygotic pairs; we can compare dizygotic co-twins with their sibs, which would give a clue to differences caused by birth order and changes in family life over the course of time; and of course, apart from twins, it is possible to compare sibs brought up together with sibs who have been separated. Work in this field has been discussed by Shields and Slater (1960) and again by Shields (1971). For our present purposes, the material can be adequately summarized in the figures of TABLE 83. The striking finding emerges that in educational attainment DZ twins brought up together are more alike than MZ twins brought up apart, but in intelligence the opposite is the case.

Correlations between Relatives

The polygenic genetical hypothesis predicts that the correlation between the intelligences of individuals with their relatives of various degree will correspond

TABLE 83
STUDIES INVESTIGATING MZ TWINS REARED APART:
INTRA-PAIR CORRELATIONS FOR INTELLIGENCE AND FOR EDUCA-
TIONAL ATTAINMENT
(From Shields, 1971, with the means added)

	MZ PAIRS		DZ PAIRS REARED TOGETHER (MOSTLY)
	REARED APART r	REARED TOGETHER r	r
Newman et al. (1937)			
Binet IQ	0·767	0·881	0·631
Educational attainment	0·583	0·892	0·691
Shields (1962)			
Combined intelligence test score (Dominoes and Mill Hill Vocabulary)	0·77	0·76	0·51
Juel-Nielsen (1965)			
Raven Matrices	0·79	—	—
Wechsler-Bellevue IQ	0·62	—	—
Burt (1966)			
Intelligence (final assessment)	0·874	0·925	0·453
Educational attainment	0·623	0·983	0·831
Means of estimates re			
Intelligence	0·76	0·85	0·53
Educational attainment	0·60	0·94	0·76

with the proportion of the genes shared in common. Thus parent and child have half their genes in common, and so do sib and sib; in these cases one expects a correlation of $+0·5$. An individual has only a quarter of his genes in common with an uncle or aunt or a half-sib; and in these relationships one expects a correlation of $+0·25$. These expectations are met fairly closely by observations [see TABLE 80]; and, naïvely considered, these findings might be thought to exclude any noteworthy contribution by the environment at all. It has to be remembered that, with homoiogamous mating the rule, on a purely genetical basis one would expect these correlations to be exceeded, and the fact they are not indicates the presence of other sources of variance (environmental contribution, dominance effects, errors in measurement, random error, etc.). However, Fisher's formulae enable one to calculate the values to be expected when due allowance has been made for the effects of both homoiogamous mating and dominance, and the estimates of the reliability further allow for some assessment of the influence of error. The correlation between the intelligence scores of MZ twins should, on the basis of genetical theory, approach $+1·0$; the fact that it reaches only $+0·87$ in MZ twins reared together, and $+0·75$ in MZ twins reared apart indicates a material contribution from non-genetical sources.

Another way of looking at the correlation between intelligence scores of index case and relative is to look at the regression equation. It will be recollected that the correlation coefficient relates the co-variance of two variables with their variances

$$r = W_{xy}/(V_x \cdot V_y)^{\frac{1}{2}}.$$

If the regression equation between the two variables is linear it takes the form

$$y = a + bx,$$

in which a and b are constants; b gives the angle of slope of the line, and if it is positive it will be because y increases as x increases. The relation between correlation coefficient and regression equation is given by the expression

$$b = W_{xy}/V_x;$$

The formula is worth noting because it indicates that, even when $r = 1 \cdot 0$, it is still possible to have a line sloping at any angle, since then $b_{xy} = (V_x/V_y)^{\frac{1}{2}}$. When the two variances are the same (as they will be as a rule in population studies of intelligence), then the regression equation is independent of them, and is identical with the coefficient of correlation.

Now, if we relate y, the deviation of the IQ of a relative from the population mean, with x, the deviation of the subject's IQ from the population mean, then b will take on different values with the class of relative chosen. In first-degree relatives b will approximate to $0 \cdot 5$. This is a figure which could be predicted on the polygenic model, and is confirmed in fact. What emerges is the well-known *regression towards the mean:* the parents (alternatively the children) of subjects will show only about half the deviation from the population mean shown by the subject. The parents of mentally subnormal children, with average IQ say 70, will tend to have IQs averaging 85; and the children of subnormal individuals will also show IQs regressing towards the population mean. The theoretical regression is not observed exactly, since it is influenced by assortative mating. One can suppose it would be more nearly exact if people, including the subnormal, mated entirely at random. Then the IQs of spouses of subnormals averaging IQ 70 would have the population mean of 100; and the children of these pairs would have IQs averaging the mid-parental value of 85.

The regression equation differs also with different kinds of mental deficiency; and by using it one can throw into sharp contrast the genetics behind high-grade subnormality and feeblemindedness on the one hand, and the genetics of low-grade subnormality, imbecility and idiocy on the other. In the first the typical regression towards the mean is observed, in the other it is not; the parents of phenylketonuric children, for instance, do not show any regression, but have their IQs averaging the population mean regardless of the IQ of the child.

The relation between the intelligence of children and that of their parents is a matter of considerable social importance. Dealing with the matter in roughly qualitative terms, Reed and Reed (1965) have provided the figures of TABLE 84. A point of special importance shown in this table is the difference between the expectations of subnormality in the children of normal × normal matings, if there is and if there is not a history of subnormality in an uncle or aunt. If subnormality were an effect produced by single genes of major effect, there would be no reason to expect such a massive difference as that shown in the

TABLE 84

FREQUENCY OF SUBNORMALITY IN SIBLINGS OF AFFECTED INDIVI-
DUALS, ACCORDING TO TYPE OF PARENTAL MATING

(After Reed and Reed, 1965; from Shields, 1971)

PARENTAL MATING	NUMBER OF SIBLINGS	PERCENTAGE SUBNORMAL
Subnormal × subnormal	76	42·1
Subnormal × normal	317	19·9
Normal × normal with subnormal uncles or aunts	139	12·9
Normal × normal	104	5·7

table. The risk when there is a subnormal parental sib, increased by a factor of 2·3 over the risk in other normal matings, is a finding which could have been predicted on the polygenic model, but is inexplicable on either the major gene or the social-cultural-environmental hypotheses.

Genetical, Environmental and other Contributions to Variance

The above discussion brings us to a final paragraph. With the aid of a very large range and amount of family and other data, it is possible to make a precise partitioning of the population variance in respect of intelligence (in British populations, in the first decades of the present century). The figures of TABLE 85 are taken from Burt (1958), and show how preponderantly important the genetical factors are.

TABLE 85

ANALYSIS OF VARIANCE FOR ASSESSMENTS OF INTELLIGENCE

(From Burt, 1958; quoted from Shields, 1970)

SOURCE	UNADJUSTED TEST SCORES	ADJUSTED ASSESSMENTS
Genetic component:		
fixable (additive)	40·51	47·92
nonfixable (dominance)	16·65	21·73
Assortative mating	19·90	17·91
Environment:		
systematic	10·60	1·43
random	5·91	5·77
Unreliability	6·43	5·24
Total	100·00	100·00

10

METABOLIC DISORDERS:
THE AMINOACIDURIAS

METABOLIC DISORDERS AND
MENTAL SUBNORMALITY

The study of disorders of metabolism is important in the history of human genetics, since the observations of Garrod at the turn of the century marked the beginning of the study of biochemical genetics. Among the first conditions studied by Garrod were alkaptonuria, pentosuria and cystinuria in which unusually high levels of substances not normally found appeared in the urine. These conditions are not as a rule accompanied by mental subnormality, but many inherited disorders of metabolism discovered later are associated with mental impairment. Indeed, it has been said that at one time or another mental impairment has been observed in association with probably all the metabolic diseases (Crome and Stern, 1967).

Garrod's observations show remarkable perception and insight considering the time at which they were made. He noted that a familial distribution of alkaptonuria showed a highly characteristic configuration, two or more sibs being affected, and other brothers and sisters, parents and other relatives showing no signs of the condition. Moreover, there was a higher rate than was to be expected of consanguinity amongst the forebears of alkaptonurics. In consultation with the geneticist Bateson, he applied the recently rediscovered laws of Mendel, and alkaptonuria was the first human trait to be demonstrated as a Mendelian recessive character. Together with other rare analogous conditions, Garrod described alkaptonuria as 'an inborn error of metabolism' (Garrod, 1908). He postulated sharply segregating biochemical variants between individuals, and put forward the idea that the underlying fault in these conditions might be the congenital lack of an enzyme, normally necessary as a catalyst at a particular point in a chain of chemical reactions in the body. This would lead to a blockage, behind which an unusually high level of metabolites would build up in the body fluids, to spill over into the urine and other excretions.

This simple but remarkable concept of a genetically determined metabolic block has stood the test of observation and investigation over the years, and holds good for many inherited disorders of metabolism discovered long after Garrod's day. This, together with the appreciation of these rare conditions as elucidating inherited individual biochemical variation, shows extraordinary perception to which we were later greatly indebted.

Many further examples of inborn errors of metabolism have been discovered since Garrod's original observations, and together they represent a group of widely differing biochemical abnormalities. They have, nevertheless, certain fundamental features in common. Important amongst these is a genetically determined specific enzyme defect in each case. Moreover, many are accompanied by mental subnormality, and it is with these that we shall be concerned in this chapter.

The constancy with which mental subnormality accompanies an inborn error of metabolism suggests a causal link. The nature of this connexion may be expected to be complex and to vary according to the disease: in some conditions the mental deficiency may be induced as a direct result of the biochemical disturbance; in others both effects may possibly arise independently from some common underlying or predisposing influence. Much has been discovered regarding the biochemical nature of the inborn errors of metabolism, but a great deal remains to be discovered about the crucial relationship of biochemical disorders and intellectual impairment.

In nearly every one of the aminoacidurias there is conclusive evidence of a Mendelian recessive pattern of inheritance. The same holds good for the lipidoses, the leucodystrophies and other neurometabolic disorders. In many conditions throughout the entire field of metabolic disorders in mental subnormality, biochemical evidence has been forthcoming to support specific enzyme defects. It is not unlikely that all the neurometabolic diseases are genetically-determined enzymopathies. There is a greater opportunity to test gene-enzyme hypotheses in this group than amongst hereditary conditions associated with mental defect in which characteristic biochemical changes are not apparent. Again, however, the study of the metabolic disorders may give a lead to the discovery of specific enzymatic changes, for example in Mendelian dominant conditions such as the phakomatoses. It may, moreover, elucidate the problems such as gene-dosage effect, that arise in connexion with the enzyme changes that have been suggested in mongolism and other conditions in which chromosome defects involve relatively large masses of genetical material.

Quite apart from the wide possibilities it opens up for future research, the rapid advance in recent years in biochemical studies of neurometabolic disorders has already gone far in increasing the scope of human genetics. For example, Hsia's demonstration of the effect of the phenylalanine-loading test in the heterozygote in phenylketonuria has led the way to a new appraisal of the heterozygous state in many conditions. Again, in phenylketonuria, the first hopes have been born of ameliorating harmful genetical effects by biochemical means (through the diet).

Numerous inborn errors of metabolism have been identified and reported. A number are represented only by a single case report in the literature. In this and following chapters we will present only those most frequently encountered, or those of particular interest from the point of view of their heredity or association with mental impairment. As our approach is not primarily from a biochemical angle we have not attempted to classify the conditions according to the biochemical mechanism involved, such as the 'overflow' and 'renal' aminoacidurias distinguished by Dent, which underlies most of the subsequent classifications of this group (see Crome and Stern, 1967). The specific enzyme defects are given, however, and their implications discussed with respect to such matters as dietary treatment.

PHENYLKETONURIA

Folling's discovery in 1934 marked the beginning of a new epoch in the scientific study of mental subnormality. In a routine survey to detect urinary ketones, this Norwegian biochemist found an unusual reaction in the case of two mentally defective sibs. Their urine gave a deep blue-green colour on the addition of ferric chloride. Folling found this to be due to the presence of phenylpyruvic acid. The finding prompted him to carry out more extensive surveys amongst mentally subnormal patients which established the existence of a syndrome which was known originally by several names, including 'phenylpyruvic oligophrenia' and 'imbecillitas phenylpyruvica', but was later designated 'phenylketonuria' by Penrose and Quastel (1937) to emphasize the biochemical nature of the abnormality and to bring the nomenclature into line with that for other inborn errors of metabolism such as alkaptonuria and cystinuria.

The discovery of phenylketonuria caught the imagination of biochemists and clinicians concerned with problems of aetiology in mental subnormality, and probably no other single condition in this field has aroused so much interest. It posed the basic question of biochemical influence upon mental function; it provided an intriguing model for the study of gene-enzyme relationships; and it held out possibilities for a therapeutic regime. Above all, it stimulated a widespread search for other conditions of mental subnormality accompanied by a specific metabolic defect.

Biochemistry

It is thought that the basic defect in phenylketonuria is a deficiency of the liver enzyme L-phenylalanine oxidase, which is normally concerned with the specific hydroxylation of the benzene ring of phenylalanine to form tyrosine. An excess of phenylalanine is found in the body fluids of phenylketonuric patients, as would be expected with such a metabolic block. Another metabolic pathway involving only the aliphatic side-chain is, however, open to phenylalanine [see FIG. 24]. This is a normal subsidiary pathway in the non-phenylketonuric subject, and by it phenylalanine is converted to phenylpyruvic acid and also to phenyllactic and phenylacetic acids. This becomes the main pathway in the phenylketonuric subject. The renal threshold for these substances is low, and they are found in large amounts in the urine in phenylketonuria.

So far, all individuals who have been discovered to excrete phenylpyruvic acid continuously in their urine have shown some degree of mental defect. The quantity of this substance excreted daily is about one gram but varies widely according to the dietary protein intake, its ultimate precursor. In one phenylketonuric subject of unusually high intelligence for the condition, a regular daily excretion of 0·5 gram was found on a normal protein intake (Cowie, 1951a) though there has been no further suggestion of a quantitative relationship between the biochemical disturbance as measured by urinary metabolites and the degree of intellectual impairment. The majority of phenylketonuric patients are severely mentally subnormal, though they are found with varying degrees of mental defect. Exceptional cases have been described in which intelligence tests have shown the subject to be of just below average intelligence and even within the normal range (e.g. Cowie, 1951b; Hsia, Knox and Paine, 1957; Coates,

Norman and Woolf, 1957). Penrose (1949) observes that there is a slight tendency for the same grade of mental defect to be repeated in affected members of the same sibship.

Although it may be supposed from genetical and clinical data that the same autosomal recessive gene is responsible for phenylketonuria in the majority of cases, there is some evidence to suggest that an alternative genetical mechanism or mechanisms may possibly operate in a small number of cases. This might explain the atypical features in some cases, such as the unexpectedly high level of intelligence, relatively low output of phenylpyruvic acid and the absence of

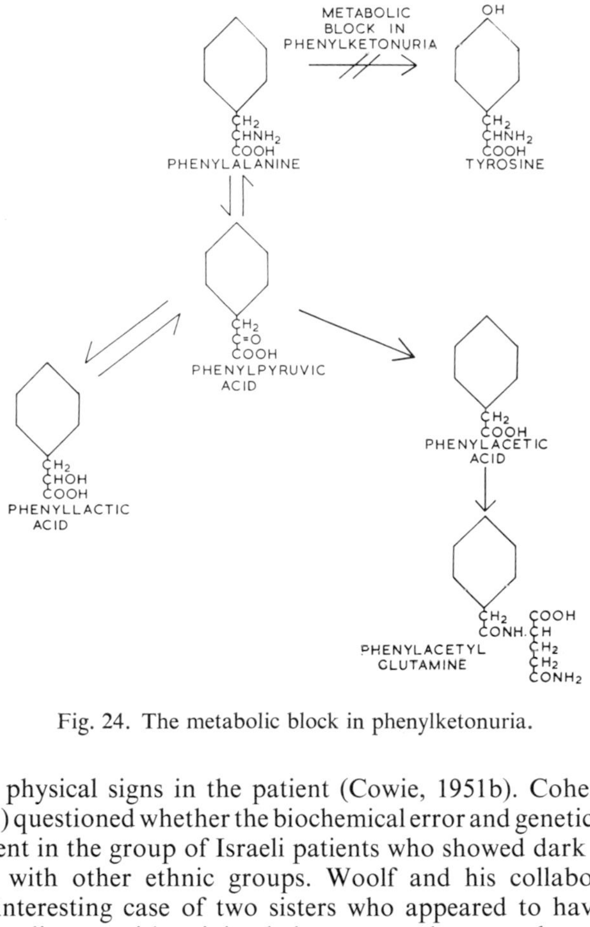

Fig. 24. The metabolic block in phenylketonuria.

characteristic physical signs in the patient (Cowie, 1951b). Cohen and his co-workers (1961) questioned whether the biochemical error and genetical mechanism may be different in the group of Israeli patients who showed dark pigmentation as compared with other ethnic groups. Woolf and his collaborators (1961) describe the interesting case of two sisters who appeared to have an unusual variant of the disease with minimal damage to the central nervous system. They considered that without doubt genetical factors were operating to render the phenylketonuria atypical in these two sisters. One possible explanation they put forward is the existence of a third allele, in addition to the normal gene and gene for phenylketonuria, which would synthesize a protein with weak enzymic properties, so that phenylalanine would be converted to tyrosine much more slowly than by the enzyme synthesized by the normal gene, but much faster than by the inactive protein synthesized by the gene for phenylketonuria, thus producing a 'partial metabolic block'.

Somatic Clinical Features

Various physical features are characteristic of phenylketonuria, although there is a wide range of pleiotropic effects (Penrose, 1951a). Thus no single clinical feature is a constant finding in patients with the condition. Physical signs frequently observed are as follows. A reduction of stature and of head measurements are not infrequent in severely affected patients. There is a dilution of pigmentation in the hair and skin. This can be shown effectively by comparison of phenylketonuric patients with their normal sibs, when the hair of the patients is seen to be lighter in colour than that of the sibs, allowing for the effect of darkening with age (Cowie and Penrose, 1951). The skin may show areas of pigmentation with *café au lait* patches and darkened moles. The eyes are usually blue. Infantile eczema and hyperidrosis are not uncommon. The upper central incisor teeth are often widely spaced. Kyphosis is common, and especially in cases with severe mental subnormality the patient adopts a 'pithecoid' stance, with slight flexion at the hips and knees, and walks on a broad base. Digital mannerisms are often seen among low-grade phenylketonuric patients. Briskness of all reflexes, superficial and deep, is a fairly constant finding. Occasionally there is a history of epileptic fits in childhood. Amelioration of the physical signs and of the mental retardation has been claimed in those cases where a special diet, low in its phenylalanine content, has been instituted early in infancy but not later.

Neuropathology

The neuropathological findings in phenylketonuria up to 1960 are well reviewed by Crome and Pare (1960). Up to that time the literature contained reports of 20 cases, in only 3 of which was the brain stated to have been normal. The findings have been diverse. Reduction in the weight of the brain was the commonest and most certain of the recorded anomalies. The second commonest anomaly was pallor of myelin staining which was present in 7 of the 20 cases. Two others showed focal defects of myelination. Similar neuropathological changes, including gliosis and demyelination of the white matter, have been observed in a recent series of 8 cases reported by Malamud (1966). The white matter of some of the brains originally described was later examined chemically (Crome, Tymms and Woolf, 1962). Compared with brains of controls, the water content was high and the cholesterol and cerebroside content of dry matter lower. This was in accordance with the view that in phenylketonuria the abnormal concentrations of phenylalanine and its metabolites in the body fluids hinder the laying down of myelin; but a gradual demyelination was not excluded. Cholesterol ester deposits and other chemical differences were found in regions of only one of the brains examined, indicating active demyelination. This patient, however, showed changes characteristic of leucodystrophy or Schilder's disease (Crome 1962a), and it was considered that actual destruction of myelin sheaths, if it occurs at all in phenylketonuria, is very slow in the majority of cases. Crome (1962a) draws attention to the occasional association of phenyl-ketonuria with leucodystrophy (in 4 out of 26 recorded cases) and considers that this rate of association of two uncommon diseases is unlikely to be fortuitous. At the present time it is still open to question whether the association is due to the presence of some attendant effect common to the two conditions or whether there is a more fundamental genetical connexion.

Genetics and Epidemiology

Phenylketonuria is inherited as a simple autosomal recessive trait. Patients with the condition are believed to account for about $\frac{1}{2}$ to 1 per cent of all cases present in hospitals for the mentally subnormal (Harris, 1959; Snyder, 1965). The frequency of the disorder in the population as a whole has been estimated in the United Kingdom as about 4×10^{-5} (Munro, 1947). A frequency of the same order was estimated for the United States (Jervis, 1937). A frequency of $2 \cdot 5 \times 10^{-5}$ was estimated for homozygotes for the phenylketonuria gene in a region of South Sweden inhabited by nearly one-half of the total population of the country (Larson, 1954). Since the Guthrie test, based on bacterial in-hibition by a phenylalanine antagonist, has supplanted the urine tests based on the ferric chloride reaction, results from large-scale surveys in the United States suggest a much higher incidence of phenylketonuria. A survey sponsored by the State Health Department using the Guthrie test for phenylketonuria, beginning in 1962, of all babies born in Massachusetts, has suggested an incidence of the order of 10×10^{-5} (births) (MacCready and Hussey, 1964). Partington and Anderson (1964) have made the suggestion that in fact the incidence of phenyl-ketonuria in North America may be very much higher than earlier estimates suggested. In their own Canadian survey based on urine testing by ferric chloride and Phenistix, an incidence of $53-92 \times 10^{-5}$ was indicated. In a survey of institutions for the mentally subnormal in Japan, 9 phenylketonuric cases were found amongst 5,419 patients screened (Tanaka et al., 1961). The incidence of the abnormality in the general population was estimated as $1 \cdot 6-1 \cdot 8 \times 10^{-5}$. The segregation ratio was lower than 25 per cent as would be expected from a simple recessive inheritance of the condition, and it was thought by the investigators that the data suggested a high infant mortality in phenylketonuric sibships, though the evidence for this was not conclusive.

Some doubt arises concerning the validity of incidence figures based upon infant screening for phenylketonuria. It is not unlikely that the assumption that all babies giving positive results in infant screening programmes are suffering from classical phenylketonuria, when in fact some are not, has accounted for some of the unusually high incidence figures that have appeared from time to time in recent surveys. At first it was thought that a positive result on infant screening would indicate definitely that any baby was suffering from phenylketonuria. It is becoming evident, however, that newborn babies giving a positive reaction on screening do not always suffer from classical phenylketonuria. Increasing evidence is accumulating of this phenomenon, and there has been growing concern about the institution of dietary treatment in the case of infants with hyperphenylalaninaemia who are not in fact phenylketonuric (Berry and Wright, 1967; Bessman, 1966).

The mistaken diagnosis of phenylketonuria in the neonate apparently may arise if the baby is a heterozygote, or even if he is completely free from the phenylketonuria gene. It is possible that the heterozygotic state, in which the carrier possesses only one phenylketonuria gene, may produce biochemical abnormalities overlapping with those characteristic of the homozygous phenylketonuric, making a definitive diagnosis in the newborn impossible (Schneider and Garrard, 1966). Secondly, and possibly more important, there might be a delay in the maturation of the enzyme phenylalanine hydroxylase even in babies of normal genotype. Stephenson and McBean (1967) have presented good evidence to support the view that this can happen. They describe temporary phenylalanine hydroxylase deficiency in a child believed to be genetically normal on the basis of his later response to phenylalanine loading. They point out that the condition is indistinguishable from phenylketonuria in early infancy and might remain unrecognized during the administration of a low phenylalanine diet.

With respect to ethnic distribution, phenylketonuria has been thought to be particularly rare in Jews, unlike several other inborn errors of metabolism. Only very occasionally have sporadic Jewish cases been reported (Cohen and Kozinn, 1949; Centerwall and Neff, 1961). Cohen, Bodonyi and Szeinberg (1961) came across two cases of phenylketonuria in two Yemenite Jewish families, which led them to examine the urine of mentally subnormal children in institutions in Israel. Their results indicated an incidence of about 0·5–1·5 per cent of the material tested, which is in line with the findings in institutions for mental defectives in the United Kingdom and the United States. All the cases found in this study belonged to the oriental non-Ashkenazi group, and it was thought that the rarity of phenylketonuria among Jews examined in Europe, the United Kingdom and the United States referred probably to the Ashkenazi group who form the majority of Jews there, and amongst whom no cases have been found in Israel either. This group of Israeli workers point out that most of their phenylketonuric patients have dark complexions, with dark and even black hair and deep brown eyes, in contrast to the blondes with fair skin and blue eyes who are commonly said to make up the vast majority of cases. The question whether the biochemical error and genetical pattern is precisely the same as in other ethnic groups remains to be examined.

Lyman (1963) in discussing the distribution of phenylketonuria in people of different national origins in the mixed population of the eastern United States, points out that there were apparently no important variations in susceptibility among the various ethnic groups with the exception of Jews and Negroes. These were not represented among phenylketonurics found in the samples discussed by Lyman, although he states that they made up a significant fraction of the populations examined. He considered that the gene is less frequent in American Negroes and Jews than in Americans of European origin, though, in contrast, he drew attention to the finding of phenylketonuria among Jews from the Middle East, mainly Yemenite, reported by Cohen et al. (1961).

Single cases of phenylketonuria occurring in American Negroes have been reported by Katz and Menkes (1964) and by Newman and Engel (1965) with a plea for more complete screening in the general population. Prior to the case-report of Katz and Menkes, phenylketonuria in only five Negroes had been

reported. Katz and Menkes estimate that if all genes determining phenylketonuria are derived from Caucasians, the disorder should be at least one-ninth
as frequent in the Negro as in the Caucasian. This estimation is based on the
calculation that the amount of Caucasian admixture in the North American
Negro is 30 per cent. Katz and Menkes feel that the rarity of Negroes with
phenylketonuria amongst patients in mental subnormality institution populations
points to a low gene frequency. The over-all finding, however, of a lower incidence
than expected of phenylketonuria amongst Negroes both in and out of institutions in North America, is due to the combined effects of a low gene frequency
and incomplete screening.

In India, Centerwall and Ittyerah (1966) surveyed 1123 patients in 26 institutions for the mentally retarded in India and found two unrelated Hindu children
with phenylketonuria. The sib of one was found also to have the condition.
These were believed to bring the number of reported cases in India up to five.
Centerwall and Ittyerah considered it of special interest that until then phenylketonuria was found in families originating from only two pockets in the Indian
subcontinent; from Mysore State, in South India, and from West Pakistan, in
both of which the rate of consanguineous marriage is relatively high.

There is little information regarding the occurrence of phenylketonuria in the
American Indians or related racial groups, such as the Mexicans. Wagner and
Littman (1967) report a Cheyenne-Arapaho Indian family with two phenylketonuric patients in a sibship. They draw attention to the fact that only three
papers in the literature (Centerwall et al., 1961; Jervis, 1939; Partington, 1961)
had previously presented the possibility of phenylketonuria occurring in families
of American-Indian or Mexican stock. They advocate that screening procedures
should include all races, as phenylketonuria appears to have a widespread
ethnic distribution and may appear in dark-skinned and dark-haired individuals.

Jervis (1937) noted in a series of phenylketonuric patients in New York, that
relatively many were of Irish extraction. Later, Penrose (1946) made the comment that he and Munro had the impression that there were many cases of
Celtic origin. Carter and Woolf (1961) took up this interesting question, and
compared the birthplaces of the parents and grandparents of a series of phenylketonuric patients with those of the parents and grandparents of three control
series of patients with Hirschsprung's disease, congenital dislocation of the hip
and coeliac disease. It was found that a high proportion of the parents and
grandparents of phenylketonuric patients were born in Ireland or western
Scotland. The findings suggested that the frequency of the gene for phenylketonuria is about four times as high in the population of these parts of the
United Kingdom as in the population of south-east England.

The Heterozygote

There is some expression of the gene in heterozygous form in that the parents
and some unaffected sibs of phenylketonuric patients who may be supposed to
carry the gene in single dose, give a response to a phenylalanine-loading test
which is intermediate between the response of the phenylketonuric subject and
that of the normal individual (Hsia et al., 1956). It seems, therefore, that
heterozygotes for phenylketonuria have some impairment of their capacity for

the metabolism of phenylalanine which is shown up under the stress of a loading dose of the substance. Even in the absence of a loading dose, differences in the blood levels of phenylalanine between heterozygotes for phenylketonuria and homozygous normal subjects have been reported (Knox and Messinger, 1958). The distribution of plasma phenylalanine levels in these two groups is shown in FIGURE 25. There is a small area of overlap, but by assessment of blood phenyl-alanine levels both fasting and after a loading dose, detection of the heterozygous state is possible in nearly all individuals. An economical formula, claimed to be the best discriminant for the carrier state in phenylketonuria, has been worked

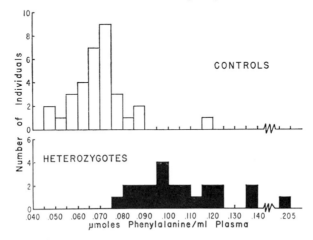

Fig. 25. Distribution of plasma phenylalanine levels in normals compared with heterozygotes (Knox and Messinger, 1958).

out by Wang, Morton and Waisman (1961). This is based on plasma levels of phenylalanine fasting and at $1\frac{1}{2}$, 2 and 3 hours following a loading dose. Apparently the slight metabolic difference from normal with respect to phenyl-alanine has no adverse effect on the heterozygotes, and they are phenotypically normal in other respects. The phenylalanine tolerance test has a place in genetic counselling as a means of detecting heterozygous carriers for the phenylke-tonuria gene.

In pursuit of the idea that there is an increased frequency of psychosis amongst the relatives of phenylketonuric patients, mainly two types of investigation have been carried out. First, the families of phenylketonuric patients have been investigated with respect to the occurrence of psychosis. Secondly, biochemical studies have been made of groups of psychotic patients, in order to detect changes which might indicate the presence of heterozygotes for the phenylke-tonuric gene.

Munro (1947) made an extensive investigation of the first kind. He found the frequency of psychosis amongst the relatives of phenylketonurics to be more than twice the expected value when compared with the frequency of psychosis in 653 control families of non-phenylketonuric mentally subnormal patients. Nevertheless, the difference was barely statistically significant. As

Penrose had done previously, Munro observed a tendency for psychosis to occur in the relatives of the phenylketonuric patients with increasing age; the expected frequency was doubled after the age of 45 years.

In a more limited study of 8 phenylketonuric patients, Thompson (1957) reported frank psychosis of aggressive and paranoid type in three males in one family and in the father of the propositus in another family. Both parents of one of the phenylketonuric patients were said to have psychopathic personalities. Mental breakdown in middle life was reported in two of the families. Some might question whether or not these diagnoses were unconditionally acceptable on the basis of the documentation provided.

An increased rate of mental disease, suicide and alcoholism amongst relatives of phenylketonuric patients was reported by Blehova and her colleagues (Blehová, Hrubcová and Bartoňová, 1963, quoted by Perry, Tischler and Chapple, 1966). They compared 15 families containing phenylketonuric patients with families containing children with severe mental defect of unclassified origin. The classes of relatives affected with mental illness or alcoholism in the phenyl-ketonuric families, however, were not specified; nor was an attempt made to relate the abnormalities found to estimated rates of heterozygosity for the phenylketonuria gene.

Perry, Tischler and Chapple (1966) investigated 1268 relatives of 34 unrelated phenylketonuric patients and a comparable number of relatives of 34 mongols for cases of mental illness and behavioural abnormalities. Not all the 1268 relatives of the phenylketonurics would, of course, be expected to be heterozygotes for the phenylketonuria gene. No significant differences were found in the incidence of psychoses, admissions to mental hospitals, personality disorders, chronic alcoholism, suicide or crime between the relatives of the phenylketonuric patients and the control group.

In another extensive and carefully designed study, Blumenthal (1967) found no difference between 108 parents of phenylketonurics, 102 parents of non-phenylketonuric mental defectives and 121 parents of children with cystic fibrosis with respect to psychiatric disorder. The last two groups were selected for controls because they were likely to be subject to similar hardships and emotional stresses as the parents of phenylketonuric patients through the disability of their children.

Further findings contrary to the view that psychosis is an expression of the phenylketonuria gene in heterozygous form have been furnished by the study in Sweden of Larson and Nyman (1968). They found that the relatives of 42 unrelated phenylketonuric patients received mental hospital care or committed suicide about as often as people in general, with 5 per cent as a likely upper limit.

Electroencephalographic abnormalities in the relatives of phenylketonuric patients have received little attention, although this would seem a worthwhile subject for study. Cowie (1951a) found that out of 22 parents and other relatives of phenylketonuric patients, 3 had epileptic features in their electroencephalo-grams. In one of these, the abnormalities could be attributed to the sequelae of a previous brain abscess and operation. Significantly abnormal electroencephalo-grams were found in 3 out of 34 parents of phenylketonurics and in 9 out of 21 non-phenylketonuric sibs in a study by Fisch *et al.* (1965). The proportion of parents with abnormal records, who were all presumably heterozygotes, was not remarkable if the abnormality were causally connected with heterozygosity for the phenylketonuria gene. The high proportion of sibs, however, with abnormal records was striking; on theoretical grounds only two-thirds of the sibs would be expected to be heterozygotes. The results may have reflected a tendency for the electroencephalogram to become more stable with age.

Passing now to the biochemical studies of psychiatric patients, elevation of blood phenylalanine levels has been found in various series of mental hospital patients, but it has not been demonstrated conclusively that this was due to the presence of heterozygous carriers of the phenylketonuria gene within these groups. Poisner (1960) found a significantly higher fasting serum phenylalanine level in a group of schizophrenics than in a group of normal controls on the same diet. The schizophrenics were not investigated for heterozygosity of the phenylketonuria gene since no known heterozygotes were available to the investigator to establish control levels for the method used.

A slightly higher mean blood phenylalanine level was found in 100 mental hospital patients as compared with 100 controls in an unpublished study by Knox, Cullen and Rosen (cited by Knox, 1966). The results indicated that most mental hospital patients were not heterozygotes. Two groups were found to contribute to the elevated phenylalanine level amongst the mental hospital patients. One group consisted of alcoholics in whom the finding may have been attributable to liver dysfunction. The other consisted of male non-alcoholics of whom one-fifth might have represented heterozygotes for the phenylketonuria gene; or in whom some other unidentified factor might have been responsible for the elevated phenylalanine level.

Although raised fasting blood phenylalanine levels have been demonstrated in these surveys, the investigation of psychiatric patients using the phenylalanine tolerance test has not indicated an excess of heterozygotes for the phenylke-tonuria gene in these groups. In a small study, no significant difference was found in the results of the phenylalanine tolerance test between a group of 14 patients after recovery from an attack of endogenous depression and 15 control patients with a variety of neurological and psychiatric diagnoses, but without a family history of endogenous depression (Pratt *et al.*, 1963). The results from the combined groups were significantly different in the direction of normality from those of a group of known heterozygotes for phenylketonuria.[1] Lippman (1958) investigated 50 schizophrenics using the phenylalanine tolerance test. In a report with meagre documentation he stated that none were clearly heterozygotes although 13 were doubtful.

Summing up, there is very little support for the view that the phenylketonuria gene in heterozygous form predisposes the carrier to psychosis or other psychiatric disorder. An interesting finding made in pursuit of this idea, however, has been the observation of an elevated fasting blood level of phenylalanine in psychiatric patients. From the evidence furnished by the various studies, the

[1] One of the depressives, No. 29 (but none of the controls), was within the heterozygote range in each of the 4 readings, Fasting, and at 1, 2 and 4 hours after ingestion of a loading dose of phenylalanine.

significance of this phenomenon is obscure, but it seems unrelated to the presence of the phenylketonuria gene.

Another interesting finding has been the high frequency of abnormal electro-encephalographic records amongst the sibs of phenylketonuric patients. This could conceivably be an effect of the phenylketonuria gene. Further study in this area would be worthwhile, especially if biochemical findings, such as the fasting phenylalanine level of the subject at the time of recording, were correlated with findings in the electroencephalogram.

Linkage

With respect to genetical linkage, a search for a relationship between the ABO agglutinogens and phenylketonuria was originally started about 1936 in England. A report was made by Munro, Penrose and Taylor (1939) on material from 25 families, showing a significant degree of linkage for the test factors A and B and for the subagglutinogen A_1. No suggestion of linkage was found when group O was taken as the test factor. A later study of material from 42 sibships supported the suggestion of genetical linkage between phenylketonuria and the agglutinogens A, B, O and A_1 (Penrose, 1945). An examination subsequently of 14 families each containing at least one case of phenylketonuria provided suggestive but not conclusive evidence of linkage (Penrose, 1951a). In this study two methods were used for testing linkage: the complete sib-pair method (Penrose, 1950) and the use of weighted u-functions (Finney, 1940). With neither method did the linkage value exceed twice its standard error, though the evidence was suggestive of linkage, as before, between phenylketonuria and the ABO agglutinogens. There was no indication of linkage with MN factors. In a still later investigation (Renwick, Lawler and Cowie, 1960) the phenylalanine tolerance test was used as a means of detecting carriers of the phenylketonuria gene through three generations of several families, thus more extensive family data were available than would have been otherwise possible. Information from this study pointed in the same direction as that from the previous studies with respect to the ABO and phenylketonuria pair of loci, but even when all the available data (from 74 informative families) were combined, the evidence for linkage was weak.

MAPLE SYRUP URINE DISEASE (MSU DISEASE)

Biochemistry

This condition was first reported by Menkes, Hurst and Craig (1954). They described it as occurring in four sibs, all of whom developed cerebral symptoms of progressive severity, appearing within the first week of life, and terminating within 3 months of onset. A characteristic feature was an odour from the urine strikingly similar to that of maple syrup. At the time biochemical investigations failed to reveal the cause of this smell, but Menkes and his co-workers rightly supposed that the condition represented a new biochemical syndrome.

Other cases were later reported, and it was established that in this condition, described originally as maple syrup urine disease, three amino acids, leucine, isoleucine and valine, accumulate in the body fluids and overflow into the urine.

Later the corresponding keto acids were also found in large quantities in blood and urine.

Three groups of workers simultaneously and independently put forward the idea that this disease was an inborn error of metabolism affecting the second stage in the metabolism of leucine, isoleucine and valine (Menkes, 1959; Mackenzie and Woolf, 1959; Dancis *et al.*, 1959). These amino acids are normally metabolized first to the corresponding α-keto acids. These then undergo oxidative decarboxylation to produce fatty acids. The enzyme or enzymes necessary for this step are apparently lacking in MSU disease and it is thought that the α-keto acids which cannot therefore follow this pathway accumulate. It is not yet clear whether one enzyme is responsible for the oxidative decarboxylation of all three keto acids, or whether there are three closely related enzyme systems under a common genetical control (Blattner, 1965). The α-keto acids are then probably partly excreted in the urine, their further decomposition products producing the characteristic odour, and partly reconverted back to leucine, isoleucine and valine. The ferric chloride reaction with urine in MSU disease is somewhat like that in phenylketonuria. There is a danger, therefore, that it may be mistaken for phenylketonuria. The two conditions can be distinguished clearly, however, by chromatography.

Clinically MSU disease is characterized by a rapid cerebral degeneration. This commonly runs a few weeks, death ensuing at a month or so after birth. In some cases the course is slower, and the child may live several months as in the original cases of Menkes, Hurst and Craig (1954). There is one unusual published case, however, of a girl with alleged MSU disease, alive and well at the age of 7 years, although mentally subnormal. There is some evidence that a late-manifesting genetical variant exists (see below). In most cases failure to suck properly and to thrive is noted 5–7 days after birth, and increased tone in the limbs, attacks of rigidity, jerking and opisthotonos are seen, with periods of apnoea and cyanosis. Marked mental retardation is obvious in those patients surviving longer. Abnormalities of the EEG have been observed, and in some patients major epileptic fits have been reported (Mackenzie and Woolf, 1959; Silberman, Dancis and Feigin, 1961). The main features at post-mortem examination are oedema of the brain and marked deficiency of myelination, demonstrated in one case by a cerebroside content only one-tenth of normal (Woolf, 1962). In the brain of one patient, dying at 20 months, almost complete absence of myelin was reported (Crome, Dutton and Ross, 1961).

A dietary treatment for MSU disease, in principle comparable to the low-phenylalanine diet for phenylketonuria, has been tried with some success in reversing the metabolic abnormalities. The diet is based on a protein hydrolysate from which leucine, isoleucine and valine have been removed by passage through a column of cationic exchange resin (Dent and Westall, 1961) and are then added in the known small amounts to enable body growth to occur. Alternatively synthetic amino acids may be added in appropriate quantities. Norton and his co-workers (1962) support the view that attention should be directed towards controlling the intake of isoleucine (as a source of alloisoleucine) as well as of leucine and valine. They investigated the plasma aminogram of four patients with MSU disease, and showed that a peak formerly identified as methionine is almost entirely composed of a ninhydrin-reacting component which has not been described previously in blood. The position of this peak was found to be identical with that of alloisoleucine.

Genetics

The occurrence of MSU disease among sibs and its absence in the parents and other relatives suggests that it is inherited as a Mendelian recessive trait. This is further supported by parental consanguinity in some of the published cases (Lonsdale, Mercer and Faulkner, 1963; Woody and Hancock, 1963). It seems that there may be expression of the gene in heterozygous form. This is suggested by the finding of a pathological hyperaminoaciduria in the relatives of two affected children, which involved in all instances small increases of valine and leucine (Müller and Schreier, 1962). Linneweh and Ehrlich (1963) on the basis of chromatographic investigation of clinically normal parents, sibs and collateral relatives of patients with maple syrup urine disease, reported that heterozygotes can be detected by the presence of alloisoleucine in fasting control blood samples and by the results of isoleucine, leucine and valine tolerance tests. Dancis, Hutzler and Levitz (1965) have, however, been cautious in coming to conclusions about the possible differences between heterozygotes and normal subjects. They have made three approaches to investigate intensively the problem of demonstrating a partial defect in the presumed heterozygote. First, they studied the effects of an oral loading test with α-ketoisocaproic acid (the keto acid of leucine). It was considered this would be superior to leucine because it was closer to the metabolic block. Secondly, they measured the enzymatic activity of the peripheral leucocyte with sodium α-ketoisocaproate-l-C^{14}. Thirdly, they compared the ability of the peripheral leucocyte to metabolize α-ketoisocaproate-2-C^{14} and sodium isovalerate-l-C^{14}. The second substrate provided a baseline of the metabolic activity of the white blood cell against which the oxidative decarboxylase activity could be measured. Only the last approach proved successful. In this the fathers of children with maple syrup urine disease were significantly different from normal males. The mothers also, as a group, had a slight reduction in enzyme activity though this was not statistically significant.

Epidemiology

It is not known how common maple syrup urine disease may be as compared with other inborn errors of metabolism such as phenylketonuria, and it may be difficult to establish any figures as death is usually very early in infancy and the diagnosis may be missed in many cases. From the point of view of ethnic distribution, it is interesting to note that the condition has been reported as occurring in Negro children (Silberman et al., 1961; Woody, Woody and Tilden, 1963) and in the Japanese (Tada, Wada and Okamura, 1963).

It has been suggested that a late-manifesting genetical variant of maple syrup urine disease exists. This idea was first put forward in connexion with the case of a girl who was reported from the age of 16 months to have recurrent spells of ataxia and semicoma. During these the urine had the characteristic odour and was found to contain large quantities of leucine, isoleucine and valine (Morris *et al.*, 1961). It was proposed that this was an apparently non-fatal variant. Later, two sibs were reported in whom the symptoms of maple syrup urine disease appeared for the first time at the ages of 15 months and 8 years respectively (Kiil and Rokkones, 1964). With an interval of 5 months, these two previously healthy sibs developed acute metabolic acidosis with cerebral symptoms, coma, tonic and clonic convulsions and respiratory distress. The 15-month-old girl recovered completely after being comatose for 3 days, but the 8-year-old boy died in respiratory and circulatory failure after 4 days in coma. Kiil and Rokkones point out that most of the reported cases of maple syrup urine disease have been in young infants, and that the three cases reported by themselves and by Morris and his colleagues are probably examples of a late-manifesting genetical variant with the possibility of recurrent clinical manifestations. They draw attention to the fact that in none of these three cases had there been a progressive neurological deterioration which is so characteristic when the disease starts in the neonatal period. They suggest the variant might be due to a partial enzyme deficiency or some other modification of the full-blown metabolic error, giving rise to less distinct symptoms or symptoms that manifest only under special provocative conditions, for example when the amount of substrate is highly increased, or under unusual catabolic stress.

ISOVALERIC ACIDAEMIA

A previously undescribed disorder of leucine metabolism associated with mental retardation has been described by Efron (1967a). She has called this isovaleric acidaemia. This is not unlikely to be an autosomal recessive condition. The patients in whom it is described are a brother and sister; neither the parents nor a normal brother show any of the abnormal features.

In addition to mild mental retardation, these sibs are described as smelling of isovaleric acid (the odour of sweaty feet). They have periodic bouts of vomiting, acidosis and lethargy or coma. These attacks are said to be usually associated with infection or immoderate protein ingestion, and are characterized by a marked intensification of the smell and an increase in the blood concentration of isovaleric acid. The attacks appear to respond to glucose and electrolyte therapy, and during the recovery phase ataxia and intention tremor have been noted. Other abnormal physical findings are a mottling of the fundus and a congenital retinal vessel tortuosity in both patients. Both children began to refuse milk, cheese and eggs at the age of about one year, at which time their odour became less noticeable.

From a biochemical point of view, this condition contrasts with maple syrup urine disease in which the degradation of all three branched chain amino acids is abnormal. It is postulated that in isovaleric acidaemia, there is basically a deficiency in the conversion of isovaleryl-Co-A to β-methylcrotonyl-Co-A. The enzyme which mediates this is distinct from those which mediate the oxidation of the branched chain keto acids of valine and isoleucine to their corresponding short chain fatty acids. Efron emphasizes that this disorder is not detectable by amino acid or keto acid chromatography. Except for the odour, no simple screening method is available.

The case of a baby with isovaleric acidaemia in the neonatal period is reported by Newman *et al.* (1967). In his case surgery for intestinal obstruction may have hastened on his death; but attention is drawn to the fact that previous reports had been of a relatively mild form of the disease. This case was taken to show that the condition associated with isovaleric acidaemia can be rapidly fatal within a few days of birth. The possibility has not been ruled out, however, that these unusual patients may in fact be atypical heterozygotes, rather than representing a genetical variant of maple syrup urine disease.

HYPERVALINAEMIA

Hypervalinaemia should be mentioned as a condition distinct from maple syrup urine disease. It was detected in a child at the age of 2 months, reported by Wada *et al.* (1963). This child showed retarded mental and physical development, and was blind and hyperkinetic. Some clinical features seen in maple syrup urine disease were observed. These included vomiting, feeding difficulties and failure to thrive. The peculiar smell of maple syrup was not present in this patient's urine. The biochemical abnormality found was an excess of valine in the blood and urine. In contradistinction to this finding, in maple syrup urine disease an excess of all three amino acids, leucine, isoleucine and valine, is found. The clinical condition of this child improved rapidly on a diet deficient in valine. Although the metabolic block has not been determined, Efron (1965a) considers it reasonable to suppose that it is between valine and its keto acid, this step being carried out by the enzyme valine transaminase which may therefore be deficient in this condition.

The mode of genetical transmission of hypervalinaemia is not known, but the finding of abnormally high amounts of valine in the urine of both parents of the patient reported by Wada *et al.* (1963) is compatible with autosomal recessive inheritance, this urinary finding being a manifestation of the single gene in the clinically normal heterozygote.

Waisman (1966) in discussing hypervalinaemia points out that his finding is of interest in that infant monkeys fed excess valine diets showed some mental retardation, convulsions and bizarre behaviour.

Investigations into the specific metabolic defect in hypervalinaemia were made by Dancis *et al.* (1967). In a study of the metabolism of the peripheral leucocytes in a child with hypervalinaemia and mental retardation, they were able to demonstrate a defect in the transamination of valine, the defective enzyme being the specific transaminase for this amino acid. The patient's leucocytes were found to be able to transaminate amino acids other than valine. Transamination of valine was shown to be demonstrable in placenta. The placenta is almost entirely foetal in origin, and the synthesis of the enzyme responsible for the transamination of valine in it is probably under the same genetical control as that in the leucocytes. Dancis and his co-workers suggest that if this proves true, it may be possible to make the diagnosis before birth by needle biopsy of the placenta.

HISTIDINAEMIA

Histidinaemia was first described in 1961 by Ghadimi, Partington and Hunter. The urine of two children with speech defects was found to produce a green colour with ferric chloride and Phenistix reagent strips. Increased amounts of histidine were found in their blood and urine. The metabolic error has been identified as a defect of the enzyme histidine α-deaminase. This enzyme is necessary for the transformation of histidine to urocanic acid. Owing to the metabolic block, histidine and its derivatives accumulate in the blood and there is raised excretion in the urine. Loading tests, in which L-histidine is given by mouth, accentuates the abnormality in blood and urine.

The clinical findings in histidinaemia are reviewed by Woody, Snyder and Harris (1965). The clinical features have been variable. Out of 11 patients

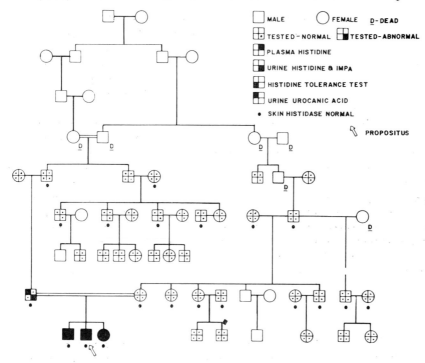

Fig. 26. Family pedigree. For this chart, histidinaemia is defined by: (1) elevated plasma histidine and (2) abnormal histidine tolerance test. Thus, the father is not affected despite occasional abnormalities of urine histidine and urocanic acid (Woody et al., 1965).

reported in the literature, 5 had fair hair, 7 had blue eyes, 5 showed growth retardation, 8 had speech difficulties and 4 were mentally retarded. Three were completely free of any such symptoms.

Berlow, Arends and Harries (1965) affirm that mental retardation must be considered a manifestation of the disease as the majority of unpublished cases, as well as a proportion of the published cases, have had mental defect. Some are said not to be retarded, but are described as having 'speech problems'. One might suspect that these problems may be part of a more generalized defect of mental functioning, though the first five published cases (four of them with speech defects) were stated to be of normal intelligence. Later reports have described patients with severe mental subnormality, some of whom had convulsions and progressive ataxia (Davies and Robinson, 1963; Holton, Lewis and Moore, 1964).

In three sibs with histidinaemia reported by Woody *et al.* (1965) a peculiar EEG pattern was found. This had not been reported previously in association with the condition. It consisted of continuous rapid activity (15–20 cycles per second) of moderate to high amplitude, upon which was superimposed random high voltage spikes. The pattern was unchanged by anticonvulsant drugs.

The mode of inheritance appears to be recessive. The condition has been reported in sibs, and parents are clinically normal. Three sibs who are children of a consanguineous marriage have been reported (Woody *et al.*, 1965; see pedigree, FIG. 26). Although in a proportion of the patients' parents, who presumably are carriers of the gene, the histidine loading test is abnormal, this is by no means an invariable finding; and in the family investigated by Woody and his co-workers histidine tolerance tests did not differentiate persons heterozygous for the trait.

Woody *et al.* (1965) put forward the interesting idea that the genetical fault which results in reduced histidine α-deaminase activity can be expressed to a different degree in different tissues. Whereas absence of histidase can be demonstrated as a rule in the skin biopsies of patients with histidinaemia, their three patients had high levels of histidine α-deaminase in the skin, which, it was suggested, might have been a means of compensation for a defect of the enzyme in the liver in these patients. It was suggested that these children might even seem to have represented a distinct variant of histidinaemia in which liver histidase activity is reduced while skin histidase activity is present.

Crome and Stern (1967) suggest that it is likely that affected children would, if treated early, benefit from a diet low in histidine; such a diet is now available commercially.

HYDROXYPROLINAEMIA AND HYPERPROLINAEMIA

These disorders, identified by Mary Efron of Boston, are very rare even compared with the other inborn errors of metabolism. Hydroxyproline and proline are non-essential amino acids, synthesized within the body. Metabolic blocks in their degradation have been identified by Efron and her colleagues in three positions, and three corresponding conditions have been delineated. All are inherited disorders associated with mental retardation.

Hyperprolinaemia I

Efron has reported hyperprolinaemia with a defect of the enzyme proline oxidase in two families affected by hereditary renal disease (Efron, 1965b). In the first family the propositus was apparently normal at birth. Early in infancy he showed signs of mental retardation, and in his second year an audiogram confirmed that he had marked hearing loss. From this time until his death in his sixth year he had a downhill course with repeated urinary tract infections. Finally he died in uraemia. During his life, he had frequent convulsions in the absence of fever, which were sometimes precipitated by flashing light. Mal-formation of the kidney was found on post-mortem examination, also some abnormalities in the central nervous system including absence of part of the inferior olive and a diffuse loss of neurones in the cortex. There was a patchy loss of ganglion cells from the organ of Corti.

All 5 sibs of this patient were of normal intelligence, but 2 had haematuria and activation of electroencephalographic seizure discharges by photic stimulation. Another sister showed EEG changes and reaction to photic stimulation but no haematuria. The patient and these 3 sibs had persistently elevated plasma proline concentrations. The mother was found to have a hypoplastic kidney, haematuria, some hearing loss and activation of an epileptiform discharge on the EEG by photic stimulation. Though she had all the abnormalities (apart, apparently, from mental retardation) shown by her affected children, her plasma proline concentration was normal on repeated measurement. There were many cases of haematuria and/or deafness among the mother's relatives throughout three generations. The ratio of males to females was approximately equal. The father was found to be free from these abnormalities, as were the paternal relatives available for testing.

In the second family, the propositus was well until the age of 30 when he noted some difficulties in micturition and increasing feelings of malaise. At 31 he developed complete urinary retention. He was found to have a large hydronephrotic kidney. A urinary chromatogram showed a specific aminoaciduria with increased excretion of proline, hydroxyproline and glycine. This patient was apparently only moderately mentally retarded. He stayed at school until 16, but only completed the fifth grade. He was rejected by the army because of low intelligence.

Three of his 5 sibs had raised plasma proline concentration, and 2 of these 3 had haematuria. The mother had haematuria and her plasma proline was at the upper limit of the normal range. The EEG effects and hearing impairment observed in the first family were not found amongst members of this family.

Four further cases of hyperprolinaemia of this type in a single family were reported by Kopelman, Asatoor and Milne (1964). The propositus was one of twin brothers (probably dizygotic) who had the nephrotic syndrome. The other twin died in renal failure. The propositus and 2 of 4 apparently normal sibs were found to have an abnormally high plasma-proline concentration, and excess urinary excretion of proline, hydroxyproline and glycine. The father had mild proteinuria, hyperprolinaemia and slight prolinuria without excess urinary hydroxyproline or glycine.

It is thought that the basic metabolic error in this form of hyperprolinaemia is a deficiency of the enzyme proline oxidase. The condition is possibly an autosomal recessive trait, with varying degrees of pleiotropic expression in the heterozygote. More data are required before the mode of inheritance can be established with certainty.

Hyperprolinaemia II

A third family was described by Efron (1965b) in whom the propositus was found to excrete large amounts of proline, hydroxyproline and glycine in the urine following an acute febrile episode at the age of 19 months.

The mother had noted before the illness that this child was developing more slowly than her other children. The febrile illness was sudden and acute, with convulsions, stupor and a right-sided paralysis. A fine erythematous rash appeared on the trunk. A diagnosis of acute encephalitis was made, but the aetiology was undetected. An EEG recorded after recovery from the acute illness was abnormal with diffuse high voltage slow delta wave activity without focal abnormality. There was no evidence of renal disease in his case but the maternal aunt and grandmother had renal disease. The paternal grandfather had renal stones.

In this patient, the plasma proline was over twice as high as any other recorded in a case of hyperprolinaemia. He also excreted $\triangle^1$-pyrroline-5-carboxylic acid, and the basic metabolic defect was considered to be a deficiency of $\triangle^1$-pyrroline-5-carboxylate dehydrogenase.

Since the report of this family by Efron (1965b) another family has been discovered in which the propositus, suffering from hyperprolinaemia of this type, was born to parents who were first cousins (Emery, Goldie and Stern, 1968). It is probable that this condition will prove to be transmitted as an autosomal recessive trait, but the study of more families is needed before a definite conclusion may be drawn as to its mode of inheritance.

Hydroxyprolinaemia

The only case described so far of this condition was reported by Efron, Bixby and Pryles (1965). This child was mentally retarded. The blood hydroxyproline levels were 20–50 times higher than normal, and large quantities were found in the urine. No hydroxyproline was detected, however, in his cerebrospinal fluid. Although this substance constitutes 14 per cent of collagen, the patient showed no signs of disturbed collagen metabolism.

This condition is probably an autosomal recessive trait. The basic metabolic error is a deficiency of hydroxyproline oxidase.

Treatment of Hydroxyprolinaemia and Hyperprolinaemia

Hydroxyproline and proline are non-essential amino acids which are readily synthesized in the body. For this reason, the three conditions associated with their defective breakdown may prove to be untreatable by dietary methods.

This problem is discussed by Efron (1967b). There is hope for treatment of an inherited inborn error of metabolism when an essential amino acid accumulates on account of a genetical defect in a degradative enzyme, as in phenylketonuria or maple syrup urine disease. In these the blood level of the accumulated amino acid can be lowered by limiting its intake in the diet. Certain disorders with blocks in the breakdown of non-essential amino acids which are intermediates in metabolic pathways may also prove amenable to a dietary regime. Efron quotes homocystinuria as an example, in which the rationale of dietary treatment is reduction of intake of the amino acid precursor, methionine. Efron mentions also citrullinaemia, argininosuccinicaciduria and ornithaemia, all of which are associated with ammonia intoxication and respond to low protein diets.

Hydroxyprolinaemia and hyperprolinaemia, however, pose a special problem owing to the fact that they are freely synthesized in the body. They may prove to be untreatable by dietary means. When the child with hydroxyprolinaemia was placed on a diet low in hydroxyproline, the plasma level did not fall.

Efron points out that such conditions present a challenge to the physician, and that means of treatment other than dietary therapy may be worth consideration. For example, it is known that the enzyme hydroxyprolinase and the two enzymes responsible for hyperprolinaemia are present in normal kidney. If hydroxyprolinaemia and hyperprolinaemia should prove a cause of mental retardation, and if the problem of survival of transplanted kidneys is eventually solved, it is within the realm of possibility that kidney transplant might prove a method of preventing brain damage in these conditions.

HOMOCYSTINURIA

Homocystinuria, an inborn error of amino acid metabolism involving the sulphur-containing compound homocystine, was first described by Field *et al.* (1962) in Belfast. The discovery was made from the analysis of urine from two mentally retarded sibs whose clinical features were thought to suggest a genetical basis. Soon afterwards other cases were described, including a series of 10 cases (from 7 families) from a survey of 2920 mentally defective individuals in Northern Ireland (Carson *et al.*, 1965). In this series the only inborn error of metabolism which occurred with greater frequency was phenylketonuria (69 cases). This suggested that homocystinuria might be one of the more common inborn errors associated with mental subnormality. It was suggested that because homocystine does not appear on phenol-lutidine paper chromatograms on account of its decomposition and because even on oxidized chromatograms homocysteic acid runs close to cysteic acid, it may have been overlooked or confused with cystine in other surveys.

The clinical features are striking and make up a picture, which, once seen, is easily recognized again. The limbs and digits are long and thin; there is genu valgum; pes cavus may be present; the patients have a shuffling gait. Kyphoscoliosis frequently develops. The hair is fair and fine, with a texture that has been likened to that of spun nylon. An intense malar flush, often with a cyanotic tinge, is characteristic; there may be marked mottling over the extensor aspects of the lower extremities. These skin changes have suggested a possible abnormality in the peripheral circulation. The eyes show characteristic signs including dislocation of the lens and a fine tremor of the iris (iridodonesis). Glaucoma, secondary to complete dislocation of the lens, and cystic retinal detachment with pigmentary changes have also been described. Most patients are severely retarded in their mental development.

This metabolic disorder appears to differ from the other aminoacidurias associated with mental subnormality, such as phenylketonuria and maple syrup urine disease, in that it follows a more slowly progressive course. Most of the patients are reported to have appeared normal at birth, and to have achieved early developmental milestones at the expected ages. Usually, however, during infancy, backwardness is noted, such as delay in learning to walk; and fits may supervene. In connexion with the progressiveness of the condition, the electroencephalographic findings in one of the patients reported by Carson and her co-workers (1965) may be of special relevance. At the age of 4 years this girl had a normal EEG record. Eight months later she had her first generalized major motor seizure, and thereafter the EEG picture progressed to diffuse generalized dysrhythmia within 3 years.

Patients with homocystinuria are prone to major thrombo-embolic episodes which may be fatal. Thus, in 2 of the 10 cases in the Northern Ireland series

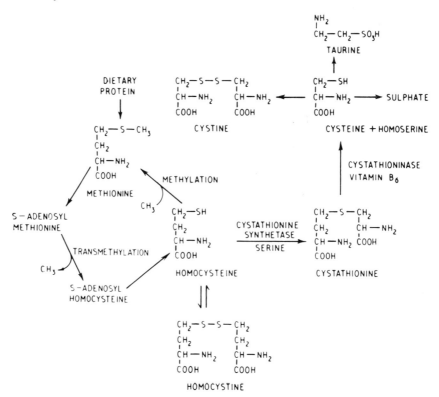

Fig. 27. The metabolism of homocystine and cystathionine (Crome and Stern, 1967).

this was the mode of death (Carson et al., 1965). In both of these children there was evidence at autopsy of previous and widespread thrombo-embolic disease, both arterial and venous. Cases of fatal coronary occlusion are reported in the series of Schimke et al. (1965).

The biochemical basis of homocystinuria has been shown to be a deficiency of the enzyme cystathionine synthetase [see FIG. 27] which has been shown to be absent from the liver and brain of patients with homocystinuria (Mudd et al., 1964; Brenton, Cusworth and Gaull, 1965a and b). This enzyme does not appear to be absent from all tissues, however, in homocystinuria. Its presence has been demonstrated, for instance, in the optic lens of a homocystinuric patient (Gaull and Gaitonde, 1966). Cystathionine synthetase converts homocysteine to cystathionine, and in homocystinuria in the brain and other tissues the level of cystathionine is low while homocysteine builds up. Some of the excess homocysteine is converted to methionine by methylation, while some is oxidized to homocystine which appears in the urine and plasma. Disappearance of methionine from the blood of patients after methionine loading is delayed, and there is increased excretion of homocystine.

When homocystinuric patients receive a normal diet, methionine accumulates in their body fluids and tissues, an abnormal amount of homocystine circulates and is excreted in the urine, and there is a lack of cystathionine in certain tissues. Therefore an approach to dietary treatment would seem justifiable along two lines. First, assuming that the excess methionine or homocystine is deleterious, the methionine intake could be cut to minimal requirements and supplementary cystine added to the diet. The addition of cystine was seen to be desirable from the work of Brenton et al. (1966). They showed that a homocystinuric child under dietary control could not be maintained in positive nitrogen balance on a diet in which methionine was provided but no cystine. Secondly, assuming that the harmful effects in the condition are related to a deficiency of cystathionine rather than to excessive methionine and homocystine, cystathionine, which is not a constituent of a normal diet, could be added to the patients' food.

These two lines of approach were considered by Komrower et al. (1966). They decided to try the low methionine-high cystine diet first. The second dietary regime was given lower priority because cystathionine is very expensive, it is rapidly excreted in the urine and no known function has been attributed to this compound.

After 2 years of experience with the low methionine-high cystine diet Komrower and his team reported encouraging results. It was possible to maintain satisfactory, if not ideal, control of plasma levels of methionine. Despite low cystine levels, growth showed signs of approaching the range of normal values. Comparison of a treated patient with her untreated sibs showed her to be brighter and closer in intelligence to her normal sisters. Apart from genu valgum, none of the more serious physical signs of homocystinuria had appeared in this child. In two cases with fits, Komrower and his team report encouraging results with the lower methionine-high cystine diet. They point out, however, that considerable reservations must still be made in respect of the long-term prognosis, in view of the fact that some of the children reported on earlier were apparently normal for the first few years of life. Obviously more experience is needed before the effects of dietary treatment in homocystinuria can be assessed fully.

Brenton et al. (1966) discuss the question of dietary treatment in homocystinuria in the light of dietary treatment that has been tried in other metabolic diseases. From information at present available it seems that the newborn infant with homocystinuria may be quite normal clinically, with the complex symptomatology including ocular defects, growth disorder and mental deficiency developing at a relatively slow rate over the next few years. Brenton and his co-workers believe that this slowness of development of pathological features may be relevant to treatment. They make a comparison with the acute catastrophic cerebral degeneration in maple syrup urine disease, in which treatment is required in the first week or two of life. The cerebral damage in phenylketonuria, probably occurs more slowly, and may still partly respond to treatment even if this is not begun until several months of age. Brenton and his colleagues point out that in homocystinuria, while it will always be the aim to diagnose the condition and begin treatment as early in life as possible on account of the ever-present threat of irreversible thrombotic damage, it is likely that some cases may benefit even if the diagnosis is not made until the child is a year or more of age.

Homocystinuria is inherited as an autosomal recessive trait. This was apparent from the earliest reports of the condition in which this mode of inheritance was indicated by the ratio of affected to unaffected sibs, by the fact that the parents

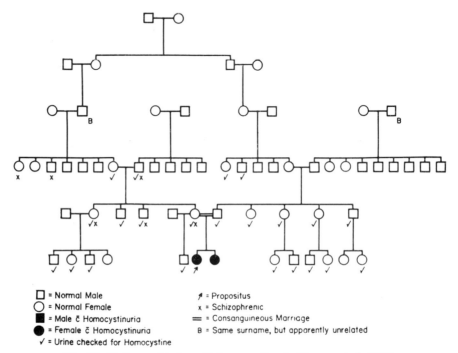

☐ = Normal Male
○ = Normal Female
■ = Male č Homocystinuria
● = Female č Homocystinuria
✓ = Urine checked for Homocystine

↗ = Propositus
x = Schizophrenic
= = Consanguineous Marriage
B = Same surname, but apparently unrelated

Fig. 28. Pedigree of twins with homocystinuria (Carson *et al.*, 1965).

were not affected, and by a history of consanguinity in 1 of the 7 families of the Northern Ireland series [see FIG. 28, from Carson *et al.*, 1965]. One pair of parents of homocystinurics in the 20 families reported by Schimke *et al.* (1965) were first cousins, and consanguinity was suspected in three other instances.

So far, detection of the heterozygote for the homocystinuria gene by clinical or biochemical means has not been conclusive. Although methionine loading tests give characteristic results in homocystinuric patients, the results in their parents have not been definitive.

Clinical abnormalities suspected of being related to the heterozygous state were found in some of the parents in the series of 20 families of Schimke *et al.* (1965). One was reported to have had electroencephalographic abnormalities.

One had a small coloboma in one eye. Mental illness and suicide were reported to have occurred in the family of one or both parents in several instances.

Homocystinuria and Marfan's Syndrome

The condition of homocystinuria has certain features in common with Marfan's syndrome. Thus 2 of the 10 cases in the Northern Ireland series had been reported previously as cases of Marfan's syndrome. There are, however, clinical, genetical and pathological features which distinguish the two conditions.

Features common to the two conditions are ectopia lentis, cardiovascular changes and skeletal characteristics including long, thin limbs and digits. Points of differentiation between the two conditions are well documented by Schimke and his co-workers who, mainly through the screening of cases of ectopia lentis, or presumed Marfan's syndrome, or both, discovered 38 cases of homocystinuria distributed in 20 families (Schimke *et al.*, 1965). It is doubtful whether the ocular changes of homocystinuria can be distinguished from those of Marfan's syndrome, though possibly downward displacement of the lens is more frequent in homocystinuria. In the skeleton, homocystinuria is distinguished from Marfan's syndrome in that generalized osteoporosis is a feature. This usually leads to the radiological sign of 'codfish vertebrae' and some degree of vertebral collapse is present in all cases. These features are not found in Marfan's syndrome. In homocystinuria, loose-jointedness is not as conspicuous as in the Marfan condition. There are differences between the two conditions with respect to the type of cardiovascular anomalies. In homocystinuria dilatation with thrombosis in medium-sized arteries and veins is a characteristic finding, whereas in Marfan's syndrome dilatation or dissection of the aorta, or both (not observed in homocystinuria), is a recognized feature. In homocystinuria the malar flush is characteristic, this is not seen in patients with Marfan's syndrome. The skin of the limbs and trunk in homocystinuria may show a cyanotic mottling (livedo reticularis); patients with Marfan's syndrome may show striae distensae, but mottling is not usual. Mental retardation, usually of severe degree, is usual in patients with homocystinuria. In Marfan's syndrome, however, mental defect is not considered to be an essential feature, and mental grades vary greatly from one patient to another (Dax, 1941).

The distinction between the two conditions that confirms their separate identity is a genetical one. Homocystinuria is inherited as an autosomal recessive trait, whereas Marfan's syndrome is an autosomal dominant condition, most instances of which are attributed to fresh mutation (Lynas, 1958).

MARFAN'S SYNDROME[1]

Attention was first drawn to this syndrome by Marfan (1896). It is a Mendelian dominant condition affecting tissues of mesenchymal origin. Affected individuals may present a striking appearance with long, thin limbs and spidery fingers, together with eye defects.

The clinical and pathological findings in Marfan's syndrome are well documented by Monz (1965). The most obvious effects are seen in the skeletal and

[1] Marfan's syndrome is not recognized as an aminoaciduria, but it is included here on account of its comparison with homocystinuria.

cardiovascular systems and in the eyes. In the skeletal system the shafts of the long bones are elongated and attenuated. Together with poorly developed musculature, this gives the limbs a slender and sometimes almost graceful appearance. The fingers and toes are long, tapering and arachnodactylic. In some cases the thorax may be narrow with marked kyphosis, and the skull may also be long and narrow. In the cardiovascular system, the heart may show enlargement, and a variety of congenital defects may be found including septal defects and coarctation of the aorta. Defects in the tunica media of the major blood vessels are characteristic, and may predispose to abnormal dilatations which in turn may lead to dissecting aneurysms and rupture. A variety of lesions may occur in the eye. Subluxation or dislocation of the lens is a characteristic feature of the condition. This is usually bilateral and appears to be associated with abnormalities of attachment or structure of the suspensory fibres. Coloboma is not infrequent. Secondary ocular defects such as glaucoma, cataract and retinal detachment may occur. In addition to these features, loose-jointedness and hypermobility of the joints are striking because of the excessive laxity of the ligaments. This effect is enhanced by muscular hypotonia.

Many of the clinical effects could be attributed directly to an abiotrophy of the connective tissue, though the specific anatomical or biochemical basis for such a weakness is not fully understood. Bolande (1963) studied the histology and histochemistry of diseased aortic and cardiac tissue in Marfan's syndrome. His findings indicated that the fundamental lesion is an over-accumulation of chondroitin sulphate, followed by disruption of the elastic fibres.

Estes, Carey and Desai (1965) reported a family in whom various members showed manifestations of Marfan's syndrome and haematological abnormalities including increased numbers of immature granulocytes, increased levels of alkaline phosphatase in peripheral blood granulocytes, giant platelets and functional platelet defects. They point out that such abnormalities have been found previously in patients with heritable disorders of connective tissue such as the Ehlers-Danlos syndrome. In the family reported the haematological defects and the manifestations of Marfan's syndrome segregated independently, and therefore could not result from a single gene defect; but Estes, Carey and Desai suggest that they may be related through loci on chromosome 21. The grounds for this supposition are somewhat tenuous, being based in turn upon the postulation that chromosome 21 is responsible for leucocyte alkaline phosphatase activity. In the family reported, the haematological abnormalities followed an autosomal dominant pattern of inheritance.

Further support for a basic pathology of connective tissue in Marfan's syndrome comes from the observations of Berenson and Dalferes (1965). They found a two- to four-fold increase in mucopolysaccharides excreted in the urine of patients with Marfan's syndrome as compared with normal controls allowing for age and sex. The mucopolysaccharides excreted in urine represent a small fraction relative to the amount metabolized in the connective tissue of the body, and an abnormal excretion of these substances is found not only in the conditions designated 'mucopolysaccharidoses', including Hurler's syndrome, but other conditions, including collagen diseases, which are essentially heritable disorders of connective tissue.

Although mental retardation is frequently seen in Marfan's syndrome, it is not considered to be an essential feature (Penrose, 1963). Cases with mental defect tend to occur sporadically in families and the degree of intellectual impairment can vary greatly from one patient to another (Dax, 1941).

The condition is transmitted as a Mendelian dominant defect. The range of variability of the clinical signs is great, and although in many instances the effects of direct transmission from parent to child can be seen clearly, the *forme fruste* may escape recognition. Nevertheless, most cases are attributed to fresh mutation. The estimated rate of mutation per generation is 6 per million gametes; and the approximate incidence of the condition is 15 per million in the general population according to Lynas (1958). Estimates of the incidence of Marfan's syndrome prior to the discovery of homocystinuria in 1962 may, however, err on the high side owing to misclassification of homocystinuric patients mistaken for cases of Marfan's syndrome. The similarities between the two conditions which may lead to a confusion in diagnosis have been discussed already [p. 225] where the clinical, pathological, biochemical and genetical differences are specified.

DISORDERS OF THE UREA CYCLE

Four disorders have been connected with enzyme defects in the Krebs-Henseleit urea cycle [FIG. 29]. These are all very rare. They are argininosuccinicaciduria, citrullinuria, hyperammonaemia and hyperlysinaemia. Certain features are common to all four of these diseases; all patients have suffered from vomiting, convulsions or other neurological symptoms, such as hyperreflexia, tremor or stupor, and some have had liver dysfunction (Crome and Stern, 1967). All four disorders have been in most cases associated with mental subnormality.

Argininosuccinicaciduria

In 1958, Allan *et al.* reported a newly recognized disease, probably hereditary, characterized by severe mental deficiency and a constant gross abnormality of amino acid metabolism. This was discovered in the course of routine testing for amino acids by paper chromatography. In this first account, a family was described in which two of four children of unrelated parents showed a severe degree of mental retardation, with grossly abnormal electroencephalograms. One had a history of epileptic convulsions followed by ataxia of several days' duration. Both had systolic murmurs. Their hair was thought to be brittle or friable in texture. An unusual substance was discovered in the urine which gave reactions typical of an amino acid or closely related compound, though at the time no suggestion could be made as to its chemical structure. The substance was also detected in the plasma and cerebrospinal fluid of the affected children. Its relatively low plasma concentration and high urinary level suggested high renal clearance. The concentration in the cerebrospinal fluid was, however, nearly three times as high as that in the plasma, suggesting that the substance was formed not by a defective enzyme in the liver or in any other organ in close relationship to the systemic blood supply, but in the brain or in some other structure closely associated with the cerebrospinal fluid. It was suggested that the abnormal substance leaked from the cerebrospinal fluid into the blood, from which it was rapidly cleared by the kidney.

The substance was later isolated and identified by Westall (1960). He established that it was argininosuccinic acid. This substance is known to be an

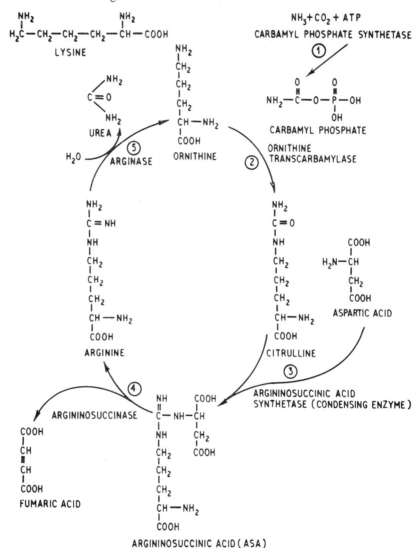

Fig. 29. The Krebs-Henseleit urea cycle (after Crome and Stern, 1967).

intermediate product in the urea cycle in the liver, though the blood urea was normal in the patient's excreting argininosuccinic acid, suggesting there was no metabolic block in this system in the liver. It has been shown, however, that urea can be synthesized by the rat brain *in vivo* (Sporn *et al.*, 1959). It is possible, therefore, that in man also urea synthesis is not limited to the liver as previously believed, but may also occur in the brain. If this is so, and if the urea cycle in the brain is similar to that in the liver, then it may be that the basic error in argininosuccinicaciduria is a deficiency of the enzyme for the break down of this substance in the brain but not in the liver.

The theory that a specific enzyme deficiency of such a kind may be responsible for the condition was given further support by the findings of Westall and Tomlinson (1961). These workers developed a simple, specific system for assaying the activity in blood cells of argininosuccinicase, (ASAase), the enzyme responsible for splitting argininosuccinic acid into arginine and fumaric acid. Using this method it was found that the level of ASAase activity in the blood cells from children with argininosuccinicaciduria was appreciably lower than that found in the blood cells of normal individuals.

It is likely that the gene is very rare. Allan et al. (1958) reported that 1,500 mentally subnormal patients were screened and no further examples discovered. Relatively few cases of argininosuccinicaciduria, about ten in all, have so far been published, but the facts available would fit in with hereditary transmission by a single autosomal recessive gene. This is supported by the evidence of apparently clinically normal parents, the occurrence of argininosuccinicaciduria in sibs in four of the families reported, the occurrence of the condition in individuals of each sex, and parental consanguinity in at least one family in which the parents were first cousins, reported by Moser et al. (1967).

In homozygous form it would seem that the gene responsible determines complete, or almost complete, inactivity of the enzyme ASAase, at least in the blood cells. The gene appears to exert some effect also in heterozygous form, as both parents (presumably heterozygotes) of the first two patients reported by Allan et al. (1958) showed reduced activity of the enzyme ASAase in blood cells to about half the normal value. In a sibship reported by Carson and Neill (1962) mental retardation, coarse friable hair and cranial nerve palsies were present in sibs of the two propositi [see pedigree, FIG. 30]. These effects may have been expressions of the abnormal gene in heterozygous form. It is not so likely that they were pleiotropic effects of the gene in homozygous form, as these sibs of the propositi did not excrete argininosuccinic acid in the urine.

A chromosome abnormality has been reported in the case of a patient with argininosuccinicaciduria (Coryell et al., 1964). This girl, with a modal number of 47 chromosomes, appeared to have trisomy involving a chromosome of the C group, possibly a number 12 chromosome. It was thought not to be an extra X chromosome because the sex chromatin pattern from a buccal smear was normal. Her mother apparently had the same chromosome abnormality, excreted argininosuccinic acid in the urine, and was mentally retarded. There have been no other reports of chromosomal abnormalities in argininosuccinic-aciduria, and the significance of the findings in this mother and daughter is not clear.

Citrullinuria

During a chromatographic screening programme for aminoaciduria, large amounts of an unidentified amino acid were found in the urine of a mentally retarded child aged 18 months (McMurray *et al.*, 1962). The amino acid was isolated and recognized as L-citrulline. Over several months chemical studies of the urine showed an output of large quantities of citrulline, though the amounts were quite variable. In a period of 10 consecutive days the quantity excreted varied from 0·48 to 2·15 g. per day. The concentration of citrulline was increased both in the plasma and cerebrospinal fluid, suggesting a defect in metabolism with an overflow into the urine, rather than a defect in renal transport. The term 'citrullinaemia' is suggested, therefore, as preferable

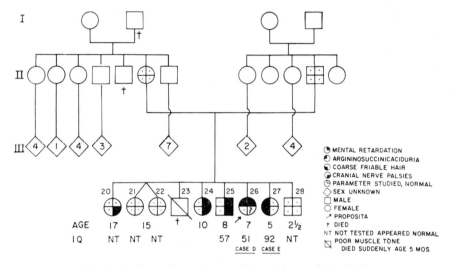

Fig. 30. Pedigree of two sisters with argininosuccinicaciduria
(Carson and Neill, 1962).

(McKusick, 1962). The presumed enzyme deficiency is of argininosuccinic acid synthetase (Crome and Stern, 1967).

There is insufficient evidence to draw conclusions as to the possible genetical mechanism in this condition. The parents of this patient were, however, first cousins, which is at least suggestive of its being inherited as a recessive trait.

Another patient, who, in the course of a screening programme for amino-aciduria, was found to excrete a large amount of citrulline, had been reported previously by Visakorpi and Hyrske (1960). This patient was mentally subnormal (IQ 32, test not specified). His electroencephalogram showed generalized dysrhythmia and he died in status epilepticus at the age of 18 years. He had two normal sibs, and it seems that the parents, too, were unaffected. The urine in this case showed a cystinuric pattern with increased amounts of cystine, lysine, arginine and ornithine. In this respect this patient differed from that described by McMurray and his colleagues, in whom the amino acid excretion pattern was not that of a typical cystinuric (McMurray and Mohyuddin, 1962). In both cases, the origin of the excessive urinary citrulline is open to question, and although in the patient of Visakorpi and Hyrske it may have been causally related to cystinuria, equally well it may have been a coincidental finding.

Citrullinuria is obviously a very rare anomaly, and it will be necessary to study more cases before the nature of the biochemical error and the genetical mechanism possibly responsible are understood.

Hyperammonaemia

Hyperammonaemia appears to be a very rare condition. It has been reported in two first cousins (Russell *et al.*, 1962) in one of whom an enzyme defect was demonstrated. Ornithine transcarbamylase activity was greatly reduced in a liver biopsy specimen. This enzyme operates in the Krebs-Henseleit urea cycle to convert ornithine together with carbamyl phosphate to citrulline. On account of its occurrence in cousins, hyperammonaemia is considered to be a genetically determined metabolic error, but its mode of inheritance has not been established.

In the two cousins reported by Russell *et al.* (1962), both girls were considered backward in early development during infancy, and mental retardation became more apparent as time went on. At the age of 6, one of the patients had an IQ 60 (Merrill-Palmer scale). The condition was accompanied by attacks of vomiting with screaming and agitation followed by lethargy and stupor. The cranial circumference was below normal in both reported cases, and on air encephalography both patients appeared to have cortical atrophy. In both, the ammonia levels in blood and cerebrospinal fluid were greatly raised, exceeding those usually found in hepatic coma.

It is interesting from a genetical point of view that one of the patients reported had a twin of normal intelligence who was free from clinical symptoms. This twin, however, had a high normal blood ammonia level. Although the twins may have been monozygous, the zygosity was not verified by blood grouping or other means.

Hyperammonaemia appears to be one of the inborn errors of metabolism whose effects can be modified by treatment. Russell *et al.* (1962) found that the ammonia concentrations in blood and cerebrospinal fluid fell to normal on a low protein diet. Efron (1966) considers it would be interesting to know whether a trial on thyroid hormone would be beneficial in this disease, as this hormone is known to influence the enzymes of the urea cycle, including ornithine transcarbamylase, in metamorphosing tadpoles.

Hyperlysinaemia

Hyperlysinaemia is the fourth disorder that has been associated with a metabolic error in the Krebs-Henseleit urea cycle. It has been suggested that it comprises more than one disease entity (Crome and Stern, 1967).

In a case reported by Woody (1964) the affected child was considered normal by her parents until she was 7 months old. She then began to have convulsions, which finally ceased at the age of 3. Weakness of ligaments with resulting instability of the joints was a prominent feature. She was hyperkinetic, irritable, quarrelsome and meddlesome in addition to being apparently mentally and physically retarded. She had a normocytic normochromic anaemia which did not respond to iron therapy, but improved when lysine intake was reduced. The levels of lysine in her plasma were 4–10 times higher than normal. Urinary lysine was 10–15 times higher than normal. She responded to a low lysine diet, though no changes could be seen in plasma or urinary amino acid patterns. On this diet her clinical condition improved; she became more amenable, and at $3\frac{1}{2}$ years of age could run and skip and say about a dozen words.

Colombo *et al.* (1964) report a child with recurrent ammonia intoxication from the early weeks of life. This was characterized by vomiting, coma, spasticity and convulsions and recovery within a few days following glucose-saline administration. The ammonia intoxication occurred only on a normal or high protein intake, and was prevented by a low protein diet. Chromatographic studies during high protein intake showed a significant increase in the concentration of lysine and arginine, and it was suggested that the child might be incapable of degrading lysine. Since lysine is a potent competitive inhibitor of arginase, it was thought that an accumulation of this amino acid possibly interfered with urea synthesis and ammonia detoxication, leading to an increase in ammonia levels and to ammonia intoxication.

Crome and Stern (1967) point out important differences between these two cases which support the view that hyperlysinaemia comprises more than one pathological entity. In Woody's case, biochemical evidence did not support a fault in the urea cycle. Excess of arginine was not found in the blood, as it was in the other case, though sometimes arginine together with ornithine, γ-amino butyric acid and cystine were increased in the urine. The biochemical anomalies in Woody's case were not affected by dietary changes, though clinically there was some improvement on reduced lysine intake.

The family history of the patient with hyperlysinaemia reported by Woody (1964) has points of particular genetical interest. The parents were consanguineous. A pattern of urinary abnormalities, similar to that of the propositus, was found in an otherwise apparently normal cousin. The pedigree [see FIG. 31] showed a distant relationship between the propositus and two infants with maple syrup urine disease. This is an extraordinary finding, considering that maple syrup urine disease and hyperlysinaemia are both very rare genetically-determined conditions. Their coincidence within one kinship by random chance is not very likely, and one is tempted to speculate whether there may be a genetical link. For example, an abnormal allele with more than one valency might be postulated, which together with either the maple syrup urine disease gene or the hyperlysinaemia gene would lead to the expression of one or other of these diseases respectively in the homozygote. Such a mechanism in an autosome might bear some analogy to the mechanism put forward by the Lyon hypothesis with respect to X chromosome activity. In the present case, the abnormal allele postulated might be relatively inactive to the gene with which it is paired to produce either hyperlysinaemia or maple syrup urine disease. This suggestion is entirely within the realms of speculation, and is not supported by the orthodox view of the highly specific action of individual genes in single gene inheritance. If, however, more families appear with genetical features such as those of the kinship reported by Woody (1964) there may be more ground on which to base new thoughts.

Hartnup Disease

Although the idea of a metabolic block determined by a gene-determined enzyme deficiency may explain the facts in a number of inborn errors of metabolism, in others it seems more likely that the basic fault lies in the transport mechanisms whereby levels and concentration gradients of various substances are maintained in cells and tissues of the body. A disturbance of this kind is seen in conditions such as cystinuria, where the high urinary levels of cystine, lysine, arginine and ornithine are due not to a metabolic block, but to a failure in

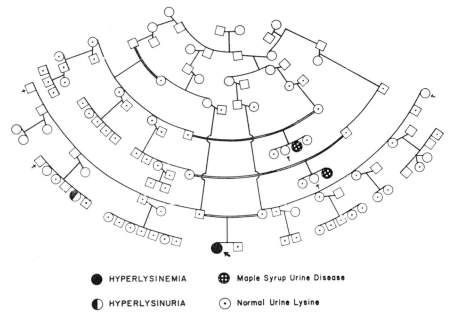

HYPERLYSINEMIA   Maple Syrup Urine Disease

HYPERLYSINURIA   Normal Urine Lysine

Fig. 31. Pedigree involving both hyperlysinaemia and maple syrup urine disease
(Woody, 1964).

reabsorption in the renal tubule. It seems not unreasonable to suppose that genetically determined faults may exist in transport mechanisms elsewhere in the body as well as in the renal tubule. It is suggested that Hartnup disease may be an example of such a failure in a transport mechanism outside the kidney (Harris, 1962).

This condition was originally described by Baron et al. (1956) as an hereditary pellagra-like light-sensitive skin rash with temporary episodes of neurological disorder characterized by variable cerebellar signs. In the various cases that have been recorded, these signs include ataxia, nystagmus and sometimes evidence of mild pyramidal involvement. Owing to the nature of the skin rash and the neurological manifestations, the condition has been mistaken for pellagra.

The condition is characterized by bizarre biochemical features. The most constant of these is generalized aminoaciduria of renal tubular origin without evidence of other defects of renal tubular function, which suggests a specific defect in the transport mechanism for amino acids from the glomerular filtrate into the capillary blood across the cells of the proximal renal tubules. The amino acid pattern in the urine is constant and one of the amino acids excreted in increased amounts is tryptophan. A constant excessive excretion in the urine of indole-3-acetic acid and a less constant large excretion of indican have been observed. These substances are metabolic products of tryptophan.

Because of the likelihood of a defect in the transfer of amino acids across the proximal renal tubule cells, and because of reports of abnormal metabolism of indolic substances in Hartnup disease, a special study was made to investigate the possibility of defects of amino acid transport, especially tryptophan metabolism and transport, elsewhere in the body (Milne *et al.*, 1960). Evidence was found for reduced absorption from the jejunum, and it was thought that this was probably due to the same unknown defect reducing absorption from the proximal renal tubular cells. The defect possibly involved the liver cells also. Although there was no proof of an actual deficiency of the enzyme, a biochemical error involving tryptophan pyrrholase was suggested, possibly a reduced contact of the enzyme with its substrate (Milne *et al.*, 1959). The biochemical peculiarities in Hartnup disease are still not fully understood, but the work of Milne and his colleagues provides the basis in theory at least for a unitary concept of the disease explicable in terms of a single specific error in the transport of amino acids.

As to psychiatric effects, the clinical picture may show considerable variation from case to case, some patients showing mental disturbances to a greater degree than others. The neurological episodes are not infrequently accompanied by mental confusion. Features which vary from case to case include emotional lability, apathy, irritability and depression. These appear to be associated mainly with active exacerbations of the disorder. A more permanent effect in some patients seems to be mental retardation, though in others there seems to be no impairment of intellectual function. Of the four sibs with no biochemical evidence of the abnormality in the first family described (Baron *et al.*, 1956), one was thought to exhibit a mixture of psychotic and backward behaviour. On psychometric testing she was assessed as having an IQ of 50 (test not specified). On the other hand, one of the affected members of the same sibship was of average intelligence (IQ 101, test not specified). This single family demonstrates a variation with respect to intelligence of affected individuals in the same sibship, and at the same time it may indicate that an effect of the gene in heterozygous form may be shown in biochemically unaffected members.

Psychiatric features may dominate the clinical picture, as in the patients described by Hersov and Rodnight (1960). One of their patients had hallucinations and delusions, a second had severe depression and depersonalization, and a third showed an anxiety reaction. These workers consider that the psychiatric symptoms in Hartnup disease are non-specific reactions which respond well to treatment, leaving no residual effects. They disagree with the view put forward by Baron *et al.* (1956) that the biochemical defect may cause slowly progressive mental deterioration, and find no support for this suggestion in their own data. The conclusion of Baron and his colleagues was based mainly on their finding that the IQs of the four affected children in their sibship diminished from 101 in the youngest to 61 in the eldest, and on the mother's impression of apparent deterioration as they grew older. Rodnight and Hersov consider this inadequate to support the conclusion that a progressive decline in intellect occurs in Hartnup disease, particularly since it fails to take into account the effects of illness and repeated periods in hospital on IQ scores and social skills.

As regards its inheritance, the first account of the disease by Baron and his co-workers in a sibship of which several members were affected and born to unaffected consanguineous parents was compatible with the hereditary transmission of Hartnup disease as an autosomal recessive trait. Further evidence supports this mode of inheritance. Jepson (1966) reviews genetical data from the 14 families reported to contain individuals with Hartnup disease. In at least 4 of these families the patients were of consanguineous parentage. All the families, except one from India, were Caucasian, coming from England, Holland, Belgium, Germany, Norway and Finland.

No biochemical method of detecting the heterozygote has been discovered. The parents and near relatives of Hartnup patients are normal when examined for aminoaciduria casein loading (Dent, 1954) and tryptophan loading tests (Halvorsen and Halvorsen, 1963) on parents and relatives have produced normal responses. As Jepson (1966) points out, the only clinical manifestation suggestive of the heterozygous condition would appear to be skin photosensitivity, seen in several biochemically normal uncles and aunts.

OCULO-CEREBRO-RENAL SYNDROME
(LOWE'S SYNDROME)

This very rare syndrome was first described by Lowe, Terrey and MacLachlan (1952) who described three children with mental retardation, renal and ophthalmological lesions and disordered metabolism. The eye lesions consisted of congenital cataracts and glaucoma; the kidneys were deficient in the production of ammonia; there was organic aciduria and systemic acidosis. Two of the children had osteomalacia or rickets.

Crome and Stern (1967) in reviewing the nature of this inborn error of metabolism, point out that the cardinal feature is the disturbance of proximal tubular function in the kidney. There is reduced tubular reabsorption of phosphate, some impairment of glucose reabsorption, and impairment of the ability of the renal tubules to form ammonia. Proteinuria, often mild, and a generalized aminoaciduria are characteristic of the condition, and mild or moderate hyperchloraemic acidosis is an almost constant feature. Children with this syndrome may suffer from inexplicable recurrent febrile episodes. These were noted by Lowe, Terrey and MacLachlan in their original cases. Early death from intercurrent infection, such as bronchopneumonia, is not unusual.

The basic inborn metabolic error in the oculo-cerebro-renal syndrome is not clear. Richards and his colleagues believe that the pathological process in the kidney is secondary rather than primary (Richards, W., et al., 1965). They suggest that this is a progressive process which begins with the deposition of proteinaceous material in the lumina of the tubules, with eventual destruction of the tubules, changes in the glomeruli and interstitial fibrosis. On the other hand, they consider the structural irregularities in the cerebral cortex, including pachygyria, pontine atrophy and possibly cerebellar hypoplasia, to be of primary congenital origin. This view, that the changes in the brain are likely to be of antenatal origin, is in agreement with that of McCance *et al.* (1960).

It seems that a number of variants of the oculo-cerebro-renal syndrome may exist. One such apparent variant, occurring in two brothers, was described by McCance *et al.* (1960). It differed from all previous recorded cases in the nature of the renal lesion. Unlike previously described patients with this condition, these boys produced highly acid urines, and did not excrete the large amounts of organic acids, probably amino acids, as reported in other cases. Changes in the brain suggested cerebral and cerebellar agenesis of prenatal origin, and the lesions as a whole were interpreted as developmental failures.

The oculo-cerebro-renal syndrome appears to be transmitted genetically as a *sex-linked* recessive trait. The evidence for this is that the condition is restricted to males; sibships may contain more than one affected male and also normal males; transmission seems to occur through unaffected females. Two infant sisters with some features reminiscent of the oculo-cerebro-renal syndrome, including congenital cataracts, encephalopathy and renal tubular pathology were described by Crome, Duckett and Franklin (1963). However, it was pointed out that no aminoaciduria was detected in one of the cases, and the renal lesions were not like those associated with the oculo-cerebro-renal syndrome. If these girls had been in fact affected by the oculo-cerebro-renal syndrome, they would have been the first female cases reported. Crome and Stern (1967) hold the view that the diagnosis of this syndrome should be reserved for cases with evidence of a sex-linked recessive mode of inheritance in addition to the established clinical and biochemical features of the disease.

The presumed heterozygous carriers of the oculo-cerebro-renal syndrome, though clinically normal, have been found to show lens changes on slit-lamp examination. Opacities in the crystalline lens were found in mothers and other female relatives of affected individuals by Richards, W., *et al.* (1965). Previously similar changes had been reported in the eyes of the mother of an affected boy by Terslev (1960). This mother was reported also to have had albuminuria and marked cystinuria though the paper chromatography of her urine gave negative results.

11

OTHER NEUROMETABOLIC DISORDERS I

GALACTOSAEMIA

The first description of galactosaemia appears to be that of von Reuss (1908). He described a grossly emaciated infant with hepatomegaly and large quantities of galactose in the urine. The present-day treatment for galactosaemia with a galactose-free diet was foreshadowed when this child was taken off a diet of milk and given only tea with glucose and a gruel of cornflour. On this regime the galactose disappeared from the urine, although the child died later. The underlying enzyme defect was not discovered until nearly 50 years later, when Isselbacher and his co-workers demonstrated using hydrolysates of red blood cells, that congenital galactosaemia represents a block that is confined exclusively to a single enzyme—galactose-l-phosphate uridyl transferase (Isselbacher *et al.*, 1956).

Chemical Pathology

Galactosaemia, a disorder of carbohydrate metabolism, is primarily a disease of early infancy, being characterized by acute gastro-intestinal symptoms including vomiting and diarrhoea, jaundice, and a failure to thrive. Mental retardation, cataracts and cirrhosis of the liver may be seen later. Anaemia may also be a prominent feature. When this occurs it appears to be partly haemolytic in nature. There may be a sudden drop in haemoglobin concentration without bleeding, followed by an increased reticulocyte count; and haemolysis may be observed *in vitro* when the patients' red cells are incubated in a medium containing galactose (Hsia and Walker, 1961). The affected individual who survives early infancy is frequently indistinguishable from a normal person, though in some hepatomegaly may persist, or cataracts provide a vital clue.

In the urine, quantities of galactose are found. Aminoaciduria of a generalized type may be present due to a relative inefficiency of the renal tubule cells with respect to the reabsorption of certain amino acids (Cusworth, Dent and Flynn, 1955). When galactose is removed from the diet the aminoaciduria disappears, and it is thought that possibly galactose itself exerts a chemical ('toxic') action on the renal tubular cells.

The diagnosis is confirmed biochemically by an abnormal galactose tolerance curve and by the presence of galactose in the urine. The demonstration of absence of the enzyme galactose-l-phosphate uridyl transferase is a biochemical test which gives further confirmation of the condition.

Of great interest is the occurrence of asymptomatic cases. These individuals have been discovered in the course of genetical studies in families containing galactosaemic members. These individuals show the typical biochemical reactions of the condition, including complete absence of galactose-1-phosphate uridyl transferase, but are symptom-free. A striking example of the asympto-matic condition was reported by Baker et al. (1966). Neither of two Negro brothers had galactose-l-phosphate uridyl transferase activity in his circulating red blood cells. Each, therefore, fulfilled the laboratory criterion for the diagnosis of congenital galactosaemia. One sib was considered to show the complete galactosaemic syndrome in infancy and responded to dietary treatment. The other, however, never showed any signs or symptoms which could be attributed to galactosaemia. Baker and his colleagues suggested the possibility of gene modifiers, still undefined, which might account for the variable expression of galactosaemia in the same family.

It seems that in some cases homozygotes for the gene may remain symptom-free for many years and isolated signs of the condition may occur late in life. For instance one such man, described by Hsia and Walker (1961) was diagnosed at the age of 63 after he had led a successful life as a business executive. In the years immediately preceding his death, he had suffered from cirrhosis of the liver and cataracts. The diagnosis of galactosaemia was not, however, considered until his grandchildren were found to have the condition.

Biochemical studies may yield further information with respect to asympto-matic galactosaemia. There is evidence for an accessory pathway of galactose metabolism through UDP-galactose pyrophosphorylase in mammalian liver (Isselbacher, 1957). Moreover, results of experiments with labelled galactose have indicated that from a group of individuals with a history of the galactosaemic syndrome in infancy, a subgroup can be delineated in childhood, characterized by the presence in certain tissues of metabolic pathways for galactose (Segal, Blair and Topper, 1963). It is not impossible that in at least some untreated homozygotes the alternative pathway becomes sufficiently well adapted for the galactosaemic effects to be overcome. Such cases would be expected to pass unnoticed. There is at present no direct evidence, however, to support this hypothesis.

In the study of 45 cases of galactosaemia by Hsia and Walker (1961) it was possible, by viewing the series as a whole, to get a composite picture of the condition which was not possible from individual case reports. These authors were impressed by the variability of the clinical manifestations, and the ability of children, after early infancy, to lead a relatively normal existence. Dent (personal communication, 1964) points out that the clinical variability is almost certainly due to a corresponding variation of the patients' milk intake. The mothers often notice their babies' sensitivity to milk and thus avoid its ad-ministration.

Galactosaemia is one of the metabolic conditions associated with mental subnormality that responds to dietary treatment as soon after birth as possible. With such treatment it can be hoped that growth and development will be normal. The biochemical error in galactosaemia is the specific inability to metabolize galactose. Galactose is a monosaccharide present with glucose in the disaccharide lactose, which is the main carbohydrate constituent of milk. The treatment is based on lactose and galactose restriction. Milk is avoided, and milk-containing foods including bread, cake and puddings are cut out of the diet. Milk substitutes of various kinds are used during infancy.

In reporting upon the effects of the diet in galactosaemia, Hsia and Walker (1961) say that there appears to be no question that the restriction of lactose in the diet has resulted in a disappearance of vomiting, diarrhoea, and a reversal of the trend towards weight-loss. In most instances observed by them jaundice, enlargement of liver and spleen and ascites diminished or completely disappeared, but cataracts tended to persist and many of these required extraction.

Diet and Intelligence

As regards the influence of the diet upon intelligence, Hsia and Walker found that the age at which the diet was started appeared to have relatively little influence on the IQ, which is quite in contrast to the impression obtained in phenylketonuria in which the age at the start of dietary treatment appears to be of prime importance, though the degree of control of the diet in galactosaemia may be of importance.

As regards mental status, in the series of 45 patients with galactosaemia studied by Hsia and Walker (1961) 60 per cent were in the normal range with an IQ 90 or over. Twenty per cent were in the borderline range (IQ 70–90) and 20 per cent were in the retarded but educable range (IQ 40–70). Some of the children in the normal intelligence range had never been treated at all. Others had been placed on a lactose-free diet at a relatively late age. It was concluded that the meagre amount of information available on the degree of dietary control in each case was, however, insufficient to draw any definite conclusions as to its significance in mental development.

Walker and his collaborators (1962) carried out psychological testing with galactosaemic patients using the Revised Stanford Binet 'Form L' and, in the case of those who were visually handicapped, the Maxfield Buchholz modification for blind children of the Vineland Social Maturity Scale. The distribution of scores given for 34 patients is shown below:

DISTRIBUTION OF IQ SCORES FOR GALACTOSAEMIC PATIENTS
(From the data of Walker, Hsia, Slatis and Steinberg (1962)

IQ	40–49	50–59	60–69	70–79	80–89	90–99	100 and over; also scored as 'Normal'
No. of patients	4	1	2	3	3	3	18

Three of the patients tested showed IQ scores as high as 119, 121 and 124 respectively. It is clear, therefore, that galactosaemia is by no means always accompanied by mental subnormality.

Neuropathology

The first report of the neuropathological findings in a case of galactosaemia was made by Crome (1962b). He summarized the neural changes as micrencephaly caused by a mainly burnt-out encephalomyelopathy. The findings were, on the whole, unspecific and encountered in the brains of mentally retarded individuals of different types. Crome points out that it is well known that established mental retardation tends to remain refractory in galactosaemia, even after the withdrawal of galactose from the diet, whereas other signs are reversible; this is not surprising in the light of the structural neural changes demonstrated. He considers that hypoglycaemia, which had once held favour as the cause of the encephalopathy in galactosaemia, is unlikely to be responsible for the changes he found. He believes that some competitive inhibition of enzymes may be the chief factor responsible for the neuropathy. For example, it is known that galactose-l-phosphate which is present in many tissues in galactosaemia, can inhibit enzymes such as phosphoglucomutase and glucose-phosphate dehydrogenase. In addition, Crome suggests that neonatal jaundice should not be discounted as a contributory cause, and that it is possibly significant that the few recorded cases of galactosaemia without neonatal jaundice have tended to be more intelligent than the rest.

Genetics

The familial incidence of galactosaemia had long been recognized, but up to the middle 1950s the mode of its inheritance had been a matter of speculation. A cardinal difficulty had been that until that time no special techniques had been consistently employed by which the specific biochemical trait could be recognized, if present, in clinically unaffected members of families of index cases.

The question of manifestation of the gene in the heterozygote was first investigated by Holzel and Komrower (1955) who carried out galactose tolerance tests on the parents of galactosaemic children [FIG. 32]. The results indicated an impaired ability to metabolize galactose after a loading dose in a number of, though not all, parents of such children. Techniques of enzyme activity assay have provided further evidence of a partial enzyme defect in the heterozygote (Kirkman and Bynum, 1959). Even with enzyme assay, however, the discrimination between normal controls and known heterozygotes still shows considerable overlap as shown by Walker and his co-workers (1962). They suggest various possible reasons for this, including on the one hand, factors pertaining to the method of assay, and on the other, the possibility of genetical heterogeneity at the galactosaemia locus or at other loci, or environmental interaction influencing the enzyme system metabolizing galactose.

There appears to be an excessive number of affected males as compared with affected females. Hsia and Walker (1961) in adding their figures for sex distribution collected from the literature by Hugh-Jones, Newcomb and Hsia (1960) and excluding duplicated cases, estimated a ratio of 91 males to 44 females, a highly significant difference ($p < 0.001$). They suggested the deficiency of affected females could result from either the condition being frequently lethal in females, possibly at an early stage of cell division, or the condition frequently not being diagnosed in affected females because of being clinically milder in the female. They postulated that this effect might be related to an ameliorating influence of progesterone on galactose metabolism.

As regards gene frequency, in an assessment from a survey by paediatricians (Schwarz et al., 1961) an estimate was made that 1 in 70,000 ($1·4 \times 10^{-5}$) individuals is born with galactosaemia, or from the Hardy-Weinberg equilibrium, one in 133 is expected to be a carrier. As many patients with galactosaemia die

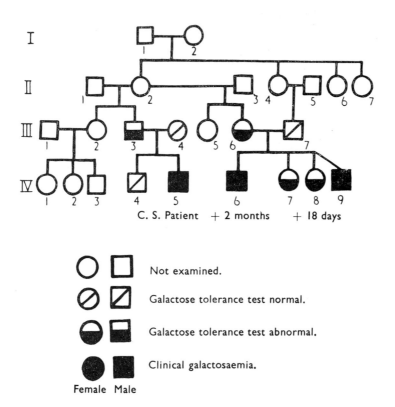

C. S. Patient   + 2 months   + 18 days

○ □   Not examined.

⊘ ▨   Galactose tolerance test normal.

◑ ◪   Galactose tolerance test abnormal.

● ■   Clinical galactosaemia.

Female Male

Fig. 32. Pedigree of two sibships with galactosaemia, showing the biochemical status of the parents (Holzel and Komrower, 1955).

suddenly, often in the neonatal period, accurate clinical diagnosis may not always be possible.

Hansen and his co-workers (1964) put the frequency much higher. From their studies of galactose-l-phosphate uridyl transferase levels in red cells, they estimated that galactosaemia may occur in as many as 1 in 18,000 ($5·6 \times 10^{-5}$) births. Since heterozygotes for the galactosaemia gene are generally asymptomatic, the identification of a heterozygote of maternal origin among the mentally retarded suggests the possibility that the symptomatology may have resulted from inadequate metabolism of galactose by the mother during pregnancy

(Hansen *et al.*, 1964). They estimate the number of homozygous diseased subjects that may be expected from chemically identified heterozygotes (i.e. individuals with levels of transferase intermediate between diseased and normal persons). Taking their estimate of 1 in 18,000 births, they suggest that galacto-saemia may be more frequent in some parts of the United States than Great Britain, where estimates of frequency were based on surveys by paediatricians (Schwarz *et al.*, 1961).

Galactokinase Deficiency

Galactokinase deficiency should be mentioned as distinct from galactosaemia. Deficiency of this enzyme in the red blood cells of a patient with galactosuria, neurofibromatosis and recurrent cataracts was reported by Gitzelmann (1965). Such a deficiency had not been found previously in mammalian species. At the age of 43 this patient appeared to be of normal intelligence. Manual work was becoming increasingly difficult for him on account of tremor, muscular weakness and pains. The link between galactokinase activity and neurofibromatosis and the importance of galactokinase in the genesis of cataracts are open to question.

FAMILIAL FRUCTOSE INTOLERANCE

Fructosuria is a characteristic sign of at least two inborn errors of metabolism. One of these, essential fructosuria, is symptomless and apparently without harmful effects. It may remain undetected or come to light by routine examina-tion for reducing substances in the urine. It is presumed that affected individuals are homozygous for a rare mutant gene (Harris, 1959). The other condition, however, is manifested by a steep rise in the level of fructose in the blood, and a sudden fall in blood glucose, following the administration of fructose by mouth or by injection. These signs may be accompanied by severe gastro-intestinal, neurological and mental effects. It has been suggested that this condition is best called *fructose intolerance* (Froesch *et al.*, 1959).

The gastro-intestinal effects of fructose intolerance include nausea, vomiting and sometimes haematemesis. The neurological and mental effects vary in different cases described. One patient complained only of mild phobic symptoms following the ingestion of food containing fruit or cane sugar (Chambers and Pratt, 1956). Froesch and his co-workers describe severe symptoms including sweating, trembling, vomiting and somnolence during fructose tolerance tests in patients with the condition. The condition has been known to be fatal in the early months of life (Sacrez *et al.*, 1962). Levin *et al.* (1963) distinguished between younger and older patients as regards clinical effects. In the younger age-group, usually less than 6 months of age, the clinical characteristics include a failure to thrive, vomiting, anorexia, hypotonia, hepatomegaly and hypoglycaemic attacks following weaning from the breast. The older patients, however, are often free from symptoms but show a marked aversion to sweetened foods.

In a female patient with fructose intolerance reported by Dormandy and Porter (1961), the psychiatric and neurological history included a nervous disposition in childhood with nocturnal enuresis, 'jerky and clumsy' move-ments, major epileptic fits from the age of 13 which persisted throughout life, several admissions to hospital in a confusional state with slurred speech, nystagmus and cerebellar ataxia. The electroencephalogram showed a mild and diffuse abnormality, and during an intravenous fructose tolerance test high altitude synchronous waves at 4 cycles per second coincided with clinical hypoglycaemia but a high total blood sugar level. A special feature of this case was galactose intolerance, which has not been reported in other cases of fructose intolerance. It was felt that both clinical and electroencephalographic evidence suggested that acute hypoglycaemic attacks were the main disability, but that some of the features including vomiting and abdominal pain reflected the toxic effects of accumulated intermediate fructose and galactose metabolites. The biochemical findings suggested at first multiple blockages in the metabolic pathways for fructose, galactose and glucose, but it was later considered that the abnormalities were secondary to a parent defect in fructose metabolism, possibly a deficiency of the enzyme fructose-l-phosphate aldolase.

It seems that on the whole in fructosaemia in fructose intolerance the brain is not as severely damaged by hypoglycaemia as in galactosaemia (Crome and Stern, 1967). However, 4 out of 12 cases reviewed by Levin *et al.* (1963) showed some degree of mental subnormality. These authors point out that although fructosaemia cannot be differentiated readily from galactosaemia on clinical grounds alone, one feature in the history may point to the correct diagnosis. In fructosaemia the infant becomes ill when taken off the breast, whereas in galactosaemia symptoms occur as soon as breast or cow's milk feeding is begun.

Evidence as to the mode of inheritance of fructose intolerance is conflicting. In some families its transmission appears to be consistent with that of a Mendelian dominant trait (Dormandy and Porter, 1961). In an Italian family with nine affected individuals, the defect is shown to be inherited as an irregular dominant trait (Missale *et al.*, 1962). In a Swiss family the pattern of transmission fits that of an autosomal recessive gene (Froesch *et al.*, 1957; Froesch *et al.*, 1959). McKusick (1962) has pointed out that in the report by Dormandy and Porter the term 'sex-linked' has been misused in referring to families with the disease affecting (probably by chance) all members of one sex.

IDIOPATHIC HYPERCALCAEMIA OF INFANCY

Although the pathogenesis of this disease remains open to question and its genetical aspects have not been investigated, it is included here because of the suggestion that it may represent an inborn error of metabolism and is, in some cases at least, associated with mental subnormality.

The syndrome, though rare, appears to be of fair importance in paediatric practice. For example, the condition accounted for 4·6 per cent of all medical admissions of children aged 6–12 months and ranked fourth in frequency after respiratory infections, feeding difficulties and otitis media in the paediatric units of Dundee hospitals over a 2-year period not long ago (Morgan *et al.*, 1956). In this sample 15 cases were diagnosed from a population of 450,000. Four of these infants died.

Mental retardation, as well as physical retardation, is found in some, but not all, cases. The condition is well reviewed by O'Brien, Peppers and Silver (1960) who mention that the condition has been divided into two varieties, a chronic, more severe form and a milder transitory variety, though it seems more likely to be a spectrum of severity rather than a clear division into specific varieties. The characteristic laboratory finding is an abnormally high serum calcium level. Clinically, the onset is often insidious, the first signs of irritability, appetite loss and a failure to thrive appearing within the first few months of life. More marked signs of polyuria, gastro-intestinal disturbances and muscular hypotonia may be directly referable to the high serum calcium level. Bony changes occur, including osteosclerosis, craniosynostosis and microcephaly, and it has been suggested that abnormal growth of the basisphenoid may contribute to the characteristic 'elfin' facies, the features of which include a

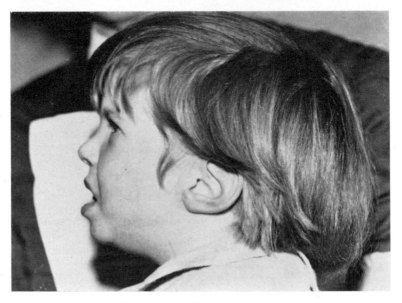

Fig. 33. Idiopathic hypercalcaemia.

short snub nose with flattened bridge, marked epicanthic folds, a rounded, bossed forehead, micrognathia and loose hanging lips [FIGS. 33 and 34].

The prognosis varies from apparently complete remission after a few months to an unrelenting course ending with death. Mental retardation has been observed amongst survivors from the severe form.

The large absorption of calcium which has been demonstrated in this condition by balance studies has been considered as probably due to overaction of vitamin D, although it is impossible to distinguish between the effects of over-dosage and of hypersensitivity (Morgan *et al.*, 1956). Fellers and Schwartz (1958) found serum vitamin D activity of infants with idiopathic hypercalcaemia to be 20 or 30 times that of normal infants. Their findings of an excess of antirachitic steroid in the serum in association with one of the lipoprotein fractions were taken as indicating a basic defect in the metabolism of vitamin D or related substance, which would lead one to include the disease in the group of inborn errors of metabolism.

A series of 4 patients aged 4, 15, 40 and 23 years respectively, were studied by Dupont and Clausen (1968). They found that the sphingomyelin fraction (also containing the phosphatidylserine fraction) seemed relatively increased. They considered these findings to suggest that the 'elfin face syndrome' with kypho-scoliosis, mental subnormality, and a history of failure to thrive in infancy and of

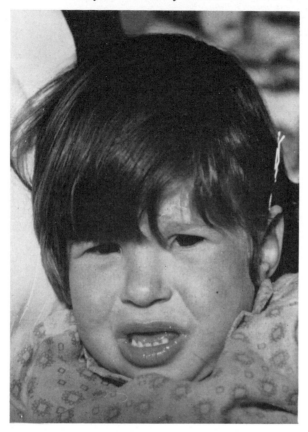

Fig. 34. Idiopathic hypercalcaemia.

early puberty in girls, is primarily or secondarily associated with sphingomyelin abnormalities.

HYPERURICAEMIA

A disorder of the nervous system in children, resulting in cerebral palsy, and associated with high levels of uric acid in the blood and urine, was reported in single cases by Catel and Schmidt (1959) and by Riley (1960). Attention was first drawn to the specific nature of this syndrome, however, by Lesch and Nyhan (1964).

This syndrome differs essentially from adult gout in that its onset is much earlier and the central nervous system is involved. Also the metabolic defect is much more severe than in adults with gout. The first signs of the syndrome are usually seen in early infancy. Characteristically, the child is backward with respect to the milestones of motor development, and is retarded in physical growth. Urinary symptoms, including haematuria and urinary calculi, may appear within the first few months of life, and the uric acid in the blood and urine rises to very high levels. In one case at the age of 4 months, uric acid stones were found in the urine and a blood uric acid level of more than 5 times the normal value (Nyhan, Oliver and Lesch, 1965). Hyperactivity of the deep tendon reflexes may be observed in the early weeks of life, but soon other neurological signs appear as well. Eventually generalized spasticity supervenes, with choreo-athetosis, dysarthria, dysphagia and profound mental retardation.

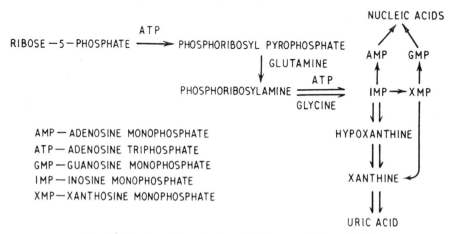

Fig. 35. The formation of uric acid (Crome and Stern, 1967).

Self-mutilation is a constant feature of the syndrome and has appeared in all cases after one year of age (Dodge, 1966). The child bites his lips and fingers, so that the tissues around the mouth are completely destroyed and the fingers may be amputated by biting. A patient of Hoefnagel's (1965) had the habit of digging deep into his eye-sockets with his fingers.

A simplified diagram of uric acid formation is shown in FIGURE 35 (after Crome and Stern, 1967). Although the basic biochemical error causing hyperuricacidaemia is still uncertain, Wyngaarden (1966) suggested a defect in the regulation of synthesis of the first specific purine precursor, phosphoribosylamine resulting in an excessive production of uric acid. This is shown in FIGURE 35, in which the double arrows mark the pathway through which, it is postulated, this is mediated. Further evidence on these lines has been provided by Seegmiller, Rosenbloom and Kelley (1967) who demonstrated a deficiency of the enzyme hypoxanthine-guanine phosphoribosyl transferase in affected individuals.

The most unusual biochemical characteristic of this syndrome is the rate of formation of uric acid from glycine. Nyhan et al. (1965) found the formation of uric acid from glycine in a patient with this disorder to exceed that in controls by 200 times. This finding was in line with those made by previous workers.

Nyhan and his co-workers suggest from their observations that intermediates of purine metabolism may be of importance for the integrity of the developing nervous system.

Neuropathological findings in the brains of two brothers with hyperuricaemia, aged 11 months and 4 years respectively at death, were reported by Crome and Stern (1967). Both were somewhat micrencephalic, with cortical neuronal loss and astrocytic hyperplasia in the molecular layer of the cortex. In one of the brains there were multiple foci of necrosis in the cerebellum.

It is possible that this rare syndrome is transmitted as a sex-linked trait, but the number of reported cases is still small and more evidence is needed

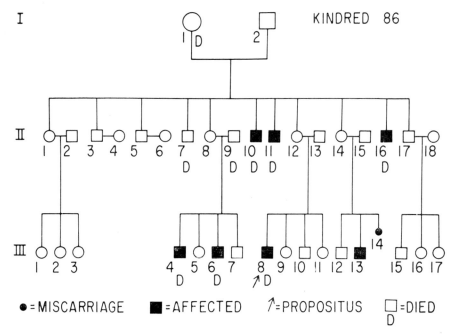

Fig. 36. Pedigree of a family with hyperuricaemia (Hoefnagel *et al.*, 1965).

before the mode of transmission can be established with certainty. The condition appears to be confined to males, and it has occurred in sibs (see pedigree of family reported by Hoefnagel *et al.* (1965) FIG. 36). The carrier state and familial transmission have not been clearly established, but a maternal uncle of the patient described by Catel and Schmidt had a neurological disorder dating from birth with choreo-athetosis and mental retardation, and typical adult gout later in life. Also 3 brothers of the maternal grandmother of the propositus were said to be mentally defective, while their 2 sisters were of normal intelligence. Two paternal uncles and the paternal grandfather of a patient described by Lesch and Nyhan (1964), had raised levels of uric acid in the blood; this finding, of course, does not fit in with a sex-linked recessive.

The syndrome is associated with death at an early age, and affected patients therefore probably do not have offspring (Hoefnagel *et al.*, 1965). A large pedigree reported by Shapiro *et al.* (1966) showed a pattern of inheritance consistent with transmission as an X-linked recessive trait. As in other reported families, only males were affected; there was no statistically significant difference between expected and observed figures for transmission of this trait to grandsons through carrier mothers.

Hoefnagel and his co-workers (1965) have attempted to test the assumption that the gene for the syndrome might be located on the X chromosome. Colour-vision studies on the families they studied were not, however, informative. Blood grouping studies did not give evidence of either non-paternity or non-maternity. In one family, typing for the Xg blood group indicated that a cross-over must have occurred between the Xg locus and the locus for the hyperuricaemia trait, if this was located on the X chromosome. It seemed therefore that close linkage between these two loci was unlikely.

ABETALIPOPROTEINAEMIA

Abetalipoproteinaemia, first observed by Bassen and Kornzweig (1950), is a rare autosomal recessive condition characterized by steatorrhoea, which is present from birth; atypical retinitis pigmentosa with macular involvement which becomes apparent later in childhood, and progressive ataxia. From birth the red blood corpuscles have a curious appearance, as if thorns are projecting from them (acanthocytosis). Mental retardation does not appear to be a constant feature. Although some of the affected children have been mentally subnormal, in the majority of cases intelligence has remained normal (Forsyth, Lloyd and Fosbrooke, 1965).

Inheritance of the condition as an autosomal recessive trait has been supported by the high rate of consanguinity amongst the parents of affected patients. The frequency is not known, but the fact that 6 of the 15 cases reported up until recently were the offspring of consanguineous matings suggests that the condition is rare (Wolff, 1965). Forsyth *et al.* (1965) make the interesting point that it is the cases (including their own reported patient) with mental retardation that came from consanguineous parents. Of those patients with normal intelligence only one has a history of consanguinity, the parents being fourth cousins (Schwartz *et al.*, 1963).

The predominant biochemical characteristic is an absence of beta-lipoprotein from the serum. The relationship between the clinical and biochemical features is not clear, but could be explained if it were assumed that the primary gene defect concerned a step, not yet elucidated, in the synthesis of beta-lipoprotein, which is the main lipid-carrying protein of the serum (Wolff, 1965). This defect could lead to the deformity of the red blood cells, as they are exposed to an abnormal plasma environment, also, conceivably to the retinal and nervous system changes as most of the proteins of nervous tissue are metabolically active lipoproteins. Treatment remains symptomatic, and a low-fat diet has been reported as helpful, with the addition of the fat-soluble vitamins A, D and E, together with vitamin K in early infancy, being administered in a water-miscible form (Wolff, 1965).

FAMILIAL DYSAUTONOMIA

Familial dysautonomia was first described as a syndrome by Riley *et al.* (1949). It is characterized by neurological deficits including changes in the autonomic nervous system and anatomical defects, and the majority of cases show some degree of psychomotor retardation, though this is not usually severe.

The characteristic features of this syndrome have been listed by Smithells (1967) as deficient lacrimation; corneal ulceration; dysphagia, salivation and vomiting; retarded speech with 'fading' of the voice; inco-ordination, hypotonia and hyporeflexia; liability to chest infections; relative insensitivity to hypercapnia and hypoxia; a labile blood pressure; skin blotching; sweating; febrile attacks; indifference to pain and defective taste discrimination; and screaming attacks with sobbing spasms. The fungiform and circumvallate papillae of the tongue are absent. Smithells points out that in clinical diagnosis the most helpful test is the response to intradermal histamine. In the normal subject this is followed by a local weal, a surrounding flare, and pain. In familial dysautonomia, there is only a weal.

A variety of neuropathological, neurochemical and neurophysiological lesions have been described in this condition. These include focal demyelination of the dorsal roots and posterior columns of the spinal cord (Fogelson, Rorke and Kaye, 1967); excess acetylcholinesterase in the nerve plexuses surrounding the sweat glands (Hutchison and Hamilton, 1962); and defective peripheral nerve conduction (Brown and Johns, 1967).

Biochemical studies which have led furthest towards an understanding of the basic biochemical defect have been in the metabolism of amines. Smith, Taylor and Wortis (1963) demonstrated high homovanillic acid and low vanillyl-mandelic acid urinary excretion rates in familial dysautonomia. Vanillyl-mandelic acid is the major acidic catabolite of norepinephrine and epinephrine, and homovanillic acid is derived from their precursors. The results supported a disturbance of catecholamine metabolism in familial dysautonomia, possibly a failure of the catecholamine precursors to be converted normally to norepine-phrine and epinephrine. A considerable amount of work has followed along the lines of catecholamine metabolism, but the exact biochemical error and the site of the dysautonomic defect are still unknown.

Familial dysautonomia is inherited as an autosomal recessive trait. It has been described in various parts of the world, but it is confined mainly to one ethnic group, the Ashkenazi Jews. Moses *et al.* (1967) studied all diagnosed cases in Israel. They found an impressive ethnic specificity, confining the occurrence of the condition to Jews originating mainly from eastern Europe. They made a tentative estimate of 0·009 for the gene frequency in the Ashkenazi population of Israel.

REFSUM'S SYNDROME

Heredopathia atactica polyneuritiformis was first defined as a clinical entity by Refsum (1946). In this syndrome the predominant clinical signs are neurological. They include polyneuritis, muscular atrophy, progressive paralysis, cerebellar ataxia, areflexia and sensory disturbances. The course is progressive but irregular, with remissions and exacerbations. Ichthyosis and deafness also occur, and there may be electrocardiographic signs of cardiac involvement. The earliest manifestations of the syndrome appear to be ophthalmological signs (Eldjarn *et al.*, 1966). These are hemeralopia and constriction of the visual fields. Anomalous pupils and retinitis pigmentosa are also seen. In addition skeletal abnormalities have been reported in association with Refsum's syndrome. These include an epiphyseal dysplasia, unusually long metacarpal and metatarsal bones and pes cavus (Reese and Bareta, 1950). As regards age of onset, the original patients described by Refsum were adults, but later he and his co-workers reported the onset of symptoms between the ages of 4 and 7 years in 4 children (Refsum, Salomonsen and Skatvedt, 1949).

In the earlier reports of the condition mental retardation did not appear as part of the syndrome, but it has been suggested that the disease may be associated with lipidosis in some cases (Richterich *et al.*, 1963). There are indications that the syndrome may be associated at least in a few cases with psychosis. One of Refsum's original patients (Refsum, 1946) suffered from an acute psychosis characterized by a paranoid confusional state with hallucinations, which cleared up, with apparent permanent improvement, after a short course of shock treatment. His father had also suffered from a psychosis which was thought to be a case of 'periodic psychosis', and the father's brother was said to present a plain picture of paranoid schizophrenia. A second brother of the father committed suicide by jumping into the sea on the way to an asylum, and a third brother of the father was alcoholic. One of the cases reported by Eldjarn *et al.* (1966), a female patient with Refsum's syndrome, developed a paranoid psychosis at about the age of 32. Refsum (1946) considers the 'general problem regarding the frequency of psychic phenomena among persons suffering from hereditary organic diseases of the nervous system' and points out that considering case records in the literature one gains the impression that psychopathological phenomena are more frequent in affected persons and their families than would be expected by random chance, and quotes examples of many authors who hold this opinion, especially as regards the heredo-ataxias. He points out that this problem is by no means solved, except for cases in which the morbid process involves the brain itself, and even then, if there is such a connexion, there is the problem of interpretation.

As regards genetics, Refsum's syndrome follows an autosomal recessive mode of inheritance. The patients originally studied by Refsum (1946) were offspring of consanguineous marriages (see pedigrees of Refsum's families, FIGS. 37 and 38). In one of his sibships a brother and sister had the syndrome in its complete form, and a sister of these patients is said to have suffered from hemeralopia with a limited field of vision and unsteady gait in the dark. It is possible that she suffered from a *forme fruste* of the condition. Although Refsum's original familial data were insufficient for him to draw definite conclusions beyond the probability that the syndrome was inherited as an autosomal recessive condition, this has been substantiated by the later reports that have appeared.

Biochemically, the syndrome appears to be associated with a block in the degradation of branched-chain fatty acids. The exact nature of this metabolic block is not yet known, nor is the role of the fatty acid in the pathogenesis of the disease. Considerable amounts of phytanic acid (3, 7, 11, 15—tetramethyl-hexadecanoic acid) have been found in various lipid fractions of serum, liver and kidneys in Refsum's syndrome (Klenk and Kahlke, 1963; Kahlke and Richterich, 1965). Phytanic acid is formed from the chlorophyll derivative phytol. In turn, it can be metabolized to mevalonic acid which is a precursor of cholesterol. Serum cholesterol levels, however, are normal in Refsum's syndrome, which suggests that mevalonic acid metabolism is not unduly disturbed (Crome and

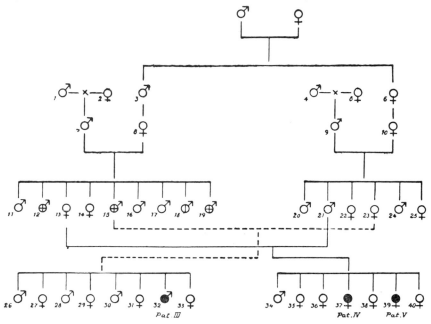

Fig. 37. Pedigree of a family with Refsum's syndrome (Refsum, 1946). ♂ Patient No. III. ♀ Patients No. IV and No. V. ⊕ insane. ♂ potator. The parents of patient No. III are second cousins. The parents of patients No. IV and No. V are likewise second cousins. Patients Nos. III, IV and V have the same grandparents. Patient No. III is also third cousin to patient No. IV and patient No. V.

Stern, 1967). Dietary treatment based on the restriction of foods containing phytol and phytanic acid has been started (Eldjarn *et al.*, 1966). In formulating this diet an attempt was made to exclude as far as possible all foods containing chlorophyll. All vegetables and fruits were excluded, also butter fats, meat fat and plant margarines. Further observation is required before the efficacy of the diet can be evaluated.

ATAXIA-TELANGIECTASIA

This rare syndrome was first described by Mme. Louis-Bar (1941) and since then a number of reports of the condition have appeared. The child usually appears normal in early infancy, and the first signs are slight choreo-athetotic movements followed by the onset of cerebellar ataxia before or during the second year of life. Telangiectasia appears in the conjunctivae, eyelids, nose, ears, neck, dorsum of hands and feet, and flexures of knees and elbows from about the fourth to sixth year. Intercurrent respiratory infections are frequent, leading to chronic bronchitis and bronchiectasis. The condition is progressive. The neurological disability is usually so severe by about the tenth year that independent locomotion is impossible, and death usually ensues at about the twelfth year. Mental retardation is not an invariable finding in this condition, and the

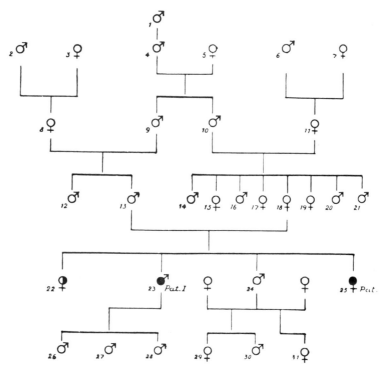

Fig. 38. Pedigree of a family with Refsum's syndrome (Refsum, 1946). ♂ Patient No. I. ♀ Patient No. II. ♀ Night-blind, constricted visual field. The parents of patients I and II are cousins.

majority of patients appear to have been at least initially of normal intelligence. Nine out of 20 cases in one review had some degree of mental retardation (Korein, Steinman and Senz, 1961). Mental deterioration, however, often takes place.

From the point of view of taxonomy, most authors have related ataxia-telangiectasia to the neuro-ectodermal phakomatoses (Hansen, 1963). It is indeed true that this condition has points in common with the phakomatoses, including the ocular lesions and the frequent appearance of cutaneous manifestations including *café-au-lait* spots and pigmented naevi. However, against classifying it with the phakomatoses is the fact that nearly all familial cases of ataxia-telangiectasia have shown a pattern of transmission consistent with autosomal recessive inheritance. A family reported by Paine and Efron (1963), showing apparent dominant inheritance was an exception, and was considered to be probably a genetical variant.

Hansen (1963) in reviewing the pathological findings in ataxia-telangiectasia considers the syndrome's relation to the phakomatoses to be based purely on clinical findings. From the clinical picture the abnormalities should be widespread, involving the cerebellum and other parts of the central nervous system, skin, lungs and possibly liver and kidneys. However, the reports of pathological findings have been few, and consist mainly of observations limited to the central nervous system. These include diffuse cerebellar degeneration, degeneration of pyramidal cells in the frontal cortex, loss of pigmentation in the substantia nigra, and possible enlargement of venules in the meninges and cerebellar white matter.

Aside from the phakomatoses, it has been suggested that ataxia-telangiectasia may be connected with quite another group of conditions: the spinocerebellar degenerations. This was suggested by Teller and Millichap (1961) who observed ocular telangiectasia in a girl with Friedreich's ataxia. This view was further supported by the findings of Paine and Efron (1963) who reported a case of ocular telangiectasia in a family with spinocerebellar degeneration transmitted as a dominant trait.

Distinctive biochemical features have been described in this condition. It appears to be associated frequently with hypogammaglobulinaemia (Gutmann and Lemli, 1963). Pelc and Vis (1960) found excessive aminoaciduria on chromatography, and the excretion of a peptide containing chiefly proline and hydroxyproline. The same substance was found in a patient reported by Paine and Efron (1963) in whom the ataxia was not apparent until the age of $4\frac{1}{2}$ years. It is possible, however, that this patient, together with another described by these authors, may have represented an atypical genetical variant with late onset of ataxia. The second case, moreover, showed the condition to be transmitted as a Mendelian dominant trait.

RARE STORAGE ABNORMALITIES WITH INVOLVEMENT OF NEURONAL TISSUE

Generalized Primary Xanthomatosis

This is a rare condition which has been noted to occur in sibships, and shows a familial pattern suggesting an autosomal recessive mode of inheritance. There appear to be three main variants of the condition, which have been outlined by Wolman and his co-workers (1961). These consist of forms involving respectively mainly bones and connective tissue; mainly skin and mucosae; and the central nervous system together with mainly tendons, bone marrow and serosae. This last form has been described by van Bogaert and his collaborators (1937) and subsequently by other workers.

It is thought that all three forms have the same basic pathology. Descriptions of affected sibs, two of whom were born of consanguineous parents, suggesting an autosomal recessive inheritance, have been made by Wolman and his co-workers (1961) and Dienst and Hamperl (1927). In these, xanthomatous changes occurred in many organs, including the adrenals so that adrenal insufficiency

together with a malabsorption syndrome dominated the picture. Death super-
vened at a few months of age. There was, in these cases, absence of clear-cut
involvement of the central nervous system, though the retinae and some
nerve cells were slightly affected. The clinical manifestations, however, bore a
striking resemblance to Niemann-Pick disease, although by the use of specific
staining methods it was shown that the storage product was not a phospholipid
as in Niemann-Pick disease.

Lipogranulomatosis

Lipogranulomatosis is described as a new lipoglycoprotein storage disease by
Farber and his colleagues (1957). This appears to be an invariably fatal storage
disease in which large quantities of lipid material are found widespread throughout the body. The exact nature of the storage product is not known. It is said
to be very like the storage product in gargoylism, but differs in its property of
solubility in organic solvents preferentially. Three patients, two of whom were
sibs, were described by these authors. This suggests a familial condition, but
clearly more evidence is required before any conclusions can be drawn concerning genetical mechanisms and the classification of the condition from a
clinical, pathological or biochemical point of view.

Progressive Familial Myoclonic Epilepsy

This condition [see also p. 169] may possibly be classed as a rare storage disease.
The condition was first described by Unverricht (1891). The histopathological
finding of amyloid bodies within the cytoplasm of nerve cells was reported by
Lafora and Glueck (1911). The discovery of basophilic material with staining
properties similar to that of the amyloid bodies in the heart and liver suggested
a disorder of metabolism to Harriman and Millar (1955). From the histochemical
reactions in tissues from their series of patients, it was thought that the cellular
inclusions contained an acid mucopolysaccharide and resembled amyloid.
In a review of the literature, however, Harriman and Millar point out that so-
called Lafora bodies have not always been found when cases of Unverricht's
syndrome have come to post-mortem. Moreover, they have been found in
conditions other than myoclonic epilepsy, including epidemic encephalitis,
Parkinsonism, choreo-athetosis and dementia with muscular atrophy. It is
suggested by them that the sequence of epilepsy and generalized myoclonus is
not a disease entity but a relatively rare symptom complex occurring in three
main clinical groups as drawn up by Hodskins and Yakovlev (1930). In this
classification there is first a Lafora body group, with diffuse distribution of these
bodies within the central nervous system. Secondly, there is a lipoid inclusions
group, with changes characteristic of amaurotic family idiocy together with
myoclonus. In this group, amyloid inclusions are not always present. Thirdly,
there is a heterogeneous degenerative group in which the common factor appears
to be involvement of brain-stem centres. Harriman and Millar point out that
recessive inheritance has been observed in some cases of all three groups, and
interpret this as an indication that the abnormal gene is responsible for either a
disorder of metabolism or an abiotrophy, and that the localization of the
disorder will determine the presence of the syndrome. The relationship of the

Lafora bodies with the myoclonus is not understood; they may represent an accumulation of storage product from disordered metabolism itself associated with the epilepsy, or they may act as an irritant.

The single fact that some cases have been described in which intracellular inclusions have not been found seems sufficient reason to question whether the basic disorder in Unverricht's syndrome is in fact one of carbohydrate metabolism. The clinical course, however, presents a well-defined picture, and may be divided into three stages, the epileptic, the myoclonic and terminal or marantic stage (Lundborg, 1913). It is therefore well established as a clinical entity.

It is usual to include under the diagnosis of progressive familial myoclonic epilepsy only those cases in which epileptic fits appear early in life (usually in puberty), in which myoclonus is a marked and persistent feature, and in which there is progressive mental deterioration. If the syndrome is limited in this way, then the genetical basis can be regarded as involving an autosomal recessive gene. This was the conclusion, based on Lundborg's data reported in his classic monograph of 1913, supported by the statisticians Weinberg and Bernstein; and this was the first demonstration of simple recessive inheritance in man. Later studies have confirmed this view. In his note on the genetic aspects, in the report by Harriman and Millar, A. C. Stevenson notes that the pattern of inheritance was typical of that met in conditions associated with a rare recessive gene, including a high incidence of consanguinity in the parents. In the three families reported there, one resulted from the mating of two first cousins, and another from two parents both of whom came from a small village where there was much intermarriage.

12

OTHER NEUROMETABOLIC DISORDERS II

THE LIPIDOSES

The lipidoses constitute a group of conditions in which there is a progressive degenerative breakdown of tissue in the central nervous system and at the same time the storage of material containing lipids in abnormal proportions or excessive amounts. They include the various forms of amaurotic family idiocy, Gaucher's disease, Niemann-Pick disease and the mucopolysaccharidoses. They nearly all show an autosomal recessive form of inheritance, except the form of gargoylism known as Hunter's syndrome, which follows a sex-linked recessive pattern.

From a clinical point of view, the lipidoses are a group characterized by progressive impairment of function of the central nervous system, which varies in rate according to the condition. Thus in the infantile form of amaurotic family idiocy (Tay-Sachs disease) the degeneration of neural tissue is rapidly fulminating leading to an early death. At the other end of the scale, the adult form (Kufs) of amaurotic family idiocy not only has its onset later in life but the degenerative process follows a slower course.

The lipidoses are, as a group, associated with mental defect of variable degree. In most of the lipidoses it is usually severe; but in some conditions the mental impairment is less marked (as, for example, in the mucopolysaccharidosis of Scheie: polydystrophic dwarfism). In Morquio's syndrome (a mucopolysaccharidosis) the classical view is that mental functioning is unimpaired. Within any one of the conditions, except perhaps the severe and rapidly fulminating ones such as Tay-Sachs disease, some degree of variability of intellectual function is to be found. Thus in gargoylism (Hurler's syndrome) although a large proportion of the patients are severely mentally subnormal, some with lesser degrees of impairment are to be found. Jackson (1951) reports a sibship of two sisters and a brother showing signs of gargoylism, including corneal clouding. The brother and one sister were of normal intelligence and the physical signs of the condition were less marked than those of the third sib who was mentally subnormal. Another patient with gargoylism, reported by Gilliland (1952), had marked physical signs including skeletal deformities and enlargement of the liver and spleen, but succeeded reasonably at school and later learned shorthand and typing. Two adult patients with gargoylism have been reported by Smith *et al.* (1952). Neither of these patients was mentally subnormal, and one had completed studies in economics and accounting.

The basic pathological defect in each of the conditions in the group of lipidoses is most likely to be a specific enzymopathy determined by a specific gene.

Much biochemical evidence has accumulated concerning the metabolic disturbances in these conditions. Although the specific enzymatic changes may still not be fully identified, a great deal is known of the body chemistry in these conditions and differential diagnosis often rests upon the biochemical findings. Crome and Stern (1967), in discussing the specificity of the chemical defects in the lipidoses, point out that the evidence suggests that these, like other pathological processes, may be regarded as a 'common abnormal' pathway which can be reached by diverse but converging metabolic processes.

IDENTITY AND POSSIBLE INTERRELATIONSHIPS

Although clinical and pathological features are sufficiently well defined to allow a single clear cut diagnosis in most individual cases, there are points in favour of regarding the lipidoses as variants which may overlap within a single heterogeneous group. The unitary concept with respect to the various forms of familial amaurotic idiocy has already been discussed, but there are indications that an even wider basis exists for relationships between the lipidoses. These indications lie in biochemical, pathological, clinical and genetical observations.

From a biochemical point of view it is difficult to draw up a systematic classification of lipid storage diseases involving the grey matter since the sphingolipids make up a chemically heterogeneous group and in some cases the chemical composition is not fully known (Leistyna, 1962). It seems not unreasonable to expect that each of the biochemical storage diseases distinguishable by clinical and pathological features eventually will be identified with specific enzyme defects and that the nosological classification will rest upon an exact knowledge of the biochemical errors involved. We are still far from this, as in some cases even the nature of the storage product is not properly understood.

The two disorders which have provoked most discussion with respect to their possible relationship have been the Tay-Sachs variety of amaurotic idiocy and Niemann-Pick disease. Crome (1957) considers them together from a pathological point of view, since their cerebral morphology is identical. Herndon (1954) lists the points of similarity between the two conditions, with respect to clinical, biochemical and pathological findings. A most potent argument in favour of genetical identity is that cases of Tay-Sachs amaurotic idiocy and Niemann-Pick disease have been reported in the same sibships (Driessen, 1953; Sorsby, 1951).

Occasional cases have been reported of familial amaurotic idiocy with other neuronal diseases. Thus patients have been described in whom it has been associated with Hallervorden-Spatz disease (Jervis, 1952; Spiegel-Adolf et al., 1959). There are grounds also for believing that genetically there may be a close relationship between familial amaurotic idiocy and metachromatic leucodystrophy. Certain morphological and biochemical observations point to this association. Lipid storage has been observed in cases of metachromatic leucodystrophy and in some cases of familial amaurotic idiocy there have been in the central nervous system large areas deficient in myelin but containing substances known as prelipids as well as neutral fat. In both familial amaurotic idiocy and metachromatic leucodystrophy increased amounts of hexosamine and neuraminic acid have been found in the brain. Mossakowski, Mathieson and Cumings

(1961) present a family in which all these findings are present in three sibs, in each of whom there was histopathological evidence of both amaurotic idiocy and metachromatic leucodystrophy. The familial data given indicates an autosomal recessive mode of inheritance.

A condition with features of Hurler's syndrome, infantile amaurotic idiocy and Niemann-Pick disease has been described as occurring in 8 patients from 6 families by Landing et al. (1964). They believe this to be the same disorder previously described by other workers (Craig, Clarke and Banker, 1959; Norman et al., 1959; Landing and Rubinstein, 1962). It had been reported variously as a Hurler variant, as Tay-Sachs disease with visceral involvement and as pseudo-Hurler disease. Landing and his team consider it to be a specific variant, characterized by mental and motor retardation. Radiological changes of the type seen early in Hurler's syndrome, an abnormal facies, peripheral oedema, vacuoles in lymphocytes and monocytes, hepatosplenomegaly, macroglossia, Reilly granules in the leucocytes, and foam cells in the marrow were observed in various of the patients. Cherry-red spots were seen in the retinae of two. Pathologically the disease produced a neural lipidosis resembling infantile amaurotic idiocy. Histochemically, the stored material was a glycolipid.

Such evidence lends strong support to the existence of genetical variants intermediate between the clearly defined lipidoses at present recognized as distinct entities. The classification of the lipidoses therefore still presents many problems, and it seems not unlikely that the ultimate solutions to these will be found by means of histochemical investigations.

FAMILIAL AMAUROTIC IDIOCY

Familial amaurotic idiocy is a diffuse cerebroretinal degeneration which may be classified according to age of onset into four types. These are the *infantile form of Tay-Sachs*, the *late infantile form of Bielschowsky*, the *juvenile form of Spiel-meyer-Vogt* and the *adult form of Kufs*.

The *infantile form* is the most common and begins usually during the first 6 months of life, progressing until death ensues between the ages of 2 and 3 years. The cardinal signs are blindness, dementia, progressive muscular weakness and paralysis. The blindness is due to a simple optic nerve atrophy. On retinoscopy a cherry-red spot is seen at the macula, surrounded by an area of pallor. The nerve cells undergo degenerative changes throughout the entire nervous system, and become distended by the accumulation of abnormal lipoid substances. The principal defect in the abnormal storage process appears to be an increase in ganglioside (Klenk, 1955). The ocular manifestations which are characteristic of the disorder were first described by a British ophthalmologist, Tay (1881). The syndrome, including its neurological signs and pathology was later described by Sachs (1887).

The *late infantile form of Bielschowsky* (Bielschowsky, 1913; Greenfield and Nevin, 1933) varies in its age of onset from 1 to 4 years. The disease runs a slower course than in the form of Tay-Sachs, and neurological signs referable to cerebellar degeneration are prominent. The neuropathological findings are similar to those seen in the Tay-Sachs form. The ocular findings are, however, less distinctive. The cherry-red spot is not seen, but optic atrophy is present together with retinitis pigmentosa.

The *juvenile form of Spielmeyer-Vogt* (Spielmeyer, 1908; Vogt, 1905), was first described by a Norwegian physician, Stengel (1826). It begins between the ages of 3 and 10 years, the commonest time of onset being about the sixth year. The progress of the disease is comparatively slow, and often death does not ensue until between the fifteenth and seventeenth years and some patients have survived until the age of 25. Again, degenerative changes in the nervous system with an accumulation of lipoid substances are characteristic. Extrapyramidal signs predominate, epileptic fits occur, and there is a progressive dementia. On retinoscopy, the signs are similar to those seen in the late infantile form of Bielschowsky, and no cherry-red spot is seen.

Kufs' adult form has an age of onset between the ages of 15 to 25 years and runs a much more slowly progressive course than the other forms (Kufs, 1925). Mental deterioration and convulsions are usually early signs in this form. Later, neurological signs, including a cerebellar type of ataxia, supervene. Usually there is no impairment of vision.

The evidence points to a common pathological basis for these various forms, and the differences between them may be related to their age of onset. It may be, for instance, that the disease process is more quickly established in the tissues of the infant, but that it meets with greater resistance in the more mature tissues of the older patient, in whom it runs a characteristically chronic course. This view is upheld by Franceschetti *et al.* (1951) who believe that the attenuation of the intensity of the pathological process, as seen in *juvenile* amaurotic idiocy, probably depends on the postponement of the age of onset. This, they consider, may be explained genetically by the fact that the further the differentiation of the nervous system has progressed, the fewer are the alterations that the pathological gene can produce. They put forward as further evidence the fact that the site of degeneration of the retina is displaced progressively from the central area towards the periphery as the age of manifestation is delayed. At the same time, there is a greater variability of the clinical picture in the *juvenile form* as compared with the *infantile type*.

Biochemistry

It is possible, though by no means established, that the basic metabolic defect in familial amaurotic idiocy may be a genetically determined deficiency of an enzyme, or enzymes, which in turn leads to an accumulation of phospholipids in the cells. A finding of altered enzyme activity was made by Aronson *et al.* (1958) during the course of serial biochemical studies on a series including 19 cases of *Tay-Sachs disease*. They found a sustained and significantly increased activity of various glycolytic, dehydrogenating and transaminating enzymes including glutamic oxalacetic transaminase and lactic dehydrogenase in the serum and cerebrospinal fluid of infants with *Tay-Sachs disease*. These raised concentrations, however, were regarded as due to the tissue degeneration rather than indicative of any fundamental metabolic defect.

A later study, however, by the same group (Aronson *et al.*, 1962) showed that the enzyme fructose-l-phosphate aldolase was absent from the sera of children with *Tay-Sachs disease*, and from the sera of 52 out of 53 parents studied, as well as in the sera of a proportion of other relatives. The findings suggest that the test for this enzyme might serve as means of detecting the carrier state. An interesting genetical finding was made by Bagh and Hortling (1948) who reported the discovery of vacuolated lymphocytes in 6 cases of *juvenile* amaurotic idiocy in Finland. The observations suggested that the percentage of vacuolated lymphocytes increased with the advancement of the disease, and by the same token, with the age of the patient. Rayner (1952) set out to investigate these findings further and undertook a pilot study to find whether vacuolization of the

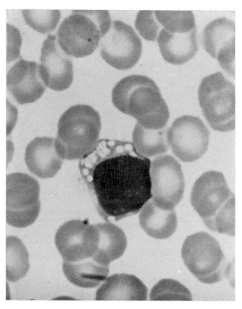

Fig. 39. Vacuolated lymphocyte from a case of juvenile amaurotic idiocy of Swedish extraction. (By kind permission of Dr. N. C. Myrianthopoulos.)

lymphocytes might occur in heterozygotes (i.e. the parents of patients with *juvenile* amaurotic idiocy). The existence of vacuolated lymphocytes was substantiated in every patient examined, though the percentage of abnormal cells was in most cases lower than that reported by Bagh and Hortling. Vacuolated lymphocytes were also found in the normal relatives (parents and some sibs) and Rayner suggested their presence as due to an expression of the gene for *juvenile* amaurotic idiocy in single dose [FIG. 39].

A similar finding has been made in connexion with the *infantile form* of familial amaurotic idiocy. The presence of vacuolated lymphocytes both in patients with *Tay-Sachs disease* and in their relatives who were apparently unaffected was reported by Spiegel-Adolf and her colleagues (1959). It would seem that these vacuoles could have been due to lipid storage, though this was not confirmed. Whatever the pathological significance of this finding, it would appear to be a feature that is worth further investigation for the detection of genetical carriers in families with amaurotic family idiocy.

Genetics: One Syndrome, or Two, Three, or Four?

It is still open to question whether the *infantile, late infantile, juvenile* and *adult* forms are distinct genetical syndromes or not, whether there are one, two, three or four different major genes involved, and whether the four forms are clinical variants of a single entity or whether they are independent diseases. Franceschetti and his colleagues (1951) review this problem and list the many advocates of the unitary theory. The dualistic conception is, however, upheld by others including Sjögren (1943), Passow (1936) and Waardenburg (1932). Klein (1953) considers that the identity of the *infantile* and *juvenile* types is suggested by the following facts. In both types similar cellular changes are observed with quantitative differences only. Secondly, there is a strong suggestion that the *late infantile* form is intermediate between the two main types, in that in some cases it resembles the *infantile* and in others the *juvenile* type. Thirdly, in the *juvenile* form the ocular findings may resemble those seen in the *infantile* type, and in some *infantile* cases the typical cherry-red spot may be lacking.

Formerly racial predisposition was a popular argument in support of a genetical differentiation between *infantile* and *juvenile* types of amaurotic idiocy. It was believed that the *infantile* type was almost if not exclusively confined to Jewish families, and the *juvenile* form to Gentile families. This argument has lost some strength since more and more reports appear of cases of the *infantile* type in families where there is no Jewish ancestry (Aronson, Valsamis and Volk, 1960). Myrianthopoulos (1962) showed that fully one-third of cases in the United States are of non-Jewish origin. However, comparative frequencies continue to show a wide disparity. The disease occurs once in about 6,000 Jewish births, and once in approximately 500,000 non-Jewish births. On this basis one of 40 Jewish persons and one of 380 non-Jewish persons is estimated as a heterozygous carrier of the gene. A survey based on the examination of death certificates referable to a period of 10 years in New York City was carried out by Kozinn, Wiener and Cohen (1957). The frequency of the heterozygotic carrier (which is about twice the gene frequency) can be estimated as about 1 in 50 Jews and about 1 in 300 non-Jews (Aronson *et al.*, 1960). The ratio of 6:1 does not differ very much (considering the errors to which the estimate is liable) from the ratio of 9·5:1 suggested by Myrianthopoulos.

Klein and Ktenidès (1954) examined 64 sibships containing Tay-Sachs disease drawn from the literature between 1933 and 1954. The resulting genetical data were compared with those of Slome (1933) collected from 1881 to 1933, and a marked preponderance was found in the observed frequency of the non-consanguineous cases in Gentile families.

Jervis (1959) draws attention to the fact that in 15 cases of the *infantile* form of amaurotic idiocy personally observed by him, all were children of unmixed Jewish families. On the other hand, he found no case in which a patient with the *juvenile* form had Jewish ancestry. The ancestry of patients with the *juvenile* form has been traced to British, Irish, Scots, German, Italian, African and Japanese families; therefore, Jervis remarks, the gene appears to be quite widespread amongst Caucasian people, and present also in African and Asiatic races. He considers the absence of any report of a Jewish case of the juvenile type as a significant argument, together with other data, in favour of a clear-cut genetic distinction between *juvenile* and *infantile* amaurotic idiocy.

Population Genetics and Mode of Inheritance

Apart from the differences between Jews and non-Jews in gene frequencies discussed above, there are also important variations between different stems of the Jewish peoples. It has been established that the birth incidence of *infantile* amaurotic idiocy is 100 times higher (and accordingly the gene frequency 10 times higher) among Ashkenazi Jews than among other Jewish groups (not to speak of non-Jewish populations) in the United States (Myrianthopoulos and Aronson, 1966). These authors do not think that this is to be explained by a differential breeding pattern, by genetical drift or a differential mutation rate; and they examine instead the possibility of differential fertility of the heterozygote.

Their findings suggested, but did not prove, that the Jewish heterozygote enjoys an over-all reproductive advantage of about 6 per cent over the presumed homozygous normal. They put forward historical evidence to corroborate this hypothesis and to place the rise of the gene for *infantile* amaurotic idiocy among the Ashkenazi Jews in historical times, perhaps during the early centuries of the Diaspora. They draw attention to the fact that this is not the only genetical disorder which has a uniquely high frequency among the Ashkenazi Jews. Gaucher's disease, Niemann-Pick disease and possibly other rare inborn errors of metabolism are known also to have a very high frequency among this group when compared with other Jewish groups and non-Jewish populations. It is possible that all three of these storage diseases and perhaps other rare metabolic conditions may be susceptible to the same selective forces and share the same polymorphic properties. The opposite holds good, however, with respect to phenylketonuria which appears to be confined in Jewish populations largely if not exclusively to non-Ashkenazi Jews (Cohen, Bodonyi and Szeinberg, 1961).

With regard to mode of inheritance, the classical investigations of Sjögren (1931, 1943) give strong support to the view that *juvenile* amaurotic idiocy is transmitted by a simple recessive mode of inheritance. Amongst the sibships he studied containing affected children, there was a high rate of parental consanguinity. Out of 145 sibships, the parents were first cousins in 23 and related in other ways in 26 instances. None of the parents was affected. Sjögren estimated the gene frequency as being of the order of 0·0062 in Sweden and the prevalence rate of the disorder in the population as 0·000038.

The pattern of inheritance for the *infantile* form is still under discussion. Slome (1933) found a high proportion of cases with consanguineous parentage in his material, which supports a recessive mode of inheritance. On the other hand, Franceschetti *et al.* (1951) quote pedigrees in which the occurrence of cases in two or three generations suggests an irregular dominant mode of inheritance. Their statistical calculations following Weinberg's method give a frequency of incidence (about 50 per cent) which likewise points to a dominant inheritance. They consider that the direct proof of the mode of inheritance will probably never be found because of the lethal character of the pathological gene.

NIEMANN-PICK DISEASE

Niemann-Pick disease was first described by Niemann in 1914 and later by Pick in 1927. It is a condition seen mainly in infants and young children, though occasionally it has been reported in older children and in adults, in whom the disease runs a slower and more chronic course (Terry, Sperry and Brodoff, 1954). The main feature is the widespread and excessive storage of sphingomyelin which may involve almost any organ. The central nervous system is not spared. Characteristic reticulo-endothelial cells, the so-called Niemann-Pick cells, which contain globules of fat in the cytoplasm, have not been found however within the brain parenchyma itself (Leistyna, 1962). As in amaurotic idiocy, only the ganglion cells appear to take an active part in the storage process. Penrose (1949a) points out that the disease causes mental deterioration but is not specially associated with mental defect. The deterioration of mental function depends on the degree of involvement of the central nervous system, though it may progress to complete dementia.

Clinically, two forms of the disease have been described, an acute infantile and a chronic form. Crome and Stern (1967) favour the subdivision into cerebral infantile, cerebral juvenile and non-cerebral variants. The infantile form, which is by far the most commonly described type, has an insidious onset usually between the third and sixth month after birth. The first sign often is a failure to thrive, which progresses to emaciation and a gross enlargement of spleen and liver. The skin may show a yellowish discoloration. As regards psychological effects, apathy is the prevailing sign at first, but progressive mental retardation soon becomes apparent. In the retina, signs of degeneration with pigmentation may occur, and sometimes a cherry-red spot has been seen.

In view of the ocular and other clinicopathological findings, the question has been raised as to whether Niemann-Pick disease and familial amaurotic idiocy are in fact variants of the same disease, differing only in the distribution of lesions. Hepatomegaly and lymph gland involvement dominate the clinical picture in Niemann-Pick disease, whilst changes in the brain and retina are more prominent in familial amaurotic idiocy. Biochemical studies of the two conditions are, however, as yet incomplete and do not justify a rigid demarcation of the two conditions (Crome, 1957). Further doubts as to a distinction between the two conditions are raised by the occurrence of both in the same family (Hilliard and Kirman, 1957).

As regards inheritance, Niemann-Pick disease appears to be transmitted as an autosomal recessive trait, although this has not yet been fully established (Herndon, 1954). More than one member of a sibship have been affected in about one-third of the reported cases. It is said that no transmission from one generation to another has been reported so far (Leistyna, 1962), though a family has been described containing two confirmed adult cases of Niemann-Pick disease in which an increase in lipoids in the blood was transmitted as a dominant trait (Pfändler, 1946). Pfändler distinguishes three grades of manifestation of the abnormal gene: first, the full clinical picture, secondly, the presence of 'latent macro-symptoms' such as hepatosplenomegaly of which the patient is unaware, and thirdly the presence of microsymptoms which Pfändler considers of primary importance for the genetical analysis of families containing the disorder. These microsymptoms include an alteration in the blood lipids. This hypothesis is based upon the findings in one family, and further bio-chemical evidence is needed from other families before it can be properly evaluated.

GAUCHER'S DISEASE

This lipidosis is named after Gaucher who described it in 1882. He believed the condition to represent an epithelioma of the spleen, but later considered the disturbance to be more widespread, characterized by connective tissue prolifera-tion. The cases described are customarily divided into two main clinical cate-gories: an acute form which shows itself within the first few months of life, and a chronic form with an insidious onset, which is usually recognized by the time the patient has reached adolescence. In the acute form signs of physical and mental retardation appear early. Clinical signs include hepatomegaly, spleno-megaly and neurological impairment. There is steadily progressive deterioration, leading in most cases to death before the age of 2 years. In the chronic form, splenomegaly due to infiltration by the typical large, pale Gaucher cells is often the first characteristic clinical sign to appear. Infiltration also occurs in the liver, lungs and bone marrow. The skin may show a patchy bronze pigmentation. Yellowish thickening of the conjunctivae (pingueculae) may appear. The general health of the patient deteriorates. Anaemia is common. Granulocytopenia and thrombocytopenia are not uncommon.

A sharp division of cases into these two clinical categories may be somewhat artificial. It seems more likely that there is a continuous gradation in severity from those cases in whom the infiltration by Gaucher cells is slight, and in whom clinical signs are absent or negligible, to the severely affected patients who die from the condition in infancy. Norman, Urich and Lloyd (1956) consider that cases may be grouped according to whether lipid storage is absent, minimal or excessive, and that non-acute specific degenerative changes are usually associated with the first two groups.

The disease is fundamentally a disorder of lipid metabolism resulting in the accumulation of cerebroside in the cells of the reticulo-endothelial system. In some cases an abnormal kerasin has been found with glucose in place of the usual galactose in the molecule, but in others the normal galactose cerebroside is found to accumulate. Stein and Gardner (1960) suggest that a defect in an epimerase enzyme may be responsible for the accumulation of the glucose cerebroside. They consider an enzymatic defect may be also responsible in those cases where galactose cerebroside accumulates.

The familial incidence of Gaucher's disease has long been observed. The first of many reports of multiple incidence within sibships was by Collier (1895). About one-third of cases reported in the literature have been familial. The pattern of inheritance has not been established beyond question, but there is good evidence for an autosomal dominant mode of transmission by a gene with variable manifestation. Groen (1948) summarizes familial cases in the literature, and draws attention to the following points. Although most of the familial cases described occurred in the members of one generation only, in sibs or cousins, in some families the disease was observed in successive generations where it was transmitted from parent to child. The cases appeared to be about equally divided between the sexes. The incidence of abortions and stillbirths among the offspring of individuals with Gaucher's disease seemed unusually high. In support of dominant transmission, Klein (1953) points out that the frequency of the disorder is sometimes very high with a sibship, though usually the proportion of those affected is about 40 per cent. On the other hand, family data have been published in which a recessive mode of inheritance is suggested, such as the Negro family reported by Herndon and Bender (1950) with 5 cases in 5 separate but closely related sibships. In this family the parents of 4 of the affected children were second cousins. Hsia, Naylor and Bigler (1959) suggest that the chronic form of the disease may be inherited as a dominant or a recessive trait and that the acute form is recessive.

A dominant mode of transmission by a gene with variable manifestation fits well the considerable variation between cases with respect to the severity of the condition, and the lateral spread (affecting cousins) in one generation with no sign of the disease in the antecedents. Individuals in which the progress is slow and the amount of accumulated kerasin too small to produce clinical signs may be apparently normal genetical carriers. They would have a 50 per cent risk of transmitting the gene to their children. It is suggested that such carriers may be detected by the presence of Gaucher cells in a smear of sternal marrow (Groen and Garrer, 1948; Zlotnick and Groen, 1961). Geddes and Moore (1953) point out, however, that frequently Gaucher cells cannot be found in the marrow of involved patients themselves, and this complicates the question of their detection in the marrow of parent carriers.

THE MUCOPOLYSACCHARIDOSES

The mucopolysaccharidoses constitute a group of conditions in which abnormal amounts of mucopolysaccharides accumulate. In addition, lipids are stored, and therefore the group is classified under the general heading of the lipidoses. There are distinct variants within the mucopolysaccharidoses that can be distinguished by their chemical pathology and by their clinical signs. This differentiation has been well reviewed by McKusick et al. (1965), McKusick (1966) and by Maroteaux and Lamy (1965). Although the classification is felt to be still incomplete, and McKusick suggests that the heterogeneity could be broken down further by investigations at a cellular level, at least five variants have been distinguished. These are Hurler's syndrome (gargoylism), Hunter's syndrome (gargoylism), Sanfillipo syndrome (polydystrophic oligophrenia), Scheie syndrome (polydystrophic dwarfism) and the Morquio syndrome. The first three are generally associated with mental subnormality of severe degree. The association with mental impairment is less regular in the Scheie syndrome. In the Morquio syndrome, however, intelligence is said to be normal or only mildly impaired, although we have observed a case in which the patient was severely subnormal. The classical clinical features of the group as a whole include skeletal deformities and dwarfing, and cardiovascular changes. An excess of urinary mucopolysaccharides is found. Many of the clinical features can be associated with an underlying defect in connective tissue metabolism.

18

Mucopolysaccharides, which are macromolecules made up of repeatedly alternating units of hexuronic acid and a hexosamine, are the non-fibrous elements of connective tissue. Hence they are widely distributed throughout the body, and are important components of cartilage, subcutaneous tissue, the cornea and the walls of blood vessels. These bear the brunt of the chemical derangement in the mucopolysaccharidoses. The chemical pathology in the mucopolysaccharidoses is fully discussed by Crome and Stern (1967) who point out that the properties of living connective tissue depend in part on the interaction of the mucopolysaccharides with collagen and other proteins. If the bonds between protein and the mucopolysaccharides are weakened, then the mucopolysaccharide may diffuse out of the tissue. The mucopolysaccharidoses have been related to disturbance in metabolism of three mucopolysaccharides. These are chondroitin sulphate B, heparitin sulphate and keratosulphate. The specific mucopolysaccharide abnormality, together with clinical and genetical features are tabulated in TABLE 86 (after Crome and Stern, 1967).

As well as underlying the physical changes, the disturbance in connective tissue metabolism may contribute indirectly to mental impairment by changes in the blood vessels supplying the brain. Intellectual function is, however, likely to be affected more directly in the mucopolysaccharidoses by the derangement of the metabolism of nerve cells. Deposits of glycolipids have been found in the brain (Cumings, 1964), but it is not understood whether the lipid and mucopolysaccharide changes are causally related, nor is it known whether one

TABLE 86

MUCOPOLYSACCHARIDOSES, THE PRINCIPAL FEATURES

(From Crome and Stern, 1967)

NAME	GENETICS	CLINICAL	MENTAL RETARDA- TION	EXCESS URINARY MPS
Hurler's syndrome (gargoylism)	Autosomal recessive	Usually severe manifestations, including early clouding of cornea, cardiovascular deficits	+++	ChSB and HS
Hunter's syndrome (gargoylism)	Sex-linked recessive	Somewhat milder course, no clouding of cornea, cardiovascular deficits	+++	ChSB and HS
Sanfillipo syndrome (polydystrophic oligophrenia)	Autosomal recessive	Mild growth disorder and somatic signs, no cardiovascular deficits	+++	HS
Scheie syndrome (polydystrophic dwarfism)	Autosomal recessive	Clouding of cornea, stiff joints, characteristic facies, aortic valve disease	+−	ChSB
Morquio syndrome	Autosomal recessive	Severe bone changes, clouding of cornea, aortic regurgitation	—	KS

Key to abbreviations: MPS, mucopolysaccharides; ChSA, Chondroitin sulphate A; ChSB Chondroitin sulphate B; HS, heparitin sulphate; KS, keratosulphate.

or the other predominates in the effect upon intelligence (Crome and Stern, 1967). Wolfe *et al.* (1964) have reported a patient of normal intelligence with gargoylism who showed deposits of mucopolysaccharide only; whereas in another patient with gargoylism who was mentally defective both mucopoly-saccharides and lipids were found in tissues including the central nervous system. They suggested that the derangements of mucopolysaccharide and lipid metabo-lism respectively were distinct, although they frequently occurred together, and that it was the lipidosis rather than the faulty mucopolysaccharide metabolism that accounted for the mental impairment.

HURLER'S SYNDROME

Attention was drawn to this condition by Hurler in 1919. It has striking charac-teristics including an unusual facial appearance with coarsened features and heavy supraorbital ridges, reminiscent of that sometimes seen in the carved

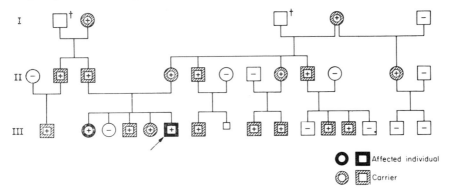

Fig. 40. Pedigree of two patients with Hurler's syndrome. The signs (positive and negative) inside the male (square) and female (circle) symbols indicate whether the skin fibroblasts in cell culture showed increased intracellular metachromasia. The small square symbol represents a male stillbirth (Danes and Bearn, 1967).

gargoyles of ancient churches. This feature, together with other clinical and biochemical signs, is common to both Hurler's syndrome and Hunter's syndrome. In consequence, the term 'gargoylism' is commonly applied to both conditions.

The facial appearance is due to a thickening of connective tissue and distortion of bony structure which are part of more widespread changes throughout the body. The skull may be rather square and box-like, or it may appear scaphoce-phalic on X-ray with premature closure of the longitudinal suture [FIG. 41]. The pituitary fossa is enlarged. There is over-all dwarfing of stature, accompanied by radiological changes which are more or less specific to the syndrome [FIGS. 42 and 43]. The most marked modification of the spine on X-ray is a hooked or spurred appearance of the first or second lumbar vertebra and sometimes of the twelfth thoracic vertebra. The vertebral bodies present an ovoid appearance, and there may also be an irregularity of the intervertebral discs. The long bones of the limbs are massive and the metacarpals show a cone-shaped deformity sometimes described as a 'sugar-loaf' appearance. Other radiological signs often seen in Hurler's syndrome are an irregularity in appearance and development of the epiphyses and ossified carpal centres; obliquity of the lower portion of the radius and of the cubitus; and coxa valga (Maroteaux and Lamy, 1965).

Other clinical features include an enlarged abdomen with umbilical and often inguinal hernias, and a progressive hepatosplenomegaly. Frequently a systolic murmur is heard. The hair is coarse; the eyebrows bushy and often meeting

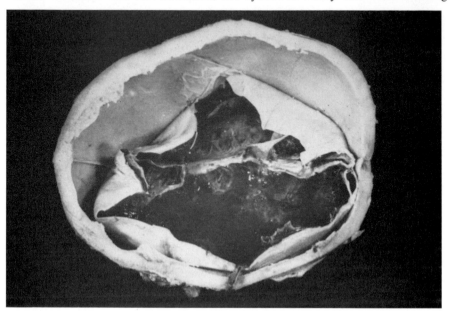

Fig. 41. Skull in Hurler's syndrome, showing thickening of skull table and meninges. (By courtesy of Dr. L. Crome.)

over the nose; there is often general hirsutism. The voice is harsh. Clouding of the cornea usually is an early sign.

The clinical course is one of progressive deterioration. Hurler's syndrome is apparently the commonest of the mucopolysaccharidoses, and the one that produces death at the earliest age. The child usually appears to develop normally for a few months, and then progressive physical and mental deterioration set in. Although delayed growth is the rule, growth may proceed at a normal rate in the first years of life, and occasionally may even be excessive in young children (Maroteaux and Lamy, 1965). Similarly, mental development may appear to be normal initially, but deterioration is usually noticed very early in life. Death supervenes usually before puberty and it is rare to see a patient with Hurler's syndrome surviving beyond the age of 20 years. Intercurrent infection or cardiac failure may be terminal events.

HUNTER'S SYNDROME

This syndrome is often referred to in the literature together with Hurler's syndrome under the single term of gargoylism. However, the syndrome to which attention was originally drawn by Hunter (1917) can be distinguished from Hurler's syndrome on genetical and clinical grounds.

Hunter's syndrome is inherited as a sex-linked recessive condition, appearing only in males, and being transmitted by apparently unaffected female carriers. The sex-linked recessive form of genetical transmission was first observed in a pedigree described by Njå (1945). Prior to this it was thought that the condition was an autosomal recessive trait. Since then, many pedigrees have appeared which substantiate the existence of the sex-linked form as a clinicogenetical entity. It is likely that about one-third of patients with gargoylism have the

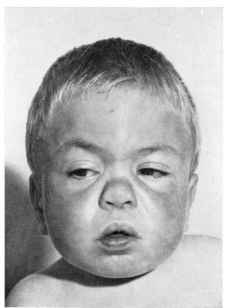 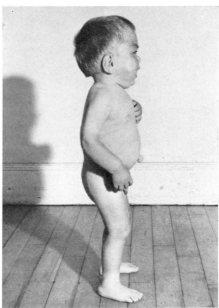

Fig. 42. Gargoylism.   Fig. 43. Gargoylism.

sex-linked recessive form, which is more frequent than had been believed previously (Maroteaux and Lamy, 1965).

Clinically, Hunter's syndrome shares many features with Hurler's syndrome. There is dwarfing of stature, a coarsened facial appearance and specific skeletal changes seen on radiological examination, though lumbar gibbus is not a feature in Hunter's syndrome. Clouding of the cornea, however, does not occur in Hunter's syndrome to a degree that is evident on ordinary clinical examination, though a very slight clouding may be seen in older patients on examination with a slit-lamp, according to McKusick and his co-workers (1965). Other ocular changes may occur in Hunter's syndrome, however, including atypical retinitis pigmentosa that may lead eventually to blindness (McKusick *et al.*, 1965). Deafness and possibly heart complications are more frequent in Hunter's syndrome than in Hurler's syndrome (Maroteaux and Lamy, 1965). The clinical course is somewhat milder and slower in Hunter's syndrome than in Hurler's syndrome.

From a biochemical point of view, Hurler's and Hunter's syndromes are indistinguishable. In both, excessive chondroitin sulphate B and heparitin sulphate are excreted in the urine. In both, accumulations of these substances are found in the connective tissue throughout the body, especially in the liver and spleen which undergo gross and progressive enlargement.

SANFILLIPO SYNDROME
(POLYDYSTROPHIC OLIGOPHRENIA)

This autosomal recessive mucopolysaccharidosis is often accompanied by severe and progressive mental retardation, but the physical signs are much less marked than in the syndromes of Hurler or Hunter. Dwarfing, skeletal changes, joint stiffness and enlargement of the spleen and liver are only slight or moderate. Corneal clouding and cardiovascular changes are not features of the Sanfillipo condition. Biochemically, the only mucopolysaccharide excreted to excess in the urine is heparitin sulphate.

SCHEIE SYNDROME
(POLYDYSTROPHIC DWARFISM)

This syndrome obtains its eponym from Scheie, who together with his co-workers described it as a newly recognized *forme fruste* of Hurler's disease (Scheie, Hambrick and Barness, 1962). Maroteaux and Lamy (1965), however, consider that the disease was probably first described by Liebenam (1938) under the name of Hurler's disease, and that other cases which appear to have been fairly similar were described still earlier. Biochemically, the syndrome is characterized by excretion of large amounts of chondroitin sulphate B.

Maroteaux and Lamy (1965) in reviewing the clinical features of the condition, draw attention to the point that in contrast to the other mucopolysaccharidoses, this illness is first noted because of lack of growth which becomes apparent between the ages of 2 and 3 years. There is dwarfism, shortening of trunk and limbs, lumbar kyphosis, genu valgum and deformity of the sternum (pectus carinatus). There are specific radiological changes. Although there is some facial resemblance to that in Hurler's and Hunter's syndromes, this is less grotesque. There is some joint stiffness, general hirsutism and hepatospleno-megaly. Slit-lamp examination shows corneal opacities, and corneal grafts become opacified (McKusick *et al.*, 1965). Retinitis pigmentosa may be a feature. Deafness is found in varying degrees. McKusick and his team have found that aortic valve disease is a feature of the syndrome, and most have aortic regurgitation, though this may be asymptomatic. There is still insufficient evidence to know the extent to which the life-span is shortened in this condition.

Mental retardation is present in variable degrees, and may not appear at all. The patients described by Scheie were of intelligence of a level of 'near genius'. McKusick and his co-workers state that one of their patients is an attorney and of at least average intelligence. Psychosis was observed in 2 out of the 4 adults they studied.

MORQUIO'S SYNDROME
(THE MORQUIO-BRAILSFORD SYNDROME)

Morquio (1929) reported a skeletal disorder in two sibs, which he described as a form of familial osseous dystrophy. Shortly afterwards, Brailsford (1929) reported a case of the same type which he termed chondro-osteodystrophy. Since these first reports, a considerable number of cases have been published with well-marked clinical and radiological features which have marked off the Morquio-Brailsford syndrome from the other forms of hereditary chondrodysplasias. More recently further means of differentiation have become possible by virtue of the biochemical findings.

Clinically, the affected child is usually normal at birth but characteristically between the first and second year of life, skeletal abnormalities become apparent. These consist of a kyphoscoliosis involving the thoracic and lumbar spine; deformities of the sternum, with pigeon-breast and barrel chest; a short neck; or reduced trunk length and a shortening of the limbs. Knock-knees are common. The joints of the long bones show swelling and limitation of movement, but there is abnormal laxity in the fingers and wrists. On X-ray examination the vertebral bodies are characteristically flat and irregular with beaking similar to that in the Hurler syndrome. The epiphyseal growth centres show severe dysplasia. The joint spaces are widened. There is general osteoporosis. In contrast to the syndromes of Hunter and Hurler, in the Morquio-Brailsford syndrome the cranium is normal. Over-all, the picture is that of a dwarf-like individual with a normal head, though McKusick and his co-workers note a characteristic facies, with broad mouth, prominent maxilla, short nose and widely-spaced teeth.

McKusick and his co-workers (1965) contend that all patients with skeletal changes identical to those described by Brailsford and Morquio develop ocular (and usually cardiac) manifestations if they survive to adolescence. This view is held also by Maroteaux and Lamy (1963) and by Robins, Stevens and Linker (1963). These extra-skeletal manifestations may appear late. The corneas become diffusely opacified, but gross obvious clouding is not usual before the age of 10. The appearance is that of a filmy haze rather than that of ground glass as in Hurler's syndrome. They differentiate this condition from the Morquio-Ullrich variant, which is characterized by variable degrees of cardiac and other visceral involvement, some mental retardation, hearing defects, Reilly granules in the leucocytes, corneal opacities and Morquio-like skeletal deformities. The Morquio-Ullrich variant has been referred to as a 'mild Hurler's' or 'atypical Morquio's' disease. In the case of patients showing corneal clouding in addition to the skeletal defects of Morquio's disease, Ullrich (1943) used the term 'Spaet-Hurler' (late Hurler).

Biochemically, Morquio's syndrome is characterized by the excretion of large amounts of keratosulphate in the urine. Observations of the cytochemical lesions associated with this condition have been made by Schenk and Haggerty (1964) who found pathological changes limited to cartilage. They consisted of cytochemically definable lesions of the matrix characterized by the presence of amorphous and fibrillar lesions and the accumulation of foam cells. An abnormal accumulation of mucopolysaccharides was found in foam cells and cartilage matrix, but there was no evidence of visceral storage of mucopolysaccharides.

INHERITANCE OF THE
MUCOPOLYSACCHARIDOSES

The mucopolysaccharidoses are all very rare. Hurler's syndrome is the most common, probably occurring once in 10,000 births although no precise information on frequency is available. Hunter's syndrome and Morquio's syndrome are each probably about a quarter as frequent, and may occur about once in every 40,000 births (McKusick *et al.*, 1965). Terry and Linker (1964) consider that Sanfillipo's syndrome may occur in one out of every 100,000–200,000 people, but McKusick *et al.* (1965) think this may well be an under-estimate in view of the relatively inconspicuous somatic features which may lead

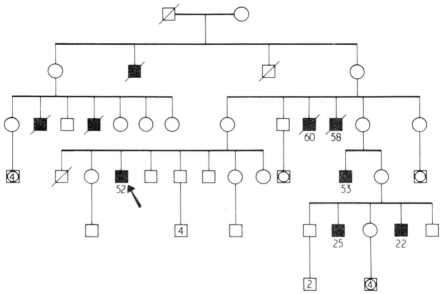

Fig. 44. Pedigree of a family with Hunter's syndrome (McKusick *et al.*, 1965). Up-dated (1963) pedigree of kindred reported by Beebe and Formel (1954). The cross bar indicates deceased persons.

to cases being missed. No estimate of frequency is available for the apparently very rare Scheie syndrome.

As regards the mode of inheritance, the syndromes of Hurler, Sanfillipo, Scheie and Morquio are all transmitted as autosomal recessive conditions. Hunter's syndrome, however, follows a sex-linked recessive pattern of inheritance. This is illustrated by the pedigree reproduced by McKusick *et al.* (1965) [FIG. 44], of a kindred reported by Beebe and Formel (1954). In this pedigree the characteristic form of transmission of a sex-linked recessive trait is seen: the affected members of the family are all males, whilst the gene is transmitted via unaffected female carriers.

Basophilic granules in the cytoplasm of polymorphonuclear leucocytes, the so-called Reilly-Alder bodies (Reilly, 1941) [FIG. 45], were the first haemato-logical abnormality described in gargoylism (Crome and Stern, 1967). However, mucopolysaccharide inclusions in the lymphocytes are a much more constant finding. These inclusions stain metachromatically with toluidine blue, and this finding has been shown to be of considerable value in the diagnosis of gargoylism (Mittwoch, 1963). The phenomenon of metachromatic staining due to the

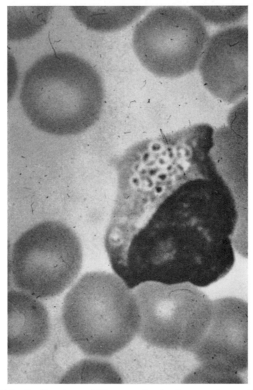

Fig. 45. Reilly-Alder bodies, basophilic granules in the cytoplasm of the polymorpho-nuclear leucocytes in gargoylism. (By courtesy of Dr. L. Crome.)

presence of increased mucopolysaccharides, has been put to valuable use in the development of a method for detecting genetical carriers.

As the mucopolysaccharidoses follow a Mendelian recessive pattern of inheritance, the carriers are characteristically symptom-free. A method for detecting heterozygotic carriers has, however, been described by Danes and Bearn (1967). Not only white blood cells, but cells from other tissues show metachromatic reactions in the case of patients with mucopolysaccharide disorders. Thus, fibroblasts from these patients, when stained with the dye toluidine-blue O, give a red staining of the cytoplasm indicating the presence of increased cellular mucopolysaccharides. Danes and Bearn extended these observations to individuals who were considered on the grounds of pedigree studies to be carriers of genes for the different types of the mucopolysacchari-doses, and found cellular metachromasia in all, except the relatives of patients with Morquio's syndrome with manifestations limited to the skeletal system. No cellular metachromasia was found in the cells of healthy controls who were not believed to be carriers of a mucopolysaccharidosis gene.

The absence of metachromasia was not unexpected in skin fibroblasts from relatives of patients with Morquio's syndrome with exclusively skeletal involvement and without the signs of Hurler's syndrome, because the patients themselves in this group showed no metachromasia in their skin fibroblasts. Danes and Bearn ascribe this to the fact that this type of Morquio's syndrome is characterized biochemically by the excretion of an increased amount of keratosulphate in the urine. As this substance is normally found only in cornea, cartilage and growing bone, it was not surprising that the skin fibroblast from an affected individual did not show increased intracellular mucopolysaccharides. Danes and Bearn conclude that intracellular metachromasia might be expected to be found in the tissues which synthesize keratosulphate, in both affected individuals with this variant and in their carrier relatives.

Although this work has been a valuable contribution in the endeavour to find new methods of detection for heterozygous carriers, it has received criticism on the grounds that cellular metachromasia may be non-specific and to some extent dependent upon the conditions in which it is observed; for example, it may appear as a random phenomenon in cells cultured over a long period. No doubt with further refinements of biochemical techniques more specific methods for detecting changes in the heterozygote will be found, possibly by the quantitative assay of enzymes of metabolites.

13

DOMINANT ABNORMALITIES

THE PHAKOMATOSES

The phakomatoses are a group of genetically-determined conditions with neuro-ectodermal lesions. They include tuberous sclerosis, von Recklinghausen's disease (neurofibromatosis), von Hippel-Lindau disease (angiomatosis), and the Sturge-Weber syndrome. Ataxia-telangiectasia is often included in the group (Hansen, 1963) but it differs genetically from the other conditions in that nearly all familial cases have shown a pattern of autosomal recessive inheritance, whereas a pattern of dominant inheritance is seen typically in families containing more than one member affected by the other conditions. Ataxia-telangiectasia is considered on page 251. Von Hippel-Lindau disease will not be considered in this book as mental subnormality or other psychological changes are not characteristically associated with it.

The name phakomata, from *phakos*, the Greek name for motherspot, was first used by van der Hoeve (1923) who described the retinal tumours in tuberous sclerosis. These are associated with other neuroectodermal lesions which may be present in the newborn child or appear later, which can be very small but can enlarge to sizeable tumours, occasionally becoming malignant.

The phakomatoses are associated with mental subnormality, but the relation-ship is not a constant one. The dominant genes responsible show considerable variation of expressivity, and the degree of intellectual impairment differs from one patient to another. A number of individuals with von Recklinghausen's disease are of normal intelligence. Although tuberous sclerosis is frequently associated with severe mental subnormality, some affected individuals have been reported as being of normal or even superior intelligence.

An approximate estimate of the prevalence of the phakomatoses amongst the severely mentally subnormal can be based on the relatively small survey of about 2000 institutionalized children by Berg and Crome (1963). Tuberous sclerosis was by far the most prevalent of the phakomatoses in this population. They found 15 patients diagnosed as having tuberous sclerosis, 2 with neurofibro-matosis, 2 with the Sturge-Weber syndrome, and one possible atypical case of tuberous sclerosis. The number of cases with tuberous sclerosis was increased even more owing to the fact that several incomplete cases remained unrecognized until pathological examination after death.

TUBEROUS SCLEROSIS (EPILOIA)

This condition, which is also known as epiloia, was first described by Bourneville (1880) who made careful observations of the neuropathology and considered the cerebral lesions to represent a kind of hypertrophic sclerosis. He also drew attention to the frequent concomitance of adenoma sebaceum of the face and of primitive-cell tumours of the kidneys.

Neuropathology

The nodules in the brain may be found in considerable numbers, scattered throughout the cortex and other regions. Their appearance at the ventricular surface has been likened to candle-gutterings, but in the main these tumours have been likened to potato tubers, which gave rise to the term tuberous sclerosis [FIG. 46]. They are slow to develop but may grow to be 2·5 cm or more in diameter. They are firm and rubbery in consistency and may even erode the

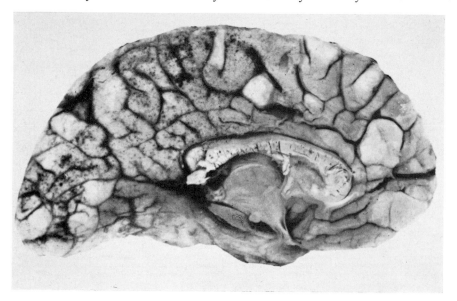

Fig. 46. Brain in tuberous sclerosis (by courtesy of Dr. L. Crome).

inner table of the skull. Histologically, they consist essentially of a proliferation of glial tissue, with scattered bizarre giant cells and undifferentiated nerve elements (Bielschowsky and Gallus, 1913). Despite the presence of these gross lesions in the brain, patients with tuberous sclerosis are usually remarkably free from severe neurological disablement apart from epilepsy.

Besides the nodules found in the brain, tumours are often found in other organs. In their excellent review of the condition, Paulson and Lyle (1966) point out that rhabdomyomata of the heart are said to occur in at least 5 per cent of cases. Renal tumours, of an embryonal mixed type which vary in histology from case to case, have been described as having been found in about 80 per cent of cases (Critchley and Earl, 1932).

Benign phakomata of the retina are frequently observed in tuberous sclerosis. These are pale, flat, opaque plaques or nodules, composed mainly of glial fibres and large cells [FIG. 47]. Sometimes they take the form of large nodular tumours, which have been likened to a glistening white mulberry (Kirby, 1951).

A great variety of skin lesions are seen in tuberous sclerosis but the most characteristic of these and the most noticeable is the permanent facial rash due to the presence of many small sebaceous adenomata. These facial lesions were first described in detail by Pringle (1890) who described them as 'indolent, firm, whitish, or yellowish, sago-grain-like, solid papules or little tumours, imbedded in the skin at different depths, or projecting from it, and varying in size from

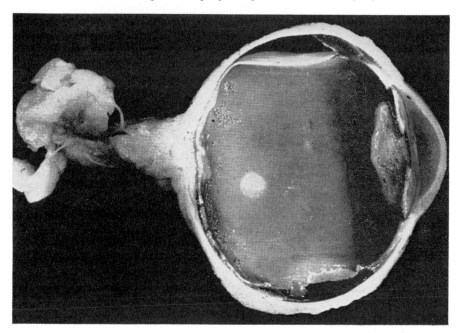

Fig. 47. Cross-section of eye of patient with tuberous sclerosis, showing phakomata in retina (by courtesy of Dr. L. Crome).

that of a pin's point to a small pea'. They are vascularized by innumerable minute capillary dilatations, giving the rash a reddish hue. The rash develops in early childhood, and is permanent. It is found on the cheeks, nose, forehead and chin. The distribution on the cheeks on either side of the nose has earned it the name of the 'butterfly' rash [FIG. 48].

Skin lesions other than the facial rash and occurring elsewhere in the body include flatter pale nodules; raised roughened plaques which may be pigmented (*peau de chagrin* patches); fibromata in the nail bed itself or beneath the nail which may cause vertical ridging of the nails; neurofibromata in the skin; and pigmented naevi.

Clinical Features

Epilepsy is almost always a concomitant of tuberous sclerosis in severe cases. Usually the patient has grand mal seizures, but focal motor seizures are also seen.

Infantile spasms may be one of the first intimations of the condition. As the patients grow older, the seizures in tuberous sclerosis usually become less frequent and more standardized, as Paulson and Lyle (1966) point out. These writers draw attention to the fact that there is no biochemical or neurophysiological explanation for the epileptic seizures, and no regular correlation between histological findings, degree of brain involvement or clinical type of seizure. It is presumed, however, that the epilepsy is causally related to the presence of

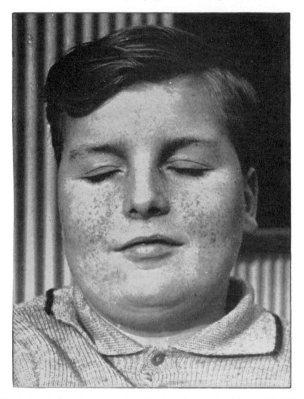

Fig. 48. Facial rash in tuberous sclerosis showing typical 'butterfly' distribution (Hilliard and Kirman, 1957).

the nodules in the brain and their interference with surrounding functioning tissue. Possibly some degree of physiological equilibrium is reached as time goes on or as the nodule stops growing, which might account for the lesser frequency of the seizures as the patient matures.

In infancy, convulsive seizures may be the only apparent manifestation of the disease, and a clinical diagnosis may be difficult. Globus and Selinsky (1935), also Brorson et al. (1961) set out this problem and discuss in very clear terms the matter of the diagnosis of tuberous sclerosis in infancy. In the typical case the diagnosis rests upon the triad of symptoms: epilepsy, mental subnormality and adenoma sebaceum. Of these three, the specific sign in tuberous sclerosis is adenoma sebaceum. This facial rash usually does not appear until the age of 4–6 years (Crome and Stern, 1967). If, however, there is a family history of the condition, and most especially if one of the parents has suggestive facial lesions, one should think of the diagnosis of tuberous sclerosis in an infant with seizures especially when there are signs of mental retardation.

Although mental retardation is regarded as one of the cardinal signs for the clinical diagnosis of tuberous sclerosis, affected individuals with normal intelligence have been described. For example, Duvoisin and Vinson (1961) reported 3 patients, of whom 2 obtained average IQ scores on psychological testing and one had a record of scholastic excellence. These writers point out that it seems likely that the literature has been biased by examples of the more severe manifestations of the disease, and that tuberous sclerosis without mental defect may be much more common than has previously been thought, as patients with less noticeable signs may frequently pass unrecognized.

The variable expressivity in a single family of the tuberous sclerosis gene with respect especially to intelligence is well demonstrated in a family reported by Scheig and Bornstein (1961). A father of normal intelligence is described; he was without a history of convulsions but exhibited most of the other signs of the disease including adenoma sebaceum and phakomata. His two children suffered from the condition in its full characteristic form. One was killed as an infant, but the other was profoundly mentally subnormal.

Attention has been drawn to the existence of abnormal psychological states other than mental subnormality in tuberous sclerosis (Paulson and Lyle, 1966). Critchley and Earl (1932) stated that the essential feature of the psychology of tuberous sclerosis is a combination of intellectual defect proper with a primitive form of psychosis, resembling a primitive type of catatonic schizophrenia. They describe the first signs of psychosis as appearing at or after the fifth year, as periods of hours or days during which the patient appears vague, preoccupied and mentally inaccessible. They specify other psychological changes that appear later, including dissociation, outbursts of motiveless excitement, echolalia, perseverative repetition of phrases, muteness, the ' "secret speech" of dementia praecox', and catatonia. Such features are, however, not uncommon amongst mentally subnormal patients irrespective of their diagnostic condition. They are seen frequently, for instance, in phenylketonuric patients. It would seem reasonable to suppose that these changes are not specifically related to tuberous sclerosis.

Kofman and Hyland (1959) attempted to assess the possible association of adenoma sebaceum with mental and neurological disorders in adults. They found only 1 case out of 10 with a psychiatric disorder. This patient was of normal intelligence, but she had a schizoid personality with long-standing hysterical and obsessional tendencies. A patient with tuberous sclerosis and fetishism is reported by Entwistle and Sim (1961), who suggest an aetiological connexion between the abnormal sexual behaviour and localized organic changes including temporal lobe effects and a lesion in the region of the caudate nucleus. However, sporadic findings of psychiatric abnormality other than mental subnormality amongst patients with tuberous sclerosis are rare, and in most cases could well be accounted for on the grounds of random chance.

Mode of Inheritance

As regards the mode of inheritance of tuberous sclerosis, difficulties have arisen on account of the great variability of signs even within the same family. Many affected individuals have no family history of the condition. Penrose (1963) is of the opinion that in about half the severe cases, or perhaps in more, it is not possible to trace any indication of familial incidence. In a number of such cases, it is likely that the condition has arisen as a new mutation, but in others it could have been transmitted by a parent in whom the signs were minimal and not noticed. Gunther and Penrose (1935) postulated that if the proportion of cases due to mutation lay between a quarter and a half, the mutation rate per individual per generation must lie between 1 in 120,000 and 1 in 60,000 (0.8 to 1.7×10^{-5}). Later, however, Penrose (1936) reconsidered the calculation which he thought to lead to too low an estimate being based solely on severe cases. On re-calculation, taking the milder cases into account, he estimated the mutation rate per individual per generation as 1 in 40,000 (2.5×10^{-5}).

With respect to incidence in the population, Gunther and Penrose (1935) suggested an approximation of 1 in 30,000 (3.3×10^{-5}) of severe cases in the general community in England. Paulson and Lyle (1966) estimate the incidence in North Carolina as probably 1 in 20,000 to 1 in 40,000 (2.5 to 5×10^{-5}), leaving out of consideration the incidence of *formes frustes* in other family members, for example, epilepsy or primary visceral tumours.

One or two families have been reported in which recessive inheritance would be postulated because parents were both normal and consanguineous (Penrose, 1963). There is no evidence, however, to suggest that the rate of consanguinity is higher amongst the parents of individuals with tuberous sclerosis than in the general population. In his study of 35 verified cases of tuberous sclerosis, Borberg (1951) found no parental consanguinity. The distribution of cases within the families he investigated was suggestive of dominant inheritance with greatly varying manifestation. This observation added weight to the already large existing body of evidence in support of a dominant hypothesis. Borberg considered that recessivity and sex-linked inheritance seemed out of the question. He found no evidence to suggest polymerism, and was of the opinion that the pronounced phenotypical variability of the disease is probably attributable to variation in the genotypic environment, or to modifying genes.

Earlier, Gunther and Penrose (1935) had expressed the view that the great variety found in the clinical manifestations in tuberous sclerosis was attributable to the influence of extraneous modifying factors, mainly a pair of independent genes, which they designated A and a. They made the assumption that when the tuberous sclerosis gene, E, was present with the independent gene A in homozygous form, the phenotype was normal; that the phenotype was mildly affected when A was heterozygous, and severely affected when A was absent. They summarized the proportions of offspring that might be expected from various matings in the form of the facing table, TABLE 87.

Marshall, Saul and Sachs (1959) studied 2 propositi with tuberous sclerosis and 14 other family members who were found subsequently to have signs of the condition. Their data were in good agreement with the Gunther and Penrose hypothesis. They made the point that the skipping of generations is to be

TABLE 87
(From Gunther and Penrose (1935))

TYPE OF MATING	PROPORTIONS OF OFFSPRING		
	NORMAL	MILDLY AFFECTED	SEVERELY AFFECTED
Ee.AA × { ee.AA, ee.Aa, ee.aa	$\frac{1}{2}+\frac{x}{2}$	$\frac{y}{2}$	0
Ee.Aa × { ee.AA, ee.Aa, ee.aa	$\frac{1}{2}+\frac{x}{4}$	$\frac{1}{4}$	$\frac{y}{4}$
Ee.aa × { ee.AA, ee.Aa, ee.aa	$\frac{1}{2}$	$\frac{x}{2}$	$\frac{y}{2}$

The genotype Ee.AA is *normal*.
The genotype Ee.Aa is *mildly affected*.
The genotype Ee.aa is *severely affected*.
The types ee.AA, ee.Aa and ee.aa are all *normal* and their frequencies in the general population are $\frac{x^2}{2}$, $2xy$ and y^2 respectively; $x + y = 1$

considered if this mode of inheritance is correct. An individual with an Ee.AA constitution would not show symptoms, but could have a child with the constitution Ee.Aa who would be affected. They recommend, therefore, that related details should be obtained concerning parents and descendants of normal relatives of patients with tuberous sclerosis; also that a periodic examination of each child of such relatives is advisable, since the possibility that the disease will develop is as high as one in four.

VON RECKLINGHAUSEN'S DISEASE (NEUROFIBROMATOSIS)

The pathological changes in von Recklinghausen's disease are multiple tumours on the peripheral nerves and in the central nervous system, and a great variety of skin lesions, including *café-au-lait* spots, pigmented naevi and areas of depigmentation. Like the gene for tuberous sclerosis, the gene for von Recklinghausen's disease shows variation of expressivity, and single families can contain individuals who differ widely with respect to the type of ectodermal manifestation and with respect to level of intelligence. Many patients are of normal intelligence. Various estimates have been made of the proportion who are mentally subnormal. Preiser and Davenport (1918) reviewed 243 cases from the literature and found 19 (7·8 per cent) to be feeble-minded. Borberg (1951) quotes Mosbacher (1925), Siemens (1926) and Heuyer and Vidart (1940) as finding varying degrees of mental deficiency in 40 per cent, 50 per cent and 33 per cent of cases respectively. The degree of intellectual impairment is usually not severe. Penrose (1963) gives a mean IQ of 67·8 (standard deviation 9·5) for 6 hospital patients with the condition. Crome and Stern (1967) point out that the central nervous system is invariably involved in cases with mental retardation, the most important change from this point of view being multifocal gliosis or glioblastomatosis of the substance of the brain and spinal cord.

Penrose (1963) lays emphasis on the fact that despite some factors common to tuberous sclerosis and to von Recklinghausen's disease, such as the appearance of giant cells in the cerebral histopathology, the two diseases are quite distinct clinically.

Like tuberous sclerosis, in many families von Recklinghausen's disease is seen to follow a pattern of genetical transmission consistent with a dominant gene of variable expressivity. Frequently, however, no family history of the condition can be elicited with respect to affected individuals, and it is likely that at least a proportion of such cases can be attributed to fresh mutation. On the other hand, affected members of families may be missed owing to the difficulty of diagnosis of *formes frustes*.

Estimation of the frequency of the condition also is made difficult by problems of diagnosis. Preiser and Davenport (1918) stated that it was found in only about 1 in 2000 cases that present themselves to medical clinics or private practitioners for skin diseases. Neel (1954) made two independent estimates of frequency of cases in the State of Michigan as 1 in 1500–1800 approximately.

STURGE–WEBER SYNDROME

This condition has also been known by the names *naevoid amentia*, *encephalofacial angiomatosis* and the *Sturge-Kalischer-Weber syndrome*. It is a rare condition associated with mental subnormality and the pathological lesions associated with it are facial and meningeal haemangiomata. The facial haemangioma is often found in the area of distribution of one of the branches of the fifth cranial nerve on one side of the face [FIG. 49]. The meningeal involvement is usually confined to the area of the parietal and occipital lobes on the side of the facial haemangioma. It is usually restricted to the soft meninges though dural involvement has been reported (Crome and Stern, 1967). On the same side, calcification of the intracranial vessels may occur, which may be seen radiologically. In some cases the distribution of the cutaneous naevus extends beyond the area described above. It may cross the midline to the other side of the face, or may extend down one side of the body, including the limbs [FIG. 50].

Patients with the Sturge-Weber syndrome are epileptic, and frequently they show signs of neurological impairment, such as ocular palsies or signs of pyramidal involvement.

Although this syndrome is classified in the group of phakomatoses, of which the other conditions are known to follow specific patterns of inheritance, the genetical aetiology of the Sturge-Weber syndrome remains to be shown. Familial recurrence of the condition has not been demonstrated; mutation in somatic cells is a theoretical possibility (Penrose, 1963). According to Koch (1960) dominant, irregularly dominant and even recessive patterns of inheritance have to be thought of, while no family is known in which there are two cases of the full syndrome. There are families which suggest a possible dominant inheritance, namely those in which the full syndrome in the proband has been

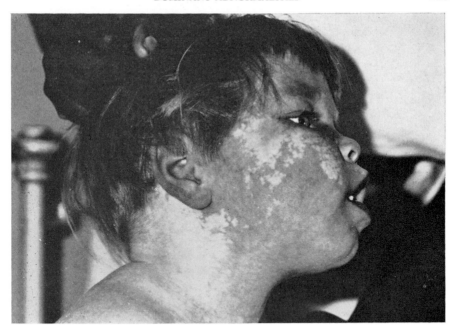

Fig. 49. Sturge-Weber syndrome.

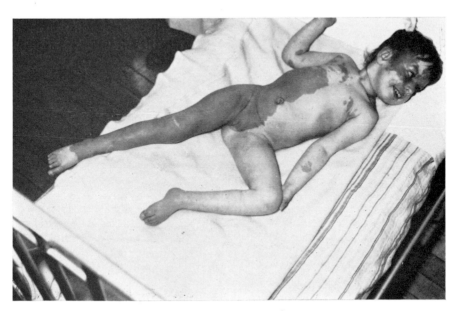

Fig. 50. Sturge-Weber syndrome.

combined with a trigeminal naevus in another member of the family. In favour of recessivity in some families is the fact that a number of workers have reported cases with consanguineous parentage.

ACROCEPHALY

A wide variety of head shapes is found among the mentally subnormal. A proportion of this may represent extreme variations of normal. The skull may

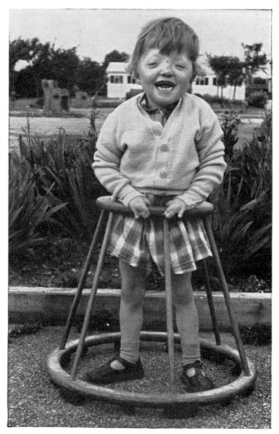

Fig. 51. Girl with Apert's syndrome (Hilliard and Kirman, 1957).

be abnormally great in its vertical measurement; this deformity is known as acrocephaly or 'tower skull'. This is concomitant with other skeletal malformations in a sufficient number of cases for syndromes to be recognizable. As a rule these are inherited as autosomal dominant traits which may show considerable variability of expression in any one family, and mental defect is not an invariable concomitant. When it does occur, it is usually not severe.

The Crouzon type of acrocephaly, or craniofacial dysostosis is characterized by an acrocephalic deformity of the skull and cranial synostosis together with hypertelorism, exophthalmos and external strabismus. The nose may be of parrot-beak shape, and the maxilla may be hypoplastic so that the lower jaw looks heavy and prominent. The dominant mode of inheritance is well documented. This is shown in an impressive pedigree with 23 affected members in 4 generations reported by Schiller (1959).

Facial abnormalities that are even more severe than in craniofacial dysostosis are seen in acrocephalosyndactyly.

Not only the skull, but also the bones of the limbs are malformed in acrocephalosyndactyly [FIG. 51]. This comprises a group of conditions with evidence of clinical and genetical heterogeneity. McKusick (1968) in discussing the various types of acrocephalosyndactyly that have been recorded, expresses the view that the association of skull and limb deformities comprises a spectrum of traits which probably represents the effects of mutations of various genes operating at different stages of differentiation and development. The hypothesis that different phenotypical variants of acrocephalosyndactyly represent effects of different gene mutations is supported by the observation that in cases of typical Apert's syndrome (McKusick's acrocephalosyndactyly type I) who reproduced, the offspring were of the same phenotype. In all the pedigrees of autosomal dominant transmission of the other types of acrocephalosyndactyly, no transition from type to type has been observed in spite of variability in expressivity of the trait within each type. McKusick classifies these conditions into at least three types of acrocephalopolysyndactyly and six types of acrocephalosyndactyly. All appear to be autosomal dominant traits except one type of acrocephalopolysyndactyly with the eponym of Carpenter's syndrome which is listed as being a recessive trait.

Blank (1960) in his observations on a British series of 39 cases, delineated two main categories of acrocephalosyndactyly. First he recognized 'typical' acrocephalosyndactyly (as originally described by Apert, 1906). A conspicuous feature of this type was interdigital osseous union, especially with a mid-digital hand mass with a single nail common to the fused digits. Secondly, he classed together other cases lacking this feature as 'atypical' forms of acrocephalosyndactyly. Blank calculated the incidence at birth of Apert's syndrome as approximately 1 in 160,000 (6.3×10^{-6}) and prevalence in the general population as 1 in 2,000,000 (0.5×10^{-6}). He attributed the difference between these estimates as being due in part to lack of ascertainment in the living population, and in part to the high mortality of these patients, particularly in early infancy. The rate of mutation at the Apert locus was estimated to be 3×10^{-6} per gene per generation. Blank found a marked parental age effect among sporadic cases of Apert's syndrome. He considered this to be probably due solely to an increase in father's age, arriving at this conclusion by studying the independent effect of father's age, mother's age and birth order using the method of total and partial correlations of Penrose (1957). Apert's syndrome and atypical acrocephalosyndactyly have never been found together in the same family, and Blank has rejected the belief that they are different manifestations of the same gene in heterozygous form or that they are due to allelic genes, although in the absence of linkage studies the precise genetical relationship of these two categories cannot be ascertained.

14

MISCELLANEOUS CONDITIONS

LAURENCE–MOON–BIEDL–BARDET SYNDROME

The cardinal features of this syndrome are retinitis pigmentosa, polydactyly, obesity, hypogenitalism and mental deficiency. The obesity and hypogenitalism are of the Fröhlich type and are hypophyseal in origin. Accessory signs observed in association with the syndrome include cataract, microphthalmia, deafness, bony deformities of the skull; other anomalies of the skeletal system including kyphoscoliosis, coxa vara, genu varum and valgum, gigantism and dwarfism; congenital heart defects and congenital malformations affecting the alimentary and genito-urinary tracts. Neurological signs have also been observed including choreo-athetosis, torticollis, facial spasm and epilepsy. One or more of the signs, without full manifestation of the whole clinical picture, have been observed amongst the relatives of patients with the full syndrome. Thus polydactyly alone or combined with retinitis pigmentosa may occur in otherwise normal relatives.

The inheritance of the syndrome is almost certainly recessive, although the gene is not completely recessive. There is no evidence of sex linkage, although there is a preponderance of affected males over affected females. Thus Cockayne, Krestin and Sorsby (1935) found a ratio of 44 males to 28 females out of 43 complete sibships recorded in the literature up to that date. Further evidence in favour of a recessive mode of inheritance is a high incidence of parental consanguinity. Streiff and Zeltner (1938) found 20 families with consanguinity out of 88, or 22·7 per cent. Panse (1938) found 15 sibships out of 61, or 24·6 per cent with consanguineous parentage. Franceschetti et al. (1951) observe that the complete syndrome arises almost exclusively in consanguineous marriages.

The partial appearance of the syndrome in relatives of patients showing the complete clinical picture is probably due to manifestation of the gene in heterozygous form. In the review by Cockayne et al. (1935) it was stated that in nearly every case in the material available to them the parents were normal. Moreover, no ascendant was recorded in these data as having the complete syndrome, though polydactyly was reported in the paternal uncle of one patient and in the maternal uncle of another. As time went on, however, and as more and more clinical and genetical material became available, it became apparent that partial manifestations were far from being uncommon amongst the relatives of patients. Thus Franceschetti et al. (1951) remark upon the appearance of a great number of partial manifestations, including polydactyly, obesity and mental disorders in the ascendant and collateral lines in pedigrees of patients with the full syndrome. They concur with the view that these partial appearances are probably due to a heterozygous phenotypic expression of the involved gene, the gene in homozygous form producing the full clinical picture.

Alternative hypotheses have been put forward to that of inheritance by a single recessive autosomal gene with partial manifestation in the heterozygote. These include the suggestion by Hanhart (1947) that very occasionally an irregular-dominant mode of inheritance may be seen in the Laurence-Moon-Biedl-Bardet syndrome, so accounting for observations of his own and of van Bogaert (1936).

Other workers consider that two genes are responsible for the syndrome. The developmental error appears to take effect between the first and second months of foetal life and to involve the mesoderm on one hand and the ectoderm on the other. The mesodermal error would lead to polydactyly and other skeletal defects, whilst the ectodermal error would lead to abnormalities of the retina and diencephalon. It has been suggested that the mesodermal and ecto-dermal parts of the syndrome are both recessive and due to mutations of two genes in the same chromosome (Rieger and Trauner, 1929; Cockayne, 1933). Bauer (1927), however, while thinking that two or even more genes may be responsible for the full clinical picture, says that polydactyly is dominant, sometimes skipping a generation, and that in this syndrome it is dominant and independent of the retinal and diencephalic effects, which are recessive. Cockayne, *et al.* (1935) disagree with this view, pointing out that pedigrees of the dominant form of polydactyly very rarely fail to show direct descent, and that it would be most improbable for all the parents of individuals with this syndrome to escape polydactyly, as did the parents in the material available to them, if it were dominant. They agree with Rieger and Trauner (1929) in believing that both parts (mesodermal and ectodermal) of the syndrome are recessive, and that it is an example of linkage.

The theory of inheritance by two or more genes is difficult to disprove, but, as Penrose (1963) points out, it cannot be regarded as probable unless sibships can be presented in which there is evidence that the separate genes are in repulsion. In other words, it would be necessary to present sibships in which some members showed one or more of the cardinal signs of the syndrome, while others, lacking these, showed one or more of the remainder, so that there was no overlap with respect to clinical signs between these sets of sibs within the sibship. Moreover, the assumption that it is not possible for a single gene to lead to both mesodermal and ectodermal changes, is without sound scientific foundation.

'TRUE' MICROCEPHALY

Microcephaly, or small-headedness, is a physical feature that is seen in many patients suffering from a variety of clinical types of mental subnormality. Unfortunately it is often spoken of in an undiscriminating way with the implica-tion, possibly unintended, that it is a clinical entity in itself instead of often being a physical finding present in a wide range of conditions. When this happens, the word 'microcephaly' assumes a significance and carries with it aetiological and diagnostic implications which do not always rightly belong to it [FIG. 52]. The clinical classification of microcephaly has been discussed by Penrose (1956b) and by Cowie (1960). It has been established that a number of microcephalic patients belong to families in which a pattern of inheritance is seen consistent with transmission by a single autosomal recessive gene. Penrose calls this form 'true microcephaly' [FIG. 53]. Several major investigations have provided evidence in support of this.

Komai, Kishimoto and Ozaki (1955) found 143 (93 male, 50 female) cases of microcephaly belonging to 78 sibships in the Japanese population. (This number included 32 cases belonging to 12 sibships reported by other Japanese investigators.) The proportion of microcephalics who were progeny of first-cousin

Fig. 52. Microcephaly due to maternal irradiation.

matings was 45 per cent. Analysis of the material according to Haldane's method indicated that an autosomal recessive gene was responsible. The recessivity was complete in the majority of cases, but in a few cases the heterozygote manifests a slight effect of the gene. They felt that since the records were made rather casually, it was difficult to make any reliable estimate of the incidence of individuals with mental retardation among the relatives of the microcephalics. It was fairly certain, however, that the incidence was considerably higher among the relatives of the microcephalics than in the general population. The great majority of the heterozygotes were of normal physique and mentality as far as could be judged by interviews with the parents of the microcephalics.

Komai *et al.* found a significantly higher percentage of males than females among the microcephalics; they remarked that this sexual disparity seemed to be a universal phenomenon. They considered it to be due in large measure to the fact that male microcephalics are generally more frequently met outside their homes, and they are more likely to become the probands of the pedigrees.

Komai *et al.*, using Dahlberg's formula, calculated the incidence of the gene for microcephaly as 0·0034–0·0063, if 0·4–0·7 per cent is accepted as the proportion of first-cousin matings in the general population. This value for the gene frequency in the Japanese population coincides closely with 0·0043–0·0062, the

Fig. 53. 'True' microcephaly.

corresponding value obtained for the Swedish population by Böök and his co-workers.

Böök, Schut and Reed (1953) expressed the view that although no extensive clinical and genetical study on an unselected material was available, nevertheless the data of the literature seemed to justify the conclusion that there is a genetical type and also the assumption that this type is an important cause of the symptom microcephaly. In their own study they made the reservation that what they tried to analyse might not be a clinical genetical entity; rather several genetical entities may be involved in producing this syndrome, each giving some variation in the clinical or pathological features.

They estimated the frequency of the syndrome 'genetic micrencephaly' as roughly between 1 in 25,000 and 1 in 50,000 (in their study on material in the

United States), and the gene frequency as between 1 in 162 and 1 in 230 (0·0043–0·0062).

They supported the view that a heterozygous expression of the gene for this syndrome might be, from the point of view of the total population, more important than the grave defect of the homozygotes. Expression in the heterozygote, they considered, showed itself as a moderate intellectual impairment. In this connexion they quote Penrose (1938a) who remarked that the incidence of 'psychopathy' among the relatives of microcephalics was above the average incidence for patients in general, and Tredgold (1949) who found a pronounced 'psychopathic family history' in most of his cases, including sibs who were often mentally abnormal. The work of Koch (1959) is also of interest. In a large study of the families of microcephalic patients, he found that amongst the relatives of the microcephalics there was a high incidence of people with small physique, smaller than average head circumference and occasional mental deficiency. These individuals were presumed to be heterozygotes.

CEREBRAL DIPLEGIA OF GENETICAL AETIOLOGY

Although exogenous factors, especially anoxia in the perinatal period, are now generally held as responsible in the majority of cases of cerebral palsy, there are indications that in at least a small proportion of cases cerebral diplegia may be determined by a recessive gene. Penrose (1963) points out that there are many instances in which the condition has all the characteristics of recessive gene determination. He gives as illustration a pedigree with two brothers, of consanguineous parentage with cerebral diplegia [see FIG. 54]. The sibships also contained three miscarriages and one child who died in infancy. It is possible that the gene may be responsible also for foetal wastage. Other published pedigrees with parental consanguinity and affected sibs include those reported by Böök (1949) and Hanhart (1936). Cerebral diplegia exemplified by these reports appears to be genetically distinct from the syndrome of spastic diplegia with congenital ichthyosis (described below).

THE SYNDROME OF SPASTIC DIPLEGIA, MENTAL SUBNORMALITY AND CONGENITAL ICHTHYOSIS

A syndrome characterized by spastic diplegia, congenital ichthyosis, mental subnormality and the less constant finding of degeneration of pigmented epithelium of the macula and its surroundings has been reported in a number of cases with a widespread geographical and ethnic distribution. Its mode of inheritance is that of a single autosomal recessive trait.

In a neuropsychiatric population study in Northern Sweden, Sjögren (1956) found a number of cases of a congenital condition characterized by severe mental subnormality, congenital ichthyosis or erythroderma ichthyosiforme, pyramidal signs which produced spasticity predominantly in the lower limbs, which was sometimes slowly progressive. In two sibs, special ophthalmological examination revealed a macular and retinal degeneration. Patients with similar constellations of symptoms had been reported previously, and in this connexion

Sjögren quotes Rud (1927), de Sanctis and Cacchione (1933), Pisani and Cacchione (1934) and Laubenthal (1938), though no genetical investigation had been made in these cases.

In a genetical analysis of his material Sjögren obtained Mendelian ratios of 31±6 per cent using Weinberg's sib method and 35±6 per cent using Haldane's method, in a material 25 cases in 10 families. These figures were reduced respectively to 19±5 per cent and 24±6 per cent if 7 atypical or uncertain cases were excluded. These figures taken in conjunction with a high frequency of consanguineous marriages indicated inheritance as a Mendelian recessive trait.

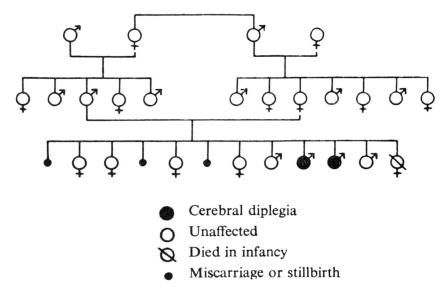

● Cerebral diplegia
○ Unaffected
◑ Died in infancy
• Miscarriage or stillbirth

Fig. 54. Pedigree of two brothers with spastic diplegia. The elder had very slight signs and was normally intelligent. The younger was typically diplegic with a Binet IQ 72 (Colchester Survey, 1938, Case No. 333). (With kind permission of Professor L. S. Penrose.)

Sjögren and Larsson (1957) reported a series of 28 cases (10 males, 18 females), 14 of whom they had examined, the remainder having died previously. With only three exceptions, the parents of these patients came from an area in Northern Sweden with a very high consanguinity rate. The gene responsible is very rare, and Sjögren and Larsson estimated its frequency in the general Swedish population as less than 0·0005. A thorough genealogical study indicated no ancestors to have shown any of the signs of the syndrome, and the single gene mutation was thought to have occurred in one common ancestor several hundred years previously.

Scarabicchi and Martino (1963) reported 3 Italian cases; Williams and Ling Tang (1960) reported 2 affected sibs of Italian ancestry. Wallis and Kalushiner (1960) reported a Jewish family in which 4 sibs (all males) were affected. The parents were first cousins. Ancestors of this family came from Or-Kasdim, which is now in Iraq, but the last four generations had been born in Israel. The first report of the syndrome in Britain was by Richards, Rundle and Wilding (1957) who observed 2 affected sisters of Greek Cypriot parentage. Other cases in Britain have been reported by Richards (1960) of a girl born to English parents who were first cousins, and by Timpany (1962) of 2 affected sibs. Link and Roldan (1958) in the United States reported an affected child born to German and Italian parents. Richards et al. (1957) believed that 3 brothers reported at a much earlier date by Pisani and Cacchione (1934) resembled the patients described by Sjögren and Larsson and by themselves.

The ichthyosis is usually apparent at birth and is generalized except for the soles of the feet. Considerable pigmentation often develops, especially in the axillae. Spasticity of the lower limbs has been observed on neurological examination in the neonatal period, and becomes clearly apparent in the child's motor development from early infancy. As a rule the mental subnormality is of severe degree. The abnormal findings on retinoscopy do not seem to be by any means a constant feature of the syndrome. Degeneration of the pigmented epithelium of the macula and its surroundings was found in only 3 out of the 28 cases reported by Sjögren and Larsson (1957). It was seen in only one of the sibs reported by Williams and Ling Tang (1960). Abnormal teeth in the syndrome were also reported by these authors and by Link and Roldan (1958); the teeth may be serrated, with dysplasia of the enamel.

RUD'S SYNDROME

The syndrome first described by Rud (1927) has some features in common with the neurological syndrome with congenital ichthyosis associated with the names of Sjögren and Larsson. However, the two syndromes appear to be clinically and genetically distinct (Richards, 1960).

Rud's first description was of a Danish male patient aged 22 with tetany, polyneuritis, hyperchromic anaemia, ichthyosis and infantilism; later he reported the case of a female who in addition showed partial gigantism and a diabetic type of hyperglycaemia. He suggested a pluriglandular disorder as the basis of the syndrome.

Van Bogaert (1935) reported his observations on 2 cases apparently suffering from the same syndrome; these patients had congenital generalized ichthyosis, mental retardation and occasional convulsions. One showed genital infantilism. He also postulated an endocrinological defect, with testicular and thyroid insufficiency predominating. He included the syndrome of Rud in his discussion of ectodermal dysplasias, considering it to be closely allied to tuberous sclerosis, neurofibromatosis and palmo-plantar keratosis.

From a clinical standpoint, the absence of spastic diplegia in reported cases of this syndrome differentiates it most distinctly from the syndrome associated with the names of Sjögren and Larsson in which it is a constant feature. In contrast, muscular hypotonia with generalized wasting of the muscles is described in Rud's syndrome.

The first case described in Britain was reported by Stewart (1939) who gave full post-mortem findings. Ichthyosis and mental defect were noted from infancy. Other features were muscular hypotonia and atrophy, sexual infantilism, dwarfism, large head, hypoplastic teeth, epilepsy, arachnodactyly and retinitis pigmentosa. McGillivray (1954) reported another case in Britain in which generalized ichthyosis, epilepsy, dwarfism (adult height 3 feet 10 inches), hypotonia and generalized wasting of the muscles were features. Richards *et al.* (1957) point out that Rud considered his patients to be of normal intelligence, but mental deficiency has been considered to be a component of this syndrome by subsequent authors and this view is generally held.

There is insufficient evidence from the reports available to draw conclusions regarding the genetics of this syndrome. It is mentioned here because of the various clinical features which it shares in common with the syndrome associated with the names of Sjögren and Larsson, which have sometimes led to mention of the two syndromes together in the literature, although it is held that they are separate clinical and genetical entities.

SEX-LINKED HYDROCEPHALUS

The aetiology of hydrocephalus is complex and in the majority of cases it is not attributable to a primarily genetical cause. There is, however, some support for the view that a sex-linked gene may account for some cases. Bickers and Adams (1949) described a family in which 3 brothers with hydrocephalus died at, or shortly after, birth. Their mother was normal, but she had 4 brothers affected in the same way as her sons. None of the females in these sibships was affected. Post-mortem findings showed an aqueductal stenosis. Later, Edwards, Norman and Roberts (1961) reported another family with congenital hydrocephalus showing a pattern of inheritance entirely consistent with recessive sex-linkage. The index case was examined *post mortem* and the aqueduct was found to be markedly reduced in calibre. In addition the pes pontis was unduly small, and there was no trace of descending corticospinal tracts. Edwards (1961) reported two other families with cases which appeared to conform to a basic pattern. The most important lesion demonstrated was aqueductal stenosis, which appeared to be related to a mutation on the X chromosome and without manifestations in the heterozygote. A number of affected individuals in these families were stillborn or died in infancy, but the survivors were severely mentally subnormal.

Crome and Stern (1967) have some reservations with respect to the interpretation of these findings. They point out that it has not been definitely proven that the cases of Edwards were hydrocephalic, even though their heads were slightly enlarged and abnormal in shape; also they consider that since hydrocephalus is one of the commonest congenital malformations of the brain, its presence occasionally in several male members of a family with unaffected females might be due to random chance.

ANHIDROTIC ECTODERMAL DYSPLASIA

This term may cover a heterogeneous group of genetical and clinical entities, and this remains to be clarified. The skin is smooth, atrophic and papery in texture; sweat glands and sebaceous glands are absent. Because they are unable to sweat, these patients suffer greatly in hot weather, and may even die due to over-heating (Lorber, 1964). The nipples are absent. Hair is scanty or even completely absent on all parts of the body. There is failure of development of the teeth, which may be small and misshapen; in some cases the patient is completely edentulous. The nails may be vestigial. Mental subnormality is by no means an invariable accompaniment of the syndrome, though this may be present and in some cases be profound (Kirman, 1955).

Penrose (1963) reviews the existing observations concerning the genetics of anhidrotic ectodermal dysplasia, and notes that there seem to be many varieties

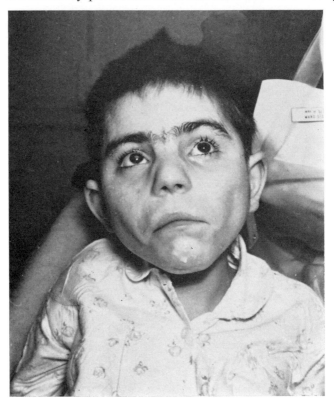

Fig. 55. De Lange syndrome.

with different modes of inheritance, including sex-linked inheritance, which may be incompletely recessive in the female. However, he points out that the possibility of autosomal inheritance with a strong tendency towards male sex limitation has not been ruled out. There are pedigrees on record with dominant inheritance in which the condition is not necessarily related to mental subnormality.

DE LANGE SYNDROME

This is a condition characterized by dwarfism, mental subnormality and multiple congenital anomalies [FIG. 55]. Patients with it are extremely hirsute. The hair grows low over the forehead; the eyebrows are bushy and meet in the midline, and there is hypertrichosis of the back and the limbs. The eyelashes are long and sweeping. The palpebral fissures slant downwards from the inner to the outer canthi. The nose is short, with a depressed bridge, and flaring forward-facing nostrils. The upper lip is thin, and usually there is some degree of micrognathia. The ears are low-set. The torso may be cylindrical in shape. There is usually micromelia of the limbs. The fingers tend to be short and tapering with short, incurved little fingers, and abnormally proximally-set thumbs. A single horizontal crease may be seen on the palm. A number of characteristic dermatographic features have been reported amongst patients with the de Lange syndrome.

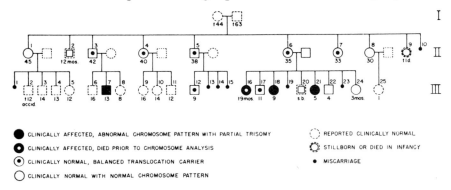

Fig. 56. Pedigree of a family with de Lange syndrome with chromosome abnormalities
(Falek *et al.*, 1966).

They are said to have an increased frequency of radial loops and whorls on the fingertips. Also there may be a characteristic zygodactylous pattern on the palms and soles, with an interdigital triradius (Berg, Smith and McCreary, 1967). An excellent review of the condition has been made by Ptacek *et al.* (1963). They draw attention to the characteristic cry, which they say alone suffices to suggest the diagnosis, when one has not yet seen the patient: it is feeble, low-pitched, raucous and growling. They also point out the invariable finding of severe mental retardation in this syndrome; the highest intelligence quotient obtained has not exceeded 25–30.

Chromosome investigations have been carried out in a number of cases of the de Lange syndrome. In some, the karyotypes have been normal. In others, however, a variety of aberrations have been reported. In several, an increased frequency of chromosomal fragments has been reported. A particularly interesting family is reported by Falek, Schmidt and Jervis (1966) in which the condition is described in 3 sibs and a maternal first cousin [Fig. 56]. All the affected children had abnormal karyotypes, with loss of a small acrocentric chromosome of the G group and an additional metacentric chromosome resembling, but smaller than, chromosome number 16 of the E group. There were 7 unaffected carriers of the balanced translocation. Berg *et al.* (1967b) review and list the various reported chromosomal abnormalities found in the de Lange syndrome and add another variant to the list from their own patient, who, together with his phenotypically normal father showed consistently an atypical medium-sized metacentric chromosome in the 6-12 group. In discussing the significance of the chromosomal findings in cases of the de Lange syndrome, these authors consider that the finding of an apparently normal karyotype in the large proportion of cytogenetically examined affected individuals, together with the inconsistent chromosomal anomalies noted in the remainder, appears to exclude a specific aberration in chromosome morphology detectable by present techniques as the aetiological basis for the syndrome. However, the various chromosomal anomalies that have been observed may be coincidental or a possible effect of some underlying causative agency which produces the clinical manifestations of the syndrome.

The possibilities of transmission of the syndrome as a recessive or a dominant trait have been considered. There is some evidence in favour of a recessive inheritance. There are insufficient data to uphold a dominant hypothesis.

Ptacek and his co-workers (1963) give pedigrees of 22 patients with the syndrome, of which 16 come from previous case reports. In these pedigrees it is seen that affected individuals occur sporadically, one in a sibship. Later, how-ever, Opitz et al. (1965) reported that they knew of a total of 7 sibships with more than one affected child per sibship, the family pattern being consistent with that of autosomal recessive inheritance. It should, however, be noted that familial incidence is unusual. Parental consanguinity appears in only two of the pedigrees of Ptacek and his co-workers, and its absence from other reports of families containing an affected individual suggests that it is not an unusually frequent finding. Berg et al. (1967a) report a finding of parental consanguinity in fewer than 20 of 200 recorded case histories. They studied the frequency of affected sibs in this material, allowing for heterozygous parents who had not produced an affected child. They found that only 8 per cent of the sibs showed the syndrome, as against the expected figure of 25 per cent if the parents were heterozygotes for a recessive trait.

There have been families reported in which relatives of the propositus have shown some of the anomalies suggestive of the de Lange syndrome. Borghi, Giusti and Bigozzi (1954) report a family in which the father and the paternal grandmother are said to have shown multiple minor anomalies of the de Lange syndrome. In another family, reported by Rodriguez-Vigil et al. (1964), the father of a boy with the de Lange syndrome is said to have shown some of the stigmata of the condition. It is conceivable that the syndrome may be transmitted as a dominant trait with variable expressivity, which could account for the minor signs in these relatives. There is, however, too little evidence at present to uphold a hypothesis of dominant transmission.

15

SEX CHROMOSOME ANOMALIES

Of the 46 chromosomes in the normal human karyotype, 44 appear to constitute pairs, matching in size and morphology. These are known as the autosomes. The other two chromosomes make up a matching pair in the normal female, and are known as the X chromosomes. They are close to the chromosomes in the C group of autosomes when compared with respect to size and morphology. In the normal male, however, only one X chromosome is present, and this is paired with a much smaller chromosome, resembling somewhat the chromosomes of the G group. This is the Y chromosome. The X and Y chromosomes are known as the sex chromosomes.

Many anomalies involving aberrations of number of the sex chromosomes have been described. In many of these cases there is evidence of more than one stem-line of cells (mosaicism). In addition to aberrations of number, less frequently cases have been reported of changes in the morphology of the sex chromosomes. Such morphological changes have been reported usually in connexion with the X rather than the Y chromosome. An example of this is the isochromosome X which is presumably formed by the fracture of the X chromosomes at the centromere and the fusion of the two long arms of the broken chromosomes at the centromere to form a large symmetrical chromosome, closely resembling a chromosome No. 3. This was first described by Fraccaro *et al.* (1960). A female with an isochromosome X and a normal X chromosome has clinical features suggestive of Turner's syndrome (sex chromosome complement XO)[1]. Another morphological change involving the X chromosome is the formation of a ring chromosome by fusion of both ends of the chromosome to each other following the loss of small terminal fragments (Lindsten and Tillinger, 1962). This is a very rare observation, and again the clinical signs are like those seen in Turner's syndrome.

Anomalies of the sex chromosomes are not usually associated with severe physical malformations as is frequent with anomalies of the autosomes. In individuals with autosomal defects it seems that all the tissues of the body are affected, but with the sex chromosome abnormalities the burden of the defect seems to lie in the genital tract (Court Brown, 1962a). From a psychiatric point of view, the autosomal anomalies are generally accompanied by mental subnormality of marked or severe degree. Sex chromosome anomalies, on the other hand, often are accompanied by some intellectual deficit, but this is of variable degree and is usually mild.

It is difficult, however, to ascertain the true distribution of intelligence amongst patients with sex chromosomal anomalies because unselected samples can only be obtained in newborn surveys, which would then have to be followed

[1]An example of this is shown in FIGURE 57.

up for psychological testing at later ages. Presumably through the effect of differential viability some cases would be lost, possibly those in the sample suffering most severely from the effects of sex chromosomal imbalance, and possibly therefore those of the lowest intelligence, although it would probably be impossible to check this. Furthermore, as Penrose (1963) points out, patients coming to notice through fertility clinics are likely to be of average intelligence and their numbers are not easily ascertained. Those, however, found in hospitals for the mentally subnormal are mainly in the mildly subnormal class. Penrose observes, moreover, that patients with one Y chromosome and three or four X chromosomes are not necessarily of lower mental level than those who have only an XXY set.

There is growing evidence, however, to suggest that in association with the sex chromosome anomalies much more important psychiatric defects may occur in the form of personality and character disorders. Indeed, these are so frequently concomitant, that the association may be regarded as characteristic. The most striking example of a sex chromosome anomaly associated with personality and character disorder is the XYY condition, which has been found associated with severely disturbed aggressive behaviour.

NUCLEAR SEX

Barr and Bertram (1949) discovered that in the resting female cell nucleus a small deeply-staining body is to be found lying close to the nuclear membrane. This was not observed in male nuclei. The discovery was made in cerebral tissue from cats, but the phenomenon is not confined to that species and the discovery has been of great service to human cytogenetics.

The Barr body is thought to consist of DNA of one condensed X chromosome (Ohno, Kaplan and Kinosita, 1959). It is also known as the sex chromatin mass, and individuals possessing it are said to be sex-chromatin positive. The number of Barr bodies in individual cells has been found to bear a constant relationship to the number of X chromosomes present. Thus, if one Barr body is present, the cell can be assumed to contain two X chromosomes; two Barr bodies denote the presence of three X chromosomes. In other words, if n is the number of Barr bodies in a cell, the number of X chromosomes present is $n+1$.

This finding has enabled the buccal smear test to be used as a screening method for detecting abnormalities involving the X chromosome. Barr bodies are easily seen in cells from the buccal mucous membrane. A scraping is taken from the inside of the cheek with a spatula, smeared on a glass slide and stained. In a specimen from a normal female one Barr body will be visible in the nuclei of a proportion of cells. This proportion is variable. It may be as high as 40 per cent, but it is sometimes as low as 25 per cent. The differences in proportion of cells with Barr bodies are partly of technical origin, although biological characteristics are no doubt involved (Barr and Carr, 1962).

The buccal smear test may be supplemented by an examination of the blood film for 'drumsticks' in the neutrophil leucocytes. Davidson and Smith (1954) discovered that in females, but not in males, an average of 3 per cent of poly-morphs have a small accessory lobule or 'drumstick' attached to the nucleus.

The buccal smear test, because it can be carried out relatively quickly and easily, has proved a useful mass survey tool in screening populations of mentally subnormal patients and in surveys of the newborn. It enables the detection of individuals in whom there is a cytogenetical aberration involving the X chromosome, or in whom the nuclear sex is at variance with the phenotypical sex.

CLINICAL SYNDROMES ASSOCIATED WITH SEX CHROMOSOME ANOMALIES

A considerable variety of karyotypes with abnormalities involving the sex chromosomes have been described, especially amongst anatomical males who may possess varying numbers of both X and Y chromosomes. This, together with a tendency for mosaicism to occur in association with abnormal sex chromosome patterns, allows a wide range of permutations and combinations. From this welter of karyotypes, however, several emerge with sufficient frequency and sufficiently constant association with specific clinical features for them to be regarded as syndromes. These include Klinefelter's syndrome and the XYY syndrome in anatomical males, and Turner's syndrome and the triple-X syndrome in anatomical females.

KLINEFELTER'S SYNDROME

In 1942 a syndrome was described by Klinefelter, Reifenstein and Albright. This occurred in males, and was characterized by gynaecomastia, aspermatogenesis without a-leydigism, and an increased excretion of follicle-stimulating hormone. At that time the present techniques for examining the karyotype or determining nuclear sex were not available, which therefore was not known until later. A proportion of patients with these clinical features have a normal autosome and sex chromosome complement, with an XY pair, and are chromatin-negative. The remainder of the patients are chromatin-positive. They usually have an XXY sex chromosome complement, and are often mosaics, with other cells, generally with a normal XY sex chromosome complement, present in the body. Sometimes a greater sex chromosome polysomy is present with multiple X chromosomes, perhaps three or four, present in addition to the Y chromosome. With such polysomy the clinical features are usually more marked and the individual may be severely mentally subnormal. On the basis of the sex chromosome complement, two main types of the condition have therefore been distinguished: on the one hand, the 'true' chromatin-positive Klinefelter's syndrome; on the other, the 'false' chromatin-negative Klinefelter's syndrome.

As regards incidence, nuclear-sex surveys amongst the newborn have shown that among live-born males one chromatin-positive male is to be found in about 490 [see TABLE 88].

This is an estimate covering all chromatin-positive karyotypes in the male. If the XXY karyotype alone is considered, its frequency among live-born males at birth would appear to be of the order of one in 600 (Polani, 1966). Of the surveys mentioned above, in only the Edinburgh survey of Maclean et al. (1964) were the sex chromosome complements of the abnormal children studied. In that survey only 16 of the 21 chromatin-positive children were investigated in this way. Of these 16 children, one had an XXYY complement, 5 were mosaics of the XY/XXY constitution and the remaining 10 had an XXY complement.

With respect to somatic development, Hornstein (1963) has distinguished three types of individuals with Klinefelter's syndrome: a tall, long-legged, eunuchoid type; a dysplastic type; and a type without distinctive somatic characteristics. The testes are descended, small and usually firm. The penis may be diminished in length. The pubic hair grows in a female distribution and is sparse. Gynaecomastia is present in variable degree, and is regarded as an optional component of the syndrome (Heller and Nelson, 1945). Sexual function appears to be normal, but individuals with Klinefelter's syndrome are usually

TABLE 88

INCIDENCE OF CHROMATIN-POSITIVE MALES IN LIVE BIRTHS

SOURCE	PLACE OF SURVEY	TOTAL LIVE BIRTHS (MALES)	NUMBER OF CHROMATIN-POSITIVE MALES	PROPORTION OF CHROMATIN-POSITIVE MALES PER 1000
Moore (1959)	Winnipeg	1911	5	2·6
Bergemann (1961)	Berne	1890	4	2·1
Weisli (1962)	Basle	1563	1	0·5
Maclean, Harnden, Court Brown, Bond and Mantle (1964)	Edinburgh	10725	21	2·0
Taylor and Moores (1967)	London	4934	12	2·4

infertile, and it is often on account of their lack of fertility that they come to notice through infertility clinics. However, it seems that infertility is a relative phenomenon in Klinefelter's syndrome. Although the characteristic microscopical changes in the testis are those of hyalinization, sclerosis and obliteration of most of the seminiferous tubules, focal hyperplasia of mostly degenerated Leydig cells and a loss of the peritubular elastic fibres (Bartalos and Baramki, 1967), spermatogenesis may still occur in a few scattered tubules, and a small number of spermatozoa have been demonstrated in the semen of patients with Klinefelter's syndrome (Ferguson-Smith et al., 1957). There is one unusual instance of a chromatin-positive male who fathered two sons (Warburg, 1963). Another case, less well-documented, has been reported in which a 70-year-old man with chromatin-positive Klinefelter's syndrome has had offspring (Kaplan et al., 1963).

THE XYY SYNDROME

The first report of the XYY syndrome was made by Hauschka et al., in 1962. Their patient was a 44-year-old man, 6 feet tall, tending towards obesity, of average intelligence and without conspicuous physical defects. He was the father of 7 living children from two marriages. His abnormal progeny from both marriages included a daughter with amenorrhoea, lacking ovaries and uterus (she was chromatin-positive with a normal female karyotype in cells from marrow and blood, but an XX/XO constitution could not be ruled out); a 'blue baby' who died aged 3 days; a mongol with autosomal trisomy G; and two miscarriages. This familial concentration of abnormal karyotypes was taken to indicate an hereditary tendency to non-disjunction. This XYY man came to notice, in fact, through the abnormalities in his progeny. His own clinical and psychological features were unremarkable. No psychiatric abnormalities were noted in his case. His only failing noted in the report was his inability to keep employers satisfied with his performance as a manual worker.

The first series of patients with the XYY syndrome to be reported, came under observation through a combination of criminal behaviour and diminished responsibility due to mental subnormality or mental illness. These were 7 men from a series of 197 patients with criminal records detained at a State mental hospital under conditions of maximum security (Jacobs et al., 1965). The clinical findings in these 7 patients and in 2 others subsequently identified in another series of patients at the same hospital were described by Price et al. (1966). Compared with 9 control patients, no distinguishing physical features were found; but the XYY males proved difficult to match for stature since 6 of the 9 were 6 feet or more in height. 8 of the XYY men were classified as high-grade mental defectives or as 'below average' in intelligence. The ninth patient was reported as being of average intelligence but had a mental illness with schizophrenic features. Most of them had frequently absconded from other mental hospitals and they had often shown aggressive or violent behaviour. A detailed psychiatric assessment of these men showed that all nine suffered from a severe degree of personality disorder (Price and Whatmore, 1967). There was no known history of brain damage, epilepsy or psychosis to account for this. Their personalities showed extreme instability and irresponsibility, and in their criminal behaviour these men did not appear to have considered any but the most immediate consequences of their actions. They showed very little depth of feeling for others in their emotional responses, and their emotional instability combined with an incapacity to tolerate the mildest frustration seemed to have been their greatest difficulty in social adjustment.

The early manifestations of behaviour disorders are an especially interesting psychiatric feature in the XYY syndrome. Three of the 9 XYY males had been convicted before the age of 10 years, and even before this first conviction at least 5 of them had been in trouble with education authorities or the police on account of minor offences or persistent truancy from school.

The first case of a prepubertal boy within the normal intelligence range with an XYY chromosome complement was reported by Cowie and Kahn (1968). His history showed that he was aggressive and violent against both property and persons from an early age, being seen first for these reasons at $4\frac{1}{2}$ years old. He would set fire to the room, destroy furniture, and attack other children. He began wandering from home at this age. Later, at school his vicious attacks on other children, his truancy and wandering and his complete lack of response to ordinary discipline called for special schooling at the age of $8\frac{1}{2}$. This boy had an EEG record with borderline non-specific abnormalities. At the age of $8\frac{1}{2}$ he was above the 97th percentile for height and weight, and had always been regarded as being large for his age. The history of this boy suggests that increased height is a feature of the XYY syndrome to appear before puberty. It confirms the retrospective evidence of early antisocial behaviour in the XYY males reported by Price and Whatmore (1967).

There is good evidence that an extra Y chromosome has a part to play in antisocial behaviour even in the absence of mental subnormality. Casey *et al.* (1966b) looked at the chromosome complement of sex chromatin-negative males 6 feet and over in height in: (1) a mentally subnormal population detained because of antisocial acts; (2) a mentally ill population detained because of antisocial acts; (3) an intermediate-sentence group of prisoners; (4) an ordinary, mentally ill, institution population; and (5) a 'normal' population sample. The results are shown in the following table, prepared by Casey and his co-workers.

GROUP	NO. OF MALES 6 FT. AND OVER	NO. WITH XYY CONSTITUTION
Detained because of antisocial behaviour:		
Mentally subnormal	50	12
Mentally ill	50	4
Criminal	24	2
Mentally ill	30	0
Normal	30	0

The striking psychiatric feature of antisocial behaviour in XYY males calls for a search for a causal link between this manifestation and the basic chromosomal defect. An obvious first step would be to look for anatomical and functional changes, such as changes in the EEG pattern, as constitutional defects. The discovery of abnormal EEG records in patients with other varieties of sex chromosome anomalies gives a lead for exploration along these lines. Moreover, EEG abnormalities have been reported in sporadic cases of the XYY syndrome, such as in the case of Cowie and Kahn (1968) and in the case of a 23-year-old male reported by Forssman (1967). This man was 6 ft. 5 in. tall, had been epileptic since aged 2 and about aged 10 began to be extremely aggressive. He had various IQ assessments at different times, between IQ 83 and IQ 69. Although the combination of the XYY constitution and epilepsy in his case may have been fortuitous, Forssman rightly points out that this finding, taken with others in sex chromatin-positive men, indicates that the possibility should be considered of the XYY complement in strikingly tall men with epilepsy.

TURNER'S SYNDROME

In 1938, Turner described a syndrome, occurring in women, in which the main characteristics were infantilism, congenital webbing of the neck and cubitus valgus [FIG. 57]. All of Turner's 7 cases were short in stature, their heights ranging from 48·5 to 55 inches. Since Turner's original report, a great variety of physical anomalies have been described in frequent association with this syndrome. These include a high-arched palate; a low hairline at the back of the neck; misshapen, protruding ears, which may be low-set; a broad short neck;

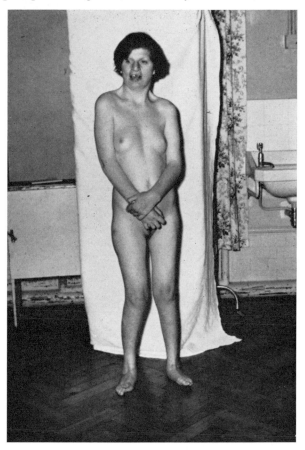

Fig. 57. Patient with isochromosome X and normal X chromosome.

a broad, flat, shield-shaped chest with widely-spaced nipples; lack of development of secondary sexual characteristics including breast development; sparseness or absence of pubic and axillary hair; broad misshapen wrists; and in the newborn especially, laxity of the neck skin, puffiness of the fingers, back of the hands and dorsum of the feet possibly as a result of congenital lymphoedema, and small, maldeveloped, hyperconvex nails. Visceral anomalies which are not uncommon in Turner's syndrome include renal malformations and coarctation of the aorta. As in the case of other chromosomal anomalies, various combinations of these signs occur. Although Turner's syndrome is characterized by more severe signs and malformations than are usual with the other sex chromosome syndromes, the clinical signs appearing in any one case may be few and slight, and the patient may not be necessarily badly handicapped from the point of view of personal appearance. Shortness of stature, however, seems to be a constant feature. Women with Turner's syndrome are amenorrhoeic and sterile.

The basic pathological lesion in Turner's syndrome is in the ovaries, which are present only as streak-like structures on the posterior surface of the broad ligament. Microscopically, the streak consists mainly of wavy fibrous tissue, devoid of primitive germ cells or follicular apparatus; though a few cases have been described with downgrowths of the covering germinal epithelium and even primordial follicles, which may account for the very occasional patient with slight breast development and the extremely rare case with a few menstrual bleedings (Bartalos and Baramki, 1967).

It seems that Turner's syndrome may represent the end of a phenotypical spectrum which can be observed in women with absence of germ cells from the gonads or gonadal dysgenesis. At least two other forms of gonadal dysgenesis, besides Turner's syndrome, are recognized as clinical entities. One is pure gonadal dysgenesis, in which there is no reduction in stature and no somatic anomalies. The other is gonadal dysgenesis in which shortness of stature is the only somatic anomaly.

In 1954 it was found on the investigation into nuclear sex that a number of women with gonadal dysgenesis were chromatin-negative (Polani, Hunter and Lennox, 1954; Wilkins, Grumbach and Van Wyk, 1954). Polani, Lessof and Bishop (1956) made the suggestion that individuals with 'ovarian agenesis' might have only one X chromosome, owing to the incidence of red-green colour blindness amongst them, as in males. They studied the colour vision of 25 cases of 'ovarian agenesis' using Ishihara tests. Of these subjects, 4 were found to be colour blind. These results differed significantly from those to be expected from testing a sample of females, but not from those to be expected in a sample of males; so that if there had been no information about the sex of the subjects, the investigators would have concluded they had tested a sample of males.

In 1959 the XO sex chromosome constitution (with a single X chromosome), which is characteristic of Turner's syndrome, was demonstrated in bone marrow cells and in a culture of skin fibroblasts from a girl of 14 years of age with gonadal dysgenesis (Ford et al., 1959). This is the most common sex chromosome pattern seen in Turner's syndrome though variants have been reported. These, when they occur, are usually mosaics, often with a stem-line of normal cells. It has been suggested that the normal XX cell line may have a diluting effect upon the phenotype in the individual with a Turner mosaic karyotype (XO/XX) and that the physical features are modified by the proportion and distribution of XO cells in the body (Ferguson-Smith, 1965).

THE TRIPLE-X CONSTITUTION

The existence of a human sex chromosome pattern with three X chromosomes was first noted by Jacobs et al. (1959). They referred to this condition as that of a 'super-female', analogous to the triple-X state in *Drosophila melanogaster* which is known by this name. The patient was a woman aged 35 years, whose menarche had been at the age of 14 years, but whose menses had stopped at 19. She was of below average intelligence. She had underdeveloped breasts and infantile genitalia. At the age of 28, on laparotomy her ovaries were found to be menopausal in appearance, and follicle formation was deficient.

Since this first report, many other examples of this syndrome have been published. No clear-cut clinical picture emerges, and the findings with respect to ovarian structure and function are variable. Thus some have anatomically deficient ovaries and menstrual irregularities or secondary amenorrhoea, while others have a normal menstrual history and are fertile. The fertility of triple-X females has been discussed by Bartalos and Baramki (1967) who remark that at least 11 cases have been reported of triple-X females who have borne children. Of these children, 31 in all (10 females; 21 males, including one pair of dizygotic twins) about half have been studied by sex chromatin and/or chromosome investigations, and have been found to be normal.

Many triple-X females are of normal appearance, and the body proportions of these patients as assessed by height, span, and upper-segment/lower-segment ratios are unremarkable (Johnston et al., 1961). In this way they differ from other groups with sex chromosome anomalies, including chromatin-positive males who may show dysplastic body proportions, XYY males who are characteristically tall, and females with XO Turner's syndrome who are abnormally short.

Some degree of mental retardation appears to be the most constant clinical characteristic in the triple-X state. This view, however, may be prejudiced at least to some extent by the detection of most cases by sex chromatin screening in mental institutions. Thus, for example, out of 595 patients in an institution for the mentally subnormal Fraser et al. (1960) found as many as 4 individuals with the triple-X chromosome constitution (6·72 per 1000). Johnston et al. (1961) found a proportion of 3·60 per 1000 in a survey of female mental defectives. This proportion was in line with that of 4·19 per 1000 found by Maclean et al. (1962) who discovered 8 XXX females out of 1907 female mental defectives. These data when pooled give a proportion of about 4·5 triple-X females per 1000 female mental defectives, which is greatly in excess of the proportion found among consecutive live female births in the general population. Twelve such females, with double-sex chromatin bodies, were found in a survey of the nuclear sex of live-born children in Edinburgh, covering 10,000 consecutive female births. This gives a proportion of only 1·20 per 1000 (Court Brown et al., 1964).

Although the physical appearance of XXX females does not usually deviate far from normal, physical abnormalities have from time to time been noted [FIGS. 58 and 59]. These are not usually gross or severe. Thus, one of the patients reported by Johnston et al. (1961) had a small head, high-arched palate, short fingers, incurved little fingers with a single interphalangeal crease on one; a single transverse palmar crease on one hand; bilateral optic atrophy and choroidoretinitis. It is our impression that gross physical defects are more often found amongst those triple-X females who are severely mentally retarded [see FIGS. 58 and 59].

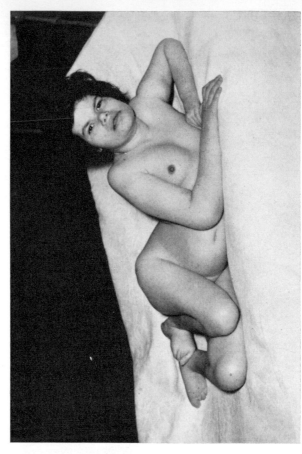

Fig. 59. XXX syndrome with cerebral palsy and mental subnormality.

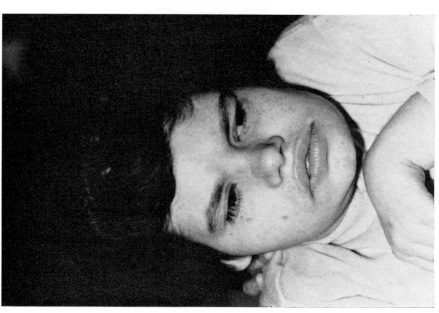

Fig. 58. XXX syndrome with cerebral palsy and mental subnormality.

SEX CHROMOSOME ANOMALIES
AND PSYCHIATRIC DISORDERS

Autosomal anomalies are usually associated with striking physical defects affecting the appearance of the patient in an obvious way; and marked or severe mental subnormality. Sex chromosome anomalies are associated with obvious physical defects to a much lesser degree. Moreover, there is usually much less intellectual impairment in association with them. As Court Brown (1962a) has pointed out, in the sex chromosome abnormalities the burden of the defect falls upon the genital tract. There is, however, growing evidence to show that the sex chromosome anomalies are often associated with profound psychological changes, most frequently in the fields of personality and character.

The most striking association of this kind has been found in the case of the XYY sex chromosome constitution. The severe character disorder leading to antisocial acts found in association with this sex chromosome complement has been discussed on page 298.

Less striking, but nevertheless fairly consistent psychological features have been found in association with other sex chromosome anomalies in both males and females. These are discussed in the following sections.

PSYCHOLOGICAL FEATURES IN
CHROMATIN POSITIVE MALES

For a considerable number of years there has been a growing impression that the sex chromosome anomalies may be associated with psychiatric disorders. As time has gone on, definite evidence has confirmed this suspicion. It seems now that although a wide variety of psychiatric conditions may accompany the sex chromosome disorders, there is a special tendency for personality and character disorders to predominate, with the particular manifestation of anti-social behaviour.

The first psychological observations of patients with Klinefelter's syndrome were made by Züblin (1953). He reported that his 6 patients, who were of less than average intelligence, showed some degree of emotional childishness, were querulous, apathetic and lacking in drive. They had difficulty in establishing relationships with others and tended to be withdrawn. They lacked sexual drive, and were sensitive about their gynaecomastia, small testes and sparse hair. Pasqualini, Vidal and Bur (1957) made psychological observations on 31 individuals with Klinefelter's syndrome. Again, the sex chromatin status of these subjects was not known. They were said to have been hypokinetic and timid from an early age. They were usually idle, slept too much, lacked vital interests, were shy and restrained, and had few friends. They showed some intellectual deficit, and a mean IQ 81 was estimated. Pasqualini *et al.* suggested that these patients had a specific pattern of psychological function, their performance IQ being superior to their verbal IQ, but this suggestion is not borne out conclusively by their observations.

Following the discovery of means to demonstrate sex chromosome anomalies by cytogenetical methods, Court Brown (1962b) first drew attention to the question of a relationship between sex chromosome abnormalities and anti-social behaviour. He noted that in adult life, a number of males with an abnormal sex chromosome complement find their way into institutions for mental defec-tives, where their frequency is about fivefold of that in the newborn population. From a study of the histories of these individuals it would seem that a high proportion are institutionalized following such antisocial acts as larceny, fire-raising and indecent exposure. Court Brown himself found that 14 out of 46 cases (30 per cent), recognized in his unit in institutions for mental defectives, were committed for these or similar reasons. This, moreover, was a minimum figure, because in 7 cases the exact reason for committal was not known. Court Brown discussed the ethics of the legal attitude that might be taken towards individuals with an abnormal sex chromosome complement who commit antisocial acts. He pointed out that clearly much work has to be done to deter-mine whether an abnormal sex chromosome complement may predispose an individual, perhaps in a suitable environment, towards delinquency, though it is difficult to escape the strong clinical impression that this is likely. Even if the proportion of such individuals, prone to clash repeatedly with the law, were only about 1 per cent in the general population, the recognition of their constitutional predisposition would be a great step forward. Furthermore, evidence that an abnormal sex chromosome complement predisposed towards delinquency would raise the whole question of whether such individuals could be held in law to suffer from a diminished responsibility by virtue of their abnormal constitution.

Wegmann and Smith (1963) took up the question of whether there was a connexion between a positive sex chromatin status in males and antisocial behaviour. They studied a combined group from two State institutions for juvenile delinquents between the ages of 12 and 18 in Wisconsin (505 indi-viduals) and an institution for criminal offenders between the ages of 16 and 30 (813 individuals). They found only 2 chromatin-positive subjects, giving a proportion of only 1:658. This is actually lower than that found in neonatal populations. Although these findings led Wegmann and Smith to conclude that there was no indication that individuals with that particular chromosomal aberration contributed disproportionately to juvenile delinquency or to felonious behaviour in the groups studied, different conclusions have been drawn from the observations in other investigations.

Forssman and Hambert (1963) followed up the work of Wegmann and Smith (1963) and made a complete buccal smear survey of 3 hospitals for criminal or hard-to-manage males of subnormal intelligence. Out of 760 males they found 15 who were chromatin-positive, or an incidence of 1:50. This was higher than the 1:100 incidence given for most mentally deficient populations (as estimated by Maclean et al. 1962). It was, however, lower than the 1:42 incidence found by Prader et al. (1958) in 336 boys in special classes for the slightly mentally retarded.

Forssman and Hambert (1963) were interested also in the question as to whether there was any correlation between mental disorders other than sub-normal intelligence, with or without social implications, and the chromatin-positive constitution in males. They screened 1625 men in 3 mental hospitals, and found 10 with positive sex chromatin (an incidence of 1:163). These 10 men had a wide variety of psychiatric disorders including episodic confusion, schizophreniform and paranoid states, manic-depressive psychosis, obsessional disorders and epilepsy. Like the 14 boys with sex chromatin-positive Klinefelter's syndrome reported by Dumermuth (1961), the majority of Forssman and Hambert's 10 patients had abnormal electroencephalograms.

Nielsen (1964a) reported findings which he put forward in evidence of a high frequency of delinquency, character disorders, alcoholism and poor social adaptation among patients with Klinefelter's syndrome. He found 4 delinquents among 10 cases of Klinefelter's syndrome in a mental hospital population. This was in accordance with the finding of Court Brown (1962b) of 30 per cent out of 46 cases of Klinefelter's syndrome with antisocial behaviour. Out of Nielsen's 4 cases of Klinefelter's syndrome, 2 were found in a mental hospital survey of 645 psychiatric patients of whom 51 had a character disorder. This gave a frequency of Klinefelter's syndrome with delinquency in this diagnostic group of 39 per 1000. Nielsen found 3 cases of Klinefelter's syndrome with character disorder or alcoholism, among a total of 98 patients with a diagnosis of either character disorder or alcoholism, giving a frequency of 31 per 1000.

Later, Nielsen (1964b) found a high proportion of chromatin-positive individuals in a buccal-smear survey of 450 male Danish mental hospital patients. He found 5 chromatin-positive cases, giving a proportion of 11·1 per 1000. An especially interesting finding in this survey was the absence of Klinefelter's syndrome among the schizophrenic patients, who made up 44 per cent of the group surveyed. This finding brought the prevalence rate for Klinefelter's syndrome among the non-schizophrenic patients to 20·8 per 1000, leaving the prevalence rate among the schizophrenics at zero. Nielsen observed that there were certain similarities in the personality and intelligence pattern of the 5 Klinefelter syndrome patients. These are reminiscent of the earlier observations by Züblin (1953) and by Pasqualini et al. (1957). Nielsen also found his patients to be immature, sensitive and lacking initiative. The IQ was within the lower limits of the normal range for 4 of his 5 patients and below the normal range for one case with a sex chromosome complement of XXXY. Of the 5 patients, 2 had psychogenic paranoid psychoses, two had depressive reactions and were classified as having character disorders, being 'unstable in their social function'. The fifth patient had been suffering from a manic state but was now senile.

This suggestion that the prevalence of Klinefelter's syndrome may be low amongst patients with schizophrenia runs counter to the idea put forward by Raphael and Shaw (1963) that sex chromosome anomalies may be more common among schizophrenics than in the general population. Out of 210 schizophrenics, Raphael and Shaw found one patient with Klinefelter's syndrome and one triple-X female.

Severe psychiatric disorders, including schizophrenia, occurred in one-third of the series of 50 patients (age range 17–66) with Klinefelter's syndrome whose records were studied by Becker et al. (1966). These patients had been seen at the Mayo Clinic from 1956 to 1962. Although intelligence was not specifically measured, only 2 were manifestly mentally deficient in comparison to a somewhat higher incidence in other studies. This was thought to be due probably to selection factors. The psychiatric disorders amongst the group were listed as follows (with numbers of patients in brackets): somatization (2); passive aggressive personality disorder (1); severe anxiety tension (8); psychogenic polydypsia and polyuria (2); depression (2); paranoid schizophrenia (2); alcoholism (1); hysterics with conversion symptoms (1); severe psychoneurosis (4); enuresis (1); sexual perversion (1).

Details of how these diagnoses were made were, however, not given in the report by Becker and his co-workers, and the mode of selection of the series is not clear in that the reasons for which the patients were seen in the first place are not discussed. This detracts from the value of the study as a demonstration of the prevalence of psychiatric disorders amongst individuals with Klinefelter's syndrome.

PSYCHOLOGICAL FEATURES IN FEMALES WITH SEX CHROMOSOME ANOMALIES

Turning now from sex chromatin-positive males to females with sex chromosome anomalies, attention has been paid to psychiatric features in patients with Turner's syndrome, and in triple-X females.

It seems that many of the psychological characteristics observed in Turner's syndrome are secondary, being reactions to oddness of appearance or physiological function. This is borne out by the psychiatric study carried out by Sabbath *et al.* (1961) of 7 adolescent girls with ovarian dysgenesis. The degree of dwarfing of stature seemed to play a considerable part in their attitudes and behaviour. Four of the girls were under 55 inches tall, which gave them the appearance of midgets. They spoke with high, thin voices and had doll-like features. Their manner ranged from tomboyishness to exaggerated prissiness. In interviews with the doctor they tended to be shy and to speak with an air of uninvolvement and vagueness. The taller girls (59–65 inches tall) looked younger than their ages but looked more like normal early adolescents than the others. They spoke more freely and spontaneously and showed a broader range of interests. A major concern in the group was their short stature. Some were concerned over the lack of feminine shape and absence of menses, others either denied that they felt a difference in these respects, or pretended not to care. Sabbath and his co-workers felt that the attitude of vagueness and relative blandness in the group was the result of a powerful sweeping denial used to handle the many conflicts their congenital abnormality produced.

Similar findings of passivity of personality, vagueness and lack of involvement were made by Hampson, Hampson and Money (1955). They studied 19 girls and women with Turner's syndrome from a psychological point of view. Though none was considered neurotic or psychotic, lack of mastery, aggressiveness and initiative was characteristic of the personality make-up. A discussion of the sex lives of girls with Turner's syndrome has been provided by Christodorescu *et al.* (1970).

A smaller and more selected group of women with Turner's syndrome was studied by Mellbin (1966). This comprised 4 psychiatric patients with an XO sex chromosome constitution. They varied greatly in their psychiatric symptomatology. One had a long-standing psychosis; another, with epilepsy, had an acute psychotic episode which disappeared leaving no trace; the third had a personality defect characterized by extreme immaturity and dependence; the fourth had anorexia nervosa. Despite the variety of psychiatric manifestations shown by these patients, they all had in common abnormal EEG records, though again, these were varied, one showing a mild, non-specific abnormality in both temporal regions; the others showing more lateralized focal or paroxysmal abnormalities.

The idea that a demonstrable organic basis might be found for the psychological features in Turner's syndrome has found support of a different kind in the work of Shaffer (1962). In psychometric studies, using the WAIS or WISC and the Benton Visual Retention Test in a series of 20 patients with an age range of 5–30 years, Shaffer found a consistent pattern of cognitive strengths and weaknesses similar to that observed in cases of brain damage. He suggested that the cognitive deficit found was characteristic of Turner's syndrome, and may stem from an organic defect related to the chromosomal anomaly. These psychometric findings were confirmed by Money (1963) who studied the IQ distribution of 37 cases of Turner's syndrome, including 16 of the patients already studied by Shaffer. He found a statistically significant difference between verbal IQ (mean $103 \pm$ S.D. 19) and performance IQ (mean $86 \pm$ S.D. 15). This discrepancy, also found by Shaffer, was attributed to a specific space-form deficit.

There has been less opportunity to study psychological features in triple-X females because these women do not usually have an obviously abnormal phenotype and they may be normal with respect to reproductive function. Hence, it is likely that many escape observation, and relatively few come to notice. This gives less opportunity for clinical and psychological study than patients with the more readily recognized Turner's syndrome. A psychiatric investigation of triple-X females receiving hospital care was, however, carried out by Kidd, Knox and Mantle (1963). They located 22 triple-X patients through the Registry of Abnormal Human Karyotypes of the Medical Research Council Clinical Effects of Radiation Unit, Edinburgh. The patients were matched with controls for age and length of admission to hospital. The triple-X patients were found to differ significantly from the matched control patients in that they demonstrated a greater intensity of impairment of interpersonal relationships and showed significantly more social withdrawal. Other prominent features of the triple-X patients were psychomotor retardation, poverty of speech, difficulty in concentration, persecutory ideas and ideas of reference. A table from the publication by Kidd, Knox and Mantle, showing the distribution of the triple-X patients by diagnosis, is given below.

A striking finding in this study was that only half of the triple-X patients were subnormal in intelligence. The remainder were of intelligence ranging from borderline average to bright. This demonstrated that mental subnormality is not an invariable psychological concomitant of the triple-X sex chromosome constitution.

The wide range of psychiatric diagnostic categories in the group of triple-X patients was broadly typical of the mental hospital populations from which these patients were drawn. This was not so, however, for those who were

	Primary subnormality	2
Subnormality	Subnormality with psychosis	4
or severe	Post-encephalitic state	3
subnormality	Epilepsy	1
	Epilepsy with psychosis	1
	Schizophrenia	4
	Paraphrenia	3
	Affective disorder, depression	1
Normal IQ range	Affective disorder, depression	
	with arteriosclerotic features	1
	Organic brain disease with psychosis	1
	Personality disorder, cyclothymia	1
All cases		22

mentally subnormal, in whom the most outstanding feature was superimposed psychosis, and the proportion of subnormal patients in the group with psychosis was considered unexpectedly high.

EEG AND NEUROLOGICAL ABNORMALITIES OBSERVED IN ASSOCIATION WITH SEX CHROMOSOME ANOMALIES

The frequent and often very striking finding of psychiatric abnormalities in patients with sex chromosome anomalies leads naturally to the speculation of an aetiological link, and how these mental effects can arise. The psychiatric changes cover a wide spectrum. Apart from mental subnormality, they include a great variety of neurotic and psychotic states. The most constant manifestations however are in the fields of character and personality. The gross character disorder associated with the XYY syndrome is a striking example; but milder changes, none the less distinct, are seen in association with other syndromes, as we have seen.

The most obvious location in which to look for a demonstrable organic change through which these psychiatric effects might be mediated, is in the central nervous system, and, more precisely, in the brain itself. With this object in view, and also sometimes by more fortuitous observation, evidence has been found supporting the presence of such organic defects. This evidence lies first in abnormal EEG records in patients with sex chromosome anomalies; secondly, in the apparent prevalence of sex chromosome anomalies amongst epileptic subjects; and thirdly the indications of a possible susceptibility to neurological disorders in patients with sex chromosome abnormalities.

The first abnormal EEG findings in individuals with a sex chromosome anomaly were made by Dumermuth (1961) who reported the electroencephalographic findings in 14 boys with chromatin-positive Klinefelter's syndrome. In 8 of these, the diagnosis had been made before puberty. Only one boy had an entirely normal EEG. In another, the EEG pattern was on the borderline. In all the 12 remaining cases pathological EEG records were obtained, which were all interpreted as indicating a disturbance in the upper brain stem. In 4, a typical epileptic pattern with generalized spikes and slow waves or focal sharp waves was recorded. These findings in prepubertal children with Klinefelter's syndrome were of special interest as they suggested a primary dysfunction of the central nervous system in association with the chromosomal defect.

Hambert and Frey (1964) point out that it is hard to judge the findings of Dumermuth (1961) as he had no control series and paroxysms of theta activity are not uncommon in childhood. Furthermore, he does not specify the mode of selection of his subjects; he does not say why they were medically examined nor why their electroencephalograms were taken. Children for whom a medical opinion is sought may have a disorder in cerebral activity for reasons other than a chromosome anomaly.

Hambert and Frey (1964), however, carried out a most careful and thorough electroencephalographic study of Klinefelter syndrome individuals, with an age range of 9 to over 70 years, and a control series. The probands were obtained by screening the inmates of various institutions. Fourteen came from mental hospitals, 17 from hospitals for the antisocial mentally retarded, and 2 from epileptic institutions. Nine came from other sources, and 3 from a mass survey of military recruits. The Klinefelter subjects showed an abnormal alpha frequency of under 7 cycles per second, random activity and foci more often than the controls, to a statistically significant degree. Thirty-three (73 per cent) of the Klinefelter subjects had abnormal readings as against 5 (or 11 per cent) of the controls. Age was taken into consideration; thus less attention was paid to theta waves when the subjects were under 20 or over 60. Because the Klinefelter subjects came mainly from mental hospitals and institutions for the mentally deficient and epileptic, their abnormalities may have been caused by other injurious factors besides genetic abnormality. But after 11 psychotic and 4 epileptic subjects were excluded from the Klinefelter group, a significantly larger proportion of the Klinefelter group (77 per cent) had abnormal records than the control group (10 per cent abnormal records). Moreover, all 3 of the Klinefelter subjects from the mass survey of military recruits had abnormal electroencephalograms; one of them had spike and wave complexes on photic stimulation. Hambert and Frey concluded that their observations indicated that the clinical features associated with excess X chromosomes in men may also cause electroencephalographic changes, particularly a low alpha frequency.

In addition to the electroencephalographic investigation of series of patients with sex chromosome anomalies, the reports of occasional patients provide additional evidence of a connexion between disorders in the EEG and these cytogenetical abnormalities. An example is found in the patient with Klinefelter's syndrome reported by Warburg (1963) who was remarkable in that it was thought likely that he had fathered two sons. He was described at the age of about 46 as a weak, non-aggressive man, suffering from 'a character neurosis with incipient intellectual impairment'. Although it was difficult to be sure of the cause, it was thought that this might be due to cerebral arteriosclerosis or to

21

'an endocrine psychosyndrome which in severe cases is indistinguishable from mild dementia'. His EEG showed a borderline pattern, with some slow waves during and after hyperventilation.

A systematic study has not yet been made of the electroencephalographic records of XYY males. In the case of the prepubertal boy with the XYY complement reported by Cowie and Kahn (1968) an EEG with borderline abnormalities was reported.

With respect to females with abnormal sex chromosome complements, the abnormal EEG records in 4 patients with Turner's syndrome reported by Mellbin (1966) have already been mentioned. Further supportive evidence of a diffuse organic brain lesion is provided by the observations of Asaka *et al.* (1967). In two triplo-X females with schizophrenic symptoms they report EEG dysrhythmia including theta waves and marked slowing on hyperventilation. Further EEG investigations of series of patients with different types of sex chromosome anomalies are much needed.

The finding of an unexpectedly high frequency of abnormal sex chromatin patterns amongst epileptic subjects complements the observation of abnormal EEG records in patients with sex chromosome abnormalities. Hambert (1964) carried out a buccal smear survey of 512 men in Swedish institutions for the epileptic. Four were chromatin-positive. The incidence was thus 0·78 per cent as against 0·27 per cent in the general male population as estimated by Maclean *et al.* (1962). The difference between these incidence figures was only on the borderline of significance $(0·05 > p > 0·025)$. Hambert emphasized that before a causal connexion between epilepsy and this unusually high rate for the incidence of positive sex chromatin can be assumed, the observation must be confirmed by series from other countries. There are not enough institutionalized cases in Sweden alone to allow a definite conclusion. That the high incidence was not due to chance is indicated by the observation that a number of Klinefelter patients in other forms of institution had epilepsy, and even more so by the observation that many chromatin-positive men have abnormal electroencephalograms.

Hambert discusses the possible ways in which the Klinefelter syndrome and epilepsy might be connected. Possibly the chromosomal aberration leads to abnormality in the tissues of the central nervous system or makes them more vulnerable than otherwise. Possibly a deficiency of testosterone is damaging to the cerebrum during development. Thirdly, it might be that aneuploidy like other forms of embryopathy leads to premature birth, predisposing to cerebral damage.

The evidence of an association between sex chromosome abnormalities and various neurological disorders is not at present very solid, but in this connexion there are 'straws in the wind'. Nielsen (1965) draws attention to the possibility that neurological disorders, other than EEG abnormalities, may be connected with Klinefelter's syndrome. He quotes Nadler *et al.* (1950) who described 2 cases of dystrophia myotonica with Klinefelter's syndrome; Bassøe (1956), who reported a case of Turner's syndrome with muscular dystrophy in a family with 5 such cases among which also a case of Klinefelter's syndrome was found; and Grumbach *et al.* (1956) who found a case of dystrophia myotonica in a series of

7 cases of Klinefelter's syndrome. In one of 5 psychiatric patients with Kline-felter's syndrome reported by Thomsen (1962), an intracranial posterior space-occupying lesion was suspected, but investigation by air-encephalography was refused. A myotonic syndrome has been described in a patient with Klinefelter's syndrome by Woollacott and Pearce (1967). The myotonia had features sugges-tive of a diagnosis of either myotonia congenita, dystrophia myotonica or paramyotonia congenita. No association between the sex chromosome anoma-lies and primary muscular disorders had been reported before.

Nielsen (1965) found 3 cases of chromatin-positive Klinefelter's syndrome in approximately 300 patients in a neurological ward. This finding suggested that the syndrome very likely may be found in a higher proportion among patients admitted to a neurological ward than in the general population. All three of these patients were considered to have hysterical conversion signs. One patient was admitted because of severe headache of hysterical conversion type, but he had a history of left-sided epileptic seizures and the development of a left-sided hemianopia and nystagmus, and it was questioned whether the neuro-logical disorder was due to birth injury or a congenital cerebrovascular abnor-mality; and it was not possible to decide whether there was in fact a connexion between the neurological disturbance and Klinefelter's syndrome. The second patient was described as having a hysterical restriction of the visual fields, super-imposed upon a slowly progressive muscular atrophy. The third patient had been admitted many times to medical, psychiatric, epileptic and neurological wards mainly because of seizures which were reported always to have been of an hysterical nature. For hypogonadism he was treated with testosterone in his late thirties, whereupon he became very aggressive and made several suicidal attempts. Nielsen draws attention to this as an indication of the possible danger of treating patients with Klinefelter's syndrome with testosterone.

SEX CHROMOSOME ANOMALIES AND DEVIANT SEXUAL BEHAVIOUR[1]

It would be natural to expect that of all types of psychiatric abnormality, disorders of sexual behaviour would be the most likely to be associated with anomalies of the sex chromosomes. Many years before the development of present techniques for chromosome investigation, the idea was put forward that at least some male homosexuals might be intersexes, with male characteristics of morphological sex, but a female chromosomal constitution. This hypothesis was put forward by Lang (1940), and was upheld for many years as being very likely true.

The theory was suggested by the experimental work of Goldschmidt (1931) who demonstrated that a range of sex intergrades in the gipsy-moth can be produced by cross-breeding races differing with respect to the strength of effect of the sex genes. In this moth, morphological sex is determined by the balance of these genes; the female sex-determining genes are carried on the sex chromo-somes, and the male sex-determining genes on the autosomes. In the male,

[1] The more general aspects of a genetical contribution to homosexuality are discussed on page 117.

the effect of the feminizing genes on the single X chromosome is outweighed by the masculinizing genes of the autosomes. In the female, on the other hand, the effect of the feminizing genes present on the two X chromosomes, overcomes the autosomal masculinizing genes. A similar means of sex determination is found in *Drosophila*. Intersexes may arise in these species by mutation, giving rise to a very powerful masculinizing recessive gene, which can, in homozygous state, overcome the feminizing genes on a pair of X chromosomes; or by polyploidy in which the number of autosomes is increased, thereby increasing the effect of masculinization because more masculinizing genes are present. For many years it was thought that a similar mechanism of morphological sex determination operated in man. According to Lang's hypothesis, in human intersex states, the chromosomal sex of the subject would be at variance with the morphological sex.

On the suggestion that at least some male homosexuals are genetical females, it followed that a higher proportion of males might be expected amongst their sibs than amongst the sibs of normal males. Lang, in fact, demonstrated a higher proportion of males than females amongst the sibs of 1015 male homosexuals, the ratio being 121:100. In a group of 1296 controls, the sibs showed a male:female sex ratio of only 107·2:100. The disproportion was even greater amongst the sibs of male homosexuals over the age of 25, the ratio of male: female in this group being 128·3:100 as compared with a ratio of 113·2:100 for sibs of male homosexuals under the age of 25. As the older group were thought to be likely to contain more 'genuine' homosexuals, the higher male: female ratio in their sibs was taken to add strength in support of Lang's hypothesis. Jensch (1941 a and b) made observations in line with those of Lang, finding a raised male:female ratio amongst the sibs of male homosexuals which was enhanced by taking the sibs of older subjects.

Other studies, however, produced less convincing results. Darke (1948) studied the sibs of 100 male homosexuals but found no statistically significant excess of males. Kallmann (1952a and b) found male:female ratios of 126·4: 100 and 125·3:100 amongst the sibs of 112 singleton and 85 twin homosexuals, but the groups were too small for the excess of males to be shown as statistically significant. Likewise, Slater (1958b) found a male:female ratio of 111:100 in the sibs of 286 male homosexuals, but the sample was not large enough for the demonstration of statistical significance.

These studies generally support the existence of an abnormally high male: female ratio amongst the sibs of male homosexuals, but this can no longer be taken as arising from a discrepancy between the morphological and chromosomal sex in the homosexuals themselves. Lang's theory was exploded by the demonstration of normal male chromosome patterns in the cells of male homosexuals, when the technique for this became available. This was first shown by Pare (1956) and from that time Lang's hypothesis has been regarded as no longer tenable. Pare carried out a nuclear-sex investigation by buccal smear of 50 male homosexuals, with a control group of 25 males and 25 females. These findings were confirmed by many later investigations by nuclear-sex typing, and by the demonstration of normal male karyotypes in the chromosomal analysis of cells from male homosexuals (Pritchard, 1962).

The main body of evidence from further studies of the nuclear sex of individuals with deviant sexual behaviour and from studies of the sexual attitudes and behaviour of individuals with abnormalities of the sex chromosome complement confirms the opinion that there is no specific link between abnormalities of chromosomal sex and sexual behaviour.

Thus, Money (1963) reported the psychological findings in 21 patients with XXY Klinefelter's syndrome, ranging in age from 12 to 69 years. The sample was obtained not by random selection, but was biased in favour of psychopathology and low IQ. Six of the patients were from mental deficiency institutions (IQ 60 down to less than 37). Of the remainder, 6 were below average, and 7 were average with respect to IQ. Two were superior, with IQs 121 and 132. All 20 of the postpubertal patients were low-powered in sexual urge. One was a transvestite. It would appear that the coincidence of transvestitism and Klinefelter's syndrome is sporadic. Money considered that the same can be said of the coincidence of homosexual behaviour and the XXY syndrome. The psychosexual pathology in such cases could best be regarded as yet another manifestation of a more general vulnerability of the XXY constitution to psychopathology of many different varieties.

In another series of patients with Klinefelter's syndrome studied by Becker et al. (1966), sexual interest and activity was apparently predominantly heterosexual in all patients but one, a mentally-retarded homosexual. Only two of the patients in this series were manifestly mentally deficient, and these authors implied that a higher rate of sexually deviant behaviour which may exist amongst mentally defective Klinefelter patients may be specifically associated with their intellectual deficit.

Certainly, a high incidence of sexually deviant behaviour was noted by Mosier, Scott and Dingman (1960) in a group of 10 institutionalized mentally deficient patients with chromatin-positive Klinefelter's syndrome as compared with a control group of mentally defective males. Seven of the 10 chromatin-positive patients had a history of sexual offences prior to admission to hospital. The offences of 6 of these patients are listed. Only 3 of the 6, however, had been accused of homosexual acts (two of paedophilia involving boys; one of sodomy with boys). The others had been accused of heterosexual acts (one of attempted rape of a married woman; one of attempted rapes of women including his mother; one of paedophilia involving girls). Mosier et al. point out that in dealing with sex offenders, Courts may unconsciously select a higher proportion of Klinefelter's syndrome men for institutionalization; these men are infertile and are less likely to be shown leniency than are fathers who are responsible for their children. Moreover, they are likely to have an abnormal personality pattern and are therefore more readily committed by the Court than individuals with apparently well-balanced personalities.

Money and Pollitt (1964) examined and compared findings from Klinefelter's syndrome and transvestitism to see the degree of overlap between cytogenetic and psychosexual ambiguity. Sixteen Klinefelter patients were studied; they lived an ordinary daily life and were not in mental deficiency institutions. There were 14 cases of Klinefelter's syndrome, 11 of transvestitism, and 2 patients with both syndromes co-existent. This overlap did not reach a level of statistical significance, and it was thought that it might well be fortuitous. On the other hand, Money and Pollitt made the reservation that the coincidence of two such rare syndromes might indicate that in certain cases of the Klinefelter syndrome, transvestitism is likely to occur more often than by chance. In previous studies the evidence weighed in favour of a normal sex chromosome complement being the usual state of affairs in both male and female patients. Thus in 5 males with transvestitism Barr and Hobbs (1954) found the epidermal nuclei from skin biopsy showed normal male morphology. A number of later accounts have appeared reporting consistency of chromosomal with anatomical sex in transvestites. Occasionally cases, however, have been reported which indicate that transvestitism may develop in patients with the XXY sex chromosome constitution (Overzier, 1958; von Walter and Bräutigam, 1958; Bishop, 1958; Davidson, 1958).

Despite the fact that cases have been reported of Klinefelter's syndrome in which the sexual leanings were contrary to the apparent sex, Davidson and Winn (1959) point out that this is the exception rather than the rule. Moreover, they emphasize that in the vast majority of cases of homosexuality and transvestitism the nuclear sex is not at variance with the anatomical sex, and it seems that chromosomal factors play little part. Overzier (1958) is of the same view, and thinks that transvestitism is absolutely independent of the chromosomal and hormonal state, but the genetically determined Klinefelter syndrome may predispose to transvestitism. He felt this was demonstrated by the case he reported of a patient with sex chromatin-positive Klinfelter's syndrome who began to show transvestite behaviour at 16, 6 months before gynaecomastia appeared.

The personality characteristics associated with Klinefelter's syndrome, including a weak libido and lack of sexual drive, are not those usually associated with a strong urge towards abnormal sexual behaviour, or indeed for any kind of sexual activity. Similarly, in females with Turner's syndrome, the libido is usually weak, and, as far as we know, no cases have been reported of deviant sexual behaviour in these patients.

In XYY males, the personality pattern is different, aggressiveness being a prominent feature. Nevertheless, the behaviour disorder does not seem to involve sexual activity to any great extent. In fact, Price and Whatmore (1967) remarked that compared with controls, XYY males in their series had committed relatively few crimes against the person; their crimes were mainly against property. Nevertheless, 2 of the 9 XYY males they studied had been convicted for sexual offences against young children. But out of 17 controls, no fewer than 9 had committed serious sexual offences. It seems reasonable to suppose that sexual offences among XYY males, when they do occur, are the outcome of the general aggression and violence to which these men are prone. So far there is no evidence that they are especially prone to homosexuality or other varieties of sexual deviation.

To sum up, the view that some male homosexuals may represent an intersex state with male characteristics of the phenotype but with female chromosomal sex, is no longer tenable. It seems likely that there is no specific link between deviant sexual behaviour and abnormalities of the sex chromosomes. Deviant sexual behaviour in individuals with abnormalities of the sex chromosomes appears to be a sporadic phenomenon, but for reasons of selection it may be noted with a greater frequency amongst special groups, such as in the mentally defective patients committed to an institution who were studied by Mosier *et al.* (1960).

SEX CHROMOSOME ANOMALIES AND MENTAL SUBNORMALITY

The association of mental subnormality with anomalies of the sex chromosomes is by no means as constant as its association with abnormalities of the autosomal chromosomes. Nevertheless, many surveys have been carried out of the incidence of sex chromosome anomalies in populations of mentally subnormal children and adults. When the figures from these are compared with those obtained from nuclear sex surveys in newborn children, the proportion of sex chromosome anomalies is seen to be strikingly higher in the mentally subnormal samples.

CHROMATIN-POSITIVE KLINEFELTER'S SYNDROME

Court Brown *et al.* (1964) point out that chromatin-positive Klinefelter's syndrome is, without doubt, often associated with a lowering of intelligence, often amounting to a major degree of mental subnormality. They pool four sets of data from surveys of male mental defectives [TABLE 89]. This gives a proportion of 9·7 sex chromatin-positive males per 1000.

This is greatly in excess of the proportion of 2·06 chromatin-positive males per 1000 from nuclear sex surveys in newborn children. The difference shows a real association between a sex chromosome abnormality in phenotypical males and

TABLE 89
(From Court Brown *et al.*, 1964)

SOURCE	MENTALLY SUBNORMAL MALES SURVEYED	CHROMATIN-POSITIVE MALES	PROPORTION OF CHROMATIN-POSITIVE MALES PER 1000
Mosier, Scott and Cotter (1960)	1252	10	7·99
Barr, Shaver, Carr and Plunkett (1960)	1506	14	9·30
Maclean, Mitchell, Harnden, Williams, Jacobs, Buckton, Baikie, Court Brown, McBride, Strong, Close and Jones (1962)	2607	28	10·74
Ferguson-Smith (1962)	916	9	9·82
Total	6281	61	9·71

mental subnormality; moreover, as Court Brown and his co-workers point out, it is assumed that these abnormal male infants experience the same mortality risks as normal male infants; if they were to experience a greater risk then the comparison would underestimate the tendency to mental subnormality.

Whereas autosomal chromosome anomalies are in the main associated with severe mental subnormality, there is a much wider range of intellectual deficit associated with the sex chromosome anomalies. It appears that many individuals with Klinefelter's syndrome, for example, are within the normal range with respect to intelligence. Israelsohn and Taylor (1961) report that Ferguson-Smith has had experience of a number of adult chromatin-positive males who were distinctly above average in intelligence. There have been indications that as regards distribution according to the level of intelligence, individuals with Klinefelter's syndrome tend to cluster in the range of mild mental subnormality. Thus, in the survey by Mosier et al. (1960) of 1252 mentally subnormal males, only 2 of the 10 patients found to have positive sex chromatin patterns were severely mentally retarded. As regards the level of intelligence, the 2 severely retarded patients had IQ 22 and IQ 28 respectively; all the others were in the range IQ 48–IQ 66. Although in the population screened there were 314 patients with IQ 20 and under, there were no sex chromatin-positive cases in that group. It was suggested that the data indicated that Klinefelter's syndrome is more likely to be found among individuals with mild rather than severe degrees of mental deficiency.

The suggested clustering of chromatin-positive males in the ranks of individuals with mild mental subnormality has not been shown to occur with any marked degree of constancy. There has been considerable variation between the findings in nuclear-sex surveys of boys attending schools for the educationally subnormal. Prader et al. (1958) in Switzerland screened 336 boys with mild mental deficiency and 390 boys of high intelligence for nuclear sex. Eight cases were found to be chromatin-positive. Klinefelter's syndrome was found in the group with mild mental deficiency and none in the group with high intelligence. These figures give a frequency of the true Klinefelter's syndrome of 2·4 per cent in males in the sample with mild mental deficiency. Ferguson-Smith (1959) found 8 cases (IQ range: 50–77) among 663 prepubertal boys attending special schools in Glasgow (1·2 per cent). A much lower proportion was found by Israelsohn and Taylor (1961) in a survey of 1556 boys attending schools in the London area for the educationally subnormal, who found only 7 subjects with chromatin-positive nuclear patterns (0·45 per cent). A somewhat higher proportion than this was found by de la Chapelle and Hortling (1960) in Finland, who detected 3 chromatin-positive males in a sample of 342 boys with mild mental defect (0·88 per cent), though this proportion was still significantly smaller than those in the surveys of Prader and his colleagues and of Ferguson-Smith.

The variation in these findings is discussed by Court Brown et al. (1964). Although it might be explained on the grounds of chance or by differences in the criteria of selection for schools for the educationally subnormal, these authors submit that there may be geographic fluctuations in the frequency of chromatin-positive males at birth. Against this, however, is the remarkable consistency in the findings of the three widely geographically separated surveys of liveborn children in Winnipeg, Berne and Edinburgh.

TRIPLE-X FEMALES

There has been a fair degree of concordance as to the proportion of triple-X females found in different samples of mentally subnormal patients:

TABLE 90

SOURCE	MENTALLY SUBNORMAL FEMALES SURVEYED	TRIPLE-X FEMALES	PROPORTION OF TRIPLE-X FEMALES PER 1000
Fraser, Campbell, MacGillivray, Boyd and Lennox (1960)	595	4	6·72
Maclean, Mitchell, Harnden, Williams, Jacobs, Buckton, Baikie, Court Brown, McBride, Strong, Close and Jones (1962)	1907	8	4·19
Johnston, Ferguson-Smith, Hand-maker, Jones and Jones (1961)	827	3	3·60 ·

Maclean and his co-workers (1962) pool these findings and compare them with the newborn surveys. Of 3000 consecutive female births in the Edinburgh survey there were 4 triple-X babies. There were none among 1383 female births in the Berne survey. Combining these results, a figure of 4 triple-X females out of 4838 births is obtained, which is significantly lower ($p < 0.001$) than the frequency of triple-X females (15 out of 3329) in the combined findings from the mental deficiency surveys. This comparison, however, leaves out of account any consideration as to whether there is any difference in mortality at any age between triple-X females and those with a normal sex chromosome complement.

Findings in smaller surveys have lent further support to the belief that there is a greater proportion of triple-X females amongst the mentally subnormal. For example, Hamerton, Jagiello and Kirman (1962) found a triple-X female in a survey of 196 female mental defectives. Ridler, Shapiro and McKibben (1963) found 2 triple-X females in a survey of 735 mentally subnormal female patients.

The wide range of intelligence amongst triple-X subjects as shown by the study of Kidd, Knox and Mantle (1963) is mentioned on pages 311–12. It appears that a proportion of triple-X females are of normal or even superior intelligence, and that mental subnormality is not to be expected in all cases.

XO FEMALES

As pointed out by Court Brown and his co-workers (1964), there are virtually no reliable data on the intelligence of women with ovarian dysgenesis. Because of their low frequency at birth, very large numbers of mentally subnormal females in institutions would have to be studied to ascertain whether amongst them there was a significant excess of individuals with the XO sex chromosome complement.

At least a proportion of XO females have been noted as being mentally subnormal (Polani, 1960; van Gemund and van Gelderen, 1961). The degree of subnormality, however, is usually mild. Thus, Cohen (1962) found only a slight decrease in mean IQ in a group of nine subjects. The hypothesis put forward by Money (1963) that a special cognitive defect may exist in association with Turner's syndrome in the nature of 'space-form blindness' is discussed on page 311.

XYY MALES

The frequency with which mental subnormality is a concomitant with the XYY sex chromosome complement has yet to be established. The first series of patients with the XYY constitution were found in a survey in a state mental hospital. Out of 342 men studied, 196 came from a hospital wing catering for the mentally subnormal, and 119 from the wing for patients with mental illness but of normal intelligence (Price and Whatmore, 1967). No fewer than 6 of the 7 XYY males detected, were, however, mentally subnormal. The seventh man was of average intelligence (IQ 93). Later, two more mentally defective patients were detected in the same hospital, increasing the excess of mentally subnormal patients in the series still more.

Subsequent findings have lent support to the association between an extra Y chromosome in the male and mental retardation. For example, on screening 942 mentally retarded and antisocial men for sex chromatin, 21 sex chromatin-positive males were discovered of whom no fewer than 7 had an XXYY sex chromosome complement (Casey et al., 1966b). Systematic surveys to detect the extra Y anomaly have, however, been carried out in groups with an excess of mentally subnormal subjects. For this reason a bias might be expected towards finding an association between this sex chromosome anomaly and mental subnormality. Besides the patient with normal intelligence described in the first series (Price and Whatmore, 1967), other males with an extra Y chromosome have been described as having intelligence within the normal range (e.g. Cowie and Kahn, 1968; Scott and Kahn, 1968). Clearly, much more extensive work will have to be done to establish the relationship between the XYY sex chromosome complement and intellectual status.

CONCLUSION

To sum up, sex chromosome anomalies are associated with severe physical malformations and profound degrees of mental subnormality to a much lesser extent than are autosomal chromosome anomalies. From a psychiatric point of view, however, it is of special interest that sex chromosome anomalies appear to exert a particular influence in the fields of personality and character. There are strong hints that these influences are mediated through organic change, as shown, for instance, by abnormalities in the EEG in some studies, and by the indications of an increased prevalence of epilepsy amongst individuals with sex chromosome anomalies.

Although there is no constant relationship between sex chromosome anomalies and severe mental subnormality, nevertheless there is a distinct relationship between these anomalies and intellectual deficit of varying degrees. It is not likely that this is due to specific genes or groups of genes present on the sex chromosomes. More probably it results from the total balance of the chromosome complement being thrown out of true by the aneuploidy. Moreover, it is likely that the relatively mild physical malformations accompanying the sex chromosome anomalies, as compared with the severe malformations seen with autosomal anomalies, are due to the relative genetic inertness of the sex chromosomes when compared with the autosomes (Hamerton and his co-workers, 1962).

The psychiatric effects associated with the sex chromosome anomalies call for intensive and extensive investigation. Although these abnormalities are relatively rare in the general population, the individuals affected by them may suffer as a result of their constitutional endowment, or may cause society to suffer. A striking example is seen in the case of XYY males. From this, many issues may spring, including that of whether such individuals, in the case of XYY males, should be considered to be of diminished criminal responsibility. The questions of management and treatment arise, and efforts to help individuals handicapped by these particular kinds of genetical abnormalities should not be thwarted by the mistaken view that nothing can be done to relieve conditions with a constitutional basis.

16

AUTOSOMAL CHROMOSOME ANOMALIES

It is possible for any of the 46 chromosomes in the human complement to undergo changes that render them abnormal in size and morphology, or by numerical over- or under-representation (e.g. trisomy or monosomy). Therefore it is not surprising that a very great variety of human chromosomal abnormalities have been reported. Many of these, mainly when an autosomal chromosome is involved, are not compatible with postnatal existence. At least four types of autosomal chromosome abnormality associated with specific clinical and pathological changes have, however, been found sufficiently frequently among survivors for them to be regarded as a genetical component of four distinct syndromes. These are: (1) autosomal trisomy G (mongolism or Down's syndrome); (2) trisomy E (Edward's syndrome); (3) trisomy D (Patau's syndrome); and (4) deletion of part of a short arm of a B group chromosome (the *cri-du-chat* syndrome).

They are all associated with striking clinical abnormalities and pathological changes which are widespread throughout the body. They are associated with severe mental subnormality, or with defects in the central nervous system compatible with severe mental impairment, even if the affected infants do not survive long enough for this to be demonstrated. They are associated with a shortened life-expectancy.

In the three trisomic syndromes, the trisomic chromosome usually exists as a separate extra chromosome, so that the total number of chromosomes in the cell is 47 instead of the usual 46. In a few cases, however, the extra chromosome (or the major part of it) is fused on to another chromosome, by the process known as *translocation* or *chromosomal fusion*. This is equivalent to trisomy; and although in these cases there are only 46 chromosomes present in the cell, one of these (the translocated chromosome) is equivalent approximately in quantity to the two chromosomes from which it is formed. Such a chromosome is recognizable by its abnormal morphology and size, which shape it so that it cannot be matched with any other chromosome in the set.

MONGOLISM (DOWN'S SYNDROME)

This is the commonest syndrome associated with an autosomal chromosome defect, and is, moreover, the commonest clinically-recognizable condition associated with mental subnormality. It can be diagnosed at birth, owing to its striking clinical features. Its incidence amongst live births has been estimated as one in 666 (Carter and MacCarthy, 1951) though this may be an under-estimate since this was based on diagnosis in the neonatal period, and some cases may escape notice until later. Allowing for this, Zappella and Cowie (1962) calculated that the incidence amongst live births may be nearer one in about 557. Mongolism seems to have a world-wide distribution, and it is likely that it occurs in all races, although Penrose (1963) thinks it is probably most frequent in populations of European origin.

Mongolism was first recognized as a clinical entity by Langdon Down in 1866. He considered that the patients bore some likeness to normal people of oriental races, and he used the term 'mongolian' in describing some of their features of appearance. It is well recognized now that any resemblance between patients with mongolism and normal members of eastern races is superficial and even fanciful. Ming-tso Tsuang and Tsung-Yi Lin (1964) report their own observations of mongolism in Chinese children and review the literature with respect to the condition in oriental races. They make the point that the characteristic features of the condition are not masked by the racial features. Apart from this scientific observation, we have heard it said by the Japanese that they think patients with mongolism look strikingly European!

Unfortunately, however, the supposed resemblance of these patients to normal Mongolians was taken up by Crookshank (1924). In his book *The Mongol in our Midst* he propounded the argument that the condition of mongolism was due to atavism. He suggested that affected individuals were descended from ancestors of the Mongolian race and that the signs they showed indicated a regression towards the orang-utang. This hypothesis is without any scientific basis whatsoever.

The Aetiology of Mongolism

For many years the only clear-cut fact to be recognized concerning the aetiology of mongolism was its relationship to maternal age. Mongols tend to be born to mothers late in the reproductive period, although mongols can be born to women of any child-bearing age. This effect is seen in the graph [FIG. 60] from the survey by Collmann and Stoller (1962) in whose Australian sample 1,134 mongol babies were born over 15 years in Victoria out of a total of 780,168 registered live births. In this graph the distribution of mongol births according to maternal age is seen to have a tendency to bimodality; the highest peak is after the age of 35 years, but there is a smaller peak between the maternal ages of 25 and 30. This smaller peak most likely arises because there is a general tendency for women to have more babies at this age-period than at other times in their reproductive period. This general tendency is seen by the distribution for all births in the general population (as shown in the graph). Although in the distribution curve for mongol births there is a sharp fall after the maternal age of 40 years, the relative incidence of mongolism still continues to rise though the peak of absolute incidence is passed. Penrose and Smith (1966) comment upon this, and say that it is not clear whether or not the incidence would continue to rise if the menopause did not bring a halt to childbearing; the shape of the distribution curve suggests that the relative increase would continue. although at a diminishing rate.

The question of whether or not birth order was of aetiological importance has received attention from a number of workers (Penrose, 1934; Malzberg, 1950;

Øster, 1953); but the difficulties in the way of finding an answer are considerable. The biggest problem is to eliminate the effect of maternal age, which is itself correlated with birth order. Then come the problems of finding an unbiased sample of mongols and balancing them with an equally unbiased sample of controls. As first born children are more likely to be born in a hospital than the later born, hospital samples of children may be unsatisfactory; and as mongols have a higher mortality than normal children soon after birth and in

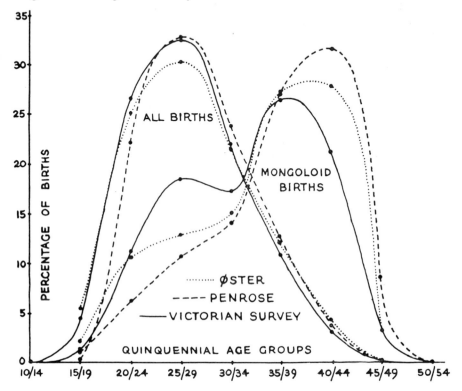

Fig. 60. Maternal age distributions, all births and mongol births, from three sources (quoted from Collmann and Stoller, 1962).

early years, one will go astray by taking as a representative sample of mongols, children who have survived for some time. All these problems and difficulties have been examined and discussed by Smith and Record (1955), and their own sampling methods appear to be as sound as practical considerations permit. They compared a series of 217 mongols born in Birmingham over a 10-year period with 1156 infants representing all births in that city in the same period. They separated the effects of maternal age and birth rank by examining the distributions of mongols and controls according to maternal age at each birth rank and according to birth rank at each maternal age-group. Their results, when the maternal age effect is removed, are shown in TABLE 91.

TABLE 91
OBSERVED AND EXPECTED DISTRIBUTIONS OF MONGOLS ACCORDING TO BIRTH RANK

BIRTH RANK	NUMBER OBSERVED (a)	NUMBER EXPECTED (b)	DIFFERENCE (a−b)
1	61	42·7	+18·3
2	50	58·1	− 8·1
3	34	34·0	0·0
4	26	27·9	− 1·9
5 and over	46	54·3	− 8·3
Total	217	217	—

When the first birth rank is compared with second and later birth ranks a highly significant excess is shown ($\chi^2 = 7\cdot91$, df 1, $p = 0\cdot005$). Observations among first born are in fact about 40 per cent higher than expectation. It would be a matter of some importance if Smith and Record's work could be repeated and confirmed. Primogeniture has been found to be associated with a wide and heterogeneous group of observations, the meaning of which is still entirely obscure.

The observation that, for whatever reason, mongols tended to occur late in sibships coupled with the striking late maternal age effect led to a belief that mongolism arose as the result of a 'tired birth'. Shuttleworth (1909) put forward a theory of 'mother-exhaustion'. Forty-three years later the notion of the aetiological effect of a worn-out reproductive system in the mother still found support. Engler (1952) expressed strong views in favour of an environmental rather than an hereditary aetiology in mongolism, and suggested a pathological condition of the uterine mucosa as the causative agent. He added, however, that 'in a number of cases genetic factors may cause havoc after an initial damage through extrinsic elements'. Briquet (1952) was another supporter of the belief that non-genetic factors at the time of conception and during gestation were strong influences in the aetiology of mongolism, and he recalled the mother-exhaustion theory of Shuttleworth and a theory of ovarian exhaustion put forward by Rosanoff and Handy (1934).

Other aetiological theories included infection by syphilis or tuberculosis, parental alcoholism, chemical contraceptives, or a familial diathesis of psychiatric disorder, mental deficiency or epilepsy. A number of endocrinological deficits were put forward as being of possible aetiological significance, including adrenal, pituitary and thymus abnormalities. Thyroid deficiency was suggested, and the treatment of mongols using thyroid extract became popular.

As early as 1932, Waardenburg suggested a chromosome abnormality in mongolism with non-disjunction as its basis. It was not, however, until 27 years later that a discovery was made that made revolutionary changes in the concept of the aetiology of mongolism. In 1959 Lejeune and his co-workers in

Paris reported the observation of 47 chromosomes in cells of tissue cultures from 3 mongols (Lejeune, Gautier and Turpin, 1959a). This report was soon followed by another, in which the finding had been repeated by the same workers in 9 mongols (Lejeune, Gautier and Turpin, 1959b). A number of reports followed this first discovery, each with similar findings confirming the presence of an extra small acrocentric chromosome of the G group.

It became widely accepted that the extra chromosome in mongolism was a chromosome No. 21 (Denver classification) but Penrose and Smith (1966) point out that precise identification of the extra chromosome is still lacking and in some cases of mongolism the smaller pair, No. 22, has been implicated rather than No. 21 (e.g. Barnicot, Ellis and Penrose, 1963). Polani (1967) discussed the problem of trisomy of autosomes in the G group, and pointed out that a definite syndrome corresponding to proved trisomy of No. 22 has not been identified, and that of the few possible cases described with this presumptive chromosome complement some have been reviewed and discovered to carry an extra Y chromosome rather than an autosomal chromosome of the G group as already suspected. It is hoped, however, that the finding of a genetic marker on one of these pairs of chromosomes may answer this question, or investigation by autoradiography. This is carried out with cell cultures grown in a medium containing tritiated thymidine. By this means it is possible to study the replication pattern of the chromosomes and to distinguish chromosomes by their characteristics of replication. Unfortunately the autosomes of the G group are very small, which leads to difficulty in investigation by this method.

For accuracy, the trisomy associated with mongolism may be referred to as *autosomal* trisomy G. The Y chromosome, which is a sex chromosome, is also a member of the G group, and the Y chromosome is not implicated in mongolism.

Although tissue cultures from most mongols show autosomal trisomy G in almost all (if not all) cells in a sample, variations from this pattern occur. Translocation, in which the major part of a trisomic autosome of the G group is fused on to the major part of another chromosome of the same group or of the D group, is seen instead of autosomal trisomy G in cells from roughly 3 per cent of mongols. Mosaicism, or a mixture of cells, some with autosomal trisomy G and some with the normal complement of chromosomes, is to be expected in roughly just over 2 per cent of mongols. Richards *et al.* (1965a) combined the figures from eleven unselected surveys. They found an over-all distribution as follows:

	PER CENT OF MONGOL SUBJECTS
Autosomal trisomy G	94
D/G translocation	1·5
G/G translocation	1·8
Mongol mosaicism	2·4

It is not within the scope of this book to go fully into the cytogenetical mechanisms by which these anomalies arise. These are discussed in detail elsewhere (e.g. Penrose and Smith, 1966). The chromosomal abnormalities in mongolism have, however, certain implications which are of great importance especially with respect to genetical counselling. With this in mind, together with other problems of importance to the doctor dealing with mongol patients and their families, these points will be discussed.

Translocation Mongolism

Occasionally mongolism occurs more than once amongst members of a family, and in some cases more than once amongst sibs. In a number of such families, the mongols are found to have a complement of 46 chromosomes, but one chromosome in the set is a large translocated chromosome of the D/G or G/G type. This kind of chromosomal pattern is approximately equivalent from a quantitative point of view to autosomal trisomy G. Apart from a very small loss of substance from the two chromosomes involved in the translocation, both chromosomes are present, even though they are fused together. Therefore the individual is virtually trisomic for an autosomal G group chromosome.

In some cases of G/G translocation, the aberrant chromosome is an isochromosome of the long arm of chromosome No. 21. An isochromosome is a perfectly metacentric chromosome with two completely homologous arms united at the centromere (Harnden, 1962). This could arise by transverse instead of longitudinal splitting in cell division.

Sometimes the translocation appears to arise *de novo*, in that the parents and other relatives of the translocation mongol do not show any detectable deviation from normal in their chromosomes. In such instances one cannot exclude the possibility of failure to detect a translocation in the relatives' chromosomes owing to some effect such as mosaicism, by which cells deviant from normal might be missed. Penrose and Smith (1966) have noted that cases of G/G translocation mongolism whose parents have normal karyotypes seem to occur about twice as frequently as cases where either the father or the mother is found to be a translocation carrier.

In a considerable proportion of cases of translocation mongols, one of the parents and other family members related to that parent, may be shown to be carriers of the translocation chromosome. However, they possess only 45 chromosomes in the cell complement, and the apparently missing chromosome in the karyotype is an autosomal chromosome of the G group. From a quantitative point of view, nevertheless, they possess the normal amount of chromosomal material, on account of the fact that the 'missing' chromosome is in fact present but fused to another chromosome. Clinically, these translocation carriers appear to be quite normal, both with respect to their mental and physical status.

The pedigrees of families with members carrying a translocation chromosome of the D/G or G/G type often show that translocation carriers are present in several generations before a mongol is born into the family. Though the reason is not clear, there are indications that the translocation carrier may possess a biological advantage in that they may outnumber family members who are not carriers [FIG. 61].

22

Another point of interest from family data is that in general mongolism of the D/G translocation type is transmitted through the mother, while patients with G/G translocations are born to parents of whom the father, rather than the mother, is the translocation carrier. Penrose (1962a) noted a significant increase in the paternal age in G/G mongolism, but there is no indication of any

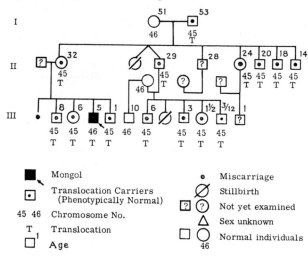

Fig. 61. Pedigree of a family with translocation mongolism
(Hamerton *et al.*, 1961).

maternal age effect for this type of mongolism or for D/G translocation mongolism.

The genetical risks of producing a mongol child for parents who have already borne a child with D/G or G/G mongolism is discussed fully by Penrose and Smith (1966). They may be summarized as follows:

TRANSLOCATION TYPE OF AFFECTED CHILD	PARENTAL KARYOTYPES	RISK OF PARENTS HAVING FURTHER AFFECTED CHILDREN
D/G or G/G	Both parents normal	Empirical risk no greater than for parents in general population, except in the case of G/G mongolism when the risk may increase with advancing paternal age; and some allowance should be made for the possibility of mosaicism in parents' gonads.
D/G	Carrier mother	Expected proportions of offspring: 1/3rd translocation mongols 1/3rd normal carriers 1/3rd entirely normal. There is a possible slight increase for trisomic mongolism.

TRANSLOCATION TYPE OF AFFECTED CHILD	PARENTAL KARYOTYPES	RISK OF PARENTS HAVING FURTHER AFFECTED CHILDREN
D/G	Carrier father	Risk probably less than 1 in 20. Chances of translocation or normal karyotype in somatically normal offspring are about equal.
G/G	Isochromosome No. 21 in either parent	All children will be affected.
G/G	Carrier of fused Nos. 21/22 chromosomes in either parent	Theoretically, risks are same as for parents who carry the D/G translocation. When father is carrier, possibly additional risk with advancing age.

Penrose and Smith (1966) point out that when the carrier parent is mosaic (i.e. when the parent has cells with a normal karyotype as well as those with the aberrant karyotype) the risks are likely to be correspondingly decreased except in rare mosaic types in which the abnormal cells are effectively trisomic.

Genetical Risk

The risk to parents who have had a translocation mongol of having another affected child has been summarized above. These parents constitute a special small group, however, and are greatly outnumbered by the parents of standard trisomic mongols.

The well-known general risk of increasing maternal age, which applies to all mothers in the population, has already been discussed. There is evidence, however, to support the view that in addition to the general risk there is an added risk for those parents who have already had a mongol child, even when that child is not a translocation mongol.

Familial cases are rare, and this fact together with the especially rare recurrence of mongolism in sibships has led some authorities to believe that familial incidence is due to random chance. Øster (1953) made a very comprehensive review of familial cases in the literature including the multiple incidence of mongolism in sibships. To this he added observations from his own survey in which 6 out of 354 mongols born alive had a younger mongol sib. He subscribes to the view of random chance, and found no evidence of familial accumulation, nor did he consider there was any evidence to suggest that a woman who had once borne a mongol child had a greater chance of bearing another than other women of similar ages.

On the other hand, pedigrees with a heavy loading of mongolism are to be found in the literature (e.g. Hanhart, 1944; Penrose, 1938a). These weigh against the random hypothesis. Moreover, Penrose (1951b) found that in familial cases consistent with genetical transmission through the maternal line, there was a weakening of the maternal age effect, the mean maternal age being significantly lower than for those cases in which transmission could be supposed to come through the paternal line, or for a control group.

A proportion of familial cases recorded before the present techniques of chromosomal analysis could be expected to have been due to chromosomal translocation. On the other hand, in more recent times, a number of familial cases have been found to be trisomic. This is well demonstrated by the work of

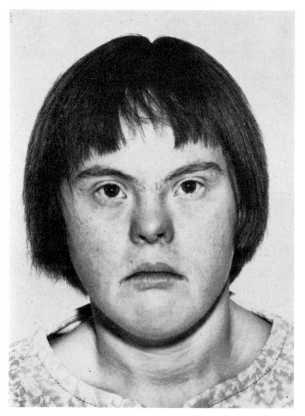

Fig. 62. D/G translocation mongolism. The first two cases of D/G translocation mongolism were described by Polani *et al.* (1960). This patient, now aged 20 years, was one of them.

Soltan, Wiens and Sergovich (1964). They presented the pedigrees of 6 pairs of sibs and 17 other families in which mongolism had occurred more than once. Chromosomal translocation was found *not* to be the underlying cause of the multiple occurrence of mongolism in any of the 21 families where chromosomal analysis was successfully carried out on at least one of the mongols. In every family either the index case or his relative or both were found to have the regular trisomic type. Translocation mongols occurred in 4 families (2 of D/G and 2 of G/G type); in each family the other mongol relative was of the regular trisomic type.

It is difficult to find an explanation for the familial occurrence of trisomy. Penrose and Smith (1966) discuss the hypothesis of a specific gene, acting independently of maternal age, which in homozygous form disturbs the process of cell division in oögenesis. Such genes have been described in *Drosophila*, also in maize. Such a gene in man could give rise to the familial incidence of non-disjunction and consequent trisomy. If this gene were rare, a detectable increase in consanguinity would be expected amongst the maternal grandparents as compared with paternal grandparents of trisomics, but a statistically significant excess of this kind has not been found. Penrose and Smith conclude that if maternal homozygous genes cause mongolism, they must be of common occurrence.

Turning from a theoretical to an empirical point of view, risk figures (not limited to translocation mongolism) have been estimated from sibship data which are of considerable value in genetical counselling. Carter and Evans (1961) collected information on the sibs of 642 index patients with mongolism. They found a striking excess of affected sibs over the expected numbers. Of 312 sibs born after the index patient, 5 also had mongolism (only 1 would have been expected from the prevalence in the general population). Of 927 earlier sibs, 4 were affected (expected number: approximately 1·5). They found the ratio of the number of sibs found affected to the number expected to be markedly influenced by the age of the mothers at the birth of the index mongol. The risk, as estimated by Carter and Evans, for mothers at various ages, may be summarized as follows:

MATERNAL AGE AT BIRTH OF MONGOL	RISK OF HAVING ANOTHER CHILD WITH MONGOLISM
Under 25 years	50-fold the random risk
25–34 years	5-fold the random risk
Over 35 years	No increase over random risk

Carter and Evans point out that the greatly increased risk amongst the younger mothers is no doubt attributable, in part at least, to a chromosome abnormality in themselves or their husbands. These estimates are empirical, and can be used when chromosome analysis is not possible.

Estimates of the risk of having a further affected child have been made by others on the basis of family records. Penrose (1956a) considers the risk to be increased by a factor of $2\frac{1}{2}$, as compared with the random risk. Berg and Kirman (1961) estimated the risk of having another mongol as being increased nearly four-fold once a mother had given birth to such a child. This was an over-all figure, since their data was not large enough to allow a subdivision of the general figure into risk figures at various maternal ages.

These estimates may be used in conjunction with absolute risk figures for the general population. These have been calculated from various surveys, and Penrose and Smith (1966) have tabulated the figures from two sources (Carter and MacCarthy, 1951: British material; Collmann and Stoller, 1962: Australian material). This is shown in TABLE 92.

TABLE 92

POPULATION RISKS OF A MONGOL BIRTH AT DIFFERENT MATERNAL AGES

(From Penrose and Smith, 1966)

AGE GROUP	CARTER AND MACCARTHY (1951) (100 CASES)		COLLMANN AND STOLLER (1962) (1119 CASES)	
15–19	0·00	—	0·43	1/2300
20–24	0·28	1/3600	0·61	1/1600
25–29	0·29	1/3000	0·82	1/1200
30–34	1·72	1/580	1·13	1/880
35–39	3·52	1/280	3·45	1/290
40–44	14·18	1/70	10·00	1/100
45–49	26·32	1/38	21·76	1/46
All	1·51	1/664	1·44	1/696

The left-hand columns show the risk per 1000 births, the right hand columns show the risks as vulgar fractions; corresponding numbers in right and left columns are in approximate but not exact agreement.

As Penrose and Smith (1966) point out, in the general population the risk of mongolism never exceeds 1/20, which may be regarded as a good risk. However, if the risks at various ages as set out in the table above are multiplied by Penrose's factor of $2\frac{1}{2}$, the risk for mothers in the last age group (45–49 years) would drop to a value 1/10 and 1/20 which could be considered as a relatively unfavourable risk.

When facilities are available for chromosomal analysis, these are of value in genetical counselling. A knowledge of the patient's karyotype provides a basis for assessment of genetical risk, and further valuable information may be obtained by examining the chromosomes of the parents. For example, when a translocation is found to be present, this information may be crucial in determining the advice that may be given.

Mortality in Mongolism

In mongolism, as in other conditions associated with autosomal chromosome defects, anatomical changes are a striking part of the clinical picture. The succinct remark of Penrose (1962b) that in mongolism 'everything in the body is morphologically a little out of the true', expresses the widespread distribution of these changes. Certain parts of the body, such as the heart, may be so severely affected, however, that the physical health and life-expectancy of the patient are at special risk.

These special aspects of this genetical syndrome deserve mention here, because the psychiatrist in counselling the parents of a mongol child is frequently asked about them. They have a direct bearing on the management of the child, and family decisions may rest upon them.

The pattern of mortality in mongolism is now changing, owing to advances in medical treatment. The greatest influence has been the advent of antibiotics, by which a good proportion of the pneumonias to which many mongols used to succumb may be treated effectively.

Life-tables for mongolism have been prepared based on various samples (e.g. Record and Smith, 1955; Carter, 1958; Collmann and Stoller, 1963). From these, and from wide general observation, it is clear that there is a markedly higher death rate in the first few weeks of life than later. In their Birmingham series, Record and Smith estimated that out of 252 mongols born over a 10-year period, nearly two-fifths were dead by the end of the first month, and that less than half survived the first year. Of Carter's series of 700 mongols attending the Hospital for Sick Children, Great Ormond Street, 30 per cent were dead one month from birth and 53 per cent by one year. In the smaller Scandinavian series of 38 mongols studied by Hall (1964) only 23 lived to attain the age of one year. It is estimated that about 10 per cent of mongols surviving the first year of life die before the age of 10 (Record and Smith, 1955; Carter, 1958).

The mortality of a sample of mongols between the ages of 1 and 63 years was studied by Forssman and Åkesson (1965). They found the mortality to be raised 6 per cent above that in the normal population for the whole group. It was highest between the ages of 1 and 5 and after the age of 40. Between 5 and 40, however, it was only a little above normal.

A higher death rate among females has been observed in mongolism by several authors. Collmann and Stoller (1963) found a higher death rate in female mongols as compared with males during the first six months of life. Record and Smith (1955) found the same effect during the first few years of life. Øster (1953) showed a trend in the same direction, in that 67 per cent of females as compared with 59 per cent of males had died in his series of 460 mongols by the time of follow-up. Penrose (1932) also found a slightly higher mortality in female mongols as compared with males; and the same finding, though not statistically significant, was made by Carter (1958). In the small series of 79 mongols observed by Cowie (1970), 13 mongols died before reaching the age of one year. Of these, no fewer than 10 were girls. The numbers in this series, however, were small, and both the relatively high survival rate and the marked excess of girls amongst those who died may have been due to chance. In their study of a mongol sample with a longer age range (up to 63 years), Forssman and Åkesson (1965) found no difference in mortality between the sexes.

With respect to the causes of death amongst mongol infants, it is generally agreed that pneumonia and congenital heart defects are the main causes. Record and Smith (1955) found that the most commonly recognized cause of death in the neonatal period was congenital heart disease, and later in the first year, infections of the respiratory tract. Infections of the gastro-intestinal tract also ranked high as a cause of death. The findings of Carter (1958) regarding the causes of death were in line with those of Record and Smith, although Carter found significantly fewer mongols died of gastro-enteritis.

Excess mortality due to leukaemia in mongols has been established. Holland, Doll and Carter (1962) found that in leukaemia in mongolism the death rate is 18 times that in the general population.

Psychological Development in Mongolism

A matter of great importance to the parents of children with mongolism is the psychological potential in the condition, and the course of psychological development that may be expected. There is diversity of opinion concerning the range of intelligence in mongolism. This is fully discussed by Penrose and Smith (1966) who quote early reports, some of which suggested that the majority were idiots with IQ below 25, while others put forward the view that most came within the imbecile range with IQs between 25 and 49. It is likely, as Penrose and Smith point out, that many of these reports may have contained some selection bias; patients who have been institutionalized for long periods are likely to have lower IQ scores.

Attempts have been made to study intelligence levels of mongols likely to be the upper end of the range of cognitive functioning. Dunsdon, Carter and Huntley (1960) selected mongol children who had attended primary schools, private schools and schools for the educationally subnormal and a few others who had seemed relatively bright at interview at the Hospital for Sick Children, Great Ormond Street. Out of 44 tested the highest IQ was 68 on the Terman-Merrill test for a boy aged 17 years 7 months. Dunsdon, Carter and Huntley considered that the upper limit of the IQ range on the Terman-Merrill test found among mongol patients is probably in the region of 70. Of 21 mongols attending a special school in New Jersey 2 cases were reported as being of borderline intelligence with IQ 71; the mean IQ of this group was 46 (Pototzky and Grigg, 1942). Wallin (1944) studied a group of 49 mongols attending special schools in Ohio and St. Louis; the mean IQ was 39 for females and 34 for males. The highest IQ scores were 63 and 53, and Wallin remarked that only one mongol, a child with a higher Binet IQ (67) had ever been examined in his clinics.

The view that the upper end of the range of intelligence in mongolism is probably in the region of IQ 60–70 is further supported by Øster's observation. In the investigation of his large unselected series in Denmark, he obtained intelligence tests results in the medical records of over 30 cases. The highest score was IQ 63 (Øster, 1953).

The general consensus of opinion is that the measured IQ or DQ tends to fall with increasing age in mongolism. A consistently downward trend in development in infancy in mongolism was demonstrated by Dameron (1963) in a longitudinal study of 12 mongol babies over a period of 3–18 months of chronological age. The test used was the California First-Year Mental Scale developed by Bayley. The performance of the subjects was compared with norms from the Berkeley Growth Study in which the same test was used. The results of Dameron's study indicated clearly that by 6 months the mongols were showing marked retardation, and thereafter there was a trend of increasing deviation from normal.

Zeaman and House (1962) in Connecticut studied the intelligence levels of a group of institutionalized mongols by cross-sectional and semi-longitudinal methods. The semi-longitudinal method was used as a less demanding procedure than a full longitudinal study. In the semi-longitudinal study, each subject was tested at least twice over a period of years, with no requirement that everyone in the sample be tested many times over a wide span of years. Since it considered pairs of measures for all individuals, the changes in performance from test to test were taken as not being due to errors of sampling producing biased cross-sections at each age. The results obtained using MA and IQ scores from the Stanford Binet (1916 Revision) on 97 mongols with an age range of approximately 6–51 years, showed that the IQ declined a few points a year when the children were young, and gradually stabilized as they became adults.

Koch *et al.* (1963) also found an apparently downward trend in development quotients in the series of 31 mongol infants they studied (age range: 2–48 months). On serial testing with the Gesell developmental scales they found an apparently progressive retardation with respect to the developmental quotient, but at the same time the maturity age for each individual viewed longitudinally showed steady developmental progress. The rate of progress, however, decelerated significantly, the average gain being 6·26 months in the first year as compared with 4·87 and 3·57 months in the second and third years respectively. The data did not indicate when a possible plateau in the mental age of mongols might be reached, or what the relationship of developmental and intelligence quotients and maturity age to mental age might be. Koch and his co-workers considered the developmental quotients obtained at 18 months to be excellent predictors of future developmental quotients at 2 or 3 years of age. Their observations supported the view held by a number of other workers, that the Gesell developmental scales are useful in establishing the presence of mental retardation in early childhood (they quote Gesell and Amatruda, 1941; Knobloch, 1959; Illingworth, 1960; and Drillien, 1961).

Gibson and Frank (1961) put forward the view that the reputed decline in mongol intelligence in the younger years might be an artefact of the infant developmental scales. These place major emphasis on psychomotor items and simple identification tasks, whereas at later ages intelligence tests stress the more truly cognitive items. Gibson and Frank are of the opinion that the near-normal infant performance of mongols cannot be taken as an adequate prediction of later cognitive ability. They suggest that there is no evidence of a statistically significant decline in the intelligence of mongols between the ages of 5 and 19 years, and during this period the intelligence becomes relatively stabilized.

Mental growth curves of institutionalized mongols over 16 years of age were studied by Durling and Benda (1952), using the Standard Revision of the Binet-Simon test. Their series of 62 patients was found to include 29 with a mental age below 3 years (47 per cent). These patients showed complete arrest in mental development or even deterioration after the age of 11 or 12 years. The 33 patients (53 per cent) with a mental age of over 3 years fell into three categories according to the age at which they reached a peak in their mental development. The peak was reached between 11 and 15 years by 16 per cent of the patients; at 18 years by 35 per cent; and after 20 years by 48 per cent.

In the foregoing studies the chromosomal types of the subjects were not taken into account. It has not been established, however, that a difference exists with respect to intellectual development between translocation and regular trisomic mongols, although Gibson and Pozsonyi (1965) report a slightly higher mean IQ for a group of 10 translocation mongols (mean IQ 43·5) when compared with 10 trisomic mongols (mean IQ 40·1). The difference was significant at a probability level of 0·05. If, on the other hand, mosaic mongols are compared with non-mosaic mongols, there is evidence to suggest that higher intelligence levels are to be found in the mosaic group (Penrose and Smith, 1966, quoting unpublished observations by Penrose, 1964).

The intelligence range in the mosaic mongols studied by Penrose rose from approximately the imbecile level to above normal average and the females were noticeably higher than the males [see TABLE 93].

TABLE 93

INTELLIGENCE LEVELS OF MOSAIC MONGOLS

(Penrose, 1964, unpublished findings, quoted by Penrose and Smith, 1966)

RATING	APPROXIMATE IQ	SEX M	F	TOTAL
S	122	0	1	1
N	100	1	3	4
M_0	78	0	4	4
M_1	56	3	1	4
M_2	34	2	2	4
Total		6	11	17
Mean IQ		56	78	70

Rosecrans (1968) lends further support to the view that an admixture of normal cells with trisomy-21 cells may ameliorate the mental defect in mongolism to some extent. He reviewed 31 cases of mosaic mongolism in the literature (normal/21-trisomy mosaicism). Of these, 20 were reported with acceptable intelligence test measures and information with respect to the proportion of aberrant cells in the karyotype. He found the mean IQ of this group (IQ 65) to be higher than that generally accepted for mongolism, and that there was a statistically significant correlation between a higher percentage of abnormal cells and lower intelligence in those cases where either blood or skin had been specified as the tissue examined. There was also a correlation in the same direction, though not statistically significant, when the source of tissue was not taken into account.

Although the evidence supports a higher level of intelligence amongst mosaic mongols, more information is needed; the view of Penrose and Smith (1966) still holds good that little is really known about the level of intelligence in mongols in relation to the degree of mosaicism that is present.

TRISOMY E SYNDROME

The first report of the syndrome associated with trisomy of a chromosome of the E group was made by Edwards et al. (1960). Their case was that of a baby girl with multiple congenital malformations. These included an odd-shaped head, which was long in its anteroposterior diameter and with wide occipito-parietal and narrow frontal diameters. The nasal bridge was broad and flat;

the mouth was triangular, small and inadequate for breast-feeding. There was micrognathia and a receding chin. The ears were low-set and malformed, with an abnormally great distance between the crus antehelicis and the helix margin, giving the ear a pixie appearance. The neck showed webbing. There was hyper-mobility of the shoulders so that they could be made almost to meet. The chest was shield-shaped with nipples almost in the anterior axillary line. The fingers and toes were short and stubby with irregular, short, flat nails. There was webbing between the second and third toes. As regards mental development, by the time of examination at 9 weeks it was obvious that she was mentally

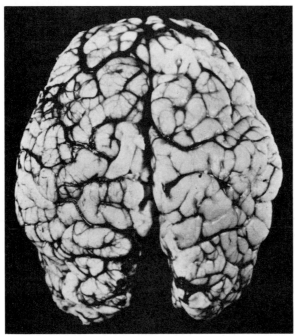

Fig. 63. Brain in trisomy E syndrome, with conjoined frontal lobes.
(By courtesy of Dr. L. Crome)

retarded; she did not smile, focus or listen to voices. From the first week of life she suffered from jaundice. This persisted and the liver was enlarged. At 4 months an exploratory operation was performed and a needle biopsy showed the appearances of giant cell hepatitis. The hepatic ducts and common bile duct were present but very small. A cholecystojejunostomy was carried out, but subsequently the jaundice deepened and shortly after operation the patient died. On post-mortem, congenital heart defects were found, including a ventricular septal defect and a patent ductus arteriosus.

In connexion with the mental retardation associated with this syndrome, the structural abnormalities found in the brain are of interest [FIG. 63]. In the original case described by Edwards and his co-workers (1960), the anterior third of the falx cerebri was narrow and did not extend for the normal distance into the longitudinal cerebral fissure. The brain was slightly underweight. In the frontal lobes and left parietal lobe the gyri were unusually prominent; the sulci were wide and there was a moderate excess of subarachnoid fluid. The neuro-pathological examination of subsequent cases of the trisomy-E syndrome have shown a range of cerebral defects from a mere shortening of the corpus callosum and a defective falx cerebri, to complete fusion of the lateral ventricles and total absence of the corpus callosum (Norman, personal communication, 1965).

Patients with the trisomy-E syndrome show a fairly constant pattern of the physical malformations reported in the first case of Edwards and his co-workers (1960). Additional defects reported in other cases include a clawing of the fingers with overriding of the index, arch patterns on at least three fingertips, renal anomalies, limited abduction of the hips, and rocker-bottom feet. Frequently, the dorsum of the feet are puffy and swollen. These infants have a somewhat longer survival than infants with the trisomy-D syndrome but most die within the first few months. Of 43 cases documented by Taylor and Polani (1964), death occurred mostly under 6 months, the mean age at death being about 90 days.

Occasionally, babies with the clinical signs of trisomy E are found to have karyotypes that are apparently normal. Out of 14 babies referred to one centre with a tentative diagnosis of trisomy 18 (though several of them not really typical), karyotypes compatible with normal were found in 9 (Ferguson-Smith, personal communication, 1969). It may be that in some such cases the possibility of mosaicism should be borne in mind. An abnormal cell line may exist only in certain tissues or in certain parts of the body, and may thereby escape detection. Apparently normal karyotypes have been found also in infants with clinical signs of the *cri-du-chat* syndrome [p. 341].

TRISOMY D SYNDROME

The multiple congenital anomalies associated with trisomy of a chromosome of the D group (chromosomes 13–15, Denver classification) were first described by Patau and his co-workers (1960). In a subsequent publication (Smith *et al.*, 1963) these workers point out that probably this syndrome had been observed on previous occasions, and quote a monograph by Kundrat (1882) in which arrhinencephalies were described as a syndrome including harelip, cleft palate, microphthalmia and failure of cleavage of the cerebral hemispheres, with absence of the olfactory bulbs as the cardinal features. It is likely that this early observer was describing the trisomy-D syndrome.

The first patient described by Patau and his colleagues was already one month old when first seen by one of them. The infant, a girl, had apparent anophthalmia, harelip, cleft palate and polydactyly of one foot. Both thumbs were maintained in a flexed position. On their passive extension, two small clicks were palpable at the metacarpal-phalangeal joint, an anomaly sometimes called 'trigger thumb'. She had single horizontal creases in both palms. There were clinical signs indicating a rotational anomaly of the heart, with marked right axis deviation on electrocardiography, and an intraventricular septal defect. Non-elevated capillary haemangiomata were present on the nasal bridge, both upper eyelids, the back of the neck, and in scattered small areas on the forehead and lower back. From the age of 3 months she had brief myoclonic seizures. She showed marked psychomotor retardation, and at the age of 5 months she performed at the developmental level of a 1-month-old.

A considerable number of cases of the trisomy-D syndrome have since been observed and reported in the literature. Features of 31 cases have been collated by Taylor and Polani (1964). The clinical picture varies somewhat from case to case according to the signs present and their severity; but the syndrome is characterized by severe physical malformations. Developmental retardation seems to be a constant component of the syndrome. In addition to the features described in the first report by Patau and his co-workers (1960), other features listed by Taylor and Polani include jitteriness and apnoeic spells, microcephaly with narrow temples, sloping forehead and frequently scalp defects, coloboma, malformed ears, cebocephaly, flexion deformity of the fingers, long hyperconvex finger-nails, distal axial triradius in the palm, a fibular S-shaped hallucal arch in the dermatoglyphics of the foot, and a prominent calcaneus. On post-mortem examination variable findings included cerebral holosphere, absent olfactory bulbs, ventricular and auricular septal defects, patent ductus arteriosus, dextroposed heart, polycystic renal cortex, hydronephrosis or hydro-ureter, undescended testes, biseptate uterus. Amongst the cases collated by Taylor and Polani, death occurred mostly before 4 months (range: 4 hours—22 months).

Because of the early death of these infants, they come to the notice of the paediatrician rather than the psychiatrist. Nevertheless, this syndrome together with the other autosomal syndromes is of relevance to psychiatric genetics, on account of the concomitant psychomotor retardation, which points to the more general implication of gross autosomal anomalies as a factor in the aetiology of mental subnormality.

THE CRI-DU-CHAT SYNDROME

The *cri-du-chat* syndrome was first described by Lejeune and his co-workers in Paris. They reported the clinical features and abnormal chromosomal findings in the case of 3 children (Lejeune *et al.*, 1963). Since then, many case-reports have been published.

Unlike the other syndromes associated with autosomal chromosome abnormalities, the *cri-du-chat* syndrome is associated with a chromosome complement with too little rather than too much chromatin. Part of the short arm of a B group chromosome is deleted. It was suggested that the chromosome involved was a No. 5 chromosome (Denver nomenclature) by autoradiographic studies using tritiated thymidine (German *et al.*, 1964). However, a child with a somewhat different pattern of congenital anomalies was found, by means of autoradiographic studies, to have a deletion of the short arm of chromosome No. 4 (Wolf *et al.*, 1965). Specific clinical features included harelip, coloboma, preauricnlar dimple and underdeveloped dermal ridges. The child, aged 11 months, had epileptic seizures. The cat-like cry was absent. It has been suggested that this case represented a different condition from the *cri-du-chat* syndrome with an abnormal No. 5 chromosome. Other reports of patients with a partially deleted chromosome thought to be a chromosome No. 4 have appeared (including reports by Hirschhorn, Cooper and Firschein, 1965; Leao, Neu and

Gardner, 1966). The findings of 5 patients of this kind have been summarized by Miller *et al.* (1966) who point out that all 5 had the non-specific features seen in patients with a partially deleted No. 5 chromosome, e.g. microcephaly, hypertelorism, low birth-weight and mental and growth retardation, and therefore at present it is questionable whether a clear correlation exists between the

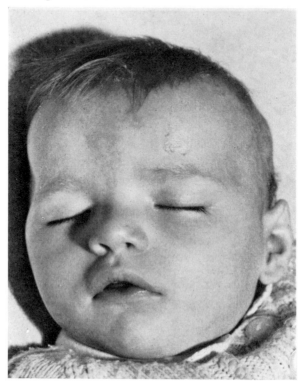

Fig. 64. *Cri-du-chat* syndrome. Note 'antimongoloid' slant of eyes and moon-shaped face.

autoradiographic replication pattern (which distinguishes chromosome No. 4 from chromosome No. 5) and the clinical features of the patient.

Let us, however, consider the *cri-du-chat* syndrome as described originally by Lejeune and his fellow workers, in which the clinical characteristics have been corroborated by many subsequent case-reports. The facial appearance is striking, with hypertelorism, sometimes strabismus, epicanthic folds and palpebral fissures that slant downwards and outwards, in contrast to the upward and outward slope in mongolism [FIGS. 64 and 65]. The nasal bridge is well developed and prominent, again in contrast with mongolism, in which the nasal bridge is flattened and depressed. The face is round and moon-shaped. The ears are low-set, and the pinna tends to be simple in configuration. Micrognathia is characteristic. The head is small. There is marked generalized hypotonia. Abnormal dermatoglyphic patterns are found, including complete or transitional single horizontal palmar creases, and sometimes an extra *t* triradius in the palm. Various abnormalities of the genitalia may be present, such as hypospadias, undescended testes. A female patient of Bergman, Flodström and Ånsehn (1965) had poorly developed secondary sexual characteristics at the age of 14, and had a hypertrophied clitoris with the urethra opening on it.

The characteristic cry is not like a cat's mew, but is more like the wailing of a kitten in distress. It is flat and toneless. Giorgi, Ceccarelli and Paci (1965)

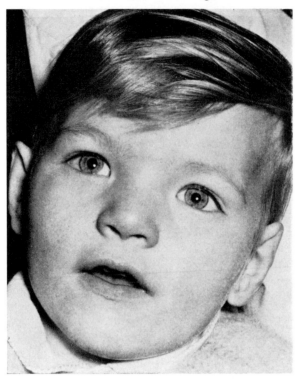

Fig. 65. *Cri-du-chat* syndrome (same patient as in Fig. 64).

regarded the absence of the cry in the patient they reported as a noteworthy feature, but it seems from subsequent literature and observation that the presence of the cry is a variable sign. For example, Berg *et al.* (1965) considered that there was no evidence that their (then adult) patient ever had produced the *cri-du-chat*. They suggested that though perhaps less elegant a name, 'partial monosomy 5 disease' might be a more accurate designation for the syndrome. The cry has been attributed to laryngeal malformations (Poncett *et al.*, 1965). It is heard in infancy, and disappears by the time the child is about a year old. Gordon and Cooke (1968) make the point that the disappearance of the cry together with a greater difficulty in distinguishing the characteristic facial appearance as the child grows older, mean that clinical diagnosis is most easily made, as a general rule, within the first 6 months of life.

The *cri-du-chat* syndrome is associated with severe mental retardation.

Berg *et al.* (1965) listed the findings of 18 reported cases including their own, and of these 16 were known to be severely mentally retarded, and the other 2 were probably severely mentally retarded. Findings suggesting specific intracranial abnormalities have been reported from time to time. An air encephalogram showed internal hydrocephalus in the $6\frac{1}{2}$-year-old girl reported by Hustinx and Wijffels (1965). Solitare (1967) reported neuropathological observations in the case of a 19-year-old girl; the brain was uniformly small and was considered an example of primary micrencephaly or micrencephalia vera.

Although failure to thrive is considered to be usually of severe degree in the *cri-du-chat* syndrome (Gordon, 1965) it seems that the condition does not preclude survival to adult years. For example, the patient reported by Berg and his co-workers (1965) was 33 years old and in good physical health.

Amongst reported cases of the *cri-du-chat* syndrome there is a preponderance of females. McGavin *et al.* (1967) counted 34 females out of 50 cases; they pointed out that a preponderance of females is also found in some of the other autosomal aberrations, notably trisomy 18. The aetiological significance of this sex preponderance is not clear; it may reflect a selective survival favouring the female at any stage, from the time of zygote formation until after birth.

A case of *cri-du-chat* syndrome with an apparently normal karyotype was reported by McGavin *et al.* (1967). Following this, Ferguson-Smith (personal communication, 1969) observed a second newborn baby with psychomotor retardation and a *cri-du-chat*, who had a normal karyotype in lymphocytes and skin fibroblasts. A similar case with normal karyotype observed by one of us (V.C., through the courtesy of Dr. Geoffrey Udall) showed the physical characteristics of the *cri-du-chat* syndrome but showed *no* psychomotor retardation. In this case, however, the cultures were from peripheral blood only and no skin culture was available. In their paper of 1967, McGavin and his co-workers discuss possible ways in which the expected deletion of a B group chromosome might be missed. This could happen if the patient were a mosaic with two cell lines, one of which is normal, and one with a deleted B group chromosome which by chance might be unrepresented in the material examined. Alternatively, the deletion might be submicroscopic, but sufficient to include enough of the relevant genetic loci to produce the syndrome. Also, because of the tendency to report positive rather than negative findings, it may be that the incidence of apparently normal karyotypes among clinically characteristic examples of the chromosomal syndromes is higher than generally suspected. In his cases, Ferguson-Smith considered the explanation to rest between a submicroscopic deletion and chromosomal mosaicism.

APPENDIXES

APPENDIX A

TWIN RESEARCH: THEORETICAL BASIS

The theoretical basis of twin research is widely known and understood. In brief it depends on the difference between monozygotic (MZ) pairs of twins and dizygotic (DZ) pairs. The former type, arising from the splitting of a single zygote early in its existence, gives us pairs of genetical duplicates of one another, invariably[1] of the same sex and usually so alike bodily (and in temperament also) that they are commonly spoken of as 'identical' or 'similar' twins. The DZ pairs arise from the fertilization of two separate ova by two separate sperms, i.e. two independent zygotes, and can be regarded as pairs of sibs who have happened to arrive in the world together.

Each member of the pair, independently of the other, may be male or female so that one may expect the various combinations: MM, MF+FM, and FF roughly in the proportions 1:2:1, and with a much higher degree of accuracy the sum of the same-sexed pairs MM+FF to equal the sum of the opposite sexed pairs.[2] This gives us a means of calculating the numbers of MZ and DZ pairs, from knowledge of the sex distribution alone, in any representative series of twin pairs.

As an example we may take the twin births in the General Register Office's returns for 1964, shown in TABLE A.1:

TABLE A.1

		LIVEBORN		STILLBORN	
		MALE	FEMALE	MALE	FEMALE
Liveborn {	male	3130	3314	181	78
	female		3046	77	175
Stillborn {	male			58	18
	female				58

There were therefore 10,225 males and 10,045 females, with sex ratio 101·8; there was in fact a much lower male sex preponderance than in the singly born. Survival rates were also practically identical for the two sexes; 9833 males survived (96·17 per cent), and 9658 females (96·15 per cent). By Weinberg's formula we estimate that there were

---

[1] Provided the individuals are not intersexes. Edwards, Dent and Kahn (1966) have reported an MZ pair of opposite sex. Both the boy and the girl were XO/XY mosaics. The girl showed Turner's syndrome, but she had a few XY lymphocytes. No XY cells were found in the boy either in blood or skin cultures, but it could be assumed that key organs, such as the endocrine cells of the testes, were predominantly of XY constitution.

[2] A sex ratio of 105 males to 100 females leads to an expectation of 100·12 same-sexed to 100 opposite-sexed pairs.

3161 MZ pairs among the 10,135 pairs born [10,135−2×(3314+78+77+18)], i.e. 31·19 per cent; among the 9490 liveborn pairs there were 2862 MZ pairs (9490−2× 3314), i.e. 30·16 per cent. The survival rate therefore favoured the DZ twins, with 95·04 per cent surviving as pairs, against a pair-survival rate of only 90·54 per cent for the MZ pairs.

A more sophisticated attack on twin mortality statistics, extending also to the end of the first year of life, has been made in the United States by Gittelsohn and Milham, 1965. Their figures are shown in TABLE A.2. In terms of individuals, the stillborn constituted 4·1 per cent of the twins, as against 1·5 per cent in the singly born; and the neonatal death rate (under 28 days) was 8·6 per cent for liveborn twin individuals, over four times the rate for single births (1·9 per cent). There was a much higher death rate in like-sexed than in opposite-sexed pairs, which could be translated into a still higher differential between DZ and MZ pairs [see TABLE A.2]. Finally, it is to be noted

TABLE A.2

OBSERVED AND ESTIMATED FOETAL AND INFANT DEATH RATES
IN TWINS

UPSTATE NEW YORK, 1950–60

(From Gittelsohn and Milham, 1965)

JOINT SURVIVORSHIP	ZYGOSITY	TOTAL PAIRS	% MZ	NUMBER DYING ONE	TWO	DEATHS PER 1000	CONCORDANCE (r)
All pairs,	DZ	13644		433	97	23	0·30
foetal death	MZ	7484	35·4	478	321	75	0·54
Both liveborn	DZ	13108		360	351	40	0·65
death 1st day	MZ	6691	33·8	235	369	73	0·72
Both survive 1st day	DZ	12395		449	102	26	0·29
death 1st month	MZ	6088	32·9	235	119	39	0·48
Both survive 1st month	DZ	11824		238	3	10	0·02
death 1st year	MZ	5734	32·7	78	1	7	0·02

that there was a high concordance rate (measured as a correlation coefficient) in the death rate at the earliest ages, a good deal higher in the MZ than in the DZ pairs. The estimated proportion of MZ pairs in the total twin pairs falls from 35·4 per cent before birth to 32·9 per cent at the end of the first day, after which it changes very little. In a representative twin series, accordingly, one should not find a much higher or lower proportion of MZ pairs than birth data would lead one to expect, though it is probable that twin-born individuals are at a slight disadvantage throughout childhood and adolescence. It is to be noted that the New York figure of 33·8 per cent MZ in liveborn pairs is significantly higher than the British figure of 30·2 per cent and Scandinavian figures are still lower.

In general one should find in a representative series of twins about 30 per cent of MZ pairs, about 35 per cent of same-sexed DZ pairs, and about 35 per cent of opposite-sexed pairs. In many twin series, the opposite-sexed twins are left uninvestigated, MZ pairs being compared only with the same-sexed DZ pairs.

The origin of any differences between members of MZ pairs has been authoritatively discussed by Darlington (1954), who shows that there must be some reservations to the usual statement that any differences between the life histories of MZ co-twins must be attributed solely to the environment. In fact there can be non-environmental causes of such differences, which Darlington classifies as:

1. *Nuclear*. If two sperm fertilize the two halves of one egg an asymmetry could arise which could lead to the misclassification of the twin pair. Gene mutations, such as those which give rise to differences of colour between the two eyes of an individual, could cause a genetic difference between the two co-twins. A difference could also be caused by chromosome errors at mitosis, such as give rise to mosaic markings and occasional structural asymmetries.

2. *Nucleo-cytoplasmic*. Some deleterious genes act asymmetrically in affecting the development of an individual; any such gene would be bound to react differently in two one-egg twins, one showing the defect and the other showing it less or not at all. The basis of the difference is cytoplasmic, although it arises from the action of a specific gene.

3. *Cytoplasmic*. The division of the cleaving egg into two is itself inherently liable to asymmetry, and the cytoplasm determines the normal asymmetry of development.

Darlington writes:

. . . differences between one-egg twins are partly like differences between two sides of an individual. They may be due to a reaction, either of an incorrect gene or genotype with a correct asymmetry of the cytoplasm, or of a correct genotype with an incorrect asymmetry of the cytoplasm (or of the young embryo). Neither of these types of difference arise between two-egg twins and it is for this reason that two-egg twins are more alike in birth weight than one-egg, or so called identical, twins. In every cytoplasmic reaction one-egg twins are bound to be, not more but less alike than two-egg twins. And likewise of course in every defect due to errors of splitting.

Darlington concludes that the one-egg twin situation by its very nature breaks down to a limited extent the distinction between heredity and environment and also between heredity and development. The embryological group of discordances are neither genetic nor environmental; they represent inherent defects of the twin experiment as a means of distinguishing genotype and environment. They are irrelevant differences, and must therefore be excluded from consideration in assessing the relative importance of heredity and environment. The cytoplasmic and embryological group of differences may very well be responsible for part of the discordances between one-egg twins, for instance according to Darlington, in birth weight, temperament and general intelligence—how great a part we do not know.

Darlington points out that the effect of this reappraisal of the twin situation is to say that some part of the differences between two MZ co-twins are likely to be non-environmental in the ordinary sense. It we put down such differences to the environment we shall be making an over-estimate, or at least stating a maximum estimate of the environmental contribution. He reaffirms the value of twin studies as the crucial means of studying genetic determination in man.

The effects to which Darlington refers, what we may perhaps call the non-genetic non-environmental effects, are not thought likely to contribute a very large part of the variance between MZ co-twins. As a general rule we shall either be in a position to ignore them, or be able to put them in the opposite scales to the effects we are endeavouring to measure. Thus, if we are interested in getting a minimal estimate of the genetical contribution to a defined estimate of intelligence, a difference between two MZ co-twins which seemed to be related to a difference in birth weight and early development could be regarded as environmental, although doing this would obviously be liable to over-estimate the effects of the environmental factors which are usually implicated.

Pace Darlington, we can use the information that twin studies provide for environmental as well as for genetical analysis, though we shall need to bear in mind the reservations described above. A research plan could be used involving the systematic investigation of discordant pairs, i.e. pairs in which the two members differ from one another in respect of the characteristic under study. We should then hope to find the presence or absence of some environmental factor, e.g. a specified environmental stress, which was correlated with the presence or absence of the criterion. The work of Pollin and his collaborators (1966, 1968) is an interesting example of this approach to schizophrenia.

More generally, we are justified in taking the degrees of concordance between MZ co-twins and DZ co-twins respectively as a guide to the relative magnitude of the genetic and environmental contributions. Where there is a high degree of concordance, or similarity, within MZ pairs and a much lower concordance within same-sexed DZ pairs, the hereditary predisposition plays a major role. Where concordance is high in pairs of both kinds (e.g. in some infections, such as measles), the environment common to both twins is the predominant factor; where concordance is low in both (e.g. multiple sclerosis) neither genetical predisposition nor early environment are important, and factors which operate more randomly in later life (e.g. poisons, infections, somatic mutation) must be the main ones. The fact that very low concordance figures for a diagnosis of 'hysteria' were found in the co-twins, both MZ and DZ, of patients so diagnosed, was used by Slater (1961) as one argument for regarding that diagnosis as without biological foundation.

It is, of course, important to determine the zygosity of a twin pair. This may be done by the method of Smith and Penrose (1955). For a full statement this paper should be consulted; but for simplicity's sake we may argue as follows, initially ignoring the fact that there are unequal numbers of DZ and MZ pairs (more DZ than MZ in Europe and more MZ than DZ in Japan).

We draw our observations from a range of anthropometric data in which degrees of similarity shown by pairs of MZ twins and DZ twins are known. We observe that, in respect of criterion 1, the degree of similarity between the two members of a pair, whose zygosity we wish to determine, is such as to be reached by a proportion d_1 of all DZ twins, and a proportion m_1 of all MZ twins. Then the probability that the pair in question is DZ is to the probability that it is MZ as d_1 is to m_1. On a second independent criterion we find the relative probabilities are d_2 and m_2. Further observations are made on the independent criteria 3, 4 etc. If we wish to take all the criteria into account, these probabilities are multiplicative; and the relative probabilities of dizygosity and monozygosity are as $d_1 . d_2 . d_3 \ldots$ etc. to $m_1 . m_2 . m_3 \ldots$ etc., in fact

$$\frac{d_1 d_2 d_3}{m_1 m_2 m_3} = p_\mathrm{D},\ \text{the probability of dizygosity relative to a probability of monozygosity of}$$

$$\frac{m_1 m_2 m_3}{m_1 m_2 m_3} = 1.\ \text{The absolute probabilities of dizygosity and monozygosity are to be}$$

obtained from the relative probabilities by writing:

$$P_\mathrm{D} = \frac{p_\mathrm{D}}{p_\mathrm{D}+1} \quad \text{and} \quad P_\mathrm{M} = \frac{1}{p_\mathrm{D}+1}.$$

It is the value of p_D that we have to calculate in the first place, and this is conveniently done by multiplying together the values of d/m from all the observational criteria available. Many of these will be the blood groups, in respect of which MZ pairs must be exactly alike, so that d/m becomes d.

In making use of blood group data, we have to take into consideration all the information available, including for instance information about the blood groups of one or both parents, or the blood groups of a sib which may throw light on the possible blood groups of the parents. Suppose we know of a pair of twins that they are blood group O, and therefore of the OO genotype. They may have come from any one of the matings OO × OO, AO × OO, BO × OO, AO × AO, BO × BO, AO × BO. If the frequency of the O gene is p, then the relative frequencies of these matings will be OO × OO p^4, OO × (A,B)O $4p^3(1-p)$, (A,B)O × (A,B)O $4p^2(1-p)^2$. The first mating provides individuals all of group O, the second individuals half of group O and half of other groups, the third individuals a quarter of whom will be blood group O, the remainder of other groups. Taking 0·6831 as the best estimate of p, for every individual of blood group O resulting from these matings we should find 0·7342 of another blood group. If then we know nothing about the genes of the parents the probability that the second of a pair of dizygotic twins will be of blood group O, given that the first twin is O, will be $1/1\cdot7342 = 0\cdot5766$. Suppose, however, that we did know the blood groups of the two parents, and that they were both blood group O, then the probability that both members of a pair of DZ twins would resemble one another in being group O would be 1.

Let us now calculate the probability that a pair of twins is dizygotic given that they are both of the same sex and are both blood group O, no further knowledge of the blood groups in the family being available. We start now with the initial probability of dizygosity (d_1/m_1). Since approximately 30 per cent of twin pairs born are MZ, this value is $70/30 = 2\cdot3333$. The probability that both members of a pair of DZ twins are of the same sex is 0·5000. The probability that two DZ twins are group O, given that one is, is 0·5766. It follows that $p_D = 2\cdot3333 \times 0\cdot5000 \times 0\cdot5766 = 0\cdot6727$. From this we calculate the absolute probability of dizygosity $P_D = 0\cdot6727/1\cdot6727 = 0\cdot4021$. There are accordingly approximately 60 chances to 40 that the pair in question is monozygotic.

All that is necessary for the calculation of the blood group probabilities and for the use of these and other marker genes is a knowledge of gene frequencies, for which appropriate books of reference may be consulted. The use of finger-prints for the diagnosis of zygosity is described in Appendix B.

Blood groups are highly efficient discriminants of zygosity, and with their help and that of finger-prints one can reduce the probability of dizygosity to very low levels in nearly all the pairs in which monozygosity is not excluded. For a positive diagnosis of dizygosity can be made with certainty, where a major gene difference can be shown to obtain, while the diagnosis of monozygosity must always be a matter of probability since dizygosity cannot be absolutely excluded. Laboratory methods of determining zygosity can be greatly strengthened by clinical comparisons between twins in such features as height, eye-colour, shape of ears, fingers, etc. The statement by relatives that the two members of the pair were different from the beginning and were never confused is by itself strong evidence of dizygosity; and the contrary statement that the two twins were so alike as to be confused by friends, teachers and even sometimes by their own parents or sibs, is practically diagnostic of monozygosity.

APPENDIX B

DIAGNOSIS OF ZYGOSITY
BY FINGER-PRINTS

The diagnosis of the zygosity of a twin pair proceeds by a process of exclusion. A difference of sex between two twins is by itself ordinarily sufficient (but see Appendix A, p. 345) to exclude monozygosity, and so also is a difference in a blood group. The investigator, accordingly, examines as many features as possible, in which a qualitative or quantitative difference may arise on a genetical basis. One can never be quite sure that a pair is not dizygotic, since chance alone might account for the similarities observed, even when they are very numerous. However, when they are very numerous, the chance of dizygosity can become vanishingly small.

Examination of the finger-prints can provide a useful discriminant. The method described below was based on finger-prints from 180 MZ and 90 DZ pairs, and was validated on an independent sample of 48 MZ and 99 DZ pairs (Slater, 1963). The discriminant Z was found to have a mean value of 0·61444 (σ 0·21855) in the MZ pairs, and a mean value of 1·00111 (σ 0·23847) in the DZ pairs. The difference between the two means is only 1·2 times its standard deviation, so that discrimination is not very good. Taking a cut-off value of Z at 0·80, there is approximately a 20 per cent misclassification both of MZ and of DZ pairs. It seems unlikely that more effective use of finger-prints for zygosity diagnosis than this is possible. Slater, P., Shields and Slater, E. (1964) used the same material to work out a quadratic discriminant, taking full account of the means, standard deviations and correlations of the 20 ridge counts provided by a pair of twins. This turned out not to give appreciably better results than the empirically obtained discriminant Z mentioned above. These authors concluded 'that there are sources of random variation limiting the reliability of evidence from ridge counts', and that both methods converged on the limit.

Despite their limitations, however, finger-prints give a probability value, which can be multiplied into the probabilities obtained by other methods of examination; in a proportion of cases, about one-third in both MZ and DZ pairs, values will be obtained which are outside the empirical range of either MZ or DZ, and so can be taken as characteristic of the opposite zygosity; and they provide an objective method of discrimination which is particularly valuable when other methods are not applicable.

Method

The most convenient method is to work on enlarged photographs of the finger-prints. However, it is also quite easy to do the ridge counting under a dissecting microscope on the original prints. The number of ridges are counted which cut or touch a straight line running from the triradius to the core or centre of the pattern. This is the method of Holt (1961), and she adds the limitation 'with the exception of the two terminal points'. This offends the logic that tells us that from Tuesday to Thursday of the same week it is two days and not one, and in the method described here the ridge number includes one of the two terminal points. The count is made to the radial triradius first, if there is one, and then to the ulnar triradius, if there is one. There will accordingly be two non-zero counts in the case of whorls, one in the case of loops, and none in the case of arches; i.e. in the total of 20 counts on each individual some are likely to be of zero magnitude.

The method of working is shown in TABLE B.1. The numbers under the rubric 'ridge count' are self-explanatory. The numbers under s in the column to the right are the differences between the value of the logs of (ridge count number + 1) for each twin. So in the first row $s = \log(25) - \log(24) = 1·3979 - 1·3802 = 0·0177$. The actual numbers of the several ridge counts have to be increased by 1, in order to obviate the appearance of log (0). These additional 1s will also go to increase the value of the total ridge counts by 20, so that in this case 285 becomes 305 and 153 becomes 173.

We calculate

$S =$ the sum of all values of s, here 11·0795;

$T =$ difference between logs of the two total ridge counts, increased by 20 as noted above, here $= \log 305 - \log 173 = 2·4843 - 2·2380 = 0·2463$:

$Z = \log_{10}(S + 30T) = \log (18·4685) = 1·2664$.

TABLE B.1

HAND	DIGIT	TWIN A PATTERN TYPE	TWIN A RIDGE COUNT	TWIN B PATTERN TYPE	TWIN B RIDGE COUNT	S
Right	1	Whorl	24	Ulnar loop	23	0·0177
			20		—	1·3222
	2	Radial loop	—	Ulnar loop	10	1·0414
			25		—	1·4150
	3	Ulnar loop	15	Ulnar loop	15	—
			—		—	
	4	Radial loop	—	Ulnar loop	14	1·1761
			23		—	1·3802
	5	Whorl	26	Ulnar loop	7	0·5283
			14		—	1·1761
Left	1	Double loop	26	Ulnar loop	23	0·0512
			13		—	1·1461
	2	Whorl	23	Ulnar loop	23	—
			24		—	1·3979
	3	Ulnar loop	16	Ulnar loop	8	0·2762
			—		—	
	4	Ulnar loop	18	Ulnar loop	16	0·0484
			—		—	—
	5	Ulnar loop	18	Ulnar loop	14	0·1027
			—		—	—
Sums			285		153	11·0795

Pattern type differences = 6. Total ridge count differences, by double count = 132, by single count = 62. $T = \log 305 - \log 173 = 0.2463$. $S = $ sum of ($\log 25 - \log 24$), etc. = 11·0795. $Z = \log (7.389 + 11.0795) = 1.2664$. $P_{MZ} = 0.022$.

Referring now to TABLE B.2, we see the relative heights of the ordinates DZ/MZ, which is going to be our estimate of p_{DZ}/p_{MZ}, at $Z = +1\cdot25$ is $10 \times 3\cdot997$ or $39\cdot97$; and at $1\cdot30$ it is $62\cdot55$. We can take p_{DZ}/p_{MZ} at the intervening value of $1\cdot2664$ as being proportionate to its distance between the two tabulated values, i.e. as $39\cdot97 + 0\cdot0164/0\cdot05 \times 34\cdot87 = 39\cdot97 + 11\cdot44 = 51\cdot41$.

In rough and ready terms, we can say that there is approximately a 50 to 1 chance that this pair of twins was dizygotic.

TABLE B.2

Z	RELATIVE HEIGHTS OF ORDINATES DZ/MZ
−0·25	$10^{-3} \times 2\cdot631$
−0·20	$3\cdot201$
−0·15	$3\cdot929$
−0·10	$4\cdot865$
−0·05	$6\cdot085$
0·00	$7\cdot653$
+0·05	$9\cdot738$
+0·10	$10^{-2} \times 1\cdot278$
+0·15	$1\cdot651$
+0·20	$2\cdot150$
+0·25	$2\cdot825$
+0·30	$3\cdot744$
+0·35	$5\cdot007$
+0·40	$6\cdot754$
+0·45	$9\cdot192$
+0·50	$10^{-1} \times 1\cdot262$
+0·55	$1\cdot748$
+0·60	$2\cdot443$
+0·65	$3\cdot438$
+0·70	$4\cdot817$
+0·75	$6\cdot961$
+0·80	$10^{0} \times 1\cdot005$
+0·85	$1\cdot455$
+0·90	$2\cdot150$
+0·95	$3\cdot195$
+1·00	$4\cdot706$
+1·05	$7\cdot092$
+1·10	$10 \times 1\cdot081$
+1·15	$1\cdot659$
+1·20	$2\cdot578$
+1·25	$3\cdot997$
+1·30	$6\cdot255$
+1·35	$9\cdot742$
+1·40	$10^{2} \times 1\cdot560$
+1·45	$2\cdot519$

APPENDIX C

THE WEINBERG PROBAND METHOD

This method of enumeration is to be used when a field investigation has been made of the frequency of trait bearers among the relatives of probands selected for being bearers of the trait under investigation, e.g. the frequency of schizophrenics among the sibs, or the co-twins, of schizophrenic index cases. The method requires one to distinguish between the primary or index cases, and the secondary or ascertained cases; but it is possible for one individual to make an appearance in each series, in which event he has to be dealt with twice over, once in each of his capacities. The application of the method can be made plain by the aid of an example.

Let us suppose that, in our enumeration of the data provided by the field study, we have now reached the sibships numbered 101, 102, 103 and 104, appertaining to the four probands so numbered, and that these four sibships are:

Proband 101 has 4 sibs, none of them schizophrenic;
Proband 102 has 3 sibs, of which one is schizophrenic;
Proband 103 has 9 sibs, of which two are schizophrenic, and of these two, one is Proband 104;
Proband 104 likewise has 9 sibs, of which two are schizophrenic, and of those two, one is Proband 103.

In our enumeration, all probands are ignored when they appear in that capacity but are counted when they appear as co-twins. So, in sibship 101 we have 4 normals, in sibship 102 we have 2 normals and 1 schizophrenic, in sibship 103 there are 7 normals and 2 schizophrenics, and in sibship 104 likewise 7 normals and 2 schizophrenics: *total*, 20 normals and 5 schizophrenics.

The fact that this method of enumeration gives a correct estimate can be illustrated on the basis of a twin material. Let us suppose that we are endeavouring to get an estimate of the 'concordance rate' for schizophrenia in a series of MZ twin pairs. We started, let us say, from a primary material of schizophrenics, of whom a certain number were born one of a MZ pair of twins, and by our field investigation we now ascertain how many of the co-twins have become schizophrenic. In the population at large, out of all the MZ pairs with a genetical predisposition to schizophrenia, there is a proportion a of pairs in which both twins are schizophrenic, a proportion b in which the first born but not the second born has become schizophrenic, an equal proportion b (assuming birth order is without effect) in which the reverse is the case, and a proportion c in which neither twin has become schizophrenic. The situation, in fact, is as shown below; and what we are aiming at is an estimate of $a/(a+b)$, i.e. the probability, given that one twin is schizophrenic, of his co-twin being so also.

SECOND BORN TWIN		FIRST BORN TWIN SCHIZOPHRENIA		TOTAL
		$+$	$-$	
schizophrenia	$+$	a	b	$a+b$
	$-$	b	c	$b+c$
Total		$a+b$	$b+c$	$a+2b+c = 1$

If we can assume[1] that the probability of ascertaining an index case is independent of the condition of the co-twin, then we can write the probability of ascertainment $= p$, the probability of non-ascertainment is $1-p$, and

$p^2 =$ the probability of ascertaining as index cases both of a concordant pair of MZ twins,

$2p(1-p) =$ the probability of ascertaining one only of a concordant pair of MZ twins, the concordant status of the co-twin being established by the field investigation,

$(1-p)^2 =$ the probability of ascertaining neither of the concordant members of the twin pair, who therefore do not appear in our series of probands at all,

$p =$ the probability of ascertaining as index case the affected twin, when the co-twin is normal.

From the a cell in the preceding table we shall ascertain ap^2 probands with concordant proband co-twins, $2ap(1-p)$ probands with concordant non-proband co-twins; and from each of the b cells, i.e. twice over, we shall ascertain bp discordant pairs.

Now, applying the Weinberg proband method, by which each independently ascertained proband is of equal status, whether or not his co-twin is a proband also, our figure of ap^2 is doubled and becomes $2ap^2$, and our final estimate of the concordance is

$$\frac{2ap^2+2ap(1-p)}{2ap^2+2ap(1-p)+2bp} = \frac{2ap}{2ap+2bp} = a/(a+b).$$

APPENDIX D

THE WEINBERG MORBIDITY TABLE

This is a method of estimating the morbidity risk among relatives of probands suffering from a disorder with an extended range of age of onset. It will be demonstrated with Kallmann's observations of the occurrence of schizophrenia in the children of schizophrenic probands (1938) as the illustrative material. What is estimated is the average risk that a child of a schizophrenic (in this proband sample) faces of becoming schizophrenic at some time in his life; it can also be used as an estimate of the 'incidence' or the 'frequency' of schizophrenia in the children of schizophrenics. The method is applicable when the numbers of relatives of probands is fairly large; and it is desired, or required, to make an estimate of the life-time morbidity risk in the relatives investigated, on the internal (observational) data alone.

The lay-out of the work-sheet is shown in the table. One needs to know the total number and age distribution of relatives, alive and dead, schizophrenic and non-schizophrenic, and the ages of onset of schizophrenia in those who became schizophrenic. This age of onset is either the age at which a first diagnosis was made at, say, a hospital admission when no past history was available; or the age of onset estimated by the clinician under whose care the relative came; or the age of onset as estimated by the investigator on the basis of retrospective information. These observational data

---

[1] Where the two affected members of a concordant twin pair are not independently ascertained, the Weinberg proband method is not applicable, and a simple 'pair-wise' estimate of concordance has to be used. As an example, this was found to be the case in a series of behaviour-disordered twins collected from the Bethlem-Maudsley Children's Department. If one of a pair of twins showed a psychiatric anomaly, the parents nearly always brought both twins up to the Children's Out-patient Department, where both were accordingly entered as patients.

provide the entries for columns b and c, from which the entries for all the other columns are obtained by addition, subtraction, division, substitution by log values, and summation.

TABLE D.1

	a	b	c	d	e	f	g	h	i
									$10^{-4} \times$
0–9	2000	971	—	971	1514·5	1514·5	1·0000	0·0000	0·0000
10–14	1029	29	3	32	1014·5	1011·5	0·9970	$\bar{1}$·9987	0·0297
15–19	997	49	33	82	972·5	939·5	0·9661	$\bar{1}$·9850	0·3608
20–24	915	93	27	120	868·5	841·5	0·9689	$\bar{1}$·9863	0·3696
25–29	795	112	19	131	739·0	720·0	0·9743	$\bar{1}$·9887	0·3569
30–34	664	125	16	141	601·5	585·5	0·9734	$\bar{1}$·9883	0·4543
35–39	523	78	10	88	484·0	474·0	0·9793	$\bar{1}$·9909	0·4367
40–44	435	126	1	127	372·0	371·0	0·9973	$\bar{1}$·9988	0·0728
45–49	308	97	2	99	259·5	257·5	0·9923	$\bar{1}$·9966	0·2990
50–59	209	152	—	152	133·0	133·0	1·0000	0·0000	0·0000
60–69	57	50	—	50	32·0	32·0	1·0000	0·0000	0·0000
70–79	7	7	—	7	3·5	3·5	1·0000	0·0000	0·0000
Totals			111	2000				$\bar{1}$·9333	2·3798

a = number of non-schizophrenics entering observation at the beginning of the age quinquennium. For a_1 we enter the total number of relatives ascertained, who entered the observation field with their birth at age 0. In subsequent rows we enter the number of those still remaining after the fall out of those who left observation, i.e. $a_2 = a_1 - d_1$.
b = number of those who ceased to be observed (otherwise than by becoming schizophrenic, e.g. by dying, emigrating, being lost sight of, still being in this age-span) during the course of the quinquennium.
c = number of those who became schizophrenic during the quinquennium (best estimate by contemporary or retrospective diagnosis).
$d = b+c$ = total of those who ceased to be observed during (or beyond the limit of) the quinquennium.
$e = a-d/2$ = estimated number of those at risk for schizophrenia during the quinquennium. The estimate is based on the assumption that those who leave observation during a quinquennium will on average have been observed over a period of half the quinquennium.
$f = e-c$ = the estimated number of those who remained non-schizophrenic.
$g = f/e$ = the estimated probability of surviving the quinquennium without becoming schizophrenic.
$h = \log(g) = \log(f) - \log(e)$.
$i = (1-g)/f$. Note that the figures in this column have for convenience been multiplied by 10^4.

We now note that the total log probability of survival to any age without developing schizophrenia is $\bar{1}$·9333; the probability Q of such survival is accordingly 0·8576. The morbidity risk of schizophrenia for the children of schizophrenics is accordingly estimated as $1-Q = 0·1424$ or 14·2 per cent.

The standard error of Q, and therefore also of $(1-Q)$ is $Q\sqrt{\Sigma i} = 0·8576\sqrt{0·00023798} = 0·8576 \times 0·015427 = 0·01323$ or 1·32 per cent.

The Weinberg morbidity table is discussed in detail in Schulz, Bruno (1936) *Methodik der Medizinischen Erbforschung*, Leipzig, Georg Thieme Verlag.

The method of estimating the standard error, due to J. O. Irwin, is described and discussed in Shrimpton, E. A. G. and Slater, Eliot (1939) Die Berechnung des Standard-fehlers für die Weinbergsche Morbiditätstafel, *Z. ges. Neurol. Psychiat.*, **166**, 715–18.

APPENDIX E

THE WEINBERG SHORTER METHOD, AND THE STRÖMGREN METHOD (SIMPLIFIED)

Weinberg pointed out that one could obtain a rough and ready estimate of the morbidity risk in the relatives of probands, if one took the limits of age for the main risk period of a lifetime, and calculated a 'Bezugsziffer', i.e. sample size corrected for age, by neglecting all those relatives who had not entered on the period of risk, counting those who found themselves between these limits as half in number, and taking those who had passed the upper age limit *in toto*. In TABLE E.1 is shown the distribution of ages of the sibs of schizophrenics, who did not themselves become schizophrenic, in the Kallmann data already shown in the TABLE 1 in Appendix D. If we assume that

TABLE E.1

AGE	NO. IN THIS AGE BRACKET	PROPORTION OF TOTAL RISK SURVIVED (M+F)	'BEZUGSZIFFER'
0–9	971	0·000	0·0
10–14	29	0·007	0·2
15–19	49	0·110	5·4
20–24	93	0·284	26·4
25–29	112	0·471	52·8
30–34	125	0·650	81·2
35–39	78	0·761	59·4
40–44	126	0·872	109·9
45–49	97	0·936	90·8
50–59	152	0·968	147·1
60+	57	1·000	57·0
Totals	1889		630·2

the main risk period for schizophrenia lies between the ages of 15 and 50, then the BZ ('Bezugsziffer') is calculated as $(971+29) \times 0 + (49+93+112+125+78+126+97) \times \frac{1}{2} + 152 + 57 = 549$, to which also must be added in whole the number of sibs who became schizophrenic at any time in the observation period (i.e. 111), so that the BZ = 660. The morbidity risk is then calculated as $111/660 = 0.168$ or 16·8 per cent. The assumptions in this method are that the risk of schizophrenia is fairly evenly distributed between the two arbitrary limits chosen, and that the ages of the relatives are also evenly distributed between these two limits. Despite its crudity, the method is a very useful one, and is often the most suitable one to use, especially when the total number of relatives observed is not a large one. It is to be noted that the figure arrived at, 16·8 per cent, is larger than, but comparable with, the figure of 14·2 per cent reached by the Weinberg Morbidity Table.

The Strömgren Method avoids the crudity of the Weinberg Shorter Method by taking into account the actual distribution of relatives between the risk limits in age and also taking into account the distribution of the risk, as obtained from independent sources, e.g. national health data. Strictly speaking, it also requires the use of information about correlation in ages of onset between relatives, and Strömgren provided this information, from his own researches, for the sibs of schizophrenics. However, the use of this additional refinement does not make much difference to the eventual result. The way the method is used can be shown by the data in the TABLE D.1, in which the second column shows, as already stated, the distribution of non-schizophrenic sibs, the third column is the estimated risk of first admission to hospital for a schizophrenic illness, averaged for both sexes, which has been accumulated by the age stated— figures which have been derived from those in the fourth and fifth columns of TABLE 2 [p. 12].

The final column in the table shown in this Appendix shows the contribution made to the 'Bezugsziffer' by the non-schizophrenic sibs, totalling 630·2. Our estimate of the morbidity risk for sibs, obtained by this method, is accordingly $111/741·2 = 15·0$. This lies between the two figures previously shown, and is somewhat nearer to that obtained by the Weinberg longer method.

It is to be noted that in all methods of calculation the number of relatives who become trait bearers, i.e. here schizophrenic, must always be included in whole, and not diminished by a weighting appropriate to their ages. If this were not done, it would be possible, in a small group of relatives of whom a very high proportion became trait bearers, to achieve a morbidity risk of over 100 per cent.

REFERENCES

The figures in square brackets indicate the page numbers in the text on which the references appear.

ABE, K., and MORAN, P. A. P. (1969) Parental age of homosexuals, *Brit. J. Psychiat.*, **115**, 313–17.   [121]

ABE, K., SHIMAKAWA, M., and KAJIYAMA, S. (1967) Interaction between genetic and psychological factors in acquisition of bladder control in children, *Psychiat. et Neurol. (Basel)*, **154**, 144–9.   [101]

ALANEN, Y. O. (1958) The mothers of schizophrenic patients, *Acta psychiat. scand.*, Suppl. 124.   [39]

ALLAN, J. D., CUSWORTH, D. C., DENT, C. E., and WILSON, V. K. (1958) A disease, probably hereditary, characterized by severe mental deficiency and a constant gross abnormality of aminoacid metabolism, *Lancet*, i, 182–7.   [227, 229]

ALSTRÖM, C. H. (1950) A study of epilepsy in its clinical, social and genetic aspects, *Acta psychiat. (Kbh.)*, Suppl. 63.   [175–6, 178]

ÅMARK, C. (1951) A study in alcoholism, *Acta psychiat. scand.*, Suppl. 70.   [111–12]

ANGST, J. (1966) *Zur Ätiologie und Nosologie Endogener Depressiver Psychosen*, Berlin.   [80]

ANGST, J., and PERRIS, C. (1968) Zur Nosologie endogener Depressionen. Vergleich der Ergebnisse zweier Untersuchungen. *Arch. Psychiat. Nervenkr.*, **210**, 373–86.   [80–2, 86]

APERT, M. E. (1906) De l'acrocéphalosyndactylie, *Bull. Soc. méd. Hôp. Paris*, **23**, 1310–13.   [285]

ARKONAC, O., and GUZE, S. B. (1963) A family study of hysteria, *New Engl. J. Med.*, **268**, 239–42.   [108]

ARONSON, S. M., PERLE, G., SAIFER, A., and VOLK, B. W. (1962) Biochemical identification of the carrier state in Tay-Sachs' disease, *Proc. Soc. exp. Biol. (N.Y.)*, **111**, 664–7.   [259]

ARONSON, S. M., SAIFER, A., KANOF, A., and VOLK, B. W. (1958) Progression of amaurotic family idiocy as reflected by serum and cerebrospinal fluid changes, *Amer. J. Med.*, **24**, 390–401.   [259]

ARONSON, S. M., VALSAMIS, M. P., and VOLK, B. W. (1960) Infantile amaurotic family idiocy: occurrence, genetic considerations and patho-physiology in the non-Jewish infant, *Pediatrics*, **26**, 229–42.   [261]

ASAKA, A., TSUBOI, T., INOUYE, E., NAGUMO, Y., HAMADA, S., and OKADA, K. (1967) Schizophrenic psychosis in triplo-X females, *Folia psychiat. neurol. jap.*, **21**, 271–81.   [314]

ASANO, N. (1967) Pneumoencephalographic study of schizophrenia, in *Clinical Genetics in Psychiatry*, ed. Mitsuda, H., Tokyo.   [36–7]

BAGH, K. VON, and HORTLING, H. (1948) Blodfynd vid juvenil amaurotisk idioti, *Nord. Med.*, **38**, 1072–6.   [260]

BAKER, L., MELLMAN, W. J., TEDESCO, T. A., and SEGAL, S. (1966) Galactosemia: symptomatic and asymptomatic homozygotes in one Negro sibship, *J. Pediat.*, **68**, 551–8.   [238]

BARNICOT, N. A., ELLIS, J. R., and PENROSE, L. S. (1963) Translocation and trisomic mongol sibs, *Ann. hum. Genet.*, **26**, 279–85.   [328]

BARON, D. N., DENT, C. E., HARRIS, H., HART, E. W., and JEPSON, J. B. (1956) Hereditary pellagra-like skin rash with temporary cerebellar ataxia, constant renal aminoaciduria and other bizarre biochemical features, *Lancet*, ii, 421–8.   [233–5]

BARR, M. L., and BERTRAM, E. G. (1949) A morphological distinction between neurones
of the male and female, and the behaviour of the nucleolar satellite during accelerated
nucleoprotein synthesis, *Nature (Lond.)*, **163**, 676–8.   [298]

BARR, M. L., and CARR, D. H. (1962) Nuclear sex, in *Chromosomes in Medicine*,
ed. Hamerton, J. L. (2nd ed. 1965), Little Club Clinics in Developmental Medicine,
published by the Medical Advisory Committee of the National Spastics Society.
[298]

BARR, M. L., and HOBBS, G. E. (1954) Chromosomal sex in transvestites, *Lancet*, i,
1109–10.   [378]

BARR, M. L., SHAVER, E. L., CARR, D. H., and PLUNKETT, E. H. (1960) The chromatin-
positive Klinefelter syndrome among patients in mental deficiency hospitals, *J.
ment. Defic. Res.*, **4**, 89–107.   [319]

BARROWS, H. S., and COOPER, W. C. (1963) Rigidity as a disease form of Huntington's
disease, *Bull. Los Angeles neurol. Soc.*, **28**, 144–7.   [137]

BARSLUND, I., and DANIELSEN, J. (1963) Temporal epilepsy in monozygotic twins,
Epilepsia (Amst.), **4**, 138–50.   [167]

BARTALOS, M., and BARAMKI, T. A. (1967) *Medical Cytogenetics*, Baltimore.
[300, 304–5]

BASSEN, F. A., and KORNZWEIG, A. L. (1950) Malformation of erythrocytes in a case of
atypical retinitis pigmentosa, *Blood*, **5**, 381–7.   [248]

BASSØE, H. H. (1956) Hypometabolisme og Menstruasjonsforstyrrelser, *Nord. Med.*,
56, 969–71.   [314]

BAUER, J. (1927) *Innere Sekretion*, Berlin.   [287]

BEADLE, G. W. (1945) Biochemical genetics, *Chem. Rev.*, **37**, 15–96.   [2]

BEARD, A. W. (1959) The association of hepatolenticular degeneration with schizophrenia, *Acta psychiat. scand.*, **34**, 411–28.   [154]

BEARN, A. G. (1960) A genetical analysis of thirty families with Wilson's disease
(hepatolenticular degeneration), *Ann. hum. Genet.*, **24**, 33–43.   [156–8]

BEARN, A. G. (1966) Wilson's disease, in *The Metabolic Basis of Inherited Disease*,
ed. Stanbury, J. B., Wyngaarden, J. B., and Fredrickson, D. S., 2nd ed., New
York.   [144–5, 159]

BECKER, K. L., HOFFMAN, D. L., ALBERT, A. UNDERDAHL, L. O., and MASON, H. L.
(1966) Klinefelter's syndrome. Clinical and laboratory findings in 50 patients,
Arch. intern. Med., **118**, 314–21.   [309, 317]

BEEBE, R. T., and FORMEL, P. F. (1954) Gargoylism: sex-linked transmission in nine
males, *Trans. Amer. clin. climat. Ass.*, **66**, 199–207.   [272]

BELL, JULIA (1934) Huntington's chorea, *Treas. hum. Inherit.*, **4**, 1–67.   [138]

BERENSON, G. S., and DALFERES, E. R. (1965) Urinary excretion of mucopolysaccharides
in normal individuals and in the Marfan syndrome, *Biochim. biophys. Acta (Amst.)*,
101, 183–92.   [226]

BERG, J. M., and CROME, L. (1963) Les phakomatoses dans la déficience mentale, in
Les Phakomatoses Cérébrales, ed. Michaux, L., and Feld, M., Paris.   [275]

BERG, J. M., DELHANTY, J. D. A., FAUNCH, J. A., and RIDLER, M. A. C. (1965) Partial
deletion of short arm of a chromosome of the 4–5 group (Denver) in an adult male,
J. ment. Defic. Res., **9**, 219–28.   [343–4]

BERG, J. M., and KIRMAN, B. H. (1961) Risk of dual occurrence of mongolism in
sibships, *Arch. Dis. Childh.*, **36**, 645–8.   [333]

BERG, J, M., SMITH, G. F., and McCREARY, B. D. (1967a) The De Lange syndrome—
the clinical picture, *Wld. Med.*, **3**, 25–6.   [295–6]

BERG, J. M., SMITH, G. F., RIDLER, M. A. C., McCREARY, B. D., FAUNCH, J. A., FARNHAM, F. N., and ALLEN, M. L. (1967b) De Lange syndrome: report of a case with an unusual karyotype, *J. med. Genet.*, **4**, 184–9.   [295]
BERGEMANN, E. (1961) Geschlechtschromatinbestimmungen am Neugeborenen, *Schweiz. med. Wschr.*, **91**, 292–4.   [300]
BERGMAN, S., FLODSTRÖM, I., and ÅNSEHN, S. (1965) Cri-du-chat, *Lancet*, i, 768–9. [343]
BERLOW, S., ARENDS, R., and HARRIES, C. (1965) Studies in histidinemia, *J.-Lancet*, **85**, 241–6   [217]
BERRY, H. K., and WRIGHT, S. (1967) Conference on treatment of phenylketonuria, Special article, *J. Pediat.*, **70**, 142–7.   [206]
BESSMAN, S. P. (1966) Legislation and advances in medical knowledge—acceleration or inhibition?, *J. Pediat.*, **69**, 334–8.   [206]
BICKERS, D. S., and ADAMS, R. D. (1949) Hereditary stenosis of the aqueduct of sylvius as a cause of congenital hydrocephalus, *Brain*, **72**, 246–62.   [293]
BIELSCHOWSKY, M. (1913) Über spätinfantile familiäre amaurotische Idiotie mit Kleinhirnsymptonen, *Dtsch. Z. Nervenheilk*, **50**, 7–29.   [258]
BIELSCHOWSKY, M., and GALLUS, K. (1913) Über tuberöse Sklerose, *J. Psychol. Neurol. (Lpz.)*, **20**, 1–88.   [276]
BISHOP, P. M. F. (1958) Discussion, in *Symposium on Nuclear Sex*, ed. Smith, D. R., and Davidson, W. M., New York.   [318]
BITTENBENDER, J. B., and QUADFASEL, F. A. (1962) Rigid and akinetic forms of Huntington's chorea, *Arch. Neurol. (Chic.)*, **7**, 275–88.   [137]
BLANK, C. E. (1960) Apert's syndrome (a type of acrocephalosyndactyly)—observations on a British series of thirty-nine cases, *Ann. hum. Genet.*, **24**, 151–64.   [285]
BLATTNER, R. J. (1965) Inborn errors of metabolism: a variant of maple syrup urine disease, *J. Pediat.*, **66**, 139–42.   [213]
BLEHOVÁ, B., HRUBCOVÁ, M., and BARTOŇOVÁ, M. (1963) (Quoted by Perry, Tischler, and Chapple, 1966) Psychické zátěže v rodinách fenylketonuriku, *Cs. Pediat.*, **18**, 701–6.   [210]
BLEULER, MANFRED (1955) Familial and personal background of chronic alcoholics, in *Etiology of Chronic Alcoholism*, ed. Diethelm, O., Springfield, Ill.   [111–13]
BLEULER, MANFRED (1963) Conception of schizophrenia within the last fifty years and today, *Proc. roy. Soc. Med.*, **56**, 945–52.   [45]
BLEULER, M., and WIEDEMANN, H.-R. (1956) Chromosomengeschlecht und Psychosexualität, *Arch. Psychiat. Nervenkr.*, **195**, 14–19.   [120]
BLUMENTHAL, MONICA D. (1967) Mental illness in parents of phenylketonuric children, *J. psychiat. Res.*, **5**, 59–74.   [210]
BOGAERT, L. VAN (1935) Les dysplasies neuro-ectodermiques congénitales, *Rev. neurol.*, **63**, 353–98.   [292]
BOGAERT, L. VAN (1936) L'hérédité hétérophène et sa valeur nosographique, *Bull. Acad. Méd. Belg.*, Series 6, **1**, 9–16.   [287]
BOGAERT, L. VAN, MAERE, M., and DE SMEDT, E. (1940) Sur les formes familiales précoces de la maladie d'Alzheimer, *Mschr. Psychiat. Neurol.*, **102**, 249–301.   [152]
BOGAERT, L. VAN, SCHERER, H. J., and EPSTEIN, E. (1937) *Une Forme Cérébrale de la Cholinestérinose Généralisée*, Paris.   [253]
BOLANDE, R. P. (1963) The nature of the connective tissue abiotrophy in the Marfan syndrome, *Lab. Invest.*, **12**, 1087–93.   [226]
BÖÖK, J. A. (1949) Inherited mental deficiency with spastic diplegia, *Commun. Inst. Genet., Univ. Lund*, No. 3.   [290]
BÖÖK, J. A. (1953) A genetic and neuropsychiatric investigation of a North-Swedish population, with special regard to schizophrenia and mental deficiency, *Acta genet. (Basel)*, **4**, 1–100; 345–414.   [14, 57–8]

BÖÖK, J. A., SCHUT, J. W., and REED, S. C. (1953) A clinical and genetical study of microcephaly, *Amer. J. ment. Defic.*, **57**, 637–60. [289]

BORBERG, A. (1951) Clinical and genetic investigations into tuberous sclerosis and Recklinghausen's neurofibromatosis: contribution to elucidation of interrelationship and eugenics of the syndromes, *Acta psychiat. scand.*, **23**, Suppl. 71. [281]

BORGHI, A., GIUSTI, G., and BIGOZZI, U. (1954) Nanismo degenerativo tipo di Amsterdam (Typus Amstelodamensis—malattia di Cornelia de Lange). Presentazione di un caso e considerazioni di ordine genetico, *Acta Genet. med. (Roma)*, **3**, 365–72. [296]

BORGSTRÖM, C. A. (1939) Eine Serie von kriminellen Zwillingen, *Arch. Rassen- und Gesellschaftsbiologie*, **33**, 334–43. [114]

BORRI, P. F., HOOGHWINKEL, G. J. M., and BRUYN, G. W. (1966) Biochemical studies in Huntington's chorea. Part 4. The fatty acid composition of plasma and erythrocyte lipids, *Psychiat. Neurol. Neurochir. (Amst.)*, **69**, 143–8. [141]

BORRI, P. F., OP DEN VELDE, W. M., HOOGHWINKEL, G. J. M., and BRUYN, G. W. (1967) Biochemical studies in Huntington's chorea. VI. Composition of striatal neutral lipids, phospholipids, glycolipids, fatty acids and amino acids, *Neurology (Minneap.)*, **17**, 172–8. [140]

BOURNEVILLE, D. M. (1880) Sclérose tubereuse des circonvolutions cérébrales; idiotie et épilepsie hémiplegique, *Arch. Neurol. (Paris)*, **1**, 81–91. [275]

BOWER, E. M., SHELLHAMER, T. A., and DAILY, J. M. (1960) School characteristics of male adolescents who later became schizophrenic, *Amer. J. Orthopsychiat.*, **30**, 712–29. [39]

BRAILSFORD, J. F. (1929) Chondro-osteo-dystrophy. Roentgenographic and clinical features of a child with dislocation of vertebrae, *Amer. J. Surg.*, **7**, 404–10. [271]

BRAIN, W. RUSSELL (1951) *Diseases of the Nervous System*, 4th ed., London. [160]

BRANTE, G. (1952) Gargoylism—a mucopolysaccharidosis, *Scand. J. clin. Lab. Invest.*, **4**, 43–6.

BRAY, P. F., WISER, W. C., WOOD, M. C., and PUSEY, S. B. (1965) Hereditary characteristics of familial temporal-central focal epilepsy, *Pediatrics*, **36**, 207–11. [167]

BRENTON, D. P., CUSWORTH, D. C., DENT, C. E., and JONES, E. E. (1966) Homocystinuria. Clinical and dietary studies, *Quart. J. Med.*, **35**, 325–46. [223]

BRENTON, D. P., Cusworth, D. C., and GAULL, G. E. (1965a) Homocystinuria. Biochemical studies of tissues including a comparison with cystathioninuria, *Pediatrics*, **35**, 50–6. [222]

BRENTON, D. P., CUSWORTH, D. C., and GAULL, G. E. (1965b) Homocystinuria. Metabolic studies on 3 patients, *J. Pediat.*, **67**, 58–68. [222–3]

BRIQUET, R. (1952) Do fator genetico do mongoloidismo, *J. bras. Psiquiat.*, **1**, 388–97. [327]

BRORSON, L. O., FREDGA, K., HULTQUIST, G. T., and LUNDBERG, P. O. (1961) Tuberous sclerosis in a mother and her newborn son, *Acta paediat. (Uppsala)*, **50**, 522–8. [278]

BROWN, F. W. (1942) Heredity in the psychoneuroses, *Proc. roy. Soc. Med.*, **35**, 785–90. [103]

BROWN, J. C., and JOHNS, R. J. (1967) Nerve conduction in familial dysautonomia (Riley-Day syndrome), *J. Amer. med. Ass.*, **201**, 200–3. [249]

BRUGGER, C. (1927) Die erbbiologische Stellung der Pfropfschizophrenie, *Z. ges. Neurol. Psychiat.*, **113**, 348–78. [22]

BRUYN, G. W. (1966) Biochemical studies in Huntington's chorea. Part 3. Aminoacids in serum and urine, *Psychiat. Neurol. Neurochir. (Amst.)*, **69**, 139–42. [140]

BRUYN, G. W., and LEQUIN, R. M. (1964) Huntington's chorea, *Lancet*, ii, 1300. [141–3]

BRUYN, G. W., MINK, C. J. K., and CALJÉ, J. F. (1965) Biochemical studies in Hunting-ton's chorea. Part I. Erythrocyte magnesium, *Neurology (Minneap.)*, **15**, 455–61.
[140]

BUCCI, L. (1963) A familial organic psychosis of Alzheimer type in six kinship of three generations, *Amer. J. Psychiat.*, **119**, 863–6.
[152]

BÜRGER, M. (1957) *Altern und Krankheit*, Leipzig.
[125]

BURKS, B. S. (1928) The relative influence of nature and nurture upon mental develop-ment, *National Society for the Study of Education, 27th Yearbook*, Part I, Bloomington.
[197]

BURT, C. (1958) The inheritance of mental ability, *Amer. Psychol.*, **13**, 1–15.
[200]

BURT, C. (1963) Is intelligence distributed normally?, *Brit. J. statist. Psychol.*, xvi, 175–90.
[191]

BURT, C. (1966) The genetic determination of differences in intelligence: a study of monozygotic twins reared together and apart, *Brit. J. Psychol.*, **57**, 137–53.
[198]

BURT, C. (1969) Personal communication.
[188, 193–4]

BURT, C., and HOWARD, M. (1956) The multifactorial theory of inheritance and its application to intelligence, *Brit. J. statist. Psychol.*, **9**, 95–131.
[195]

BYERS, R. K., and DODGE, J. A. (1967) Huntington's chorea in children, *Neurology (Minneap.)*, **17**, 587–96.
[137]

CAINE, T. M. (1970) Personality and illness, in *The Psychological Assessment of Mental and Physical Handicaps*, ed. Mittler, P., London.
[94]

CARSON, N. A. J., DENT, C. E., FIELD, C. M. B., and GAULL, G. E. (1965) Homo-cystinuria. Clinical and pathological review of ten cases, *J. Pediat.*, **66**, 565–83.
[221]

CARSON, N. A. J., and NEILL, D. W. (1962) Metabolic abnormalities detected in a survey of mentally backward individuals in Northern Ireland, *Arch. Dis. Childh.*, **37**, 505–13.
[229]

CARTER, C. O. (1958) A life-table for mongols with the causes of death, *J. ment. Defic. Res.*, **2**, 64–74.
[335]

CARTER, C. O. (1965) The inheritance of common congenital malformations, in *Progress in Medical Genetics*, Vol. IV, ed. Steinberg, A. G., and Bearn, A. G., London.
[46]

CARTER, C. O. (1969) Genetics of common disorders, *Brit. med. Bull.*, **25**, 52–7. [90]

CARTER, C. O., and EVANS, K. A. (1961) Risk of parents who have had one child with Down's syndrome (mongolism) having another child similarly affected, *Lancet*, ii, 785–7.
[333]

CARTER, C. O., and MACCARTHY, D. (1951) Incidence of mongolism and its diagnosis in the newborn, *Brit. J. soc. Med.*, **5**, 83–90.
[324, 333]

CARTER, C. O., and WOOLF, L. I. (1961) The birthplaces of parents and grandparents of a series of patients with phenylketonuria in south-east England, *Ann. hum. Genet.*, **25**, 57–64.
[208]

CASEY, M. D., BLANK, C. E., STREET, D. R. K., SEGALL, L. J., McDOUGALL, J. H., McGRATH, P. J., and SKINNER, J. L. (1966) YY chromosomes and antisocial behaviour, *Lancet*, ii, 859–60.
[302, 322]

CASEY, M. D., SEGALL, L. J., STREET, D. R. K., and BLANK, C. E. (1966) Sex chromo-some abnormalities in two state hospitals for patients requiring special security, *Nature (Lond.)*, **209**, 641–2.
[302, 322]

CATEL, W., and SCHMIDT, J. (1959) Über familiäre gichtische Diathese in Verbindung mit zerebralen und renalen Symptomen bei einem Kleinkind, *Dtsch. med. Wschr.*, **84**, 2145–7.
[245, 247]

CATTELL, R. B. (1953) Research designs in psychological genetics with special reference to the multiple variance method, *Amer. J. hum. Genet.*, **5**, 76–93.
[99]

CATTELL, R. B., STICE, G. F., and KRISTY, N. F. (1957) A first approximation to nature-nurture ratios for eleven primary personality factors in objective tests, *J. abnorm. soc. Psychol.*, **54**, 143–59. [100]

CENTERWALL, W. R., CENTERWALL, S. A., ARMON, V., and MANN, L. B. (1961) Phenylketonuria. II. Results of treatment of infants and young children. A report of 10 cases, *J. Pediat.*, **59**, 102–18. [208]

CENTERWALL, W. R., and ITTYERAH, T. R. (1966) Phenylketonuria among the mentally retarded in India, *Lancet*, ii, 193–4. [208]

CENTERWALL, W. R., and NEFF, C. A. (1961) Phenylketonuria—a case report of Jewish ancestry, *Arch. Pediat.*, **78**, 379–84. [207]

CHAMBERS, R. A., and PRATT, R. T. C. (1956) Idiosyncrasy to fructose, *Lancet*, ii, 340. [242]

CHANDLER, J. H. (1966) EEG in prediction of Huntington's chorea: an eighteen year follow-up, *Electroenceph. clin. Neurophysiol.*, **21**, 79–80. [144]

DE LA CHAPELLE, A., and HORTLING, H. (1960) Frekvensen av Klinefelters syndrom och gonadal dysgenesi vid oligophreni, *Nord. Med.*, **63**, 256–8. [320]

CHHUTTANI, P. N., CHOPRA, H. L., and SINGH, S. (1959) Huntington's chorea. A biochemical study, *J. Indian med. Ass.*, **32**, 401–2. [139]

CHRISTODORESCU, D., COLLINO, S., ZELLINGHER, R., and TĂUTU, C. (1970) Psychiatric disturbances in Turner's syndrome, *Psychiat. Clin.*, **3**, 114–24. [310]

COATES, S., NORMAN, A. P., and WOOLF, L. I. (1957) Phenylketonuria with normal intelligence and Gowers' muscular dystrophy, *Arch. Dis. Childh.*, **32**, 313–17. [203]

COCKAYNE, E. A. (1933) *Inherited Abnormalities of the Skin and its Appendages*, London. [287]

COCKAYNE, E. A., KRESTIN, D., and SORSBY, A. (1935) Obesity, hypogenitalism, mental retardation, polydactyly and retinal pigmentation; the Laurence-Moon-Biedl syndrome, *Quart. J. Med.*, n. s. **4**, 93–120. [286]

COHEN, B. E., BODONYI, E., and SZEINBERG, A. (1961) Phenylketonuria in Jews, *Lancet*, i, 344–5. [207, 262]

COHEN B. E., SZEINBERG, A., BIOCHIS, H., POLLACK, S., HIRSCHHORN, N., and BAR-OR, R. (1961) Phenylketonuria among Jews, *Israel Soc. clin. Path*, **9E**, 93. [207, 262]

COHEN, H. (1962) Physiological test findings in adolescents having ovarian dysgenesis, *Psychosom. Med.*, **24**, 249–56. [322]

COHEN, M. E., BADAL, D. W., KILPATRICK, A., REED, E. W., and WHITE, P. D. (1951) The high familial prevalence of neurocirculatory asthenia (anxiety neurosis, effort syndrome), *Amer. J. hum. Genet.*, **3**, 126–58. [103]

COHEN, P., and KOZINN, P. J. (1949) Phenylpyruvic oligophrenia in a Jewish child, *J. Pediat.*, **34**, 76–9. [204, 207]

COLLIER, W. (1895) Case of enlarged spleen in a child aged six, *Trans. path. Soc. Lond.*, **46**, 148–50. [264]

COLLMANN, R. D., and STOLLER, A. (1962) A survey of mongoloid births in Victoria, Australia, 1942–57, *Amer. J. publ. Hlth*, **52**, 813–29. [325–6, 334]

COLLMANN, R. D., and STOLLER, A. (1963) Data on Mongolism in Victoria, Australia. Prevalence and life-expectation, *J. ment. Defic. Res.*, **7**, 60–8. [335]

COLOMBO, J. P., RICHTERICH, R., DONATH, A., SPAHR, A., and ROSSI, E. (1964) Congenital lysine intolerance with periodic ammonia intoxication, *Lancet*, i, 1014–15. [232]

COMFORT, ALEX (1956) *The Biology of Senescence*, London. [122]

COMFORT, ALEX (1963) Mutation, autoimmunity, and ageing, *Lancet*, ii, 138–40. [122]

COMFORT, ALEX (1965) *The Process of Ageing*, London. [122]

CONNELL, P. H. (1958) *Amphetamine Psychosis* (Maudsley Monograph No. 5), London. [45]

CONRAD, H. S., and JONES, H. E. (1940) A second study of familial resemblance in intelligence, *National Society for the Study of Education*, Pt. II, 97–141, Bloomington. [194]

CONRAD, K. (1935) Erbanlage und Epilepsie. I. Untersuchungen an einer Serie von 253 Zwillingspaaren, *Z. ges. Neurol. Psychiat.*, **153**, 271–326. [170–2]

CONRAD, K. (1936a) Erbanlage und Epilepsie. II. Ein Beitrag zur Zwillingskasuistik. Die konkordanten Eineiigen, *Z. ges. Neurol. Psychiat.*, **155**, 254–97. [172]

CONRAD, K. (1936b) Erbanlage und Epilepsie. III. Ein Beitrag zur Zwillingskasuistik. Die diskordanten Eineiigen, *Z. ges. Neurol. Psychiat.*, **155**, 509–42. [172]

CONRAD, K. (1937) Erbanlage und Epilepsie. IV. Ergebnisse einer Nachkommenschaft-suntersuchung an Epileptikern. (Zur empirischen Erbprognose der Epilepsie), *Z. ges. Neurol. Psychiat.*, **159**, 521–81. [174]

CONRAD, K. (1938) Erbanlage und Epilepsie. V. Beitrag zur Frage der 'epileptoiden' Psychopathie, *Z. ges. Neurol. Psychiat.*, **162**, 505–50. [183]

CONRAD, K. (1939) Der Erbkreis der Epilepsie, in *Handbuch der Erbpathologie des Menschen*, Bd. V/2, ed. Just, G., Berlin. [183]

CONSTANTINIDIS, J. (1967) Étude de quelques facteurs épidémiologiques et génétiques de la psychose maniaco-dépressive, *J. Génét. hum.*, **16**, 156–73. [84]

CONSTANTINIDIS, J., GARRONE, G., and DE AJURIAGUERRA, J. (1962) L'hérédité des démences de l'age avancé, *Encéphale*, **51**, 301–44. [151]

CONSTANTINIDIS, J., GARRONE, G., TISSOT, R., and DE AJURIAGUERRA, J. (1965) L'incidence familiale des altérations neurofibrillaires corticales d'Alzheimer, *Psychiat. et Neurol. (Basel)*, **150**, 235–47. [151]

COPPEN, A. (1967) The biochemistry of affective disorders, *Brit. J. Psychiat.*, **113**, 1237–64. [75]

COPPEN, A. (1969) The biochemistry of affective disorders, in *The Future of Brain Sciences*, proceedings of a conference held at the New York Academy of Medicine, May 2–4, 1968, ed. Bogoch, S., New York. [75–6]

COPPEN, A., COWIE, V., and SLATER, E. (1965) Familial aspects of 'neuroticism' and 'extraversion', *Brit. J. Psychiat.*, **111**, 70–83. [101, 104]

CORSELLIS, J. A. N. (1962) *Mental Illness and the Ageing Brain*, Maudsley Monograph No. 9, London. [127]

CORYELL, M. E., HALL, W. K., THEVAOS, T. G., WELTER, D. A., GATZ, A. J., HORTON, B. F., SISSON, B. D., LOOPER, J. W., and FARROW, R. T. (1964) A familial study of a human enzyme defect, argininosuccinicaciduria, *Biochem. biophys. Res. Commun.*, **14**, 307–12. [229]

COURT BROWN, W. M. (1962a) in *Cytogenetics in Medicine*, R.C.P.E., No. 18. [297]

COURT BROWN, W. M. (1962b) Sex chromosomes and the law, *Lancet*, ii, 508–9. [307, 309]

COURT BROWN, W. M., HARNDEN, D. G., JACOBS, P. A., MACLEAN, N., and MANTLE, D. J. (1964) Abnormalities of the sex chromosome complement in man, *Spec. Rep. Ser. med. Res. Coun. (Lond.)*, No. 305. [305, 319–21]

COURT BROWN, W. M., JACOBS, P. A., BUCKTON, K. E., TOUGH, I. M., KUENSSBERGE, E. V., and KNOX, J. D. E. (1966) *Chromosome Studies on Adults. Eugenics Laboratory Memoirs XLII*, London. [123]

COURVILLE, C. B., NUSBAUM, R. E., and BUTT, E. M. (1963) Changes in trace metals in brain in Huntington's chorea, *Arch. Neurol. (Chic.)*, **8**, 481–9. [139]

COWIE, J., COWIE, V., and SLATER, E. (1968) *Delinquency in Girls*, London. [117]

COWIE, J., and KAHN, J. (1968) The XYY constitution in a pre-pubertal child, *Brit. med. J.*, **1**, 748–9. [301–2, 322]

COWIE, V. A. (1951a) Phenylpyruvic oligophrenia, *J. ment. Sci.*, **97**, 505. [203, 210]

COWIE, V. (1951b) An atypical case of phenylketonuria, *Lancet*, i, 272. [203–4]

COWIE, V. (1960) The genetics and sub-classification of microcephaly, *J. ment. Defic. Res.*, **4**, 42–7.   [287]

COWIE, V. (1961) The incidence of neurosis in the children of psychotics, *Acta psychiat. scand.*, **37**, 37–87.   [192–3]

COWIE, V. (1969) Serum protein changes (particularly gamma globulins) in Hunting-ton's chorea, *Proc. Second Internat. Cong. Neuro-Genetics and Neuro-Ophthalmology of the World Federation of Neroulogy* (Montreal).   [142]

COWIE, V. (1970) *A Study of the Early Development of Mongols*, Oxford.   [335]

COWIE, V., COPPEN, A., and NORMAN, P. (1960) Nuclear sex and body-build in schizo-phrenia, *Brit. med. J.*, **2**, 431–3.

COWIE, V., and GAMMACK, D. B. (1966) Serum proteins in Huntington's chorea, *Brit. J. Psychiat.*, **112**, 723–6.   [142]

COWIE, V. A., and PENROSE, L. S. (1951) Dilution of hair colour in phenylketonuria, *Ann. Eugen. (Lond.)*, **15**, 297–301.   [205]

COWIE, V., and SEAKINS, J. W. T. (1962) Urinary alanine excretor in a Huntington's chorea family, *J. ment. Sci.*, **108**, 427–31.   [141]

CRAIG, J. M., CLARKE, J. T., and BANKER, B. Q. (1959) Metabolic neuro-visceral disorder with accumulation of unidentified substance: a variant of Hurler's syndrome?, *Amer. J. Dis. Child.*, **98**, 577.   [258]

CRAWFURD, M. D'A. (1961) Multiple congenital anomaly associated with an extra autosome, *Lancet*, ii, 22–4.

CRESSERI, A. (1948) l'Ereditarietà della Demenza Senile, *Boll. Soc. ital. Biol. sper.*, **24**, 200–1.   [132]

CRITCHLEY, M., and EARL, C. J. C. (1932) Tuberose sclerosis and allied conditions, *Brain*, **55**, 311–46.   [276, 279]

CRITCHLEY, M., and WILLIAMS, D. (1939) Identical twins, one suffering from petit mal, both with abnormal electroencephalograms, *Proc. roy. Soc. Med.*, **32**, 1417.   [166]

CROME, L. (1957) as quoted in *Mental Deficiency* by Hilliard, L. T., and Kirman, B. H., at numerous places, London.   [257, 263]

CROME, L. (1962a) The association of phenylketonuria with leucodystrophy, *J. Neurol. Neurosurg. Psychiat.*, **25**, 149–53.   [205–6]

CROME, L. (1962b) A case of galactosaemia with the pathological and neuropatho-logical findings, *Arch. Dis. Childh.*, **37**, 415–21.   [240]

CROME, L., DUCKETT, S., and FRANKLIN, A. W. (1963) Congenital cataracts, renal tubular necrosis, and encephalopathy in two sisters, *Arch. Dis. Childh.*, **38**, 505–15.   [236]

CROME, L., DUTTON, G., and ROSS, C. F. (1961) Maple syrup urine disease, *J. Path. Bact.*, **81**, 379–84.   [213]

CROME, L., and PARE, C. M. B. (1960) Phenylketonuria: a review and a report of the pathological findings in four cases, *J. ment. Sci.*, **106**, 862–83.   [205]

CROME, L., and STERN, J. (1967) *Pathology of Mental Retardation*, London. [153, 201–2, 218, 227–8, 230–2, 235–6, 243, 246, 251, 257, 263, 266–7, 272, 279, 282, 293]

CROME, L., TYMMS, V., and WOOLF, L. I. (1962) A chemical investigation of the defects of myelination in phenylketonuria, *J. Neurol. Neurosurg. Psychiat.*, **25**, 143–8.   [205]

CROOKSHANK, F. G. (1924) *The Mongol in our Midst*, London.   [325]

CUMINGS, J. N. (1964) Metabolic diseases of the nervous system, in *Diseases of Metabolism*, 5th ed., ed. Duncan, G. C., Philadelphia.   [266]

CUSWORTH, D. C., DENT, C. E., and FLYNN, F. V. (1955) The amino-aciduria in galactosemia, *Arch. Dis. Childh.*, **30**, 150–4.   [237]

DAMERON, L. E. (1963) Development of intelligence of infants with mongolism, *Child Develop.*, **34**, 733–8.   [336]

DANCIS, J., HUTZLER, J., and LEVITZ, M. (1965) Detection of the heterozygote in maple syrup urine disease, *J. Pediat.*, **66**, 595–603. [214]

DANCIS, J., HUTZLER, J., TADA, K., WADA, Y., MORIKAWA, T., and ARAKAWA, T. (1967) Hypervalinemia: a defect in valine transamination, *Pediatrics*, **39**, 813–17. [216]

DANCIS, J., LEVITZ, M., MILLER, S., and WESTALL, R. G. (1959) Maple syrup urine disease, *Brit. med. J.*, **1**, 91–3. [213]

DANES, B. S., and BEARN, A. G. (1967) Cellular metachromasia, a genetic marker for studying the mucopolysaccharidoses, *Lancet*, i, 241–3. [273]

DARKE, R. A. (1948) Heredity as an etiological factor in homosexuality, *J. nerv. ment. Dis.*, **107**, 251–68. [316]

DARLINGTON, C. D. (1954) Heredity and environment, *Caryologia* 6 (Suppl.) (Proc. IXth Conf. Genet.), 370–81. [346]

DAVIDSON, W. M. (1958) Discussion, in *Symposium on Nuclear Sex*, ed. Smith D. R., and Davidson, W. M., p. 91, New York. [318]

DAVIDSON, W. M., and SMITH, D. R. (1954) A morphological sex difference in the polymorphonuclear neutrophil leucocytes, *Brit. med. J.*, **2**, 6–7. [298]

DAVIDSON, W. M., and WINN, S. (1959) The relationship between genetic, nuclear and social sex, *Postgrad. med. J.*, **35**, 494–500. [318]

DAVIES, H. E., and ROBINSON, M. J. (1963) A case of histidinaemia, *Arch. Dis. Childh.*, **38**, 80–2. [218]

DAVIS, H., and DAVIS, P. A. (1936) Action potentials of the brain in normal persons and in normal states of cerebral activity, *Arch. Neurol. Psychiat. (Chic.)*, **36**, 1214–24. [162]

DAVISON, K., and BAGLEY, C. R. (1969) Schizophrenia-like psychoses associated with organic disorders of the central nervous system: a review of the literature, in *Current Problems in Neuropsychiatry: Schizophrenia, Epilepsy, the Temporal Lobe*, ed. Herrington, R. N., Ashford, Kent. [29–30, 54, 153]

DAX, E. C. (1941) Arachnodactyly (dolichosténomélie of Marfan), *J. ment. Sci.*, **87**, 434–8. [225, 227]

DEIWICK, H. J., and OEPEN, H. (1964) Hauptkettenenzyme in Serum bei Huntingtonscher Chorea, *Hum. Genet.*, **1**, 103–4. [141]

DELBRÜCK, A., and OEPEN, H. (1964) Mucopolysaccharidstoffwechsel bei Huntingtonscher Chorea, *Hum. Genet.*, **1**, 105–6. [141]

DENT, C. E. (1954) The renal amino-acidurias, *Exp. Med. Surg.*, **12**, 229–32. [235]

DENT, C. E. (1964) Personal communication. [238]

DENT, C. E., and WESTALL, R. G. (1961) Studies in maple syrup urine disease, *Arch. Dis. Childh.*, **36**, 259–68. [213]

DIENST, H., and HAMPERL, H. (1927) Über einen Fall von lipoidzelliger Splenohepatomegalie vom Typus Niemann-Pick, *Wien. klin. Wschr.*, **40**, 1432–3. [253]

DODGE, J. A. (1965) De Lange's Amsterdam dwarfs syndrome: a case report, *Develop. Med. Child Neurol.*, **7**, 31–4.

DODGE, P. R. (1966) Disordered uric acid metabolism and neurologic abnormalities, *Develop. Med. Child Neurol.*, **8**, 89–91. [246]

DOOSE, H., GERKEN, H., PETERSEN, C. E., and VÖLZKE, E. (1967) Electroencephalography of epileptic children's siblings, *Lancet*, i, 578–9. [166]

DORMANDY, T. L., and PORTER, R. J. (1961) Familial fructose and galactose intolerance, *Lancet*, i, 1189–94. [242–3]

DRIESSEN, O. A. (1953) De l'identité de la maladie de Tay-Sachs et de Niemann-Pick, *Acta paediat. Uppsala.*, **42**, 447–52. [257]

DRILLIEN, C. M. (1961) A longitudinal study of the growth and development of prematurely and maturely born children, *Arch. Dis. Childh.*, **36**, 1–10 (quoted by Koch, R., Share, J., Webb, A., and Graliker, B. V., 1963). [337]

DUMERMUTH, G. (1961) EEG-Untersuchungen beim jugendlichen Klinefelter-Syndrom, *Helv. paediat. Acta*, **16**, 702–10.   [309, 313]

DUNSDON, M. I., CARTER, C. O., and HUNTLEY, R. M. C. (1960) Upper-end of range of intelligence in mongolism, *Lancet*, i, 565–8.   [336]

DUNSDON, M. I., and ROBERTS, J. A. FRASER (1957) A study of the performance of 2,000 children on four vocabulary tests. II. Norms with some observations on the relative variability of boys and girls, *Brit. J. Statist. Psychol.*, **10**, 1–16.   [192]

DUPONT, A., and CLAUSEN, J. (1968) The elfin-face syndrome, *Lancet*, i, 209.   [245]

DURLING, D., and BENDA, C. E. (1952) Mental growth curves in untreated institutionalized mongoloid patients, *Amer. J. ment. Defic.*, **56**, 578–88.   [337]

DUVOISIN, R. C., and VINSON, W. M. (1961) Tuberous sclerosis: report of three cases without mental defect, *J. Amer. med. Ass.*, **175**, 869–73.   [279]

EDGAR, G. W. F. (1963) Progressive myoclonus epilepsy as an inborn error of metabolism comparable to storage disease, *Epilepsia (Amst.)*, **4**, 120–37.   [170]

EDWARDS, J. H. (1960) The simulation of Mendelism, *Acta genet. (Basel)*, **10**, 63–70.
                                                                               [46–7, 55]

EDWARDS, J. H. (1961) The syndrome of sex-linked hydrocephalus, *Arch. Dis. Childh.*, **36**, 486–93.   [293]

EDWARDS, J. H. (1963) The genetic basis of common disease, *Amer. J. Med.*, **34**, 627–38.
                                                                               [46–7, 55]

EDWARDS, J. H., DENT, TESSA, and KAHN, J. (1966) Monozygotic twins of different sex, *J. med. Genet.*, **3**, 117–23.   [345]

EDWARDS, J. H., HARNDEN, D. G., CAMERON, A. H., CROSSE, V. M., and WOLFF, O. H. (1960) A new trisomic syndrome, *Lancet*, i, 787–9.   [338–40]

EDWARDS, J. H., NORMAN, R. M., and ROBERTS, J. M. (1961) Sex-linked hydrocephalus, *Arch. Dis. Childh.*, **36**, 481–5.   [293]

EFRON, M. (1965a) Amino-aciduria (Parts I and II), *New Engl. J. Med.*, **272**, 1058–67 and 1107–13.   [216]

EFRON, M. (1965b) Familial hyperprolinemia. Report of a second case, associated with congenital renal malformations, hereditary hematuria and mild mental retardation, with demonstration of an enzyme defect, *New Engl. J. Med.*, **272**, 1243–54.
                                                                               [218–20]

EFRON, M. (1966) Diseases of the urea cycle, in *The Metabolic Basis of Inherited Disease*, ed. Stanbury, J. B., Wyngaarden, J. B., and Fredrickson, D. S., 2nd ed., New York.   [231]

EFRON, M. L. (1967a) Isovaleric acidemia, *Amer. J. Dis. Child.*, **113**, 74–6.   [215]

EFRON, M. L. (1967b) Treatment of hydroxyprolinemia and hyperprolinemia, *Amer. J. Dis. Child.*, **113**, 166–9.   [220]

EFRON, M. L., BIXBY, E. M., and PRYLES, C. V. (1965) Hydroxyprolinemia. II. A rare metabolic disease due to a deficiency of the enzyme 'Hydroxyproline oxidase', *New Engl. J. Med.*, **272**, 1299–1309.   [220]

ELDJARN, L., TRY, K., STOKKE, O., MUNTHE-KAAS, A. W., REFSUM, S., STEINBERG, D., AVIGAN, J., and MIZE, C. (1966) Dietary effects on serum-phytanic-acid levels and on clinical manifestations in heredopathia atactica polyneuritiformis, *Lancet*, i, 691–3.
                                                                               [250–1]

ELSÄSSER, G. (1952) *Die Nachkommen geisteskranker Elternpaare*, Stuttgart.   [24]

ELSTON, R. C., and GOTTESMAN, I. I. (1968) The analysis of quantitative inheritance simultaneously from twin and family data, *Amer. J. hum. Genet.*, **20**, 512–21. [100]

EMERY, F. A., GOLDIE, L., and STERN, J. (1968) Hyperprolinaemia type 2, *J. ment. Defic. Res.*, **12**, 187–95.   [220]

ENGLER, M. (1952) A comparative study of the causation of mongolism, peristatic amentia, and other types of mental defect, *J. ment. Sci.*, **98**, 316–25.   [327]

ENTRES, J. L. (1921) Über Huntingtonscher Chorea, *Z. ges. Neurol. Psychiat.*, **73**, 541–51. [143]

ENTWISTLE, C., and SIM, M. (1961) Tuberous sclerosis and fetishism, *Brit. med. J.*, **2**, 1688–9. [279]

EPILEPSIA (1969) Symposium on Epilepsy and Heredity held at the Meeting of the French League against Epilepsy, Paris, 3 Oct. 1967, *Epilepsia (Amst.)*, **10**, No. 1. [174]

ERLENMEYER-KIMLING, L. (1968) Mortality rates in the offspring of schizophrenic parents and a physiological advantage hypothesis, *Nature (Lond.)*, **220**, 798–800. [70]

ERLENMEYER-KIMLING, L., and JARVIK, L. F. (1963) Genetics and intelligence: a review, *Science*, **142**, 1477–9. [192]

ERLENMEYER-KIMLING, L., and PARADOWSKI, W. (1966) Selection and schizophrenia, *Amer. Naturalist*, **100**, 651–65. [67]

ESSEN-MÖLLER, E. (1941) Psychiatrische Untersuchungen an einer Serie von Zwillingen, *Acta psychiat. scand.*, Suppl. 23. [17–18, 20]

ESSEN-MÖLLER, E. (1946) A family with Alzheimer's disease, *Acta psychiat. scand.*, **21**, 233–44. [152]

ESSEN-MÖLLER, E. (1955) The calculation of morbid risk in parents of index cases, as applied to a family sample of schizophrenics, *Acta genet. (Basel)*, **5**, 334–42. [15]

ESSEN-MÖLLER, E. (1963) Über die Schizophreniehäufigkeit bei Müttern von Schizophrenen, *Schweiz. Arch. Neurol. Psychiat.*, **91**, 260–6. [15, 40]

ESTES, J. W., CAREY, R. J., and DESAI, R. G. (1965) Marfan's syndrome. Haematological abnormalities in a family, *Arch. intern. Med.*, **116**, 889–93. [226]

EYSENCK, H. J. (1968) Genetics and personality, in *Genetic and Environmental Influences on Behaviour*, ed. Thoday, J. M., and Parkes, A. S., Edinburgh. [101]

FALCONER, D. S. (1965) The inheritance of liability to certain diseases, estimated from the incidence among relatives, *Ann. hum. Genet.*, **29**, 51–76. [48–50]

FALCONER, D. S. (1967) The inheritance of liability to diseases with variable age of onset, with particular reference to diabetes mellitus, *Ann. hum. Genet.*, **31**, 1–20. [51–3]

FALCONER, D. S. (1970) Personal communication. [51]

FALEK, A., SCHMIDT, R., and JERVIS, G. A. (1966) Familial de Lange syndrome with chromosome abnormalities, *Pediatrics*, **37**, 92–101. [295]

FARBER, S., COHEN, J., and UZMAN, L. L. (1957) Lipogranulomatosis: a new lipo-glyco-protein 'storage' disease, *J. Mt Sinai Hosp.*, **24**, 816–37. [254]

FELDMAN, R. G., CHANDLER, K. A., LEVY, L. L., and GLASER, G. H. (1963) Familial Alzheimer's disease, *Neurology (Minneap.)*, **13**, 811–24. [152]

FELLERS, F. X., and SCHWARTZ, R. (1958) Etiology of the severe form of idiopathic hypercalcemia of infancy. A defect in vitamin D metabolism, *New Engl. J. Med.*, **259**, 1050–8. [244]

FERGUSON-SMITH, M. A. (1959) The prepubertal testicular lesion in chromatin-positive Klinefelter's syndrome (primary micro-orchidism) as seen in mentally-handicapped children, *Lancet*, i, 219–22. [320]

FERGUSON-SMITH, M. A. (1962) Sex chromatin anomalies in mentally defective individuals, *Acta cytol. (Philad.)*, **6**, 73–83. [319]

FERGUSON-SMITH, M. A. (1965) Karyotype-phenotype correlations in gonadal dysgenesis and their bearing on the pathogenesis of malformations, *J. med. Genet.*, **2**, 142–55. [305]

FERGUSON-SMITH, M. A. (1969) Personal communication. [340, 344]

FERGUSON-SMITH, M. A., LENNOX, B., MACK, W. S., and STEWART, J. S. S. (1957) Klinefelter's syndrome: frequency and testicular morphology in relation to nuclear sex, *Lancet*, ii, 167–9. [300]

FEUCHTWANGER, E., and MAYER-GROSS, W. (1938) Hirnverletzung und Schizophrenie, *Schweiz. Arch. Neurol. Psychiat.*, **41**, 17–99. [28]

FIELD, C. M. B., CARSON, N. A. J., CUSWORTH, D. C., DENT, C. E., and NEILL, D. W. (1962) Homocystinuria. A new disorder of metabolism, *Abstr. Xth Internat. Congr. Pediat.*, Lisbon, p. 274. [221]

FINNEY, D. J. (1940) The detection of linkage, *Ann. Eugen. (Lond.)*, **10**, 171–214. [212]

FISCH, R. O., SINES, L. K., TORRES, F., and ANDERSON, J. A. (1965) Studies on families of phenylketonurics: observations on intelligence and electroencephalographic changes, *Amer. J. Dis. Child.*, **109**, 427–31. [211]

FISCHER, M., HARVALD, B., and HAUGE, M. (1969) A Danish twin study of schizophrenia, *Brit. J. Psychiat.*, **115**, 981–90. [17, 19–20]

FLEMING, L. W., BARKER, M. G., and STEWART, W. K. (1967) Plasma and erythrocyte magnesium in Huntington's chorea, *J. Neurol. Neurosurg. Psychiat.*, **30**, 374–8. [140]

FOGELSON, M. H., RORKE, L. B., and KAYE, R. (1967) Spinal cord changes in familial dysautonomia, *Arch. Neurol. (Chic.)*, **17**, 103–8. [249]

FÖLLING, A. (1934) Utskillelse av fenylpyrodruesyne i urinen som stoffskifteanomali i forbindelse med imbecillitet, *Nord. med. T.*, **8**, 1054–9. [203]

DA FONSECA, A. F. (1959) *Análise Heredo-Clínica das Perturbações Afectivas*, Faculdade de Medicina, Oporto. [84]

FORD, C. E., JONES, K. W., POLANI, P. E., DE ALMEIDA, J. C., and BRIGGS, J. H. (1959) A sex-chromosome anomaly in a case of gonadal dysgenesis (Turner's syndrome), *Lancet*, i, 711–13. [304]

FORSSMAN, H. (1967) Epilepsy in an XYY man, *Lancet*, i, 1389. [302]

FORSSMAN, H., and ÅKESSON, H. O. (1965) Mortality in patients with Down's syndrome, *J. ment. Defic. Res.*, **9**, 146–9. [335]

FORSSMAN, H., and HAMBERT, G. (1963) Incidence of Klinefelter's syndrome among mental patients, *Lancet*, i, 1327. [308]

FORSYTH, C. C., LLOYD, J. K., and FOSBROOKE, A. S. (1965) A-β-lipoproteinaemia, *Arch. Dis. Childh.*, **40**, 47–52. [248]

FOULDS, G. A. (1965) *Personality and Personal Illness*, London. [94]

FOULDS, G. A. (1971) Personality deviance and personal symptomatology, *Psychol. Med.* (in the press) [94]

FRACCARO, M., IKKOS, D., LINDSTEN, J., LUFT, R., and KAIJSER, K. (1960) A new type of chromosomal abnormality in gonadal dysgenesis, *Lancet*, ii, 1144. [297]

FRANCESCHETTI, A., KLEIN, D., FORNI, S., and BABEL, J. (1951) The tapeto-retinal degenerations and corneal dystrophies, *Acta 16th Internat. Congr. Ophthalmol. London*, July 1950, B.M.A. [259, 261, 286]

FRASER, J. H., CAMPBELL, J., MacGILLIVRAY, R. C., BOYD, F., and LENNOX, B. (1960) The XXX syndrome frequency among mental defectives and fertility, *Lancet*, ii, 626–7. [321]

FROESCH, E. R., PRADER, A., LABHART, A., STUBER, H. W., and WOLF, H. P. (1957) Die hereditäre Fructoseintoleranz, eine bisher nicht bekannte kongenitale Stoffwechselstörung, *Schweiz. med. Wschr.*, **87**, 1168–71. [242–3]

FROESCH, E. R., PRADER, A., WOLF, H. P., and LABHART, A. (1959) Die hereditäre Fructoseintoleranz, *Helv. paediat. Acta*, **14**, 99–112. [243]

FULLER, J. L., and THOMPSON, W. R. (1960) *Behavior Genetics*, New York. [100]

GALTON, F. (1869) *Hereditary Genius*, London. [188]

GARROD, A. E. (1908) Croonian lectures on inborn errors of metabolism, *Lancet*, ii, 1–7, 73–9, 142–8, 214–20. [201]

GAUCHER, P. C. E. (1882) *De l'Épiéthéliome Primitif de la Rate*, Paris, Thèse. [264]

GAULL, G., and GAITONDE, M. K. (1966) Homocystinuria. An observation on the inheritance of cysthionine synthase deficiency, *J. med. Genet.*, **3**, 194–7. [222]

GEDDES, A. K., and MOORE, S. (1953) Acute (infantile) Gaucher's disease; report of a case, the second in a family, *J. Pediat.*, **43**, 61–6.   [265]

VAN GEMUND, J. J., and VAN GELDEREN, H. H. (1961) Gonadale dysgenesie bij Kinderen, *Ned. T. Geneesk*, **105**, 1678–83.   [322]

GERMAN, J., LEJEUNE, J., MACINTYRE, M. N., and DE GROUCHY, J. (1964) Chromosomal autoradiography in the cri du chat syndrome, *Cytogenetics*, **3**, 347–52.   [341]

GESELL, A., and AMATRUDA, C. S. (1941) *Developmental Diagnosis*, New York (quoted by Koch, R., Share, J., Webb, A., and Graliker, B. V., 1963).   [337]

GHADIMI, H., PARTINGTON, M. W., and HUNTER, A. (1961) A familial disturbance of histidine metabolism, *New Engl. J. Med.*, **265**, 221–4.   [216]

GIBBONS, J. L. (1968) Biochemistry of depressive illness, in *Recent Developments in Affective Disorders. A Symposium*, ed. Coppen, A., and Walk, A., Ashford, Kent.
                    [75]

GIBSON, D., and FRANK, H. F. (1961) Dimensions of mongolism. I. Age limits for cardinal mongol stigmata, *Amer. J. ment. Defic.*, **66**, 30–4.   [337]

GIBSON, D., and POZSONYI, J. (1965) Morphological and behavioral consequences of chromosome subtype in mongolism, *Amer. J. ment. Defic.*, **69**, 801–4.   [337]

GILLILAND, I. C. (1952) Chondrolipodystrophy (Gargoylism), *Proc. roy. Soc. Med.*, **45**, 594–6.   [256]

GIORGI, P. L., CECCARELLI, M., and PACI, A. (1965) Su un caso di sindrome del 'cri du chat' con peculiari anomalie fenotipiche, *Minerva pediat.*, **17**, 1972–5.   [343]

GITTELSOHN, A. M., and MILHAM, S. (1965) Observations on twinning in New York State, *Brit. J. prev. soc. Med.*, **19**, 8–17.   [346]

GITZELMANN, R. (1965) Deficiency of erythrocyte galactokinase in a patient with galactose diabetes, *Lancet*, ii, 670–71.   [242]

GLOBUS, J. H., and SELINSKY, H. (1935) Tuberous sclerosis in the infant, *Amer. J. Dis. Child.*, **50**, 954–65.   [278]

GOLDBERG, E. M., and MORRISON, S. L. (1963) Schizophrenia and social class, *Brit. J. Psychiat.*, **109**, 785–802.   [39]

GOLDSCHMIDT, R. (1931) Analysis of intersexuality in the Gipsy-moth, *Quart. Rev Biol.*, **6**, 125–42.   [315]

GOODMAN, N. (1957) Relations between maternal age at parturition and incidence of mental disorders in the offspring, *Brit. J. prev. soc. Med.*, **11**, 203–13.   [15]

GORDON, R. R. (1965) The cri du chat syndrome, *Develop. Med. Child Neurol.*, **7**, 423–5.
                    [344]

GORDON, R. R., and COOKE, P. (1968) Facial appearance in cri du chat syndrome, *Develop. Med. Child Neurol.*, **10**, 69–76.   [343]

GOTTESMAN, I. I. (1962) Differential inheritance of the psychoneuroses, *Eugen. Quart.*, **9**, 223–7.   [98]

GOTTESMAN, I. I. (1963) *Heritability of Personality: A Demonstration*, Psychological Monographs, ed Gimble, G. A., No. 572, Vol. 77, No. 9, 1–21.   [98]

GOTTESMAN, I. I., and SHIELDS, J. (1966a) Schizophrenia in twins: 16 years' consecutive admissions to a psychiatric clinic, *Brit. J. Psychiat.*, **112**, 809–18.   [17]

GOTTESMAN, I. I., and SHIELDS, J. (1966b) Contributions of twin studies to perspectives on schizophrenia, in *Progress in Experimental Personality Research*, ed. Maher, B. A., New York.   [18]

GOTTESMAN, I. I., and SHIELDS, J. (1967) A polygenic theory of schizophrenia, *Proc. nat. Acad. Sci. (Wash.)*, **58**, 199–205.   [55]

GOWERS, W. R. (1906) On tetanoid chorea and its association with cirrhosis of the liver, *Rev. Neurol. Psychiat.*, **4**, 249–58.   [153]

GREENFIELD, J. G., and NEVIN, S. (1933) Amaurotic family idiocy: study of a late infantile case, *Trans. ophthal. Soc. U.K.*, **53**, 170–200.   [258]

GROEN, J. (1948) The hereditary mechanism of Gaucher's disease, *Blood*, **3**, 1238–49.
[264]

GROEN, J., and GARRER, A. H. (1948) Adult Gaucher's disease, with special reference to the variations in its clinical course and the value of sternal puncture as an aid to its diagnosis, *Blood*, **3**, 1221–37. [265]

GRUMBACH, M. M., ENGLE, E. T., BLANC, W. A., and BARR, M. L. (1956) (Quoted by Nielsen, J., 1965) The sex chromatin pattern in testicular disorders: relationship to pathogenesis and true hermaphrodism, *J. clin. Endocr.*, **16**, 923. [314]

GRÜNTHAL, E., and WENGER, O. (1939) Nachweis von Erblichkeit bei der Alzheimer'-schen Krankheit nebst Bemerkungen über den Altersvorgang im Gehirn, *Mschr. Psychiat. Neurol.*, **101**, 8–25. [152]

GUNTHER, M., and PENROSE, L. S. (1935) The genetics of epiloia, *J. Genet.*, **31**, 413–30.
[6, 280–1]

GUTMANN, L., and LEMLI, L. (1963) Ataxia-telangiectasia associated with hypo-gammaglobulinemia, *Arch. Neurol. (Chic.)*, **8**, 318–27. [253]

HALL, B. (1964) Mongolism in newborns. A clinical and cytogenetic study, *Acta paediat. (Stockh.)*, Suppl. 154. [335]

HALLGREN, B., and SJÖGREN, T. (1959) A clinical and genetico-statistical study of schizophrenia and low-grade mental deficiency in a large Swedish rural population, *Acta psychiat. scand.*, Suppl. 140. [22, 31–2]

HALVORSEN, K., and HALVORSEN, S. (1963) Hartnup disease, *Pediatrics*, **31**, 29–38.
[235]

HAMBERT, G. (1964) Positive sex chromatin in men with epilepsy, *Acta med. scand.*, **175**, 663–5. [314]

HAMBERT, G., and FREY, T. S. (1964) The electroencephalogram in the Klinefelter syndrome, *Acta psychiat. scand.*, **40**, 28–36. [313]

HAMERTON, J. L., COWIE, V. A., GIANNELLI, F., BRIGGS, S. M., and POLANI, P. E. (1961) Differential transmission of Down's syndrome (mongolism) through male and female translocation carriers, *Lancet*, ii, 956–8. [330]

HAMERTON, J. L., JAGIELLO, G. M., and KIRMAN, B. H. (1962) Sex chromosome abnormalities in a population of mentally defective children, *Brit. med. J.*, **1**, 220–3.
[321, 323]

HAMERTON, J. L., TAYLOR, A. I., ANGELL, R., and MCGUIRE, V. M. (1965) Chromosome investigations of a small isolated human population: chromosome abnormalities and distribution of chromosome counts according to age and sex among the inhabitants of Tristan Da Cunha, *Nature (Lond.)*, **206**, 1232–4. [124]

HAMPSON, J. L., HAMPSON, J. G., and MONEY, J. (1955) The syndrome of gonadal agenesis (ovarian agenesis) and male chromosomal pattern in girls and women: psychologic studies, *Bull. Johns Hopk. Hosp.*, **97**, 207–26. [310]

HANHART, E. (1936) Eine Sippe mit einfach-rezessive Diplegia Spastica Infantilis (Littlescher Krankheit) aus einem Schweizen Inzuchtgebiet, *Erbarzt*, **11**, 165.
[290]

HANHART, E. (1944) Neue familiäre Fälle von mongoloiden Schwachsinn als Beweis für die Mitwirkung von Erbfaktoren, *Arch. Klaus-Stift. Vererb.- Forsch.*, **19**, 549–50.
[331]

HANHART, E. (1947) Neue Sonderformen von Keratosis palmo-plantaris, *Dermatologica (Basel)*, **94**, 286–308. [287]

HANSEN, E. (1963) Ataxia-telangiectasia, *Develop. Med. Child Neurol.*, **5**, 63–5.
[252–3, 275]

HANSEN, R. G., BRETTHAUER, R. K., MAYES, J., and NORDIN, J. H. (1964) Estimation of frequency of occurrence of galactosemia in the population, *Proc. Soc. exp. Biol. (N.Y.)*, **115**, 560–3. [241]

HANZAWA, M. (1957) Elektroencephalogramm bei Zwillingen, in Genetische Studien an Zwillingen: A. Morphologischer Teil, Osato, S. and Awano, I., *Acta Genet. med. (Roma)*, **6**, 283–366. [163]

HARE, E. H., and PRICE, J. S. (1969) Birth order and family size: bias caused by changes in birth rate, *Brit. J. Psychiat.*, **115**, 647–57. [120]

HARE, E. H., and PRICE, J. S. (1970) Birth rank in schizophrenia: with a consideration of the bias due to changes in birth rate, *Brit. J. Psychiat.*, **116**, 409–20. [120]

HARNDEN, D. G. (1962) Normal and abnormal cell division, in *Chromosomes in Medicine*, ed. Hamerton, J. L., London, National Spastics Society. [329]

HARRIMAN, D. G. F., and MILLAR, J. H. D. (1955) Progressive familial myoclonic epilepsy in three families: its clinical features and pathological basis—with an appendix on the genetic aspects by A. C. Stevenson, *Brain*, **78**, 325–49. [254–5]

HARRIS, H. (1959) *Human Biochemical Genetics*, Cambridge. [206, 242]

HARRIS, H. (1962) Metabolic defects and mental retardation, *Res. Publ. Ass. nerv. ment. Dis.*, **39**, 87–96. [233]

HARVALD, B. (1954) *Heredity in Epilepsy. An Electroencephalographic Study of Relatives of Epileptics*, Copenhagen. [176, 178, 183]

HARVALD, B., and HAUGE, M. (1965) Hereditary factors elucidated by twin studies, in *Genetics and the Epidemiology of Chronic Diseases*, ed. Neel, J. V., Shaw, M. W., and Schull, W. J., Washington, U.S. Department of Health, Education and Welfare. [84]

HAUSCHKA, T. S., HASSON, J. E., GOLDSTEIN, M. N., KOEPF, G. F., and SANDBERG, A. A. (1962) An XYY man with progeny indicating familial tendency to non-disjunction, *Amer. J. hum. Genet.*, **14**, 22–30. [300]

HAYASHI, S. (1967) A study of juvenile delinquency in twins, in *Clinical Genetics in Psychiatry*, ed. Mitsuda, H., Tokyo. [114]

HELLER, C. G., and NELSON, W. O. (1945) Hyalinization of the seminiferous tubules associated with normal or failing Leydig cell function. Discussion of relationship to eunuchoidism, gynecomastia, elevated gonadotrophins, depressed 17-ketosteroids and estrogens, *J. clin. Endocr.*, **5**, 1–12. [300]

HERNDON, C. N. (1954) Genetics of the lipidoses, *Res. Publ. Ass. nerv. ment. Dis.*, **33**, 239–58. [257, 263]

HERNDON, C. N., and BENDER, J. R. (1950) Gaucher's disease; cases in five related negro sibships, *Amer. J. hum. Genet.*, **2**, 49–60. [265]

HERSOV, L. A., and RODNIGHT, R. (1960) Hartnup disease in psychiatric practice: clinical and biochemical features of three cases, *J. Neurol. Neurosurg. Psychiat.*, **23**, 40–5. [234]

HESTON, L. L. (1966) Psychiatric disorders in foster home reared children of schizophrenic mothers, *Brit. J. Psychiat.*, **112**, 819–25. [41–2]

HESTON, L. L. (1970) The genetics of schizophrenic and schizoid disease, *Science*, **167**, 249–56. [62]

HESTON, L. L., LOWTHER, D. L. W., and LEVENTHAL, C. M. (1966) Alzheimer's disease: a family study, *Arch. Neurol. (Chic.)*, **15**, 225–33. [152]

HESTON, L. L., and SHIELDS, J. (1968) Homosexuality in twins; a family study and a registry study, *Arch. gen. Psychiat.*, **18**, 149–60. [117]

HEUSCHERT, D. (1963) EEG-Untersuchungen an eineiigen Zwillingen im höheren Lebensalter, *Z. menschl. Vererb.-u Konstit.-Lehre*, **37**, 128–72. [163]

HEUYER, G., and VIDART, G. L. (1940) Le syndrome mental de la maladie de Recklinghausen, *Ann. méd.-psychol.*, **98**, 218–33. [281]

HIGGINS, J. V., REED, E. W., and REED, S. C. (1962) Intelligence and family size: a paradox resolved, *Eugen. Quart.*, **9**, 84–90. [195]

HILLBOM, EERO (1960) After-effects of brain injuries, *Acta psychiat. scand.*, **35**, Suppl. 142. [28]

HILLIARD, L. T., and KIRMAN, B. H. (1957) *Mental Deficiency*, London.   [263]

HIRSCHHORN, K., COOPER, H. L., and FIRSCHEIN, I. L. (1965) Deletion of short arms of chromosome 4–5 in a child with defects of midline fusion, *Hum. Genet.*, 1, 479–82.   [341]

HODSKINS, M. B., and YAKOVLEV, P. I. (1930) Anatomico-clinical obervations on myoclonus in epileptics and on related symptom complexes, *Amer. J. Psychiat.*, 9, 827–48.   [254]

HOEFNAGEL, D. (1965) The syndrome of athetoid cerebral palsy, mental deficiency, self-mutilation and hyperuricemia, *J. ment. Defic. Res.*, 9, 69–74.   [246]

HOEFNAGEL, D., ANDREW, E. D., MIREAULT, N. G., and BERNDT, W. O. (1965) Hereditary choreoathetosis, self-mutilation and hyperuricemia in young males, *New Engl. J. Med.*, 273, 130–5.   [247–8]

VAN DER HOEVE, T. (1923) Eye diseases in tuberose sclerosis of the brain and in Recklinghausen's disease, *Trans. ophthal. Soc. U.K.*, 43, 534–41.   [275]

HOLLAND, W. W., DOLL, R., and CARTER, C. O. (1962) The mortality from leukaemia and other cancers among patients with Down's syndrome (mongols) and among their parents, *Brit. J. Cancer*, 16, 177–86.   [335]

HOLLINGSHEAD, A. B., and REDLICH, F. C. (1954) Social stratification and schizophrenia, *Amer. sociol. Rev.*, 19, 302–6.   [38]

HOLT, S. B. (1961) Inheritance of dermal ridge patterns, in *Recent Advances in Human Genetics*, ed. Penrose, L. S., London.   [350]

HOLTON, J. B., LEWIS, F. J. W., and MOORE, G. R. (1964) Biochemical investigation of histidinaemia, *J. clin. Path.*, 17, 671–5.   [218]

HOLZEL, A., and KOMROWER, G. M. (1955) A study of the genetics of galactosaemia, *Arch. Dis. Childh.*, 30, 155–9.   [240–1]

HOOGHWINKEL, G. J. M., BORRI, P. F., and BRUYN, G. W. (1966a) Biochemical studies in Huntington's chorea, Part II. Composition of blood lipids, *Acta neurol. scand.*, 42, 213–20.   [140]

HOOGHWINKEL, G. J. M., BORRI, P. F., and BRUYN, G. W. (1966b) Biochemical studies in Huntington's chorea. V. Erythrocyte and plasma glyco-lipids and fatty acid composition of erythrocyte gangliosides, *Neurology (Minneap.)*, 16, 934–6.   [140]

HOPKINSON, G. (1964) A genetic study of affective illness in patients over 50, *Brit. J. Psychiat.*, 110, 244–54.   [86]

HOPKINSON, G., and LEY, P. (1969) A genetic study of affective disorder, *Brit. J. Psychiat.*, 115, 917–22.   [86–9]

HORNSTEIN, O. (1963) Zur Klinik und Histopathologie des männlichen primären Hypogonadismus. II. Mitteilung. Kastratismus und sogenanntes Klinefelter-Syndrom als Krankheitsformen mit bekannter Ätiologie, *Arch. klin. exp. Derm.*, 217, 149–95.   [30]

HSIA, D. Y-Y., DRISCOLL, K. W., TROLL, W., and KNOX, W. E. (1956) Detection by phenylalanine tolerance tests of heterozygous carriers of phenylketonuria, *Nature (Lond.)*, 178, 1239–40.   [202, 208]

HSIA, D. Y-Y., KNOX, W. E., and PAINE, R. S. (1957) A case of phenylketonuria with borderline intelligence, *Amer. J. Dis. Child.*, 94, 33–9.   [203]

HSIA, D. Y-Y., NAYLOR, J., and BIGLER, J. A. (1959) Gaucher's disease: a report of two cases in father and son and a review of the literature, *New Engl. J. Med.*, 261, 164–9.   [265]

HSIA, D. Y-Y., and WALKER, F. A. (1961) Variability in the clinical manifestations of galactosemia, *J. Pediat.*, 59, 872–83.   [237–41]

HUGH-JONES, K., NEWCOMBE, A. L., and HSIA, D. Y-Y. (1960) The genetic mechanism of galactosemia, *Arch. Dis. Childh.*, 35, 521–8.   [240]

HUNTER, CHARLES (1917) A rare disease in two brothers, *Proc. roy. Soc. Med.*, **10**, 104–16.   [269]

HURLER, G. (1919) Über einen Typ multipler Abartungen, vorwiegend am Skelett-system, *Z. Kinderheilk.*, **24**, 220–34.   [267]

HUSTINX, T. W. J., and WIJFFELS, J. C. H. M. (1965) 'Cri du chat' syndrome, *Lancet*, ii, 135–6.   [344]

HUTCHISON, J. H., and HAMILTON, W. (1962) Familial dysautonomia in two siblings, *Lancet*, i, 1216–18.   [249]

IBER, F. L., CHALMERS, T. C., and UZMAN, L. L. (1957) Studies of protein metabolism in hepatolenticular degeneration, *Metabolism*, **6**, 388–96.   [155]

ILLINGWORTH, R. S. (1960) *The Development of the Infant and Young Child*, Edinburgh (quoted by Koch, R., Share, J., Webb, A., and Graliker, B. V., 1963).   [337]

INOUYE, E. (1960) Observations on forty twin index cases with chronic epilepsy and their co-twins, *J. nerv. ment. Dis.*, **130**, 401–16.   [173]

INOUYE, E. (1963) Similarity and dissimilarity of schizophrenia in twins, *Proc. Third World Congress of Psychiatry, June 1961*, Vol. I, 524–30, Montreal.   [18, 22, 36]

ISRAELSOHN, W. J., and TAYLOR, A. I. (1961) Chromatin-positive presumed Klinefelter's syndrome, *Brit. med. J.*, **1**, 633–5.   [320]

ISSELBACHER, K. J. (1957) Evidence for an accessory pathway of galactose metabolism in mammalian liver, *Science*, **126**, 652–4.   [238]

ISSELBACHER, K. J., ANDERSON, E. P., KURASHI, K., and KALCKAR, H. M. (1956) Congenital galactosemia, and single enzymatic block in galactose metabolism, *Science*, **123**, 635–6.   [237]

JACKSON, W. P. U. (1951) The clinical features, diagnosis, and osseous lesions of gargoylism exemplified in three siblings, *Arch. Dis. Childh.*, **26**, 549–57.   [256]

JACOBS, P. A., BAIKIE, A. G., COURT BROWN, W. M., MACGREGOR, T. N., MACLEAN, N., and HARNDEN, D. G. (1959) Evidence for the existence of the human 'super female', *Lancet*, ii, 423–5.   [304]

JACOBS, P. A., BRUNTON, M., MELVILLE, M. E., BRITTAIN, R. P., and McCLEMONT, W. F. (1965) Aggressive behaviour, mental subnormality and the XYY male, *Nature (Lond.)*, **208**, 1351–2.   [301]

JAMES, WILLIAM H. (1971) Sex ratios of half-sibs of male homosexuals, *Brit. J. Psychiat.* **118**, 93–4.   [119]

JARVIK, L. F. (1963) Senescence and chromosomal changes, *Lancet*, i, 114–15.   [124]

JENSCH, K. (1941a) Zur Genealogie der Homosexualität, *Arch. Psychiat. Nervenkr.*, **112**, 527–40.   [118–19, 316]

JENSCH, K. (1941b) Weiterer Beitrag zur Genealogie der Homosexualität, *Arch. Psychiat. Nervenkr.*, **112**, 679–96.   [118–19, 316]

JEPSON, J. B. (1966) Hartnup disease, in *The Metabolic Basis of Inherited Disease*, ed. Stanbury, J. B., Wyngaarden, J. B., and Fredrickson, D. S., 2nd ed., New York.
[235]

JERVIS, G. A. (1937) Phenylpyruvic oligophrenia: introductory study of 50 cases of mental deficiency associated with excretion of phenylpyruvic acid, *Arch. Neurol. Psychiat. (Chic.)*, **38**, 944–63.   [206, 208]

JERVIS, G. A. (1939) The genetics of phenylpyruvic oligophrenia, *J. ment. Sci.*, **85**, 719–62.   [208]

JERVIS, G. A. (1950) Gargoylism (lipochondrodystrophy): a study of ten cases with emphasis on the formes frustes of the disease, *Arch. Neurol. Psychiat. (Chic.)*, **63**, 681–712.

JERVIS, G. A. (1952) Hallervorden-Spatz disease associated with atypical amaurotic idiocy, *J. Neuropath. exp. Neurol.*, **11**, 4–18.   [257]

JERVIS, G. A. (1959) Juvenile amaurotic idiocy, *Amer. J. Dis. Child.*, **97**, 663–7.   [261]

JERVIS, G. A. (1963) Huntington's chorea in childhood, *Arch. Neurol. (Chic.)*, **9**, 244–57. [137]

JOHNSTON, A. W., FERGUSON-SMITH, M.A., HANDMAKER, S. D., JONES, H. W., and JONES, G. S. (1961) The triple-X syndrome; clinical, pathological, and chromosomal studies in three mentally retarded cases, *Brit. med. J.*, **2**, 1046–52. [305, 321]

JONES, H. E. (1929) Homogamy in intellectual abilities, *Amer. J. Sociol.*, **XXXV**, 369–82. [194]

JUEL-NIELSEN, N. (1965) Individual and environment. A psychiatric psychological investigation of monozygotic twins reared apart, *Acta psychiat. scand.*, Suppl. 183. [98, 198]

JUEL-NIELSEN, N., and HARVALD, B. (1958) The electroencephalogram in uniovular twins brought up apart, *Acta genet. (Basel)*, **8**, 57–64. [163]

KAHLKE, W., and RICHTERICH, R. (1965) Refsum's disease (heredopathia atactica polyneuritiformis): an inborn error of lipid metabolism with storage of 3, 7, 11, 15-tetramethyl hexadecanoic acid, *Amer. J. Med.*, **39**, 237–41. [251]

KAIJ, L. (1960) *Alcoholism in Twins: Studies on the Etiology and Sequels of Abuse of Alcohol*, Stockholm. [110–11]

KAIJ, L. (1967) Atypical endogenous psychosis: report on a family, *Brit. J. Psychiat.*, **113**, 415–22. [24]

KALLMANN, F. J. (1938) *The Genetics of Schizophrenia*, New York. [31, 32, 354]

KALLMANN, F. J. (1950) The genetics of psychoses: an analysis of 1,232 twin index families, *Internat. Congr. Psychiat.*, *Rapports*, **6**, 1–27, Paris. [84, 132]

KALLMANN, F. J. (1952a) Comparative twin study on the genetic aspects of male homosexuality, *J. nerv. ment. Dis.*, **115**, 283–98. [117, 316]

KALLMANN, F. J. (1952b) Twin and sibship study of overt male homosexuality, *Amer. J. hum. Genet.*, **4**, 136–46. [117,316]

KALLMANN, F. J. (1956a) The genetics of aging, *J. Chron. Dis.*, **4**, 140–52. [132]

KALLMANN, F. J. (1956b) Genetic aspects of mental disorders in later life, in *Mental Disorders in Later Life*, ed. Kaplan, O. J., 2nd ed., Stanford. [132]

KALLMANN, F. J. (1959) The genetics of mental illness, in *American Handbook of Psychiatry*, ed. Arieti, S., Vol. 1, New York. [77]

KALLMANN, F. J., and JARVIK, L. F. (1959) Individual differences in constitution and genetic background, in *Handbook of Aging and the Individual*, ed. Birren, J. E., Chicago. [132]

KALLMANN, F. J., and SANDER, G. (1948) Twin studies on aging and longevity, *J. Hered.*, **39**, 349–57. [122, 132]

KALLMANN, F. J., and SANDER, G. (1949) Twin studies on senescence, *Amer. J. Psychiat.*, **106**, 29–36. [122, 132]

KAMIDE, H. (1957) Observations on 42 twin pairs with epilepsy, *Psychiat. Neurol. jap.*, **59**, 1259–1302. [173]

KAPLAN, H., ASPILLAGA, M., SHELLEY, T. F., and GARDNER, L. I. (1963) Possible fertility in Klinefelter's syndrome, *Lancet*, i, 506. [300]

KARLSSON, JON L. (1966) *The Biologic Basis of Schizophrenia*, Springfield, Ill. [64]

KATZ, H. P., and MENKES, J. H. (1964) Phenylketonuria occurring in an American negro, *J. Pediat.*, **65**, 71–4. [207–8]

KAY, D. W. K. (1959) Observations on the natural history and genetics of old age psychoses: a Stockholm material, 1931–7, *Proc. roy. Soc. Med.*, **52**, 791–4. [86]

KAY, D. W. K. (1963) Late paraphrenia and its bearing on the aetiology of schizophrenia, *Acta psychiat. scand.*, **39**, 159–69. [45, 53, 55]

KENYON, F. E., and HARDY, S. M. (1963) A biochemical study of Huntington's chorea, *J. Neurol. Neurosurg. Psychiat.*, **26**, 123–6. [139]

KETY, S. S., ROSENTHAL, D., WENDER, P. H., and SCHULSINGER, F. (1968) The types and prevalence of mental illness in the biological and adoptive families of adopted schizophrenics, in *The Transmission of Schizophrenia*, ed. Rosenthal, D., and Kety, S. S., Oxford.   [42]

KIDD, C. B., KNOX, R. S., and MANTLE, D. J. (1963) A psychiatric investigation of triple-X chromosome females, *Brit. J. Psychiat.*, **109**, 90–4.   [311, 321]

KIIL, R., and ROKKONES, T. (1964) Late manifesting variant of branched-chain keto-aciduria (maple syrup urine disease), *Acta paediat.* (*Uppsala*), **53**, 356–64.   [215]

KIMBALL, O. P., and HERSH, A. H. (1955) The genetics of epilepsy, *Acta Genet. med.* (*Roma*), **4**, 131–42.   [168]

KIND, HANS (1966) The psychogenesis of schizophrenia: a review of the literature, *Brit. J. Psychiat.*, **112**, 333–49.   [39]

KIRBY, T. J. (1951) Ocular phakomatoses, *Amer. J. med. Sci.*, **222**, 227–39.   [277]

KIRKMAN, H. N., and BYNUM, E. (1959) Enzymic evidence of a galactosemic trait in parents of galactosemic children, *Ann. hum. Genet.*, **23**, 117–26.   [240]

KIRMAN, B. H. (1955) Idiocy and ectodermal dysplasia, *Brit. J. Derm.*, **67**, 303–7.[294]

KISHIMOTO, K., NAKAMURA, M., and SOTOKAWA, Y. (1957) On population genetics of Huntington's chorea in Japan, Annual Report of the Research Institute of Environ-mental Medicine, Nagoya Univ.   [143, 145]

KLEBANOFF, L. B. (1959) Parental attitudes of mothers of schizophrenic, brain-injured and retarded and normal children, *Amer. J. Orthopsychiat.*, **29**, 445–54.   [40]

KLEIN, D. (1953) Metabolic disorders, in *Clinical Genetics*, ed. Sorsby, A., London.
                                                                                       [261, 265]

KLEIN, D., and KTENIDÈS, M-A. (1954) Au sujet de l'hérédité de l'idiotie amaurotique infantile (Tay-Sachs), *J. Génét. hum.*, **3**, 184–202.   [261]

KLENK, E. (1955) The pathological chemistry of the developing brain, in *Biochemistry of the Developing Nervous System*, ed. Waelsch, H., New York.   [258]

KLENK, E., and KAHLKE, W. (1963) Über das Vorkommen der 3.7.11.15-Tetra-methylhexadecansäure (Phytansäure) in den cholesterinestern und anderen Lipoidfraktionen der Organe bei einem Krankheitsfall unbekannter Genese [Ver-dacht auf Heredopathia atactica polyneuritiformis (Refsum-syndrom)], *Hoppe-Seylers Z. physiol. Chem.*, **333**, 133.   [251]

KLINEFELTER, H. F., REIFENSTEIN, E. C., and ALBRIGHT, F. (1942) Syndrome charac-terized by gynecomastia, aspermatogenesis without a-Leydigism, and increased excretion of follicle-stimulating hormone, *J. clin. Endocr.*, **2**, 615–27.   [299]

KNOBLOCH, H. (1959) Pneumoencephalograms and clinical behaviour, *Pediatrics*, **23**, 175–8 (quoted by Koch, R., Share, J., Webb, A., and Graliker, B. V., 1963).
                                                                                            [337]

KNOX, W. E. (1966) Phenylketonuria, in *The Metabolic Basis of Inherited Disease*, 2nd ed., ed Stanbury, J. B., Wyngaarden, J. B., and Fredrickson, D. S., New York.   [211]

KNOX, W. E., CULLEN, A. M., and ROSEN, B. (1966) Unpublished results, cited by Knox, W. E. (1966) Phenylketonuria, in *The Metabolic Basis of Inherited Disease*, 2nd ed., ed Stanbury, J. B., Wyngaarden J. B., and Fredrickson, D. S., New York.
                                                                                            [211]

KNOX, W. E., and MESSINGER, E. C. (1958) The detection in the heterozygote of the metabolic effect of the recessive gene for phenylketonuria, *Amer. J. hum. Genet.*, **10**, 53–60.   [209]

KOCH, G. (1959) Genetics of microcephaly in man, *Acta Genet. med.* (*Roma*), **8**, 75–85.
                                                                                            [290]

KOCH, G. (1960) Neuere Betrachtungen über die Erblichkeit der Sturge-Weberschen und von Hippel-Lindauschen Krankheit, *Med. Welt* (*Berl.*), **40**, 1955–61.   [282]

KOCH, G. (1965) Die Bedeutung genetischer Faktoren für das menschliche Verhalten, *Ärzt. Praxis*, **17**, 823 and 839–46. [118, 120]

KOCH, G. (1967) Epilepsien, in *Humangenetik. Ein kurzes Handbuch in fünf Bänden*, Band V/2. Psychiatrische Krankheiten, Stuttgart. [161–2, 172, 174, 177]

KOCH, R., SHARE, J., WEBB, A., and GRALIKER, B. V. (1963) The predictability of Gesell developmental scales in mongolism, *J. Pediat.*, **62**, 93–7. [337]

KOFMAN, O., and HYLAND, H. H. (1959) Tuberous sclerosis in adults with normal intelligence, *Arch. Neurol. Psychiat. (Chic.)*, **81**, 43–8. [279]

KOMAI, T., KISHIMOTO, K., and OZAKI, Y. (1955) Genetic study of microcephaly based on Japanese material, *Amer. J. hum. Genet.*, **7**, 51–65. [288–9]

KOMROWER, G. M., LAMBERT, A. M. CUSWORTH, D. C., and WESTHALL, R. G. (1966) Dietary treatment of homocystinuria, *Arch. Dis. Childh.*, **41**, 666–71. [223]

KOPELMAN, H., ASATOOR, A. M., and MILNE, M. D. (1964) Hyperprolinaemia and hereditary nephritis, *Lancet*, ii, 1075–9. [219]

KOREIN, J., STEINMAN, P. A., and SENZ, E. H. (1961) Ataxia-telangiectasia. Report of a case and review of the literature, *Arch. Neurol. (Chic.)*, **4**, 272–80. [252]

KOZINN, P. J., WIENER, H., and COHEN, P. (1957) Infantile amaurotic family idiocy. A genetic approach, *J. Pediat.*, **51**, 58–64. [261]

KRANZ, H. (1936) *Lebensschicksale Krimineller Zwillinge*, Berlin. [115]

KRINGLEN, E. (1967) *Heredity and Environment in the Functional Psychoses*, Norwegian Monographs on Medical Science, Oslo. [17, 20, 84–5]

KRINGLEN, E. (1968) An epidemiological-clinical twin study on schizophrenia, in *The Transmission of Schizophrenia*, ed. Rosenthal, D., and Kety, S. S., Oxford. [19]

KUFS, H. (1925) Über die Bedeutung der optischen Komponente der amaurotischen Idiotie in diagnostischer und erbbiologischer Beziehung und über die Existenz 'spätester' Fälle bei dieser Krankheit, *Z. ges. Neurol. Psychiat.*, **95**, 169. [259]

KUNDRAT, H. (1882) Arrhinencephalie als typische Art von Missbildung, Graz. von Leuschner and Lubensky (quoted by Smith, Patau, Therman, Inhorn, and de Mars, 1963). [340]

KURLAND, L. T. (1959) The incidence and prevalence of convulsive disorders in a small urban community, *Epilepsia (Amst.)*, **I**, 143–61. [161]

LABHARDT, F. (1963) *Die schizophrenieähnlichen Emotionspsychosen: ein Beitrag zur Abgrenzung Schizophrenia-artiger Zustandsbilder*, Berlin. [42–3]

LAFORA, G. R., and GLUECK, B. (1911) Beitrag zur Histopathologie der myoklonischen Epilepsie, *Z. ges. Neurol. Psychiat.*, **6**, 1–14. [254]

LANDING, B. H., and RUBINSTEIN, J. H. (1962) Biopsy diagnosis of neurologic diseases in children, with emphasis on the lipidoses, in *Cerebral Sphingolipidoses: a Symposium on Tay-Sachs' Disease and Allied Disorders*, ed. Aronson, S. M., and Volk, B. W., New York. [258]

LANDING, B. H., SILVERMAN, F. N., CRAIG, J. M., JACOBY, M. D., LAHEY, M. E., and CHADWICK, D. L. (1964) Familial neurovisceral lipidosis, *Amer. J. Dis. Child.*, **108**, 503-22. [258]

LANG, T. (1940) Studies on the genetic determination of homosexuality, *J. nerv. ment. Dis.*, **92**, 55–64. [315]

LANG, T. (1960) Die Homosexualität als genetisches Problem, *Acta Genet. med. (Roma)*, **9**, 370–81. [118–20]

LANGDON DOWN, J. (1866) Observations on an ethnic classification of idiots, *Clinical Lectures and Reports, London Hospital*, **3**, 259–62. [325]

LANGE, J. (1931) *Crime as Destiny* (Originally published in 1929, trans. Charlotte Haldane in 1931) London. [114]

LARSON, C. A. (1954) An estimate of the frequency of phenylketonuria in South Sweden, *Folia hered. path. (Milano)*, **4**, 40–6. [206]

LARSON, C. A., and NYMAN, G. E. (1968) Phenylketonuria: mental illness in heterozygotes, *Psychiat. clin.*, **1**, 367–74.   [210]
LARSSON, T., and SJÖGREN, T. (1960) Essential tremor. A clinical and genetic population study, *Acta psychiat. scand.*, Suppl. 144.   [135]
LARSSON, T., and SJÖGREN, T. (1961) Dystonia musculorum deformans. A clinical
and genetic population study. Communication No. 196 at the Second International
Conference of Human Genetics, Rome.   [134]
LARSSON, T., SJÖGREN, T., and JACOBSON, G. (1963) Senile dementia: a clinical socio-
medical and genetic study, *Acta psychiat. scand.*, Suppl. 167.   [127–35]
LAUBENTHAL, F. (1938) Über einige Sonderformen des 'angeborenen Schwachsinns',
Z. ges. Neurol. Psychiat., **163**, 233–88.   [291]
LEAO, J. C., NEU, R., and GARDNER, L. I. (1966) Hypospadias and other anomalies
associated with partial deletion of short arms of chromosome No. 4, *Lancet*, i,
493–4.   [341]
LE GRAS, A. M. (1933) Psychose und Kriminalität bei Zwillingen, *Z. ges. Neurol.
Psychiat.*, **144**, 198–222.   [114]
LEISTYNA, J. A. (1962) Lipid storage disorders of the central nervous system, *Amer.
J. Dis. Child.*, **104**, 680–94.   [257, 263]
LEJEUNE, J., GAUTIER, M., and TURPIN, R. (1959a) Les chromosomes humains en
culture de tissus, *C.R. Acad. Sci. (Paris)*, **248**, 602–3.   [328]
LEJEUNE, J., GAUTIER, M., and TURPIN, R. (1959b) Étude des chromosomes somatiques
de neuf enfants mongoliens, *C.R. Acad. Sci. (Paris)*, **248**, 1721–2.   [328]
LEJEUNE, J., LAFOURCADE, J., BERGER, R., VIALATTE, J., BOESWILLWALD, M., SERINGE,
P., and TURPIN, R. (1963) Trois cas de deletion partielle du bras court d'un chromo-
some 5, *C.R. Acad. Sci. (Paris)*, **257**, 3098–102.   [341]
LENNOX, W. G., GIBBS, E. L., and GIBBS, F. A. (1945) The brain-wave pattern, an
hereditary trait: evidence from 74 'normal' pairs of twins, *J. Hered.*, **36**, 233–43.
                                                                                           [162]
LENNOX, W. G., and LENNOX, M. A. (1960) *Epilepsy and Related Disorders*, London.
                                                                                           [173]
LEONHARD, K. (1957) *Aufteilung der Endogenen Psychosen*, Berlin.   [78]
LEONHARD, K. (1959) *Aufteilung der Endogenen Psychosen*, Berlin.   [24]
LEONHARD, K., KORFF, I., and SCHULZ, H. (1962) Die Temperamente in den Familien
der monopolaren und bipolaren phasischen Psychosen, *Psychiat. et Neurol. (Basel)*,
143, 416–34.   [79–80]
LESCH, M., and NYHAN, W. L. (1964) A familial disorder of uric acid metabolism and
central nervous system function, *Amer. J. Med.*, **36**, 561–70.   [247]
LEVIN, B., OBERHOLZER, V. G., SNODGRASS, G. J. A. I., STIMMLER, L., and WILMERS,
M. J. (1963) Fructosaemia. An inborn error of fructose metabolism, *Arch. Dis.
Childh.*, **38**, 220–30.   [242–3]
LEWIS, A. (1935) Problems of obsessional illness, *Proc. roy. Soc. Med.*, **29**, 325–36. [105]
LIEBENAM, LEONORE (1938) Beitrag zur Dysostosis multiplex, *Z. Kinderheilk.*, **59**,
91–123.   [270]
LINDSTEN, J., and TILLINGER, K.-G. (1962) Self-perpetuating ring chromosome in a
patient with gonadal dysgenesis, *Lancet*, i, 593–4.   [297]
LINK, J. K., and ROLDAN, E. C. (1958) Mental deficiency, spasticity and congenital
ichthyosis. Report on a case, *J. Pediat.*, **52**, 712–14.   [292]
LINNEWEH, F., and EHRLICH, M. (1963) Heterozygoten—Test für die Ahornsirup-
krankheit (maple syrup urine disease), *Klin. Wschr.*, **41**, 255–7.   [214]
LIPPMAN, R. W. (1958) The significance of heterozygosity for hereditary metabolic
errors related to mental deficiency, (oligomentia), *Amer. J. ment. Defic.*, **63**, 320–4.
                                                                                           [211]

LJUNGBERG, L. (1957) Hysteria: a clinical, prognostic and genetic study, *Acta psychiat. scand.*, Suppl. 112.   [106–7]

LOISEAU, P., and BEAUSSART, M. (1969) Hereditary factors in partial epilepsy, *Epilepsia* (*Amst.*), **10**, 23–31.   [167]

LONSDALE, D., MERCER, R. D., and FAULKNER, W. R. (1963) Maple syrup urine disease: report of two cases, *Amer. J. Dis. Child.*, **106**, 258–66.   [214]

LORBER, J. (1964) Hereditary ectodermal dysplasia, *Proc. roy. Soc. Med.*, **57**, 116–17.   [294]

LOUIS-BAR, D. (1941) Sur un syndrome progressif comprenant des télangiectasies capillaires cutanées et conjonctivales, symétriques, à disposition naevoide et des troubles cérébelleux, *Confin. neurol.* (*Basel*), **4**, 32–42.   [251]

LOWE, C. U., TERREY, M., and MACLACHLAN, E. A. (1952) Organic-aciduria, decreased renal ammonia production, hydrophthalmos, and mental retardation, *Amer. J. Dis. Child.*, **83**, 164–84.   [235]

LOWENBERG, K., and WAGGONER, R. W. (1934) Familial organic psychosis (Alzheimer's type), *Arch. Neurol. Psychiat.* (*Chic.*), **31**, 737–54.   [152]

LUNDBORG, H. (1913) *Medizinisch-biologische Familienforschungen innerhalb eines 2232-köpfigen Bauerngeschlechtes in Schweden*, Jena.   [255]

LUXENBURGER, H. (1930) Heredität und Familientypus der Zwangsneurotiker, *Arch. Psychiat.*, **91**, 590–4.   [105]

LYMAN, L. F. (1963) *Phenylketonuria*, Springfield, Ill.   [207]

LYNAS, M. A. (1958) Marfan's syndrome in Northern Ireland: an account of thirteen families, *Ann. hum. Genet.*, **22**, 289–309.   [225, 227]

MCCANCE, R. A., MATHESON, W. J., GRESHAM, G. A., and ELKINTON, J. R. (1960) The cerebro-ocular-renal dystrophies: a new variant, *Arch. Dis. Childh.*, **35**, 240–9.   [236]

MACCREADY, R. A., and HUSSEY, M. G. (1964) Newborn phenylketonuria detection program in Massachusetts, *Amer. J. publ. Hlth*, **54**, 2075–81.   [206]

MCGAVIN, D. D. M., CANT, J. S., FERGUSON-SMITH, M. A., and ELLIS, P. M. (1967) The cri-du-chat syndrome with an apparently normal karyotype, *Lancet*, ii, 326–30.   [344]

MACGILLIVRAY, R. C. (1952) Gargoylism (Hurler's disease), *J. ment. Sci.*, **98**, 687–96.

MACGILLIVRAY, R. C. (1954) The syndrome of Rud, *Amer. J. ment. Defic.*, **59**, 67–72.   [293]

MCINNES, R. G. (1937) Observations on heredity in neurosis, *Proc. roy. Soc. Med.*, **30**, 895–904.   [103]

MACKENZIE, D. Y., and WOOLF, L. I. (1959) 'Maple Syrup Urine Disease', an inborn error of the metabolism of valine, leucine and isoleucine associated with gross mental deficiency, *Brit. med. J.*, **1**, 90–1.   [213]

MCKUSICK, V. A. (1962) Medical genetics, 1961, *J. chron. Dis.*, **15**, 417–572.   [230, 243]

MCKUSICK, V. A. (1965) The genetic mucopolysaccharidoses, *Circulation*, **31**, 1–4.   [265]

MCKUSICK, V. A. (1966) Heritable disorders of connective tissue: newer aspects, *Birth Defects Orig. Art. Ser.*, **2**, 58–65.   [265]

MCKUSICK, V. A. (1968) *Mendelian Inheritance in Man. Catalogs of Autosomal Dominant, Autosomal Recessive and X-linked Phenotypes*, 2nd ed., Baltimore. [285]

MCKUSICK, V. A., KAPLAN, D., WISE, D., HANLEY, W. B., SUDDARTH, S. B., SEVICK, M. E., and MAUMENEE, A. E. (1965) The genetic mucopolysaccharidoses, *Medicine* (*Baltimore*), **44**, 445–83.   [265, 269–72]

MACLEAN, N., HARNDEN, D. G., COURT BROWN, W. M., BOND, J., and MANTLE, D. J. (1964) Sex-chromosome abnormalities in newborn babies, *Lancet*, i, 286–90.   [300]

MACLEAN, N., MITCHELL, J. M., HARNDEN, D. G., WILLIAMS, J., JACOBS, P. A., BUCKTON, K. A., BAIKIE, A. G., COURT BROWN, W. M., McBRIDE, J. A., STRONG, J. A., CLOSE, H. G., and JONES, D. C. (1962) A survey of sex-chromosome abnormalities among 4514 mental defectives, *Lancet*, i, 293–6.   [305, 308, 314, 319, 321]

McMENEMEY, W. H. (1961) Immunity mechanisms in neurological disease, *Proc. roy. Soc. Med.*, **54**, 127–36.   [142]

McMENEMEY, W. H., WORSTER-DROUGHT, C., FLIND, J., and WILLIAMS, H. G. (1939) Familial presenile dementia: report of case with clinical and pathological features of Alzheimer's disease, *J. Neurol. Psychiat.*, **2**, 293–302.   [152]

McMURRAY, W. C., and MOHYUDDIN, F. (1962) Citrullinuria, *Lancet*, ii, 352.   [230]

McMURRAY, W. C., MOHYUDDIN, F., ROSSITER, R. J., RATHBUN, J. C., VALENTINE, G. H., KOEGLER, S. J., and ZARFAS, D. E. (1962) Citrullinuria: a new aminoaciduria associated with mental retardation, *Lancet*, i, 138.   [230]

MAHLER, M. S. (1961) On sadness and grief in infancy and childhood, in *The Psychoanalytic Study of the Child*, Vol. 16, London.   [40]

MALAMUD, N. (1966) Neuropathology of phenylketonuria, *J. Neuropath. exp. Neurol.*, **25**, 254–68.   [205]

MALZBERG, B. (1950) Some statistical aspects of mongolism, *Amer. J. ment. Defic.*, **54**, 266–81.   [325]

MARFAN, A. B. (1896) Un cas de déformation congénitale des quatre membres, plus prononcée aux extrémités, caractérisée par l'allongement des OS avec un certain degré d'amincissement, *Bull. Soc. med. Hôp. Paris*, **13**, 220–6.   [225]

MARKS, I. M., CROWE, M., DREWE, E., YOUNG, J., and DEWHURST, W. G. (1969) Obsessive compulsive neurosis in identical twins, *Brit. J. Psychiat.*, **115**, 991–8. [105]

MAROTEAUX, P., and LAMY, M. (1963) La maladie de Morquio. Étude clinique, radiologique et biologique, *Presse méd.*, **71**, 2091–4.   [271]

MAROTEAUX, P., and LAMY, M. (1965) Hurler's disease, Morquio's disease, and related mucopolysaccharidoses, *J. Pediat.*, **67**, 312–23.   [265, 268–70]

MARSHALL, D., SAUL, G. B., and SACHS, E. (1959) Tuberous sclerosis: a report of 16 cases in two family trees revealing genetic dominance, *New Engl. J. Med.*, **261**, 1102–5.   [280]

MAUGHAN, E., and WILLIAMS, J. R. B. (1966) Huntington's chorea, *Lancet*, i, 491.   [142–3]

MAYER-GROSS, W., SLATER, E., and ROTH, M. (1969) *Clinical Psychiatry*, 3rd ed., ed. Slater, E., and Roth, M., London.   [77, 127, 136]

MEDAWAR, P. B. (1946) Old age and natural death, *Mod. Quart.*, **1**, 30.   [122]

MEEHL, P. E. (1962) Schizotaxia, schizotypy, schizophrenia, *Amer. Psychol.*, **17**, 827–38.   [21, 62]

MEGGENDORFER, F. (1925) Über familiengeschichtliche Untersuchungen bei arteriosklerotischer und seniler Demenz, *Zbl. ges. Neurol. Psychiat.*, **40**, 359.   [130]

MELLBIN, G. (1966) Neuropsychiatric disorders in sex chromatin negative women, *Brit. J. Psychiat.*, **112**, 145–8.   [310, 314]

MENKES, J. H. (1959) Maple syrup disease: isolation and identification of organic acids in the urine, *Pediatrics*, **23**, 348–53.   [213]

MENKES, J. H., HURST, P. L., and CRAIG, J. M. (1954) A new syndrome; progressive familial infantile cerebral dysfunction associated with an unusual urinary substance, *Pediatrics*, **14**, 462–7.   [212–13]

MESNIKOFF, A. M., RAINER, J. D., KOLB, L. C., and CARR, A. C. (1963) Intrafamilial determinants of divergent sexual behaviour in twins, *Amer. J. Psychiat.*, **119**, 732–8.   [118]

METRAKOS, J. D. (1961) The centrencephalic EEG in epilepsy, *Proc. 2nd Internat. Congress hum. Genetics*, iii, 1792–5, Istituto Mendel, Rome, 1963.   [165]

METRAKOS, J. D., and METRAKOS, K. (1960) Genetics of convulsive disorders. I. Introduction, problems, methods, and baselines, *Neurology (Minneap.)*, **10**, 228–40. [165]

METRAKOS, K., and METRAKOS, J. D. (1961a) Genetics of convulsive disorders. II. Genetic and electro-encephalographic studies in centrencephalic epilepsy, *Neurology (Minneap.)*, **11**, 474–83. [165]

METRAKOS, K., and METRAKOS, J. D. (1961b) Is the centrencephalic EEG inherited as a dominant?, *Electroenceph. clin. Neurophysiol.*, **13**, 289. [165]

MILLER, O. J., BREG, W. R., WARBURTON, D., MILLER, D. A., DeCAPOA, A., and CHUTORIAN, A. M. (1966) Deleted late-replicating chromosome 4/5, *Lancet*, ii, 105–6. [342]

MILNE, M. D., CRAWFORD, M. A., GIRÃO, C. B., and LOUGHRIDGE, L. (1959) The metabolic abnormality of Hartnup disease, Proc. of the Biochemical Society, *Biochem. J.*, **72**, 30P. [234]

MILNE, M. D., CRAWFORD, M. A., GIRÃO, C. B., and LOUGHRIDGE, L. W. (1960) The metabolic disorder in Hartnup disease, *Quart. J. Med.*, **29**, 407–21. [234]

MINISTRY OF HEALTH (1969) Statistical Report Series No. 4, Psychiatric Hospitals and Units in England and Wales In-patient Statistics from the Mental Health Enquiry for the years 1964, 1965 and 1966, London, H.M.S.O. [72–4, 129]

MISSALE, G., COCCONI, G., CONTERIO, F., MAINARDI, D., and CANALETTI, R. (1962) Fruttosuria familiare con intolleranza al fruttoso. Indagini clinico-metaboliche, *Ateneo parmense*, **33**, Suppl. I, 25–42. [243]

MITSUDA, H. (1967) *Clinical Genetics in Psychiatry*, Tokyo. [34, 35]

MITTWOCH, U. (1963) The demonstration of mucopolysaccharide inclusions in the lymphocytes of patients with gargoylism, *Acta haemat. (Basel)*, **29**, 202–7. [273]

MONEY, J. (1963) Cytogenetic and psychosexual incongruities with a note on spaceform blindness, *Amer. J. Psychiat.*, **119**, 820–7. [311, 317, 322]

MONEY, J., and POLLITT, E. (1964) Cytogenetic and psychosexual ambiguity: Klinefelter's syndrome and transvestism compared, *Arch. gen. Psychiat.*, **11**, 589–95. [317–18]

MONZ, W. (1965) The Marfan syndrome: clinical and necropsy findings in the A. family, *Med. J. Aust.*, i, 571–7. [225]

MOORE, K. L. (1959) Sex reversal in newborn babies, *Lancet*, i, 217–19. [300]

MORAN, P. A. P. (1965a) Class migration and the schizophrenia polymorphism, *Ann. hum. Genet*, **28**, 261–8. [70]

MORAN, P. A. P. (1965b) Schizophrenia and maternal age at parturition, *Ann. hum. Genet.*, **28**, 269–72. [70]

MORAN, P. A. P. (1969) Statistical methods in psychiatric research, *J. roy. statist. Soc.*, **132**, 484–517. [68–70]

MORAN, P. A. P., and ABE, K. (1969) Parental loss in homosexuals, *Brit. J. Psychiat.*, **115**, 319–20. [121]

MORGAN, H. G., MITCHELL, R. G., STOWERS, J. M., and THOMSON, J. (1956) Metabolic studies on two infants with idiopathic hypercalcaemia, *Lancet*, i, 925–31. [243–4]

MORQUIO, L. (1929) Sur une forme de dystrophie osseuse familiale, *Bull. Soc. Pediat. Paris*, **27**, 145–52. [271]

MORRIS, M. D., LEWIS, B. D., DOOLAN, P. D., and HARPER, H. A. (1961) Clinical and biochemical observations on an apparently non-fatal variant of branched-chain keto aciduria (maple syrup urine disease), *Pediatrics*, **28**, 918–23. [215]

MOSBACHER, F. W. (1925) *Über Recklinghausen-Kranke und deren Verwandte*, München. [281]

MOSER, H. W., EFRON, M. L., BROWN, H., DIAMOND, R., and NEUMANN, C. G. (1967) Argininosuccinic aciduria. Report of two new cases and demonstration of intermittent elevation of blood ammonia, *Amer. J. Med.*, **42**, 9–26. [229]

25A—

MOSES, S. W., ROTEM, Y., JAGODA, N., TALMOR, N., EICHHORN, F., and LEVIN, S. (1967) A clinical, genetic and biochemical study of familial dysautonomia in Israel, *Israel J. med. Sci.*, **3**, 358–71. [249]

MOSIER, H. D., SCOTT, L. W., and COTTER, L. H. (1960) The frequency of the positive sex-chromatin pattern in males with mental deficiency, *Pediatrics*, **25**, 291–7. [319–20]

MOSIER, H. D., SCOTT, L. W., and DINGMAN, H. F. (1960) Sexually deviant behaviour in Klinefelter's syndrome, *J. Pediat.*, **57**, 479–83. [317]

MOSSAKOWSKI, M., MATHIESON, G., and CUMINGS, J. N. (1961) On the relationship of metachromatic leucodystrophy and amaurotic idiocy, *Brain*, **84**, 585–604. [257–8]

MOTULSKY, A. G., SCHULTZ, A., and PRIEST, J. (1962) Werner's syndrome: chromosomes, genes, and the ageing process, *Lancet*, i, 160–1. [126]

MUDD, S. H., FINKELSTEIN, J. D., IRREVERE, F., and LASTER, L. (1964) Homocystinuria: an enzymatic defect, *Science*, **143**, 1443–5. [222]

MÜLLER, W., and SCHREIER, K. (1962) Die Ahorn-Sirup-Krankheit, *Dtsch. med. Wschr.*, **87**, 2479–81. [214]

MÜLLER-KÜPPERS, M., and STENZEL, K. (1963) Zum Problem der Frühmanifestation der Erbchorea, *Acta paedopsychiat.*, **30**, 348–55. [137]

MUNRO, T. A. (1947) Phenylketonuria: data on 47 British families, *Ann. Eugen. (Lond.)*, **14**, 60–88. [22, 206, 209]

MUNRO, T. A., PENROSE, L. S., and TAYLOR, G. L. (1939) A study of the linkage relationship between the genes for phenylketonuria and the ABR allelomorphs in man, p. 224 (abstract) *Proc. Seventh Internat. Genet. Congress*, Cambridge, 1941. [212]

MYRIANTHOPOULOS, N. C. (1962) Some epidemiologic and genetic aspects of Tay-Sachs' disease, in *Cerebral Sphingolipidoses: a Symposium on Tay-Sachs' Disease and Allied Disorders*, ed. Aronson, S. M., and Volk, B. W., New York. [261]

MYRIANTHOPOULOS, N. C. (1966) Huntington's chorea, *J. med. Genet.*, **3**, 298–314. [139, 144–5]

MYRIANTHOPOULOS, N. C., and ARONSON, S. M. (1966) Population dynamics of Tay-Sachs disease. I. Reproductive fitness and selection, *Amer. J. hum. Genet.*, **18**, 313–27. [262]

NADLER, C. S., STEIGER, W. A., TRONCELLETI, M., and DURANT, T. M. (1950) (quoted by Nielsen, J., 1965) Dystrophia myotonica, with special reference to endocrine function (Klinefelter's syndrome), *J. clin. Endocr.*, **10**, 630–6. [314]

NEALE, F. C., and FISCHER-WILLIAMS, M. (1958) Copper metabolism in normal adults and in clinically normal relatives of patients with Wilson's disease, *J. clin. Path.*, **11**, 441–7. [158]

NEEL, J. V. (1954) Problems in the estimation of the frequency of uncommon inherited traits, *Amer. J. hum. Genet.*, **6**, 51–60. [282]

NEUMAYER, E., and RETT, A. (1966) Eine Choreasippe mit rigider Form. (A rigid form of Huntington's chorea in three generations of a family), *Wien. Z. Nervenheilk*, **23**, 74–85. [137]

NEWMAN, C. G. H., WILSON, B. D. R., CALLAGHAN, P., and YOUNG, L. (1967) Neonatal death associated with isovalericacidaemia, *Lancet*, ii, 439–41. [216]

NEWMAN, H. A., and ENGEL, L. (1965) Phenylketonuria in a negro infant, *J. Pediat.*, **67**, 329–30. [207]

NEWMAN, H. H., FREEMAN, F. N., and HOLZINGER, K. J. (1937) *Twins: a Study of Heredity and Environment*, Chicago. [98]

NIEDERMEYER, E. (1966) Considerations of the centrencephalic (generalized) type of epilepsy, *Delaware med. J.*, **38**, 341–8. [166, 179]

NIELSEN, J. (1964a) Klinefelter's syndrome and behaviour, *Lancet*, ii, 587–8. [309]

NIELSEN, J. (1964b) Prevalence of Klinefelter's syndrome in patients with mental disorders, *Lancet*, i, 1109. [309]

NIELSEN, J. (1965) Klinefelter's syndrome in a neurological ward, *Acta neurol. scand.*, **41**, 197–214.   [314–15]

NIELSEN, J., (1968) Chromosomes in senile dementia, *Brit. J. Psychiat.*, **114**, 303–9.
                                                                                  [127]

NIEMANN, A. (1914) Ein unbekanntes Krankheitsbild, *Jb. Kinderheilk*, **79**, 1–10. [263]

NJÅ, A. (1945) A sex-linked type of gargoylism, *Acta paediat. (Uppsala)*, **33**, 267–86.
                                                                                  [269]

NORMAN, R. M. (1965) Personal communication.   [340]

NORMAN, R. M., URICH, H., and LLOYD, O. C. (1956) The neuropathology of infantile Gaucher's disease, *J. Path. Bact.*, **72**, 121–31.   [264]

NORMAN, R. M., URICH, H., TINGEY, A. H., and GOODBODY, R. A. (1959) Tay-Sachs disease with visceral involvement and its relationship to Niemann-Pick's disease, *J. Path. Bact.*, **78**, 409–21.   [258]

NORRIS, VERA (1959) *Mental Illness in London*, Maudsley Monographs No. 6, London.
                                                                                 [12, 13]

NORTHCUTT, R. C. (1962) Multiple congenital anomalies in a Negro infant with 13–15 trisomy, *Sth. med. J.*, **55**, 385–9.

NORTON, P. M., ROITMAN, E., SNYDERMAN, S. E., and HOLT, L. E. Jr. (1962) A new finding in maple-syrup-urine disease, *Lancet*, i, 26–7.   [213]

NOVELLETTO, A. (1958) Problèmes actuels de la myoclonie-épilepsie progressive de Unverricht-Lundborg. Revue bibliographique et critique, *Encéphale*, **47**, 223–52.
                                                                                  [169]

NYHAN, W. L., OLIVER, W. J., and LESCH, M. (1965) A familial disorder of uric acid metabolism and central nervous system function. II, *J. Pediat.*, **67**, 257–63. [246–7]

O'BRIEN, D., PEPPERS, T. D., and SILVER, H. K. (1960) Idiopathic hypercalcemia of infancy, *J. Amer. med. Ass.*, **173**, 1106–10.   [243]

ØDEGAARD, Ø. (1963) The psychiatric disease entities in the light of a genetic investigation, *Acta psychiat. scand.*, Suppl. 169, **39**, 94–104.

ØDEGAARD, Ø. (1970) The multifactorial theory of inheritance in predisposition for schizophrenia, in *Genetic Factors in Schizophrenia*, ed. Kaplan, A. R., Springfield, Ill.   [54, 63]

OEPEN, H., and BICKEL, H. (1964) Aminosäuren- und Zuckerbestimmung im Urin bei Huntingtonscher Chorea, *Hum. Genet.*, **1**, 98–100.   [141]

OEPEN, H., and KREUTZ, F. H. (1964) Orientierende Untersuchung des Fettstoffwechsels bei Huntingtonscher Chorea, *Hum. Genet.*, **1**, 101–2.   [141]

OHNO, S., KAPLAN, W. D., and KINOSITA, R. (1959) Formation of the sex chromatin by a single X-chromosome in liver cells of Rattus Norvegious, *Exp. Cell Res.*, **18**, 415–18.   [298]

OPITZ, J. M., SEGAL, A. T., LEHRKE, R. L., and NADLER, H. L. (1965) The etiology of the Brachmann-de Lange syndrome, *Birth defects reprint series*, the National Foundation, March of Dimes, New York.   [296]

ØSTER, J. (1953) *Mongolism. A clinicogenealogical investigation comprising 526 mongols living on Seeland and neighbouring islands in Denmark*, Copenhagen.
                                                                       [326, 331, 335–6]

OUNSTED, C. (1955) The hyperkinetic syndrome in epileptic children, *Lancet*, ii, 303–11.
                                                                                  [168]

OVERZIER, C. (1958) Transvestitismus und Klinefelter-syndrom, *Arch. Psychiat. Nervenkr.*, **198**, 198–209.   [318]

PAINE, R. S., and EFRON, M. (1963) Atypical variants of the 'ataxia telangiectasia' syndrome, *Develop. Med. Child Neurol.*, **5**, 14–23.   [252–3]

PANSE, F. (1938) Über erbliche Zwischenhirnsyndrome und ihre entwicklungsphysiologischen Grundlagen, *Z. ges. Neurol. Psychiat.*, **160**, 1–72.   [286]

PANSE, F. (1942) *Die Erbchorea. Eine Klinisch-genetische Studie*, Leipzig.
[136, 138, 143]

PARE, C. M. B. (1956) Homosexuality and chromosomal sex, *J. psychosom. Res.*, **1**, 247–51. [316]

PARTANEN, J., BRUUN, K., and MARKKANEN, T. (1966) *Inheritance of Drinking Behaviour*, Helsinki. [109–10]

PARTINGTON, M. W. (1961) Observations on phenylketonuria in Ontario, *Canad. med. Ass. J.*, **84**, 985–91. [208]

PARTINGTON, M. W., and ANDERSON, R. M. (1964) Case finding in phenylketonuria. I. Report of a survey by the College of General Practice of Canada, *Canad. med. Ass. J.*, **90**, 1312–15. [206]

PASQUALINI, R. Q., VIDAL, G., and BUR, G. E. (1957) Psychopathology of Klinefelter's syndrome: review of 31 cases, *Lancet*, ii, 164–7. [307, 309]

PASSOW, A. (1936) *Handbuch der Neurologie*, ed. Bumke and Foerster, Vol. 16, 908, Berlin. [261]

PATAU, K., SMITH, D. W., THERMAN, E., INHORN, S. L., and WAGNER, H. P. (1960) Multiple congenital anomaly caused by an extra autosome, *Lancet*, i, 790–3. [340–1]

PATAU, K., THERMAN, E., SMITH, D. W., and DEMARS R. I. (1961) Trisomy for chromosome No. 18 in man, *Chromosoma (Berl.)*, **12**, 280–5.

PATTERSON, R. M., BAGCHI, B. K., and TEST, A. (1948) The prediction of Huntington's chorea. An electroencephalographic and genetic study, *Amer. J. Psychiat.*, **104**, 786–97. [144]

PAULSON, G. W., and LYLE, C. B. (1966) Tuberous sclerosis, *Develop. Med. Child Neurol.*, **8**, 571–86. [276, 278–80]

PELC, S., and VIS, H. (1960) Ataxie familiale avec telangiectasies oculaires (Syndrome de D. Louis-Bar), *Acta neurol. belg.*, **60**, 905–22. [253]

PENROSE, L. S. (1932) On the interaction of heredity and environment in the study of human genetics (with special reference to mongolian imbecility), *J. Genet.*, **25**, 407–22. [335]

PENROSE, L. S. (1934) A method of separating the relative aetiological effects of birth order and maternal age, with special reference to mongolian imbecility, *Ann. Eugen. (Lond.)*, **6**, 108–22. [325]

PENROSE, L. S. (1935) Inheritance of phenylpyruvic amentia (phenylketonuria), *Lancet*, ii, 192–4. [22]

PENROSE, L. S. (1936) Autosomal mutation and modification in man with special reference to mental defect, *Ann. Eugen. (Lond.)*, **7**, 1–15. [280]

PENROSE, L. S. (1938a) Some genetical problems in mental deficiency, *J. ment. Sci.*, **84**, 693–707. [290, 331]

PENROSE, L. S. (1938b) A clinical and genetic study of 1280 cases of mental defect, *Spec. Rep. Ser. med. Res. Coun. (Lond.)*, No. 229, London, H.M.S.O. [185]

PENROSE, L. S. (1945) A search for linkage between the A, B, O agglutinogens and phenylketonuria, *Amer. J. ment. Defic.*, **50**, 4–7. [212]

PENROSE, L. S. (1946) Phenylketonuria. A problem in eugenics, *Lancet*, i, 949–53.
[208]

PENROSE, L. S. (1949a) *The Biology of Mental Defect*, London. [263]

PENROSE, L. S. (1949b) The Galton Laboratory: Its work and aims, *Eugen. Rev.*, **41**, 17–25. [53]

PENROSE, L. S. (1950) Data for the study of linkage in man: red hair and the ABO locus, *Ann. Eugen. (Lond.)*, **15**, 243–7. [212]

PENROSE, L. S. (1951a) Measurement of pleiotropic effects in phenylketonuria, *Ann. Eugen. (Lond.)*, **16**, 134–41. [205, 212]

PENROSE, L. S. (1951b) Maternal age in familial mongolism, *J. ment. Sci.*, **97**, 738–47. [331]

PENROSE, L. S. (1956a) Some notes on heredity counselling, *Acta genet.* (*Basel*), **6**, 35–40. [333]

PENROSE, L. S. (1956b) Microcephaly, *Folia hered. path.* (*Milano*), **5**, 79–86. [287]

PENROSE, L. S. (1957) Parental age in achondroplasia and mongolism, *Amer. J. hum. Genet.*, **9**, 167–9. [285]

PENROSE, L. S. (1962a) Paternal age in mongolism, *Lancet*, i, 1101. [330]

PENROSE, L. S. (1962b) Biological aspects, in *Proceedings of the London Conference on the Scientific Study of Mental Deficiency, 1960*, Vol. I, 11–18, ed. Richards, B. W. Dagenham. [334]

PENROSE, L. S. (1963) *The Biology of Mental Defect*, 3rd ed,. London. [227, 280–2, 287, 291, 294, 298, 325]

PENROSE, L. S. (1966) *The Biology of Mental Defect*, 2nd rev. ed., London. [6]

PENROSE, L. S., and QUASTEL, J. H. (1937) Metabolic studies in phenylketonuria, *Biochem. J.*, **31**, 266–74. [203]

PENROSE, L. S., and SMITH, G. F. (1966) *Down's Anomaly*, London. [325, 328–31, 333–4, 336, 338]

PERRINE, G. A. Jr., and GOODMAN, R. M. (1966) A family study of Huntington's chorea with unusual manifestations, *Ann. intern. Med.*, **64**, 570–4. [137]

PERRIS, C., ed. (1966) *A Study of Bipolar (Manic-depressive) and Unipolar Recurrent Depressive Psychoses*, *Acta psychiat. scand.*, Suppl. 194, Copenhagen. [81]

PERRIS, C. (1968) Genetic transmission of depressive psychoses, *Acta psychiat. scand.*, Suppl. 203, 45–52. [83]

PERRY, T. L. (1961) Urinary excretion of trace metals in Huntington's chorea, *Neurology* (*Minneap.*), **11**, 1086–90. [139]

PERRY, T. L., TISCHLER, B., and CHAPPLE, J. A. (1966) The incidence of mental illness in the relatives of individuals suffering from phenylketonuria or mongolism, *J. psychiat. Res.*, **4**, 51–7. [210]

PETERSÉN, I., and ÅKESSON, H. O. (1968) EEG studies of siblings of children showing 14 and 6 per second positive spikes, *Acta genet.* (*Basel*), **18**, 163–9. [164]

PFÄNDLER, U. (1946) Etude clinique et génétique de la maladie Niemann-Pick, *Arch. Klaus-Stift. Vererb.- Forsch.*, **21**, 311–15. [263]

PICK, L. (1927) Über die lipoidzellige Splenohepatomegalie Typus Niemann-Pick als Stoffwechselerkrankung, *Med. Klin.*, **23**, 1483–8. [263]

PISANI, D., and CACCHIONE, A. (1934) Frenastenia e dermatosi, *Riv. sper. Freniat.*, **58**, 722–36 (quoted by Richards, Rundle, and Wilding, 1957). [291–2]

POISNER, A. M. (1960) Serum phenylalanine in schizophrenia: biochemical genetic aspects, *J. nerv. ment. Dis.*, **131**, 74–6. [211]

POLANI, P. E. (1960) Chromosomal factors in certain types of educational subnormality, in *Mental Retardation*, ed. Bowman, P. W., and Mautner, H. V., New York. [322]

POLANI, P. E. (1966) Sex chromosome anomalies, *Proc. VI Congresso Internazionale di Patologie Clinica, Rome, 1966*, 361–3. [299]

POLANI, P. E. (1967) Occurrence and effect of human chromosome abnormalities, in *Social and Genetic Influences on Life and Death*, Eugenics Society Symposium, ed. Lord Platt, and Parkes, A. S., Edinburgh. [384]

POLANI, P. E., BRIGGS, J. H., FORD, C. E., CLARKE, C. M., and BERG, J. M. (1960) A mongol girl with 46 chromosomes, *Lancet*, i, 721–4.

POLANI, P. E., HUNTER, W. F., and LENNOX, B. (1954) Chromosomal sex in Turner's syndrome with coarctation of the aorta, *Lancet*, ii, 120–1. [304]

POLANI, P. E., LESSOF, M. H., and BISHOP, P. M. F. (1956) Colour-blindness in 'ovarian agenesis' (gonadal dysplasia), *Lancet*, ii, 118–20. [304]

POLLACK, M., WOERNER, M. G., GOODMAN, W., and GREENBERG, I. M. (1966) Childhood development patterns of hospitalized adult schizophrenic and nonschizophrenic patients and their siblings, *Amer. J. Orthopsychiat.*, **36**, 510–17.   [39]

POLLIN, W., and STABENAU, J. R. (1968) Biological, psychological and historical differences in a series of monozygotic twins discordant for schizophrenia, in *The Transmission of Schizophrenia*, ed. Rosenthal, D., and Kety, S. S., Oxford. [17, 348]

POLLIN, W., STABENAU, J. R., MOSHER, L., and TUPIN, J. (1966) Life history differences in identical twins discordant for schizophrenia, *Amer. J. Orthopsychiat.*, **36**, 492–509.   [348]

PONCETT, E., LAFOURCADE, J., ZHA, J., and AUTIER, C. (1965) Les troubles de la voix et les malformations laryngées dans la maladie par aberration chromosomique de 'Maladie du cri du chat', *Ann. Oto-laryng.* (*Paris*), **82**, 865–8.   [343]

POND, D. A., BIDWELL, B. H., and STEIN, L. (1960) A survey of epilepsy in fourteen general practices. I. Demographic and medical data, *Psychiat. Neurol. Neurochir.* (*Amst.*), **63**, 217–36.   [161]

POTOTZKY, C., and GRIGG, A. E. (1942) A revision of the prognosis in mongolism, *Amer. J. Orthopsychiat.*, **12**, 503–10.   [336]

PRADER, A., SCHNEIDER, J., ZÜBLIN, W., FRANCÉS, J. M., and RÜEDI, K. (1958) Die Häufigkeit des echten, chromatin-positiven Klinefelter-Syndroms und seine Beziehungen zum Schwachsinn, *Schweiz. med. Wschr.*, **88**, 917–20.   [308, 320]

PRATT, R. T. C. (1967) *The Genetics of Neurological Disorders*, London.   [169]

PRATT, R. T. C., GARDINER, D., CURZON, G., PIERCY, M. F., and CUMINGS, J. N. (1963) Phenylalanine tolerance in endogenous depression, *Brit. J. Psychiat.*, **109**, 624–8.   [211]

PREISER, S. A., and DAVENPORT, C. B. (1918) Multiple neurofibromatosis (von Recklinghausen's disease) and its inheritance, description of a case, *Amer. J. med. Sci.*, **156**, 507–40.   [281–2]

PRICE, J. (1968) The genetics of depressive behaviour, in *Recent Developments in Affective Disorders*, ed. Coppen, A. J., and Walk, A., British Journal of Psychiatry Spec. Publ. No. 2, Ashford, Kent.   [108]

PRICE, W. H., STRONG, J. A. WHATMORE, P. B., and McCLEMONT, W. F. (1966) Criminal patients with XYY sex-chromosome complement, *Lancet*, i, 565–6.   [301]

PRICE, W. H., and WHATMORE, P. B. (1967) Behaviour disorders and pattern of crime among XYY males identified at a maximum security hospital, *Brit. med. J.*, **1**, 533–6.   [301–2, 318, 322]

PRINGLE, J. J. (1890) A case of congenital adenoma sebaceum, *Brit. J. Derm.*, **2**, 1–14.   [277)

PRITCHARD, M. (1962) Homosexuality and genetic sex, *J. ment. Sci.*, **108**, 616–23.   [316]

PROUT, C. T., and WHITE, M. A. (1956) The schizophrenic's sibling, *J. nerv. ment. Dis.*, **123**, 162–70.   [39]

PTACEK, L. J., OPITZ, J. M., SMITH, D. W., GERRITSEN, T., and WAISMAN, H. A. (1963) The Cornelia De Lange syndrome, *J. Pediat.*, **63**, 1000–20.   [295–6]

RABOCH, J., and NEDOMA, K. (1958) Sex chromatin and sexual behavior: a study of 36 men with female nuclear pattern and of 194 homosexuals, *Psychosom. Med.*, **20**, 55–9.   [120]

RAPHAEL, T., and SHAW, M. W. (1963) Chromosome studies in schizophrenia, *J. Amer. med. Ass.*, **183**, 1022–8.   [309]

RAYNER, S. (1952) Juvenile amaurotic idiocy: diagnosis of heterozygotes, *Acta genet.* (*Basel*), **3**, 1–5.   [260]

RECORD, R. G., and SMITH, A. (1955) Incidence, mortality and sex distribution of mongoloid defectives, *Brit. J. prev. soc. Med.*, **9**, 10–15.   [335]

REED, E. W., and REED, S. C. (1965) *Mental Retardation: a Family Study*, Philadelphia. [199–200]

REED, T. E. (1959) The definition of relative fitness of individuals with specific genetic traits, *Amer. J. hum. Genet.*, **11**, 137–55. [144]

REED, T. E., and CHANDLER, J. H. (1958) Huntington's chorea in Michigan, 1. Demography and genetics, *Amer. J. hum. Genet.*, **10**, 201–25. [138, 143]

REED, T. E., and NEEL, J. V. (1959) Huntington's chorea in Michigan. 2. Selection and mutation, *Amer. J. hum. Genet.*, **11**, 107–36. [144]

REESE, H., and BARETA, J. (1950) Heredopathia atactica polyneuritiformis, *J. Neuropath. exp. Neurol.*, **9**, 385–95. [250]

REFSUM, S. (1946) Heredopathia atactica polyneuritiformis. A familial syndrome not hitherto described, *Acta psychiat. scand.*, Suppl. 38. [249–50]

REFSUM, S., SALOMONSEN, L., and SKATVEDT, M. (1949) Heredopathia atactica polyneuritiformis in children. A preliminary communication, *J. Pediat.*, **35**, 335–43. [250]

REICH, T. (1970) Personal communication. [51]

REICH, T., CLAYTON, P. J., and WINOKUR, G. (1969) Family history studies: V. The genetics of mania, *Amer. J. Psychiat.*, **125**, 1358–69. [83]

REILLY, W. A. (1941) The granules in the leukocytes in gargoylism, *Amer. J. Dis. Child.*, **62**, 489–91. [272]

RENWICK, J. H., LAWLER, S. D., and COWIE, V. A. (1960) Phenylketonuria: a linkage study using phenylalanine tolerance tests, *Amer. J. hum. Genet.*, **12**, 287–322. [212]

RESEARCH COMMITTEE OF THE COLLEGE OF GENERAL PRACTITIONERS (1960) A survey of the epilepsies in general practice, *Brit. med. J.*, **2**, 416–22. [161]

VON REUSS, A. (1908) Zuckerausscheidung im Säuglingsalter, *Wien. med. Wschr.*, **58**, 799–804. [237]

RICHARDS, B. W. (1960) Congenital ichthyosis, spastic diplegia, and mental deficiency, *Brit. med. J.*, **2**, 714. [292]

RICHARDS, B. W., RUNDLE, A., and WILDING, A. ST. J. (1957) Congenital ichthyosis, spastic diplegia and mental deficiency, *J. ment. Defic. Res.*, **1**, 118–29. [292–3]

RICHARDS, B. W., STEWART, A., SYLVESTER, P. E., and JASIEWICZ, V. (1965) Cytogenetic survey of 225 patients diagnosed clinically as mongols, *J. ment. Defic. Res.*, **9**, 245–59. [328]

RICHARDS, W., DONNELL, G. N., WILSON, W. A., STOWENS, D., and PERRY, T. (1965) The oculo-cerebro-renal syndrome of Lowe, *Amer. J. Dis. Child.*, **109**, 185–203. [235–6]

RICHTERICH, R., KAHLKE, W., MECHELEN, P. VAN, and ROSSI, E. (1963) Refsums syndrom (heredopathia atactica polyneuritiformis): Ein angeborener Defekt im Lipid-Stoffwechsel mit Speicherung von 3, 7, 11, 15-Tetramethyl-Hexandecansäure, *Klin. Wschr.*, **41**, 800–1. [250]

RIDLER, M. A. C., SHAPIRO, A., and McKIBBEN, W. R. (1963) Sex chromatin abnormalities in female subnormal patients, *Brit. J. Psychiat.*, **109**, 390–4. [321]

RIEGER, H., and TRAUNER, R. (1929) Über einen Fall von Biedl-Bardetschem Syndrom und die Erblichkeitsverhaltnisse dieses Zustandes, *Z. Augenheilk*, **68**, 235–43. [287]

RILEY, C. M., DAY, R. L., GREELEY, D. M., and LANGFORD, W. S. (1949) Central autonomic dysfunction with defective lacrimation, *Pediatrics*, **3**, 468–78. [249]

RILEY, I. D. (1960) Gout and cerebral palsy in a 3-year-old boy, *Arch. Dis. Childh.*, **35**, 293–5. [245]

DE RISIO, C., CONTERIO, F., and RIDOLO, P. (1965) Il problema dell' ereditarietá nella demenza presenile di Alzheimer. (Analisi clinica e genetica della forma familiare della malattia), *Sist. nerv.*, **17**, 188–96. [152]

ROBERTS, J. A. FRASER (1937) Sex-linked microphthalmia sometimes associated with mental deficiency, *Brit. med. J.*, **2**, 1213–16. [187]

ROBERTS, J. A. FRASER (1945) On the difference between the sexes in dispersion of intelligence, *Brit. med. J.*, **1**, 727–30.   [193]

ROBERTS, J. A. FRASER (1952) The genetics of mental deficiency, *Eugen. Rev.*, **44**, 71–83.   [186]

ROBINS, M. M., STEVENS, H. F., and LINKER, A. (1963) Morquio's disease: an abnormality of mucopolysaccharide metabolism, *J. Pediat.*, **62**, 881–9.   [271]

RODIN, E. A. (1964) Familial occurrence of the 14 and 6/sec. positive spike phenomenon, *Electroenceph. clin. Neurophysiol.*, **17**, 566–70.   [164]

RODIN, E. A., and WHELAN, J. L. (1960) Familial occurrence of focal temporal electroencephalographic abnormalities, *Neurology (Minneap.)*, **10**, 542–5.   [167]

RODRIGUEZ-VIGIL, L. E., LAGUNILLA, M. F. L., SÁNCHEZ, B. J. L., JIMÉNEZ, P. F., and ANTŨNA, F. E. (1964) Typus degenerativus amstelodamensis de Cornelia de Lange, *Rev. esp. Pediat.*, **20**, 463–76.   [296]

ROHR, K. (1961) Beitrag zur Kenntnis der sogennannten schizophrenen Reaktionen, Familienbild und Katamnesen, *Arch. Psychiat. Nervenkr.*, **201**, 626–47.   [43]

ROSANOFF, A. J., and HANDY, L. M. (1934) Etiology of mongolism, with special reference to its occurrence in twins, *Amer. J. Dis. Child.*, **48**, 764–79.   [327]

ROSANOFF, A. J., HANDY, L. M., and PLESSET, I. R. (1935) The etiology of manic-depressive syndromes with special reference to their occurrence in twins, *Amer. J. Psychiat.*, **91**, 725–62.   [84]

ROSANOFF, A. J., HANDY, L. M., and PLESSET, I. R. (1941) The etiology of child behavior difficulties, juvenile delinquency and adult criminality with special reference to their occurrence in twins, *Psychiat. Monogr. (California) No. 1*, Sacramento, Department of Institutions.   [114–16]

ROSECRANS, C. J. (1968) The relationship of normal/21-trisomy mosaicism and intellectual development, *Amer. J. ment. Defic.*, **72**, 562–6.   [338]

ROSENBERG, C. M. (1967) Familial aspects of obsessional neurosis, *Brit. J. Psychiat.*, **113**, 405–13.   [106]

ROSENTHAL, D. (1963) *The Genain Quadruplets. A Study of Heredity and Environment in Schizophrenia*, New York.   [37–8]

ROSENTHAL, D., WENDER, P. H., KETY, S. S., SCHULSINGER, F., WELNER, J., and ØSTERGAARD, LISE (1968) Schizophrenics' offspring reared in adoptive homes, in *The Transmission of Schizophrenia*, ed. Rosenthal, D., and Kety, S. S., Oxford.
                                                                                                                          [42]

ROTH, M. (1955) The natural history of mental disorder in old age, *J. ment. Sci.*, **101**, 281–301.   [127]

ROTH, M. (1957) Interaction of genetic and environmental factors in the causation of schizophrenia, in *Schizophrenia: Somatic Aspects*, ed. Richter, D., New York.   [27]

RUD, E. (1927) Et tilfaelde af infantilisme med Tetani, Epilepsi, Polyneuritis, Ichthyosis og Anaemi af pernicios type, *Hospitalstidende*, **70**, 525–38.   [291–2]

RÜDIN, E. (1953) Ein Beitrag zur Frage der Zwangskrankheit, insbesondere ihrer hereditären Beziehungen, *Arch. Psychiat. Nervenkr.*, **191**, 14–54.   [105]

RUSSELL, A., LEVIN, B., OBERHOLZER, V. G., and SINCLAIR, L. (1962) Hyperammonaemia: a new instance of an inborn enzymatic defect of the biosynthesis of urea, *Lancet*, ii, 699–700.   [231]

SABBATH, J. C., MORRIS, T. A., MENZER–BENARON, D., and STURGIS, S. H. (1961) Psychiatric observations in adolescent girls lacking ovarian function, *Psychosom. Med.*, **23**, 224–31.   [310]

SACHS, B. (1887) On arrested cerebral development with special reference to its cortical pathology, *J. nerv. ment. Dis.*, **14**, 541–53.   [258]

SACREZ, R., JUIF, J.-G., METAIS, P., SOFATZIS, J., and DOUROF, N. (1962) Un cas mortel d'intolérance héréditaire au fructose, *Pédiatrie*, **17**, 875–89.   [242]

DE SANCTIS, C., and CACCHIONE, A. (1933) L'idiozia xerodermica, *Zbl. ges. Neurol. Psychiat.*, **65**, 386–7. [291]

SASS-KORTSAK, A., CHERNIAK, M., GEIGER, D. W., and SLATER, R. J. (1959) Observations on ceruloplasmin in Wilson's disease, *J. clin. Invest.*, **38**, 1672–82. [158]

SCARABICCHI, S., and MARTINO, A. M. (1963) La sindrome di Sjögren e Larsson. Revisione critica e presentazione di tre casi, *Minerva med.*, **54**, 1603–9. [291]

SCHARFETTER, C. (1970) On the hereditary aspects of symbiontic psychoses: a contribution towards the understanding of the schizophrenia-like psychoses, *Psychiat. clin.*, **3**, 145–52. [44]

SCHEIE, H. G., HAMBRICK, G. W. JR., and BARNESS, L. A. (1962) A newly recognised *forme fruste* of Hurler's disease (gargoylism), *Amer. J. Ophthal.*, **53**, 753–69. [270]

SCHEIG, R. L., and BORNSTEIN, P. (1961) Tuberous sclerosis in the adult. An unusual case without mental deficiency or epilepsy, *Arch. intern. Med.*, **108**, 789–95. [279]

SCHEINBERG, I. H., and STERNLIEB, I. (1959) The liver in Wilson's disease, *Gastroenterology*, **37**, 550–64. [154]

SCHENK, E. A., and HAGGERTY, J. (1964) Morquio's disease: a radiologic and morphologic study, *Pediatrics*, **34**, 839–50. [271]

SCHENK, V. W. D. (1959) Re-examination of a family with Pick's disease, *Ann. hum. Genet.*, **23**, 325–33. [150, 153]

SCHILLER, J. G. (1959) Craniofacial dysostosis of Crouzon. A case report and pedigree with emphasis on heredity, *Pediatrics* **23**, 107–12. [285]

SCHIMKE, R. N., MCKUSICK, V. A., HUANG, T., and POLLACK, A. D. (1965) Homocystinuria. Studies of 20 families with 38 affected members, *J. Amer. med. Ass.*, **193**, 711–19. [222, 224–5]

SCHNEIDER, A. J., and GARRARD, S. D. (1966) Diagnostic and therapeutic implications of persistent hyperphenylalaninemia in an infant heterozygous for the gene of phenylketonuria, *J. Pediat.*, **68**, 704–12. [207]

SCHÖNFELDER, T. (1966) Kindliche Chorea Huntington, *Z. Kinderheilk*, **95**, 131–42. [137]

SCHULZ, B. (1929) Über die hereditären Beziehungen der Hirnarteriosklerose, *Z. ges. Neurol. Psychiat.*, **120**, 35–67. [132]

SCHULZ, B. (1932) Zur Erbpathologie der Schizophrenie, *Z. ges. Neurol. Psychiat.*, **143**, 175–293. [27–8]

SCHULZ, B. (1934) Versuch einer genealogisch-statistischen Überprüfung eines Schizophreniematerials auf biologische Einheitlichkeit, *Z. ges. Neurol. Psychiat.*, **151**, 145–70. [27, 55–6]

SCHULZ, B. (1936) *Methodik der Medizinischen Erbforschung*, Leipzig. [355]

SCHULZ, B., and LEONHARD, K. (1940) Erbbiologisch-klinische Untersuchungen an insgesamt 99 im Sinne Leonhards typischen beziehungsweise atypischen Schizophrenien, *Z. ges. Neurol. Psychiat.*, **168**, 587–613. [33–4]

SCHWAB, HANS (1938) Die Katatonie auf Grund katamnestischer Untersuchunge. II. Die Erblichkeit der eigentlichen Katatonie, *Z. ges. Neurol. Psychiat.*, **163**, 441–506. [32]

SCHWARTZ, J. F., ROWLAND, L. P., EDER, H., MARKS, P. A., OSSERMAN, E. F., HIRSCHBERG, E., and ANDERSON, H. (1963) Bassen-Kornzweig syndrome: deficiency of serum β-lipoprotein, *Arch. Neurol. (Chic.)*, **8**, 438–54. [248]

SCHWARZ, V., WELLS, A. R., HOLZEL, A., and KOMROWER, G. M. (1961) A study of the genetics of galactosaemia, *Ann. hum. Genet.*, **25**, 179–88. [241–2]

SCOTT, P. D., and KAHN, J. (1968) An XYY patient of above average intelligence as a basis for review of the psychopathology, medico-legal implications of the syndrome, and possibilities for prevention, in *Psychopathic Offenders*, ed. West, D. J., Cambridge. [322]

SCOTTISH COUNCIL FOR RESEARCH IN EDUCATION (1949) *The Trend of Scottish Intelligence*, London.   [192]

SEEGMILLER, J. E., ROSENBLOOM, F. M., and KELLEY, W. N. (1967) Enzyme defect associated with sex-linked human neurological disorder and excessive purine synthesis, *Science*, **155**, 1682–4.   [246]

SEGAL, S., BLAIR, A., and TOPPER, Y. (1963) Congenital galactosaemia with normal galactose metabolism, *Clin. Res.*, **11**, 228.   [238]

SHAFFER, J. W. (1962) A specific cognitive deficit observed in gonadal aplasia (Turner's syndrome), *J. clin. Psychol.*, **18**, 403–6.   [311]

SHAPIRO, S. L., SHEPPARD, G. L., DREIFUSS, F. E., and NEWCOMBE, D. S. (1966) X-linked recessive inheritance of a syndrome of mental retardation, *Proc. Soc. exp. Biol.* (*N.Y.*), **122**, 609–11.   [248]

SHIELDS, J. (1954) Personality differences and neurotic traits in normal twin school-children, *Eugen. Rev.*, **45**, 213–46.   [21, 102]

SHIELDS, J. (1962) *Monozygotic Twins Brought up Apart and Brought up Together*, London.   [98–9, 198]

SHIELDS, J. (1968a) Summary of the genetic evidence, in *The Transmission of Schizophrenia*, ed. Rosenthal, D., and Kety, S. S., Oxford.   [23, 32]

SHIELDS, J. (1968b) Personal communication.   [106]

SHIELDS, J. (1971) Heredity and psychological abnormality, in *Handbook of Abnormal Psychology*, 2nd ed., ed. Eysenck, H. J., London.   [97, 99, 197–8]

SHIELDS, J., and SLATER, E. (1960) Heredity and psychological abnormality, in *Handbook of Abnormal Psychology*, 1st ed., ed. Eysenck, H. J., London.   [196–7]

SHIELDS, J., and SLATER, E. (1966) La similarité du diagnostic chez les jumeaux et le problème de la spécificité biologique dans les névroses et les troubles de la personnalité, *Évolut. psychiat.*, **31**, 441–51.   [103]

SHRIMPTON, E. A. G., and SLATER, ELIOT (1939) Die Berechnung des Standardfehlers für die Weinbergsche Morbiditätstafel, *Z. ges. Neurol. Psychiat.*, **166**, 715–18.
                                                                                      [356]

SHUTTLEWORTH, G. E. (1909) Mongolian imbecility, *Brit. med. J.*, **2**, 661–4.   [327]

SIEMENS, H. W. (1926a) Zum Studium der Abortivformen der Recklinghausenscher Krankheit, *Derm. Z.*, **46**, 168.   [281]

SIEMENS, H. W. (1926b) Klinisch-dermatologische Studien über die Recklinghausensche Krankheit, *Arch. Derm. Syph.* (*Berl.*), **150**, 80.   [281]

SIEMENS, H. W. (1926c) Über Pigmentflecke bei Recklinghausen-Kranken, *Arch. Derm. Syph.* (*Berl.*), **151**, 382.   [281]

SILBERMAN, J., DANCIS, J., and FEIGIN, J. (1961) Neuropathological observations in maple syrup urine disease, *Arch. Neurol.* (*Chic.*), **5**, 351–63.   [213–14]

SINGER, M. T., and WYNNE, L. C. (1965) Thought disorder and family relations of schizophrenics, *Arch. gen. Psychiat.*, **12**, 201–12.   [40]

SJÖGREN, T. (1931) *Die juvenile amaurotische Idiotie*, Lund.   [261–2]

SJÖGREN, T. (1935) Vererbungsmedizinische Untersuchungen über Huntingtons Chorea in einer schwedischen Bauernpopulation, *Z. menschl. Vererb.-u. Konstit.-Lehre*, **19**, 131–65.   [143–5]

SJÖGREN, T. (1943) Klinische und erbbiologische Untersuchungen über die Heredoataxien, *Acta psychiat. scand.*, Suppl. 27.   [261–2]

SJÖGREN, T. (1956) Oligophrenia combined with congenital ichthyosiform erythrodermia, spastic syndrome and macular-retinal degeneration, *Acta genet.* (*Basel*), **6**, 80–91.   [291]

SJÖGREN, T. (1959) The genetics of schizophrenia, Congress Report of the 2nd International Congress for Psychiatry, 1957, Vol. 1, Zürich.   [38]

SJÖGREN, T., and LARSSON, T. (1957) Oligophrenia in combination with congenital ichthyosis and spastic disorders. A clinical and genetic study, *Acta psychiat. (Kbh.)*, Suppl. 113, **32**, 1–112.   [291–2]

SJÖGREN, T., SJÖGREN, H., and LINDGREN, Å. G. H. (1952) Morbus Alzheimer and Morbus Pick. A genetic, clinical and patho-anatomical study, *Acta psychiat. scand.*, Suppl. 82.   [148–51]

SLATER, E. (1938) Zur Erbpathologie des manisch-depressiven Irreseins. Die Eltern und Kinder von Manisch-Depressiven, *Z. ges. Neurol. Psychiat.*, **163**, 1–147.   [89]

SLATER, E. (1943) The neurotic constitution. A statistical study of two thousand neurotic soldiers, *J. Neurol. Psychiat.*, **6**, 1–16.   [95]

SLATER, E. (1953) Psychotic and neurotic illnesses in twins, *Spec. Rep. Ser. med. Res. Coun. (Lond.)*, No. 278, London, H.M.S.O.   [17–18]

SLATER, E. (1958a) The monogenic theory of schizophrenia, *Acta genet. (Basel)*, **8**, 50–6.   [58–60]

SLATER, E. (1958b) The sibs and children of homosexuals, in *Symposium on Nuclear Sex*, ed. Smith, D. R., and Davidson, W. M., London.   [316]

SLATER, E. (1961) The thirty-fifth Maudsley lecture: 'Hysteria 311', *J. ment. Sci.*, **107**, 359–81.   [106–7, 348]

SLATER, E. (1962) Birth order and maternal age of homosexuals, *Lancet*, i, 69–71. [120]

SLATER, E. (1963) Diagnosis of zygosity by finger prints, *Acta psychiat. scand.*, **39**, 78–84.   [350]

SLATER, E. (1965) Diagnosis of 'Hysteria', *Brit. med. J.*, **1**, 1395–9.   [107]

SLATER, E. (1966) Expectation of abnormality on paternal and maternal sides: a computational model, *J. med. Genet.*, **3**, 159–61.   [63, 90]

SLATER, E. (1968) A review of earlier evidence on genetic factors in schizophrenia, in *The Transmission of Schizophrenia*, ed. Rosenthal, D., and Kety, S. S., Oxford.

SLATER, E., BEARD, A. W., and GLITHERO, E. (1963) The schizophrenia-like psychoses of epilepsy, *Brit. J. Psychiat.*, **109**, 95–150.   [180]

SLATER, E., and GLITHERO, E. (1963) The schizophrenia-like psychoses of epilepsy. iii. Genetical aspects, *Brit. J. Psychiat.*, **109**, 130–3.   [28]

SLATER, E., and GLITHERO, E. (1965) A follow-up of patients diagnosed as suffering from 'hysteria', *J. psychosom. Res.*, **9**, 9–13.   [107]

SLATER, E., and ROTH, M. (1969) *Clinical Psychiatry*, 3rd ed., London.   [77]

SLATER, E., and SHIELDS, J. (1969) Genetical aspects of anxiety, in *Studies of Anxiety*, ed. Lader, M. H., Brit. J. Psychiat. Spec. Publn No. 3, Ashford, Kent.   [103–5]

SLATER, E., and SLATER, P. (1944) A heuristic theory of neurosis, *J. Neurol. Psychiat.*, **7**, 49–55.   [94–5]

SLATER, E., and TSUANG, M.-t. (1968) Abnormality on paternal and maternal sides: observations in schizophrenia and manic-depression, *J. med. Genet.*, **5**, 197–9.   [63, 90–1]

SLATER, E., and WOODSIDE, MOYA (1951) *Patterns of Marriage. A Study of Marriage Relationships in the Urban Working Classes*, London.   [194]

SLATER, P., SHIELDS, J., and SLATER, E. (1964) A quadratic discriminant of zygosity from fingerprints, *J. med. Genet.*, **1**, 42–6.   [350]

SLOME, D. (1933) The genetic basis of amaurotic family idiocy, *J. Genet.*, **27**, 363–72.   [261]

SMITH, A., and RECORD, R. G. (1955) Maternal age and birth rank in the aetiology of mongolism, *Brit. J. prev. soc. Med.*, **9**, 51–5.   [326]

SMITH, A. A., TAYLOR, T., and WORTIS, S. B. (1963) Abnormal catecholamine metabolism in familial dysautonomia, *New Engl. J. Med.*, **268**, 705–7.   [249]

SMITH, D. W., PATAU, K., THERMAN, E., and INHORN, S. L. (1962) The No. 18 trisomy syndrome, *J. Pediat.*, **60**, 513–27.

SMITH, D. W., PATAU, K., THERMAN, E., INHORN, S. L., and DE MARS, R. I. (1963)
The D_1 trisomy syndrome, *J. Pediat.*, **62**, 326–41.   [340]

SMITH, E. B., HEMPELMANN, T. C., MOORE, S., and BARR, D. P. (1952) Gargoylism
(dysostosis multiplex). Two adult cases with one autopsy, *Ann. intern. Med.*, **36**,
652–67.   [256]

SMITH, J. C. A. (1925) Atypical psychoses and heterologous hereditary taints, *J. nerv.
ment. Dis.*, **62**, 1–32.   [24]

SMITH, S. M., and PENROSE, L. S. (1955) Monozygotic and dizygotic twin diagnosis,
Ann. hum. Genet., **19**, 273–89.   [348]

SMITHELLS, R. W. (1967) Familial dysautonomia or the Riley-Day syndrome, *Develop.
Med. Child Neurol.*, **9**, 234–5.   [249]

SNYDER, C. H. (1965) Phenylketonuria and allied metabolic diseases, *J. La med. Soc.*,
117, 330–5.   [206]

SOLITARE, G. B. (1967) The cri du chat syndrome: neuropathologic observations,
J. ment. Defic. Res., **11**, 267–77.   [344]

SOLTAN, H. C., WIENS, R. G., and SERGOVICH, F. R. (1964) Genetic studies and
chromosomal analyses in families with mongolism (Down's syndrome) in more
than one member, *Acta genet. (Basel)*, **14**, 251–64.   [332]

SORSBY, A. (1951) *Genetics in Ophthalmology*, London.   [257]

SPIEGEL-ADOLF, M., BAIRD, H. W., KOLLIAS, D., and SZEKELY, E. G. (1959) Cerebrospinal fluid, serum, and blood investigations in amaurotic family idiocy, *Amer.
J. Dis. Child.*, **97**, 676–83.   [257, 260]

SPIELMEYER, W. (1908) Histologische und histopathologische Arbeiten über die
Grosshirnrinde. Klinische und anatomische Untersuchungen über eine besondere
Form von familiarer amaurotischen-Idiotie, *Nissl Arbeit.*, **2**, 193–213.   [259]

SPORN, M. B., DINGMAN, W., DEFALCO, A., and DAVIES, R. K. (1959) Formation of
urea from arginine in the brain of the living rat, *Nature (Lond.)*, **183**, 1520–1.   [228]

STEIN, M. H., and GARDNER, L. I. (1960) Possible site of biochemical error in Gaucher's
disease, *Lancet*, ii, 1254.   [264]

STEINBERG, A. G., and MULDER, D. W. (1951) Review of *A study of Epilepsy in its
Clinical, Social, and Genetic Aspects*, 1950, by Alström, C. H., *Amer. J. hum. Genet.*,
3, 79–81.   [176]

STENGEL, C. (1826) Reprinted in: Nissen, A. J. Juvenil amaurotisk idioti i Norge,
Nord. Med., **52**, 1542–6 (1954).   [259]

STENSTEDT, Å. (1952) A study in manic-depressive psychosis: clinical, social and
genetic investigations, *Acta psychiat. scand.*, Suppl. 79.   [85]

STENSTEDT, Å. (1959) Involutional melancholia, *Acta psychiat. scand.*, Suppl. 127.   [86]

STENSTEDT, Å. (1966) Genetics of neurotic depression, *Acta psychiat. scand.*, **42**, 392–409.
                                                                                                 [108]

STEPHENSON, J. B. P., and MCBEAN, M. S. (1967) Diagnosis of phenylketonuria
(phenylalanine hydroxylase deficiency, temporary and permanent), *Brit. med. J.*,
3, 579–81.   [207]

STERNLIEB, I., MORELL, A. G., BAUER, C. D., COMBES, B., STERNBERG, S. DE B., and
SCHEINBERG, I. H. (1961) Detection of the heterozygous carrier of the Wilson's
disease gene, *J. clin. Invest.*, **40**, 707–15.   [158]

STEWART, R. M. (1939) Congenital ichthyosis, idiocy, infantilism and epilepsy: the
syndrome of Rud, *J. ment. Sci.*, **85**, 256–63.   [292]

STREIFF, E. B., and ZELTNER, C. (1938) Le syndrome de Laurence-Moon-Bardet-
Biedl, *Arch. Ophtal (Paris)*, n.s. **2**, 289–321.   [286]

STRELETZKI, F. (1961) Psychosen im Verlauf der Huntingtonschen Chorea unter
besonderer Berücksichtigung der Wahnbildungen, *Arch. Psychiat. Nervenkr.*,
202, 202–14.   [136]

STRÖMGREN, E. (1967) Neurosen und Psychopathien, in *Humangenetik: ein kurzes Handbuch in fünf Bänden*, Band V/2, ed. Becker, P. E., Stuttgart. [109]

STUMPFL, F. (1936) *Die Ursprünge des Verbrechens dargestellt am Lebenslauf von Zwillingen*, Leipzig. [115]

SUZUKI, T. (1960) EEG studies on epileptic twins, *Psychiat. Neurol. jap.*, **62**, 35–9. [173]

TADA, K., WADA, Y., and OKAMURA, T. (1963) A case of maple sugar urine disease, *Tohoku J. exp. Med.*, **79**, 142–7. [214]

TANAKA, K., MATSUNAGA, E., HANDA, Y., MURATA, T., and TAKEHARA, K. (1961) Phenylketonuria in Japan, *Jap. J. hum. Genet.*, **6**, 65–77. [206]

TAY, W. (1881) Symmetrical changes in the region of the yellow spot in each eye in an infant, *Trans. ophthal. Soc. U.K.*, **1**, 55–57. [258]

TAYLOR, A. I., and MOORES, E. C. (1967) A sex chromatin survey of newborn children in two London hospitals, *J. med. Genet.*, **4**, 258–9. [300]

TAYLOR, A. I., and POLANI, P. E. (1964) Autosomal trisomy syndromes, excluding Down's, *Guy's Hosp. Rep.*, **113**, 231–49. [340–1]

TELLER, W. M., and MILLICHAP, J. G. (1961) Ataxia-telangiectasia (Louis-Bar syndrome), with prominent sinopulmonary disease, *J. Amer. med. Ass.*, **175**, 779–82. [253]

TERRY, K., and LINKER, A. (1964) Distinction among four forms of Hurler's syndrome, *Proc. Soc. exp. Biol. (N.Y.)*, **115**, 394–402. [272]

TERRY, R. D., SPERRY, W. M., and BRODOFF, B. (1954) Adult lipidosis resembling Niemann-Pick's disease, *Amer. J. Path.*, **30**, 263–79. [263]

TERSLEV, E. (1960) Two cases of aminoaciduria, ocular changes and retarded mental and somatic development (Lowe's syndrome), *Acta paediat. (Uppsala)*, **49**, 635–44. [236]

THOMPSON, J. H. (1957) Relatives of phenylketonuric patients, *J. ment. Defic. Res.*, **1**, 67–78. [210]

THOMSEN, O. (1962) Klinefelter's syndrom hos 5 patienter med psykiatriske Lidelser, *Ugeskr. Laeg.*, **124**, 1276–85. [315]

TIENARI, P. (1963) Psychiatric illnesses in identical twins, *Acta psychiat. scand.*, Suppl. 171. [17]

TIENARI, P. (1966) On intrapair differences in male twins with special reference to dominance-submissiveness, *Acta psychiat. scand.*, Suppl. 188, **42**.

TIENARI, P. (1968) Schizophrenia in monozygotic male twins, in *The Transmission of Schizophrenia*, ed. Rosenthal, D., and Kety, S. S., Oxford. [19, 20]

TIMPANY, M. M. (1962) Congenital ichthyosis, spastic diplegia and mental deficiency, *Lancet*, i, 1132. [292]

TJIO, J. H., and LEVAN, A. (1956) The chromosome number of man, *Hereditas (Lund)*, **42**, 1–6. [1]

TREDGOLD, A. F. (1949) *A Textbook of Mental Deficiency*, 7th ed., London. [290]

VON TROSTORFF, S. (1968) Über die hereditäre Belastung bei den bipolaren und mono-polaren phasischen Psychosen, *Schweiz. Arch. Neurol. Neurochir. Psychiat.*, **102**, 235–43. [79–80]

TSUANG, MING-TSO (1969) Huntington's chorea in a Chinese family, *J. med. Genet.*, **6**, 354–6. [137]

TSUANG, MING-TSO, and LIN, T-Y. (1964) A clinical and family study of Chinese mongol children, *J. ment. Defic. Res.*, **8**, 84–91. [325]

TURNER, H. H. (1938) A syndrome of infantilism, congenital webbed neck and cubitus valgus, *Endocrinology*, **23**, 566–74. [302]

ULLRICH, O. (1943) Die Pfaundler-Hurlersche Krankheit, *Ergebn. inn. Med. Kinder-heilk.*, **63**, 929–1000. [271]

UNVERRICHT, H. (1891) *Die Myoclonie*, Leipzig.   [254]

UZMAN, L. L. (1955) Chemical nature of the storage substance in gargoylism, Hurler-Pfaundler's disease, *Arch. Path.*, **60**, 308–18.

UZMAN, L. L., IBER, F. L., CHALMERS, T. C., and KNOWLTON, M. (1956) Mechanism of copper deposition in the liver in hepatolenticular degeneration (Wilson's disease), *Amer. J. med. Sci.*, **231**, 511–18.   [155]

VANDENBERG, S. G. (1967) Hereditary factors in normal personality traits (as measured by inventories), in *Recent Advances in Biological Psychiatry*, Vol. 9, ed. Wortis, J., New York.   [97]

VERNER, JR., J. V., JOHNSON, J. H., and MERRITT, F. L. (1966) Café au lait spots, temporal dysrhythmia, and emotional instability, *Int. J. Neuropsychiat.*, **2**, 179–87.   [167]

VISAKORPI, J. K., and HYRSKE, I. (1960) Urinary amino acids in mentally retarded patients, *Ann. Paediat. Fenn.*, **6**, 112–18.   [230]

VOGEL, F. (1957) Elektroencephalographische Untersuchungen an gesunden Zwillingen, *Acta genet. (Basel)*, **7**, 334–7.   [163]

VOGEL, F. (1958) *Über die Erblichkeit des normalen Elektroenzephalogramms. Vergleichende Untersuchungen an ein- und zwei-eiigen Zwillingen.* Stuttgart.   [163]

VOGEL, F. (1965) '14 and 6/s positive spikes' im Schlaf-EEG von jugendlichen ein- und zwei-eiigen Zwillingen, *Hum. Genet.* **1**, 390–1.   [163–4]

VOGEL, F. (1966a) Zur genetischen Grundlage fronto-präzentraler beta-Wellen-Gruppen im EEG des Menschen, *Hum. Genet.*, **2**, 227–37.   [164]

VOGEL, F. (1966b) Zur genetischen Grundlage occipitaler langsamer beta-Wellen im EEG des Menschen, *Hum. Genet.*, **2**, 238–45.   [164]

VOGEL, F., and GÖTZE, W. (1959) Familienuntersuchungen zur Genetik des normalen Elektroencephalogramms, *Dtsch. Z. Nervenheilk*, **178**, 668–700.   [164]

VOGEL, F., and HELMBOLD, W. (1959) Koppelungsdaten für zwei Wahrscheinlich einfach mendelnde EEG-Merkmale des Menschen, *Z. menschl. Vererb. -u. Konstit.-Lehre*, **35**, 28.   [164]

VOGEL, F., and KRÜGER, J. (1967) Multifactorial determination of genetic affections, *Proc. 3rd internat. Congress hum. Genet.*, *Chicago*, 1966, pp. 437–45.   [56, 63]

VOGT, H. (1905) Über familiäre amaurotische Idiote und verwandte Krankheitsbilder, *Mschr. Psychiat. Neurol.*, **18**, 161–71, 310–57.   [259]

WAARDENBURG, P. J. (1932) *Das menschliche Auge und seine Erbanlagen*, Haag.   [261, 327]

WADA, Y., TADA, K., MINAGAWA, A., YOSHIDA, T., MORIKAWA, T., and OKAMURA, T. (1963) Idiopathic hypervalinemia, *Tohoku. J. exp. Med.*, **81**, 46–55.   [216]

WAGNER, M. G., and LITTMAN, B. (1967) Phenylketonuria in the American Indian, *Pediatrics*, **39**, 108–10.   [208]

WAISMAN, H. A. (1966) Some newer inborn errors of metabolism, *Pediat. Clin. N. Amer.*, **13**, 469–501.   [216]

WALKER, F. A., HSIA, D. Y-Y., SLATIS, H. M., and STEINBERG, A. G. (1962) Galactosemia; a study of 27 kindreds in North America, *Ann. hum. Genet.*, **25**, 287–311.   [239–40]

WALKER, S., and HARRIS, R. (1962) Investigation of family showing transmission of a 13–15 chromosomal translocation (Denver classification), *Brit. med. J.*, **2**, 25–6.

WALLIN, J. E. W. (1944) Mongolism among school children, *Amer. J. Orthopsychiat.*, **14**, 104–12.   [336]

WALLIS, K., and KALUSHINER, A. (1960) Oligophrenia in combination with congenital ichthyosis, spastic disorders and macular degeneration (Sjögren-Larsson syndrome), *Ann. paediat. (Basel)*, **194**, 115–24.   [291]

WALSHE, J. M. (1961) The movement of copper through membranes, in *Wilson's Disease: Some Current Concepts*, ed. Walshe, J. M., and Cumings, J. N., Oxford. [155]

WALSHE, J. M. (1962) Wilson's disease: the presenting symptoms, *Arch. Dis. Childh.*, **37**, 253–6. [154]

WALTER, K., and BRÄUTIGAM, W. (1958) Transvestitismus bei Klinefelter-Syndrom, *Schweiz. med. Wschr.*, **88**, 357–62. [318]

WANG, H. L., MORTON, N. E., and WAISMAN, H. A. (1961) Increased reliability for the determination of the carrier state in phenylketonuria, *Amer. J. hum. Genet.*, **13**, 255–61. [209]

WARBURG, E. (1963) A fertile patient with Klinefelter's syndrome, *Acta endocr. (Kbh.)*, **43**, 12–26. [300, 313]

WARREN, C. B. M., and BROUGHTON, P. M. G. (1962) Wilson's disease, *Arch. Dis. Childh.*, **37**, 242–52. [154]

WATSON, J. D., and CRICK, F. H. C. (1953a) Molecular structure of nucleic acids. A structure for deoxyribose nucleic acid, *Nature (Lond.)*, **171**, 737–8. [2]

WATSON, J. D., and CRICK, F. H. C. (1953b) Genetical implications of the structure of deoxyribonucleic acid, *Nature (Lond.)*, **171**, 964–7. [2]

WEGMANN, T. G., and SMITH, D. W. (1963) Incidence of Klinefelter's syndrome among juvenile delinquents and felons, *Lancet*, i, 274. [308]

WEINBERGER, H. L. (1926) Über die hereditären Beziehungen der senilen Demenz, *Z. ges. Neurol. Psychiat.*, **106**, 666–701. [132]

WEISLI, B. (1962) Vergleich des phänotypischen und zellkernmorphologischen Geschlechtes bei 3029 Neugeborenen, *Acta anat. (Basel)*, **51**, 377–83. [300]

WELNER, J., and STRÖMGREN, E. (1958) Clinical and genetic studies on benign schizophreniform psychoses based on a follow-up, *Acta psychiat. scand.*, **33**, 377–99. [43]

WENDT, G. G., LANDZETTEL, H. J., and UNTERREINER, I. (1959) Das Erkrankungsalter bei der Huntingtonschen Chorea, *Acta genet. (Basel)*, **9**, 18–32. [138]

WENDT, G. G., LANDZETTEL, I., and SOLTH, K. (1960) Krankheitsdauer und Lebenserwartung bei der Huntingtonschen Chorea, *Arch. Psychiat. Nervenkr.*, **201**, 298–312. [138]

WESTALL, R. G. (1960) Argininosuccinic aciduria: identification and reactions of the abnormal metabolite in a newly described form of mental disease, with some preliminary metabolic studies, *Biochem. J.*, **77**, 135–44. [228]

WESTALL, R. G., and TOMLINSON, S. (1961) Argininosuccinase activity in argininosuccinic aciduria, *Proc. 5th Internat. Cong. Biochem.* (Moscow, Aug. 1961) p. 366. [229]

WHEELAN, LORNA (1959) Familial Alzheimer's disease, *Ann. hum. Genet.* **23**, 300–10. [152]

WILKINS, L., GRUMBACH, M. M., and VAN WYK, J. J. (1954) Chromosomal sex in 'ovarian agenesis', *J. clin. Endocr.*, **14**, 1270–1. [304]

WILLIAMS, R. D. B., and LING TANG, I. (1960) Mental defect, quadriplegia and ichthyosis, *Amer. J. Dis. Child.*, **100**, 924–9. [291–2]

WILSON, S. A. K. (1912) Progressive lnticular degeneration: a familial nervous disease associated with cirrhosis of the liver, *Brain*, **34**, 295–509. [153]

WILSON, S. R. (1970) The determination of the mode of inheritance from the correlation between relatives, Personal communication. [70]

WINOKUR, G. (1967) Genetic principles in the clarification of clinical issues in affective disorder, Am. Assoc. for the Advancement of Science, Convention. [82]

WINOKUR, G., and CLAYTON, P. (1967) Family history studies. I. Two types of affective disorders separated according to genetic and clinical factors, in *Recent Advances in Biological Psychiatry*, Vol. 9., ed. Wortis, J., New York. [84]

WINOKUR, G., and PITTS, F. N. JR. (1965) Affective disorder. VI. A family history study of prevalences, sex differences and possible genetic factors, *J. psychiat. Res.*, **3**, 113–23.
[84]
WISSFELD, E. (1954) Epilepsieverdächtige EEG-Befunde bei Psychopathen (Zur Frage der epileptoiden Psychopathie), *Nervenarzt*, **25**, 30–6.   [182]
WISSFELD, E., and KAINDL, E. (1961) Über die Deutung und den Wert abnormer EEG-Befunde bei psychopathischen Persönlichkeiten, *Nervenarzt*, **32**, 57–66. [182, 184]
WOERNER, P. I., and GUZE, S. B. (1968) A family and marital study of hysteria, *Brit. J. Psychiat.*, **114**, 161–8.   [108]
WOLF, U., REINWEIN, H., PORSCH, R., SCHROTER, R., and BAITSCH, H. (1965) Defizienz an den kurzen Armen eines Chromosoms Nr. 4, *Hum. Genet.*, **1**, 397–413.   [341]
WOLFE, H. J., BLENNERHASSET, J. B., YOUNG, G. F., and COHEN, R. B. (1964) Hurler's syndrome. A histochemical study. New techniques for localization of very water-soluble acid mucopolysaccharides, *Amer. J. Path.*, **45**, 1007–27.   [266]
WOLFF, O. (1965) A-beta-lipoproteinaemia, *Develop. med. Child Neurol.*, **7**, 430–1. [248]
WOLMAN, M., STERK, V. V., GATT, S., and FRENKEL, M. (1961) Primary familial xanthomatosis with involvement and calcification of the adrenals, *Pediatrics*, **28**, 742-57.   [253]
WOODY, N. C. (1964) Hyperlysinemia, *Amer. J. Dis. Child.*, **108**, 543–53.   [231–3]
WOODY, N. C., and HANCOCK, C. D. (1963) Maple syrup urine disease: further observations, *Amer. J. Dis. Child.*, **106**, 578–85.   [214]
WOODY, N. C., SNYDER, C. H., and HARRIS, J. A. (1965) Histidinemia, *Amer. J. Dis. Child.*, **110**, 606–13.   [217–18]
WOODY, N. C., WOODY, H. B., and TILDEN, T. D. (1963) Maple syrup urine disease in Negro infant, *Amer. J. Dis. Child*, **105**, 381–6.   [214]
WOOLF, L. I. (1962) Recent work on phenylketonuria and maple syrup urine disease (leucinosis), *Proc. roy. Soc. Med.*, **55**, 824–6 (Section of Neurology, 36–8).   [213]
WOOLF, L. I., OUNSTED, C., LEE, D., HUMPHREY, M., CHESHIRE, N. M., and STEED, G. R. (1961) Atypical phenylketonuria in sisters with normal offspring, *Lancet*, ii, 464–5.   [204]
WOOLLACOTT, S., and PEARCE, J. (1967) A myotonic syndrome associated with Kline-felter's syndrome, *J. med. Genet.*, **4**, 299–301.   [315]
WYNGAARDEN, J. B. (1966) Gout, in *The Metabolic Basis of Inherited Disease*, 2nd ed., ed. Stanbury, J. B., Wyngaarden, J. B., and Fredrickson, D. S., New York.   [246]
YAMADA, T. (1967) Heterogeneity of schizophrenia as demonstrable in electro-encephalography, in *Clinical Genetics in Psychiatry*, ed. Mitsuda, H., Tokyo.   [36]
YANOFF, M., and SCHWARZ, G. A. (1965) Lafora's disease—a distinct genetically determined form of Unverricht's syndrome, *J. Génét. hum.*, **14**/2–3, 235–44. [170]
YOSHIMASU, S. (1961) The criminological significance of the family in the light of the studies of criminal twins, *Acta Criminol. et Med. Legal. Japon.*, **27**, 117–41. [116]
YOSHIMASU, S. (1965) Criminal life curves of monozygotic twin-pairs, *Acta Criminol. et Med. Legal. Japon.*, **31**, 5–6.   [116]
ZAPPELLA, M., and COWIE, V. (1962) A note on the time of diagnosis in mongolism, *J. ment. Defic. Res.*, **6**, 82–6.   [325]
ZAWUSKI, G. (1960) Zur Erblichkeit der Alzheimerschen Krankheit, *Arch. Psychiat. Nervenkr.*, **201**, 123–32.   [152]
ZEAMAN, D., and HOUSE, B. J. (1962) Mongoloid MA is proportional to log CA, *Child Develop.*, **33**, 481–8.   [336]
ZERBIN-RÜDIN, E. (1967a) Hirnatrophische Prozesse, in *Humangenetik, ein Kurzes Handbuch*, V/2, ed. Becker, P. E., Stuttgart.   [150, 152]
ZERBIN-RÜDIN, E. (1967b) Endogene Psychosen, in *Humangenetik, ein Kurzes Hand-buch*, V/2, ed. Becker, P. E., Stuttgart.   [14, 56, 60, 76–8, 86, 90]

ZERBIN-RÜDIN, E. (1969) Zur Genetik der depressiven Erkrankungen, in *Das Depressive Syndrom*, Internat. Sympos. Berlin, Feb. 1968, ed. Hippius, H., and Selbach, H., Munich.   [85]

ZLOTNICK, A., and GROEN, J. J. (1961) Observations on a patient with Gaucher's disease, *Amer. J. Med.*, **30**, 637–42.   [265]

ZÜBLIN, W. (1953) Zur Psychologie des Klinefelter-syndroms, *Acta endocr. (Kbh.)*, **14**, 137–44.   [307, 309]

INDEX

Note. Figures in *italics* denote illustrations.

Abetalipoproteinaemia, 248
Accident of evolution, senescence as, 122
Acrocephalosyndactyly, *284*, 285
Acrocephaly, 284
Adenine, 2
Adenoma sebaceum, 276, 278
Alanen, on schizophrenia, 39
Alanine, serum, in Huntington's chorea, 141
Alcoholism, 109
  amount, 110
  bout drinking, 111
  classification, Jellinek, 109
  density, 110
  heritability, 110
  in relatives of,
    chronic alcoholics, 113 (*table*)
    hysterics, 108
    schizophrenics, 23
  in twins, 110, 111 (*table*)
  intellectual impairment in, 110
  lack of control, 110
  morbidity risk, in sibs of chronic alcoholics, 112 (*table*)
  sex distribution, 113
Alkaptonuria, 201
Alleles, 2, 204
Alloisoleucine, 213, 214. *See also* Leucine
Alström, on children of epileptics, 183
Alzheimer's disease, 127, 133, 147
  age of onset, 149 (*table*)
  and Pick's disease, differential diagnosis, 147
  clinical picture, 148 (*table*)
  epidemiology, 149
  genetics, 150
  incidence, compared with that of Pick's disease, 152
  mode of inheritance, 152
  pathology, 148
  sex distribution, 149
Åmark, on alcoholism, 111, 112 (*table*)
Amaurotic family idiocy, 256, 258
  adult form of Kufs, 259
  and Niemann-Pick disease, interrelationship, 257, 263
  biochemistry, 259
  classification, 258

Amaurotic family idiocy (*cont.*)
  ethnic distribution, 261
  genetics, 261
  heterozygotic carriers, 261
  infantile form, 258
    late, of Bielschowsky, 258
  juvenile form, of Spielmeyer-Vogt, 259
  mode of inheritance, 262
  parental consanguinity, 262
  population genetics, 262
  relationship with other lipidoses, 257
Amines, in affective psychoses, 75
Amino acids, in Huntington's chorea, 140, 141
—transport, defects of, 234
Aminoacidurias, 201
Amphetamine intoxication, associated with schizophrenia, 28, 45
Anaemia, in galactosaemia, 237
Aneuploid constitution, and criminality, 113
Angst, on affective psychoses, 80
  on schizophrenic illnesses, 32
Anhidrotic ectodermal dysplasia, 293
Antibiotics, in mongolism, 335
Antisocial behaviour. *See* Behaviour: antisocial. *See also* Personality: disorder
Anxiety states, 103
  in co-twins of patients with anxiety states, 104 (*table*)
Apert's syndrome, *284*, 285
Arginase, 232
Arginine, 230, 232, 233
Argininosuccinic acid synthetase deficiency, 230
Argininosuccinicaciduria, 220, 227
  pedigree of two sisters, *230*
Arteriosclerotic psychosis and senile dementia, clinical and pathological features, 128 (*table*)
Asano, on classification of schizophrenias, 36
ASAase, 229
Assortative mating, 192, 194
Ataxia-telangiectasia, 251
  and the phakomatoses, 277
  relation to phakomatoses, 252
  spinocerebellar degenerations, 253
Autistic children, mothers of, 40

Auto-immune processes, in senescence, 123
Autoradiography, in mongolism, 328
Autosomal chromosome anomalies. *See* Chromosomes: anomalies: autosomal

Banse, on manic-depressive illness, 77
Barr body, 298
Bateson, on alkaptonuria, 201
Behaviour, antisocial. *See also* Personality: disorder
  criminal. *See* Criminality
  in Klinefelter's syndrome, 309
  in sex chromosome disorders, 307, 308
    XYY syndrome, 302 (*table*), 307
  difficulties, twin concordance, 114 (*table*)
  sexual, disordered, in sex chromosome anomalies, 315
  traits of childhood, 101
Bel-Air clinic, and Alzheimer-Pick diseases, 151
Bernreuter, on personality traits, 99
—Personality Inventory, 100
Bernstein, on progressive familial myoclonic epilepsy, 255
Bezugsziffer, 78, 87, 89, 356
Bielschowsky's amaurotic family idiocy, 258
Binet, intelligence tests, 188
Biochemical disorder, and intellectual impairment, 202
Birthweight in twins, and subsequent development, 96
Bladder control, 101
Bleuler, Manfred, on tuberculosis and schizophrenia, 22
Blood groups
  gene determination, 7
  in twin research, 348
Body, constitution, effect on manifestation of hereditary predisposition, 27
Böök, single gene theory of schizophrenia, 57
Brain disease, organic, in aetiology of schizophrenia, 29, *30*
  in Huntington's chorea, biochemical studies, 141
  in trisomy E syndrome, *339*
  in tuberous sclerosis, *276*
  lesion, and epilepsy, 179
  tumour, associated with schizophrenia, 28, 29
  weight of, 125
Buccal smear test, 298
Burghölzli, Zurich, 112
Burt, Sir Cyril, 193
Butterfly rash, in tuberous sclerosis, 277, *278*

Caeruloplasmin, in Wilson's disease, 155, 158

Café-au-lait spots in ataxia-telangiectasia, 252
  in epilepsy, 167
  in phenylketonuria, 205
  in Von Recklinghausen's disease, 6, 281
Carter, C. O., work on multifactorial inheritance, 8
Catecholamine metabolism, in dysautonomia, 249
Cells
  aneuploid, 124
  division, 1
  hypomodal, 1 23
  proportion of, as function of advancing age, 124 (*table*), 125 (*graph*)
Celtic peoples, phenylketonuria in, 208
Central nervous function, and gene manifestation, 27
Cerebral diplegia of genetical aetiology, 290
—disorders, associated with schizophrenia, 28
—pathology, in schizophrenia, 37
—vascular disease, causing dementia in the aged, 127
Children
  behaviour traits in, 101
  neurotic symptomatology in, 102
  of psychotics, 92, 93 (*table*)
Cholesterol, in Huntington's chorea, 141
Chondroitin sulphate, 266, 267, 270
Chromatids, 1
Chromatin-positive males, incidence, 300 (*table*)
Chromosomes
  anomalies. *See also under* Chromosomes: sex
    and personality deviations, 92
    autosomal, 324
      physical defects, 307
    causing pathological mental defect, 186
    in argininosuccinicaciduria, 229
    in De Lange's syndrome, *295*
    in homosexuality, 120
    in Marfan's syndrome, 229
  B. *See* Cri-du-chat syndrome
  definition, 1
  deletions, 4
  Denver classification, 340, 341
  fusion. *See* Chromosomes: translocation
  G, in mongolism, 328, 329
  in intersex states, 316
  in male homosexuals, 316
  in senescence, 124
  isochromosome, in mongolism, 329
  numbers, 1
  sex. *See also specific sex chromosomes*
    anomalies, 297
      and mental subnormality, 319

Chromosomes: sex: anomalies (*cont.*)
 and psychiatric disorders, 307
 associated EEG abnormalities, 310
 —with personality disorders, 298
 clinical syndromes associated with, 299
 deviant sexual behaviour in, 315
 females with, psychological features in,
  310
 neurological abnormalities, 314
 personality disorder in, 307
 morphology, changes in, 297
 polysomy, 299
 —chromatin status, and antisocial
  behaviour, 308
 —distribution, 1
 structure, and genes, 2
 translocations, 4, 324, 328, 329
 trisomy. *See under specific syndromes, e.g.,*
  Trisomy E syndrome
 X, 297 *et seq.*
  in hyperuricaemia, 248
  isochromosome X, 297
  loss of, in females, 127
  Lyon hypothesis on, 232
  patient with isochromosome X and
   normal X chromosome, *303*
  ring, 297
 XO constitution, 304. *See also* Ovarian
  dysgenesis
 XXX (triple X) constitution, 304. *See also*
  XXX syndrome
 XXXY, 309
 XXYY, 299, 322
 Y, 297 *et seq.*
Citrullinaemia, 220
L-citrulline, 230
Citrullinuria, 229
Coffee consumption, hereditary factors, 110
Cohen, Sydney, on Huntington's chorea, 142
Colour blindness, red-green, in ovarian
 agenesis, 304
Connective tissue metabolism, 266
Conrad, Klaus, on epilepsy, 170, 174
Convulsions, due to extracerebral causes, 179
 in tuberous sclerosis of infancy, 278
Copper metabolism, 139, 155
Copying processes, in senescence, 123
Cousin marriage, 5
Cowie, on children of psychotics, 92
Craike, in schizophrenia, 41
Craniofacial dystosis, 284
Cri-du-chat syndrome, 341, *342, 343*
 clinical features, 342
 karyotypes, normal, in, 340
 mental retardation in, 343
 mosaicism in, 344
 sex distribution, 344

Criminality, 113
 adult, serious, stemming from juvenile
  delinquency, 116
 classification, 116
 family history of, 115
 in relatives of schizophrenics, 23
 in twins, 113, 114 (*table*)
 in XYY syndrome, 301
 morbidity risk, in sibs of chronic alcoholics,
  112 (*table*)
 sex incidence, 115
Crossing over, in meiosis, 1
Crouzon acrocephaly, 284
Cry, in cri-du-chat syndrome, 343
Cyclothymia, leading to affective psychoses,
 79
Cyclothymic personality, relation to endogenous affective psychoses, 92
Cystathionine, metabolism, *222*
Cystine, 230, 232, 233
Cystinuria, transport mechanism disturbance
 in, 233
Cytosine, 2

Da Fonseca, on manic-depressive illness, 85
Dahlberg's method, 158
De Lange syndrome, *294*
 parental consanguinity, 296
 pedigree, *295, 296*
Delinquency, twin concordance, 114 (*table*)
Delirious pictures, in the elderly, 127
Dementia, senile, 127
 age of onset, 129 (*table*)
 arteriosclerotic psychosis and, clinical and
  pathological features, 128 (*table*)
 autonomy, 134
 clinical features, 127
 definition, 127
 distribution, 130
 epidemiology, 129
 familial factor, 134
 first admission rates, 131 (*graph, table*)
 genetics, 130
 incidence in relatives of senile dements, 132
 morbidity risk, 130 (*table*), 134
 pathology, 127
 polygenic inheritance, 134
 risk of, in sibs of index patients, 133 (*table*)
 single gene hypothesis, 135
 sociomedical factors, 134, 135
 twin studies, 132
Dent, classification of inborn errors of
 metabolism, 202
Denver classification, of chromosomes, 340,
 341
Deoxyribonucleic acid. *See* DNA

26

Depression, reactive, 102, 108
Depressive syndromes, in Huntington's chorea, 136
Deviations of personality. *See* Personality: deviations
Diabetes, heritability, 51, 52
Diet
  in abetalipoproteinaemia, 248
  in galactosaemia, 238
    effect on intelligence, 239
  in Refsum's syndrome, 251
  low-methionine, 220
  —high-cystine, 223
Diplegia, cerebral, of genetical aetiology, 290
DNA (deoxyribonucleic acid), 2
  in mutations, 3
Dominant abnormalities, 277
—inheritance, 4
  characteristics, 5 (*table*), 6
  delayed harmful effects, 7
  in neurometabolic disorders, 202
  incidence, 6
Down's syndrome. *See* Mongolism
Drosophila melanogaster, 304, 316
Dysautonomia, familial, 249

Educability, hereditary contribution to, 196
Education, fitness of, for individual child, 189
Edwards, polygenic hypothesis of schizophrenia, 58
EEG anomalies
  in association with sex chromosome anomalies, 310
  in chromatin-positive constitutions, 309
  in homocystinuria, 221, 224
  in relatives of hyperprolinaemics, 219
  in sibs of histinaemics, 218
  in Turner's syndrome, 311
  in XYY syndrome, 302
Electrolyte metabolism, in affective psychoses, 76
Elfin face syndrome, of idiopathic hypercalcaemia, 245
Elsässer, on psychotic matings, 24
Encephalofacial angiomatosis. *See* Sturge-Weber syndrome
Endocrines, in affective psychoses, 76
Entres, on manic-depressive illness, 77
Enuresis, 102
Environment and heredity, in MZ twin differences, 346
  in causation of schizophrenia, 38
  intra-uterine, 95
Environmental accident, and pathological mental defect, 186
—stress, effect on manifestation of hereditary predisposition, 27

Enzymes
  defects, in neurometabolic disease, 202
  genes in synthesis of, 2
  in amaurotic family idiocy, 259
Epilepsy, 160. *See also* Pyknolepsy
  age of onset, 162, 163 (*graphs*)
  and chronic paranoid psychoses, 180
  and Klinefelter's syndrome, 314
  Bray and Wiser syndrome, 167
  café-au-lait spots, 167
  centrencephalic, 178, 179
    and mental subnormality, 181
  children of probands, abnormal personalities of, 183 (*table*)
  chronic, convulsive symptomatology causing, 179
  definition, 160
  EEG phenomena, 162, 164, 165 (*graph, table*)
    in relatives, 176 (*table*), 177 (*table*)
  EEG-clinical syndromes, 165
  familial temporal-central focal, 167
  family investigations, 164, 174
  fitness, 178
  hypersocial traits, 184
  in relatives, 176 (*table*), 177 (*table*)
  in tuberous sclerosis, 277
  mental subnormality, 181
  mode of inheritance, 175, 177
  morbidity risk, 161, 162 (*table*)
  pedigrees, *168*
  petit mal, 166
    autosomal dominant, 166
    theta rhythmicity, 166
  photogenic, 169
  prevalence, 161 (*table*)
  progressive familial myoclonic, 254
  psychic equivalents, 182
  psychoses. *See* Psychoses: epileptic
  public attitude towards, 176
  risk of, in relatives, 175 (*table*)
  schizophrenia-like psychoses associated with, 28
  sex chromatin patterns in, 314
  symptomatic, 179
  symptomatic-idiopathic classification, 171 (*table*)
  temporal lobe, associated with schizophrenia, 28
  'trichotomized' classification, 179
  twin investigations, 162, 170, 173 (*table*)
    concordance rates, 172 (*table*), 173 (*table*), 174 (*table*)
  Unverricht-Lundborg's myoclonic, 169
    mode of inheritance, 177
Epileptic-like manifestations in normal individuals, 160

Epileptoid personality, 181
Epiloia. *See* Tuberous sclerosis
Essen-Möller, on schizophrenia, 10, 18 (*table*), 20, 29, 41
Evolution, senescence as accident of, 122
Examinations, justification for, 189
Extraversion-intraversion and neuroticism, correlation, 101
Eysenck, on personality traits, 99, 101

Falconer, model of heritability in schizophrenia, 48, *49 et seq.*
Fears, 102
Ferraro, on schizophrenia, 29
Fertility, and intelligence, 195
Finger-prints, in diagnosis of zygosity, 349, 351 (*table*), 352 (*table*)
Fischer, on schizophrenia, 17, 19 (*table*)
Fisher's formulae, 198
Food fads, 102
Foster children
    and place of heredity and environment in intelligence, 196
    psychiatric disorders in, 42 (*table*)
Freeming, on alcoholism, 111
    on schizophrenia, 13
Fructosaemia, differential diagnosis from galactosaemia, 243
Fructose intolerance
    EEG, 243
    familial, 242
    mode of inheritance, 243
Fructose-l-phosphate aldolase, 243, 259
Fructosuria, 242

Galactokinase deficiency, 242
Galactosaemia, 5, 237
    asymptomatic 237, 238
    chemical pathology, 237
    dietary treatment, 238
    differential diagnosis, 243
    gene frequency, 241
    genetics, 240
    heterozygotes, 240, 241
    intelligence in, and diet, 239
    mode of inheritance, 240
    neuropathology, 240
    pedigree of two sibships, *241*
    sex distribution, 240
Galactose
    intolerance, 243
    loading test, 240
    metabolism, accessory pathway, 238
    tolerance curve, 237
Galactose-l-phosphate uridyl transferase, 237, 238, 241

Galton, Francis, on human variability in intelligence, 188
    twin studies, 170
Gamete, 1
Ganglioside, 258
Gargoylism, 256, 268, *269. See also* Hurler's syndrome, Hunter's syndrome
Garrod, on biochemical genetics, 201
Gaucher's disease, 256, 264
    in Jews, 262
    mode of inheritance, 264
Genain quadruplets, and schizophrenia, 38
Gene-dosage effect, 202
Genes and chromosome structure, 2
    autosomal recessive, in phenylketonuria, 204, 206
    contribution to IQ, 190
    determining blood groups, 7
    effect on general body functions, 190
    frequency, 4, *59*
    in enzyme synthesis, 2
    in protein synthesis, 2
    single, inheritance, 3
        dominant type, 4
        recessive type, 4
Genetic factors and personality variables, 97
Genetics, principles, 1
Genotypic milieu, 26
Glucose-phosphate dehydrogenase, 240
Glutamic acid metabolism, in Huntington's chorea, 141
Glycine, formation from, of uric acid, 246
Goldschmidt, on homosexuality, 118
Gonadal dysgenesis, 304
Gottesman, on schizophrenia, 17, 19 (*table*)
Gout, differential diagnosis from hyperuricaemia, 245
Grueneberg's quasi-continuous characteristics, 46
Gruhle, on schizophrenia, 10
Guanine, 2
Guthrie test for phenylketonuria, 206

Hallervorden-Spatz disease, 257
Hardy-Weinberg equilibrium, 241
Hare-lip, cleft-palate syndrome, 8, 46
Hartnup disease, 233
    biochemical features, 233
    clinical features, 234
    decline in intellect in, 235
    heterozygote, 235
    psychiatric features, 234
Harvald, on epileptoid personality, 183
    on manic-depressive illness, 85
Hauge, on manic-depressive illness, 85

Heparitin sulphate, 266, 267
Hepatic illness, in Wilson's disease, 154
Hepatolenticular degeneration. *See* Wilson's disease
Heredity and environment, in MZ twin differences, 346
Heredopathia atactica polyneuritiformis. *See* Refsum's syndrome
Heston, on schizophrenia, 62
Heterogeneity, in schizophrenia, 30
Heterozygosis, 123
Heterozygote, definition, 5
Histidinaemia, 216
   clinical findings, 217
   EEG pattern in sibs of patients, 218
   family pedigree, *217*
   recessive inheritance, 218
Histidine α-deaminase, 217
Histidine, low diet, 218
Hoffman, on manic-depressive illness, 77
Homocystine, metabolism, *222*
Homocystinuria, 220, 221
   and Marfan's syndrome, 225
   clinical features, 221
   consanguinity, 224
   dietary treatment, 223
   EEG abnormality, 221
   heterozygote, 224
   pedigree of twins with, *224*
   recessive inheritance, 224
Homoiogamy, 194
   variability in intelligence caused by, 195
Homosexuality, 117
   and XXY syndrome, 317
   birth order, 120
   chromosome anomaly in, 120
   —patterns in, 316
   in Ancient Greece, 121
   maternal age, 120, 121
   paternal age, 121
   sex ratio, 118, 119 (*table*)
   twin concordance rate, 118
Homovanillic acid, 249
Homozygote, 4
   definition, 5
Hopkins, Frederick Gowland, 2
Hsia's phenylalanine-loading test, 202
Hunter's syndrome, 256, 265, 266 (*table*), 268
   differential diagnosis from Hurler's syndrome, 269
   incidence, 272
   mode of inheritance, 272
   pedigree, *272*
Huntington's chorea, 7, 92, 135
   age of onset, 138, 144
   akinetic, 137
   biochemical studies, 139

Huntington's chorea (*cont.*)
   clinical syndrome, 135
   EEG changes in, 144
   epidemiology, 145
   fitness, 144
   genetics, 143
      counselling, 145
      heterozygotic frequency, 145
      pleiotropic effect of gene, 144
   mutation, 144
   pedigree, *146*
   penetrance concept in, 47
   personality changes in, 144
   schizophrenia-like psychoses associated with, 28, 29
   selection, 144
Hurler's syndrome, 256, 265, 267
   differential diagnosis, 269
   — — Morquio's syndrome, 271
   incidence, 272
   mode of inheritance, 272
   prognosis, 268
   skull in, *268*
Hybrid vigour, 123
Hydrocephalus, sex-linked, 293
5-Hydroxyindoles, in affective psychoses, 76
Hydroxyprolinaemia, 220
5-Hydroxytryptamine, in affective psychoses, 76
Hyperammonaemia, 231
Hypercalcaemia, 244
   of infancy, idiopathic, 243, *244*, *245*
Hyperlysinaemia, 231
   and maple syrup urine disease, in one kinship, 232, *233*
   parental consanguinity, 232
Hyperphenylalaninaemia, 206
Hyperprolinaemia, treatment, 220
   I, 218
   II, 219
Hyperuricaemia, 245
   chromosome X in, 248
   mode of inheritance, 247
   neuropathology, 247
   pedigree, *247*
   self-mutilation in, 246
Hypervalinaemia, 216
Hypoxia, cerebral, and epilepsy, 179
Hysteria, 106
   morbidity risk in relatives, 106
   polygenic determination, 107
   sex incidence, 107
Hysterical conversion signs, in Klinefelter's syndrome, 315
Hysteroid-Obsessoid Questionnaire, 94

Ictal anxiety, 34

Ichthyosis, 290 *et seq.*
Immunity, in Huntington's chorea, 142
Immunoglobulins, in Huntington's chorea, 142
Inborn errors of metabolism, 201 *et seq.*
  causing mental subnormality, 202
  transport mechanism anomalies, 233
Indolic substances, in Hartnup disease, 234
Infants, birth factors and subsequent development, 96
Inouye, classification of schizophrenia, 36 (*table*)
  on schizophrenia, 18 (*table*), 22
Insomnia, 101
Intellectual deterioration, in alcoholism, 110
Intelligence
  and assortative mating, 192, 194
  and fertility, 195
  children's, of ordinary elementary and special MD schools, distribution, 191 (*graph*)
    relation with that of parents, 199, 200 (*table*)
  correlations between relatives, 197
    regression equation, 198
  environmental factor, in co-variance between relatives, 192
  heredity and environment in, 196
    twin investigations, 197, 198 (*table*)
  human variability, 188
  in foster children, 196
  in mongolism, 336
  in sex chromosome anomalies, 297
  in Von Recklinghausen's disease, 281
  normal (Gaussian) curve, 189
    expectations derived from polygenic hypothesis, 190
    sex differences, 190, 192, 193 (*tables*)
    variation in, 188
  range of, in Klinefelter's syndrome, 319
  tests, 188
    correlation coefficients in family, twin and foster-child studies, 192 (*graph*)
    factor analysis, 188
    general factor, 188
    genetic-environmental factors, 189
    group factors, 189
  Type IV frequency curve, 194
  variance,
    analysis of, for assessments of intelligence, 200
    environmental contribution, 200
    genetical contribution, 200
    in the phakomatoses, 277
    in tuberous sclerosis, 279
    polygenic factors, 7, *8*
  quotient, 7, 190 (*table*)

Intersex state, 315
Involutional melancholia, 86
IQ. *See* Intelligence: quotient
Irradiation, causing mutations, 3
Isochromosome. *See under* Chromosomes
Isoleucine, 212, 213, 214, 216
Isovaleric acidaemia, 215

Jacobson, on senile dementia, 129 *et seq.*
Jaspers, on schizophrenia, 10
Jaundice, neonatal, and galactosaemia, 240
Jellinek, classification of alcoholism, 109
Jensch, on homosexuality, 118
Jewish race
  amaurotic family idiocy in, 261, 262
  and Wilson's disease, 156
  phenylketonuria in, 207
Juvenile delinquency, 114 (*table*), 117
  leading to serious adult criminality, 116
  sex incidence, 116

Kahn, on psychotic matings, 24
Kaij, on alcoholism, 111
Kallmann, on manic-depressive illness, 77, 78, 85
  on schizophrenia, 10, 18 (*table*), 22, 41
  on schizophrenic illnesses, 32
Karlsson, on monogenic theory of schizophrenia, 64, *65, 66*
Kay, on schizophrenic illnesses, 32
  polygenic hypothesis of schizophrenia, 55
Kayser-Fleischer ring, in Wilson's disease, 154
Keratosulphate, 266, 267, 271
Kety, on schizophrenia, 10
Kidney transplant, in hyperprolinaemia, 221
Kleist, on classification of schizophrenias, 33
Klinefelter's syndrome, 125, 299 *et seq.*
  and epilepsy, 314
  and schizophrenia, 309
  and transvestism, 317
  antisocial behaviour in, 309
  chromatin-positive, 319
  deviant sexual behaviour in, 317
  EEG abnormality in, 310
  incidence, 299
  intelligence range in, 319
  psychological features, 307
  somatotypes, 300
  testosterone treatment, dangers of, 315
Knoll, on schizophrenic illnesses, 32
Krebs-Henseleit urea cycle, *228,* 231
Kringlen, on manic-depressive illness, 85
  on schizophrenia, 17, 19 (*table*), 20, 22, 41
Kufs' amaurotic family idiocy, 256, 259

Lafora bodies, 170, 254, 255
Landolt's 'forced normalization,' 182
Larsson, on senile dementia, 129 *et seq.*
Laurence-Moon-Biedl-Bardet syndrome, 286
Lennox, on epilepsy, 173, 174 (*table*)
Leonhard, classification of schizophrenias, 33
  on manic-depressive illness, 78, 81
  on schizophrenic illness, 32
Leucine, 212 *et seq.* See also Alloisoleucine;
  Isoleucine
Leucodystrophy, 205, 206
Leukaemia in mongols, 335
Lewis, classification of mental defect, 185
  on obsessive-compulsive states, 105
Lipid metabolism, in Huntington's chorea,
  140
Lipidoses, 256
  identity, 257
  interrelationships, 257
  mental defect in, 256
Lipogranulomatosis, 254
Lithium, in affective psychoses, 76
Liver, in Wilson's disease, 153
Ljungberg, on hysteria, 106
Loading tests. See under specific substances.
Lobstein, on manic-depressive illness, 77
Longevity, 122
Lowe's syndrome (oculo-cerebro-renal syn-
  drome), 235
Luxenburger, Hans, on manic-depressive
  illness, 77, 78, 85
  on obsessive-compulsive states, 105
  on schizophrenia, 10, 18 (*table*)
Lyon hypothesis on X chromosome activity,
  232
Lysine, 230, 232, 233

Magnesium metabolism, in Huntington's
  chorea, 139
Manic-depressive illness
  and schizophrenia: distribution in pairs of
    secondary cases, 91 (*table*)
  definition, 75
  expectation in relatives, 77
—sex ratio, 77 (*table*)
  in twins, concordance rates, 85 (*table*)
  incidence in first-degree relatives of manic-
    depressive patients, 78 (*table*)
  multifactorial inheritance, 54
  relatives, risk of affective psychoses in, 84
    (*table*)
  sex distribution of affected relatives, 83
    (*tables*)
  sex-linked gene theory, 82
—matings, 24

Maple syrup urine disease (MSU disease), 212
  and hyperlysinaemia, in one kinship, 232,
    233
  biochemistry, 212
  clinical picture, 213
  differential diagnosis from, 213
  enzyme deficiency, partial, 215
  epidemiology, 214
  ethnic distribution, 214
  genetical variant, late-manifesting, 214, 215
  genetics, 214
  heterozygotes, 214
  loading test, 214
  parental consanguinity, 214
Marfan's syndrome, 225
  autosomal dominant inheritance, 225
  chromosome abnormality, 229
  clinical picture, 225
  haematological abnormalities, 226
  mutation rate, 227
  parental consanguinity, 229
  recessive inheritance, 229
Maudsley Personality Inventory, 93, 101
Mayo Clinic, 309
McKusick's acrocephalosyndactyly type I.
  See Apert's syndrome
Meehl, on schizophrenia, 62
Megimide, 36
Meiosis, 1
Mendelian dominant inheritance. See
  Dominant inheritance
—ratio, 4
—recessive inheritance. See Recessive inheritance
Mental defect
  in the lipidoses, 256
  low-grade, 190
  pathological, 186
    due to chromosomal anomaly, 186
    due to rare single gene, 186
    non-genetic factors, 187
  physiological, 185
  subcultural, 185, 186
  subnormality
—and epilepsy, 181
    and metabolic disorders, 201
    and schizophrenia, 22
    and sex chromosome anomalies, 319
    frequency in sibs of affected individuals,
      200 (*table*)
    genetics, 185
Metabolic disorders, and mental subnormality, 201
Metabolism, inborn errors of, 201 *et seq.*
  transport mechanism anomalies, 233
Metachromatic leucodystrophy, 257
—staining, 273

Methionine, 214
  loading tests, 224
  metabolism, 223
  reduced intake, 220
Meyer, Adolf, twin studies of epilepsy, 170
Microcephaly
  autosomal recessive gene, 288
  due to maternal irritation, *288*
  gene frequency, 289
  heterozygotic expression, 290
  sex ratio, 289
  true, 287, *289*
Minnesota Multiphasic Personality Inventory
  (MMPI), 98
Mitosis, 1
Mitsuda, conceptual scheme of schizophrenias, 34
  on schizophrenia, 23, 34, 41
Monoamines, and affective psychoses, 75
Mongolism, 324
  aetiology, 325
  autoradiography in, 328
  birth order, 325, 327 (*table*)
  chromosome structure in, 328, 329
  familial incidence, 331
  genetical risk, 331
  incidence, 324
  intelligence range, 336
  leukaemia in, 335
  maternal age and, 325, 326 (*graph*), 331
    risk of having another mongol child, 333
      (*table*), 334 (*table*)
  mortality, 334
    in infancy, causes, 335
    sex distribution, 335
  mosaic, intelligence in, 337, 338 (*table*)
  'mother exhaustion' theory, 327
  psychological development, 336
  translocation, 329
    D/G, 329, *332*
    intelligence in, 337
    parental transmittance, 330
    pedigree, *330*
    risk of, in later sibs of affected children,
      330–1 (*table*)
  trisomy
    familial occurrence, 333
    intelligence in, 337
    risk of, in later sibs of affected children,
      333
Monosomy, definition, 324
Moran, heterozygotic advantage theory of
  schizophrenia, 69
Morbidity, Weinberg table, 354
Morquio's syndrome, 256, 265, 266 (*table*),
  271
  incidence, 272

Morquio's syndrome (*cont.*)
  metachromasia, absence of, 2'4
  mode of inheritance, 272
Morquio-Brailsford syndrome. *See* Morquio's syndrome
Morquio-Ullrich syndrome, 271
Mosaicism, 297, 299, 328, 340
Mother, schizophrenogenic, 39
Mucopolysaccharidoses, 256, 265
  heterozygotic carriers, detection of, 273
  principal features, 267 (*table*)
Multifactorial inheritance, 8
Multiple sclerosis, associated with schizophrenia, 29
Mutation, 3
  processes, in senescence, 123
  rates, 6

Naevoid amentia. *See* Sturge-Weber syndrome
Nail-biting, 102
Narcolepsy, associated with schizophrenia, 29
Natural selection, 6
  and single gene inheritance, 4
  effects of, and homoiogamy, 195
Neuroectodermal lesions, in the phakomatoses, 277
Neurofibromatosis. *See* Von Recklinghausen's disease
Neurological abnormality, in association
  with sex chromosome anomalies, 314
Neuronal tissue involvement, in rare storage
  abnormalities, 253
Neurosis
  and psychosis, relationship, 93
  family studies, 102
  in relatives of neurotics, 103
  symptomatology, genetical factors, 101
  twin concordances, 102 (*table*)
  —studies, 102
  working model, 94
Neuroticism
  and extraversion-intraversion, correlation,
    101
  correlation between mother of male patient
    and her children, 101
  intrafamilial correlations, *100*
Niemann-Pick disease, 256, 263
  and amaurotic family idiocy, interrelation-
    ship, 257, 263
  in Jews, 262
Night terrors, 102
Norrie's disease, 187

Obsessive-compulsive states, 105

Oculo-cerebro-renal syndrome (Lowe's syndrome), 235
Ødegaard, on schizophrenia, 23, 54 (table), 63
Oneirophrenia, 34
Ornithaemia, 220
Ornithine, 230 et seq.
Ovarian dysgenesis (XO syndrome), 304, 310, 321

Paranoia, in Huntington's chorea, 136, 137 (table)
Paraphrenia, late, in the elderly, 127
Paresis, general, associated with schizophrenia, 28
Parkinson's disease, 139
  and Huntington's chorea, 142
  associated with schizophrenia, 29
Partanen, on alcoholism, 109
Patau's syndrome. See Trisomy D
Payne-Whitney Clinic, New York, 112, 120
Pearson's coefficient of variability, 193
Pellagra, differential diagnosis from Hartnup disease, 233
Perinatal accident, affecting development and maturation, 96
Perris, on affective psychoses, 81
Personality
  change,
    in Huntington's chorea, 135, 144
    in Wilson's disease, 153
    post-traumatic, 95
  deviations
    and neurotic reactions, 92
    qualitative/quantitative variations, 94
    relationship to other psychiatric disorders, 92
    schizoid, 24
    working model, 94
  differences, in twins, 99 (tables)
  disorder. See also Behaviour: antisocial
    accompanying sex chromosome anomalies, 307
    associated with sex chromosome anomalies, 298
    in parents of schizophrenics, 23
    in XYY syndrome, 301
    transience of, 93
  epileptoid, 181
  in XYY males, 318
  social extraversion-introversion type, 97
  traits
    and symptoms, correlation, 94, 95 (table)
    genetical contribution to, 98, 99 (tables)
    MMPI, heredity loadings, 98 (table)
    twin concordances, 97 (table)

Personality trait: (cont.)
  type of, effect on manifestation of hereditary predisposition, 27
  variables, and genetic factors, 97
Petit mal. See under Epilepsy
Pfropfschizophrenie, 22
Phakomata, retinal, 276, 277
Phakomatoses, 277
  enzyme defect in, 202
  incidence among the mentally subnormal, 277
  neuropathology, 276
  similarity to ataxia-telangiectasia, 252
Phenylactic acid, 203
Phenylalanine
  blood levels in mental hospital patients, 211
  loading test, 202, 208
  plasma levels, 209 (graph)
  —hydroxylase, 207
  —oxidase, 203, 204
Phenylketonuria, 5, 6, 22, 202, 203. See also Hyperphenylalaninaemia
  and epilepsy, 181
  biochemistry, 203
  differential diagnosis from maple syrup urine disease, 213
  EEG abnormalities in relatives, 210
  epidemiology, 206
  ethnic distribution, 207
  genetics, 206
  heterozygote, 208
  infant mortality, 206
  —screening, 206
  IQ of parents, 199
  linkage, 212
  metabolic block, 203, 204, 205
  neuropathology, 205
  physical signs, 205
  pleiotropic effects, 205
  psychological changes in, 279
  psychosis among relatives, 209
  somatic clinical features, 205
Phenyllactic acid, 203
Phenylpyruvic acid, 203, 204
Phosphoglucomutase, 240
Phytanic acid, 251
Pick's disease, 133, 147
  age of onset, 149 (table), 150 (table)
  and Alzheimer's disease, differential diagnosis, 147
  clinical picture, 148 (table)
  epidemiology, 149
  genetics, 150
  pathology, 148
  pedigree, 153
  sex distribution, 149
  single gene hypothesis, 152

Poisoning, schizophrenia following, 45
Polydystrophic dwarfism. *See* Scheie syndrome
oligophrenia. *See* Sanfillipo syndrome
Polygenic inheritance, 7
Pre-psychotic drift, in schizophrenia, 39
Primogeniture, in mongolism, 327
Proband method of analysis, 19
  Weinberg, 353
Progesterone, effect on galactose metabolism, 241
Proline oxidase, 218, 219
Protein synthesis, and genes, 2
Psychasthenic personality, 106
Psychiatric disorders, and sex chromosome anomalies, 307
Psychogenesis, and schizophrenia, 37
Psycho-infantile personality, 106
Psychopath, epileptoid, 182 (*table*)
Psychopathy
  in alcoholism, 111
  in relatives of microcephalics, 290
  morbidity risk, in sibs of chronic alcoholics, 112 (*table*)
Psychoses
  acute, in Huntington's chorea, 136
  affective, 72
    admission rates, 72 (*table*)
      age incidence, 74 (*table*)
      sex incidence, 74 (*table*)
    age of onset, 82
    biochemistry, 75
    cyclic, 80
    cyclothymic personality traits, 79
    definition, 72, 75
    diagnostic distribution of affected relatives, 81 (*table*)
    endocrinological aetiology, 76
    expectation in the general population, 76
    in parents of schizophrenics, 23
    in the elderly, 127
    incidence in first-degree relatives of affective psychotics, 89 (*table*)
    —in relatives of bipolar and unipolar affective psychotics, 80 (*table*)
    involutional melancholias, 80
    mode of inheritance, 89
    monophasic depression, 80
    morbidity risk among relatives, 90 (*table*)
    of later life, and involutional melancholia, 86
    risk of, in relatives
      of bipolar and unipolar index patients, 79 (*table*)
      of involutional melancholia, age-related incidence, 86 (*table*) *et seq.*
      of manic-depressives, 84 (*table*)

Psychoses: affective (*cont.*)
    sex distribution, 82
    temperamental types among relatives, 79, 80 (*table*)
    twin research, 84
    unipolar and bipolar studies, 78
  and neurosis, relationship, 93
  arteriosclerotic, and senile dementia, clinical and pathological features, 128 (*table*)
  atypical
    and schizophrenia, 34
    familial factors, 24
    family pedigree, 24, 26
  due to cerebrovascular disease, in the elderly, 127
  epileptic, 180
  in Refsum's syndrome, 250
  in relatives of phenylketonurics, 209
  in Scheie syndrome, 270
  in tuberous sclerosis, 279
  paranoid, 136, 180
  schizo-affective, 34
Psychotic parents, children of, 24, 25 (*table*)
Purine metabolism, in hyperuricaemia, 247
Pyknolepsy, 169
Pyruvate metabolism, in Huntington's chorea, 142

Reactive depression, 102, 108
Recessive inheritance, 4
  characteristics, 5 (*table*)
  in aminoacidurias, 201, 202
  in neurometabolic disorders, 202
Recombination, in meiosis, 1
Refsum's syndrome, 249
  consanguinity in, 250
  dietary treatment, 251
  metabolic block, 250
  pedigree, 251, 252
  psychosis in, 250
Reilly-Alder bodies, 272, 273
Renal disease, in hyperprolinaemia, 218 *et seq.*
Reticulo-endothelial system, and schizophrenia, 22
Retina, phakomata of, 276, 277
RNA (ribonucleic acid), 3
Rohr, on schizophrenic illnesses, 32
Röll, on manic-depressive illness, 77
Rosanoff, on epilepsy, 170
  on manic-depressive illness, 85
  on schizophrenia, 18 (*table*)
Rosenthal, on schizophrenia, 10, 37
Roth, diagnostic scheme, 132
  on schizophrenic illnesses, 32, 41

Rüdin, Ernst, on obsessive-compulsive states, 105
  on schizophrenia, 10
Rud's syndrome, 292

Sanfillipo syndrome (polydystrophic oligo-phrenia), 265, 266 (*table*), 270
  incidence, 272
  mode of inheritance, 272
Scheie syndrome (polydystrophic dwarfism), 256, 265, 266 (*table*), 270
  incidence, 272
  mode of inheritance, 272
Schilder's disease, 205
Schizo-affective psychoses, 34
Schizoid personality, 21, 92
  —traits, 54
Schizophrenia
  acute, 11, 136
  admission rate, 11 (*table*)
  aetiology, 37
  age distribution, 12 (*table*)
  and Klinefelter's syndrome, 309
  and manic-depressive illness: distribution in pairs of secondary cases, 91 (*table*)
  and mental subnormality, 22
  and psychogenesis, 37
  and the reticulo-endothelial system, 22
  as a balanced polymorphism, 68
  association with cerebral disorders, 28
  — —tuberculosis, 22
  atypical, 23, 35
  biochemical threshold phenomenon, 47
  brain disease in aetiology of, 29, *30*
  catatonic, 31, 32
  childhood, 10
  chronic, 36
  definition, 10
  diathesis, and stress, 45
  EEG studies, 36
  exogenous cases, 28
  expectancy, 11
    in different countries, *13* (*table*)
    for parents of schizophrenics, 15, 40
    for relatives of schizophrenics, 14 (*table*)
  familial incidence, 'typical' and 'atypical', 34
  fertility, 68
    class differences, 69
  fitness rate, 64, 67, 69
  following trauma, 27
  genetic basis, 16
  —heterogeneity in, 26
  genetical models, 45
  hebephrenic, 31
  hereditary predisposition, 27

Schizophrenia (*cont.*)
  heredity, in Inouye's classification, 36 (*table*)
  heritability, 46 *et seq.*
    Falconer's estimates, 50 (*table*)
    for first cousins, 51
    polygenic model, 48, *49*
      arguments for and against, 53
    similarity to diabetes, 52
  heterogeneity, 30
  heterozygote, manifestation rate, 67
  —advantage theory, 69
  homogeneity, 27, 55
  in both parents, risks for children, 16 (*table*)
  in children of schizophrenics, incidence, 32 (*table*)
  in foster-children, 41
  in one twin, observational data, 18 (*table*)
  in sibs of schizophrenics, 28 (*table*), 56 (*table*)
  in twins
    concordance, 18, 19, 41
      and severity of psychosis, relationship, 20
      by sex and sampling, 21 (*table*)
      pairwise, 20
      sex ratio, 20, 21
    earlier studies of, 17, 18 (*table*)
    MZ co-twins, other psychiatric conditions in, 21
  — —reared apart, 40, 41 (*table*)
    pairwise rates, 19
    recent studies, 19 (*table*), 20 (*table*)
  incidence, in relatives of schizophrenics, 14
  Inouye classification, 36 (*table*)
  mode of inheritance, 16
  morbidity risk, 11
    and Falconer's incidence, 51
    for general population, 47
    in relatives of schizophrenics, 15 (*table*)
  multifactorial inheritance, 48
  mutation rate, 68
  nuclear, 36
  organic factors, 29
  paranoid, 31
  paraphrenia, late, 53
  PEG studies, 36
  penetrance, 47
  peripheral, 36
  personality change in, 11
  phenocopies, 28, 30, 38
  polygenic inheritance, 46
  population risks, 11
  proband, diagnosis, 31 (*table*)
  psychogenic psychoses resembling, 42

Schizophrenia (*cont.*)
psychotic drift, 69
relapsing, 36
relation to other disorders, 22
risk of, for twins of schizophrenics, 17
  sex ratio, 20
sex ratio, 12
sibs of schizophrenics, investigations on, 16
single gene hypothesis, 57
  arguments for and against, 62
  expectations in offspring by type of parental mating, 61 (*table*)
  observational data, fitness to theoretical expectations, 60 (*table*), 62 (*table*)
  predictive properties, 61
  under mathematical test, 70
stress, and diathesis of, 45
survival rate, 12
symptomatic, 43
transient, 36
types, 31
'typical', 35
Schizophrenia-like psychosis, 28, 153
Schizophrenia-paranoia, admission rates, 73 (*table*)
Schizophrenic illnesses
familial differences between types, 34, 35 (*table*)
genetical predisposition, 32 (*table*)
—matings, 24
phenotype, fitness of, 53
reaction, 43
spectrum disorders, 22
Schizophreniform psychoses, benign, 43
Schizophrenogenic mother, 39
Schneider's symptoms, 29, 34
School problems, 102
Schulz, Bruno, on homosexuality, 120
on psychotic matings, 24
on schizophrenia, 10
on schizophrenic illnesses, 32, 33
Segregation, of characteristics, 2
Self-mutilation, in hyperuricaemia, 246
Senescence, 122. *See also* Werner's syndrome
Senile dementia. *See* Dementia, senile
—chromatin screening, 305
status and antisocial behaviour, 308
—chromosomes. *See* Chromosomes: sex
Sex-limitation, 4
Sex-linkage, 4
Sex, of sibs of male homosexuals, 316
Sexual behaviour disorders, in sex chromosome anomalies, 315
Shields, on personality traits in MZ twins, 98, 99 (*tables*)
on schizophrenia, 17, 19 (*table*), 41
Sickle-cell anaemia, 4

Sjögren, on affective psychoses, 82
on manic-depressive illness, 77
on senile dementia, 129 *et seq.*
on spastic diplegia-mental subnormality-congenital ichthyosis syndrome, 291
Skin lesions, in tuberous sclerosis, 277
Skull, abnormal, 284
Slater, extension of Böök's hypothesis, 58
on hysteria, 106, 107
on manic-depressive illness, 77, 85
on schizophrenia, 18 (*table*), 22, 41
Sleep-talking, 101
Sleep-walking, 101
Sociopathy, in relatives of hysterics, 108
Sodium metabolism, in affective psychoses, 76
Somatic illness, schizophrenia following, 27
Spastic diplegia-mental subnormality-congenital ichthyosis syndrome, 290
Spearman, on intelligence, 185
Sphingomyelin, 245, 263
Spielmeyer-Vogt's amaurotic family idiocy, 259
Spinocerebellar degenerations, relation to ataxia-telangiectasia, 253
Stenstedt, on manic-depressive illness, 77
Stevenson, on progressive familial myoclonic epilepsy, 255
Storage abnormalities with involvement of neuronal tissue, 253
Stress, 42, 96
Strömgren, method (simplified), 356
on manic-depressive illness, 77
on obsessive-compulsive states, 105
on schizophrenia, 10
Sturge-Kalischer-Weber syndrome. *See* Sturge-Weber syndrome
Sturge-Weber syndrome, 282, *283*
Suicide, in relatives of schizophrenics, 23

Tay-Sachs disease. *See* Amaurotic family idiocy
Teacher's Report Form, 93
Teeth-grinding, 101
Temperament, cyclothymic, in schizophrenia, 54
Testicular feminization syndrome, 4
Testosterone, in treatment of Klinefelter's syndrome, 315
Thalassaemia, 4
Threshold effects, 8
Thymine, 2
Tienari, on schizophrenia, 19, 22, 41
Torsion dystonia, 134
Tortoise, longevity, 122
Tower skull, 284
Transvestism, and Klinefelter's syndrome, 317

Trauma, schizophrenia following, 27
Triple-X females. See XXX syndrome
Trisomy, definition, 324
—D syndrome, 340
—E syndrome, 338
    brain in, *339*
Tristan da Cunha inhabitants, in studies on
    ageing, 124
Tryptophan, 234
Tsuang, on schizophrenia, 23
Tuberculosis, association with schizophrenia,
    22
Tuberous sclerosis (epiloia), 6, 277
    abnormal sexual behaviour in, 279
    brain in, *276*
    butterfly rash in, 277, *278*
    clinical features, 277
    consanguinity of parents, 280
    diagnosis, in infancy, 278
    gene, variable expressivity, 279
    incidence, 280
    mode of inheritance, 280
    mutation rate, 280
    proportions of offspring from various
        matings, 280
    skin lesions in, 277
Tumours, in the phakomatoses, 276
Turner's syndrome, 125, 302
    ovaries in, 304
    psychological features, 310
        organic basis for, 311
Twins. *See also under individual disorders*
    birthweight and subsequent development,
        96
    blood groups, 348
    concordance, in genetic-environmental
        contributions, 348
    death rates, 346 (*table*)
    discordant pairs, 17
    DZ, definition, 345
    intra-pair correlations for personality
        questionnaire scores, 99 (*table*)
    longevity in, 122
    MZ
        definition, 345
        differences in, non-environmental causes,
            346
        personality traits in, 99 (*tables*)
            concordances, 97 (*table*)
            heritability, 97
    psychiatric diagnosis and concordance in,
        103
    research on, theoretical basis,
    sex distribution, 345 (*table*)
    survival, sex distribution, 345 (*table*)
    work on, 16
    zygosity, diagnosis by finger-print, 349

Twins: zygosity (*cont.*)
    method of determination, 348, 350, 351
        (*table*), 352 (*table*)
Tyrosine, 203, 204

Unverricht-Lundborg's myoclonic epilepsy.
    See under Epilepsy
Urea cycle, disorders of, 227
Uric acid, *246*
Urocanic acid, 217

Vacuolated lymphocytes, *260*
Valine, 212, 213, 214, 216
Vandenberg, on twin research, 97
Verbality, sex differences in, 193
Vigour, 123
Vitamin D activity, in hypercalcaemia, 244
Von Recklinghausen's disease (neurofibro-
    matosis), 281
    gene manifestations, 6
    incidence, 282

Watson and Crick, structure of DNA, 2
Weinberg
    morbidity table, 354
    on manic-depressive illness, 77
    on progressive familial myoclonic epilepsy,
        255
    proband method, 353
    shorter method, 356
Werner's syndrome, 126
Wilson's disease (hepatolenticular degenera-
    tion), 139, 153
    age of onset, 154
    clinical course, 154
    consanguinity rate, 156 (*table*), 158
    copper metabolism, 155
    genetical carriers, detection of, 158
—genetical modifiers, 158
    genetics, 156
    Geographical origins of parents, *157*
    Kayser-Fleischer ring, 154
    pathology, 153
    personality changes in, 153
    schizophrenia-like psychosis in, 153
    sex incidence, 158
Winokur, on manic-depression, 82
Wittermans, on schizophrenic illnesses, 32

Xanthomatosis, generalized primary, 253
XO syndrome. *See* Ovarian dysgenesis
XXX syndrome, 304, 321
    EEG abnormality in, 314

XXX syndrome (*cont.*)
  incidence, in the mentally subnormal, 321
    (*table*)
  psychological features, 311
  with cerebral palsy and mental sub-
    normality, 306
XXY syndrome, and homosexuality, 317
XXYY chromosome complement, 322
XYY syndrome, 300, 322, 323
  antisocial behaviour, 302 (*table*), 307
  behaviour disorder, early manifestation, 301

XYY syndrome (*cont.*)
  criminal behaviour in, 301
  males, personality characteristics in, 318

Zerbin-Rüdin, on manic-depressive illness, 77
  on monogenic theory of schizophrenia, 60,
    70
  twin research in manic-depressive illness, 85
    (*table*)
Zygote, 1